ALTERNATIVES TO ATHENS

Alternatives to Athens

*Varieties of Political Organization
and Community in Ancient Greece*

EDITED BY

ROGER BROCK
and
STEPHEN HODKINSON

OXFORD
UNIVERSITY PRESS

OXFORD

UNIVERSITY PRESS

Great Clarendon Street, Oxford OX2 6DP

Oxford University Press is a department of the University of Oxford.
It furthers the University's objective of excellence in research, scholarship,
and education by publishing worldwide in

Oxford New York

Auckland Bangkok Buenos Aires Cape Town Chennai
Dar es Salaam Delhi Hong Kong Istanbul Karachi Kolkata
Kuala Lumpur Madrid Melbourne Mexico City Mumbai Nairobi
São Paulo Shanghai Taipei Tokyo Toronto

Oxford is a registered trade mark of Oxford University Press
in the UK and in certain other countries

Published in the United States
by Oxford University Press Inc., New York

© Oxford University Press 2000

First published 2000
First published in paperback 2002

British Library Cataloguing in Publication Data

Data available

Library of Congress Cataloging in Publication Data

Data available

ISBN 0-19-815220-5
ISBN 0-19-925810-4 (pbk.)

1   3   5   7   9   10   8   6   4   2

Typeset by John Waś, Oxford
Printed in Great Britain
on acid-free paper by
Biddles Ltd., Guildford and King's Lynn

Acknowledgements

THE seminar series which led to this volume was originally devised and organized jointly with our former colleagues David Whitehead and the late John Smart and owes much to their ideas and input. We should like to add to the thanks of individual contributors our appreciation of the contribution made by the audiences present at the original versions of these papers, and especially by Peter Rhodes and Lynette Mitchell, who commuted for three years from Durham to Leeds and Manchester to attend almost all of them.

We are grateful to E. J. Brill for permission to reuse in Antony Keen's chapter material from his book *Dynastic Lycia: A Political History of the Lycians and their Relations with Foreign Powers, c. 545–362 BC*, published by them in 1998. Other publishers have kindly granted permission to reproduce figures: see the List of Illustrations below.

We are also grateful to Mogens Hansen for encouragement and advice, to referees for the Press for suggestions and criticisms which improved the volume, to John Waś for his copy-editing and typesetting, to Georga Godwin for seeing the book through the press, and to Hilary O'Shea for her support through a lengthy process of preparation. We should finally like to thank all those who assisted us and our contributors by drawing maps specially for the volume or advising on computing and bibliographic problems.

April 2000

R.B.
S.H.

Acknowledgements (Paperback Edition)

WE are very pleased that Oxford University Press has decided to issue a paperback edition which, as well as making the contents accessible to a wider readership, has given us the opportunity to tidy up some typographical slips and to update the bibliography. We are particularly grateful to Paul Cartledge for his assistance with the latter.

July 2002

R.B.
S.H.

Contents

The Alternative Polis

List of Illustrations

Illustration Acknowledgements

Line illustrations have been redrawn by Paul Simmons, Oxford.

Fig. 4.2 (*a*) is from R. J. Scranton, *Greek Walls* (Harvard: Harvard University Press, 1941). Reproduced by kind permission of Harvard University Press and the American School of Classical Studies at Athens.

Fig. 4.3 is from R. Koldewey, *Die antiken Baureste der Insel Lesbos* (Berlin: G. Reimer, 1890).

Fig. 4.4 is from Philip Betancourt, *The Aeolic Style in Architecture* (Princeton: Princeton University Press, 1977). Reproduced by kind permission of Princeton University Press.

Fig. 11.3 was originally drawn by Y. Rizakis and is included by courtesy of A. Rizakis.

Fig. 11.4 was originally drawn by J. Travlos for the American School of Classical Studies at Athens: Agora Excavations, and is included by kind permission of the School.

Fig. 12.1 is based on a map in D. Westlake, *Thessaly in the Fourth Century* BC (London: Methuen, 1935).

Fig. 12.4 is based on A. Fol and T. Spiridonov, *Historical Geography of the Thracian Tribes up to the Third Century* BC [in Bulgarian] (Sofia, 1983), pl. III.

Fig. 15.1 is from an original in A. G. Keen, *Dynastic Lycia* (Leiden: E. J. Brill, 1998), and is included by kind permission of E. J. Brill.

List of Contributors

ZOSIA HALINA ARCHIBALD is a Senior Research Fellow in the Department of Classics and Ancient History at the University of Liverpool. She has made a special study of the dynamics of inter- and intra-community contacts during the hellenistic period under a Leverhulme Special Research Fellowship (1995–7) at Liverpool, which will shortly be published as a monograph. Her most recent book is *The Odrysian Kingdom of Thrace: Orpheus Unmasked* (1998). Dr Archibald is director of the British team at the excavations at Vetren-Pistiros, an emporium in inland Thrace. She is currently writing a book about archaeology for ancient historians.

MICHAEL ARNUSH is an Associate Professor of Classics and History at Skidmore College in Saratoga Springs, NY. He has published on Delphic political history in the fourth and third centuries BC, the early stages of Athenian democracy, and Greek international diplomatic relations.

DAVID BRAUND is Professor of Black Sea and Mediterranean History, University of Exeter; his recent publications include *Georgia in Antiquity* (1994). He is preparing a new book, entitled *Greeks, Scythians and Amazons*, on Greek attitudes and entanglements in the Black Sea region.

ROGER BROCK is Lecturer in Classics at the University of Leeds. He has published on Greek history and historiography and on wine in ancient Greece, and is preparing a book on Greek political imagery.

PIERRE CARLIER is a graduate of the École Normale Supérieure and 'Docteur ès lettres', and Professor of Greek History at the University of Paris X—Nanterre. His publications include *La Royauté en Grèce avant Alexandre* (1984), *Démosthène* (1990), and *Le IVème siècle avant J.-C.* (1995), and he is currently preparing a book on Homer.

JOHN K. DAVIES, Rathbone Professor of Ancient History and Classical Archaeology at Liverpool since 1977, is the author of *Athenian Propertied Families, 600–300 BC* (1971), of *Democracy and Classical Greece* (2nd edn. 1993), and of many scholarly papers on Greek history.

W. G. (GEORGE) FORREST (1925–97) was Fellow and Tutor in Ancient History at Wadham College, Oxford, for many years before becoming the Wykeham Professor of Ancient History at Oxford in 1977. He is best known for his books *The Emergence of Greek Democracy* (1966) and *A History of Sparta* (1968) and for many articles on Greek history, Aristophanes, and the inscriptions of Chios.

STEPHEN HODKINSON is Lecturer in History at the University of Manchester, and also Special Lecturer in Classics at the University of Nottingham. He is author of many articles on Classical Spartan society and on pastoralism in the ancient economy. He is co-editor of *The Shadow of Sparta* (1994) and of *Sparta: New Per-*

spectives (1999). He has recently published a monograph on *Property and Wealth in Classical Sparta* (2000).

ANTONY G. KEEN is an Associate Lecturer at the Open University and a contributor to the Copenhagen Polis Centre. He has written widely on the subject of Lycia, including his book *Dynastic Lycia*, published in 1998.

ROBIN LANE FOX is Fellow and Tutor of New College, Oxford and University Reader in Ancient History.

ANDREW LINTOTT studied at Oxford and taught for some years at King's College, London and at the University of Aberdeen, before returning to Oxford, where he is a Reader in Ancient History and Fellow of Worcester College. He has written a number of books on ancient history, the first of which was *Violence in Republican Rome* (1968) and the most recent *The Constitution of the Roman Republic* (1999).

KATHRYN LOMAS is part-time Lecturer at the University of Newcastle upon Tyne. She is the author of *Rome and the Western Greeks* (1993) and of numerous articles on Roman Italy, Greek colonization, and urban development in the Graeco-Roman world, and is co-editor (with T. J. Cornell) of *Urban Society in Roman Italy* (1995).

BARBARA MITCHELL is Emeritus Fellow of St Anne's College, Oxford, where she taught Ancient History from 1959 to 1989.

CATHERINE MORGAN is Lecturer in Classical Archaeology at King's College, London. She has excavated in Greece, Albania, and Russia (where she is currently engaged in publishing Attic black- and red-figured pottery from Phanagoria). Her published work focuses on early Greek politics and religion.

P. J. RHODES is Professor of Ancient History at the University of Durham. His most recent book is *The Decrees of the Greek States* (with D. M. Lewis; 1997).

JAMES ROY is Senior Lecturer in Classics at the University of Nottingham and has written on various aspects of classical Greek history, often concerning Arcadia. He is currently working on studies of Arcadia and Elis in collaboration with the Copenhagen Polis Centre.

KEITH RUTTER is Reader in the Department of Classics, University of Edinburgh. His principal research interest is in the history and coinage of the Greeks in the western Mediterranean, and his publications include *Campanian Coinages 475–380 BC* (1979) and *Greek Coinages of Southern Italy and Sicily* (1997).

NICHOLAS SEKUNDA studied ancient Cretan mercenary archers for his doctoral thesis at the University of Manchester. His main academic field of interest is the history and archaeology of ancient (especially Greek) warfare, but he retains an interest in ancient Crete. He currently lives and works in Poland.

NIGEL SPENCER is Research Associate at the Institute of Archaeology in Oxford. He is currently conducting research into the north-east Aegean and western Anatolia, including acting as Director of the Madra Çay Delta Archaeological Project, an interdisciplinary research project, conducted in collaboration with scholars from the United States and Turkey, investigating the long-term cultural and environmental history of the coastal region opposite Lesbos' eastern shore (the Mytilenean *peraea*).

HANS VAN WEES is Lecturer in Ancient History at University College, London. He is the author of *Status Warriors: War, Violence and Society in Homer and History* (1992) and joint editor, with Nick Fisher, of *Archaic Greece: New Approaches and New Evidence* (1998).

Abbreviations

For standard abbreviations see *L'Année philologique*

AAA	*Athens Annals of Archaeology*
AEMTh	*Το Αρχαιολογικό Έργο στη Μακεδονία και Θράκη*, vols. i–vi (1987–92). Thessaloniki, 1989–95
Arch. Rep.	*Archaeological Reports* published by the Society for the Promotion of Hellenic Studies
Achaia und Elis	A. D. Rizakis (ed.), *Achaia und Elis in der Antike*. Athens and Paris: KERA/De Boccard, 1991
Archaia Thrake	*Αρχαιά Θράκη· Πρακτικά 2ου Διεθ. Συμποσίου Θρακικών Σπουδών*. Komotini, 1997
Buck	C. D. Buck, *The Greek Dialects*, 2nd edn. Chicago, Ill.: University of Chicago Press, 1955 (numbers refer to Part II: Selected Inscriptions)
CEG	P. A. Hansen, *Carmina Epigraphica Graeca*. 2 vols.; Berlin: de Gruyter, 1983–9
CID	*Corpus des inscriptions de Delphes*, i. *Lois sacrées et règlements religieux*, ed G. Rougemont (1977); ii. *Les Comptes du quatrième et du troisième siècle*, ed. J. Bousquet (1989); iii. *Les Hymnes à Apollon*, ed. A. Bélis (1992). Paris: de Boccard
Coulson *et al.*, *Archaeology*	W. D. E. Coulson, O. Palagia, T. L. Shear Jr., H. A. Shapiro, and F. J. Frost (eds.), *The Archaeology of Athens and Attica under the Democracy*. Oxford: Oxbow, 1994
CPC Acts 1	M. H. Hansen (ed.), *The Ancient Greek City-state*. Acts of the Copenhagen Polis Centre, 1; Copenhagen: Royal Danish Academy of Sciences and Letters, 1993
CPC Acts 2	M. H. Hansen (ed.), *Sources for the Ancient Greek City-state*. Acts of the Copenhagen Polis Centre, 2; Copenhagen: Royal Danish Academy of Sciences and Letters, 1995
CPC Acts 3	M. H. Hansen (ed.), *Introduction to an Inventory of Poleis*. Acts of the Copenhagen Polis Centre, 3; Copenhagen: Royal Danish Academy of Sciences and Letters, 1996
CPC Acts 4	M. H. Hansen (ed.), *The Polis as an Urban Centre and as a Political Community*. Acts of the Copenhagen Polis Centre, 4; Copenhagen: Royal Danish Academy of Sciences and Letters, 1997
CPC Acts 5	M. H. Hansen, *Polis and City-state: An Ancient Concept and its Modern Equivalent*. Acts of the Copenhagen Polis Centre, 5; Copenhagen: Royal Danish Academy of Sciences and Letters, 1998
CPC Acts 6	T. H. Nielsen and J. Roy (eds.), *Defining Ancient Arkadia*.

	Acts of the Copenhagen Polis Centre, 6; Copenhagen: Royal Danish Academy of Sciences and Letters, 1999
CPC Papers 1	D. Whitehead (ed.), *From Political Architecture to Stephanus Byzantius: Sources for the Ancient Greek Polis*. Papers from the Copenhagen Polis Centre, 2 (Historia Einzelschriften, 87); Stuttgart: Steiner, 1994
CPC Papers 2	M. H. Hansen and K. Raaflaub (eds.), *Studies in the Ancient Greek Polis*. Papers from the Copenhagen Polis Centre, 2 (Historia Einzelschriften, 95); Stuttgart: Steiner, 1995
CPC Papers 3	M. H. Hansen and K. Raaflaub (eds.), *More Studies in the Ancient Greek Polis*. Papers from the Copenhagen Polis Centre, 3 (Historia Einzelschriften 108); Stuttgart: Steiner, 1996
CPC Papers 4	T. H. Nielsen (ed.), *Yet More Studies in the Ancient Greek Polis*. Papers from the Copenhagen Polis Centre, 4 (Historia Einzelschriften, 117); Stuttgart: Steiner, 1997
Figueira and Nagy, *Theognis*	T. J. Figueira and G. Nagy (eds.), *Theognis of Megara: Poetry and the Polis*. Baltimore, Md., and London: Johns Hopkins University Press, 1985
Ergon	Τὸ Ἔργον τῆς Ἀρχαιολογικῆς Ἑταιρείας
FdD	*Fouilles de Delphes*
Fornara	C. W. Fornara, *Translated Documents of Greece and Rome*, i. *Archaic Times to the End of the Peloponnesian War*. Baltimore, Md., and London: Johns Hopkins University Press, 1977 [followed by item number]
FGrH	F. Jacoby, *Die Fragmente der griechischen Historiker*. Leiden: Brill, 1923– [followed by author number and fragment number]
GVI	W. Peek, *Griechische Vers-Inschriften*, i. *Grab-Epigramme*. Berlin: Akademie-Verlag, 1955
Harding	P. Harding, *Translated Documents of Greece and Rome*, ii. *From the End of the Peloponnesian War to the Battle of Ipsus*. Cambridge: Cambridge University Press, 1985 [followed by item number]
JRGZM	*Jahrbuch des Römisch-Germanischen Zentralmuseums, Mainz*
ICret.	M. Guarducci (ed.), *Inscriptiones Creticae*. Rome: Libreria dello Stato, 1935–50
IG	*Inscriptiones Graecae*
KA	*Poetae Comici Graeci*, ed. R. Kassel and C. Austin. Berlin: de Gruyter, 1983– (7 vols. to date)
Michel, *Recueil*	C. Michel, *Recueil d'inscriptions grecques*. Hildesheim: Olms, 1976 (reprint of 1st edn., Paris: Leroux, 1900)
Mitchell and Rhodes, *Development*	L. G. Mitchell and P. J. Rhodes (eds.), *The Development of the Polis in Archaic Greece*. London and New York: Routledge, 1997
ML	R. Meiggs and D. M. Lewis, *A Selection of Greek Historical Inscriptions to the End of the Fifth Century B.C.* Ox-

	ford: Clarendon Press, 1969 [followed by inscription number]
PA	J. Kirchner, *Prosopographia Attica*. 2 vols.; Berlin: Reimer, 1901–3 [followed by entry number]
PMG	D. L. Page (ed.), *Poetae Melici Graeci*. Oxford: Clarendon Press, 1962
Praktika	Πρακτικά· Διεθνές Συνεδρίο για την Αρχαία Θεσσαλία στη Μνημή του Δημήτρη Ρ. Θεοχάρη. Athens: ΤΑΡΑ
RE	A. Fr. von Pauly, rev. G. Wissowa *et al.*, *Real-Encyclopädie der klassischen Altertumswissenschaft*. Stuttgart and Munich: Metzler/Druckenmüller, 1894–1980
SEG	*Supplementum Epigraphicum Graecum*
SGDI	H. Collitz and F. Bechtel (eds.), *Sammlung der griechischen Dialekt-Inschriften*. Göttingen: Vandenhoeck & Ruprecht, 1885–1915
*Syll.*³	W. Dittenberger, *Sylloge Inscriptionum Graecum*, 3rd edn. 4 vols.; Leipzig: Hirzel, 1915–24
Structures rurales	P. Doukelis and L. Mendoni (eds.), *Structures rurales et sociétés antiques: Actes du colloque de Corfou, 14–16 mai 1992*. Annales littéraires de l'Université de Besançon, 508; Paris and Besançon: Les Belles Lettres, 1994
TAM	E. Kalinka *et al.*, *Tituli Asiae Minoris*. Vienna: Österreichische Akademie der Wissenschaften, 1901–
Thessalia	Θεσσαλία· Δεκαπέντε χρόνια αρχαιολογικής έρευνας 1975–1990. Αποτελέσματα και προόπτικες/*Actes du Colloque, la Thessalie: Quinze années de recherches archéologiques, 1975–1990. Bilan et perspectives, Lyon 17–22 avril 1990*. Athens: Kapon, 1994
*TLE*²	M. Pallottino (ed.), *Testimoniae Linguae Etruscae*, 2nd edn. Florence: Nuova Italia, 1968
Tod	M. N. Tod, *A Selection of Greek Historical Inscriptions*. 2 vols.· Oxford: Clarendon Press, 1948 [followed by inscription number]
Urbanization	H. Damgaard Andersen, H. W. Horsnaes, and S. Houby-Nielsen (eds.), *Urbanization in the Mediterranean in the Ninth to Sixth Centuries* BC. Acta Hyperborea, 7, Danish Studies in Classical Archaeology; Copenhagen: Museum Tusculanum, 1997

Note on Transliteration

An attempt has been made to standardize transliteration throughout the volume along fairly familiar principles: in general, proper names and technical terms are given in modernized form, but common and familiar Latinized forms have been retained (e.g. Pericles, Cleon). Individual contributors are not responsible for any residual inconsistency.

I

Introduction: Alternatives to the Democratic Polis

ROGER BROCK AND STEPHEN HODKINSON

In the second half of the fourth century BC Aristotle's school undertook a major research project: a collection of 'constitutions' (*politeiai*) of Greek states. The project's primary purpose was to underpin Aristotle's writing of his *Politics* (as the transitional passage at the end of his *Nicomachean Ethics* makes clear); but the 'constitutions' clearly also circulated independently, since the ancient lists of the works of Aristotle mention a collection of 158 constitutions of states 'democratic, oligarchic, tyrannic, and aristocratic'.[1] The project covered the full range of constitutional forms; and from the surviving fragments of eighty-odd individual studies known to us, we can see that it also covered communities of widely differing types and locations.[2] The major Greek poleis ('city-states' or, perhaps better, 'citizen-states')[3] of the mainland and islands—places such as Athens, Sparta, Corinth, Miletos, Samos, Naxos, and Aegina—were there, together with Syracuse, Akragas, Taras, Croton, and other major powers of Magna Graecia; but so too were small poleis such as Troizen, Cythnos, Melos, and Tenedos. Indeed, the project clearly embraced the whole Greek world, from Massalia (modern Marseilles) in the western Mediterranean, via Cyrene in Libya, to Soli in Cilicia, as well as cities whose Greek nature was marginal, such as Adramyttion and Kios in Mysia, and, most famously, Carthage, which was not Greek at all.[4] It included communities not regarded as poleis, and even some which were not unitary states. There were studies of a number of communities

---

[1] The quotation is from Diogenes Laertius 5. 27, item 143; what Hesychius means by a *polis idiōtikos* in his parallel list is anyone's guess. It is interesting that Diogenes' list excludes the 'good forms' of democracy and monarchy, namely polity and kingship, which complete the list of six types of constitution in Aristotle's *Politics* 3. 7.

[2] For a recent edition of the fragments see Gigon (1987) 561–722, though his list of 148 constitutions identifiable by title or fragment is probably rather optimistic.

[3] 'City-state' is the orthodox English translation of the Greek term 'polis'. The alternative term, 'citizen-state', on which see Hansen (1993), lays stress on the polis as a community of citizens. For a succinct account of the polis see the article 'Polis' in the *Oxford Classical Dictionary* (3rd edn.) by O. Murray. The meaning and reference of the term 'polis' are the subject of a major research project by the Copenhagen Polis Centre. One important qualification of the traditional view to emerge from their researches is the argument that autonomy was not an essential feature of a polis: see Hansen (1995*a*).

[4] That there was a *Carthaginian Constitution* is an inference from the lengthy discussion in book 2 of the *Politics*; it is not otherwise attested (Gigon 1987: 648–9).

known as ethnē, such as the Aetolians, Acarnanians, Ambrakians, Arcadians, Achaeans, Bottiaeans, Epeirotes, Lycians, and Thessalians, several of which are discussed in this volume; and the islands of Cyprus and Crete were dealt with *en bloc* rather than in terms of the various local political communities which they contained.[5] The complete project must have painted a marvellously diverse picture of political organization and activity over the Greek world of the Mediterranean, a picture reflected, albeit often dimly, in the illustrations Aristotle drew from it for the *Politics*.

Sad to say, little of this diversity is reflected in the picture of ancient Greek politics current in popular perceptions or presented in many educational syllabuses, which for the most part concentrate on one particular political system—the Athenian democracy (*dēmokratia*) of the fifth and fourth centuries BC. Even within the world of specialist academic research, although recent years have witnessed a burgeoning number of studies of other Greek communities, democratic Athens remains the central focus of historical studies of ancient Greece, especially in the study of politics.[6] In 1992 and 1993 this concentration on Athenian politics reached a climax as a consequence of the celebrations of the 2,500th anniversary of what many interpret as the birth of Athenian *dēmokratia*, the reforms of Kleisthenes in 508/7 BC. These celebrations were marked by a variety of academic and popular events, ranging from specialist scholarly colloquia and publications on democratic Athens, through broader conferences on democracy embracing participants from both academic and political life, to cultural events open to the general public such as exhibitions and multi-faceted occasions like the 'Democracy Week' held in London in June 1993.

It was against this background, and at the very time of the democracy celebrations, that (in concert with our former colleagues John Smart and David Whitehead) we resolved, as organizers of the Leeds–Manchester Greek History Research Seminar, to initiate a series bearing the title 'Alternatives to the Democratic Polis'. The thinking behind the series, as advertised in the initial call for papers, was to combat the 'danger of tunnel vision, a perspective which ignores the variety of ancient Greek state forms and the plurality of constitutional patterns'. Instead, we aimed 'to give the variety and plurality their due by examining alternatives (theoretical and actual) to the polis and/or to democracy in archaic, classical, and early hel-

---

[5] On ethnē see the section below on 'Communities other than the polis'. On the Achaeans, Thessalians, Epeirotes, and Lycians see the respective chapters by Morgan, Archibald, Davies, and Keen. For the argument that the local Cypriot kingdoms should be regarded as poleis see Demand (1996). Aristotle's treatment of Crete as a unity was founded on misconception: Perlman (1992); for elements of confederacy in one region of Crete, however, see the chapter by Sekunda below.

[6] Besides the books mentioned in the next section of this introduction, one might note the wealth of studies by M. H. Hansen, culminating in Hansen (1991), textbooks such as Sinclair (1987) and Stockton (1990), and more theoretical discussions like Farrar (1988) and Ober (1989).

lenistic Greece'. Our aim, in short, was to provide a counterbalance to the then current democracy celebrations, to redirect attention to the range of political systems and communities beyond that of the democratic polis, and particularly Athenian *dēmokratia*, and to encourage a more rounded analysis of Greek political life. One of our intentions was to bring together into a common forum work being done, sometimes in isolation, by scholars of different generations from a range of academic institutions both in Britain and elsewhere. The outcome exceeded even our expectations. Such was the response of colleagues wishing to place their work within the series that it ran for three academic years, commencing in October 1992 and culminating in a day conference at Manchester in May 1995. Our theme had clearly answered to a need felt by these scholars for a view of the ancient Greek state which was not dominated by democratic Athens. The response also testifies to the reality of modern historical research, which, contrary to popular presentation, has for some years past extended its horizons to the full range of ancient state formations. It is hardly coincidence, moreover, that our own initiative should have coincided with the inauguration of the massive collective research effort of the Copenhagen Polis Centre, whose work, though focused upon study of the polis, both concurs with ours in examining the range of such communities throughout the ancient Greek world and has embraced in practice the study of communities other than the polis.[7]

In this volume we present a selection of papers from the seminar series under the title *Alternatives to Athens: Varieties of Political Organization and Community in Ancient Greece*. 'Athens' stands here as the prime representative of the forms of constitution and state (democracy and the polis) which have dominated the attention of most modern observers of ancient Greece. The term 'alternatives' is intended in several overlapping senses. Some of the political ideas and systems discussed in the following chapters were directly contemporaneous with democratic Athens and were either projected alternatives to her democratic system or external powers, possessing a variety of different political formations, with whom the Athenians had to compete or negotiate. Other chapters discuss 'alternatives to Athens' in the looser sense of ways of organizing politics and society other than through democracy or the polis: providing, as our subtitle suggests, case studies of the widely varying forms of political or social organization, community, and identity which developed within the Greek world and among neighbouring peoples between the archaic and hellenistic periods. Finally, 'alternatives to Athens' is also intended in the historiographical sense to signal the broader perspective and more flexible approach we should adopt both to the study of ancient society and politics and to the political heritage we derive from Greek antiquity.

[7] For the publications of the Copenhagen Polis Centre see *CPC Acts* 1–5; *CPC Papers* 1–4.

The domination of Athens

The world of Greek politics represented in this volume differs so vastly from the Athenocentric image which so powerfully informs modern perceptions that it is worth considering the reasons for this divergence between image and reality. There are, it seems to us, two principal reasons for the modern over-concentration on Athenian *dēmokratia*: the overwhelming one-sidedness in the amount and quality of our information, and the tendency of modern liberal democratic society to look back to its supposed predecessor in the ancient past. Both reasons deserve some scrutiny.

It is obvious and undeniable that Athens is much the best-documented political community of ancient Greece. In part, this is due to the fact that, of all the 158 'constitutions' referred to above, only the *Athenian Constitution* survives in anything more than a fragmentary condition, following its discovery on a papyrus recovered from the sands of Egypt in the late nineteenth century. In part, it is a reflection both of Athens' size and power, which made her a dominant force in Greek affairs, and of her role as the leading cultural centre, which made the greatest contribution to the Greek literary and artistic heritage. Hence, to a wealth of contemporary writings there was added an abiding interest throughout antiquity in matters Athenian; and many works relating to her affairs were subsequently copied or at least cited in later periods. Even before the discovery of the papyrus text of the *Athenian Constitution*, the work was already much the best known of all the Aristotelian constitutions owing to its frequent citation by other ancient writers (Gigon 1987: 581). The rich documentation of Athenian political life, however, is also due to the link between Athenian democracy and the 'epigraphic habit': the Athenians had an ideological commitment to the publication of records of public business, normally in the form of inscriptions on stone. Whatever view one takes of the use which they themselves made of this material,[8] the extensive surviving remains of the archive which they created leave us uniquely well informed on the detailed working of Athenian democracy. It is easy for such a wealth of material to create what is sometimes called 'the tyranny of the evidence'. Since we can answer a much wider range of questions about Athens in much fuller detail than is possible for other states, there is sometimes a tendency to concentrate upon these richer sources of material, which offer a more secure niche for academic specialization.

To say this is not to ignore the increased attention which has undoubtedly been given by a number of recent scholars to the history and archaeology of other Greek states (as is evident from the Recommended Reading below). However, the sheer paucity of detailed information about their political

---

[8] Since the publication of Thomas (1989), many scholars have become more sceptical about the role played in Athenian public life by records and written documents.

systems inevitably restricts the depth of analysis on this subject in relation to other aspects of their societies.[9] Moreover, the existence of particular local studies has hardly produced a general reassessment of Greek politics upon a less Athenocentric model such as would hold sway in basic courses and textbooks on Greek political history.[10]

At first sight, these observations might appear to be contradicted by the case of Sparta. The quantity of information about Spartan public affairs is indeed slight compared with that concerning Athens.[11] The Aristotelian *Constitution of the Lakedaimonians* (as the Spartans called themselves) survives only in brief fragments; the Spartans' cultural contribution was negligible; and extant inscriptions recording their public business in the classical period can be counted on the fingers of one hand. Yet recent years have witnessed several studies of the operation of Spartan politics;[12] and her constitution is often discussed as a working alternative to Athenian *dēmokratia* (Powell 1988; Finer 1997: i. 336–40). The case of Sparta is, however, less of an exception than it might seem. First, modern scholarly study of Sparta is by no means as universal a phenomenon as the study of democratic Athens. The subject is comparatively neglected in scholarship in the United States, in marked contrast with the veritable industry of recent American studies of Athenian democracy. Secondly, there is a vast gulf between the character of modern studies of Athenian and of Spartan politics. In contrast to recent in-depth studies of the detailed operation of Athenian democratic institutions and ideology, studies of Spartan politics are frequently reduced to elementary, and often controversial, debates concerning basic 'facts' of political procedure.[13] Thirdly, our capacity to engage in more substantive discussion of Spartan politics, as of most other aspects of her society, is to a considerable extent a spin-off from the political and

[9] J. B. Salmon (1984), for example, devotes only 8 pages (232–9) out of 464 to the constitution of Corinth, for want of evidence.

[10] For example, in Buckley (1996), a valuable textbook for the requirements of UK 'Advanced' level syllabuses in Ancient History, nine out of eleven chapters on the internal politics of Greek states relate to Athens. With the exception of a chapter on tyranny and one on 7th- and 6th-cent. Sparta, the histories of Greek states other than Athens are discussed primarily in terms of their *foreign* policies. Among works by academics aimed at a popular audience, Murray (1988*b*) devotes only two pages to oligarchy in classical Greece as a whole compared with sixteen on Athenian democracy in the 5th and 4th cents.

[11] Compare the slender scale of MacDowell's book on Spartan law (1986) with the mountain of publications on Athenian law.

[12] e.g. Andrewes (1966); Ste Croix (1972) 124–50; W. E. Thompson (1973); Lewis (1977) 27–49; D. H. Kelly (1981); Forrest (1983); Cartledge (1987) esp. 99–138.

[13] e.g. the debate between Rahe (1980) and Rhodes (1981*b*) regarding the procedures for electing the executive officials known as ephors. Note the comments of Ste Croix (1972: 131) regarding Spartiate voting procedures: 'It is a sobering reflection that our knowledge of the persistence of these extraordinary procedures depends upon an aside of six words in Thucydides, a couple of isolated remarks in Aristotle, and a single passage in Plutarch. There may well have been other unique features of Spartan constitutional procedure which our sources have failed to record.'

cultural prominence of Athens and from the perceived opposition between the two states in classical Greek politics and ideology. The prominence of Sparta in the contemporary classical literary record is largely an Athenian phenomenon, the majority of our evidence coming from writers who were either Athenians themselves (Thucydides, Euripides, Aristophanes, Critias, Xenophon, Plato) or persons, such as Herodotus and Aristotle, who were deeply influenced by Athens. The Athenians' preoccupation with Sparta was the product of their own self-representation, with Sparta serving the role of the archetypal opposite or 'Other', her institutions presented in stark contrast—either positively or negatively in accordance with the writer's attitude—to those of Athens (Powell and Hodkinson 1994; Greenstein Millender 1996). The sources' presentation of Spartan politics often shares these concerns. Indeed, they have not been entirely absent from modern scholarship: it is notable that the main subject of recent debate has been the extent to which Spartan decision-making was open and democratic. The case of Sparta is indeed the proverbial exception which proves the rule about the dominance of the Athenian perspective in both the surviving historical record and the modern study of Greek political systems.

The second reason for the current focus of study is the role of Athenian *dēmokratia* in twentieth-century political and cultural discourse. This differs in important respects from its role in earlier centuries. The early modern period's attitude to Athenian democracy was largely one of contempt for and horror at the evils of mob rule. Even the democratic movements of the late eighteenth and early nineteenth centuries were concerned to avoid what they saw as the excesses of Athenian direct democracy through the creation of representative bodies to balance and dilute the element of popular participation (J. T. Roberts 1994; cf. Loraux and Vidal-Naquet 1979). A positive evaluation of Athenian democracy emerged only in the mid-nineteenth century, a development fostered by a historical rather than philosophical approach to the subject and commonly associated with the work of George Grote.[14]

It was when modern democratic ideas gained general acceptance as a legitimate principle of government, however, that democratic Athens came—above all in English-speaking countries—to be regarded as an ancestor of, and a source of identification for, modern political regimes. In consequence, Athenian *dēmokratia* became involved in contemporary debates about the nature and success of modern states which called themselves democracies. One source of involvement was disillusion at the limited degree of popular participation and commitment within contemporary democratic regimes and at the dominance of 'élite theories' within Western democra-

---

[14] Grote was not working in isolation, but reflected wider trends (Hansen 1992: 20–1; J. T. Roberts 1994: ch. 11).

tic thought.[15] For example, Moses Finley's *Democracy Ancient and Modern* (1973) used the example of Athenian democratic practice as an argument against the conviction that the active involvement of the mass of citizens was an unobtainable ideal for modern democracies. The political thrust of Finley's lectures, delivered in 1972, can be seen as part of a wider defence of classical democratic theory among political scientists which had begun in the 1960s in reaction to the increasing assimilation of élite theories into mainstream democratic thought (Parry 1969: 149–52). Doubts about the feasibility of effective popular participation in Western democracies still remain, and at least one current major American project on Athenian democracy, which commenced in the 1980s, is in part a reaction against élitist models of ancient Greek and modern politics.[16]

A second source has been the widespread collapse of non-democratic regimes around the globe during the last quarter of a century. This process commenced in southern Europe, starting—appropriately enough—in Greece itself, with the overthrow of the Colonels' regime in 1974, an event soon followed by the institution of democratic regimes in place of long-standing dictatorships in both Portugal and Spain. It developed through the 1980s in several countries in Latin America and South-east Asia, climaxed in the collapse of Communist regimes in Eastern Europe in 1989, and has continued to a certain extent in the 1990s on the African continent. Although not all of these changes led to the establishment of stable democratic regimes, by 1990 the number of the world's liberal democracies had more than doubled, according to one calculation (Fukuyama 1992: 49–50), in the course of only fifteen years. This growth has been underpinned by the growing ideological dominance of liberal democratic premises, themselves buttressed by the increasing penetration of free-market economics throughout the global economy. Although some theorists of the success of liberal democracy have declined to appeal to the Athenian precedent,[17] a common response has been to view it as the starting-point of the democratic journey.[18] Indeed, some have seen the possibility, particularly in the concept of 'teledemocracy', of using advances in computer technology as a means of returning to a direct participatory democracy on the Athenian model.[19]

When Athenian democracy is linked into the long-term development of a seemingly unchallengeable principle of human government, it is that much

[15] For a useful conspectus of the range of élite theories see Parry (1969).

[16] On the relation of the various democratic projects of Josiah Ober, Charles Hedrick, J. Peter Euben, and John Wallach to the alternative political model of the school of Leo Strauss see J. T. Roberts (1994) 300.

[17] For example, for Fukuyama (1992: 48) there were no democracies before 1776; Athenian democracy 'does not qualify, because it did not systematically protect individual rights'. It is, of course, a commonplace in this sort of discussion that, while the issue of definition is crucial, the essential nature of democracy is very hard to pin down.

[18] We draw here upon the title *Democracy: The Unfinished Journey. 508 BC to AD 1993* (Dunn 1992). [19] Hansen (1992) 24 and nn. 74–5.

easier to slip into over-magnification of the role of *dēmokratia* in the spectrum of ancient Greek politics, and even into a teleological approach which views it as the culmination of Greek political development. This tendency was exemplified in certain quarters during the recent celebrations of the 2,500th anniversary of the 'foundation' of Athenian democracy. The senior editors of one conference volume justified their enterprise on the grounds that 'since the American governmental system was inspired by the *Greek* democratic ideal, it was particularly appropriate that the American School organize a conference in Greece to commemorate . . . the democratic reforms of the *Greek* statesman, Kleisthenes' (our italics).[20] This statement involves two unfortunate misrepresentations: first, an exaggeration of ancient Greek and modern democratic connections, in that the American Founding Fathers in fact took their classical inspiration not from Greece but from Rome and were generally dubious that they had much to learn from the tiny republics of antiquity (Hansen 1992: 18; J. T. Roberts 1994: 175–93); secondly, the magnification of Kleisthenes' local Athenian achievement into a broader 'Greek' phenomenon, of which democracy was the ideal.

In reality, attempts to claim the heritage of Athenian *dēmokratia* as a charter for Western liberal democracies fall down because of the vastly different nature of the two kinds of regime. Modern liberal democracies are representative governments—elected oligarchies, as the ancient Greeks might have called them—whose rule is tempered by the selective recognition of individual rights. Athenian *dēmokratia*, in contrast, was a direct democracy in which decisions were made by the voting of citizens who were political equals in mass meetings of the assembly (*ekklēsia*), legislators (*nomothetai*), and judges (*dikastai*). The context of this political system, moreover, was fundamentally alien to modern democratic values. Although the liberty of citizens was a fundamental ideal, membership of the citizen body was restricted by descent group (after 451/0 BC to men whose parents were both Athenian) and by gender. All women were excluded and acquisition of citizenship by naturalization was only rarely possible for resident non-Athenian males.[21] Democratic Athens was also critically dependent upon its exploitation of a large population of chattel slaves.[22] As Robin Osborne has recently remarked, 'Athenian democracy went part and parcel with an Athenian way

---

[20] Coulson *et al.*, *Archaeology*, p. v.

[21] The exclusive nature of Athenian *dēmokratia* was remarked on by David Hume (J. T. Roberts 1994: 159; cf. ch. 12) and has been a central element in recent debates over the relationship between *dēmokratia* and democracy (Meier and Veyne 1988; Hansen 1989a). On *dēmokratia* and women see Slater (1968); duBois (1988); Keuls (1993). On the rarity of citizenship grants to non-Athenians see M. J. Osborne (1981–3), esp. i. 5–6; iii. 204–9, who notes that a large proportion of such grants were made as a token of recognition to high-ranking foreign benefactors—some of them monarchs such as Evagoras of Salamis, discussed in David Braund's chapter—who (were) never expected to move to Athens and actually take up citizen rights.

[22] The connection between the growth of chattel slavery and of Athenian *dēmokratia* was

of life which we would judge illiberal, culturally chauvinist and narrowly restrictive. It was, essentially, the product of a closed society. As such it cannot offer us much of a model for the running of an open society' (Osborne 1994: 57).

Athens in the context of other poleis

The dominance of Athens in modern discourse is all the more misleading when one considers how extremely unrepresentative she was of ancient Greek poleis. Her population was much greater than that of any other polis, leading also to abnormally great military power and the possibility of an unusually expansive foreign policy. Exploitation of her advantages in foreign policy, both militarily and commercially, combined with her native resources (above all the silver mines of Laurion), made her also much the wealthiest Greek state before the rise of Macedon. At the same time the extent of her territory made for a social and political organization of unusual complexity. Sheer size generates statistics which can be misleadingly impressive: ostracism required a quorum of 6,000, several times the population of most Greek states, but in fact this represented the participation of at most 20 per cent of the citizen population.[23] Even so, Athens' financial and human resources (especially the existence of a large and densely concentrated urban population) must greatly have facilitated a system of mass political participation. Not many other cities could have afforded political pay on such a scale, for example (though we should not underestimate Athens' ideological commitment to the system: assembly pay was introduced only in the more straitened circumstances of the fourth century).[24] Finally, democratic Athens was unusual in her relative political stability, since it was not uncommon for cities to oscillate between oligarchy and democracy. The firm commitment of the great majority of Athenian citizens to democracy meant that her two episodes of tyranny were (and perhaps could only have been) brief hiatuses in a smooth democratic continuum, despite the persistence of a minority oligarchic view discussed below by P. J. Rhodes and Robin Lane Fox. Consequently, it is easy for Athenian politics to be interpreted (as the Aristotelian *Athenian Constitution* does) as a gradual and more or less teleo-

---

argued by Finley (1959). On their interrelationship in the functioning of Athenian economy and politics see R. Osborne (1995).

[23] The population of Athens is a notoriously contentious topic: in general, see Hansen (1985), Patterson (1981) for some estimates for the 5th cent., and, recently, Sallares (1991) 51–60, 94–9; Meiggs (1964) 2–3 suggested that the Athenians worked with a notional estimate of 30,000 for the citizen body.

[24] For a brief estimate of the costs of the Athenian system see Hansen (1991) 315–16. Ste Croix (1975) argued that Aristotle implies in the *Politics* that other democracies also provided payment for attendance at the assembly and for other political activity; however, the only specific instances known to him were Rhodes from the 4th cent. BC onwards and Iasus (interestingly, a small polis) in the 3rd cent.

logical evolution towards developed democracy, and then for this model, in
which full popular democracy is the highest constitutional condition, to be
applied to other poleis, which are judged to fall short of this condition to a
greater or lesser degree.

The position in reality was very different. First, the majority of poleis
were fairly small, with a citizen population measured in hundreds rather
than thousands: Plataea in Boeotia, for example, though not unimportant,
could only raise a maximum of around 600 soldiers and will have had a total
population of only a few thousand.[25] The fourth-century Boeotian constitution, in which (excluding Thebes) 16 named communities provided 9,000
infantry and 900 cavalry (*Hell. Oxy.* 16 [19]. 3–4), suggests that Plataea
was not far from the Boeotian norm, Thebes apart. A citizen population
of, say, 750 is also at the high end of the range proposed as typical of the
Greek world by one scholar.[26] Even if numerical estimates of this sort must
inevitably be regarded with caution, since reliable data are so sparse, the
essential point remains, that large and wealthy poleis were relative anoma-
lies among a much greater number of more modest-sized communities with
limited resources.[27] Lack of resources will have circumscribed the options
available to these communities in all kinds of ways, including the cost and
complexity of the political machinery which they could support. The idea
that smaller communities could not sustain more than an oligarchic form of
government and that democracy followed naturally from increased size is
a prominent feature of Aristotle's political thought (*Pol.* 1286^{b}20; 1292^{b}41;
1297^{b}22; 1320^{a}17; cf. Thuc. 6. 39). Our estimation of the reality of a system which from a constitutional viewpoint we might consider an oligarchy
could perhaps be altered by considering the activity of those involved as
'voluntary political service'.[28] At all events, we should not automatically
assume that day-to-day administration and direction of policy by a minority implies crowds of other people protesting at their exclusion. Even in
non-democratic systems, the assembly still met periodically and served to
provide some degree of participation for ordinary citizens, as well as a means
by which information could be conveyed and decisions ratified. At the very
least, assemblies were necessary so that popular opinion could be mobilized
in favour of policies already determined by the minority, an essential process
in small communities where that minority could not avoid daily interaction

[25] In their own territory at the battle of Plataea in 479 BC they fielded about 600 (Hdt. 9.
28. 6). In the Archidamian War their forces, excluding the old and infirm, were about 450
(212 escapers (Thuc. 3. 24. 2), over 200 executed by the Spartans, plus some allowance for
casualties; cf. 2. 78. 3, where the total is rounded down to 400).

[26] Ruschenbusch (1985) estimated that a typical polis had 133–800 citizens living in an area
of 25–100 km.²; he also counted at least 750 poleis in the Greek mainland and the Aegean
alone.   [27] See the important study by Nixon and Price (1990).

[28] Cf. Aristotle, who speaks of *leitourgia* in the politics of earlier times and of holding office
as *leitourgein* (*Pol.* 1279^{a}10–13; 1291^{a}33–8; cf. 1321^{a}33).

with the rest of the community. Hence persuasion and the cultivation of rhetorical ability were an essential part of political leadership from the time of 'Homeric' society onwards (*Il*. 3. 204–24; 9. 53–4, 440–3). While we moderns tend to regard politics as a matter of domination and control, for the Greeks issues of power were often balanced by the need to create a general will to action and consensus within the community. Though Herodotus and Thucydides were writing in the heyday of democratic developments, the essential political distinction for both was between those communities which were ruled by monarchs or tyrants and those which ruled themselves, whatever the precise form of their self-government. Decisions and actions taken by self-governing communities of varying political characteristics are therefore uniformly attributed to 'the Athenians', 'the Corinthians', or 'the Thebans'. Regardless of differences in constitution or in the composition of the decision-making body, the perception is that 'the supreme command resides in "the citizens"'. Hence the fact that decisions of a minority were viewed as embodying the will of the entire community.[29] Only tyranny and the junta-like form of oligarchy called *dynasteia* were excluded from this principle. A polis which wanted to deny responsibility for previous policy could do so only on the grounds that it had been the work of such an extreme regime.[30]

This consensual aspect of Greek political communities tends to be somewhat obscured in certain studies which address citizenship in terms of political 'rights' exercised through bodies such as the assembly and the courts— particularly in the case of Athens, where the great majority of the Athenian male population were citizens in this sense. An alternative approach, which has gained ground in Athenian studies in recent years, lays greater emphasis on the interplay between the public/polis and the private/*oikos* (household) aspects of the community, thereby drawing attention to the function and status of women. When citizenship depends on the mother's descent as well as the father's, women are in an important sense included within the political community, despite their lack of active political rights. We should adopt a similar approach to those not 'fully enfranchised' in poleis ruled by minority regimes. Such men are likely to have perceived themselves as embraced by ethnic self-definitions like 'the Corinthians' by virtue of descent, hereditary residence in and occupation of the land, privileged access to religious and judicial functions, and so on. It is perhaps not surprising

---

[29] For the contrast between ancient and modern views of politics see Murray (1988*b*) 440; for the essential antithesis between autocracy and self-government see Pope (1988) 281–3 (quotation from p. 281).

[30] Cf. the Thebans' argument in 427 that at the time of their support for the Persians their government was neither an oligarchy nor a democracy but a *dynasteia* (Thuc. 3. 62. 3). Similarly, in 395 they excuse their earlier vote for the destruction of Athens on the grounds that it was not the polis which had so voted but merely one man who happened at the time to hold the seat at the council of the Peloponnesian League (Xen. *Hell.* 3. 5. 8).

that our sources, with their particular interest in active politics, especially political conflict, and, (in the case of the philosophers), a perennial concern with who is to be regarded as a true citizen, tend to neglect this outlook.[31]

Secondly, constitutional stability was by no means the norm in classical Greece. Aristotle's extended discussion, in book 5 of the *Politics*, of constitutional change and of techniques for avoiding the dissolution of each form of constitution bears witness to the frequency of the phenomenon. Numerous examples could be adduced. Take the case of fifth-century Samos: in 440 BC the existing constitution was replaced by an Athenian-sponsored democracy, which was itself briefly overthrown by an oligarchic counter-coup and then restored (Thuc. 1. 115–17), but subsequently probably replaced by some sort of oligarchy of landowners at some time before 411, when this oligarchy too was brought down by a democratic uprising (Thuc. 8. 21).[32] Even then some of the former revolutionaries plotted to subvert the new democracy, though this plan was thwarted with Athenian assistance (Thuc. 8. 63. 3, 73. 3–6); this regime, however, lasted only until 404, when it was replaced after Athens' defeat by a narrow oligarchy favourable to Sparta. There is more to such cases than political instability: changes of constitution in the fifth and fourth centuries were usually tied up with foreign-policy issues, since hegemonic powers like Athens and Sparta tended to favour governments friendly to themselves (democracies in the former case, oligarchies in the latter) and would support changes in their interest. By the same token, would-be revolutionaries would look to a strong external power for support; and external support, combined with a protracted rivalry between leagues jockeying for advantage, increased the frequency of coups and the likelihood that they would, at least in the short term, succeed.[33] However, the example of the Samian democrats turned would-be oligarchs should put us on our guard against supposing that all such revolutions were primarily ideologically motivated. The leaders of both tendencies will have come from the leisured élite, and it is not unduly cynical to suggest that those prevented from exercising power under a democracy might be inclined to promote an oligarchy of their own supporters, and vice versa.

Furthermore, the difficulty of determining the nature of the constitution of Samos before the popular uprising of 411 warns us how slippery and malleable constitutional labels could be in antiquity, as now: if it was

---

[31] For a survey of the two approaches to citizenship see Scafuro (1994); Mossé (1979) discusses 'active' and 'passive' citizenship and the theoretical reasons for Aristotle's neglect of the latter.

[32] The nature of the Samian constitution between 439 and 411 is elusive: for recent discussions see Gomme, Andrewes, and Dover (1945–81) v. 44–9 on Thuc. 8. 21; Quinn (1981) ch. 2; Lintott (1982) 101–3, 116–17; Shipley (1987) 112 ff.; Hornblower (1991) on Thuc. 1. 117. 3.

[33] The rise of Thebes as a hegemonic power in the 4th cent. created a much more complex position in which a variety of permutations of external adherence and internal constitutional preference became possible: see James Roy's discussion of affairs in Achaea and Sicyon in the 360s (ch. 18).

an oligarchy, it may well have had a constitutional arrangement similar to democracy; while if it was formally a democracy, it was not democratic enough for the dēmos, the common people. Much depended on who was making the judgement, and from what perspective.[34] In the case of Samos, it was mainly a question of practical ideological positions, of what one party or another considered acceptable. In other cases, however, our judgement can be made difficult through the perceptions of our sources. This is above all true in the case of Aristotle, since he seeks to impose his own typological scheme, shaped by his philosophical outlook and preferences, on the material he presents; and owing to his stature as a thinker, his definitions have proved particularly influential.[35] Andrew Lintott's paper deals with Aristotle's original contribution, the hybrid of democracy and oligarchy which he calls 'polity', showing how fine distinctions could be on such borderlines (if indeed they are meaningful at all). Keith Rutter in his discussion of the Syracusan democracy demonstrates not only the impact of Aristotle's particular constitutional definitions, but also the way in which his use of historical examples may be shaped by his immediate agenda. This case study also brings out well the impact of source outlook on our perceptions: for Thucydides, Syracuse is in some sense a *Doppelgänger* of Athens, the reflection which brings about her downfall in a way that Sparta, her antithesis, cannot. Hence she must resemble (or come to resemble) Athens as a democracy as well as a naval power. Diodorus, our other major source, also calls the post-466 Syracusan constitution a democracy. He too has his own moral agenda, but he is also writing in a later period, the first century BC, when constitutional labels have taken on rather different valuations. By Diodorus' period it was not so much that democracy had been eliminated, as used to be argued: paradoxically, while the beginning of the hellenistic period is usually seen as the end of authentic radical democracy at Athens, it also marks the beginning of a period (down to the coming of the Romans) in which some sort of authentic democracy was the norm for Greek city-states.[36] Such shifts in the application of labels were, however, nothing new. The principle is already neatly expressed in Aristotle's comment—whether true or not—that 'what we now nowadays call "polities" were formerly called democracies' (*Pol.* 1297[b]24–5).

---

[34] On the slipperiness of constitutional labels see Brock (1989).

[35] This is particularly true of studies of democracy: good recent examples are O'Neil (1995) and E. W. Robinson (1997). For the impact of Aristotle's outlook on his account of Sparta see Schütrumpf (1994).

[36] See Gauthier (1993), esp. 217–25, and Gruen (1993); this is also the underlying theme of Rhodes with Lewis (1997), esp. 531–6.

Constitutional diversity

We need to bear in mind both the difficulty of reliable definition and the impact of the Athenian outlook and agenda when we examine the range of constitutions found in classical Greece. In the case of democracy, the Athenian model can be particularly unhelpful, and we should be wary of assuming that it is to be inferred wherever we hear of a democracy. It is certainly true that Athens 'exported' democracy in the period of her fifth-century empire, and that she acted as a model for other democracies, not all of them her subjects (Lewis 1997: 51–9). Yet even the Athenians were aware that their model would not work everywhere without modification. When in the mid-fifth century they imposed a democratic regime on Erythrae, they made concessions not only to a smaller population, establishing a council of 120 rather than 500, but also to a less widespread commitment to participation throughout the citizen body by allowing individuals to serve (perhaps unpaid) one year in four, whereas Athenians were limited to twice a lifetime.[37] Likewise, poleis might share the same ideology, yet arrive at different mechanisms. One perennial concern of democracies was control of the executive, including those who presided over the assembly, to prevent them from gaining a position of authority. At Athens this was achieved by stipulating that no citizen could preside over the assembly for more than one day in his life; at Corcyra, on the other hand, the same safeguard was put in place by dividing responsibility for presiding between two boards of officials who could act as mutual checks. Similarly, Athens subjected its magistrates to a process of strict accountability, but it did not require them to lay down office at the end of their year's term on pain of death, as fourth-century Boeotia did to its Boeotarchs (O'Neil 1995: 33, 92).

Certainly, there were numerous other democracies, even if an Athenian might have disputed the claim of some to the title.[38] On the other hand, we should be cautious about seeing democracy everywhere. Although it is tempting to argue that whenever we find a citizen assembly or decrees of the people or dēmos there is a democracy, such an approach can be misleading. Much depends on the regularity and frequency with which the assembly meets, whether it debates motions or simply approves them, whether initiative rests only with officials or with any citizen, whether proposals or amendments can be made from the floor of the assembly, and on other details of procedure.[39] It is easy to be misled by the formal aspects of a constitution, particularly if it is not of a radical type. We should equally bear in mind how it operated in practice, and where power lay. Sparta of-

[37] ML 40; cf. Rhodes (1992) 93–4.
[38] There is a useful list of democracies mentioned by Aristotle in *CPC Acts* 5: 190 n. 548.
[39] Rhodes with Lewis (1997) pt. III. Note also Aristotle's recommendation in *Pol.* 1298^{b}32–3 that, as an aid to constitutional stability, oligarchic assemblies be allowed to pass only motions identical to, or compatible with, motions brought before them.

fers an excellent example: formally, since she had kings, she ought to have been seen as a monarchy (or rather a dyarchy), and it was possible, if mildly paradoxical, to describe her as a democracy (Isoc. 7. 60–1; 12. 178); but any close examination of Sparta in action could hardly fail to identify her as an oligarchy.[40]

As far as Athenian ideology was concerned, the antithesis of democracy was tyranny.[41] This was largely the product of their historical experience in being freed from tyranny rather later than many of their neighbours, and then having been threatened with its return under first Spartan and then Persian sponsorship. As a result, the bulk of our source material is extremely hostile to tyranny and tends to conceal the benefits for which it had in many cases been responsible (J. B. Salmon 1997). Modern scholarship avoids this pitfall, but frequently treats tyranny as a transitional political phase belonging to the archaic period which facilitated the change to constitutional government, whether of the few or the many, and which lingered thereafter only in fringe or backward areas of the Greek world. Indeed, the same attitude is often applied to monarchy in general.[42] This marginalization of monarchy and tyranny, however, produces a somewhat distorted perspective on Greek politics. It is true that one-man rule often flourished in areas with a less firmly rooted tradition of constitutional government and, in the case of Sicily in particular, of settlement and citizenship—an issue discussed in this volume by Kathryn Lomas. The striking resurgence which monarchy enjoys in the fourth century is, however, surely principally the product of its efficacy in providing strong leadership, above all military leadership, in states which were threatened by their neighbours and/or which had hitherto been unable to have much impact on affairs beyond their borders. Dionysius I at Syracuse, Philip II in Macedon, and Jason of Pherai in Thessaly are leading examples; but it is tempting to see the affection of the dēmos of Sicyon for their tyrant Euphron (whom, after his assassination, they buried in the agora of their city like a founder) as engendered by his success in freeing them from a Spartan-sponsored oligarchy.[43] Sicyon, on the north coast of the Peloponnese, was hardly a fringe area. Similar factors may lie

---

[40] Ste Croix (1972) 124–51 is a classic example of this pragmatic approach to the Spartan constitution; cf. also Andrewes (1966). We should remember, too, how much political influence could be derived from other elements of the state, especially religious ones. Aristotle has acute observations on possible disparity between the formal and practical character of constitutions (*Pol.* 1292^{b}11–21).

[41] Eur. *Supp.* 429–55 is an archetypal statement; there is also clear Athenian influence in the speech of Otanes at Hdt. 3. 80.

[42] It could be argued that the distinction between the unconstitutional tyrant and constitutional monarch is something of a red herring, since even notionally constitutional kings like the later rulers of Cyrene had in practice to reconsolidate their power and behave in a distinctly autocratic manner, as Barbara Mitchell demonstrates in her contribution.

[43] On the efficacy of 4th-cent. monarchy see Davies (1993) ch. 13. For Euphron see James Roy's discussion in this volume and Mossé (1969) 125–8.

behind the crop of tyrants in the later fourth century in Euboea, an island
sandwiched between the hegemonial powers of Athens and Thebes; to be
sure, a number of them were sponsored by Macedon as part of Philip's
intrigues against Athens;[44] but that does not fully explain why there should
have been such a series of them. Moreover, Callias of Chalcis, who finally
united the island under his leadership, was a strikingly non-aligned figure.
Again, as Barbara Mitchell's paper shows, the resilience of monarchy in
Cyrene owed much to Persian sponsorship, but the fact that monarchy was
congenial to the neighbouring Libyans and the absence of a hoplite peasantry were also significant factors. Finally, although some fourth-century
monarchs were undoubtedly opportunists, as Davies (1993) styles them—
Dionysius I is perhaps the best example—many of them began their careers
from an orthodox constitutional position (Philip as king, Jason as *tagos*; the
position of Mausolus in Caria was also hereditary), the potential of which
they then developed.

Despite Athenian abhorrence of monarchs in theory, their relationship
with the reality was much more complex, something David Braund explores
in his contribution. Monarchy was part of the city's past on a mythological
level, an era annually re-examined in drama. It was also a feature of the
real world in both the fifth and fourth centuries, and one of which imperial
Athens needed to take advantage. In the fifth century Athens was allied to
Echekratides, *tagos* of Thessaly, and made an abortive attempt to restore
his exiled son Orestes (Thuc. 1. 111); she also co-operated closely with
Perdiccas and Archelaos of Macedon (*SEG* x. 86; ML 91). In the fourth
century she courted Dionysius I and enjoyed an enduring relationship with
the Spartocids, hereditary rulers of the Bosporan kingdom in the Black
Sea. Her involvement with the royal house of the Molossians is discussed
in this volume by John Davies. Athenian writers found it hard to ignore
the resurgence of monarchy in the fourth century: witness Plato's critical
engagement with the king of Persia following his successful interference in
Greek affairs in the Peace of Antalcidas (*Rep.* 553 C–D, *Laws* 694 A–695 E; cf.
his theoretical interest in monarchy in the *Politicus*); Isocrates' encomium
of Evagoras of Salamis and his orations and letters addressed to various
sole rulers, including Dionysius, Philip, and Alexander; and Demosthenes'
ambivalent presentation of the strengths and weaknesses of Philip's position
in the *Olynthiacs*.

Monarchy, then, remained an effective and appropriate constitutional option for a significant part of the Greek world, rather than existing merely as
a theoretical possibility or, in the form of tyranny, as the ideological antithesis of democracy for the Athenians. Nevertheless, both for the Athenians
and in many other parts of Greece, oligarchy was the practical alternative

---

[44] Although, as Berve notes (1967: 300–3), the dominance of Athenian orators among our
sources presents problems of definition.

to democracy. The antithesis between the rule of the few and the rule of the many runs throughout Thucydides' accounts and analysis of political activity in the later fifth century. Likewise, Aristotle observes that it is commonly supposed that there are only two constitutions, democracy and oligarchy, and that this is in practice generally the case (*Pol.* 1290^{a}13–19; 1301^{b}39–1302^{a}2). In reality, though, the simple label 'oligarchy' covers a remarkable diversity of political organization, united only by the restriction of active participants to some fraction—usually though not necessarily a minority—of the total citizen population. The restriction which delimited the enfranchised citizens could be based on a variety of factors. Wealth is the one which particularly preoccupies Aristotle, and which he considers more fundamental even than the issue of numbers (esp. *Pol.* 1279^{b}11–1280^{a}6). It normally took the form of a property qualification, though not necessarily a very high one: Aristotle recommends 'index-linking' the requirement as a means of preserving oligarchies.[45] Ancestry (whether real or invented) was equally significant: many cities, especially in the archaic period, were ruled by a hereditary oligarchy composed of a group of families, such as the Eupatrids (the 'well-born') in Athens before Solon, or a single family like the Bacchiads of Corinth or the Penthelidai at Mytilene; while in colonial cities descendants of the original settlers naturally tended to occupy a privileged position.[46] In the cases mentioned above the chosen family or families formed the deliberative body and the pool of candidates for office; but in others, as for a time at Massalia described below, each family was represented by the head of the household alone.

In practice, of course, wealth and birth often went together, though that was not inevitable. Indeed, Hans van Wees in his contribution to this volume argues from the evidence of the poetry of Theognis that in archaic Megara, often supposed to be ruled by an embattled hereditary aristocracy, the exercise of power was dependent simply on possession of wealth ('timocracy'), often acquired illegitimately by violent means. Other bases for limitation were also possible. One method was to impose a numerical limit: the figure 1,000 crops up with some regularity, though lower numbers are also attested.[47] Another was to restrict the franchise to those who defended the state by serving as hoplites or cavalrymen, a *de facto* property quali-

---

[45] Our sources usually fail to distinguish between land and other forms of wealth, though Aristotle sometimes explicitly discusses landholding, which in practice will have been the major source of income in most cases. According to Aristotle (*Pol.* 1319^{a}14–19), Aphytis, in Chalkidike, subdivided landholdings so as to enfranchise everyone. For oligarchies based on land, see Whibley (1896) 111–15; on wealth in general, ibid. 126–32. For 'index-linking' see Arist. *Pol.* 1308^{a}35–^{b}9; cf. 1306^{b}6–16.

[46] Aristotle identifies hereditary oligarchy as one of his four types of oligarchy (*Pol.* 1292^{b}3–4; 1293^{a}28–30).

[47] 1,000: (e.g.) Opuntian and Epizephyrian Locri, Croton, Rhegium, and Colophon; lower figures: 600 at Massalia and 180 at Epidaurus, for example (Whibley 1896: 134–8); cf. also Rhodes with Lewis (1997) 510–12 on the related issue of quorums.

fication, though one which acknowledged the value of wealth to the state. This motif of 'service with persons and property' was very much to the fore in the Athenian oligarchic coup of 411 (*Ath. Pol.* 29. 5; Thuc. 8. 65. 3). Of course, it was possible to combine more than one principle (besides birth and wealth). At Massalia power was restricted to 300 families, each represented in early times by its head, thereby also reflecting the oligarchic preference for higher age in office-holders.[48] The Athenian oligarchs who seized power in 411 attempted to combine an inclusive hoplite-based constitution with an exclusive numerical limit ('the Five Thousand'), but ran into difficulties since the number of hoplites eligible for the franchise greatly exceeded that limit. In the later oligarchy of 404 a simpler (and lower) numerical limit of 3,000 was deployed instead. Finally, the restriction might sometimes be based not on structural criteria such as those already considered but on contingent historical circumstance. At Megara, for example, only those who had taken part in the (probably mid-sixth-century) oligarchic coup were eligible for office, a criterion based upon participation in group violence which was highly appropriate in the Mafioso-like society described by van Wees.[49]

It would be easy to take a cynical view and suggest that oligarchy had no ideological basis beyond the concern of those exercising power to retain it. Certainly, for anyone taking a pragmatic rather than a strictly moral view, it is hard to perceive any palpable distinction between oligarchy and aristocracy. Analytically, the former term is perhaps best regarded as a functional description, the latter as a persuasive definition. The formulation of Megabyzos, advocate of aristocracy in Herodotus' 'Persian debate' (3. 81. 3), is revealing: 'let us select a gathering of the best men and entrust power to them, for we ourselves shall be among them'. Indeed, Aristotle appears to treat aristocracy mainly as a theoretical option, and notes at one point that it is quite possible for the dēmos *en masse* to be better (and richer) than the few (*Pol.* 1283^b33-5).[50] It is true that the exercise of power is part of the

---

[48] Whibley (1896) 148–9; the select body at Sparta was called *gerousia* (council of elders), comprising 28 men aged 60 or over, plus the two kings. After agitation at Massalia, however, other family members were admitted to participation (Arist. *Pol.* 1305^b2-10).

[49] Megarian coup: Arist. *Pol.* 1300^a16-19 with 1304^b34-9; for the date see E. W. Robinson (1997) 114–17, Lane Fox and van Wees (below, pp. 37–44 and 52 n. 2). On all the varieties of oligarchy see Whibley (1896) ch. 4, still the standard text after a century. On fixed number at Athens see Brock (1989).

[50] Aristotle seems to concede up to a point the claims of Sparta and Carthage that their use of election for office reflects a concern to select the best men (1293^b7-18)—though he is famously scathing about the Spartan mechanism of election—while remaining clear that they are oligarchic in operation (and Sparta formally a mixed constitution: 1294^b18-34). Matters are further complicated by the proximity of aristocracy to 'polity' in his constitutional schema (on which see Andrew Lintott's contribution) and by an ambiguous definition which also embraces constitutions directed towards what is best for the state and its members (1279^a35-7). In that sense, even Athenian democracy could be presented (albeit tendentiously) as *aristokratia* (Pl. *Menex.* 238 c–d; Isoc. 12. 131).

aristocratic ideal, but it is not coextensive with it: minority regimes must often have excluded men who considered themselves in social and economic terms among the *kaloi k'agathoi* ('handsome and good', i.e. gentlemen) or *aristoi* ('the best people'). Theognis at Megara is a case in point. We can see in his poetry that, even when they were excluded from power, especially by those they considered their inferiors, the self-perceptions of such *aristoi* did not alter. As Robin Lane Fox and P. J. Rhodes both demonstrate, those who considered themselves among the *aristoi* did not abandon their ideology even when compelled to live under a democracy. However, competitiveness was also part of the aristocratic ideal, hence the fact that, as Aristotle notes, oligarchies are especially prone to faction (*Pol.* 1305^{b}22–1306^{b}5; cf. Hdt. 3. 82. 3; Thuc. 8. 89. 3), a phenomenon of which the collapse of the rule of the Four Hundred at Athens and the career of Alcaeus furnish familiar examples. The former is discussed here by Rhodes, while Nigel Spencer analyses the disintegration of the aristocratic oligarchy of Mytilene brought about by the influx of wealth from foreign ventures.

This is not to say that there was no such thing as oligarchic ideology. Indeed, in its original form it was very much concerned precisely with personal excellence and success, since it seems to have focused on the character or quality of those participating in politics. This embraced not only one's personal qualities but also a desire for the approbation of, and success in competition against, one's peers. Hence the importance to such men of election, rather than the democratic random choice of the lot—which opponents of democracy ridiculed as just as likely to pick out an enemy of the dēmos as a friend (Xen. *Mem.* 1. 2. 9; *Dissoi Logoi* 7. 5; Isoc. 7. 23).[51] In the later fifth century, perhaps in response to the development of a democratic ideology which made use of abstract ideals, the rule of the few came to be justified in more general terms centred on their other common characteristic: wealth. The claim took two forms: that the rich were more capable and trustworthy stewards of public affairs and assets; and that they were entitled to a greater share in political power because of their greater contribution to the commonwealth—the idea of 'proportional equality'.[52] The argument from contribution to the state also of course underlay hoplite or military oligarchies, as noted above.

Oligarchies could also offer the attractions of greater efficiency, especially for smaller and less prosperous states. Unhindered by democratic concerns about control of delegated authority, they could assign multiple administrative roles to the same individual (Arist. *Pol.* 1299^{a}31–^{b}30; 1321^{b}8–12)

---

[51] Cf. Xen. *Hell.* 2. 3. 25 for the oppressiveness of democracy for such people, and Thuc. 8. 89. 3 on the capacity of oligarchs to laugh off even defeat in democratic elections because it was not at the hands of their peers. Nevertheless, many of the Athenian élite clearly opted out of democratic politics: L. B. Carter (1986) chs. 1–3.

[52] For 'proportional equality' see Harvey (1965–6); for *isonomia* ('political equality') in oligarchic ideology see Cartledge (2000); for the battle of ideology see Brock (1991).

and be more relaxed about iteration, or even life tenure, which—it could be argued—allowed poleis to retain competent men in office and benefit from the expertise they had acquired, something Athenian democracy regarded as potentially dangerous. In practice, too, peer pressure among a competitive élite probably served as an effective substitute for the more formal mechanism of scrutiny and accountability imposed by democracies. Competence and expertise were considerations which even democratic Athens acknowledged in permitting the re-election of generals and, in the fourth century, financial administrators (at least *de facto*). As already noted, the claim to be the best managers of money was also part of the oligarchic claim (Thuc. 6. 39. 1), although it would have been naïve to regard the wealthy as less prone to corruption, despite Theramenes' snide reference to the dēmos as 'those who would sell the state for a drachma' (Xen. *Hell.* 2. 3. 48). More to the point, the wealthy had assets which could temporarily cover or guarantee state needs, and which could be distrained upon in case of conviction for embezzlement. Even democratic Athens appointed the Treasurers of Athena from the highest property class (*Ath. Pol.* 8. 1; 47. 1). It was probably also easier for oligarchies to do away with parts of the administrative mechanism and so simplify it: small states could make do without a council—as oligarchic Cnidos did in the fourth and third centuries BC—and indeed in extreme cases, according to Aristotle, without a regular assembly.[53] Even large oligarchic states tended to operate with small bodies: the council at Corinth numbered eighty (ten men per tribe), the *gerousia* at Sparta a mere thirty. It is a common and not unreasonable perception that smaller decision-making bodies are more effective. A willingness to serve without payment or profit was, as we have already noted, also an attraction (cf. Arist. *Pol.* 1308^{b}31–1309^{a}14); indeed, Aristotle counsels that oligarchic magistrates should be seen to incur expense (1321^{a}33). In contrast, as noted above, the Athenian democratic system was expensive; hence the fact that in the straitened circumstances of the late Peloponnesian War restriction of pay for political activity was an important aspect of the oligarchic programme of 411 (*Ath. Pol.* 29. 5; 30. 6).

In a limited space we cannot do more than sketch a little of the constitutional variety in which classical Greece abounded, but the foregoing should serve to demonstrate the diversity which existed within the broad constitutional labels, and the possibility of change, whether gradual or sud-

[53] Rhodes with Lewis (1997) 330; Arist. *Pol.* 1275^{b}7–8; Plutarch (*Dion* 53. 4) claims that Corinth made little use of her assembly in the 4th cent., and there is no mention of assemblies in the account in the *Hellenica Oxyrhynchia* (19. 2–4 in Chambers's numeration) of constitutional arrangements in federal Boeotia *c*.395 BC. Some sort of probouleutic body was the norm for all Greek states, and the evidence is much too fragmentary to establish any general principle behind the (apparent) presence or absence of councils in documents: community size and expense may have been more significant factors than ideology (Rhodes with Lewis 1997: 475–8).

den, within both democracy and oligarchy, as well as between them, and hence across a broad spectrum of constitutional options. These are points on which Aristotle is most emphatic,[54] and the examples he cites are more than adequate to justify him. As his analysis indicates, there was throughout Greek history a fluctuating balance between ideological consciousness and pragmatism, and between structural and contingent factors, in the choices and alterations which Greek communities made regarding their political systems. Radical change at the state level could be precipitated not only by ideological concerns but also by personal ones, often financial, familial, or sexual: the fifth book of the *Politics* contains a rich selection of examples. The implication for modern views of the Greek polis is that we should abandon the angle of vision in which classical Athenian *dēmokratia* appears as the central point of Greek political experience for a perspective which sees it within a much broader context—a context very unlike the present-day ideological dominance of liberal democracy in which a range of political regimes could lay claim to legitimacy both as viable systems in their own right and as potential models for imitation by their neighbours.

Communities other than the polis: ethnē and ethnos-states

Besides a plurality of constitutional patterns within the polis, Greek anti-quity also possessed various different kinds of communities, of which the polis was only one form.[55] One important form of community was the eth-nos (plural, ethnē), which features in the second part of this volume. In terms of geographical area, an ethnos typically embraced a broad region of Greece such as those studied in this volume, Achaea, Arcadia, Macedonia, Thessaly. Indeed, ethnē covered a large part of the northern and central Peloponnese, and the bulk of the central and northern Greek mainland.[56] Yet 'in many studies of ancient Greece the ethnos is almost ignored, either as being an embarrassing legacy of a more primitive era, or . . . because its contribution to the great intellectual revolution of the fifth century seems so marginal when compared to that of the polis' (Snodgrass 1980: 42). When considered at all, ethnē have often been addressed by default in studies focused mainly on the polis (e.g. Sakellariou 1989) and defined in terms of

---

[54] Variety: *Pol.* 1289ᵃ8–11; 1316ᵇ25–7 (and cf. the typologies of oligarchy and democracy in 4. 5–6); change: 1301ᵇ6–17; 1306ᵇ17–21.

[55] John Davies has recently recommended use of the term 'microstate' in place of 'polis', to direct attention towards the full range of ancient Greek polities (Davies 1997: 27).

[56] In addition, there were geographically dispersed ethnē or pseudo-ethnē, such as the Dorians and Ionians, which, as R. Parker has reminded us (1998: 19), were viewed by con-temporaries in the same terms as ethnē located in particular regions. One sign of this attitude is the inclusion of the Ionians and Dorians (the latter separated into two geographically based groups, one from the metropolis, the other from the Peloponnese: cf. the inscriptions cited by Daux 1957: 108–11) among the ethnē represented within the Delphic amphiktyony (on which see further below).

contrasting negatives to the polis: as primitive, 'tribal', pre-polis forms of organization, suited to societies settled in homesteads or villages rather than cities, and marked by only a limited range of collective functions (Ehrenberg 1960: 24–5). This approach perpetuates in many respects the distorted perspective of those classical polis-centred writers who viewed ethnē as inferior types of communities, characteristic of less developed parts of Greece which were not yet split up into poleis but settled by villages (e.g. Thuc. 3. 94; Arist. *Pol.* 1261ª28; cf. Hansen 1997a: 11–12). Alternatively, those modern studies which have taken non-polis communities more seriously have generally viewed ethnē in terms of conditions in the later classical and hellenistic periods, when a number of them had been transformed into confederacies (on which see below) which challenged the political and military dominance of the leading poleis. Even among these studies the tendency has been to search for the roots of these confederacies in earlier times and to infer that already in these early periods ethnē were a distinct, though relatively undeveloped, form of state organization, alternative to the polis, often referred to as 'tribal states'.[57]

In recent years a growing body of work by a number of archaeologists and historians, including contributors to this volume, has done much to rescue ethnē from the worst excesses of such stultifying images.[58] Early Greek ethnē are nowadays increasingly viewed, not as a form of state alternative to the polis, but rather as a different tier of identity (cf. J. M. Hall 1997) which could coexist with the presence of various types of local communities, including poleis. The constituent communities of ethnē varied in character both in different periods and from region to region; but polis communities could develop and exist within ethnē without any necessary lessening of their affiliation to a common ethnic or regional identity. For some poleis, indeed, ethnic identity was not just single but multiform. Many of the smaller poleis of classical Arcadia, such as Gortys, Oresthasion, and Trapezus, acknowledged not only their identity as Arcadians but also a narrower ethnic identity as—respectively—Kynourians, Mainalians, and Parrhasians (Nielsen 1996a; Roy 1996). Far from being primitive or simple political organisms, therefore, ethnē were complex, multi-layered

---

[57] e.g. Larsen (1968) 4–7, who also postulates the existence of earlier monarchic or confederate governments within several ethnē in which confederacies are later attested in historical times (ibid. 12–13, 28, 44, 83).

[58] The study of ethnē has been transformed in particular by the impact of extensive recent excavation and survey by Greek and Bulgarian archaeologists: see e.g. the research reported in Rizakis (1991) on the northern and central Peloponnese; in the 1992 *Praktika* and 1994 *Thessalia* colloquia on Thessaly; in Bouzek, Domaradzki, and Archibald (1996) and in the 1997 *Archaia Thrake* colloquium on Thrace; and in *AEMTh*, the journal of record for excavations in northern Greece (with summaries in English and French). For recent synthetic discussions of particular regions see e.g. Archibald (1998); Blum *et al.* (1992); Flensted-Jensen (1995); Hatzopoulos (1996); Helly (1995); McInerney (1995); Morgan and Hall (1996); Nielsen (1996a, b, c; 1997; 1999); Nielsen and Roy (1999); Rizakis (1995); Roy (1996). General discussions can be found in J. M. Hall (1997); Morgan (1991; 1997; 2001).

entities which constituted, as Zosia Archibald argues in her contribution, not so much an alternative *mode* of organization to the polis as a different *plane* of organization in which 'the state entity was a complex web of social groups, cities, and other settlements'. It is hardly surprising that, contrary to traditional perceptions, such complex social formations were often at the forefront of early Greek socio-political developments—for example, in developments at religious sanctuaries and in the growth of urban centres (Morgan 1997; 2001). The development of ethnē was, however, by no means uniform in time across the whole of Greece: in some regions ethnē become evident at an early date; in others regional identity is first attested only in later times. Despite much common ground in recent scholarship, views also differ regarding both the period when strong regional power structures first developed in the more politically precocious ethnē and the criteria by which such developments can be detected in the archaeological record. (These differences are evidenced to a certain extent in this volume in the respective contributions of Zosia Archibald and Catherine Morgan.) It is clear, however, that in some regions, such as Achaea and Arcadia, ethnic identities existed for significant periods before the creation of regional political organizations in the late fifth and early fourth centuries, respectively (Morgan and Hall 1996: 193–9; Nielsen 1996*b*). In other cases, such as that of the Triphylians of the western Peloponnese in the early fourth century, the creation of an ethnic identity and a regional confederacy took place side by side within a very short period of time, driven in the Triphylian case by the need for unity in maintaining their recent liberation from Elis (Nielsen 1997). The development of confederacies, moreover, took place at different times in different ethnē, and was by no means irreversible. The classical Achaean confederacy was dissolved some time in the fourth century before its revival in 281/0. The Arcadian confederacy of the 360s, as James Roy indicates in his paper, soon split apart into two hostile camps and probably ceased existence altogether after 324/3, but without any alteration in the common ethnic identity felt by members of its politically divided communities. Indeed, for the vast bulk of their history the Arcadians were an ethnos, possessing a strong common identity, without being an ethnos-state (Nielsen 1999).

In her contribution to the volume Catherine Morgan, one of the leading exponents of newer approaches to the study of ethnē, considers, through a case study of the early Achaean ethnos in the north-western Peloponnese, another aspect of early Greek development normally treated only from a polis perspective: the relationship between cities (or, more neutrally, large nucleated settlements) and the growth of complex political relations. Big sites, she notes, are found in ethnē as well as poleis; but extent of urbanization, she insists, is not a necessary indicator of political development. The constituent areas of the early Achaean ethnos exhibit considerable diversity in their degree of settlement nucleation; yet the archaeological record evinces signs of highly structured socio-political relationships and of drastic organizational change in the Pharai valley, in which major settlement centres were comparatively slow to develop.

The presence of large population centres is also noted by Zosia Archibald in her comparative study of ethnē in archaic and classical Macedonia, Thessaly and Thrace.[59] In contrast to Achaea, strong regional power structures developed, in her view, in all three regions—even in non-monarchic Thessaly—at comparatively early dates. Her study accordingly poses the central issue of the relationship between regional authority and urban centres. The existence of civic officials in fourth- and third-century Thessaly and Macedonia is attested by an increasing quantity of epigraphic evidence. For earlier periods the main available evidence comes from archaeological survey, which presents the challenge and opportunity of examining long-term developments in the relationship between settlement histories, the use of space, and political organization. The longevity of many bigger and smaller sites in Macedonia and Thessaly suggests, she argues, that, far from the traditional image of ethnē as loose-knit societies, these were states in which the regional and civic identity and institutions evident in later periods were developing strongly and in parallel from an early date.

These studies of ethnē in earlier periods are complemented by John Davies' essay on the development of the previously little-studied Molossian/ Epeirote ethnos in north-western Greece during the late fifth and fourth centuries. A body of new epigraphic documentation is utilized to construct a fascinating picture of a state and society undergoing a sustained phase of political and territorial transformation, as the Molossian polity engaged in the process of incorporating other Epeirote ethnē. As Davies shows, despite its 'barbarian' image in the minds of Athenian writers, the Molossian polity in the late classical period exhibits important parallels with the history of certain Greek poleis—especially with the cases of Cyrene (as discussed in this volume by Barbara Mitchell) and of Sparta—in the functioning of a 'constitutional' and contractual kingship within a *politeia* marked by a defined citizenship, with all the tensions over their respective powers to which that combination frequently gave rise. Yet there are equally parallels with other ethnē: in the existence of local governing bodies as in Macedon and, evidently therefore, of structured local relationships in a largely pre-urban context, as already noted for archaic Achaea; in the comparability of the stories of Greek origins of the Molossian and Macedonian royal houses; and in the similarity of their expansionist activities in the classical period.

The question of Macedonian kingship is addressed in this volume by Pierre Carlier. Older interpretations have often assimilated Macedonian kingship to the 'traditional' Greek kingship of the Homeric poems. In

---

[59] On the last of which see, more fully, Archibald (1998).

parallel with 'tribal' interpretations of Greek ethnē, some have viewed both Macedonian and Homeric kings as tribal military leaders. The Homeric situation, Carlier argues, can illuminate certain Macedonian phenomena, such as the coexistence of kingship with well-entrenched poleis and civic institutions. Yet, although Macedonian kings in the classical period were not absolute monarchs, they enjoyed considerably more autocratic powers than did Homeric kings, or indeed the kings of neighbouring Molossia. These powers, Carlier suggests, were not present *ab initio* but developed owing to a number of factors particular to Macedonian society and history. In this important respect Macedonian political evolution under the Temenid kings diverged significantly from that of the poleis of southern Greece, although certain elements of constitutionality did later take hold during the Antigonid monarchy of the hellenistic period. Once again we are reminded that ethnē, far from their traditional static image, were dynamic polities whose histories present a complex and varying amalgam of continuity and change which, in spite of certain common institutional factors, often led to widely divergent political outcomes. Among ethnē, as among poleis, there was no single dominant trend.

It is now widely recognized that Greek political developments must be viewed in the broader context of parallel developments in other regions of the Mediterranean. Hence the final paper in this section concerns a non-Greek people, the Lycians of southern Anatolia, who were subjects of the Persian empire. Antony Keen's analysis of Lycian political formations in the late archaic and classical periods indicates several parallels to the bipartite regional/local structure of several Greek ethnē.[60] In terms of identity, there is a marked preference for use of the regional Lycian ethnic, but evidence also for the use of local ethnics. In terms of settlement, the region as a whole contained a number of significant population centres, some of which minted their own coinage. In terms of political structure, there are clear signs of a dominant regional dynast, probably based on the town of Xanthos, but also indications of lesser dynasts who issued coins in their own names or were buried in monumental pillar or hērōon-type tombs.

Amphiktyonies and confederacies

Ethnic affiliations were also linked to other political formations in which individual communities bonded together in common association, some of which are considered in the last four chapters of the volume. One form of association was the amphiktyony, a grouping of independent communities around a common sanctuary. The late George Forrest's paper assembles a tantalizing, albeit fragmentary, range of evidence which suggests the prevalence of such associations among the embryonic poleis of archaic Greece.

---

[60] For a more detailed analysis see Keen (1998).

He argues that the activities of these amphiktyonies were from the start political (and military) as well as religious, but notes that an essential point was the location of the common sanctuary in a neutral setting away from the territory of the amphiktyony's most powerful members. A certain connection between these associations and ethnē is evident from the fact that some of these amphiktyonies, such as the Dorian hexapolis and the Panionian league, were based upon ethnic affiliation and that common cult (though not always one single cult) was also a prime vehicle for the shared identity of most ethnē. Nevertheless, unlike the ethnē considered earlier, the significance and coherence of most of these early groupings appear to have declined with the growing crystallization of the polis institutions of their constituent members.

One amphiktyony, however, which originated around the sanctuary of Demeter at Anthela near Thermopylae and later extended its orbit to embrace the panhellenic sanctuary of Apollo at Delphi, did become of increasing importance during the Classical period. Unusually, its membership was structured neither around individual poleis nor around a common ethnic identity but on the basis of the representation of several different ethnē, mainly from central Greece (Daux 1957). During the fifth and fourth centuries the amphiktyons increasingly came to exploit the importance of the Delphic sanctuary as a means of intervening in external affairs. In return, the amphiktyony was itself visited with increasing efforts at control by outside powers which manipulated its guardianship of the sanctuary for their own purposes. The amphiktyony's close involvement in some of the most significant political developments of the fourth century, including the rise of Macedon, is well known to students of Greek history. In the midst of this political maelstrom lay the tiny polis of Delphi, situated close by the sanctuary, whose relationship to the amphiktyony in the 330s and 320s BC is the subject of Michael Arnush's contribution. Through close examination of a neglected class of inscriptions, the proxeny decrees, he charts the changing rhythms of the Delphians' policy, sometimes sounding their own melody, but more often in harmony with that of the amphiktyony, as both polis and amphiktyony together played an increasingly anti-Macedonian and pro-Aetolian political tune. This mutual accord stemmed, as he notes, from Delphi's position as a self-governing polis, but one thoroughly implicated in the amphiktyony's affairs as permanent member of its biannual council (*synedrion*), local administrator of its finances, and supplier of the sanctuary's administrative officials.

Other forms of association between individual states were also of major importance at various periods of Greek history. One long-standing form of multi-state political organization, the hegemonic *symmachia*, or military alliance (often translated as 'league') dominated by its leading power, has been much studied by historians. Its first incarnation was in the form of the 'Pelo-

ponnesian League' (more properly, 'the Lakedaimonians and their allies'),
dominated by Sparta between the mid-sixth and mid-fourth centuries,
followed by Athens' development of the fifth-century 'Delian League'/
Athenian empire and the fourth-century 'Second Athenian League'. Like
the amphiktyonies, these major hegemonic *symmachiai* typically possessed
a common council (of varying degrees of political influence *vis-à-vis* the
hēgemōn) which was attended by delegates from their member states, although not always by the league *hēgemōn*. Besides these major alliances,
which dominate the history books on ancient Greece, there existed at different times and places a considerable number of smaller hegemonic *symmachiai* (whose institutional procedures, however, were not necessarily as
developed or consultative in character as those already mentioned). There
is evidence for at least three different small-scale hegemonic *symmachiai*
during the classical period within the region of Arcadia alone (Nielsen
1996c: 79–87).

There was, however, another form of association which involved an altogether closer form of mutual co-operation. This was what an eminent
modern comparative political scientist (a former Manchester Professor of
Government)[61] has called the 'second great political innovation' of ancient
Greece: the 'confederation' or 'confederacy', often—perhaps somewhat
inaccurately—referred to as the 'federal league' or 'federal state'.[62] These
confederacies most frequently arose in ethnē, although their constituent
members were most often poleis—a further indication of the compatibil-
ity of local polis status with recognition of a common regional identity.
Notwithstanding misguided attempts to read confederacies back into the
earliest periods of Greek history, they nevertheless had a long and distinguished history, commencing (probably) in the late sixth century in Boeotia.

[61] The late S. E. Finer, Professor of Government at the University of Manchester 1966–74;
subsequently Gladstone Professor of Government and Public Administration at Oxford.

[62] Finer (1997) i. 317. Finer disallows use of the term 'federal' for ancient Greek confederacies, with specific comment on the inadequacy of Larsen's oft-cited definition of a federal
state as one 'in which there is a local citizenship in the smaller communities as well as a joint or
federal citizenship and in which the citizens are under the jurisdiction of both the federal and
local authorities' (1968: xiv–xv). He argues that federalism is a juristic concept, one of whose
essential characteristics (as understood by political scientists since the 1787 constitution of the
United States) is that the federal and local authority 'each formulates and executes its decisions
through its own organs neither of which—unless by mutual free agreement—may invade or
obstruct or override those of the other'. This 'carries the implication that the central government acts *directly* on the population of the state *through its own agencies* with no reference to
the governments of the constituent regional authorities'. Ancient Greek confederacies do not
meet this criterion since 'there was *no central machinery of administration* bearing directly on all
citizens, only that of the cities'; they are rather 'composite' or '*confederate* states' (Finer 1997:
i. 377–80, with quotations at 378 and 379; italic original). Neither did the Greeks have any
concept of 'federalism', the most frequent descriptive terms for confederacies being ethnos or
koinon, the latter a term also used of other types of polities. Note that on Finer's definition
'confederacy' and 'federal state' should not be treated as synonyms, as they are in much ancient historical discussion. For a comparable case of an 'unhelpful gulf' between the usage of
political scientists and classicists, regarding the term 'sovereignty', see Davies (1994a).

Despite periodic dissolutions, in the early and middle years of the fourth century the Boeotian confederacy played a major role in undermining the position of Sparta and the Peloponnesian League and exercised a temporary hegemony over central and southern Greece. It was in the third century, however, that confederacies came to dominate mainland Greek politics (through the Aetolian and Achaean confederacies) as the most effective form of organized response to Macedon and the other hellenistic monarchies. The essence of most confederacies was that, while remaining internally self-governing, the member communities established for the purpose of common action in war and diplomacy a set of central officials and institutions, including one or more generals in command of a confederate army, a common council and/or assembly, and sometimes a small body of executive officers, and even judges. In contrast to hegemonic *symmachiai*, confederacies typically involved the existence of some kind of double citizenship of both local community and regional entity. The details, however, differed quite widely in the extent of popular participation and in the precise relationship between the confederacy and individual member states (Beck 1997: 165–211). Indeed, in the Aetolian confederacy the more distant poleis were incorporated not as full members but through grants of *isopoliteia*, whereby their citizens could acquire citizen rights within the wider body but the poleis themselves had no active participation in confederate decision-making. Some confederacies, moreover, possessed one dominant member—such as Thebes in the Boeotian confederacy or Olynthos in the Chalcidic confederacy (Xen. *Hell*. 5. 2. 11–19)—which made their operation, at least in terms of foreign policy-making, closer to that of hegemonial leagues.

James Roy's paper deals with another mainland Greek confederacy, the Arcadian confederacy of the 360s, which (in alliance with the Boeotian confederacy) played an important, if short-lived, role in the demise of Sparta. The confederacy, as in several other regions, built upon the prior existence of an Arcadian ethnic identity, which is attested already by the fifth century but had not previously been translated into any common political organization.[63] Likewise, as Roy's paper demonstrates, the confederacy displayed the standard organizational features found elsewhere: a central military commander, council, assembly, and executive officials. As in Boeotia, its constituent members were largely poleis and, despite attempts to lessen their influence, the individual ambitions of the most important poleis (there being no single dominant member) remained important and were implicated in the confederacy's rapid split. The Arcadian confederacy's distinctive fea-

---

[63] On the absence of a 5th-cent. Arcadian confederacy, in spite of the existence of the *Arkadikon* coinage, which is best interpreted as a festival coinage for the pan-Arcadian games at the sanctuary of Zeus Lykaios, see Nielsen (1996*b*). That the 4th-cent. confederacy nevertheless built upon pre-existing ethnic identity is shown by the desire of the Tegean democrats in 370 to 'unite the whole *Arkadikon*' (Xen. *Hell*. 6. 5. 6).

ture, however, was the democratic character of its institutions and polices: in Roy's words, an 'original attempt to transplant democracy from the polis to a supra-polis structure'. For several years this attempt was a remarkable success and its ultimate failure was perhaps less due to its inherent unfeasibility than to the continuing impact of the oligarchic connections which Sparta had established within the various Arcadian poleis over the previous two centuries.

By comparison with the cases mentioned above, our information about the western Cretan confederacies discussed by Nicholas Sekunda is extremely sparse. We have no precise details of their organization, institutions, or political character. Yet there are just sufficient indications in the fragmentary evidence for a sensitive interpreter, armed with a long-term understanding of Cretan history, to essay a tentative yet revealing reconstruction of the attempts of the Polichnitai in the later fifth century and of the Oreioi in the third to band together, the former in response to the threat of Aeginetan Kydonia, the latter in the context of the particular economic and environmental conditions of the White Mountains in the hellenistic period. As in Arcadia, both confederacies were ultimately overtaken by competing political developments. The common identity of the Polichnitai appears to have become submerged under the emergence of polis structures; although one of these poleis, Polyrrhenia, subsequently pursued tendencies towards regional unification in a different, more hegemonial, form. Similarly, the disappearance of the confederacy of the Oreioi from the historical record was followed by the appearance of its constituent communities as separate members of an even larger, pan-Cretan, confederation.

A striking aspect of the picture which emerges from these papers on ethnē, amphiktyonies, and confederacies is the sheer variety of communities in the ancient Greek world, a variety every bit as broad as the diversity of internal regimes within the Greek polis. (Sometimes, indeed, as in the case of Arcadia in the 360s, developments in forms of communities and in constitutional arrangements were closely connected.) Equally striking features, however, are the remarkable fluidity with which in a given region political formations could change from one type of polity to another (and sometimes back again) and the flexibility of perceptions of identity, which could gravitate from one corporate locus to another, or remain firmly committed to both. The inhabitants of Thessaly could develop both their regional and their local identities apace. The ethnē of north-western Greece could merge their separate identities within a larger Epeirote *koinon*. Both poleis and ethnē could participate in amphiktyonies and acknowledge broader commitments than those to their individual communities. The polis of Delphi could devote its energies both to local community needs and to those of both sanctuary and amphiktyony. In Achaea and Boeotia confederacies could form, dissolve, and then re-form. In Crete regional confederacies could emerge for finite periods before giving way to polis structures or to a pan-Cretan association. Poleis in Arcadia could acknowledge a common *Arkadikon* for at least a century before giving it a political shape, then quickly split it along ideological lines. Mantineia, which led this split, had just a few years earlier—during the events of 370/69, as Roy explains—moved from a state of division into several discrete polities (following its *dioikismos* by the Spartans in 385), through the status of a unitary polis, to membership of the confederacy, all in the course of barely twelve months!

A few years ago John Davies remarked that 'to those of us who are watching with compassion and anxiety the *dioikismos* of what was Jugoslavia it perhaps comes as a surprise to see how such processes could occur in either direction in archaic or classical Greece with so little violent disruption'.[64] These comparative comments are no less relevant today as we write these words in the aftermath of intransigent and bloody conflict in Kosovo over the separatist aspirations of the Albanian population of the Serb Republic. This is not to deny that fierce passion and bloodshed were ever a part of similar changes in ancient Greece. Witness the events in 370 at Tegea during the creation of the Arcadian confederacy (Xen. *Hell.* 6. 5. 6–10) or those which preceded the Union of Argos and Corinth in the late 390s (ibid. 4. 4. 1–6). We should not present too anodyne a picture of ancient Greek political change. Nevertheless, the comparative flexibility of political arrangements was a significant phenomenon in a world which did *not* possess, as does our own, a single dominant political formation like the nation-state whose citizens lack direct control of its differentiated decision-making institutions and armed forces. The challenge for us moderns is to develop an interpretative framework for ancient Greek politics and polities which matches the flexibility of the Greeks themselves.

RECOMMENDED READING

General works

Amit (1973); Finley (1983); Gehrke (1985; 1986); Grant (1988); N. F. Jones (1987); Lintott (1982); Murray (1988*b*).

Theory and ideology

Brock (1989); Harvey (1965–6); Raaflaub (1983); J. T. Roberts (1994).

Monarchy and tyranny

Adcock (1953); Andrewes (1956); Barceló (1993); Berve (1967); Carlier (1984);

---

[64] Davies (1994*a*) 64. He ascribed the phenomenon to the fact that the basic socio-political building-block was below the level of the unitary polis.

Caven (1990); Chamoux (1953); Drews (1983); Finley (1978); Hammond (1989); Hornblower (1982); McGlew (1993); van Wees (1992); F. W. Walbank (1984).

Aristocracy and oligarchy

Donlan (1980); Greenhalgh (1972); Whibley (1896).

Democracy outside Athens

Buckler (1980) ch. 6; Lewis (1997) 51–9; Lintott (1982) ch. 5; (1992); O'Neil (1995); E. W. Robinson (1997); Tomlinson (1972) ch. 19.

Alternatives to the polis

Beck (1997); Buck (1994); Foresti *et al.* (1994); Larsen (1955; 1968); Lewis (1962); Morgan (1990; 1991); Rhodes (1994); Sordi (1958); Tausend (1992).

Regional studies (excluding Athens and Sparta)

Bommeljé and Doorn (1987); Borza (1990); Buck (1979); Cherry, Davis, and Mantzourani (1991); Figueira (1981); Finley (1987); Griffin (1982) 34–77; Hammond (1967); Hammond, Griffith, and Walbank (1972–88); Jameson, Runnels, and van Andel (1994); Legon (1981); Renfrew and Wagstaff (1982); Roesch (1965); J. B. Salmon (1984); Sherwin White (1978); Shipley (1987); Snodgrass (1990); Tomlinson (1972); van Andel and Runnels (1987); Westlake (1935).

BIBLIOGRAPHICAL SUPPLEMENT TO THE PAPERBACK EDITION

p. 5: On the Spartan ephorate see N. Richer, *Les Éphores: Études sur l'histoire et sur l'image de Sparte* (*VIIIᵉ–IIIᵉ siècle avant Jésus-Christ*) (Paris: Publications de la Sorbonne, 1998), and P. Cartledge, *Sparta and Lakonia*, 2nd edn. (London: Routledge, 2001), ch. 3. There is now a second edition (2001) of Powell (1988); Vidal-Naquet and Loraux (1979) (p. 6) is accessible in English (as 'The Formation of Bourgeois Athens: An Essay on Historiography between 1750 and 1850') in P. Vidal-Naquet, *Politics Ancient and Modern* (Cambridge: Polity, 1995) 82–140. On the issue of 'rights' as applied to Greek politics (pp. 7, 11), see F. D. Miller, *Nature, Justice and Rights in Aristotle's* Politics (Oxford: Clarendon Press, 1995); on democracy, D. Held, *Models of Democracy* (Cambridge: Polity, 1996); and on prospects for 'teledemocracy' (p. 7), M. H. Hansen, 'Direct Democracy, Ancient and Modern', in P. McKechnie (ed.), *Thinking Like a Lawyer: Essays on Legal History and General History for John Crook on his Eightieth Birthday* (Leiden: Brill, 2002) 135–49. On classical influences on the American constitution (p. 8) see Carl J. Richard, *The Founders and the Classics: Greece, Rome, and the American Enlightenment* (Cambridge, Mass.: Harvard University Press, 1994), and on the differences between ancient and modern politics and the issue of whether ancient Greek poleis were states in the modern sense (p. 11), see P. Cartledge, 'La politica', in S. Settis (ed.), *I Greci: Storia, cultura, arte, società*, vol. i (Turin: Einaudi, 1996) 39–72; 'The Historical Context', in M. Schofield and C. Rowe (eds.), *The Cambridge History of Ancient Political Thought* (Cambridge: Cambridge University Press, 2000) 11–22; M. Berent, 'Collective Rights and the Ancient Community', *Canadian Journal of Law and Jurisprudence*, 4/2 (1991) 387–99; 'Hobbes and the "Greek Tongues"', *History of Political Thought*, 17 (1996) 36–59; 'Stasis, or the Greek Invention of Politics', *HPT* 19/3 (1998) 331–62; 'Anthropology and the Classics: War, Violence and the Stateless *Polis*', *CQ*, NS 50 (2000) 257–89; 'Sovereignty Ancient and Modern', *POLIS* 17/1–2 (2000) 2–34; and, in contrast to Berent's view of the 'stateless polis', M. H. Hansen, 'Was the Polis a State or a Stateless Society?', in T. H. Nielsen (ed.), *Even More Studies in the Ancient Greek Polis* (Papers from the Copenhagen Polis Centre, 6; Stuttgart: Steiner, 2002) 17–47. On oligarchy (p. 17) see M. Ostwald, *Oligarchia: The Development of a Constitutional Form in Ancient Greece* (*Historia* Einzelschriften, 144; Stuttgart: Steiner, 2000), and 'Oligarchy and Oligarchs in Ancient Greece', in P. Flensted-Jensen, T. H. Nielsen, and L. Rubinstein (eds.), *Polis and Politics: Studies in Ancient Greek History Presented to Mogens Herman Hansen on his Sixtieth Birthday, August 20, 2000* (Copenhagen: Museum Tusculanum, 2000) 385–96.

VARIETIES OF
POLIS ORGANIZATION

2

Theognis: An Alternative to Democracy

ROBIN LANE FOX

Lax epiba dēmōi: my fellow contributors have discussed many Greek alternatives to democracy, from confederacy to monarchy, but none has considered trampling it underfoot. Trampling, however, is the recommended treatment for the 'empty-headed dēmos' in verses ascribed to the poet Theognis (847–50). Trample on them, poke them with a sharp goad, burden them with a heavy yoke, and in the Theognidean view, you will never find a 'dēmos' so fond of its master. Our democratic age can only marvel at advice which seems politically so incorrect. 'Die Bezeichnung "Landjunker" wäre nicht ganz falsch' ('The description "Landed Gentry" would not be altogether wrong'), Jacoby suggested (1931: 147), trying to characterize the author. His recent Budé editor has been more forthright: 'un farouche aristocrate, ombrageux et vindicatif' ('a fierce aristocrat, touchy and vengeful') (Carrière 1975: 8).

In this paper I wish to answer two questions: was the author of this poetry voicing an 'alternative to democracy' and, if not to democracy, to what? Secondly, did his poetry live on and contribute to such an alternative anywhere after his lifetime? The second question is one of reception, but there is a time and place in which I think we have evidence to make it worth asking. The first question presupposes answers to other vexed questions, the author's identity, place, and date, with which, then, I must begin.

Corpus and authorship

Our 'Theognis' corpus poses particular problems of origin and authenticity. What we now read as *Theognidea* has four separate passages of invocation, some groups of lines which are elsewhere ascribed to Solon, Mimnermus, and Euenus, a segregated 'book 2', and several lines in book 1 which refer to events much later than others in the collection. Many of the 'poems' are extremely brief and sometimes they are repeated in more or less the same form later in our same collection. No other early Greek poet has reached us in such a curious condition and historians cannot afford to ignore the probable reasons for this disorder.

The scholarship on this question from 1921 to 1989 has been helpfully

I have been greatly helped by E. L. Bowie, K. Hoekstra, and Martha Lovell in the refinement of the arguments in this paper.

assembled and surveyed (Gerber 1991). From Jacoby's important study
in 1931 to M. L. West's clear synthesis and further proposals in 1974
(West 1974: 40–64), separate 'blocks' of material have been detected in the
Theognid books which survive. Like West and many of his predecessors,
I accept that our lines 19 to 254 are a solid block of verses by the original
Theognis, although they have been arranged by a later editor. As E. L.
Bowie has emphasized during his important adjustment to West's history
of the text (Bowie 1997), these lines are not necessarily complete poems.
In most cases they have been abbreviated first by an editor, then by his
copyists, who left out bits and pieces of the poems which they encountered.
We do not know when the first editor worked on these lines, but perhaps
the block existed before c.300 BC.

The second block runs from lines 255 to 1002. Its contents and origins are
more varied and we cannot be sure how much of it is by Theognis himself.
The third block runs from line 1002 to the end of our book 1. Authentic
verses by Theognis are uncertain here too. It might seem safe to accept only
those verses addressed to Cyrnus, Theognis' addressee, but even here we
should be cautious: later poems might have imitated the Cyrnus-address, as
the poet's own seal-poem, or *sphragis*, anticipated.[1] The evidence of P.Oxy.
2380 shows that the lines from the first and second block existed as a unit at
least by c. AD 200. Probably, something like our book 1 existed much earlier,
perhaps in the first century BC. Both the second and third block repeat
verses which are known in an earlier block. They, too, include verses which
are known from other sources as the work of another poet. Bowie sums up
the likeliest reason for these curious facts: editors of blocks one, two, and
three were working from anthologies in which Theognis poems were only
one constituent. Unwittingly, they included, and abbreviated, verses which
were sometimes not Theognis' own. As for book 2, I accept that verses from
it were still mixed up in what is now book 1 as late as c. AD 500 and were not
segregated until c. AD 800, as M. L. West and the Budé editor, J. Carrière,
have each argued (Carrière 1975: 23–7).

What survives, then, is a range of verses which are mostly abbreviations
of longer poems. They were excerpted from anthologies in which Theognis
was only one poet among several. The original poet's date, home, and
identity are more than usually difficult questions when the evidence has been
excerpted and confused. We can only work with what we have, recognizing
that it is incomplete and sometimes of uncertain authorship.

The opening seal, or *sphragis*, begins the reliable first block of verses: it
calls the author a man of Megara (22–33). In the *Laws*, however, Plato calls
Theognis a man of Megara Hyblaea in Sicily.[2] It is very hard to believe that
Plato is correct. Nothing in the first block or the Cyrnus poems which follow

---

[1] Discussion in Edmunds (1997) esp. 30–40.
[2] *Laws* 630 A; Figueira (1985) §§ 17–20.

implies that the poet was familiar with the western Mediterranean. Perhaps Plato was misled by lines in a Theognid anthology with a different scope from ours. References to places in our collection fall outside the blocks or verses which are likeliest to be Theognis'. Lines 891–4 are, however, early and lament the mishaps of Euboean Cerinthus and the Lelantine plain, local affairs which are rather unlikely to have concerned a poet in Sicily. Lines 783 ff. refer to a journey in the first person to Sicily, another to Euboea, another to Sparta, and then contrast all three with 'home': unfortunately, they may not be by Theognis himself. Lines 774 ff. invoke Apollo's protection for Alcithous' city, mainland Megara. Again, those lines are not demonstrably Theognis', but an editor certainly thought them appropriate in this collection. The *Suda* (s.v. Theognis) does credit Theognis with an elegy on 'those of the Syracusans saved in the siege'. This siege should be the great siege of 415–3 and it is a neat conjecture that the author was the Athenian Theognis, known at that time as a tragic poet and later as a member of the Thirty (*PA* no. 6736). Perhaps this poem confused Plato, but the confusion remains surprising.

Among this crossfire by historians, literary critics may prefer to be less fundamentalist. Is the first person of the poems necessarily Theognis himself (Ford 1985)? Are not the references to a 'polis' and its troubles an imagined context to which audiences could respond anywhere in the Greek world without needing knowledge of Megara (Nagy 1985: § 9)? Neither strategy is adequate. Perhaps no Cyrnus existed and perhaps the real Theognis was a man of very different views from those given in the first person in his poems. However, this poetic Theognis is the only one of whom we know anything. Local Megarian colour is almost imperceptible (Figueira 1985: esp. § 15), but it is wrong to argue that poetry addressing local circumstances could not be widely received elsewhere: we need only think of Alcaeus or Attic comedy. A balanced view is preferable. The poems do sometimes refer to events in the poet's own city and to specific mishaps elsewhere, but not so pervasively that they could not travel and appeal beyond their context. This quality will be relevant to my second question, their influence.

The question of date

At the core is a poet in Megara, but when? The issue is crucial to our interpretation of the poems, and has to be addressed at length. Chronographers dated him to the Olympiads of 552–41,[3] but we can suspect the pull of synchronisms on their date and wonder whether it rests on more than hellenistic inference from what was then thought 'Theognid'. The early to mid-sixth century has appealed to most modern scholars, but in 1974 M. L. West argued for a much earlier date for the early core, and if he

---

[3] Hieron.: Ol. 59; *Chron. Pasch.*: Ol. 57; *Suda*: Ol. 59; Cyril., Euseb.: Ol. 58.

is right, historians need to take more notice (West 1974: 65–8). In West's view, Theognis was composing on the eve of Theagenes' tyranny in Megara and continued during its duration, in which he was exiled. We know that the Athenian Cylon married a daughter of Theagenes before the tyranny which he attempted to impose on Athens at some point between 636 and 628 (Jeffery 1976: 87). If we assume that Theagenes was already tyrant in Megara, West's dating requires Theognis' poetry to have begun *c*.640 to 630. If so, it becomes a primary source for the early tyrannies, one of Greek history's most challenging black holes.

Unfortunately, the verses in the main Theognis block (lines 19 to 254) contain no references to external events which we can locate from other evidence. Beyond them, we can turn with some confidence to other Cyrnus verses and look for a date for Theognis there. More speculatively, we can also look for any reference to an early external event in the entire collection and see if it supports West's unusually early dating, while remembering that the lines may not in fact be by Theognis himself.

In this second speculative category only one group of verses takes us back to a date before *c*.580. Lines 891–4 lament the spoiling of the Lelantine plain, the ruin of Cerinthus, and the replacement of *agathoi* by *kakoi*. They execrate the Cypselids for their intervention. The Cypselids must be Corinthians, not members of the Athenian Philaid clan.[4] No source reports an attack by a Corinthian Cypselid on southern Euboea and the plain, but the most plausible context is a Cypselid expedition northwards. The obvious reason for making one was their foundation of Potidaea. Periander's son, Gorgos, is said to have died founding Potidaea before Periander reached old age.[5] A date of *c*.600–590 is about right for the foundation and on the way north, I suggest, this Cypselid venture attacked Euboea. On any view, the verses refer to stasis, not to the great Lelantine war of the later eighth century. The curse on the Cypselids implies a date after Cypselus' own death *c*.625, and the lines certainly belong after the emergence of Theagenes at Megara.[6] By 600–590 his tyranny was over: if the lines are Theognis' own, they tell strongly against West's dating.

At the very least they do not refer to an event before *c*.630 and they lend no support to West's suggestions. Among the verses to Cyrnus, a more solid category, only one couplet is relevant. Lines 1103–4 refer to the effects of *hybris*: '*hybris* destroyed the Magnesians and Colophon and Smyrna: it will utterly destroy you too, Cyrnus.' From Archilochus, we can date the destruction of Magnesia securely to *c*.650 BC (fr. 20 West): it was connected in the tradition with excessive licence, and earlier in the collections lines 603–4 have already referred to it in its own right. West's distinctive sugges-

---

[4] Despite Hudson-Williams (1910) 231, on 891–4.

[5] J. B. Salmon (1984): 211–13. Cf. Nic. Dam. *FGrH* 90 F 59. 1.

[6] Cf. Jeffery (1976) 66.

tion is that the accompanying 'destructions' of Colophon and Smyrna refer right back to events of the late eighth century (West 1974: 66–7). Herodotus mentions the capture of Aeolian Smyrna by exiles from Ionian Colophon:[7] West cites Mimnermus fr. 9, which calls the settlers in Colophon 'leaders in grievous *hybris*'. He suggests that the seizure of Aeolian Smyrna by hybristic Colophonians *c.*700 BC is the ruin which Theognis mentions. As for the ruin of Colophon, he suggests that it followed soon afterwards and that Mimnermus mentioned it in lines now lost to us.

None of these proposals is cogent. In Mimnermus, the *hybris* is attributed to the first settlers at Colophon: it is not mentioned in the taking of Smyrna. No early 'ruin' of Colophon is attested, either, and the Colophonians' seizure of Smyrna was a change of personnel, not the 'destruction' of a polis. West's dating of Theognis needs a date for these ruinations before *c.*640, but it fails to find one.[8]

There is a neat, simple alternative. The famous destruction of Smyrna was the work of Alyattes the Lydian, *c.*600 BC, attested both by texts and by archaeology.[9] As for Colophon, Gyges, according to Herodotus (1. 14. 1), had already captured the '*asty*' of Colophon, but Bowra's much-cited paper on Xenophanes and Colophon justly decides that 'this must mean that he took the lower town: he did not take the citadel' (Bowra 1941: 119). Colophon survived and its luxury became proverbial. According to Aristotle (*Pol.* 1290^{b}16–17), the rich 'became very rich before the war with the Lydian'. Xenophanes' famous lines on their perfumed, purpled luxury refer to this same era,[10] despite Bowra's attempts to connect them with the later Persian conquest. Theopompus links this luxury with the city's ruin in further comments which are probably based on lines of Xenophanes in the same context: 'because of this *agōgē* (way of life), they fell into tyranny and stasis and were destroyed' (*FGrH* 115 F 117). If we add in Aristotle's remark, a war with the Lydians had intervened: do we know of one?

Polyaenus 7. 2. 2 tells of Colophon's treaty with Alyattes, who then deceived the city's famous cavalry and caused them all to be murdered: he is also said to have promised them double pay and a new agora. This same cavalry class included the luxurious rich known to Xenophanes and Aristotle: Alyattes, it seems, destroyed them and, to judge from Theopompus (using Xenophanes), a tyrant, stasis, and destruction were connected, although the exact details escape us. We have no evidence of a later Persian destruction of Colophon, whereas the Lydian intervention is attested. The destruction

---

[7] Hdt. 1. 150; cf. Huxley (1966); 59.   [8] Discussion in Nagy (1995) § 4.

[9] Huxley (1966) 77: Hdt. 1. 16. 2; for dating of the destruction cf. Cook (1958–9) 23–7; Anderson (1958–9) 148.

[10] Xenophanes fr. 3 West, quoted by Athen. 12, 526 A, to illustrate Phylarchus on Colophonian luxury (*FGrH* 81 F 66).

known to Theopompus from Xenophanes surely occurred, like Smyrna's, in the reign of Alyattes, *c*.600–590.

In Bowra's view (1941: 125), the destruction was the work of the Persians and Xenophanes saw from the inside (*c*.545) the destruction which startled Theognis. In my view, Xenophanes' lines looked back to a destruction by Lydia, not Persia, which had occurred more than a generation before 546. Bowra was wrong to connect the event with Persia, just as West was wrong to postulate it in the late eighth century, as his view of Theognis' own date required. Magnesia had fallen *c*.650 BC, Smyrna and Colophon *c*.600–590. When Theognis wrote his verses to Cyrnus, they were the most conspicuous examples of ruin through *hybris*. As a result, they are important for his dating. They rule out a Theognis composing *c*.640 and they rule out a Theognis in the mid-540s or later. By then the fall of Sardis and other examples would have deserved mention instead.[11]

The only two references in the corpus to events before *c*.550 which we can date externally thus turn out to be consistent with each other. Both the Lelantine lament and the lines on *hybris* belong in the early sixth century. They tell strongly against a Theognis writing with Theagenes' rise before his eyes. The dates of Theagenes' tyranny are most obscure, but he was not mentioned by Aristotle among long-lasting tyrants and he is most unlikely to have continued from *c*.640–635 to as late as 605. The only datable points from this period in the Theognid corpus thus fall when West's suggested 'life and times' are past. Only if we give Theognis an earlier, undated output and extend his poetry from *c*.640 to *c*.590 can we fit him to West's scheme. It is much easier to reject it, split Theognis from Theagenes, and place him *c*.600–*c*.560.

Theognis' Megara

To what, then, was Theognis reacting in this period? His stance is unmistakably the stance of an *agathos*, a true aristocrat, true to aristocratic values. The central core of his poetry communicates these values to Cyrnus at a time when they are under challenge. Cyrnus is evidently younger, the beloved of his older poet. His personal name is extremely rare.[12] According to Hesychius, the word *kyrnos* means a *nothos* or bastard:[13] it is a delicious possibility that Theognis is addressing his wisdom to a young *nothos*, in need of advice because his own birth is only half blue-blooded.

Perhaps Cyrnus existed, perhaps his name is his only reality. Certainly, lines addressed to him are most likely to be Theognis' own and lines 39–52 are most relevant to the crisis which is presented as his setting. 'Cyrnus,

---

[11] Van Wees (this volume) n. 2 argues for retention of the traditional date.
[12] Cf. Fraser and Matthews (1987–) i. 277.
[13] Schmidt (1858–64) 942; discussion in Nagy (1985) § 43.

this polis is pregnant and I fear that it may bring forth a man to chasten our wicked insolence.' This man (a *euthyntēr*) is presumably a tyrant, but it need not be Theagenes: a new tyrant could be feared *c.*580 or later. The poet fears one because of the insolence of *kakoi* who corrupt the dēmos and give judgements to the unjust for the sake of personal gain. We can, of course, compare Solon in the 590s, observing how great men can ruin a city and a dēmos can be enslaved to a *mounarchos* through ignorance (fr. 9 West). Theognis does not mention Theagenes as a lesson from history, but Solon does not mention Cylon either. Theognis, however, concludes, 'from these things come *stasies* and internecine killings and *mounarchoi*: may they never please this city' (51–2). West (1974) 68 argues that Theognis was warning here too about tyranny and that he could pray for it never to please Megara only if Megara had not yet had a tyranny and Theognis was writing before Theagenes.

This last point is not to be pressed. Forty years, maybe more, could have passed (on my dating) since Theagenes' fall and Theognis did not need to state specifically 'never again'. His opening verses fear a 'corrector', but the closing ones pray for no *stasies* or *mounarchoi*: the latter may be a generalized plural, but they may, alternatively, express something less specific. *Stasies* are not revolutions, but factions who take a stand; Herodotus reminds us that the exclusive Bacchiad *genos* were also called *mounarchoi*, though they were not a tyrant.[14] We have a slight knowledge of Megarian affairs apart from tyranny. In Plutarch's *Greek Questions* an era of *sōphrosynē* among sober-minded citizens is said to have followed Megara's tyranny.[15] Perhaps Plutarch drew on Aristotle's lost *Constitution*, which also (perhaps) drew on hints discerned in Theognis. Clues to this era of *sōphrosynē* can be sought in the institutions of Megarian colonies sent out in the seventh and sixth centuries.[16] The epigraphic sources are later, but they attest *dēmiourgoi* as magistrates (we should not be surprised in those Doric communities) and *aisymnoi* at Chalcedon and Callatis.[17] These *aisymnoi* are suggestive. On his later travels Pausanias (1. 43. 3) gives a fascinating glimpse of Megara's Aesymnion, built over the graves of supposed heroes and commemorating the just 'Aesymnoi' and the rotating rule of elected magistrates in Megara after the ending of kingship. The myth and the building make sense as reflections of an era of rule by *aisymnoi*, taking turns after monarchic government.[18] Tyranny, I suggest, was followed at Megara by an era of lawful oligarchy, headed by *aisymnoi* rotating in office, the officials whom we find in contemporary Megarian colonies. Theognis' fear, then, may be faction and monarchical rule by a group like his city's *aisymnoi*: 'may it never please this

---

[14] Hdt. 5. 92. 2; in general, see Aurenche (1974) 10–43.
[15] *Quaest. Graec.* 18 (=*Mor.* 295 D). Cf. Figueira (1985) 130; Oost (1973); Legon (1981) 104–35.
[16] Cf. N. F. Jones (1987) 94–7.
[17] Cf. Jeffery (1973–4).
[18] Cf. Bohringer (1980).

city'. Out of these evils a single tyrant, or corrector, might then be born, but not if these evils are kept at bay. It is not, then necessary to date the closing verses to a time before Theagenes put tyranny on the Megarian map.

It is not even necessary for Theognis to have coincided with a tyrant at home. Lines 1203 ff. do begin, 'I will not go, nor will a tyrant be lamented by me or mourned at his tomb'. However, they may well not be by Theognis himself, as they occur in a block of mixed origins. Even if they are, the first person need not be autobiographical. Even as it is, the 'tyrant' need not be a 'tyrant' in the poet's home city. It would be most unwise to see a reference to Theagenes here.

Theognis is also troubled by changes among the dēmos. Lines 53–60 complain memorably how they used to roam like deer outside the city, but now they are *agathoi* ('good'), although they do not even know what is noble and what is not. The former *agathoi* are now *deiloi* ('worthless') and the jumped-up *kakoi* ('bad') deceive and mock one another. The lines address Cyrnus; the likely view is that they are Theognis' own. What is this unwelcome alternative, evident *c.*590–560?

Previous scholars have suspected that already it must be democracy, ascribed to Megara by bits of Aristotle's *Politics* and Plutarch's *Greek Questions*.[19] The word 'democracy', however, is not used exactly by either author and the date to which they are referring is not clear. More important is Aristotle *Poetics* 3. 3: the Megarians, no less, were the inventors of comedy 'in the time of the democracy among them'. This 'invention' of comedy preceded the Athenians' in 486: did Aristotle believe that a Megarian democracy had also preceded Cleisthenes' in 508? If he did, we can perhaps see why. Not only did he use the word rather freely: Megarians themselves, perhaps, were claiming priority. The origins of comedy certainly became an inter-city issue. The Parian Marble credits Athens with the invention and, as Jacoby also recognized, the credit was phrased polemically: 'at *Athens*', it begins, 'Susarion introduced the comic chorus' between 580 and 560 (*FGrH* 239 A 39). The entry answered the counter-claims of Megara. Did Megarians also claim against Athens the credit for democracy, a false 'anniversary' whose influence shows in Aristotle's mistaken acceptance of the word for their early constitution?

Before 508, democracies did not exist in mainland Greece and the alternative which troubled Theognis must be something else. Our knowledge of the Megarian citizenry is thin and based on late sources, but Plutarch knows of the 'five villages' in the early Megarid, one of which was called Kynosoureis (*Quaest. Graec.* 17). Epigraphically, 'hundreds' or *hekatostyes* are also attested, late in Megara itself but also in Megarian colonies founded in the seventh and sixth centuries, where it is safe to consider them original to the settlements. What is attested separately at Byzantium, Chalcedon,

[19] Plut. *Quaest. Graec.* 18; Arist. *Pol.* 1302[b], 1304[b].

and Heraclea on the Pontus can presumably be ascribed to their Megarian metropolis at the time of foundation (N. F. Jones 1987: 96). In 221/0 BC a Megarian inscription happens to attest the name of one such 'hundred' at Megara itself: *hekatostys Kynosuris*.[20] The 'hundred' here has the very name of one of the five early villages. We cannot date its receipt of this name, but the overlap does remind us of the shifts in the number and nature of tribal and 'kinship' units in other Greek cities after or during their tyrannies, at Athens, naturally, but also at Cleisthenes' Sicyon (as L. H. Jeffery 1976: 162–6 acutely suggested) and Corinth (where the three Doric tribes became eight).[21] Not 'democracy' but some such reshuffling could neatly explain Theognis' discontent: the old 'hundreds' of kinship (dominated by the *agathoi*) had turned into hundreds based on locality (even bearing the names of the ancient villages). The change gave a new prominence to outlying villagers, the 'animal kingdom' of Theognis' past, and diluted his own social equals in the units which previously ran Megara.

Theognis also complains how the *hybris* of the *kakoi* is corrupting the dēmos and how they give judgments to the unjust. In the wake of tyranny, Megarian nobles no longer dominated the process of justice, but by looking at Megarians abroad we can add spice to Theognis' complaints. In 602 the Samians had founded Perinthus (Shipley 1987: 51): according to Plutarch's *Greek Questions* (again, using Aristotle's lost *Constitution*?), Megarians attacked this intrusive city on the Propontis: the Samians won, but persuaded their Megarian captives to attack the noble Geōmoroi on Samos, the island's landed aristocracy (*Quaest. Graec.* 57). As captives in war, why should the Megarians care? But Theognis would see it as the ultimate 'badness' to attack a fellow nobility, even after a defeat.

The Megarians' assault on the Geōmoroi is undated, but Barron and Shipley argue for a date in the 590s.[22] Several decades later, probably *c.*560–555, the Megarians, with help from Boeotians, founded Heraclea on the Pontus (Burstein 1976: 15–18). Thanks to Aristotle's *Politics*, we are slightly informed about its politics. Aristotle describes how 'the dēmos was put down immediately after the city's foundation because of the demagogues. The notables were unjustly treated by them and banished, but then they gathered, returned, and destroyed the dēmos' (*Pol.* 1304[b]31–7). Again, Aristotle is wrong to imply a democracy in Heraclea at its foundation. Presumably the original constitution was a broad oligarchy, but it must have included some of Theognis' skin-clad *bêtes noires*. Abroad, they and their leaders showed the mettle which Theognis feared.

Perhaps they showed it at home too in his lifetime. Plutarch also describes

[20] *IG* iv². 1. 42.
[21] Nic. Dam. *FGrH* 90 F 60. 2; J. B. Salmon (1984) 231–9, although I do not accept his dating of the change to the Cypselid era.
[22] Shipley (1987) 52–4, with reference to Barron (1961) 187–8.

the notorious *palintokia*, or compulsory repayment of interest paid on loans, at Megara (*Quaest. Graec.* 18, 59), and perhaps Aristotle is also describing events of the sixth century when he passes from Heraclea to a similar stasis at Megara (*Pol.* 1300^{a}17–18, 1304^{b}35–6): there, demagogues expelled the notables, and confiscated their goods, but were overthrown when the exiles returned and fought them. Lines 1197–1202 complain how others 'have taken my possessions, plundering them by force', how poverty afflicts 'me', how 'others possess my flowery fields'. These verses are addressed to Cyrnus and may be Theognis', despite their position so late in our book 1. If so, it is tempting to take them as biographical and to link them with the upheavals at Megara described, but not dated, by Aristotle.

If this is correct, Theognis' political fears and laments make sense without the existence of tyranny. Theognis saw the social and political base of his Megara broaden; perhaps the old 'hundreds' were diluted and renamed; hints of non-noble activity by Megarians abroad gave substance to his fears at home: if they would attack a Geōmoros and the leaders of their own colony, how could an *agathos* feel entirely safe? In Megara itself upheavals followed and, like other men of property, Theognis perhaps found himself driven into exile. Nothing in the surviving poetry suggests that he lived to take revenge.

Theognis' poems, then, are not in themselves an 'alternative to democracy', despite Aristotle's loose use of the term. Nor are they an 'alternative to Theagenes'. His alternative, however, is singularly interesting. It is not to counter stasis with stasis, like Alcaeus in Mytilene, nor for the nobles to strike back. In his view of the world, an ideal core of *agathoi* exists and endures, as it always does in a self-styled *agathos*'s mind, but other *agathoi* are no longer true to their class. It is not only that they rush to marry rich, common heiresses, and dilute the noble blood-line. They let down their friends and cannot be trusted to be straight. In an age of *anamixis* ('social flux'), high society could not be sure that a man born *kalos* would behave like an *agathos*. The answer, most strikingly, is to adopt a stance of superior non-involvement, combined with 'protective mimicry', as Jaeger well described it (1939: i. 199). Imitate the action of the polypus, which resembles the rock to which it clings: suit your colour to the circumstances; practise a 'friendship from the tongue', whatever your true thoughts (213–18). Theognis is the first known advocate in world history of what Sartre and his existentialists have called 'bad faith'.

Dissimulation had been execrated in earlier Greek poetry, most notably by Homer's Achilles: Hera might deceive Zeus, but when gods or heroes resorted to pretence, they usually pretended to be somebody else altogether. The distinctive fact about Theognis' pretence is that it arises from an era of social change. Born *agathoi* no longer remain *agathoi*, and those who do so must practise dissimulation because of the company they must keep. A true *agathos* will overlook a casual injustice, but there can be no mercy for the *agathos* who turns rotten. Like the best of them, Theognis himself can repay betrayal in kind, a bastard (in one sense) to a bastard (perhaps) in another. 'To you I have given wings, Cyrnus,' he tells us of his pupil in nobility, 'with which your fame will cross the seas and resound at banquets and in song.' A long promise of immortal fame is followed by a sting in the poem's tail. 'You will be the subject of song for ever, as long as earth and sun endure, but here is your memorial, Cyrnus: you treat me with scant respect and you cheat me as if I were a child' (237–54). Even a Cyrnus, it seems, could not be trusted, but Theognis knew exactly how to throw him.

Theognis' heirs

The 'farouche aristocrate' of the earlier sixth century continued to find an audience way beyond the crisis of his home city. In contrast to Solon or Alcaeus, his poems stood for superior values expressed in general terms, not in personal invective or specific political action. They were elegies, poetry which modern scholars have set overwhelmingly in the context of sympotic recitation, 'for the most part nothing else than normative poetry for the symposium' (Pellizer 1990: 180 n. 11). Jan Bremmer has even concluded that 'the inference seems reasonable that in archaic Greece, the symposion was also the stage for didactic poetry addressed to boys' (1990: 137), although the second book of our 'Theognis' is perhaps not best called 'didactic'. The symposium is often seen nowadays as the primary location for the recital of archaic Greek poetry; but even if all that is ascribed to symposia is true, we must also give weight to early poems' independent, written circulation, even in the sixth century. Theognis promises Cyrnus fame abroad, not only in distant feasts and banquets, and obviously this fame assumes that the poem will travel, surely not just by word of mouth. Just as Solon could cap a poem written by Mimnermus (Solon fr. 27 West), just as Semonides of Amorgos knew his Hesiod (fr. 7 West), so texts by Theognis and others circulated freely round the early Greek world. The problem was to limit what was Theognis' own and what was by somebody else. The *sphragis*-poem, or 'seal', is addressed to Cyrnus and is explicitly concerned to prevent plagiarism or alteration. Its author, surely Theognis himself, must already be thinking of safeguarding a written text. The *sphragis* assumes that the poems' audience, therefore, goes beyond sympotic occasions (Edmunds 1997: 30–40).

As Greek political history altered, Theognis' views survived in writing and continued to speak to an appropriate audience. In the odes of Pindar, in the early fifth century, we see Theognis' class from another angle: 'at this height', wrote Jaeger (1939: 205), 'we can forget the problems and conflicts of Theognis's world and be content to marvel at the power and beauty

of that noble and distant ideal'. Envy and the contrary views of the *kakoi*
are present, but only as occasional background touches. Yet, there is no
commendation of 'protective mimicry' and in Pindar the main problem of
lying is the problem of not doing justice to noble repute.

Beyond the victory ode, however, we can sense that Theognis' warnings
had lost none of their relevance. The city where we can sense it best is
Athens, where it was particularly easy for *kaloi* by birth to be far from
agathoi in conduct. Those born in the 520s found themselves living under
a democracy after 508 (Forrest 1960: 233), but Theognis' words on *agathoi*,
kakoi, and 'protective mimicry' were general enough to apply in the face
of the new political alternative. In the 480s ostracisms turned born *agathoi*
against each other and set friend against friend (Davies 1993: 23–36). There
was a place for the polypus and 'friendship from the tongue', intensifying
in the late 460s to 440s, as the Pindaric era ended and those who stood for
it, like Thucydides the son of Melesias, found themselves out in the cold.[23]

We know that Theognis and his corpus led an active life in the Athens
which followed, from Pericles to Critias. The golden age of Attic drama
is not, for us, an age of new personal poetry. The older lyrics helped to
meet this need, as we know from testimonies and quotations. Xenophon,
it was believed, wrote a book *On Theognis*, denying the majority view that
the poet had spoken out against marrying for money and contaminating
noble birth (Stob. *Flor*. 88.14). The author is not certainly Xenophon, as
posterity believed, but he belongs in the contemporary Socratic climate: he
tried to argue that Theognis' concern was the contrast of knowledge and
ignorance, a fine case of forcing the evidence to suit a tutor's views.

What did a young man in Periclean Athens read and know by Theognis'
name? We cannot be sure, but recent scholarship has made us much clearer
where the answer lies. In 1960 A. R. Burn still thought of an inner core
and an outer grey, or rather 'blue', area: he suggested that young Athenians
knew 'an abridged Theognis for schools', perhaps extending only to our line
775 and certainly excluding book 2 because Athens, in Burn's view (1960:
252–4), was 'not a society rotten with homosexuality'. It is clear, however,
from the *Suda* that the contents of our erotic book 2 were mixed up among
what we read as book 1 at least as late as AD 500 and probably until *c*.800,
as M. L. West (1974: 44–5) and the Budé editor Carrière (1975: 23–7) have
each independently observed. It is also clear from the 'Xenophon' quotation
that by the late fifth century collections of Theognid verse were arranged
differently from ours. It was not even that the order closely resembled
ours, but merely left a few bits out: Xenophon's collection evidently began
with our lines 183 ff. on noble birth. The contents of book 2 were not kept
separate: there were no individual 'books': texts varied and began at different

[23] Wade-Gery (1958) 251. For the polypus in other Pindaric poetry see Athen. 12, 513 C;
for its habits ibid. 7, 317.

points; some people's scrolls probably included lines which are known to us as Solon's or Mimnermus', while others did not: perhaps there were texts of 'mixed *gnōmai*', moralizing lines of which Theognis' were only a part. Quite a bit of our Theognid corpus still led a separate existence, and we cannot infer that it had an earlier, slimmer shape from our cluster of fifth- and fourth-century citations. The philosophers Xenophon and Isocrates quoted only the more uplifting 'ethical' fragments, and their choice was necessarily narrow. Texts which contained these verses also contained some horrors: lines about the 'witless' dēmos, 'bad faith', false friendship, and the infidelity of boys. In certain cases, verses known in our corpus may have been followed by more lines than ours. It is evident that we have only the opening lines or excerpts of well-known, longer poems.

Henri Marrou (1965: 69) suggested that 'le cercle aristocratique de Callias' in late fifth-century Athens was the milieu which put the *gnōmai* of our book 1 together with the pederasty of book 2. He was wrong to think that such a compilation was necessary: the two types of verse had already grown up together and no 'book 2' had been separated. He was right, however, in his belief that Theognid poetry appealed to this milieu. We meet it in the dialogues of Socrates, both Plato's and Xenophon's.[24] The Socrates of Xenophon's *Memorabilia* adopts Theognid verses as a starting-point in some of his little lessons to prominent Athenians; he uses them when discussing how only the *esthlos* can teach noble *esthla* or how there can be no friendship between the 'good' and the vulgar 'bad'.[25] Like the Xenophontic *On Theognis*, Socrates then reinterprets the meaning of these words. The old verses, however, were plainly a first resort as a source of wisdom in the circles in which he moved.

We can sense this same starting-point in the brief Platonic *Lysis* and in a well-known debate in the *Republic*. The *Lysis* is an intellectual version of one of Theognis' great concerns: who are friends and can friendship exist between 'good' and 'bad'? (Glidden 1981). Socrates discusses the poet's saying that 'happiness is horses, dogs, and a friend abroad' (212 E), the verse which we know from Solon but which is also present in our Theognid book 2. Menexenus accepts it as 'self-evident', but when Socrates bewilders him, he withdraws to the ancient saying 'the fair is *philon*' (216 C). These words, too, are embedded in Theognis, as the words sung by the Muses at the wedding of Cadmus and Harmony (Thgn. 15–18).

In the *Lysis* the young participants begin with proverbial notions to be found in the Theognid corpus. Like Xenophon's Socrates and Xenophon himself, Plato's Socrates then redefines them. Aristotelian views on friendship can also be read in this light, especially in the *Eudemian Ethics*,[26] but for Athenian circles *Republic* 331 E is more pertinent. Polemarchus, the metic

---

[24] Xen. *Mem.* 1. 2. 20; 2. 6; cf. *Symp.* 2. 4.   [25] *Mem.* 1. 2. 20; 2. 6.

[26] *EE* 1237^{b}15, 1230^{a}12, 1243^{a}18.

in high Athenian society, begins with Simonides' description of justice, and
then refines 'what is due' into 'doing good to friends and harm to enemies'.
Socrates's first move is to ask him if 'friends' are those who seem to be
'good' or those who really are? This same maxim of just requital and this
same dilemma of 'apparent friends' are evident in the Theognid poems.
The maxim was widely familiar, but in this context the Theognid poems,
I suggest, are the body of wisdom to which Polemarchus turns and from
which Socrates begins.

The setting of these Socratic exchanges, both in Plato and in Xenophon,
lies in very high society indeed. The guests at Xenophon's *Symposium* are
guests of the grand Callias whose circle Marrou credited with collecting a
Theognid corpus. In his *Memorabilia*, the Critobulus who discusses friendship between 'good' and 'bad' is the son of Criton, the very rich landowner
and farmer.[27] Plato's Lysis is born to a nobility which would comfort even
a Theognis, with an ancestry which runs back to Zeus and a family cult of
Heracles in the deme Aixonē (Davies 1971: no. 9574). Though not a citizen,
the Polemarchus of the *Republic* is a man with rich and noble friends.

In the mentality of Athenian high society in the later fifth century, much
has been made of new forces, the impact of sophists, the teaching of newly
invented political theory, the evident sense of a 'generation gap'.[28] Members of old or very rich families were prominent in the two coups against the
democracy in 411 and 404/3 and an interest in political alternatives is naturally inferred from their participation.[29] However, there was, I suggest, an
older anti-democratic bedrock to these people which was not to be found in
trendy new theories of the relationship between military and political power
or ideas for reshaping the boulē.[30] The Platonic and Xenophontic dialogues
give hints of the opinions which a gilded young man would bring to his first
encounter with a tutor in philosophy. The maxims of aristocratic poetry,
the very maxims known to us in the Theognid corpus, are unmistakably in
attendance.[31] They spoke to these young men's innate sense of superiority,
some of them true *agathoi* by birth, some of them also *kaloi* by appearance,
some of them *agathoi* by recent family tradition and riches which had lost
their first, post-Eupatrid lustre. They knew these poems by heart, not just
because their fathers and first teachers had passed them on. They had also
sung them and recited them at parties since their youth.

Singing was a prominent feature at Greek symposia, which recent scholarship has done so much to illuminate. In Athens of the later fifth century
a few allusions in comedy help us to pick up some of the fashions. Specific

[27] *Mem.* 2. 6, esp. 2. 6. 35; cf. Davies (1971) no. 8823.
[28] As in the brilliant study by Forrest (1975).
[29] Ostwald (1986) 537–50 (appendix C) on the relationship between the *jeunesse dorée* and
political coups.   [30] Thuc. 8. 97. 2; *Ath. Pol.* 31.
[31] Pl. *Meno* 95 D.

songs can be inferred from Aristophanes' evidence, although the modish young Pheidippides prefers to recite a speech from Euripides rather than sing a song by Simonides to the accompaniment of the lyre (*Clouds* 1353–76). Recitations of speeches did become popular, but we would be wrong to imply that they squeezed out older, lyric song. Alan Cameron's fine book on Callimachus and his circle begins by stating that 'it is not surprising that young men who had grown up in the age of sophists preferred Euripidean speeches in their cups' (A. Cameron 1995: 72), but he goes on to illustrate very aptly how 'despite the popularity of dramatic recitation at Hellenistic symposia singing was not entirely a thing of the past' (ibid. 74). Despite the comic young Pheidippides, it was not so in classical Athens, either. Parties give vent to various forms of fun, and fashion was never one-sided.

If we attend to the 'wisdom' encountered by Socrates, we can add a further range of songs to those made explicit in bits of comedy. The sophists' young pupils knew these wise verses because they had learnt them, recited them, and sung them. The bits which are quoted in our texts, both then and later, were only the polite and more abstract outcrops of a broader and richer songsheet. Those who knew the verses on friendship will also have known the verses on *kakoi*, on the dēmos and even (despite A. R. Burn) the fickle charm of boys.

As the lamps burned low in the sympotic space of a Callias or Pyrilampes, young voices would raise a chorus of choice Theognid wisdom. What was good enough for Cyrnus was still good enough for a Charmides. The same stance of detached superiority befitted any young *agathos* who found himself living under the post-Periclean democracy. They began by singing their own alternative Acropolis Refrain: *akropolis kai pyrgos eōn* . . ., 'Acropolis and tower to the witless dēmos, Cyrnus, the good man receives scant honour' (Thgn. 233–6). They went on to the Plight of the Polis: 'The polis is still the polis, but its people are not the same' (Thgn. 53), as each of them felt in his bones after spending days in the assembly, surrounded by history's new *kakoi* and Cleon grinding on and on. The youthful voice of our 'Old Oligarch' was no doubt prominent, along with the enigmatic Critias, who capped it with the lines on Noble Breeding. It was time to put the boot in: *lax epiba dēmōi keneophroni. Lax epiba demōi* ('trample down the dēmos'): particular guests could enjoy a personal jibe, as Pyrilampes' son was called Demos (Davies 1971: no. 8792 § VIII). He too was notoriously 'witless', annoyingly handsome in the late 420s and no doubt better for a kick. All could enjoy the alternative political advice. Trample on Demos, great and small: such prejudice was best sung in private and Thucydides would have roared with the best of them. In many cases we know only an excerpt of the opening lines of the song. 'Fine is the answer of noble men, fine the deeds, but as for the ignoble, the winds bear their wretched words away' (Thgn. 1167–8): who is to say with what delicious incorrectness such verses were continued round the table? Among all the new theory and intellectual 'corruptions', an older songsheet bound these younger *chrēstoi* to the wisdom of the past. Democracy was not an alternative which Theognis had foreseen, but his verses and the accretions of the next hundred years still spoke to those who were not at home with their *politeia*.

In the 420s, however, the problems of apparent *philoi* and of *agathoi* who went *kakoi* were more acute than ever. There were too many political options and there was too little except a passé snobbism to hold all 'true' *agathoi* together. The highest Greek society had been remarkably prone to faction, even in its golden age, and Theognis had already given Cyrnus a lasting taste of a double-cross in verse. The inscrutability of man's character was a commonplace of other Attic drinking-songs:[32] if only we could see inside each other, the old songs said, we could judge each other's true character. Theognis, however, had linked this old theme to social change and the plight of a superior class under stress. In Athens of the late fifth century 'friendship from the tongue' had lost none of its relevance in the company of a Phrynichus (Thuc. 8. 50–1) or among drinking companions of Andocides, the born *agathos* who betrayed the *kaloi* in 415 and expected to be forgiven when the dust had settled: 'he has this skilled ability', according to his rhetorical attacker, most probably Meletus, 'to do his enemies no harm, but his friends as much harm as he can' (Lys. 6. 7). Theognis already knew his type. As for the earnest, theoretically committed, Theramenes, I sometimes think that contemporaries had torn the verses on treacherous friends and *agathoi* out of his Theognid songsheet. He soon grew out of singing, but the experience had not forewarned him about Peisander or Critias's capacity to double-cross.

According to Philodemus, it was the sentiments, rather than the music, of Ibycus, Anacreon, and others which corrupted the young.[33] He was discussing the value of music, but his comment can apply very well to the Athens of Pericles and Socrates. Superior birth and riches struck up a duet of sympathy with the moral poetry of old Theognis. Suspicions about its relevance can be grounded more firmly by observing Alcibiades. Every one of the songsheet's themes was admirably suited to this aristocrat's behaviour, a chameleon and polypus in one. In Thucydides' great speech for him at Sparta (6. 89–92) we catch some highly reminiscent echoes. This past master of 'protective mimicry' defends his fellow-travelling with democracy by pleading 'necessity': at Athens an aristocratic 'polypus' had no option. Others, according to Alcibiades, both now and among 'those from the past', had 'roused the dēmos to "more wicked" behaviour': Theognis had foreseen it, the *agathoi* turning *kakoi* and corrupting a dēmos which really needed a good, hard boot. 'As for love of my polis' says Alcibiades,

---

[32] Anonymous party songs translated in West (1993) 177–9, esp. v. 889.
[33] *De musica* XIV. 8–13.

'I am not going against a polis which is still mine, but trying to recover one which is no longer so' (6. 92. 4): Theognis again had shown the way, how 'the people are different though the polis is still (just) the same polis' (Thgn. 53). Theognis was writing when the lower classes first came out of the woods: would the polis still be the same if they actually took total control? As for friendship, the 'worst enemies are not those like you Spartans who do harm to their enemies, but those who force their friends to become enemies instead' (Thuc. 6. 92. 3). The old maxim in the background must not be missed, here: 'do the maximum good to friends and the maximum harm to enemies'. Alcibiades is defending his treachery by appealing to widely quoted wisdom,[34] but it is wisdom which the Theognid poems had also voiced and refined.

My argument, then, proceeds in stages: Theognis, a man from Megara, composed in the earlier sixth century and wrote when the ideal of aristocracy was being shaken by populist oligarchy. His poems circulated in writing and were known in variously organized collections at Athens, where they were read and sung by a new age of *agathoi* under stress. Those who 'found themselves living under a democracy' responded to Theognis' alternative voice, but that voice also warned why their own alternative would fall apart in faction and double-crossing.

---

[34] Blundell (1989) esp. 26–59; L. G. Mitchell (1997*b*) and L. G. Mitchell and Rhodes (1996) nicely illustrate the maxim's continuing life in Attic oratory of the 4th cent., but by then the 'friends and enemies' are drawn from the wider citizenry, not an old noble clique. For a similar extension of *kaloi kai agathoi* to the citizenry in the 4th cent. see Ste Croix (1972) 371–6.

3

Megara's Mafiosi: Timocracy and Violence in Theognis

HANS VAN WEES

BIRTH and wealth were the two criteria by which political power was restricted in the many Greek states which did not adopt democracy. How wealth came to replace birth as the more important of these criteria is one of the key questions in the history of archaic Greece, to which the usual answer is that it was down to economic expansion. New opportunities in trade and overseas settlement—to which some would add developments in agriculture—made some common men rich and made many more independent of aristocratic patrons. In the face of new propertied élites and newly prosperous 'middle classes', hereditary power and status declined.[1]

The elegies of 'the unacceptable face of aristocracy', Theognis of Megara,[2] are generally regarded as vital evidence for this process. A fresh look

---

[1] See e.g. Andrewes (1956) 31–8, 78–81; Forrest (1966) 67– 97; Murray (1993) 140–5, 220–1; Ste Croix (1981) 278–80; Donlan (1997); also Spencer (this volume). Agricultural developments: e.g. Starr (1977); Hanson (1995). The other major cause of change usually cited, the rise of the hoplite phalanx, has been losing ground: e.g. van Wees (1995b); Raaflaub (1997). The contrary view that there were no hereditary aristocracies to overthrow (Stahl 1987: esp. 83–4; Stein-Hölkeskamp 1989: esp. 86–93, 134–8) offers a largely convincing interpretation of later archaic society, but does not do justice to Homeric, Hesiodic, and other evidence for early aristocracies (cf. van Wees 1992: 73–4, 81–3, 158, 274–94).

[2] Murray (1993) 221. For the views adopted here on the various Theognidean questions see Robin Lane Fox in this volume (and e.g. Legon 1981: 106–11), but note the following differences. (1) I attribute to Theognis not only all verses addressed to Cyrnus, and the verses 11–14 and 429–38 (attributed to Theognis in the 4th cent. BC), but also 'unsigned' verses contained within the 'Cyrnus' blocks identified by West (1974: 42–6), i.e. *all* the verses 19–254 (including 153–4 and 227–32, adapted from Solon—see nn. 21 and 36 below), 319–72, 539–56, 805–22, and 1171–84b. The heavy concentration of addresses to Cyrnus suggests that these blocks were in their entirety excerpted from Theognis' elegies. This paper draws only on the verses so attributed, unless otherwise indicated (in brief references 'cf.' indicates that the lines which follow may not be by Theognis), and many well-known 'Theognidean' passages are thus excluded from consideration; none of these would pose a problem for my arguments. (2) Lane Fox is right to argue against West (1974: 65–71) that the reference to the capture of Smyrna implies a 6th-cent. date for Theognis, but I am not convinced by the argument that this reference precludes the dates offered by the ancient sources (between 552 and 541 BC) because the sack of Sardis and the Ionian cities by the Persians in 546–545 BC ought to have been mentioned by that date. Apart from the obvious possibility that the reference predates these events by a few years, it would not be surprising if, even after the Persian conquest, the example of a few cities which suffered an exceptional fate some generations ago carried more weight than the collective subjection (not destruction) of all Asian Greek cities in recent years. The ancient date in the 540s may not be reliable, but we have no grounds for rejecting it.

at Theognis' picture of society and politics in archaic Megara, however, will show that there is no sign of a hereditary élite, in decline or otherwise. There is a ruling class, of course, and Theognis himself belongs to it—he is a man who judges disputes (543–6), rides to battle on horseback in the company of his squire, Cyrnus (549–54),[3] and resents social climbers (53–8)—but this is no aristocracy of birth. Theognis' world is characterized, rather, by violent competition for power and property, and drastic changes of fortune, which made it impossible to sustain any kind of closed élite.[4] It was endemic violent conflict, more than economic expansion, which created such a degree of social mobility that hereditary aristocracy had to give way to timocracy as the only viable alternative.

Whereas the common interpretation of the shift from birth to wealth models itself, with suitable modifications, on the way in which the old aristocracy was gradually supplanted by bourgeois traders and industrialists in modern European history, we shall be drawing for inspiration on a very different model. George Forrest once suggested that 'the Cosa Nostra of the American Underworld' might be a suitable analogy for certain aspects of Dark Age Greek society, but added that the Greeks 'grew out of all such foolishness well before the days of detailed history' (Forrest 1966: 50). I venture to suggest that they did not. The violent world of the Sicilian and American Mafia has a good deal in common with the world of Theognis, and a study of it may help us understand better the nature of archaic Greek society and politics.[5]

The struggle for power

The death of Rosario 'The Terrorist' Riccobono might almost have been designed to illustrate Theognis' dictum that 'it is hard to deceive an enemy, but easy for a friend to deceive a friend' (1219–20). In 1982 two of the top men in the Sicilian Mafia invited many of their colleagues to a lavish Christmas lunch. Riccobono, having been treated as 'one of the most pampered guests', dozed off after the meal. His hosts had him strangled in his sleep.[6] Mafiosi insist that they are friends and family to their associates. 'You know, Frankie, I don't like you—I love you. I don't like Sammy—I love him,' John Gotti assures two of his under-bosses in a conversation taped by the FBI, 'I love you guys. I don't fabricate no part of it'. Loyalty is

[3] Theognis' order to Cyrnus to 'bridle the horses' (551) means that he fights as a mounted hoplite accompanied by a squire (*contra* van Groningen 1966: 219, 311).

[4] Stahl (1987: esp. 63–5, 89–93) is exceptional in giving the consequences of endemic élite violence their full weight (*contra* Von Der Lahr 1992: 59–72, esp. 61). The political rather than social significance of internal conflict has recently been stressed by R. Osborne (1996: esp. 185–97), and Raaflaub (1997: 57).

[5] The parallels are not complete or perfect, of course, but in many respects work remarkably well: see also van Wees (1999).

[6] Follain (1995) 127 (cf. 119); Stille (1994) 96, 112.

the highest ideal. A Sicilian hitman proudly declares: 'That's what I was: a man to be trusted . . . loyal through and through.'[7] All the same, the annals of the Mafia are littered with stories of betrayal. Many of the best-known figures—John Gotti included—came to power by having their bosses murdered.[8] Megara may not have reached quite such levels of violence, but the deep mistrust of friends which characterizes Theognis' poetry shows a society which, like the Mafia, is held together by friendship and torn apart by ambition.

Friendship is more than an emotional bond for Theognis; it is also, and primarily, an instrumental relationship in which benefits are shared and reciprocated. 'What use is a worthless man as friend (*philos*)?', he asks, counting the ways in which such a man falls short: when you are in trouble, he will not help; when he is in luck, he will not share; when you do him a favour, he will give nothing in return; however much you do for him, the relationship will always remain precarious, 'for the bad have a mind that cannot be satisfied, and if you make one mistake, the friendship is drained from everything that happened before' (102–10). The opening line of this passage warns against letting a third party persuade one to 'make friends with a bad man' (101), which suggests the sort of manoeuvring associated with political intrigue, in which the instrumental side of friendship would have been of particular importance.[9]

Theognis complains that the citizens of Megara are worse than worthless as friends: they are positively treacherous. 'They deceive one another and laugh at one another' (59=1113), adding insult to injury by ridiculing their victims (van Groningen 1966: 33 ad 59). His advice is therefore not to 'make friends with any of these townsmen' (61), and not to 'join with anyone in any serious matter', since 'they cannot be trusted at all in what they do, but they love tricks and convoluted deceptions' (64–8). The deceivers seek 'evil gains' (κακοκερδείη, 221–6)—a single ship could carry all men in the entire world 'who are not driven to shameful things by gain' (83–6)—and the deceived suffer 'grief beyond healing' (75–6). These references to serious matters and serious consequences show that Theognis is talking about a sphere of action in which the stakes are high, and he once specifically refers to private feuding or political rivalry: 'a trustworthy man is worth as much as gold and silver in a hard conflict' (διχοστασία, 77–8). In Megara treachery for the sake

---

[7] *The Gotti Tapes*, 25, 28; Anon. (1991) 192. Bonanno (1983: 'Family', 'friends', not 'organization' and 'business associates': 147–9; 'Father', not 'boss': 85).

[8] Usurpation as structural to Mafia politics: Arlacchi (1986) 15–16; Blok (1974) 172–4.

[9] 'Politicized' friendship in Theognis: Konstan (1997) 49–52; Donlan (1985); Sartori (1957) 20–3. Konstan is right to reject the view of Nagy (1985: e.g. 27–8, 56), picked up by Donlan (1985: 243–4), that Theognis means all members of the community when he speaks of *philoi*: fellow citizens are *astoi*, *philoi* are friends.

of personal advantage has poisoned the competition for power and prestige.[10]

Deceit lurks especially among friends. 'Few companions' will stand by you when times are bad (79–82). The poet wishes for a companion (*hetairos*) who does remain loyal 'like a brother'(97–99), but he later asserts that not even a brother will be friends with a man in trouble (299–300). Within his own circle of friends, too, solidarity is limited: 'when you suffer, Cyrnus, we all grieve with you; but remember that other people's troubles last but a day' (655–6). Again, while sadly noting that exiles are deserted by their friends (209–10 = 332ab), Theognis recommends taking no chances with such people: 'Never befriend an exile for the sake of his prospects, Cyrnus, for when he goes home he is no longer the same man' (333–4). The instrumental nature of these relationships means that friends are quickly dropped when they no longer have the resources to make themselves useful.[11]

There is also constant anxiety about being betrayed by friends 'in serious matters': 'Do not fully share your affairs with all your friends; of many, few have a mind that can be trusted. Trust in few men when you embark upon important actions' (73–5); 'Many are companions over drinks and dinner, but only a few in serious matters' (115–16; cf. 641–4). Theognis worries about 'dangerous' (δεινός) companions who say one thing but think another, who praise you to your face but speak ill of you behind your back (91–6, 117–26), but even as he bemoans the untrustworthiness of friends, he comes perilously close to recommending that his friends should be deceitful—to everyone but him (Konstan 1997: 50):

Do not make any of these townsmen your friend from the heart, son of Polypaos, not for any reason, but in what you say give the impression of being a friend to all, while in matters of importance you join with no one. (61–5)

Cyrnus, take a subtle attitude towards all friends, adopting the temperament of each. You must have the temperament of the wily octopus, which appears to the eye like whatever rock it hovers around. Attach yourself to this rock now, turn a different colour next. Intelligence is better than inflexibility. (213–18; 1071–4)

None of this advice is supposed to apply in relations with Theognis himself. 'Do not show *me* respect in words while your mind and heart are elsewhere,' he says; 'a fine man' should 'ever have an unchanging attitude towards a friend, until the end' (87–90; 1082c–1084). Logically inconsistent as these pieces of advice are, they make perfect sense in the poet's paranoid universe, where treachery is always just around the corner: it is equally vital to trust no one and to have friends who can be trusted implicitly.

In practice, it seems, Theognis' relationships with his friends were

---

[10] So Donlan (1985) 239; *contra* van Groningen (1966) 45–6 and Jacoby (1931) 60, who oddly insist that Theognis is speaking of social or economic, not political, life.
[11] Donlan (1985) 230; Foxhall (1998) 56.

fraught. 'My friends have betrayed me,' he tells Cyrnus (811–13), and another time he complains that not even Cyrnus shows him 'the slightest respect' but deceives him 'with words, as if I were a little boy' (253–4), perhaps because someone has given him 'advice' about his mentor and told him to break off the friendship (1101–2 = 1278ab).

Stark evidence of the general atmosphere of suspicion is the fact that Theognis finds it necessary to argue that 'one must never *destroy* a friend for a *petty* reason, Cyrnus, giving credence to harsh slander; if a man becomes angry at every mistake made by his friends, they will never be dear or close to one another' (323–7; 1133–4). Errors and rumours are evidently liable to provoke a fierce response. Theognis himself, while advocating tolerance in minor matters, responds ferociously to more serious transgressions. He switches allegiance, joining forces with former enemies (813–14), and seeks revenge. 'When great harm is done to a man, his heart shrinks, Cyrnus, but after avenging himself it grows big' (361–2). In revenge, too, deception is the key to success: 'Talk nicely to your enemy, but when he falls into your hands, make him pay without making excuses' (363–4).

The level of violence in these confrontations is high. Theognis lost all his farm land (1197–201) to 'men who hold my possessions, having seized them by force' (346–7). One passage, unfortunately garbled, appears to connect this with a sea voyage (1202), another refers to the poet as 'a dog who crossed the water course in winter flood and shook everything off' (347–8). Both suggest that the property was lost as a result of a hasty flight abroad, which in turn suggests that Theognis abandoned his estate fearing for his life.[12] His vengeful prayers are: 'may I have greater power than my enemies' (337), 'may I give pain in return for pain, for that is the right thing' (344), and 'may I drink their dark blood' (349). Allowing for a rhetorical flourish in this last phrase, it nevertheless seems clear that he has lethal retaliation in mind. Should he succeed, he will gloat at his enemy's funeral—if that is what is meant by the startling exhortation to laugh and enjoy oneself in the presence of 'one who weeps' (1217–18; cf. 1041–2).[13]

As in the world of the Mafia, lives and possessions are at risk in struggles for power conducted with the help of close companions and friends. Fierce competition and high stakes mean extreme demands on loyalty, great rewards for disloyalty, and therefore constantly changing alliances. Like many a Mafioso, Theognis may call others aggressive and treacherous while thinking of himself as pragmatic and adaptable in holding his own and avenging

---

[12] The interpretation of 347–8 by van Groningen (1966: 139–40) and West (1974: 153) is preferable to Nagy's (1985: 71–2). The sea voyage in 1202 has alternatively been explained as a trading venture: Jacoby (1931) 60; Nagy (1985) 64–8; Erbse (1998) 240–1 (who misunderstands the ingenious emendation proposed by West 1974: 164–5).

[13] Adopting the reading of 1217–18 in West's edition, which deletes 'never' as a misguided emendation by a pious excerptor; the sentiment is clear in 1041–2, but that couplet may not be by Theognis. On the level of violence see Stahl (1987) 64–5.

his wrongs, but in reality the fine line between flexibility and duplicity is bound to have been frequently crossed by both sides.

The exercise of power

Theognis' picture of the ruling classes of his city is drawn in black and white. The élite is divided between 'good' or 'fine' men (*agathoi*; *esthloi*), like himself, and 'bad' or 'worthless' men (*kakoi*; *deiloi*) who use their power aggressively. Just how distorted an image of power relations in Megara this may have been is brought home by a glance at the similarly black-and-white world of the Mafia.

The adjective *mafioso* describes someone or something admirable, and Mafiosi are fond of admitting that they *are* Mafiosi, 'if by mafioso one means, as I mean, be good to your neighbour . . . and give help to people in difficulty'.[14] The Calabrian equivalent *'ndranghetista* derives from *andragathia*, 'being a good man', and two of the Mafioso's favourite epithets, 'man of honour' (*uomo d'onore*) and 'man of order' (*uomo di ordine*), also stake his claim to represent what is right and proper. One Sicilian-born New York boss claims that 'we considered our code of ethics stricter and fairer than any we encountered in America'.[15]

The use of violence is played down or conveniently ignored. 'All the things that I have known inside Cosa Nostra are beautiful,' gushes supergrass Tommaso Buscetta, 'with the exception of murder, which is a necessity.' Another informer reminisces: 'the mafiosi were . . . the wise ones. You never thought of the violence.' The rosiest picture comes from a hitman with about a dozen killings to his name who likes to think that his boss 'was against bloodshed and had always been able to command respect without using violence, which is how it used to be years ago'.[16]

Rivals, by contrast, are painted in very dark colours, especially when they are more successful. The New York don who speaks of the fairness of his own code complains that an old opponent attained his position of dominance 'through a combination of intimidation, strong-arm tactics, bullying and tenacity'. The hitman who waxes nostalgic about a peaceful past accuses a new generation of having 'neither rules nor principles': they 'became successful in only a year or two by using fear. No one trusted them . . . They were wild beasts.' Yet even this new generation, associated with the notorious Mafia of Corleone under Totò 'The Beast' Riina, took pains to eliminate their enemies 'in a formally correct way so that not even the victims' closest friends could react, being formally in the wrong'. They did

[14] Follain (1995) 3. Variations on this theme: ibid. 54 (Buscetta); Arlacchi (1986) 181 (a cabinet minister); Bonanno (1983) 31.
[15] Bonanno (1983) 223 (cf. 404). *'Ndrangheta*: Arlacchi (1986) 4–5 (Anton Powell alerted me to the significance of this word).
[16] Informers: Follain (1995) 3–4. Hitman: Anon. (1991) 59–60 (his tally: 231).

so 'to fortify their own men in the belief that they were upholding the laws of Cosa Nostra rather than violating them'.[17]

Neither the high ideals claimed for 'us' nor the low violence attributed to 'them' can be taken at face value. The reality of Mafia politics falls somewhere in between—or combines—the two extremes.[18]

Theognis denounces the regime in Megara in strong terms. 'These townsmen are still sensible', he says, 'but the leaders are set to sink into deep trouble' (41–2 = 1082ab). For now, all is 'very quiet', but 'civil conflicts' and 'internecine killings' will soon shatter the calm and the city will end up governed by 'sole rulers' (47–52). The implied scenario is that the people will eventually turn against the ruling class and support men seeking to establish themselves as dictators, 'tyrants': 'this polis is pregnant, Cyrnus, and I fear that she may give birth to a chastiser of our bad *hybris*' (39–40). *Hybris*—wilful humiliation of the weak by the powerful[19]—is thus singled out as the key characteristic of the regime. As a member of the élite, Theognis speaks of 'our' *hybris*, but he immediately goes on to dissociate himself from it, explaining that 'good men have never yet destroyed a single polis' and that the *hybris* of the élite is perpetrated by its 'bad' members (43–4).[20]

Theognis' warnings grow ever more dire. 'I fear, son of Polypaos, that *hybris* will destroy this polis, just as it did the raw-meat-eating Centaurs' (541–2). '*Hybris* destroyed the Magnesians, and Colophon, and Smyrna; it will certainly destroy you people too, Cyrnus' (1103–4; 235–6; cf. 603–4). He reminds us that wealth produces 'surfeit', which inspires *hybris*, which leads to disaster. These lines borrow heavily from Solon, but introduce a characteristic twist: in Solon, the rule applies to all mankind; in Theognis, it applies specifically 'to a bad man' (151–4).[21] He further alleges that 'the bad men . . . ruin the people and give judgments in favour of the unjust, for the sake of private gains and power' (44–6), and that they like 'gains accompanied by public misery' (49–50):[22] 'All this has gone to the dogs and

---

[17] Quotations from, respectively, Bonanno (1983) 85–6 (cf. 123–4); Anon. (1991) 95–6; Follain (1995) 97, 119; Stille (1994) 119.

[18] Also Follain (1995) 45; and van Wees (1999).

[19] That this is the meaning of *hybris* has been definitively established by Fisher (1992: esp. 208–16 for *hybris* in Theognis); further observations in Cairns (1996).

[20] A variation on this passage (1081–4) attributes the *hybris* to the future tyrant, not to the present élite; this is a very different sentiment, and despite the address to Cyrnus this is likely to be the work of a different poet, whether a later poet trying to 'amend' Theognis (Von Der Lahr 1992: 87–9) or an earlier author (Nagy 1985: 50). For the status of the 'leaders' see n. 22 below.

[21] To my mind, the manuscripts of Theognis are right to treat the whole of 151–4 as a single poem. Editors treat 153–4 as distinct because they are almost identical to two verses from Solon (fr. 6. 3–4 West), but I would argue that these lines were taken from their Solonic context and deliberately adapted by Theognis (so also Donlan 1980: 84; see nn. 2 above and 36 below). That Theognis believes a good man, unlike a bad man, capable of avoiding *hybris* even when he becomes rich is clear from 319–22.

[22] The view that the 'bad leaders' are demagogues trying to 'corrupt' (not 'ruin') the people

lies in ruins, and the blessed immortal gods are not at all to blame, Cyrnus, but the violence and low gains and *hybris* of men have knocked us from much prosperity into misery' (833–6; cf. 289–92).

The moral standards of our poet himself, by contrast, are so demanding that some of his precepts acquired the status of proverbial wisdom. The very first lesson he imparts to his young friend Cyrnus is a blanket rejection of all injustice: 'Be sensible, and do not by shameful or illegitimate means pull in honours or excellences or wealth' (27–30). Against *hybris* he sets 'good sense' (γνώμη), 'the best thing gods can give to mortal men, Cyrnus' and 'much better than destructive *hybris*' (1171–6; cf. 895–6). Against coercion, he sets 'bestowing benefactions' (εὐεργεσία): 'there is nothing better for a just man' (547–8). Against greed, he counsels that 'you should want to live with little property, a respectful man, rather than become rich by acquiring property unjustly' (145–6). Lasting possessions can be acquired only 'from Zeus, with justice, and in a pure manner'; anything obtained 'illegitimately, before time, in a spirit of greed' or 'under oath against what is right' will be lost sooner or later (197–208).

Against corruption in the administration of justice, he sets his own scruples, which he urges his friends to imitate:

I must judge this case with a carpenter's rule and square, Cyrnus, and be fair to both sides, with the aid of seers and bird omens and burnt offerings, in order to avoid the shameful accusation that I have made a mistake. (543–6; cf. 945–6)

Walk the middle of the road, calm like me, and do not give to one side, Cyrnus, what belongs to the other. (331–2; cf. 219–20).

Theognis even offers a striking definition of what it means to be 'good', to have 'excellence' (*aretē*). Justice alone matters: 'All excellence is contained in righteousness, and every man is good, Cyrnus, if he is just' (147–8). 'If you could be neither victim nor perpetrator of shameful deeds, Cyrnus, you would experience the greatest excellence' (1177–8). These are potentially radical sentiments, but Theognis did not intend to issue an egalitarian manifesto.[23] The tacit assumption, voiced elsewhere in the corpus, is that the poor cannot help behaving badly (383–92), and, as we shall see, Theognis does not believe that anyone born bad can learn to be good. To him, only men born into prosperity *can* ever be righteous and achieve excellence.

This image of a ruling class divided into a group without any faults and a group without any merits is hardly realistic. It is significant that the population of Megara failed to appreciate the self-proclaimed virtues of Theognis and his like: 'when he is citadel and bulwark to an empty-headed people,

---

(van Groningen 1966: 29; West 1974: 68–9; Legon 1981: 113–14; Von Der Lahr 1992: 41–5, 49–50) is rightly rejected by Nagy (1985: 43–4) and Fisher (1992: 208–9).

[23] So Donlan (1980) 94. One of these lines is also attributed to Phocylides (fr. 10 Diels).

Cyrnus, it is a fine man's lot to get little respect' (233–4).[24] It is equally significant that the Megarians, it seems, did not rise up against their oppressors, as Theognis thinks they should have done. His acknowledgement that for the moment all remained 'very quiet' and the frequent repetition of his prophecies of disaster suggest that nothing happened. Frustration at seeing the power of 'the bad men' unchallenged may have sparked this outburst: 'Stamp on the empty-headed people, hit them with a sharp stick, and put them under a heavy yoke, for among all mankind upon whom the sun looks down you will not find a people who love their masters so much' (847–50).[25] If the Megarians did not respect 'the good' and did not resist 'the bad', it was surely not because they were stupid or slavish, as Theognis would have it, but because they did not think highly of the former and did not particularly resent the latter.

What we have in Theognis' poetry is thus analogous to what we have found among Mafiosi: a highly favourable self-image of one section of the elite contrasted with a deeply hostile image of their political rivals—who are apparently in the majority or, at any rate, enjoying greater success. In reality, the behaviour of both sides is likely to have combined, and ranged between, the extremes. The strains created were apparently not so unbearable as to provoke a popular uprising, but powerful enough to be exploited for the purposes of Theognis' political propaganda. *Hybris*, coercion, greed, and corruption in the administration of justice thus featured prominently in Megarian politics, and this is hardly surprising in view of the picture painted for us of fierce and often violent competition for wealth and power.

Violence and social mobility

Coercion and deception can be effective shortcuts to success: when crime pays, it really pays. In a violently competitive society, therefore, one may expect to find considerable social mobility, as successful perpetrators of violence and deceit rise while their victims' fortunes decline in proportion. This is certainly true of the world of the Mafia, and it appears to be true also of Theognis' Megara.

The situation in the traditional agricultural communities of Sicily offers the closest parallels to ancient Greece. Most rural Mafiosi were respected members of the local landowning élite, which controlled most political offices. They were in the habit, however, of employing the 'muscle' of poor agricultural labourers and shepherds, for whom the rewards of a violent career meant—sometimes spectacular—social advancement. 'Mafiosi kept restive peasants in submission, while opening up avenues for upwardly

---

[24] And not all the townsmen are 'pleased' with him: 24–6, 367–8 = 1184ab, 369–70.

[25] These verses contain no address to Cyrnus, but it is tempting to attribute them to Theognis on the strength of the recurring phrase 'the empty-headed people'.

mobile peasants who qualified in the use of violence.'[26] Among those who seized the opportunity were the three men who dominated the Sicilian Mafia in the first half of the twentieth century: Vito Cascio Ferro, son of a peasant, 'Uncle' Calò Vizzini, son of a day labourer, and Giuseppe Genco Russo, shepherd. Recent leaders have come from the same background: Luciano Liggio was from 'a poor and illiterate peasant family, and one of the most violent lieutenants in the local mafia clan', as was Totò Riina, whose mother could not even afford the train fare to visit him in jail.[27]

As these social climbers seized property and muscled in on sources of income, others inevitably lost both wealth and influence. Influence, in particular, was easily lost, and Mafia leadership was often short-lived, rarely passed on from father to son. Despite the general mobility and instability, established Mafiosi despised parvenus. Liggio and Riina 'were snootily referred to as the *viddani*', the 'peasants', by the bosses in Palermo, and even Liggio's own boss in Corleone is said to have spoken of him as a 'tramp' and 'a jumped-up nobody who didn't know his place and needed to be taught a lesson'.[28]

This may throw some light on Theognis' attitudes towards social mobility. In Megara, he complains, the most marginal members of society have risen to the top, while the most prominent families have sunk low: 'Cyrnus, this polis is still a polis but its people now are other men, who previously knew no courts or laws, but wore threadbare goatskins on their backs and grazed like deer outside this city. And now, son of Polypaos, they are good men, and those who used to be fine men are now worthless' (53–8). It is obvious that 'good', 'fine', and 'worthless' are here not primarily ethical terms, but have a social connotation, as they so often do in Greek literature: rustics becoming 'good' means that they attain a high status, fine men becoming 'worthless' means that they lose their former social standing. Another passage makes this even clearer: 'Cyrnus, the good men of the past are now bad men, and those who used to be bad men are now good men. Who could bear to see such things: the good men less respected, worse men treated with respect? And the fine man courts the offspring of the bad one' (1109–12).[29]

This last comment reveals that social climbers are assimilated into the established élite through marriage, a practice denounced at length elsewhere: 'A fine man does not mind marrying a bad daughter of a bad man so long as he is given much wealth, nor does a woman refuse to be the wife of a wealthy bad man, but she wants riches instead of a good man. They respect

---

[26] Blok (1974) 75 (cf. 96 and, for a case study, 148–9).

[27] Follain (1995) 14–15; also 101 (on Liggio) and 15, 96, 98, 115 (on Riina). The anonymous hitman of *Man of Respect* is also the son of a very poor agricultural labourer (see van Wees 1999); he ends up as a prosperous farmer.

[28] Palermo bosses: Follain (1995) 104. Corleone boss: Anon. (1991) 49, 51.

[29] It may be, as West suggests (1974: 150), that 1110–14 are a fuller extract from the same original text as 58–60, with 1109 a variation on 57 (or a condensation of 53–7).

wealth: fine man marries bad man's offspring and bad man marries the off-spring of good' (185–90). Marrying a rich man's daughter meant receiving a large dowry, while there will have been less direct advantages in marrying off one's own daughter to a rich man. As a result, 'wealth and birth [γένος] mingle', and 'the birth of the townsmen is obscured' (190–2). Theognis could hardly have been more emphatic that the 'bad' owe their new-found status to nothing but wealth. The 'good', he implies, have been born into their position, a claim to which we shall return.

The poet's disapproval of associations between 'good' and 'bad' extends beyond intermarriage to *any* kind of contact with 'bad' men. 'Do not so-cialize with bad men, but always deal with the good: drink and eat among them, and sit among them, and please them, whose power is great. For you will learn fine things from fine people, but if you mix with the bad, you will ruin even what sense you have. Now that you know these things, socialize with the good' (31–7; also 113–14). The ostensible emphasis here is on the morally corrupting influence of bad company, but the remark about the power of 'good men' indicates a hidden agenda. Moral excellence and pol-itical clout appear together again later: 'inferior to no one, it would seem, is a companion who has good sense, and who has power' (411–12). The powerful 'good men' with whom one must associate must be members of the established élite while the 'bad men' to avoid are social climbers.[30]

However exaggerated, Theognis' claims that high and low had changed places and his warnings against making friends with men of humble social origins do indicate considerable social mobility, both upwards and down-wards. Where did new wealth come from, and how was old wealth lost? Despite a good deal of interest in the unpredictability of life,[31] there is in Theognis no hint of fortunes made or lost in trade, of agricultural disasters or windfalls, or of wealth wasted in conspicuous consumption. What we do find are abundant references to violent and deceitful acquisition. The only concrete instance of wealth changing hands may be the forcible seizure of the poet's land by unspecified enemies, but, as we have seen, Theognis presents a Megara full of 'bad' men who are driven by *hybris* and greed to use their power violently and corruptly, and who will betray their closest friends for personal gain. Allowing once again for exaggeration and distor-tion, one may reasonably conclude that Theognis' fate was far from unique: much property was acquired and lost as a result of violence, intimidation, and deceit.

This conclusion is strengthened if the two groups of 'bad' men we have encountered in Theognis—those who are morally 'bad' in their abuse of power, and those who are 'bad' in terms of their humble origins—are the

[30] The warning never to 'lay plans with a bad man' when it concerns 'something important' (69–70) is surely also directed against political ties with social climbers.

[31] See 129–30, 133–42, 155–72.

same group, as they surely must be. Theognis would hardly regard many men of 'bad' social origins as morally 'good' yet refuse to have anything to do with them, or accuse members of the established élite of being morally 'bad' while insisting that one should socialize and marry only within this group.[32] Theognis' view is, rather, that Megara's upwardly mobile—so far from becoming popular leaders against the establishment[33]—constitute the most aggressive and oppressive element of the ruling class. This is a hostile view, but the connection it makes is not implausible: one can see why new members of the ruling class would be particularly aggressive if they had made careers of violent acquisition.

If we further assume that even the poorest had opportunities to enrich themselves by means of force, either independently or, more probably, as 'muscle' for competing factions within the élite, there might be some truth even in another of Theognis' seemingly wild exaggerations: some of the new rich might indeed once have been very poor shepherds or agricultural labourers living on the margins of society.

Theognis' image of 'the bad men' is close to the lurid image which an established Mafioso tends to have of new rivals—low-born, violent, untrustworthy, bestial—and I would suggest that both perceptions are the product of a similar social structure, in which violence is widespread and social mobility extensive. This has implications for Theognis' claim to speak for an élite which was born to its eminent status.

Timocracy and 'aristocracy'

If it is true that social status and property ownership were in constant flux as a result of violent competition, no élite could have remained closed for long. The result would have been a *de facto*, if not *de jure*, timocracy. Theognis' groans about 'obscured' birth may make him sound like a spokesman for an aristocracy trying to defend its privileges against a new propertied elite, but one should neither overestimate the importance of 'birth' in his thought nor make too much of his rejection of wealth.

Every generation of Mafiosi deplores the growing importance of money, even as they rake it in. It is clear that, from the moment the Mafia began to take shape in the 1860s, the acquisition of wealth was its *raison d'être*, yet mafiosi always seem to think that money used to matter less in the past. In 1909 the shooting of an American policeman in Palermo was seen as a sign that the Mafia 'was turning into a more violent and ruthless organization in which the accumulation of wealth had become the key objective'. The same complaint was heard in 1931, when Charlie 'Lucky' Luciano rose to power

[32] West, however, dissociates the two sets of 'bad men', by positing a drastic change of regime between the composition of 39–52 and 53–68 (1974: 69–70).

[33] See n. 22 above for the mistaken view that they become 'demagogues', and see Stein-Hölkeskamp (1989: 90–1) and Stahl (1987: 83–4) on absorption into the élite.

in New York. Again, in 1963 the arrest of Giuseppe Genco Russo prompted one of his men to complain that 'money had destroyed the old ideals of respect'; this same man, by his own admission, none the less disobeyed his next boss's orders and struck out on his own to make a fortune from heroin dealing.[34] It is true that Mafiosi have been competing for ever greater financial rewards, and it does seem that disputes over matters of 'honour' have declined in favour of even more disputes over money (Arlacchi 1986: 57–61), but grumbling about the undue influence of money is evidently a constant in Mafia history. Behind it surely lies a clash between ideology and practice. Wealth was never supposed to be more than a by-product of competition for honour, respect, and power (Bonanno 1983: 162), but in fact was always a prime objective in its own right.

'Excellence' (*aretē*), as we have seen, is defined by Theognis as purely a matter of righteousness. The implication that wealth is irrelevant to being 'good' or 'bad' is spelt out elsewhere. 'A divine power may give wealth even to an utterly bad man, Cyrnus, but a share of excellence is allotted to few' (149–50). The best 'treasury' to bequeath to one's children is not of a material nature, but the 'respect accorded to good men' (409–10; cf. 1161–2). Wealth supposedly does not matter.

The significance attributed to birth, while greater than that of wealth, is remarkably limited. It is certainly not a pervasive concern, but addressed only in the context of marriage and procreation (183–96). Even in this context, there is no explicit reference to more than a single generation of ancestors: the poet speaks of 'a bad daughter of a bad man' (κακὴν κακοῦ, 186), 'the offspring of a bad (or good) man' (ἐκ κακοῦ, ἐξ ἀγαθοῦ, 198–90, 1112), and 'a woman with a bad father' (κακόπατρις, 193), rather than using phrases indicating a longer line of descent, such as 'the offspring of bad men' in the plural, or 'of good family'. As with one's own qualities, excellence in one's parents is a matter of righteousness, not wealth or power or descent: 'there is nothing better among mankind, Cyrnus, than a father and mother who give heed to holy justice' (131–2). And even being the child of good parents is no guarantee that one will be a good man oneself, for 'if good sense were something that could be created and put into a man, no bad man would ever be born from a good father, since he would be persuaded by wise words. But by teaching you will never make a bad man good' (429–38). If some children of good people are born bad, and if the bad remain beyond educating, then excellence is evidently a moral quality which is neither innate nor passed down through a long, noble lineage, but which by some combination of heredity and education *may* be derived from one's parents.

What Theognis attributes to the established élite is thus a moral superiority completely divorced from wealth and only partially related to birth. This

---

[34] Wealth always the main objective: Blok (1974); 1909: Follain (1995) 27–9; 1931: Bonanno (1983) 162–3 (also 290–1, 404); 1963: Anon. (1991) 88 and 156–9, 185 (drug trade).

hardly amounts to a legitimation of 'aristocratic' power, as scholars would have it.[35] On the contrary, the criteria of excellence advocated by Theognis are *in principle* egalitarian: the poet felt that few met them, but the criteria in themselves contain nothing that is peculiarly aristocratic, nothing beyond the aspirations of common men.

Theognis thus offers neither an aristocratic ideology nor evidence for an endangered hereditary aristocracy. He speaks as a member of an established élite which is 'established' only in the sense that it has been in power rather longer—perhaps no more than a generation longer—than the rivals who have recently gained the upper hand. He claims in justification of this élite no hereditary privileges or innate superiority, but only that its members have been raised to live up to the highest moral standards to which all citizens aspire, while their rivals and inferiors are driven by the lowest and most selfish of impulses.

In reality, being a righteous man and having righteous parents was clearly never enough to ensure prestige and power, and Theognis elsewhere admits that wealth mattered a great deal. He ruefully acknowledges, in lines adapted from Solon, that 'to wealth there is no apparent limit for mankind, because those of us who now have the greatest livelihood are eager to have twice as much' (227–9).[36] What is more, he concedes that 'a man of good repute' may find himself forced to marry beneath him (193–6), since poverty is to be avoided at all costs: 'On the run from poverty one must even throw oneself into the sea with its great monsters, Cyrnus, and jump from steep cliffs . . . For a poor man, dear Cyrnus, it is better to die than to live while harsh poverty grinds him down' (175–6, 181–2).

Poverty is relative, of course, and any man who could not afford a life of leisure on the income from his property might be called 'poor' (*penēs*) in Greek. Having to scrape a living is accordingly not primarily what Theognis is worried about. To him, the greatest horror of poverty lies in a loss of *power*: 'Poverty, more than anything else, including grey old age and fever, Cyrnus, subdues a good man . . . and a man subdued by poverty can neither say nor do anything; his tongue is tied' (173–4, 177–8). Presumably the reference is not only to a muted role in social life, but also to the exclusion of the poor from politics. A later poem, which may or may not be by Theognis himself, says so explicitly: 'You recognize poverty even when she belongs to someone else, for she attends neither assembly nor legal proceedings

---

[35] e.g. Donlan (1985) 77–95; Stein-Hölkeskamp (1989) 92; Von Der Lahr (1992) 103.

[36] The change from Solon's text is small in these lines, but significant in what follows: whereas in Solon the gods give 'gains' only to take them away again (fr. 13. 75–6 West), Theognis introduces the element of human 'foolishness' (ἀφροσύνη) into the equation, which fits well with the importance he attaches to 'good sense' everywhere else, making it the greatest good of all in 1171–6, cited above (cf. Donlan 1980: 92–3). Again we have a deliberate adaptation of Solon by Theognis (see nn. 2 and 21 above).

[δίκαι]' (267–8).[37] If poverty was a fate worse than death, if power depended on wealth, and if few among the established élite had qualms about bonding with the newly wealthy, we can only conclude that the Megarian regime of Theognis' day was indeed a timocracy, in which property determined political and social status regardless of social origins.

When a New York godfather concludes his autobiography with the sentence 'I have learned that true wealth comes from good family and good friends' (Bonanno 1983: 406), we do not conclude that he is a defender of aristocracy against timocracy, and we should not draw that conclusion from similar sentiments in Theognis either. All we can safely infer from his work is, on the one hand, an ideology according to which the longer-established element of the élite possessed a far greater measure of 'good sense' and 'righteousness' than recent recruits; and, on the other hand, a world of violent competition, extensive social mobility, and timocracy, in which no élite group could long retain unchallenged dominance, and no one could claim to have a monopoly on sense and righteousness—or on *hybris* and greed, for that matter.

Conclusion: violence, wealth, and birth in archaic Greece

The purpose of drawing comparisons between the worlds of Theognis and the Mafia has been to highlight the culture of violent competition which they have in common. If Mafiosi, all engaged in fierce struggles for power and wealth, can see themselves as paragons of virtue while accusing their rivals of unprincipled greed and violence, we need to look beyond Theognis' black-and-white imagery, and give full weight to the evidence which suggests that in his community violence and greed were structural phenomena, rather than aberrations which could be blamed on 'the bad men'.

This conclusion should in turn alert us to the significance of other archaic evidence which attests to the prevalence of violent competition for power. It is in the nature of the surviving evidence that we hear most about the *coups d'état* and violent reigns of tyrants, but we should not assume that such men were exceptional in resorting to force. Poetry—notably the remainder of the Theognid corpus and the work of Alcaeus—and oral tradition both suggest that violent struggles among the élite were common and invariably involved groups of people going into exile or fighting their way back. In many parts of Greece, as in Megara, therefore, power and property must have changed hands constantly as it was abandoned, seized, and recovered.

The Mafia analogy has also drawn to our attention the possibility of a high degree of social mobility where violent conflict is endemic. Theognis shows that this was true in Megara, and his near contemporary Anacreon actually tells us of the remarkable ascent of Artemon, once a petty criminal,

---

[37] Van Groningen (1966) 110 ad 267–70 points out the significance of this passage.

now a rich man with all the trappings of the leisure class (fr. 388 Page). In this light, we should also take seriously the many poets who comment on the changeability of fortune and the high hopes of men, such as the late-seventh-century Semonides, who notes that 'there is no mortal who does not think that, this time next year, he will be a friend to wealth and the good people' (fr. 1. 9–10 West). As well as reflecting on the vanity of ambition, lines like these may reflect real possibilities of social advancement.

Finally, the way in which Mafiosi habitually deplore the importance of wealth even though they are prepared to kill for money has warned us against reading a traditional aristocratic ideology opposed to timocracy into Theognis' rejection of wealth in favour of moral excellence. Similar sentiments are strewn throughout what survives of archaic poetry. Already around 600 BC Alcaeus can quote 'a man is what he owns' as a well-known saying (fr. 360 LP). The poets evidently felt that in a perfect world wealth would play less of a part in society, and timocracy was clearly not their ideal. On the other hand, there is little to suggest that hereditary aristocracy was any more of an ideal. Few poets after Homer and Hesiod[38] gave birth as much of a place in their scheme of values as Theognis did—which is not much at all. All we can infer from their grumbling and moralizing about the significance of wealth is that, in practice, timocratic regimes were widely prevalent in the archaic age. While violent conflict and its attendant upheavals remained common, it could hardly be otherwise.[39]

---

[38] See n. 1 above.

[39] It is surely no coincidence that classical Athens, the most democratic of Greek states, had a notably low level of violence in social and political life: see Herman (1994); van Wees (1998). See Fisher (1998) for channels of social mobility in classical Athens.

4

Exchange and Stasis
in Archaic Mytilene

NIGEL SPENCER

Introduction

THE papers presented in the Leeds–Manchester seminar series, which now
constitute the chapters of this volume, are an indication of the increasing
debate in recent years concerning the plurality of constitutional forms in
ancient Greece. Scholars have signalled a growing awareness that in certain
regions there developed social and political systems which might have fundamentally differed from one another (a polarity represented most clearly
by the contrasting notion of polis or ethnos),[1] with the discussions trying
to assess what these differences might have meant in terms of an area's
settlement and society.

The present chapter also focuses upon this theme of variation in state-
forms, but does so on a scale different from many other studies, comparing
not simply states from different regions, but also neighbouring ones within
the same region. In the same way that few people now would assume that
a polis (or indeed an ethnos) in one region of Greece was necessarily like
another elsewhere, it is proposed here that no such assumption should be
made simply because the geographical scale is smaller and one is dealing
with independent polities which shared borders, in this case within a single
island, Lesbos in the north-east Aegean (Figure 4.1, inset).

For a study of possible variation between neighbouring states, Lesbos is
a particularly useful subject to choose because throughout antiquity it was

This paper is a revised version of that given in both the Leeds–Manchester seminar series
'Alternatives to the Democratic Polis' in Jan. 1995 and the 1995 joint AIA/APA colloquium in
San Diego (USA) on Early Greek Culture and Society entitled 'Approaches to Greek State-
formation', organized by John Lenz (Drew University, New York). I thank the editors of the
present volume and those present at both sessions where the paper was presented for many
constructive comments on earlier versions, although the responsibility for all the arguments put
forward here of course remains with the author. My attendance at the AIA/APA conference in
San Diego was made possible by generous grants from the Paisner Fund of Worcester College,
Oxford, the Board of Literae Humaniores in Oxford, and an Overseas Conference Grant from
the Humanities Research Board of the British Academy. The research for the paper was carried
out during a British Academy Major State Studentship and a British Academy Postdoctoral
Fellowship (generously funded by Swan Hellenic/P&O). All dates to which reference is made
are BC unless otherwise stated.

[1] This contrast between polis and ethnos, often seen by Greek writers as the quality distinguishing Greek and non-Greek states, is clearly stated in Aristotle (*Pol.* 1324^{b}10).

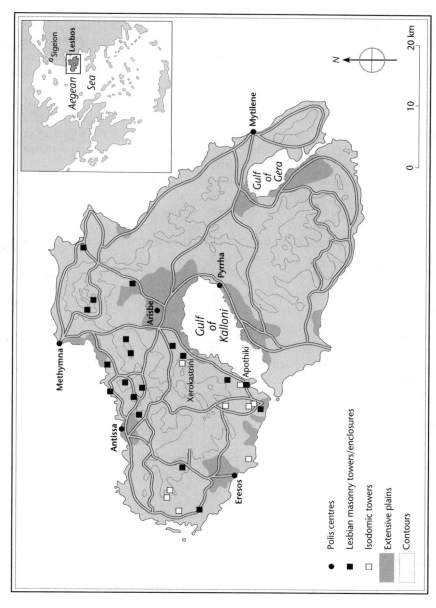

FIG. 4.1. Map of Lesbos indicating polis centres, towers, enclosures, and cult places. Shaded areas represent extensive plains. Contours at 300 m.

one of those few islands which was divided politically between a relatively large number of cities.[2] Our earliest source for this phenomenon, Herodotus, notes in his short treatment of the area of Aiolis that six poleis had once coexisted in Lesbos, but that in the fifth century only five remained because at some point before his time Methymna, located on the north coast of the island, had moved south beyond the Lepetymnos mountain range and enslaved the Arisbeans, who dwelt in the large alluvial plain at the head of the Gulf of Kalloni (Figures 4.1, 4.2*b*).[3] This reduction in the number of poleis in the island continued later also, with Mytilene absorbing the lands of Pyrrha after the latter was devastated by an earthquake, probably that of 231 (Kontis 1978: 345), and Methymna acquiring the territory of Antissa after its destruction by the Romans in 167.[4]

I have discussed in detail elsewhere this interaction of the Lesbian poleis,[5] and the focus of the present paper will be on the related issue mentioned above, namely the possible differences between the states in Lesbos during the archaic period. Using archaeology as well as the historical sources, I shall propose that one polis in the island (Mytilene) actually seems to have differed fundamentally from the others, and shall go on to suggest why this might have been the case. I begin with the archaeological evidence.

Archaeological evidence

In the archaic period one way in which Mytilene seems to be contrasted clearly with the other cities in Lesbos is in terms of its comparative lack of monumental construction work both in the *chōra* of the city in the south-east corner of the island and also at the city centre itself. In the centre and west of the island the more affluent members of the other five cities arranged the construction of a series of elaborate tower and enclosure complexes built in the decorative Lesbian style of polygonal masonry at marginal locations in their polis *chōra* (Figure 4.2*a*).[6] These structures are to be found largely at spectacular sites on or above the main communication routes in central

---

[2] Other examples of Aegean islands similarly divided between more than one state include Keos (four poleis), Amorgos (three poleis), Rhodes (three poleis), and Euboea (five poleis). It is notable that none of these (not even the larger Euboea) possessed as many poleis as Lesbos once did.

[3] Hdt. 1. 151. 2. For the site of Arisbe near modern Kalloni see the collected historical and archaeological references in Spencer (1995*a*) 25–6 (site 116).

[4] For summaries of the respective histories of these two cities see Kontis (1978) 342–6 (Pyrrha), 303–6 (Antissa). For the destruction of Antissa see also the recent article by Mason (1995).

[5] Spencer (1993) 85–205; Schaus and Spencer (1994) 411–20; Spencer (1994) 207–13; (1995*b*) 28–42.

[6] Ibid. (all references). For the dating of the structures see the detailed discussion in Spencer (1995*a*) appendix 2 (pp. 53–64).

(a)

(b)

FIG. 4.2. (a) The Lesbian masonry enclosure wall at Xirokastrini.
(b) View east from Xirokastrini over the Arisbe plain.

FIG. 4.3. The terrace wall at Apothiki.

and western Lesbos, often just beyond the edge of the large coastal plains
in which the polis centres are situated (Figure 4.2*b*).[7]

As well as the towers and enclosures, other remote areas of the polis *chōra*
in this same central and western region of Lesbos were marked out in the
archaic period by monumentally built cult-places. At Apothiki in the west
of the island a cult site is located on what must have been the outer edge of
the territory of Eresos, in the form of a large platform 41.0 × 45.5 m. (with a
ramp at one end) supported by an enormous polygonal terrace wall (Figure
4.3), first located and drawn in the nineteenth century by Koldewey and
Kiepert.[8] And nearer the centre of the island, also in a marginal location
between the cities of Arisbe and Methymna, two temples stand side by side,
2 km. north-west of the village of Ayia Paraskevi at the location known
as Klopedi.[9] The larger of the two temples which employed the famous
Aeolic column capitals (Figure 4.4) dates from the late sixth century, with
the smaller, squatter structure beside it probably dating from the earlier
archaic period.[10]

---

[7] This distribution is illustrated in Schaus and Spencer (1994) fig. 5; Spencer (1995*b*) fig. 3.1.

[8] Koldewey (1890) 38, 43–4, 87, and pl. 15.1–4. The colossal scale of the terrace wall (which
has great similarities to the archaic Lesbian masonry terrace wall of the Apollo temple at
Delphi) led Koldewey to identify the site as a centre of cult practice (ibid., 44). The scatter of
fine wares (of archaic through Roman date) on and around the platform at the site, together
with large fragments of glazed tiles apparent, seem conclusive proof of this assertion; see
Schaus and Spencer (1994) 416 and n. 31; Spencer (1995*a*) 28 (site 130).

[9] For a summary of the discussions concerning the date of both temples see Spencer (1995*a*)
24 (site 111). For a third possible large-scale cult-place opposite Apothiki near the east shore
of the gulf of Kalloni see Schaus and Spencer (1994) figs. 4–5 and n. 55 (p. 420); Spencer
(1995*a*) 18–9 (sites 83, 87).   [10] See n. 9.

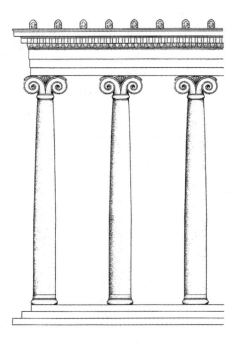

FIG. 4.4. The Aeolic column capitals
of the sixth-century temple at Klopedi.

I have suggested elsewhere that the functions performed by all these
rural structures are quite complex, and that at different times they served
a whole range of purposes if one examines them on various levels. One
can see them as manifestations of peer competition and emulation among
the élites; a symbolic way in which the upper orders of society tried to
distinguish themselves above the lower members by conspicuous display
of consumable wealth; also, on a wider scale, in times of tension between
the states, the structures could have served as symbols of possession at the
outer limits of a city's territory.[11] In the latter scenario, the substantially
built towers and enclosures (many at strategic locations) were suitable also
to act as foci for defence of border areas at a time when sought-after natural
resources and/or territory may have been in dispute.

On a more fundamental level, however, if one considers simply the *distribution* of all this monumental construction work in the archaic period in
Lesbos, one is struck by the fact that for Mytilene in the south-east of the
island there is an almost complete blank (see Figure 4.1). Mytilene exhibits
no towers and enclosures, and the only possible archaic extra-urban cult-

---

[11] An idea first discussed in detail by de Polignac (1984).

place (approximately 11 km. to the south of the city) seems a particularly small-scale example, exhibiting no architectural remains at all (Schaus and Spencer 1994: fig. 4). And it is not that the area of Mytilene has been less well explored than that of the other cities: in south-eastern Lesbos there has been exhaustive fieldwork carried out by archaeologists, and there simply does not seem to be any large-scale construction work in the hinterland which might date from the archaic period.[12]

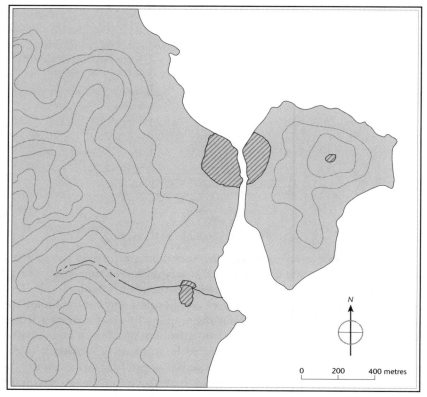

FIG. 4.5. Archaeological plan of archaic Mytilene. Shaded areas
represent main foci of archaic settlement. Contours at 20 m.

Not even the remains at the city of Mytilene itself are particularly impressive. Although the modern town lies on top of the ancient city, the piecemeal excavations carried out over many years have made it clear where the focus of the archaic settlement lay, with the remains clustered mainly

[12] See e.g. the immensely detailed field research presented in Axiotis (1992), covering the whole of south-east Lesbos, including even the forested uplands near Ayiasos between ancient Mytilene and Pyrrha. Cf. Spencer (1995*a*).

around the north harbour (Figure 4.5). In this area, the sum total of discoveries comprises groups of modest structural remains; a number of (not
particularly rich) graves; a small, rather curious, oval shrine to the Anatolian mother goddess Cybele; and from the acropolis nothing except a few
column fragments which might either be votive columns or come from a
more substantial structure (although since no foundations were found with
them it is impossible to know the precise original location of the columns).[13]
But the remains are hardly those which you would expect from the famous
city which was the home of Alcaeus and Pittacus, and the comment of
Thucydides (1. 10. 2) about Sparta's low-key architecture which would not
impress future visitors and archaeologists rings just as true for the remains
so far uncovered of Mytilene in what was supposed to be its prime, the
archaic period.

This lack of visible investment in both the archaic city and the *chōra* of
Mytilene in the south-east of the island raises the question of why there
is such a perceptible difference from the other states. The uplands of the
Olympus mountain range may have cut Mytilene off from the other poleis,
so that perhaps there was less need for the city to define its outer limits.
Nevertheless, it is the one polis in the island where we do know (from lyric
poetry) that there was a group of aristocratic genē in the archaic period
which controlled between them what seems to have been a fairly restricted
oligarchy (which sources suggest had developed from a system of hereditary
rule)[14] and had available at least a reasonable amount of disposable income. If
these groups were not investing their capital either in their city or in its hinterland, where was their investment going? Elsewhere? Furthermore, if, as
I have suggested from the archaeology of the island, Mytilene seems distinguished from the other poleis in Lesbos, is this borne out by other sources?

Literary evidence

A careful reading of the historical sources reveals that Mytilene is indeed distinguished from the other cities in Lesbos in the archaic period—repeatedly
so, especially in terms of having very wide horizons and looking abroad.

First, Herodotus, in his account of the East Greek poleis involved in the
establishment of the pan-Greek 'Hellenion' at Naukratis in the reign of
Amasis, lists the Ionian and Dorian states which joined forces in setting up
the shrine and then picks out Mytilene, not just as the only polis in Lesbos,

---

[13] The archaeological evidence for protogeometric–archaic Mytilene is summarized in Spencer (1995c) 277–81, 295, 296–9, 301–3, and figs. 3, 11.

[14] Aristotle (*Pol.* 1311[b]23–31) states that the ruling genos of archaic Mytilene, the Penthil-
idai, had exercised a βασιλικὴ δυναστεία before its overthrow by a certain Megakles (an event
which probably took place in the 7th cent.). This was a form of government which Aristotle
defined elsewhere as a type of oligarchy which was hereditary, and where the rulers made
decisions not necessarily based upon the law (*Pol.* 1292[b]6–10). Concerning the constitution of
7th/6th-cent. Mytilene, see also the recent discussion of Kurke (1994: 76–7 and n. 18).

but as the only polis of all Aeolis among those which helped in its foundation (Hdt. 2. 178. 2). This testimony has been backed up by epigraphical
finds at Naukratis, where on some distinctive votive vessels of Aeolic grey
ware dedicated to Aphrodite (and probably Apollo also) there are indeed
inscriptions indicating that they were dedicated by Mytileneans (where the
inscriptions are specific, they are the dedications of 'Mytileneans', not 'Les-
bians' or 'Aeolians' more generally).[15]

To put this activity by Mytilene in context, we are informed by Strabo
that a generation earlier Sappho's brother had traded wine down to Naukratis (Str. 17. 1. 33), and Strabo also notes that Alcaeus visited Egypt.[16]
Furthermore, Egypt is one area where sixth-century Lesbian grey-ware
amphorae have been found (Figure 4.6),[17] and at least some of them must,
in all probability, have been brought by these visiting traders from Mytilene, given the city's well-attested presence at the port noted above.[18] It
is probably no coincidence either that later, during the invasion of Egypt
by Cambyses in 525, prominent among his forces of Ionians and Aeolian
Greeks was a ship from, of all places, Mytilene (Hdt. 3. 13. 1–2).

Another example from Herodotus of Mytilene's being distinguished from
the other cities in the island in the archaic period is the role which Lesbos
played in the Ionian revolt. Indeed, Mytilene seems to be the only city
which is heavily involved. At six places Herodotus refers to the ships of the
island, and where a specific origin is given, the only city named is Mytilene.[19]
Furthermore, when Histiaeus was visiting the Ionian and Aeolian states to

[15] Petrie (1886) pl. 32 no. 185; Gardner (1888) 65–6 and pl. 21 (graffiti 786–93 on Aeolic
bucchero; see esp. nos. 788 and 790 for the preserved dedications by 'Mytileneans'). For the
dating of these inscriptions (to the second quarter of the 6th cent.) see Jeffery (1990) 360.

[16] Str. 1. 2. 30. It should be noted that there is no evidence at all to suggest that the reason for
this visit by Alcaeus to Egypt was that in a period of exile 'the party of Alcaeus was driven out
into foreign lands'; cf. Page (1955) 223. During other banishments, Alcaeus clearly attempted
to stay as close as possible to the political action in Mytilene, and had no difficulty in taking
refuge simply in the borderlands of the polis: see Alcaeus fr. G 2 LP. Given the politically
divided nature of the island, which would have made local asylum possible, it seems absurd to
suggest that he would have resorted to going all the way to Egypt without some other reason.

[17] For the typological definition of archaic Lesbian amphorae see Clinkenbeard (1982);
Dupont (1982).

[18] Of course, it need not have been Mytileneans who were responsible for taking *all* these
'Lesbian' amphorae to Egypt. First, it is clear from the evidence of the Giglio shipwreck that
in the archaic period ships carried mixed cargoes, so that, for example, Mytilenean wares could
have been carried to their final destination by sailors from elsewhere who had simply put in
at Lesbos during their voyage; see Bound (1991). Second, as Herodotus explicitly states (3.
6–7), reuse and redistribution of amphorae were common, so that the modern find-spots of
the vessels are not necessarily the locations to which they were taken initially by their original
carriers.

[19] Hdt. 6. 5. 2–3 (Histiaeus visits Mytilene and gains eight triremes, which sail with him to
the Hellespont); 6. 6. 1 (the Mytilenean triremes in action with Histiaeus in the Hellespont); 6.
8. 2 and 6. 14. 3 (two references to the detachment of ships at the battle of Lade made up of the
'Aeolians of Lesbos', where it is not specified from which Lesbian cities the ships came); 6. 26.
1–2 and 6. 27–8 (two more references to the Mytilenean ships of 6. 5. 2, although Herodotus
refers to them here simply as 'Lesbian').

Fig. 4.6. The distribution of Lesbian grey-ware amphorae in the archaic period.

Pantikapaion
Chersonesos
Simagre △?
Istros △
Thasos
Chios △/○
Old Smyrna ◇?
Athens
Kamarina
Tocra
Naukratis
Daphnae
Thebes

◇ 8th-century finds
□ 7th-century finds
△ 6th-century finds
○ Early 5th-century finds

seek additional forces after being turned away by Miletus, in Lesbos he chose to visit Mytilene and no other polis.[20] That choice alone indicates where he expected to receive the best offer of help.

Yet another episode in the archaic period which not only distinguishes Mytilene from the rest of the island but also emphasizes once again the foreign interests of this polis in comparison with the others of Lesbos is the dispute with the Athenians over the area of Sigeion in the Troad in the last decade of the seventh century (Figure 4.1, inset).[21] If one were not aware of evidence such as the wide distribution of the Lesbian amphorae in the archaic period (which, as is indicated in Figure 4.6, included the Black Sea) or the other involvement of Mytilene overseas (especially in Egypt), this event at Sigeion would not really be very striking. But when one considers these latter activities, remembering also that our present archaeological knowledge suggests that Mytilene was a small settlement with probably a few rich families, then the conflict over Sigeion becomes more intriguing. For Mytilene mobilized, equipped, and sent out a group of soldiers a long way north to the Troad to challenge the intervention of the large, rival city of Athens, and was prepared to continue the struggle for a long period (to judge from the accounts of Strabo and Herodotus).[22] Once again, it is significant that Mytilene took this action alone, and was not helped by any of the other poleis in the island. This episode further emphasizes, therefore, that of all the Lesbian cities Mytilene alone was sufficiently concerned with this corner of a foreign field to resort to military action, implying that for some people of the city there were some very significant interests outside Lesbos (in this case a strategic location on the coast of the Troad and Asia Minor), which were worth going to a lot of trouble to protect.

These three historical episodes from different times during the seventh and sixth centuries show two things. Not only do they support the view I put forward earlier when I looked at the archaeology within the island, that Mytilene is differentiated from the other cities in Lesbos (and I emphasize again that in the literary sources it has been constantly differentiated), but the episodes also indicate repeatedly that the richer members of society in Mytilene had wide horizons, perhaps wider than those elsewhere in the

[20] Hdt. 6. 5. 2–3. On the only other occasion that Histiaeus visited Lesbos (after abandoning the blockade of Thasos) Herodotus states (6. 28. 1–2) that he went back to the island before 'crossing opposite to the mainland [of Asia Minor] . . . in the plain of Atarneus and . . . that of the Caïcus'. Both these areas are east and south-east of Lesbos, so the only place 'opposite' (i.e. on the east coast of Lesbos) from where Histiaeus could logically have landed with his fleet would again have been Mytilene, a city which, after all, had been friendly to him before.

[21] The main accounts of the conflict are those in Str. 13. 1. 38–9; Hdt. 5. 94–5; D.L. 1. 74; D.S. 9. 12. 1. The Troad had been settled extensively by Lesbos from the late 8th cent. For the historical references to this tradition see Str. 13. 599, 610, and Thuc. 3. 50. 3, and for the archaeological evidence suggesting an Aeolian presence at a number of sites see the summaries in Cook (1973) 59 and pl. 3a (Dardanos), 75 and pl. 3a (Ophryneion), 80 and pl. 3b (Rhoiteion), 98, 101 (Troy), 206–7 (Neandria), 217 (Kolonai), 231 and pl. 22c (Hamaxitus), 246 (Assos), 261–4 (Lamponia).   [22] Str. 13. 1. 38–9; Hdt. 5. 94–5.

island, where the more affluent citizens seem to have been content to invest in the hinterlands of their cities, building temples and/or a large number of elaborate towers and enclosures, as if their own sphere of interest was limited chiefly to the island itself.

In Mytilene, however, the aristocratic genē of the archaic period were uninvolved in these conflicts and rivalries in central and western Lesbos. Instead, they were looking abroad to foreign ventures, participating in overseas territorial disputes, setting up shrines (or simply trading) in places as far away as Egypt. From all these episodes (especially that of the Ionian revolt) it is clear that Mytilene possessed a well-equipped navy. It would no doubt have been the more affluent element of society which possessed the capital to provide the hardware for all these enterprises in the first place, namely the boats themselves,[23] and also had a desire to bring in exotic orientalia in order to boost their prestige and standing (as has recently been re-emphasized by Leslie Kurke and Ian Morris).[24] To judge from the importance placed upon these exotica by the symposiast poets in Lesbos, their investment in such activity may well have been a heavy one,[25] and they may have been personally involved in the transport, or, as is perhaps more likely, they probably leased the boats to entrepreneurs (dependants or impoverished nobles), thus freeing themselves of the more risky venture of making the long-distance voyages themselves.[26]

If this was the case—if in the archaic period, as I suggest, Mytilene was a very different, 'international' polis (for want of a better term) with the élite investing much more of their consumable wealth in these ventures outside the island and experiencing more prolonged exposure to other cultures— can one tell what the consequences might have been for the constitution and society of Mytilene?

As Kurke and Redfield determined from their respective studies of such activity in archaic Greece,[27] the evidence of archaic poets on this point is that the consequences (both for the élites themselves and for the polis as a whole) are very clear. Kurke (1994: 78–9) judged that contact with other cultures (especially the East) in archaic Lesbos speeded the challenge to

---

[23] I note in passing that the large forest of the black pine (*Pinus nigra*) in south-east Lesbos, a wood particularly useful for shipbuilding, would have provided plentiful raw material for ship construction in Mytilene. See Meiggs (1982) 44 for the ancient use of this timber, and Paraskevaides (1983) 77, 87, 113, 160, for the use made of this forest's wood in the 18th and 19th cents.

[24] Kurke (1992) 92–6; I. Morris, pers. comm. (1993). See also Morris (1986) for gift-exchange among the archaic élite.

[25] Kurke (1992); Spencer (1995c) 304 and n. 227. The Mytilenean activity at Naukratis seems a probable example of aristocratic exchange in luxury goods being underlain by commodity trade: see Morris (1986) 5.

[26] For a discussion of both these models of archaic Greek trade (proposed originally by Bravo and Mele) see Cartledge (1983).

[27] Kurke (1994); Redfield (1986); cf. von Reden (1995).

the oligarchic orthodoxy which had prevailed hitherto, leading ultimately to conflict in the existing social order.

Redfield (1986: 52–8), focusing specifically on the influence of the market in archaic Greece, came to much the same conclusion. In short, if the likes of Alcaeus had bound themselves to exchange-led activities in the archaic period in the hope that by gaining rare foreign trinkets they would emphasize their superior position in society, they had not bargained for the other, completely opposite, consequence which this policy would also bring, the *threat* to the very social order they were trying to preserve. For the archaic poets emphasize one point above all for the market at this time: it was irrational, something to be feared; it could subvert the usual order of society, making *agathoi* poor and *kakoi* rich; and those who suddenly became wealthy by it (such as those who had leased the boats from the aristocrats, gone abroad, and made a fortune) would, when they returned, inevitably be a threat to the pre-eminent social position claimed for generations by people such as Alcaeus. The new coined forms of wealth also played an important catalytic role in this breakdown of the previously unquestioned aristocratic positions, as is clear from the suspicion voiced by both Alcaeus and Theognis of this new system as a means for reckoning power and status.[28]

Given that the suggested result of overseas activity would have been to create acute social stasis, it is surely not coincidental that Mytilene, a state heavily involved in such activity abroad, also came to be the paradigm of such discord. After all, for centuries afterwards, even down to the time of Strabo, some of the best-remembered facts about early Lesbos were the party disputes and short-lived tyrannies in archaic Mytilene recounted by Alcaeus, verses which came to be known simply as the *Stasiōtika*.[29]

These models concerning the effects of involvement in international exchange during the archaic period are therefore one way to interpret not only the contrast between Mytilene and the other cities in Lesbos but also the famous (or rather, infamous) instability of Mytilene. In the other poleis the lower horizons for the politai, together with the type of investment and status symbols employed by the élite, slowed the tide of social change. The symbols which the upper ranks invested in (the enclosures, towers, and monumental cult-places) may well have served some communal purposes, but their permanence in the landscape also symbolically established those

---

[28] For Alcaeus see Kurke's commentary on Alcaeus fr. D 11 LP in Kurke (1991) 252–4; for Theognis see Redfield (1986) 54–6 and Lane Fox (this volume). Von Reden (1995) 174–84 argues, however, that the suspicion of the latter author was not directed specifically towards 'money', and suggests that the term χρήματα (as used by Theognis) should not be understood as 'coinage'.

[29] Str. 13. 2. 3. Kurke (1994) 79 noted the irony of this term given that Alcaeus' rhetoric was an attempt to preserve the old order in which no such 'division' existed.

who arranged their construction above the more humble orders much more securely and permanently than in Mytilene; for these élites any threat was less immediate. In Mytilene, however, the problems were always in high relief, since there was continual tension and suspicion with the possibility that the profits (or simply the ideas) gained by others in distant emporia would lead to the adventurous seafarers returning to challenge the eminence of the more 'established' members of society, and it is this emphasis on external contacts which I suggest was the essential difference in Mytilene.

To sum up, Mytilene was certainly different from the other poleis in the island, and (internally) the expressions of power and status were negotiated in a fundamentally different way. Unfortunately for Mytilene, this negotiation was carried out on a potentially very unstable base, one which relied upon maintaining access to foreign exchange networks and controlling strategic places where investment had been made (such as Sigeion in the Troad), activities which hastened the challenge to the existing notions of one's social position. The symbolic functions proposed for the elaborate towers and enclosures, including peer competition and emulation, can very easily be accommodated into this model, the boasts at Mytilenean symposia being the distant network of one's ships and the incoming luxurious goods from exotic resorts. Yet there was always the possibility that the traditional divisions of status (preserved more successfully in other Lesbian poleis by élite investment in the *chōra* itself) were more vulnerable and often inverted in Mytilene. Consequently, the continual (and unique) stasis which came to dominate the latter's domestic politics by the late seventh century is, perhaps, no surprise.

5
Cyrene: Typical or Atypical?

BARBARA MITCHELL

THE object of this paper is to examine the history of the Theran colony of
Cyrene during the two centuries or so from its foundation about 630 BC to
the end of the Battiad monarchy, and to discuss how far politically it was
similar to or differed from other contemporary Greek colonies. Its especially
distinguishing feature is the long-lasting Battiad monarchy, which will be
my central focus.

The colony and early monarchy

Monarchy as a form of government existed in a considerable number of
archaic Greek city-states, including Cyrene's mother city Thera.[1] Kings
continued in a constitutionalized form in Sparta, whence Thera claimed to
be an early colony. In Argos, the Temenid dynasty probably ruled until the
sixth century, in the third generation after Pheidon, a 'king who became a
tyrant' (Arist. *Pol.* 1310^b25); kings continued to exist in classical times, but
were not hereditary, perhaps elected and only holding office for life (Carlier
1984: 385–6). In other cities monarchy left traces in some religious and
dynastic titles, e.g. the *archōn basileus* in Athens, and the name *basileidai*
for clans at Ephesus and Erythrai (*Suda* s.v. 'Pythagoras'), implying the
existence of an earlier monarchy. Similarly, at Corinth the closely interre-
lated Bacchiad ruling clan are called 'monarchs' (μούναρχοι) by the Delphic
oracle which predicted their overthrow by the first tyrant, Cypselus (Hdt.
5. 92. 2).

In the archaic period monarchy in its narrowest form[2] can be roughly
described as a form of government in which the king had overall power in
religious, constitutional, and military spheres, and could decide matters of
peace and war, usually with a council of advisers. It was normally dynastic, succession passing to the eldest son of a deceased king or near male
relative, and could sometimes be shared by two families each inheriting

I should like to thank Joyce Reynolds, John Lloyd, and the editors for their assistance.

[1] Chamoux (1953) is still the best account of the Battiad monarchy. Cf. the comparative
study of Carlier (1984: esp. pp. vi–viii and pt. III). For the period 479– 323, Hornblower (1983)
ch. 5. Applebaum (1979) gives an excellent account of the economic background. R. Osborne
(1996) 8–17 with 357 compares the literary traditions for the foundation of Cyrene with the
archaeological evidence. Malkin (1994a) chs. 5–6 identifies areas of Spartan interest in North
Africa.   [2] As Carlier shows (1984: *passim*), it varied according to city and period.

similarly. Their religious authority tended to survive when they were deprived of political power. Apart from Sparta, where the two kings survived primarily as generals, it is not a form of government prevalent in Greece during the classical period. Kings still tended to rule over ethnos states on the fringes of the polis societies of Greece, as in Macedon, and similarly in Caria, where the dynasty of Lygdamis and Artemisia ruled at Halicarnassus in the fifth century and the Hecatomnid Mausolus flourished in the fourth.

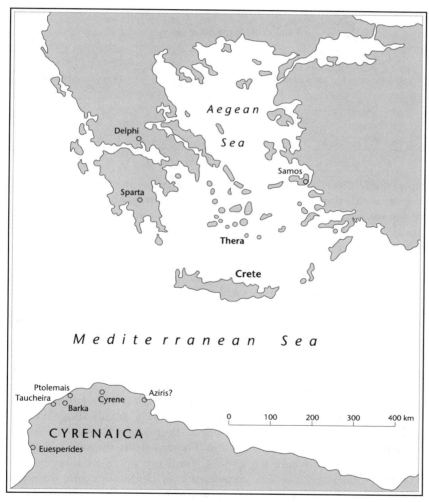

FIG. 5.1. Map of Greece and Cyrenaica.

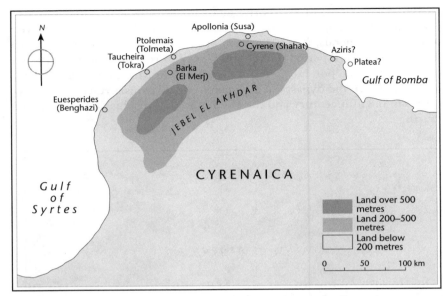

F IG. 5.2. Map indicating early Greek settlement in Cyrenaica.

However, at Cyrene, founded around 630 BC as a colony of Thera (also a monarchy at this time) under an oikist and king, Battos, a monarchy survived until the mid-fifth century as a ruling dynasty. I shall examine the social, political, and constitutional conditions which could have contributed to the atypical length of the dynasty and suggest comparisons and contrasts with other contemporary cities. External relations with non-Greeks need to be taken into account: first, with the local Libyan tribes, second, with Egypt, and finally, after Egypt became a satrapy of the Persian empire in the 520s, with Persia.

The story of the colony's foundation and the subsequent history of the Battiad monarchy are derived from Herodotus book 4, the earliest narrative source, and also the only detailed account we have of any archaic Greek colonial foundation. Herodotus first (150–3) gives a Theran version in which Grinnos, king of Thera, takes his city's offering to Delphi, consults the oracle about 'other matters', and is told to found a city in Libya. There follows a Cyrenaean version (154–6) giving different details about the origins and name of Battos. Grinnos indicates Battos as a younger and more appropriate oikist than himself, but the Therans delay the sending of the colony, 'not knowing where Libya was', until prompted by a seven-year drought on Thera and a second consultation of Delphi bringing the same response. After this delay the Therans sent messengers to Crete for information about Libya and obtained the services of Korobios, a sea captain who traded in purple, who took a few Therans to investigate. He showed them Platea, identified either with Bomba, a small almost uninhabitable island out in the Gulf of Bomba off the coast of Libya, or, as Boardman thinks (1966: 149–50), a promontory now joined to the coast by a neck of sand.[3] Here Korobios was left with provisions for a few months while the Therans returned home for instructions. Running out of provisions, he was fortunately visited by a Samian merchant ship captain Kolaios, on his way from Samos to Egypt, who left him sufficient provisions for a year. Meanwhile, the Therans organized a small colonial expedition, two pentekonters manned by men only. The number was probably 200, or only 100 if all were oarsmen.[4]

The colonists returned to Platea under their appointed oikist, called by Herodotus 'Battos' but, as we know from Pindar (*Pyth*. 5. 87), originally named Aristoteles. Herodotus too was aware that he had another name which was changed to 'Battos' (155. 2). The Cyrenaean version makes Battos an illegitimate son of a Theran noble, Polymnestus, and Phronima, a Cretan princess rescued from an unjust death by a visiting Theran merchant who had been ordered to drown her. High but illegitimate birth would make him a suitable choice for the founder of a colony and has parallels in other colonial enterprises, including Syracuse. Menekles, the third-century historian of Barka, makes Battos the leader of a political faction, but this seems to be a later conventionalized version (*FGrH* 270 F 5).[5]

The Theran and Cyrenaean accounts overlap chronologically up to the point at which the colonists in the two pentekonters are sent, if we identify the 'misfortunes' at the beginning of chapter 156, which prompt Battos to consult Delphi a second time, with the drought, the reason for the second consultation of Delphi in the Theran account. From chapter 157 Herodotus' source is Cyrenaean. After two years on Platea the colonists moved to the African-named Aziris on the mainland, but after six years there some Libyans persuaded them to move westwards up to the site of

---

[3] Greek sailors had probably obtained some knowledge of the North African coast before the foundation of Cyrene. R. Osborne (1996) 8–17, 357, finds support for earlier interest in the variety of later 7th- and early 6th-cent. pottery now recorded from Cyrenaean sites. He argues convincingly that the mid-5th-cent. oral traditions of Thera and Cyrene would not have revealed to Herodotus that other cities had an interest in the potential colonization of Libya, but restricted it to the Battiad foundation of Cyrene. Delphi's insistence on a Libyan colony suggests in itself that the oracle already had information from other cities. Cf. Malkin (1994*a*) ch. 5 and Boardman (1966) 13–15.

[4] Mahaffy's supplement ⟨σ´⟩ (200) has usually been accepted but Cawkwell (1992) defends 100. Herodotus (4. 153) quotes the Theran decree laying down the method for their selection: men with brothers living chosen by lot from each of the seven districts of Thera. A similar but not identical source lies behind the early document cited in the 4th-cent. 'Founders' Stele', see ML 5; against genuineness of the latter, Dušanić (1978*b*) 55.

[5] Archias, founder of Syracuse, was a Bacchiad noble stained by blood-guilt (Plut. *Mor.* 772). On the multiple and complex causes of colonization see Jeffery's admirable discussion (1976: ch. 4).

Cyrene on the plateau, where the land was better and 'the sky leaked'; but
the Libyans led them past the best land (at Irasa) at night 'so that the Greeks
should not see it as they passed' (158), though this may be a Cyrenaean excuse for not settling there, since after six years they should have known
where it was. Evidently, some Libyans were already anxious about being
deprived of land by the Greeks. Even so, the site of Cyrene was fertile and
the colony prospered.

The appointment of an oikist who was also intended to be a hereditary
king is a unique feature of the colony. It was derived from both Thera
and her 'mother city' Sparta, but took off in a different direction, since the
powers of the king were combined with those of the oikist, which, as in other
colonies, included supervision of religious cults and land distribution, but,
in contrast to other colonies, became hereditary since oikist and king were
one and the same.

Monarchy was a convenient form of government for a colony and the
Cyrenaean monarchy was stronger than that of its mother city Thera.[6]
If mother cities were not monarchies (like Corinth in the late eighth and
seventh centuries, they were usually aristocracies), the oikist or oikists appointed in their colonies had extensive powers. They were sometimes buried
within the city and had heroic cults founded in their honour, as did Battos
(Pind. *Pyth.* 5. 93), so their names often survived.[7] They had power to
divide available land for the first colonists, whose allotments seem to have
been inalienable and constituted a title to citizenship of the new polis. This
function was inherited by later kings of Cyrene, who used it to carry out land
distributions and to found or refound other colonies in Libya.[8] The kings
were hereditary, and so inherited the powers which had been conferred in
Thera on the first king, Battos the oikist. The combination gave them more
extensive legitimate power than the earlier kings of Thera.

After its false starts, the colony prospered, and in the reign of the third
king, Battos II, 'the fortunate', extra colonists from elsewhere in Greece
were sent out (perhaps around 580), again on the advice of Delphi. The
Cyrenaeans, Herodotus says, invited them to participate in a division of
land (4. 159. 2). Neighbouring Libyans, friendly to begin with, were then
deprived of lands and appealed for help to Apries, king of Egypt, but Egyp-
tians and Libyans were badly defeated by the Cyrenaeans at Irasa (159).
Apries lost his throne to Amasis as a result, which indicates that Irasa
was fought not long before 570 BC, when Amasis became Pharaoh. At an
unknown date after Irasa Battos II died and was succeeded by his son Ar-

---

[6] Grinnos performs the religious office of taking the Therans' offering to Delphi, but takes
Battos and other citizens with him when he consults Delphi (Hdt. 4. 150) and does not behave
like an absolute monarch. See Carlier (1984) 419–21.

[7] Cf. Jeffery (1976) 52–3, 59 n. 7.

[8] See below, this page (Battos II), p. 89 (Arkesilas III), and pp. 94–5 (Arkesilas IV).

kesilas II. He had dynastic trouble with his brothers, who departed and founded Barka (Hdt. 4. 160. 1),[9] causing the Libyans in the area to revolt from Cyrene. Arkesilas' attempt to take revenge on his brothers' Libyan allies led to his serious defeat in a battle at Leukon, whose site is unknown. The Cyrenaeans are said by Herodotus to have lost 7,000 hoplites; this may, like many casualty figures, be an exaggeration, but if it is from a Greek source it may not be grossly wrong unless it comes from a strongly anti-Battiad tradition. If it is anything like the truth, it reflects a very large expansion of population in the reign of Battos II. The land allotments for them both east and west of Cyrene would have occupied cultivable land over a wide area, and the 'eastern Libyans' with whom the rebels sought protection from Arkesilas (Hdt. 4. 160. 2) should be beyond Cyrene. The Libyan victory at Leukon brought revenge for Irasa. It must have decimated Cyrenaean hoplite power.

Arkesilas II was assassinated not long afterwards, probably blamed for the defeat. Herodotus says he was strangled by a brother, Learchos. Dynastic rivalry was a natural weakness of monarchies and, as in oriental despotisms and like Pheretima later, a royal woman took vengeance. Learchos was killed (without, apparently, succeeding his brother) through a plot of Arkesilas' widow Eryxo, and Arkesilas' son Battos III succeeded to the throne, a weak king who was also physically lame (Ogden 1997: ch. 9).

The reforms of Demonax

With the monarchy weakened, the Cyrenaeans applied, probably around 550, to Delphi for further advice. The oracle recommended them to appoint Demonax from Mantinea as arbitrator. Either the king concurred in the decision to send to Delphi, or he had insufficient influence to prevent it. Delphi suggested that Cyrene should grant political privileges to the recent colonists, who already had land, and that the powers of the monarchy should be reduced. Demonax organized the population into three local tribes. The first consisted of the original Theran (i.e. Dorian) colonists and the surrounding *perioikoi* (Hdt. 4. 161). The latter are puzzling: they have been taken to be Libyan, as they are at 159. 4, where *perioikoi* is used adjectivally with 'Libyan' and they are not under Greek control but ruled by their own king, Adikran. Here (161) the *perioikoi* are likely to be an under-privileged class not eligible by birth to be enrolled in the three Dorian tribes to which the original Theran settlers will have belonged; they may have included some Libyans, but this is uncertain. They could have been in origin a serf class back on Thera (where Aristotle says the 'few' who were free ruled over 'many' who were not: *Pol.* 1290^{b}10–11) who followed their masters

---

[9] At El Merj, about 100 km. WSW of Cyrene, about 18.5 km. behind its port, the later Ptolemais.

to Libya, or they could have been settled Libyans who had become hell-enized.[10] Peloponnesians and Cretans (i.e. also Dorians) formed the second tribe and 'islanders', who will have been mainly Ionians, the third. It is not known what the tribal status of the new settlers was before Demonax: whether they adhered to the systems of their mother cities, or whether, as seems less likely, they were incorporated in the three traditional Dorian tribes of the original Theran colonists. Either way, they would have been politically inferior to the Theran settlers. Under Demonax's reorganization all three tribes will have been theoretically on an equal footing.[11] As their names indicate, they were based on the local origins of the inhabitants, which must have been replicated in the new settlements. Herodotus' description of the first tribe as 'Therans and *perioikoi*' implies that it was local, and the same must be true of the other two. They cannot have been defined by descent, since the Peloponnesians and Cretans of the second tribe were Dorian, but separated from the lands of the original Theran colonists. By the tribal reform, the new settlers will have gained constitutional uniform-ity with the original Theran colonists but the latter will have been left united, with their land tenure and social organization untouched and with the *perioikoi* added to their local tribe, that of their masters, which would have discouraged their democratization. The Therans would therefore have been strengthened rather than weakened as a landed aristocracy and enabled to oppose the monarchy.

Demonax also stripped the monarchy of its powers, except for control of sacred lands (τεμένεα or precincts of the gods) and priesthoods, and put its earlier authority in the hands of the dēmos (Hdt. 4. 162). The Therans, who formed the first tribe along with their *perioikoi*, will have been of higher status, derived from their longer occupation of richer land closer to the city and with control over their *perioikoi*. They therefore had local power, analogous to the influence of Athenian families with estates in the Attic plain before Cleisthenes' tribal reform split them up between the ten new Attic tribes. The tribal reform of Demonax and his reduction of the king's power must therefore have worked in favour of the Theran aristocracy; and the dēmos which took over the political powers of the monarchy would have had an aristocratic bias, though we do not know what this meant in detail (Chamoux 1953: 139–42). But there is archaeological evidence for an early agora and also a public building or meeting-place east of the larger, later

[10] See O'Neil (1995) 170 n. 33. For other views see E. W. Robinson (1997) 105 n. 148.

[11] Cf. Jeffery (1976) 186–7, 197–8, 202 n. 6. Her interpretation of the tribal reform, however, takes the three ethnic 'parts' to have been divided between the three tribes, not identified with them (more like the ten tripartite Cleisthenic tribes at Athens), so that the original settlers will have been represented, like the new colonists, in all three tribes. This seems too radically democratic for the period. O'Neil (1995: app. 1, pp. 170–1) thinks they were incorporated in the old Dorian tribes. He aptly compares the local origins of the new tribes with those of the mid-5th-cent. Athenian colony of Thourioi (Diodorus 18. 19–20).

agora, dated to the third quarter of the sixth century, so possibly associated with Demonax.[12]

The τεμένεα, however, were a very important exception, since they will have continued to provide the king with great wealth, as appears from the records of the revenues from their produce kept by public officials, the *dēmiourgoi*, after the fall of the monarchy.[13] In addition, Demonax did not remove from the king the revenues for the export of silphion, the now extinct medicinal plant which was Cyrene's characteristic export and emblem. It was evidently a royal monopoly, perhaps shown on the Laconian cup of *c*.560 representing Arkesilas II weighing some kind of produce usually taken to be silphion. It was mentioned by Solon and was known as 'the silphion of Battos' as late as Aristophanes.[14] It grew wild in the semi-desert hinterland of the plateau (Hdt. 4. 169–71); Theophrastus (*HP* 9. 1. 7) says only the Libyans knew how to treat it, so it may have been given by them as tribute.

Battos' son, Arkesilas III (who succeeded him probably around 530), wanted to recover the full powers of his ancestors. Not unexpectedly, he was opposed, and eventually went in exile to Samos, an old ally of Cyrene, to appeal for help, while his mother Pheretima appealed to Euelthon, the king of Cyprus. She was unsuccessful, but Arkesilas raised Samian troops by promising them land allotments. He went to consult Delphi about his return (Hdt. 4. 163), and was told obscurely not to heat the jars fiercely if he found any in the furnace (in other words, to be lenient towards his enemies), and to avoid 'the place surrounded by water', otherwise 'he and the beautiful bull' would die. On returning to Cyrene, Arkesilas regained his full powers, but ignored the oracle's warning and took harsh revenge on his opponents. These were primarily the aristocrats who had benefited from Demonax's reforms. Some fled the country, but some he captured and sent to Cyprus to be executed. These were blown off course to Cnidos, where they were rescued by the Cnidians and sent to Thera, but another group were not so lucky: they took refuge in a large tower (*pyrgos*) owned by one Aglomachos (4. 164), evidently the fortified farm of a rich aristocratic landowner. They were burnt to death when Arkesilas set fire to it, ignoring the oracle's advice 'not to burn the jars in the oven'. In addition, Arkesilas unfortunately took 'the place surrounded by water' to be Cyrene, and went instead to Barka, where he was murdered by Cyrenaean exiles along with his father-in-law Alazeir, the 'beautiful bull' of the oracle's reply.

Part at least of the Delphic oracle must be *post eventum*, since it prophesied that only eight kings should rule Cyrene, and was therefore invented

---

[12] Stucchi (1965) 69–77; Bacchielli (1981) 25–34; Vickers and Reynolds (1971–2) 33–4.

[13] Inscriptions in Oliverio (1933) 15 and 16 (mid-5th cent.); *SEG* ix. 11–44; discussion in Applebaum (1979) 87–129.

[14] Solon fr. 39; Ar. *Plutus* 925 and scholiast, citing Aristotle (fr. 528 Rose); Chamoux (1953) 247–63; (1985) 165–72. The Arkesilas cup: Simon, Hirmer, and Hirmer (1990) 38 and pl. xv; Jeffery (1990) 199 no. 8 and pl. 35.

after the fall of the last Battiad, but Delphi may well have counselled moderation, and the end of the response is so obscure that it might be genuine. Alternatively, it may be thought that the prophecy of Arkesilas' death and that of Alazeir is too neatly fulfilled and that the whole is a later invention in suitably oracular style.

The *pyrgos* of Aglomachos was characteristic of a noble's large landholding. Although its location is unknown, it is good evidence for the system of land tenure in operation around Cyrene. Remains of many similar fortified farmhouses have survived from the fourth century and later in the *chōra*, the fertile land surrounding Cyrene, both on the coast and inland on the plateau. They would have served as refuges against raids by nomadic Libyans (see below) or as granaries, and they perhaps provided collecting-points for silphion.[15]

The Persian factor

Arkesilas' appeal to Samos and his short-lived recovery of the powers of the monarchy probably came late in his reign, since in Herodotus' narrative it leads on to other events surrounding his death which indicate that Cyrenaean politics were moving along lines similar to those of other Greek states: his mother Pheretima's appeal to Aryandes, the Persian satrap of Egypt, and Aryandes' expedition against Cyrene in 514 to avenge Arkesilas' death (4. 164–5).[16] Already in 525, during Cambyses' attack on Egypt, the Cyrenaeans had abandoned their friendship with the Egyptian king Amasis and Medized along with the Barkans and Libyans (Hdt. 3. 13). Although the Cyrenaeans provided only a small amount of tribute, which Cambyses scattered derisively among his troops, we learn elsewhere (Hdt. 2. 181) that Cambyses sent home the Cyrenaean princess or noble lady Ladike, who had earlier become a wife of Amasis to cement an alliance between Egypt and the Cyrenaeans. Cambyses' generous act, not uncharacteristic of the Persian kings towards enemies who were potential allies, perhaps affected the Cyrenaeans' submission. In any case, Arkesilas' mother Pheretima was able in 514 to claim this credit for him when she asked Aryandes for help in avenging his murder, saying he had been killed 'because of his Medism' in 525, though the real reason for his death was the political opposition of the aristocrats. By 514 Cyrene had moved even closer to Persia because Egypt was now firmly governed by a Persian satrap with an army.

Similarly, Samos had fallen under Persian control in stages: first in 525 when Polycrates (previously, like Cyrene, an ally of Amasis) sent a herald

---

[15] For the locations of some *pyrgoi* and the extent of the *chōra* see Laronde (1990) 169–80; for a comprehensive survey, Laronde (1987) 257–347.

[16] Cf. B. M. Mitchell (1966) 99–103; (1975) 85–7; Shipley (1987) 96–107; M. M. Austin (1990) 298–302; for an earlier date in his reign, arguing that Arkesilas appealed to Polycrates: Chamoux (1953) ch. 6: Noshy (1968) 53–78; Laronde (1988) 38–50; Carlier (1984) 475 n. 697.

secretly to Cambyses, asking him not to omit to ask for help on the Persian expedition against Egypt (Hdt. 3. 44). Both Samos and Cyrene were shaken by Cambyses' acquisition of the Phoenician fleet just before he conquered Egypt. Cyprus had also moved into the Persian camp (Hdt. 3. 19). Later, under the pro-Persian tyrants, Syloson and his son Aeaces, Samos moved decisively on to the Persian side and Aeaces was among the pro-Persian tyrants who took ships to the Danube to assist Darius' Scythian expedition (Hdt. 4. 138). At the end of his reign Arkesilas, with the help of the Samians, had recovered the powers of the monarchy which had been lost through the reforms of Demonax and was behaving in very similar fashion to the pro-Persian tyrants of Asia Minor and the islands.[17] The reliance of the Battiad monarchy on Persian support and its survival under Battos IV and Arkesilas IV dates from Pheretima's use of Arkesilas' submission in her appeal to Aryandes and his response.

After Egypt had fallen under the authority of a Persian satrap the power and status of the Battiad monarchy were to some extent dependent on the Great King, but to what degree is difficult to determine. When Pheretima begged Aryandes to avenge her son's murder, she was able to rely on the good relations of Arkesilas with Persia. He had evidently become in some sense a pro-Persian vassal, though not under such direct control as the cities of the eastern Aegean which brought ships to aid Darius' Scythian expedition in 514 (Hdt. 4. 83, 89, 138). This may have been because of their proximity, since the Phoenician ships were not at the Danube either, although they were Persia's main sea power. Neither Cyrene nor Barka nor any of the other Greek cities in Libya is listed separately from the Libyans in the Persian lists of subject peoples; but Herodotus' list of satrapies, from whatever date and source it derives, has both Libya and the Greek cities Cyrene and Barka combined with Egypt in the 'sixth satrapy' (Hdt. 3. 91. 3). This suggests that they were treated administratively as the responsibility of the satrap of Egypt and that all were tributary. The Libyans (Putaya) appear for the first time *c*.513, in a list of subject peoples on the hieroglyphic list on one of Darius' 'Suez Canal' stēlai (as a result of Aryandes' expedition) but not on the foundation stone, also *c*.513, at Persepolis, though they are found on Darius' tomb at Naksh-i-Rustum *c*.490.[18] The absence of the Libyans, Cyrene, and Barka on Darius' list at Bisutun (521 BC) confirms the view argued above that Arkesilas III's Medism in 525 was half-hearted and that closer links with Persia followed Darius' systematic organization of the satrapies, including Egypt, after he succeeded Cambyses in 522 (early in his reign, since Aryandes was satrap before 514). Unlike the Greek tyrants of the Ionian cities, Cyrene was not called on to provide land or sea forces under

[17] M. M. Austin (1990) 298–302 compares the position of the Greek pro-Persian tyrants to that of the Battiads.

[18] Kent (1943) 302–6; G. G. Cameron (1943) 307–12; Wade-Gery (1958) 159 nn. 2–3.

either Darius or Xerxes, though the 'Libyans' are listed in Xerxes' army list at Hdt. 7. 71, an unreliable source for participation in his 480 campaign. A realistic list of Xerxes' army and navy would not have included them or the Greek cities of Cyrenaica, if only for geographical reasons. In return, however, for the submission of Cyrene, Persia backed the Battiad monarchy.

The response of Aryandes to Pheretima was to send a punitive expedition against Barka but to leave Cyrene alone. Having destroyed Barka after a nine-months siege, he made a demonstration of force as far as Euesperides. Menekles of Barka, the third-century local historian, says that the Persians attacked Cyrene (*FGrH* 270 F 5), but Herodotus reveals that the Cyrenaeans gave them safe conduct.

Arkesilas III's successor Battos IV probably owed his throne to the Persian intervention. The role of Pheretima is remarkable. During the absence of Arkesilas III in Barka and after his murder she acted as regent, exercising full royal powers and attending the boulē (council). If she was really the daughter of Battos II, as Herodotus surprisingly says (4. 205, assuming the text is not corrupt), she was a sister (or possibly half-sister) of Arkesilas II, and therefore the aunt (or step-aunt) of her husband Battos III, and both great-aunt and mother of Arkesilas III. Her age and status may explain her regency while Arkesilas was in Barka. Her position is somewhat like that of Atossa, daughter of Cyrus and wife of Darius, but incestuous. Such close intermarriage in a royal family is contrary to normal Greek custom and is comparable to the brother–sister marriages of the Egyptian Pharaohs and the Carian Hekatomnids, though nephew–aunt marriages are obviously biologically more unexpected than uncle–niece and brother–sister unions. The need for concentration of power within a royal dynasty was responsible, and it is worth remembering that in Corinth the ruling aristocratic Bacchiad family always intermarried (Hdt. 5. 92. 2). It could well have suited the Battiads for Battos 'the lame' to have a powerful wife, daughter of the 'fortunate' Battos II, when the family was threatened during the troubled reign of Arkesilas II. The practice of incestuous endogamy may have spread to Cyrene from Egypt. There are, however, parallels in the Spartan kingship. In the mid-sixth century King Anaxandridas lived with two wives, the first being his niece (Hdt. 5. 39–41). There is a closer parallel in the fifth century when King Leotychidas, whose only son (by his first wife) predeceased him, married his daughter Lampito (by his second wife) to his grandson, later King Archidamus II (Hdt. 6. 71), who thus married his step-aunt as Battos III may have done. So the irregularity conceivably has a Spartan as well as eastern parallels, although Herodotus depicts Pheretima, an arch-Medizer, as a typically cruel oriental-style queen, as indicated by the vengeance she took on the Barkan enemies of Arkesilas, crucifying the men and cutting off the breasts of their wives (4. 202. 1).[19]

[19] On incestuous royal marriages see Hornblower (1982) 358–63. For discussion of the

The pro-Persian monarchy continued and prospered under Battos IV. Persian control was fairly easygoing so long as tribute was paid and military service available when called upon. Otherwise, the Persian kings left cities and tribes mainly with their own forms of government, intervening only to prevent internecine quarrels. We have no information about the reign of Battos IV, but it is likely that he followed the precedent of Demonax to the extent of leaving the tribal reform in place but retaining the royal powers which had been recovered by Arkesilas III. There is no evidence for revolts during his reign and Cyrene was not called upon to send military aid to Xerxes against mainland Greece in 481–480, as earlier Darius had not asked for her help on the Scythian expedition, possibly for geographical reasons. Ample coinage and the building of the great temple of Zeus suggest that his reign was peaceful and prosperous (Chamoux 1953: ch. 7; 320–31). The prosperity of the Greek cities of Asia Minor under Persian rule, both before and after the Ionian revolt, provides a comparison. After the fall of Miletus and the end of the Ionian revolt in 494, the Persian satrap of Ionia, Artaphernes, imposed a *Pax Persica* on the Ionian cities from which they benefited materially in the absence of internecine wars (Hdt. 6. 42). Soon afterwards the Persian general Mardonius put down tyrannies and established 'democracies' in Ionia, evidently because the Ionians disliked their tyrants (Hdt. 6. 43).[20] However, no such action was taken against Battos IV, which suggests that in his reign the monarchy was not unpopular with the majority of the dēmos, though the aristocrats may have been biding their time. The wealth of the king from the τεμένεα and the silphion revenues will have contributed to the apolitical nature of the reign, and the Persian power to which Battos IV owed his throne still lay in the background in the potential protection of the satrap of Egypt.

The end of the monarchy

It is not known when Arkesilas IV succeeded Battos IV, but he too was wealthy and powerful. Pindar (*Pyth.* 5. 15) calls him 'king of great cities'. It is unclear what kind of control the kings of Cyrene exercised over the other Greek cities within their orbit. At this time these were Barka, Teuchira (Tokra), Euesperides, probably Antipyrgos (Tobruk), and naturally Apollonia, the port of Cyrene. It must have been flexible, but although they were self-governing there was a common coinage before 450 BC, with the Cyrenaean emblems silphion on the obverse and the head of Zeus Ammon

dynastic and property reasons for the Lampito–Archidamus marriage see Hodkinson (1986) 401; and for the frequency of close-kin marriages among the Spartan royal families, Hodkinson (1989) 92, 115 n. 12. (I owe the Spartan parallels to the editors.)

[20] Cf. M. M. Austin (1990); Graf (1985) 79–123 goes too far in denying that the Asian Greeks resented their tyrants; see also Murray (1988a) 473–80. Note the decline of Ionia *after* its liberation from Persia: Cook (1961).

on the reverse, on the same standard and with the names of a city or two
cities indicated. Similar issues continued after the fall of the monarchy,
probably about 450.[21] Some cities had a joint coinage, not necessarily including Cyrene. The coinages represented are: Cyrene, Barka, Cyrene and
Euesperides, Barka and Teuchira, and (possibly slightly later), Barka and
Cyrene. The priority of Barka in the last two issues may indicate that the
predominance of Cyrene declined in the period after the fall of the monarchy.
Perhaps convenience for exchange was a stronger factor than the political
supremacy of Cyrene, but the common standard and emblems nevertheless
suggest a league or confederacy.[22]

Arkesilas IV's reign is likewise undocumented until the late 460s, when he
competed in and won victories in the four-horse chariot races at the Pythian
games in 462 and the even more prestigious festival at Olympia in 460.
In competing, Arkesilas surpassed the precedent of a Cyrenaean aristocrat
Telesicrates, who won the foot race at the Pythian games in 474. Like
another ruler, Hieron of Syracuse, whose power in some ways resembled
his own, Arkesilas commissioned Pindar to celebrate his Pythian victory
(*Pythian* 5). Competing at the major festivals of the Greek mainland and
commissioning Pindar were deliberate moves by Arkesilas IV away from
Persia in the wake of the Persian defeats at Salamis, Plataea, and Mykale,
the campaigns of Cimon against the Persians in the Hellespont and more
recently his victory at the river Eurymedon, near Antalya in south-west
Turkey. In 465 Xerxes had been murdered and the empire weakened in
the ensuing power-struggle between his three sons, from which Artaxerxes
emerged as his successor (Cook 1983: 127). With the centre weakened by
the accession struggle, Egypt revolted in 460. This was provoked by the
Libyan border-king Inaros, who brought over to aid him a force of 200
Athenian and allied ships which were then campaigning in Cyprus (Thuc.
1. 104). If the eastern Libyans had already become restive, Arkesilas would
no longer have been able to rely on help from the satrap of Egypt against his
political enemies. This consideration could well have persuaded Arkesilas
to heighten his profile in mainland Greece by making use of the well-known
Cyrenaean skill in horsemanship at the games.

A second reason for competing was a domestic one: the need to excel at
the games in which his potential enemies, the Cyrenaean aristocrats, who
were also well-endowed with horses and wealth, were able to compete and
rival his prestige. Already seeing trouble ahead, he sent a four-horse chariot
to compete at the Pythian festival of 462 under a manager Euphemus with
Charrotus, his wife's brother, as charioteer. He aimed not only at winning

[21] See below, pp. 100–2.
[22] See G. F. Hill, Meiggs, and Andrewes (1951) C 12, p. 333; Kraay (1976) 297–9 (cf. 1964).
For the problematic functions of ancient coinage see Howgego (1990), a cogent case against
the view that all ancient coinage was minted for state purposes, arguing that exchange and
other motives have to be admitted.

the victor's crown for Cyrene but at enrolling a colony of Greek soldiers to be settled at Euesperides. The military colonists were virtually his mercenaries and would provide a loyal refuge there if he needed it, as he eventually did. In the event his chariot won, but Euphemus died and Charrotus led the colony.[23]

It is clear from the text of *Pythian* 5 that there was hostility in 462 between Arkesilas IV and the aristocrats. At the beginning of the ode the storms of winter have passed and at the end Pindar prays that no stormy blast of autumn may blight the flower—the same metaphor for internal trouble as at the beginning. *Pythian* 4, a long ode in praise of Arkesilas and Cyrene on his return home from the same victory, ends with a plea to him to maintain calm in the city and to recall the exiled Damophilus, a Cyrenaean aristocrat whom Pindar met in Thebes and who may have commissioned the ode to help bring about his return.

Arkesilas continued to thrive until after 460, when he won first prize in the four-horse chariot race at Olympia. Soon after, faced with renewed opposition, he fled Cyrene and took refuge at Euesperides, where his colonists were now established. In his reinforcement of Euesperides with Greek colonists[24] he was repeating a solution for obtaining external military power for the monarchy which was similar to Arkesilas III's earlier recruitment and settlement of Samians as mercenaries to restore the privileges of the kingship against aristocratic opposition. Arkesilas IV's settlement of colonists shows that he still retained the original power of the kings to divide and distribute land, inherited from the oikist Battos, and that the sway of Cyrene extended westwards as far as Euesperides. This may be why Aryandes had gone no further back in 514 but upheld the claim of Cyrenaean authority thus far.

A combination of the scholiast on *Pythian* 4 and Aristotle (fr. 611 Rose, from Herakleides—where 'Battos' seems to be a mistake for 'Arkesilas' since he is described as the seventh king after the first) shows that Arkesilas was murdered in Euesperides.[25] The parallel with Arkesilas III's murder in Barka is remarkable, but this time no force from Egypt came to Arkesilas IV's aid or to avenge him.

When was Arkesilas IV murdered? In my view the monarchy did not last till *c*.439, the date usually accepted.[26] It is based on the traditional 200 years for the length of the Battiad dynasty, but this could be a round figure, perhaps based on 8 generations of 25 years. It gives Arkesilas or Battos IV,

[23] Schol. Pind. *Pyth.* 5. 26, referring to the hellenistic historian Theotimus. Cf. B. M. Mitchell (1966) 108–10.
[24] The city existed by 514 BC, when Aryandes made his demonstration of force (Hdt. 4. 204); a fortification wall dating back to *c*.600 has now been revealed: Buzaian and Lloyd (1996) esp. 143–4.
[25] Ogden (1997) 60 attempts to defend 'Battos', but the eight kings prophesied by the *post eventum* Delphic oracle (Hdt. 4. 163. 2) seem conclusive.
[26] e.g. Chamoux (1953) 206–10; *contra*, B. M. Mitchell (1966) 110; Hornblower (1983) 61.

or both, unusually long reigns to fill the period from the accession of Battos IV in 514. He was probably dead before c.454, when Cyrene helped the Athenian refugees who returned through Libya when the revolt of Egypt ended in disaster (Thuc. 1. 110). Arkesilas would hardly have helped enemies of Persia.

Social factors, predominantly the lack of a hoplite class of small farmers, would have contributed to the support of Persia in enabling the monarchy to survive so long, but its survival was due to Aryandes' intervention, which ensured the accession of Battos IV after the crisis of the murder of Arkesilas III. It was ended by a 'democratic' revolution, according to Aristotle (fr. 611 Rose), but this was probably not a radical democracy on the Athenian model. Its power was more likely to have been based on the aristocratic opposition to Arkesilas IV, who had caused the 'storm' of Pindar *Pyth.* 5. 10. This, says the scholiast, hints at revolution, and *stasis* broke out between him and the 'dēmos'. But it is clear that the 'dēmos' here must have been dominated by the aristocratic opposition. Cyrene lacked a large peasant hoplite class of small farmers with an even distribution of wealth, as in Attica. In addition, owing to a lack of suitable harbours, Cyrene did not develop naval power, which might have supported a politically active class. As it was, Cyrenaic land tenure, based mainly on large estates, implies that the opposition to the monopoly of power by the monarchy finally came from the aristocratic landowners. The tribal reform of Demonax gave social status to the more recent settlers, who would have included some peasantry, but, as argued above, it left political power with a dēmos dominated by the aristocracy. Perhaps the loss of hoplites at Leukon was not easily recovered (see above, p. 87). The recruitment of soldier farmers as colonists, from Samos by Arkesilas III and the Greeks enrolled as mercenaries at the Pythian games in 462 by Arkesilas IV, also suggests a scarcity of local hoplite small farmers, if the new colonists were thought by the kings to be sufficient support for them against the aristocratic opposition. They provided an external force which succeeded temporarily for Arkesilas III, though not for his grandson.[27]

In the Cyrenaean agrarian system labouring work on the big estates was probably done by *perioikoi*. These may have included non-nomadic, Hellenized Libyans, who had been tribalized and given a stake in the state by Demonax, but did not demand a political voice. For whatever reason, a large hoplite class did not emerge. In Syracuse too, where the Sikels as serfs provided agricultural labour, the hoplite class was small. The absence of small farmers in both states made the democracies which succeeded the

[27] Applebaum (1979) 32 takes the lack of a politicized small peasantry (i.e. a hoplite class) as one reason for the long survival of the monarchy; but though this undoubtedly delayed democracy, Applebaum ignores the major part played by the aristocracy in opposing Arkesilas III and Arkesilas IV.

autocratic rulers unstable and short-lived and not as radical or established as the Athenian democracy. They both lasted only about fifty years.[28]

These factors could have contributed to the survival of the monarchy in Cyrene during a period in which it had long been effectively superseded in most other states. But the succession of Battos IV after the murder by aristocrats of Arkesilas III and hence the survival of the monarchy till the mid-fifth century was due entirely to the support of Persia via Egypt. The monarchy under the last two kings was still wealthy owing to the revenues from the sacred lands and the silphion monopoly, which had survived or was recovered by Arkesilas III. As argued above, the eventual failure to resist political opponents was probably caused by the lack of support from Persia at some unknown date during the Egyptian revolt.

The Libyan factor

Relations between Cyrene and the neighbouring Libyan tribes were generally friendly, with the exception of the quarrel over land after the arrival of the new colonists, which led to the battle of Irasa. Though the extent of Libyan influence on Cyrene in the archaic and classical periods is problematic, both geographically and socially, the proximity of the Libyan tribes and the interrelationships of the Greeks with them are likely to have contributed to the longevity of the monarchy. There is evidence for Libyan influence in the cultic and social rather than the political or central cultural and artistic spheres, and also in some practical skills connected with land usage.

The Cyrenaeans certainly learnt about animal husbandry from the Libyans, including the use of the four-horse chariot (Hdt. 4. 189). The tribe most expert in this, the Asbystai, says Herodotus (4. 170), closely imitated the customs of their neighbours the Cyrenaeans. This may have included a more sophisticated form of agriculture and arable farming, and may have encouraged some Libyans to lead a settled rather than a nomadic existence where the land was suitable. Both peoples seem to have learnt from their neighbours, and some Libyans may already have been transhumant, as they have been up to modern times. Geographically, it is difficult to be certain how much territory (*chōra*) each of the Greek cities controlled, but it is likely to have been the areas on the fertile well-watered plateau which were suitable for growing cereals, vegetables, and the vines and olives characteristic of Mediterranean agriculture. The less fertile surrounding areas both to the north towards the coast and south towards the desert would have been utilized by Libyans and were more suited to a pastoral way of life. The pattern of settlements and zones of different types of cultivation have been located and analysed in detail for the hellenistic period by Laronde.[29] The

---

[28] See Rutter (this volume) for 'democracy' at Syracuse, and cf. Hornblower (1983) 54–5, 59–62.   [29] Laronde (1987) ch. 13, esp. 285–6 and fig. 87.

geographical features (especially rainfall and wells), traces of ancient field systems, and relative frequency of Graeco-Roman remains led him to define the central *chōra* of Cyrene as the land between the ancient villages of Messa to the west and El-Gubba to the east, about 60 km. overall and roughly 35 km. from north to south. The boundaries cannot have been exactly defined, but this area was probably determined in principle in the archaic period. The monopoly of silphion, which grew wild in the Libyan area and was worked only by Libyans, contributed greatly to the wealth of the Battiad kings (Hdt. 4. 169), as noted above, and the Libyans also probably sold or bartered wool from their flocks, from which the Cyrenaeans could have exported a surplus. The wealth of the monarchy which helped to perpetuate it thus partly depended on the Libyans, as did the skill in horsemanship which Arkesilas IV made use of when he competed in the Pythian and Olympic chariot races. The wealth and prestige of the Battiads generally commanded respect from the Libyan tribes, some of whom were also ruled by kings such as Adikran.

There was intermarriage with Libyan women from the beginning. Such links must go back to the beginning of the colony, since no women came on the original expedition, and Battos, as well his fellow colonists, would have taken a Libyan wife. She was presumably of high birth and might have been royal, since some Libyan tribes were themselves ruled by kings. However, intermarriage with Greeks continued. In Barka there was an interesting mixture: the royal house was related to a Libyan family, since Arkesilas III married the daughter of the king Alazeir, who was Greek but whose African name suggests a Libyan mother, and might have been called after his grandfather, perhaps some unknown royal Libyan. The Barkan royal family was also related by marriage to the Battiads, since the daughter of Alazeir was already related to Arkesilas (Hdt. 4. 164. 4).[30] The Libyan influence on Barkan women was, however, stronger than at Cyrene itself. Herodotus notes that, unlike the Cyrenaean women, they abstained from pork as well as beef (4. 186). Intermarriage with Libyans would have made for racial and social integration in Cyrene and the other Greek cities in Cyrenaica, unlike, for example, the situation in Syracuse, where the native Sikels and Greeks were entirely separated socially and the Greek landowners had Sikel serfs (cf. Rutter, this volume). The respect of the Libyans for the Cyrenaean monarchy, a system they understood, may have owed something to this fusion.

The resulting symbiosis survived the demise of the monarchy. Ptolemy I's *diagramma* (ordinance) of 321 allowed citizens of Cyrene to have Libyan

---

[30] There were Battiads in Barka at the end of Arkesilas III's reign who were spared by Pheretima and to whom she gave over the city after Arkesilas' murder (Hdt. 4. 202). Possibly they were descended from the dissident brothers of Arkesilas II (4. 160) and later made up their quarrel with the Battiads of Cyrene.

mothers from between the limits of Katabathmos, the boundary with Egypt, and Automalax, at the Altars of the Philainoi, the border between Cyrenaica and Carthage (Tripolitania).[31] This measure clarified the status of those of mixed parentage, so there must have been some for whom it was necessary. Naturally it did not apply to unions between Cyrenaean women and Libyan men, which would not have been recognized as marriages. The legitimizing of mixed marriages will have encouraged cultural assimilation.

Signs of admixture are noted by Laronde (1990). He emphasizes the distinction between Libyan nomadic and non-nomadic tribes, a distinction Herodotus was aware of, although his divisions in the excursus at the end of book 4 are not geographically credible since he locates all the non-nomadic Libyan tribes to the west of 'Lake Tritonis'—that is, to the west of Cyrenaica (4. 186–97)—and the nomads between here and Egypt. Diodorus (3. 49) gives a more realistic division of the Libyans into three groups: those who were settled agriculturalists, the nomadic shepherds (like the transhumant Bedouin of recent times), and the raiding nomads from the southern desert. Laronde convincingly argues that the last group were a threat to settled Libyans and Greeks equally. *Pyrgoi* of Cyrenaean nobles outside Cyrene, towers like that of Aglomachos in Hdt. 4. 164, have been located both north and south of the plateau, the Jebel-al-Akhdar (Green Mountain) of Cyrenaica. They date from the hellenistic era and attempts have been made to explain their location and relation to the *chōra* of Cyrene.[32] That they were built for defence against the threat of raids is a likely explanation. Nomadic tribes, among whom the Garamantes were prominent, were a feature of North Africa from east to west in the desert, south of the cultivable areas; they were a danger to the wealthier settled peoples till the early Roman imperial period.[33] This meant that the interests of Greeks and settled Libyans tended to be similar, determined by the same need for defence.

The evidence from surviving lists of names from the *chōra* of Cyrene suggests that there was more Libyan influence in its more distant parts, as do the representations of Libyan dress and pastoral Greek divinities.[34] The distinction between nomadic and non-nomadic and semi-nomadic Libyans was as important as that between Greek and non-Greek racial groups. Most of the time, as Laronde concludes (1990: 180), contacts and exchanges between Greeks and Libyans were the rule rather than the exception, and the Greek cities of Cyrenaica generally lived in harmony with their Libyan

[31] *SEG* ix. 1. 1–5; trans. M. M. Austin (1981) no. 264. 1–5.

[32] Laronde (1990) 173–4; (1987) ch. 13. For an excellent account of the Jebel and transhumance in ancient and recent times see Johnson (1973).

[33] Laronde (1990) *passim*); Reynolds (1981) 379–83 makes the same point concisely for both Greek and Roman periods: 'Serious hostility was due to pressures from Libyans further afield.'

[34] For nomenclature, see Laronde (1987) 338–40; Reynolds (1981); all the attested names from Cyrenaica: Fraser and Matthews (1987–) vol. i; for Libyan dress and pastoral divinities see Fabbricotti (1981).

neighbours. Cyrenaean control over the *chōra* remained constant under both the monarchy and the constitutional government, although Libyan religious and cultural influence became stronger further from the city. Good relations with the neighbouring Libyans contributed to the wealth of Cyrene both during and after the monarchy. Its wealth depended mainly on the products of the land in the form of flocks, horses, and crops, and land was plentiful. The monarchy during its existence and the landowners were the main beneficiaries of the system. Indeed, the fall of the monarchy probably meant that its wealth and revenues fell largely into the hands of the wealthy landowning class which had been responsible for its downfall. There was no redivision of land, and although some sort of democracy followed the downfall of Arkesilas IV the lack of a more equal distribution of wealth among the citizen body meant that it tended to instability, as later events show.

After the monarchy

Cyrene after the fall of the monarchy is less well documented, and also less prominent. As noted above, the ensuing constitution is called a 'democracy' by Aristotle but the dēmos was probably still dominated by the landowning class. Aristotle may refer to this democracy in the *Politics* (1319ᵇ), but several other contexts have been suggested.[35] That there was a democracy of some kind after the fall of the monarchy is supported by archaeological evidence: Lidiano Bacchielli (1985) saw signs of democracy in the public building in the agora in the second half of the fifth century, which he suggests provided public spaces for a democratic assembly, drawing parallels with Athenian buildings of this period.

A further sign of change towards a democratic system, whatever its exact form, can be seen in the inscriptions of the *dēmiourgoi*, three annual state magistrates, evidently one from each tribe, who managed sacred lands for the polis and were accountable to the dēmos. They record produce of the various crops from these estates (barley, wheat, grapes, olives, olive oil, etc.). The earliest go back to the mid-fifth century. The sacred lands would have included the τεμένεα which Demonax had reserved for Battos III (Hdt. 4. 161) and which must therefore have yielded revenues which remained under the control of the monarchy throughout its existence. This wealth would have made it possible for Arkesilas IV to compete at Delphi and Olympia. It is tempting to connect the beginning of the records of the *dēmiourgoi* (though the office itself might be earlier) with the democratic changes which took

[35] Various contexts have been suggested for Arist. *Pol.* 1319ᵇ6–27: the reform of Demonax (E. W. Robinson (1997) 105–8); the fall of the monarchy (O'Neil (1995) 170–1); some extra enfranchisements which provoked the *stasis* of 401 (D.S. 14. 34) (B. M. Mitchell (1966) 112), which I still think the most likely. None is at all certain, and it could refer to some later otherwise unrecorded *stasis* in the early 4th cent. (see below). Hornblower (1983) ch. 5 charts the known constitutional changes which followed the monarchy down to the Ptolemaic period.

place after the fall of the monarchy, and if so this would be another reason for dating its end to around 450 rather than later.[36]

However, in spite of these constitutional features, which imply a citizen assembly and a degree of public accountability, Cyrene veered more towards Sparta than towards Athens. This is understandable in view of her Theran background and the predominance of the landowning class in the dēmos. Under Ptolemy's ordinance of 321 BC she had, like Sparta, five ephors and a gerousia (council of elders) as well as a council, prytaneion, and assembly, but how early they were instituted is not known.[37] The policy of Cyrene during the Peloponnesian war was pro-Spartan, since in 413 she sent two triremes to guide a Peloponnesian force under Gylippos, blown off his course to Libya on his way to Sicily in 413 (Thuc. 7. 50); though, as Hornblower notes, a Cyrenaean individual, Epikerdes, gave money to aid the Athenian prisoners in Syracuse, also in 413.[38] Diodorus (14. 34) and Pausanias (4. 26. 2) record in 401 a *stasis* in which 500 of the upper class (*dunatōtatoi*: 'most powerful') were killed and many of the *chariestatoi* ('most refined') fled. This latter term, surely a word from an oligarchic source, is always a term of approval in Diodorus, as Rutter notes (this volume). They returned with 3,000 Messenian mercenaries, who had been expelled by Sparta from Cephallonia and Naupactos after the defeat of Athens. After a fierce battle, in which the Messenians were killed almost to a man,[39] the two sides agreed to live in the city together, probably under a more liberal regime but not a radical democracy. More democratic changes may have followed in the early fourth century, since the Therans sent an embassy to Cyrene to confirm the rights of Therans resident in Cyrene and the 'Founders' Oath' stele affirming the grant contains the democratic formula 'it seemed good to the dēmos'.[40] However, a narrow oligarchy was in control again by the end of the fourth century since the more liberal Ptolemaic settlement, the *diagramma* of 321 BC, provides that the citizen body of '10,000' are to do what the '1,000' had done hitherto.

These developments cannot be called atypical in a Greek polis of the fifth to fourth centuries, although they stand in contrast to the more stable

---

[36] *SEG* ix. 11–44 (5th–2nd cents. BC); Oliverio (1933) nos. 15 and 16 (perhaps before 450 BC), and pp. 90–1, 99. For their functions and a detailed analysis see Applebaum (1979) 33, 87–129.

[37] *SEG* ix. 1 = M. M. Austin (1981) no. 264 (*c*.320 BC) line 35: Ptolemaic and pre-Ptolemaic boulai, neither democratic; ibid. 44–6: prytaneion. For the prytaneion see S. G. Miller (1978) no. 270; Hansen and Fischer-Hansen (1994) 31.

[38] Hornblower (1983) 62; *IG*: i³. 125 (the Athenian decree honouring Epikerdes); Dem. 20. 42.

[39] Roger Brock interestingly suggests that the employment of the Messenians may be due to Spartan collusion, perhaps engineered to get rid of them? It is certainly odd to find them fighting for the aristocrats, who were presumably pro-Spartan.

[40] ML no. 5. 11 (cf. 3–4) (= Fornara no. 18). Applebaum (1979) 35–6 (followed by Hornblower (1983) 62) takes Arist. *Pol.* 1319[b] to refer to an (otherwise unknown) Kleisthenic type of democracy accompanied by moves in the direction of Athens, including increased coinage and participation in the Panathenaia, in about 375 BC.

but not altogether typical Athenian democracy. Other cities provide closer parallels with Cyrene: equally balanced dēmos and *oligoi* are seen in action in Corcyra in 427 (Thuc. 3. 70–83, ending with his famous analysis of *stasis*), or at Megara in 424 (Thuc. 4. 66–73). In Samos during 411 'democrats' and 'oligarchs' became no more than interchangeable political labels for the two factions (Thuc. 8. 73). Syracuse reverted to tyranny in 405 after 60 years of democracy.

Modern scholars have followed Aristotle's example in the *Politics* (especially book 6), in attempting to classify different constitutions as 'democratic' by observing the distinctions between kinds of democracy. At Cyrene Demonax's reforms can be called an early type of democracy even though the aristocracy benefited from them, since the dēmos to whom he handed over power must have included all Cyrenaeans outside the monarchy. However, between this and the Athenian democratic model there are many variations.[41] The democratic polis was neither a uniform nor a stable form of government. We know virtually nothing of how the post-monarchic democracy at Cyrene worked, but although the poorer citizens seem to have allied themselves with the wealthy in replacing the monarchy with democracy, which would have been in their interest too, it was probably the unequal division of landed wealth which led to the bitter civil strife of 401 and was responsible for the instability of the fourth century before the moderate constitution of Ptolemy I.

Under the sway of Alexandria the city of Cyrene produced many distinguished men in the mainstream of Greek intellectual and creative tradition, among them the poet Callimachus, Eratosthenes, who calculated the circumference of the earth and got it almost right, the Middle Academy philosopher Carneades, and a school of medicine. In the post-Battiad period Cyrene developed along lines that were fundamentally Greek and followed patterns of constitutional change which are paralleled in many other Greek cities.

[41] O'Neil (1995) has classified them into three basic types: first, early (in which he includes that of Demonax, p. 25); second, a numerous and varied middle group of cities which tend to instability; and third, 'final' or radical democracies on the Athenian model. Aristotle's analysis of different types of democracy in the *Politics* is discussed by Lintott (1992) and summarized by Keith Rutter in this volume.

6

Friends and Foes: Monarchs and Monarchy in Fifth-century Athenian Democracy

DAVID BRAUND

THE fifth-century Athenian democracy had to negotiate relationships with the many states of its world which were ruled by monarchs of one type or another. However, the democracy had inherent difficulties in dealing with monarchs. A single incident illustrates the point. In 411 BC Athenian oligarchs set about persuading the democratic assembly to change its democracy: from this beginning they succeeded in establishing the oligarchical rule of the Four Hundred. According to Thucydides, their rhetoric centred upon a key argument:

> Peisander and the other envoys sent from Samos reached Athens and addressed the people with a summary of many arguments, but especially that, if they were to recall Alcibiades and were to cease maintaining the same form of democracy, they could have the King as their ally and achieve victory over the Peloponnesians. Many protested . . . Then Peisander came forward in the face of great protest and insults and personally asked each one of those who protested what hope he had for the salvation of the city: the Peloponnesians had as many ships to oppose them at sea and a greater number of allied cities, while the King and Tissaphernes gave funds to the Peloponnesians, which they themselves no longer possessed. What hope, unless someone should persuade the King to come over to the Athenian side? And when Peisander's opponents could not answer him, he told them plainly that 'This cannot happen unless we conduct more prudent politics and put our government into fewer hands, so that the King may trust us.' (Thuc. 8. 53. 2–3)

The argument is that the King (of Persia)[1] cannot be expected to form an alliance with Athens while Athens is a democracy, as at present. At the same time, the King can be expected to do so if Athens abandons democracy in favour of a more oligarchical regime. According to Thucydides, it was this

I am grateful to participants in the Leeds–Manchester seminar, where an earlier version of this paper was delivered, especially to Peter Rhodes and the editors. I have further benefited from discussion with colleagues at Exeter. All responsibility remains with me, of course.

[1] Persia might be deemed to have both good and bad kings: E. Hall (1989) 97–8. However, note here the absence of any expression of concern about Persia as such, on which more below. It is worth remembering also that Athens and Persia could align (however unsatisfactorily and temporarily) against Sparta in the 390s, when mutual interest suited: Hornblower (1994a) 75.

argument that persuaded the Athenians to change a constitution that had
been in place for almost a century (cf. Thuc. 8. 68. 4). Certainly, there was
the supporting argument that the change could be reversed in the future,
if so desired; there was also the superior organization of the oligarchical
conspirators. However, the key point must be that in democratic Athens the
alienation of monarchy from democracy was a notion sufficiently familiar
and sufficiently accepted as powerful fact to permit its use as compelling
grounds for fundamental constitutional change.

In what follows I first explore the Athenian democracy's ambivalence
towards the institution of monarchy. We shall see that, while monarchy was
widely regarded as at odds with democracy, the existence of good kings
could also be accepted and such kings could even be accommodated within
the Athenian democracy's past. In the second section I seek to elucidate the
fifth-century democracy's concern (1) with the notion of the establishment
of one-man rule at Athens, (2) with the personal power of its individual
politicians, and (3) with its own imperial rule as a monarch or tyrant. In
the third section I explore the actual relationships which Athenian democracy formed and maintained with a range of monarchs, largely through
the agency of individuals. Such foreign connections might bring benefits
to individual Athenians (including a possible place of refuge in times of
trouble), but they also made them vulnerable to attack at Athens. Wise individuals stressed that their personal links were deployed entirely for the
communal advantage of the democracy. Meanwhile, the collective mytho-
logy of the Athenian democracy facilitated its relationships with at least
some monarchs. However, the issue of monarchy remained a conundrum
for fifth-century Athenian democracy on all fronts, while monarchy became
still more pressing as an issue in the aftermath of the Peloponnesian War.

Tensions between democracy and monarchy

Democracy (the rule of the many) could not be further removed from
monarchy (the rule of one): in 411 the adoption of something closer to oligarchy (the rule of the few) seemed to offer a possible *rapprochement* with
monarchy. About 430 Herodotus encapsulated many of the issues at stake
in his famous debate on the various merits and demerits of democracy, oligarchy, and monarchy.[2] Whatever the historicity of this particular debate,
abstract exchanges on the relative merits of constitutions were to be found
also in other sorts of writing, including writing for performance on the
Athenian stage. Indeed, Thucydides himself all but returns to the comparison of constitutions in book 8, when he describes the constitution of the
5,000 as a 'measured mixture', for the notion of such a mixture implies an
assessment of the relative merits and appropriate ratio of its ingredients.[3]

[2] Hdt. 3. 80–2, on which see now Asheri (1996).   [3] Thuc. 8. 97. 2: μετρία ξύγκρασις.

The first speaker in Herodotus' debate, Otanes, stresses that the problem with monarchy is that it gives absolute power to a single person. Such power corrupts absolutely: the king preys upon his subjects without legal redress. By contrast, claims Otanes, democracy brings equality under the law: its magistrates, unlike the monarch, are chosen by lot and are answerable under the law. The second speaker, Megabyzus, agrees with Otanes' damning analysis of monarchy, but objects to his support for democracy. Megabyzus stresses that the masses lack knowledge, which even the tyrant has, for all his drawbacks. Rather, he urges, they should choose a few good men (including himself and those conspiring with him). The third speaker is Darius, soon to be king and supporting monarchy. He agrees with Megabyzus against democracy, but opposes him on oligarchy. Offering the most abstract of the three analyses, Darius claims that an examination of the three forms of constitution at their respective best shows conclusively that monarchy at its best is better than the other constitutional forms. On Darius' argument, the goodness of the king informs his whole regime, while he can deal efficiently with wrongdoers. In any event, he claims, monarchy emerges naturally from failing oligarchy or democracy. As well as being natural in that sense, Darius observes that it is also traditional in Persia (Hdt. 3. 80–2). Darius' arguments carry the day, to the dismay of Otanes in particular.

Of course, Herodotus' narrative is replete with instances that show the limitations of Darius' sophistic case: indeed, in the debate itself Herodotus has Otanes point to the dysfunctional monarchies of Cambyses and the Magus, which formed the immediate background to the very debate itself. The fundamental problem with monarchy is that, in the absence of external controls, such as law, it depends so heavily upon the character of the individual monarch. In developing his case on the assumption that the king will have a very good character, Herodotus' Darius is begging the question. Moreover, on Otanes' view no man—not even the very best of men—will be able to resist the corruption of absolute power: Herodotus' Darius does not offer a response to that. Meanwhile, oligarchical Megabyzus' objections to democracy are undercut by his rhetorical wish that the enemies of Persia be ruled by democracy. Herodotus' audience knows full well that Darius' Persians will be defeated at Marathon by the forces of democratic Athens, not to mention the subsequent defeat of Xerxes. To that extent, Megabyzus had his wish and was shown to be wrong (cf. Aesch. *Pers.* 230–1).

There is no closure to the debate beyond the unsatisfactory decision to choose monarchy, for there is no sense that one of the three forms of constitution is clearly better than the others. Rather, the debate serves to ventilate issues that run through Herodotus' narrative and which indeed had a range of relevances for his audience, both Athenian and non-Athenian. As Gould boldly observes of the debate, 'The language and arguments of Otanes' speech clearly derive from the language of Athenian political debate in Herodotus' own day and have numerous parallels in contemporary literature.'[4] In so far as Herodotus' own political preferences surface in his text, they seem ambivalent. Beside his mad kings, such as Cambyses or Cleomenes, there are apparently sound kings, such as Idanthyrsus of the Scythians or the unnamed king of the Ethiopians. Moreover, he can explicitly observe the superiority of judgement by a (Spartan) king over an (Athenian) democracy.[5]

One may wonder whether Herodotus' Darius pointedly gives the game away in his speech by introducing the notion of a constitution at its best. A percipient audience might conclude that in the abstract each form of constitution has its particular strengths and weaknesses. The important issue is how those are negotiated in particular concrete instances: what matters is not whether monarchy is good or bad, but whether a particular monarch is good or bad. Herodotus' Darius says enough to encourage the thought, which is played out throughout Herodotus' narrative, where his audience is invited to form judgements of particular rulers. Even if one were to accept that monarchy at its best is the superior form of constitution, one might still hold that monarchy at its worst (or even when averagely good or bad) is the inferior form. Moreover, as we have seen, Otanes' claim goes unanswered: even the best king may deteriorate under the corrupting influence of his absolute power.

The absences in the debate are also worth observing. Throughout, beyond simple notions of good and bad, there is no attempt to draw distinctions between different forms of monarchy: in particular, kingship and tyranny are not distinguished here, as they were to be in philosophical works of the fourth century.[6] As in the crucial oligarchic argument of 411, the issue is primarily a matter of numbers: the rule of one, a few, or many. After all, any attempt to disentangle kingship and tyranny would not advance the understanding of that issue, but would tend to obstruct it, not least because the terms are replete with value judgements and other difficulties of definition.[7] At the same time, there is no consideration of ethnicity until Darius seeks to invoke Persian tradition on his side. Rather, the broad applicability of the debate across peoples is indicated not only by the lack of such specifics before Darius makes his observation, but also by the fact that when Herodotus introduces the discussion he draws attention to its

[4] Gould (1989) 15, though he proceeds properly to stress that Herodotus' primary audience and, still more so, his influences ranged beyond Athens; Rhodes (this volume) notes such constitutional language elsewhere, in Athens and beyond.

[5] Hdt. 5. 97. On the kings of the Scythians and Ethiopians see Braund (1998).

[6] On tyranny and kingship in the 5th-cent. Athenian discourse see Barceló (1993); Georgini (1993); Lanza (1977); Seaford (forthcoming).

[7] Even a discussion as abstract as that of Plato's *Gorgias* shows scant concern with distinctions between kingship and tyranny: e.g. 470 D–E and 525 D; 492 B comes closest to some such distinction. Of course, this is not to say that theoretical distinctions could not be drawn: cf. *Polit.* 291 D–E, *Rep.* 543–4.

doubtful historicity: the debate is as applicable to Greeks as to Persians or indeed any other people. Again, comparison with the argument of 411 is instructive. There too there is no sign of the issue of ethnicity: where one might have anticipated some concern about dealing with the Persian, there is no mention of such. Presumably the opponents of the shift to oligarchy would have raised the issue, but it does not appear in Thucydides' account.

In one sense, of course, monarchy was understood by Greek authors as a barbarian institution and especially a Persian one: unless otherwise contextualized, the word 'king' indicated the Persian king. Further, Greek authors could claim that there existed an intimate relationship between the acceptance of absolute monarchy and the very nature of barbarians, whereby each was a function of the other. Barbarians accepted monarchy because they were servile, it was argued, while their servility was expressed in their having a monarchy.[8] Yet Greek authors could also allow that barbarian monarchs might be good as well as bad. As we have seen, Herodotus seems to present the Scythian king Idanthyrsus and the unnamed Ethiopian king as admirable monarchs, not to mention Amasis and Rhampsinitus of Egypt. Even among the Persians, Cyrus has much to recommend him in Herodotus (for all his imperialist folly), no doubt an inspiration for Xenophon's philosophizing idealization in the *Cyropaedia* and the tradition that developed thereafter, wherein the Greek Pausanias can praise the emperor Antoninus Pius as a second Cyrus.[9]

However, monarchy was also a Greek issue, as perhaps indicated by the sustained Greek interest in the institution. There were Greek kings in abundance. The dual kingship of Sparta was idiosyncratic, but for all that its kings could be treated as monarchical, especially when a forceful individual held the kingship. Agesilaus, in particular, rather as Persian Cyrus, could receive an idealizing monograph from Xenophon. If the Persian king would find it difficult to do business with the Athenian democracy, then he might find much less difficulty with the quasi-monarchical constitution of Sparta: that was an unspoken context for the oligarchs' argument in 411.[10]

Not that the Spartan kings were the only monarchs of Greece. The king of Macedon was Greek enough, as were, further afield, the rulers of the Bosporan kingdom. There were also the kings of the mythical past, whose currency at Athens was maintained by key texts, particularly Homer, by drama, and by religion, over which the King (Archon) presided at Athens.[11] The gods themselves had a monarchical structure under Zeus. And Zeus'

[8] Unlike Herodotus, for example, Aristotle does draw a distinction in this context between kingship and tyranny: Garnsey (1996) 115–16.
[9] Braund (1998) on the kings of Herodotus. On Pius, Paus. 8. 43. 6.
[10] See Lewis (1977) 148–52; L. G. Mitchell (1997a) 108–33 on the use of personal links in Spartan foreign relations.
[11] Cf. Thuc. 1. 9 on Homer; R. Parker (1996) 22. On the emergence of the King (Archon) see Rhodes (1981a) 98–102.

use and abuse of monarchical power were explored on stage in fifth-century Athens, as in the *Prometheus Bound*. The very origins of the Athenian state were set in a world of kings, notably Erechtheus and Cecrops: here too was the stuff of drama, such as Euripides' *Erechtheus*.[12] Here the king might be imagined as a monarchical champion of democracy, as is Theseus in Euripides' *Suppliants*. In a well-known scene in that play, valuably discussed by Rhodes elsewhere in this volume, the Herodotean debate finds many an echo. In the play the debate is between Theseus himself and a Theban herald, who expresses confidence in the superiority of (Theban) monarchy over (Athenian) democracy. In Euripides there is no Greek–barbarian antithesis: as noted above, the tension between democracy and monarchy is no less powerful in an entirely Greek context, as here between Athens and Thebes.[13]

As in the Herodotean debate, so in *Suppliants* the weakness of democracy is perceived as lack of knowledge with consequent susceptibility to deceptive rhetoric (Eur. *Supp.* 409–25). Theseus' response echoes the arguments of Herodotus' Otanes. He claims that under monarchy there is no law beyond the ruler's will, when the ruler preys upon his subjects without legal redress. By contrast, democracy means law and equality under which those in the state can flourish (ibid. 426–62). Also, as in the Herodotean debate, Euripides shows no interest in distinguishing kingship from tyranny. That was a matter for theorists like Aristotle.[14] Euripides has Theseus use the terminology of kingship and tyranny together, without distinction, it seems: 'Where a dēmos guides the land, it delights in the youths of the city. But the man that is king (*basileus*) considers them an enemy thing and the best, whom he deems have ideas, he kills, fearing for his tyranny (τυραννίδος πέρι)' (*Supp.* 442–6).

Theseus' rebuttal is firm and comprehensive; it offers a clarity of resolution lacking in Herodotus' debate. Democracy is best. After all, the audience of the play was the democracy itself, Theseus was Theseus, and the Theban herald was no more than an opinionated nobody, unnamed and going beyond his brief, from a hostile city with an alien constitution. In play after play, Athenian tragedy presented its audience with the follies, failures, and dangers of monarchs and monarchy, both Greek and non-Greek. By implication, and directly on occasion as in the *Suppliants*, the superiority of democracy is affirmed and celebrated. In this respect at least, I can find no indication of the subversion that has occasionally been claimed for Athenian tragedy.[15]

The peculiar case of Theseus highlights the central ambivalence about monarchy within Athenian democratic ideology. He was king, potentially

---

[12] Saïd (1985); Loraux (1993). [13] See Zeitlin (1990).
[14] *Pol.* 1310ᵃ39–1311ᵃ23, where Greek and non-Greek are not distinguished.
[15] For subversion see Goldhill (1987); contrast Brock (1991).

the enemy of democracy. Yet he could be constructed as a good king who ruled under the law, indeed as a democratic king (R. Parker 1996: 170). He was also a figure of the past, who had served a crucial function in the creation of the Athenian state, together with other kings, like Cecrops and Erechtheus. Kingship might be acknowledged as characteristic of an early phase of development, before democracy proper at Athens, with an intervening period of tyranny: such seems to be Thucydides' assessment (1. 13–18). Athenian kings in that sense were no threat to present democracy, but rather the contrary.

Monarchy in the democracy and the democracy as a monarchy

By contrast, Athenian tyrants were perceived as a significant threat. The Athenian democracy had developed very much in the context of the rejection of tyranny and there abided under fifth-century democracy a keen anxiety that tyranny might be restored. In wrestling with the socio-economic and political problems of the developing Athenian state at the beginning of the sixth century, Solon himself explicitly rejected the position of tyrant which he claimed to have been offered.[16] Later in the sixth century and thereafter, although Peisistratus acquired the reputation of a 'good king', after the fashion of Theseus, tyranny was damned in the person of his sons. The assassination of Peisistratus' son Hipparchus by Harmodius and Aristogeiton seems to have been regarded in the fifth century as a defining moment in the history of Athenian democracy, even though the tyranny subsisted for a few years after the killing.[17] In Thucydides' view at least, Athenian awareness of that affair played a large part in the summoning of Alcibiades from Sicily in 415 under suspicion of aiming at tyranny.[18] Shortly afterwards, Thucydides has the fugitive Alcibiades hold forth at Sparta on the hostility between democracy and tyranny. And, despite Alcibiades' slipperiness and his particular situation at this juncture in Sparta, famously hostile to tyrants (Thuc. 1. 18), his generalized observation seems close enough to the position of Herodotus' Otanes, namely that 'democracy is the name given to any force that opposes absolute power' (Thuc. 6. 89).

The suspicion of tyranny was raised by any form of social or political prominence at Athens. As Cartledge has demonstrated, even the keeping of pea-fowl might be taken as a hint of tyrannical outlook and ambitions. So too the conspicuous consumption of fine fish. So too overt expressions of patronage, which were avoided accordingly.[19] It is no surprise that a figure as prominent as Pericles found himself lampooned as a kind of tyrant. As Rhodes observes elsewhere in this volume, there is every reason to suppose

[16] Solon frr. 32–4 West; E. Hall (1989) 13–14.
[17] Taylor (1981); E. Hall (1989) 58–9, 67–8.   [18] Thuc. 6. 60; cf. 6. 15.
[19] Ar. *Wasps* 493–5, with Davidson (1993); Davidson (1997) ch. 9; Cartledge (1990); Millett (1985).

that attacks upon Pericles were at their height in the 430s, though there was ample scope for it in earlier decades too. Plutarch's *Life*, though written much later, preserves much that is drawn from the political invective of Pericles' day, not least from that in the comic drama of Cratinus. The radical flavour of Pericles' early democratic politics is said to have been generated by his fear of ostracism for aiming at tyranny (Plut. *Per.* 7. 3). His much-criticized building programme was 'tyrannizing' over Greece (*Per.* 12. 2). Such had been the desire of the Persian king, whose attributes are echoed in Pericles' case: his Odeum recalls the king's pavilion,[20] his Aspasia rivals the king's courtesans (*Per.* 24). After all, in Athenian history the Persian king might be remembered as the would-be restorer of Peisistratid tyranny in the person of Hippias (e.g. Hdt. 6. 107). At the same time, Pericles can be plotted against the Homeric tradition, as being better than King Agamemnon (Plut. *Per.* 28. 5), an Olympian king (*Per.* 39). As for Peisistratus, Pericles even looked like him (*Per.* 7. 1). In his later career, on Plutarch's assessment, Pericles established a 'kingly constitution' ($\beta\alpha\sigma\iota\lambda\iota\kappa\grave{\eta}\ \pi\omega\lambda\iota\tau\epsilon\acute{\iota}\alpha$) in democratic Athens (*Per.* 15. 5) with more power than many a king or tyrant (ibid.). Plutarch concludes that Pericles' position was at odds with democracy, but was a force for good.[21]

Such too was the expressed opinion of Thucydides, namely that in Pericles' later years 'there came about in name a democracy, but in practice rule by the first man' (Thuc. 2. 65. 9). While democrats might regard Pericles' pre-eminence with suspicion, the less democratic sensibilities of Plutarch and Thucydides might well interpret his position as the exercise of the judicious control that democracy required in the view of its critics. Indeed, Thucydides seems to have been responding to an ongoing debate on the role of Pericles. In the fourth century, exploring issues of power and morality, Plato offers a discussion in the *Gorgias* which not only indicates the existence of such discourse, but also suggests that this debate was a facet of a broader discussion of the strengths and weaknesses of the Athenian democratic system itself.[22] Of course, Thucydides stresses Pericles' personal qualities, which centre upon his knowledge. As Herodotus' Darius recommends, the best man guides the state in the interest of its members and can resist the corruption which Otanes had declared inevitable. It is in this kind of analysis that Plato's concept of the philosopher-king has its intellectual roots, as also Xenophon's imagined picture of the great Cyrus in his *Cyropaedia*.

Pericles' alleged tyranny was not only internal to Athens, but also external, exercised over Greece (cf. Plut. *Per.* 12. 2). In the *Gorgias* Plato has the Sicilian Polus declare: 'Do they [sc. the orators of the democracy]

[20] *Per.* 13. 5–6; M. C. Miller (1997) 218–42.   [21] *Per.* 39. 5; cf. 16.
[22] *Gorg.* 515 E, for example; 517 C allows that some democratic politicians (including Pericles) were better than others.

not, just as tyrants, slay whoever they might wish and take away property and expel from cities whomsoever they might choose?' (*Gorg.* 466 B–C). Although the dialogue ranges between generalized discussion and the particular critique of Athens, Polus' assertion here has a direct bearing upon the Athenian democracy. Whilst the charge of aiming at tyranny might be levelled against élite individuals (not least anti-democrats), Plato's Polus can turn the charge so as to suggest that democratic politicians are all akin to tyrants, whether in internal or external affairs. At the same time, Polus' analysis reminds us that, while distinctions between Pericles and his successors (so-called 'demagogues') might be made by Thucydides, they are seldom apparent in the expressed views of other Athenians.[23]

As politicians of the Athenian democracy might be regarded as tyrants, so too the democracy itself was readily represented as such, by virtue of its absolute rule over others. Thucydides has Pericles himself declare to the Athenians that they hold their empire like a tyranny (2. 63. 2). Such also was the complaint of Athens' enemies, it seems: Thucydides has the Corinthians conclude their rousing harangue at Sparta on that very note: 'As for the tyrant city established in Greece [sc. Athens], let us see that it threatens us all alike, so that it rules some and plans for the rest; let us set forth and oppose it; let us live without danger in the future; and let us liberate the Greeks who are now enslaved' (Thuc. 1. 124. 3).[24]

Later, Thucydides has Cleon acknowledge as much, for his own ends. Repeating Pericles' point, Thucydides' Cleon advises the assembly that it is so generous-spirited in its democratic outlook that it fails to appreciate its allies' perception of its empire as a tyranny, to be plotted against and overthrown (3. 37). More overtly cynical, the Old Oligarch observes with appreciative disapproval the tyrannical behaviour of the Athenian dēmos in ruling its empire, especially through killing, expropriation, and exile.[25]

Meanwhile, Aristophanes portrays a personified Demos as a tyrant with an empire.[26] The image, both in Thucydides and in Aristophanes, entails an oxymoron which gives it much of its force: the People itself, it is claimed, is a tyrant. A tyrant, it seems, in that a single Athens rules in its own interests, not in the interest of its many subjects. Like the tyrannical democrats of Plato's *Gorgias*,[27] the Athenian dēmos itself can be seen as killing, expropriating, and exiling according to its whim. The criticism, in the *Knights* at least, is not directed against Athenian imperial rule as such, but against the manner of that rule. For in the *Knights* the

---

[23] See Finley (1985) esp. 41, where he points out that Thucydides (unlike modern scholars) makes little use of the term 'demagogue'. Cf. Xen. *Symp.* 4. 32, where the impoverished Charmides claims now to be like a tyrant, thanks to the democracy, whereas he had been a slave when he had been wealthy. This was the internal tyranny of the Demos, as imagined by its enemies: e.g. Xen. *Mem.* 1. 2. 40–6.   [24] Cf. Tuplin (1985) 352–3.

[25] Notably ps.-Xen. *Ath. Pol.* 1. 14.

[26] Ar. *Knights* 1111 ff. with Tuplin (1985) 357–8.   [27] *Gorg.* 466 B–C, quoted above.

contrast is not with a pre-imperial Athens, but with an imperial Athens which had once ruled as a good monarch, in the good old days when the dēmos of Athens was the *monarkhos* of all Greece (*Knights* 1329–30). Those were the days when Athens was engaged in war with the Persians, before the tribute was tyrannically abused and misappropriated (cf. *Ach.* 673–4, *Wasps* 1098–101). If Athens was to have an empire, it could only be rule by the single city: in that sense Athenian imperial rule could only be monarchical, but it could be the rule of a 'good king', not the rule of a tyrant.

The destructive force of imagery which projected Athens as a tyrant was all the stronger because Athenians evidently attempted to justify their pre-eminence with reference to their role in the defeat of the Persian king.[28] They certainly urged the need to pursue the conflict with Persia. However, from an allied perspective, while a 'good king' might be tolerable, Athenian tyranny might well seem no better than the rule of the Persian king, or of the local tyrants through whom he ruled. From the perspective of oligarchs among the allies, the sponsorship offered by Persia can only have made the Athenian defeat of Persia seem a change for the worse. As for the future, why fight for Athens against the Persian king, when Athens itself was a tyrant? Thucydides has Hermocrates explore that very issue in his speech at Kamarina in Sicily; having stressed Athens' unjust use of power, Hermocrates concludes:

So, in making this stand against Persia, Athens was not fighting for the freedom of Hellas, nor were the Hellenes fighting for their own. What Athens wanted was to substitute her own empire for that of Persia, and the other Hellenes were simply fighting to get themselves a new master whose intelligence was not less but who made a much more evil use of it than did the old. (Thuc. 6. 76)

In reply, Euphemus the Athenian recalls Athens' role against the Persians only to stress that he does not base his case on that role (Thuc. 6. 83). Apparently, Athenian allusion to the defeat of Persia had become a commonplace in justifications of Athenian imperialism: accordingly, at the beginning of the Melian Dialogue the Athenians explicitly reject elaborate arguments for their empire based upon their defeat of the Persians (Thuc. 5. 89). The argument was all too familiar. It had probably been a key theme of Aristophanes' *Babylonians* a decade before, in 426.[29] It is aired again in his *Peace* of 421 (107–8). For all sides, the discourse of monarchy was a primary medium for debate about the exercise of power both within the democracy and also by the democracy.

---

[28] Thuc. 1. 73, with Meiggs (1972) 378–9.
[29] See Meiggs (1972) 393.

The accommodation of friendly kings

Well before the Peloponnesian War, the Athenian democracy had shown itself capable of establishing successful connections with kings. Alexander I of Macedon is said to have established good relations with Athens by the time of the Persian Wars, apparently formalized in a treaty (Hdt. 8. 136). In 445/4 a King Psammetichus, evidently ruler of Egypt, saw fit to send a gift of grain to Athens.[30] In the late 430s Athens formed links with rulers in the Black Sea region and may well have played a significant role in the contemporary establishment of the Spartocids as rulers of the Crimean Bosporus.[31] Also in the late 430s the Athenian democracy, which had previously had a friend and ally in King Perdiccas of Macedon, switched its allegiance to his brother and his associates, who no doubt sought to replace Perdiccas on the throne. Evidently Athens was actively engaged in the politics of kingdoms, internal as well as external (Thuc. 1. 57). A *rapprochement* of sorts could even be achieved with the Persian king, as the Peace of Callias indicates. Small wonder that 'the friendships of kings' could be cited as a constituent part of the power of the Athenian democratic state.[32]

As usual in ancient diplomacy, such state relations were facilitated and underpinned by personal links between individual Athenians and foreign kings, whether Greek or non-Greek, sometimes formalized as *proxenia*.[33] The position of such intermediaries was uncomfortable under the democracy, for it gave them a pre-eminent role which was prone to criticism, especially in the context of the shifting sands of diplomacy wherein foreign friends might soon become foreign enemies. Moreover, their links with foreigners might well have been gained through inheritance, a problematic course for a democracy. Pericles was wise to pre-empt the criticism that he anticipated upon the outbreak of the Peloponnesian War as a result of his personal links with King Archidamus of Sparta:

he announced to the Athenians in the Assembly that Archidamus was his guest-friend, but that this would not be to the detriment of the city, and further that, with regard to his own lands and houses, if the enemy did not ravage them like those of others, he would make them public property and on their account he should come under no suspicion. (Thuc. 2. 13. 1)

Pericles had himself, we are told, launched a prosecution against Cimon on the basis of Cimon's links with a king. According to Plutarch, Pericles was among those who accused Cimon of having taken bribes from King Alexander I of Macedon in return for not seizing part of his kingdom in

---

[30] Plut. *Per.* 37. 4, with Meiggs (1972) 268–9.

[31] Plut. *Per.* 20, with Braund (1994a) 124–5.

[32] Plut. *Per.* 15. 1–2. On the *rapprochement* with Persia see M. C. Miller (1997) 21–2; cf. L. G. Mitchell (1997a) 111–33.

[33] Gauthier (1985); Herman (1987); L. G. Mitchell (1997a); cf. Konstan (1997).

the aftermath of the Thasian revolt *c*.463 (Plut. *Cimon* 14. 2). Cimon's reported response to the charge, very possibly from the broadly contemporary Stesimbrotus of Thasos, further indicates the kind of reproaches that an Athenian with active foreign connections might have to tolerate:

Defending himself before the jurors, he said that he was not *proxenos* of wealthy Ionians or Thessalians, as were others, so that they might be courted and take money; rather, he was *proxenos* of Spartans, emulating and admiring their austerity and temperance, a virtue to which he preferred no wealth, but instead he seized wealth from the enemy and adorned the city. (Plut. *Cimon* 14. 3)

Evidently, it was not only ambassadors who might be accused of personal enrichment through their diplomatic activities, but also *proxenoi*. Moreover, Cimon's role as *proxenos* of Sparta was shortly to lead to his ostracism, once relations between Athens and Sparta had soured, a convenient indication of the dangers of foreign connections for the individual Athenian under the democracy. And while all foreign connections carried a risk, associations with kings were problematic by their very nature.

The individual was wise to stress that his personal connections brought benefit to the city, or else to take the more drastic measures of Pericles in 431. Andocides, who had much to do to establish his democratic credentials, argued that in 411 he had done just this by using his inherited guest-friendship with King Archelaos of Macedon to bring oar-spars from Macedon to the democratic forces on Samos.[34] Yet such arguments, even where accepted, missed some of the point: there remained something uncomfortable for the democracy in the very ability of an individual to achieve so much. Such links were part of an élite lifestyle, which was ultimately at odds with the central concept of democratic equality. Moreover, they had a particular association with tyranny at Athens, much more overt than the conspicuous consumption of fine fish. After all, Cylon had attempted to establish himself as tyrant with the support of Theagenes, tyrant of Megara (Thuc. 1. 126). Later, Peisistratus had finally established himself as tyrant with the support of foreign resources and manpower, including the tyrant Lygdamis of Naxos and the aristocracy of Eretria.[35]

Marriage had long been a means of forming and confirming such external connections. Cylon had married Theagenes' daughter (Thuc. 1. 126). Peisistratus made extensive political use of marriage, notably in his dealings with Argos. Cimon, whose family had long-established connections in the region of Thrace, had a Thracian mother, for Miltiades his father had married the daughter of a Thracian king, attested under the Greek name Hegesipyle.[36] Pericles' citizenship law of 451/0 seems best understood not as a personal attack on Cimon (it was not retrospective) but as an attempt to restrict the

[34] Andoc. 2. 11, with Herman (1987) 82–3.   [35] Hdt. 1. 61–2; *Ath. Pol.* 15. 2.
[36] On Peisistratus and Miltiades see Davies (1971) 445–50; 234–6.

marriages of the Athenian élite to Athens itself. By so doing, the law limited the potential of the élite to engage in the personal foreign diplomacy that seemed to threaten democracy.[37]

Yet, for all that, the pressures of the Peloponnesian War in particular required that Athens maximize available links, friendships, and alliances, not least with kings. The situation had become more desperate by 411 and the latter stages of the war, but it is worth stressing that Athens had been seeking to develop alliances from the very outbreak of war, as to a degree in the years before the conflict also. In particular, although the Persian king remained an object of easy suspicion and hostility, there are enough hints in our sources to confirm that Athens sought his help very early in the war. The topicality of Persia in 426 is indicated by the performance of Aristophanes' *Babylonians* in that year. It is confirmed by the explicit testimony of his *Acharnians* in 425, where, characteristically, the Athenian ambassadors sent to deal with the Persian king are lampooned as deceitful and grasping. Thucydides gives us no more than glimpses of the feverish diplomatic campaigns directed at the Persian king both by Athens and by Sparta in these years.[38] It was also in these years, after *c*.430, that Herodotus completed his *Histories*: the Persian Wars had a new and rather peculiar relevance at a time when Athenians and Spartans were vying for the Persian king's friendship. Even in these early years, the impact of the Peloponnesian War upon Athenian attitudes to barbarians, to kings, and to both was doubtless significant, though we need not suppose that its impact was entirely in one direction. But there is no sign that the attitudes of Persian kings had changed: throughout the war, it was Sparta whose diplomacy was the more successful with regard to Persia. Given the long years of Athenian imperial hostility towards Persia, the Persian king's preference for Sparta seems readily comprehensible, whether or not Athens was a democracy. Sparta's more monarchical regime can only have encouraged the Persian. Both recent history and broad constitutional considerations pointed the Persian king in the same direction, towards Sparta.

It was also in the early years of the war that the Athenian democracy pursued the friendship and alliance of the Thracian king, Sitalces. No doubt personal Athenian connections were exploited by the state, such as those of Thucydides the historian. However, we hear only of ambassadors and Nymphodorus of Abdera, Athens' unreliable *proxenos*.[39] Thucydides provides a short disquisition:

The Athenians . . . sent for Nymphodorus . . . wishing that Sitalces, son of Teres, king of the Thracians, become their ally. This Teres, the father of Sitalces, first established for the Odrysians the great realm including much of the rest of Thrace

---

[37] The argument is congruent with Patterson (1981).   [38] Thuc. 2. 67; 4. 50.

[39] The ambassador Theorus is named: Ar. *Ach.* 134–73; Thuc. 2. 29 with L. G. Mitchell (1997a) 134–47; Archibald (1998).

(for a great part of the Thracians are autonomous). This Teres bears no relation to the Tereus who took his wife from Athens, Procne the daughter of Pandion. Nor did they come from the same Thrace. Rather, one lived in Daulia, in the land now called Phocis, then inhabited by Thracians; and it was in this land that the women did the deed concerning Itys (and in many of the poets, where the nightingale is mentioned, the bird is called 'Daulian'). And it is probable that Pandion made the marriage link with his daughter over this sort of distance, permitting mutual aid, rather than over a journey of many days to the Odrysians. And Teres, who did not have the same name, was the first king in power over the Odrysians. It was his son, Sitalces, that the Athenians made their ally, wishing to join with him in controlling the lands of Thrace and Perdiccas himself. Nymphodorus came to Athens and established the alliance of Sitalces and undertook that Sadocus his son, an Athenian, would put an end to the war in Thrace. For he would persuade Sitalces to send a Thracian army of cavalry and peltasts to the Athenians. He also brought Perdiccas over to the Athenians and persuaded them to return Therme to him. And Perdiccas immediately marched against the Chalcidians with the Athenians and Phormio. In this way, Sitalces the son of Teres became an ally of the Athenians and also Perdiccas, the son of Alexander, king of the Macedonians. (Thuc. 2. 29; cf. 67)

Thucydides' insistence on the lack of any link between Odrysian Teres and Athenian Procne may be traced to his particular knowledge of matters Thracian, which he is willing to claim and display elsewhere also.[40] However, the myth had a particular relevance to Athens' attempt to woo Sitalces: for all Thucydides' insistence, Athens had a real interest in exploiting the supposed mythical link with Teres to underpin the developing alliance with Sitalces. In particular, the myth offered the notion of kinship between the Athenians and the family of Sitalces, which facilitated the otherwise extraordinary award of Athenian citizenship to a Thracian prince.[41]

The great advantage of this myth for the Athenian democracy was that it stressed the central significance of the prince's relationship not with individual Athenians,[42] but with the dēmos as a whole. Of course, Nymphodorus did not count in this regard, for he was an outsider, an Abderite. We are left to speculate about the apparent absence of any award of Athenian citizenship to Sitalces, whose claim to kinship was at least as strong: perhaps the king himself considered citizenship to be less honorific than might an Athenian, for it might be interpreted as a diminution of his kingly eminence. King Evagoras of Salamis on Cyprus evidently took a different view when he accepted Athenian citizenship in c.407, but he was very much a

[40] Thuc. 2. 97; 7. 29; cf. Badian (1993) 171–85.

[41] R. Parker (1996) 170–5 (with bibliography) puts this in the context of Thracian–Athenian cultural relations; cf. Archibald (1998); L. G. Mitchell (1997a) 142–7.

[42] No doubt individual Athenians did play particular roles in the city's relationship with Sitalces, including perhaps the envoys at Thuc. 2. 67 (where Sitalces' lack of citizenship seems to be confirmed). Hornblower (1991) 286 suspects that Thucydides himself had a role, though Thucydides' insistence on the falseness of the mythical link with Athens seems to tell against it, unless he had been willing to maintain the diplomatic fiction until it came to his writing.

self-made ruler who had only recently taken power (in 411), unlike the inherited regime of Sitalces. In Evagoras' case too, however, a communal myth seems to have been relevant, for Evagoras evidently claimed kinship with the mythical rulers of Athenian Salamis. A similar process may be imagined in the award of Athenian citizenship to Tharyps, king of the Molossians, though our knowledge of his case is inadequate.[43] Communal myths allowed the democracy to exploit the genealogies which could put it on a par not only with aristocracy, as Loraux and others have noted, but even with kings.[44]

Elsewhere in this volume, Rhodes has argued plausibly that a key effect of the long years of the Peloponnesian War was to enhance the attractions of oligarchy for Athenians who may not have been so well-disposed towards this form of government before 431. Moreover, the oligarchical arguments advanced in 411 seem to indicate new Athenian attitudes towards monarchy, and Persian monarchy at that: the exigencies of war were a powerful stimulus, especially where present difficulties could be laid at the door of democracy.

It seems reasonable also to infer that those Athenians who enjoyed personal connections with kings were overwhelmingly those who were themselves outstanding in Athenian society: these were the men who were particularly susceptible to the charge of aiming at tyranny. As usual, Alcibiades offers an idiosyncratic example. Under suspicion of tyrannical ambitions,[45] Alcibiades was also able to move around the Greek world and beyond to Thrace and the courts of Persian satraps. Alcibiades had family and personal connections with Sparta[46] and no doubt with others besides: in addition to his more personal resources, it was links such as these, I suggest, that enabled him to survive and even prosper as an exile. Certainly in 411 there were Athenians who were very ready to believe that he had managed to win substantial influence in the Persian empire.

It is in this context that we should probably understand the tendency that becomes observable in the latter stages of the war, whereby individual Athenians took refuge with kings. The search for refuge lays bare for us the existence of relationships which would otherwise have remained unknown. King Archelaos I of Macedon may have seemed a particularly attractive resort: his regime certainly attracted attention and admiration at Athens, and not only for its hellenism.[47] It was to Archelaos that Euripides travelled

---

[43] On Evagoras: *IG* i³. 113; Dem. 12. 10; Isoc. *Evag.* 54, with Maier (1994) 313. On Tharyps, *IG* ii². 226; cf. on his Athens-orientated hellenism, notably Justin 17. 3; Plut. *Pyrrhus* 1, with Hammond (1967) 506–7, who takes the view that he received his Athenian citizenship *c.*428–424 BC, though a date in the 390s remains possible. On King Tharyps and the Molossians see Davies (this volume).

[44] Loraux (1986); Thomas (1989); Braund (1994*b*).

[45] Seager (1967); Davidson (1997) 298–30.   [46] Thuc. 6. 89; 8. 6.

[47] Thuc. 2. 100; cf. Plato, *Gorg.* 470–1, typically debunking.

near the end of the war in search of royal patronage.[48] So too did Agathon (Ar. *Frogs* 83–5). The kingdom of the Crimean Bosporus was another option. A court case happens to inform us that the young Mantitheus took refuge there before the end of the war: he was evidently from a wealthy and possibly oligarchical (so his enemies said) family (Lys. 16. 4). He is unlikely to have been the only Athenian there: Aeschines' denunciation of Demosthenes' family (3. 172–3) leads him to suggest that Gylon, Demosthenes' grandfather, had also taken refuge in the Bosporan kingdom before the end of the war, though the chronology and circumstances remain obscure: only Aeschines' hostility is clear. Evidently, Andocides was not the only Athenian to seek out Evagoras: certainly Conon made his way there after Aegospotami (Xen. *Hell.* 2. 1. 29). However, as is evident from Xenophon's experiences in the early 390s, the lives of those who sought refuge at foreign courts might be hazardous, not least if they chose to seek refuge among the Odrysians of Thrace, for all their king's exuberant claims to good will towards Athens. The significance of kings, for good and ill, in the latter stages and immediate aftermath of the war may help to account for the emergence of a taste for philosophical works on monarchy and monarchs that has been noted in the early decades of the fourth century.[49]

Monarchy was an abiding conundrum for the Athenian democracy. The dēmos sought to build links with monarchs in its own right, asserting its own genealogy and perhaps aware of the monarchical overtones of its imperial rule, whether positive or negative. It might also benefit from the links of Athenian individuals, though there remained a substantial risk for those individuals in that their special connections were at odds with democratic ideology. No doubt the fact that many of these kings were barbarian (or arguably so) and even Persian (cf. Plato, *Gorg.* 524 E) made the conflict no easier. The best strategy for the individual Athenian in self-defence was that attempted by Andocides, stressing that his personal links with the king of Macedon were exploited not for some selfish or tyrannical purpose but for the communal benefit of the democratic city. That was the tenor of the oligarchs' (baseless) argument in 411. Alcibiades had established special relationships in Persia, they argued, which could bring benefit to the Athenian community—but only if democracy were replaced by something more controlled, discreet, and (from the Persian king's perspective) trustworthy: that meant something closer to monarchy than democracy, its polar opposite.

---

[48] Harder (1985). Aeschylus' sojourn with Hiero in Sicily offered a precedent: Dougherty (1993) 88.

[49] On those with Evagoras see Isoc. *Evag.* 51, with Maier (1994) 313. For Thracian 'enthusiasm' see e.g. Xen. *Anab.* 7. 3. 39. On the taste for works on monarchy see Eder (1995).

7
Oligarchs in Athens

P. J. RHODES

My object in this paper is to look for oligarchs, and more generally for opponents of democracy, in Athens; to see who they were, what opinions and objectives they held, and why. Limits on space will allow me to go only as far as the end of the fifth century.

I begin with men better described as ur-oligarchs, those who were active before the concepts of democracy and oligarchy were formulated in the first half of the fifth century (cf. below), but who were on the side of the upper class and were opposed to developments which would be detrimental to the power and position of the upper class.

In the beginning we can identify issues, but few of the men who were opposed to reform on those issues. There will have been rich landowners threatened by Solon's economic reforms, in particular overlords of *hektēmoroi* (men bound to hand a sixth of their produce to an overlord) who stood to lose wealth and dependants when Solon liberated the *hektēmoroi*; and, probably an inner circle within that group, there will have been the members of the families that had been running Athens, who did not want to share power with others, even with the other rich men who might aspire to power when Solon made wealth the sole criterion of eligibility for office. *Ath. Pol.* 3 states twice that before Solon appointments were made 'on the basis of excellence and wealth' (*aristindēn* and *ploutindēn*) and chapter 1 uses *aristindēn* of the jurors who tried the men charged with killing Cylon's supporters. We happen to have independent evidence that to characterize appointments as *aristindēn* was contemporary usage: Draco's homicide law uses the word of the phratry members who in some circumstances would be appointed to consider a pardon for an unintentional killer,[1] and it may well be that the word was used also of the appointment of the fifty-one *ephetai* (the judges in some homicide cases).[2] Solon in his poems used *dēmos* ('people') at least once of the whole community (fr. 36. 2 West), but there

Versions of this paper were read to the Oxford Philological Society and to the seminar on Alternatives to the Democratic Polis. I am grateful to all who listened to me and discussed the subject with me, and to the editors for their help in the preparation of this version. I plan to pursue this enquiry into the fourth century on another occasion; I have said something about the hellenistic and Roman period in Rhodes with Lewis (1997) 35–61.

[1] *IG* i³. 104 = ML 86 = Fornara 15 B 19, restored from [Dem.] 43. 57.
[2] Poll. 8. 125, cf. what may be a misunderstanding of ἀριστίνδην in Phot., *Suda* (E 3877) ἐφέται, *Lex. Seg.* 188. 30–2, with MacDowell (1963) 48–50. ἀριστίνδην is used of appointments

are passages where he seems to have used it of the ordinary people as opposed to the ruling class;[3] for the ruling class he used paraphrases: 'those who had power and were admired for their wealth' (οἳ δ' εἶχον δύναμιν καὶ χρήμασιν ἦσαν ἀγητοί), 'those who are greater and better in strength' (ὅσοι δὲ μείζους καὶ βίαν ἀμείνονες);[4] he also used the terms 'good' (*esthlos/agathos*) and 'bad' (*kakos*) to contrast men of the upper and lower class.[5] In neighbouring Megara Theognis lamented the claim of those who were merely rich to equality with those who were truly *agathoi*.

From the century before Solon we have a scattering of names, mostly of archons. Many of these men cannot be linked reliably to families which we know were prominent after Solon, but of course this may reflect only our shortage of evidence: it does not prove that there were many families in the oldest ruling class which died out or withdrew from politics after Solon. Megacles the Alcmaeonid had resisted Cylon's attempt to become tyrant:[6] we do not know any opponents or any supporters of Solon, but we may assume that to gain acceptance for his measures he must have had some supporters from within the ruling class, just as we may assume that to be appointed archon he must himself have belonged to the ruling class.

There is one man who can perhaps be identified as an opponent after the event: Damasias, the man who was archon in 582/1 and refused to retire at the end of the year. Since the name is rare in Athens, it is more likely than not that he was related to the Damasias who was archon in 639/8 and therefore belonged to one of the families which ruled Athens before Solon's reforms; and in that case it is possible that his refusal to retire represents unwillingness by a member of that group to share power with men outside the group, and that the 'ten archons' who follow, whatever precise arrangement lies behind *Ath. Pol.*'s account, represent an attempt to guarantee that men outside the group will have a genuine chance of being appointed.[7]

For Peisistratus' rise to power we have the three parties, given simply regional characteristics by Herodotus (1. 59. 3), but ideological stances in addition by *Ath. Pol.* and by Plutarch.[8] Of the three leaders, we know that Megacles and Peisistratus were both related to men who had held the archonship before Solon; Lycurgus happens to be the first attested member of what appears in the classical period as an aristocratic family, but it is

---

in two decrees from Ozolian Locris, of the late sixth and early fifth centuries: *IG* ix². 1. 609, 717 = Buck 58, 59 = ML 13, Tod 34 = Fornara 33, 87.

[3] Frr. 5. 1; 6. 1; 36. 22; 37. 1, 7.   [4] Frr. 5. 3; 37. 4.

[5] Frr. 34. 9; 36. 8. For this use of the words see e.g. Adkins (1960) 30–40, 75–9, 159–63; (1972) 12–21.   [6] Stated most explicitly by Plut. *Sol.* 12. 1.

[7] *Ath. Pol.* 13. 1–2, with Wade-Gery (1931) 79 = (1958) 102–3, and Rhodes (1981*a*) ad loc. However, Figueira in a very speculative study (1984) makes Damasias a populist going beyond Solon and the ten the result of aristocratic reaction.

[8] *Ath. Pol.* 13. 4–5; Plut. *Sol.* 13. 1–3, cf. 29. 1.

unlikely that he had a less good pedigree than his rivals. On the surface, *Ath. Pol.*'s characterization of the three parties is clearly anachronistic: we cannot believe that in the first half of the sixth century the men of the plain wanted an oligarchy or the men of the coast wanted the middle constitution. Beneath the surface, however, we can detect a measure of truth: Peisistratus in aiming to become tyrant must himself have been dissatisfied and have had supporters who were dissatisfied with the status quo; Lycurgus, who consistently opposed him, may have been satisfied and have had supporters who were satisfied with the status quo; Megacles was in the middle at least in the sense that he could co-operate with Peisistratus at one time and with Lycurgus at another. A topographical point may be added: the plain surrounding Athens (Lycurgus' region) is likely to have contained the largest number, and the east of Attica (Peisistratus' region) the smallest number, of families which were not only rich but influential in the politics of Athens.

Peisistratus' position as tyrant brought him power and, no doubt, wealth, and it will presumably have been opposed by all upper-class Athenians for whom a subordinate position was too great a price to pay for the benefits to be obtained by co-operating with him: they may well have thought of themselves not as champions of upper-class rule but as champions of freedom and lawful government.[9] We cannot identify many of the men who went into exile or had their children deported as hostages (Hdt. 1. 64. 1). In the Philaid family the departure of the elder Miltiades to the Chersonese is represented by Herodotus as the withdrawal of an opponent (Hdt. 6. 35. 3), but in going to this place so vital to Athens' interests he must surely in some sense have gone as an agent of Athens and of the ruler of Athens: his half-brother Cimon is said to have gone into exile, to have been allowed back after giving Peisistratus the credit for an Olympic victory, and to have been killed after not giving Peisistratus' sons the credit for another victory (Hdt. 6. 103. 3); Cimon's son, the younger Miltiades, was archon in 524/3[10] and later went to take over the family position in the Chersonese (Hdt. 6. 103. 4). Herodotus' belief that the Alcmaeonids were in exile throughout the main period of the tyranny (6. 123. 1) was shown to be wrong by the discovery that Cleisthenes was archon in 525/4:[11] the standard reaction to that has been to believe in two shorter periods of exile, one after Pallene and one after the murder of Hipparchus; Rosalind Thomas has wondered if the claim that the Alcmaeonids went into exile under the tyranny is in fact simply a back-projection from their brief period of exile in 508/7 (1989: 148–51), but that seems to me too sceptical. We have no information on

---

[9] The *skolia* (drinking-songs) celebrating the murder of Hipparchus in 514 claimed that Athens was thereby made a place of legal equality (*isonomia*): *PMG* 893, 896 ap. Ath. 15. 695 A–B. Cf. below, n. 14.   [10] ML 6 = Fornara 23 C 4, with D.H. *Ant. Rom.* 7. 3. 1.
[11] ML 6 = Fornara 23 C 3.

what became of Lycurgus and his family, either under the tyranny or on its overthrow.

Harmodius and Aristogeiton were *Gephyraioi*, whose family had come from Tanagra, we do not know how long before.[12] Notoriously, Thucydides insists that in 514 they killed Hipparchus not for ideological but for personal reasons;[13] yet even in Thucydides' account their original target was not Hipparchus, the object of their grudge, but Hippias, and they already had supporters, who presumably did not share their personal motive, and they expected to gain popular backing when they had struck the first blow. Davies remarks that members of the family are to be found on the democratic side in the fifth century (1971: 472), but that need not tell us anything about their attitudes in the late sixth. It is possible that *isonomia* was used at first by all opponents of the tyranny, to denote the kind of equality that would prevail when there was no tyrant, and that afterwards Cleisthenes tried to appropriate the term for his reforms.[14]

In the political vacuum created by the expulsion of Hippias we have the rivalry of Cleisthenes and Isagoras. When Isagoras had the upper hand, 'Cleisthenes added the dēmos to his following, though he had totally spurned it before',[15] and Isagoras appealed to Cleomenes of Sparta—because they were *xenoi* ('guest-friends'), but presumably not because Cleomenes was interested in Isagoras' wife (Hdt. 5. 70. 1). To add the dēmos to his following and outdo Isagoras in popularity, Cleisthenes must at least have given some indication of his plans for reform, and it is likely enough that he said things about eliminating unfairness which seemed unpalatable to those who thought he might eliminate kinds of unfairness from which they benefited. It is surely anachronistic to suppose that Isagoras complained that Cleisthenes was setting up a democratic kind of regime of which Cleomenes as an oligarchic Spartan ought to disapprove: I suspect he argued that Cleisthenes was in danger of becoming another tyrant and Sparta should not expel one tyrant to let another take his place. Cleomenes 'tried to dissolve the council and put the offices in the hands of three hundred supporters of Isagoras, but the council resisted and refused to obey' (Hdt. 5. 72. 1–2): for those of us who believe in Solon's council of four

[12] Hdt. 5. 57. 1 with Davies (1971) 472–3.   [13] Thuc. 6. 54–59. 1, cf. 1. 20. 2.
[14] Cf. n. 9, above, citing the *skolia* celebrating the murder of Hipparchus. Ehrenberg argued that *isonomia* was first used to denote the equality among the aristocrats which was restored by the overthrow of the tyranny: (1940: 296; 1950: 530, 535 = 1965: 279, 284–5). That view of *isonomia* as an aristocratic ideal was attacked by Vlastos (1953) 339–44; and Ehrenberg announced his conversion: (1956: 67–9 = 1965: 261–3). Ostwald has argued for *isonomia* as Cleisthenes' slogan (1969: esp. 96–136). Meier regards *isonomia* and the other iso- words used by Herodotus as an extension, c.500, of the older ideal of *eunomia* (1980: 281–4 = 1990: 161–2). I am prepared to believe that, although *isonomia* cannot be regarded as a specifically aristocratic state of affairs, the word was first used to refer to Athens' equality after the overthrow of the tyranny before it came to be used for Cleisthenes' particular kind of equality.
[15] Hdt. 5. 69. 2, cf. 66. 2.

hundred, that will be the body which Cleomenes tried to dissolve but which backed Cleisthenes; we cannot penetrate a short-lived plan never put into effect, and say who the three hundred were or what role was envisaged for them.[16]

In the years that followed it is hard to see much sign of disagreement on how Athens should be governed. I regard the institution of the council's oath and of the ten generals, in 501/0, as the completion of Cleisthenes' system, not as a modification of it.[17] The change in the appointment of the archons, in 487/6 (*Ath. Pol.* 22. 5), whether it is the first use of allotment for this purpose or a reversion to Solon's practice,[18] is one stage in the process by which the archons became routine officials and the generals became the leading officials of fifth-century Athens; but we have too little information to say whether it represents an adjustment to a new reality or an attempt to bring about a new reality or something between the two.[19]

Plutarch has stories about Aristides. At the time of the battle of Plataea, in 479, some men of distinguished family, impoverished by the war, conspired to dissolve the dēmos (ἄνδρες ἐξ οἴκων ἐπιφανῶν . . . συνωμόσαντο καταλύσειν τὸν δῆμον); Aristeides decided to arrest just a few of the conspirators, and two of those escaped (Plut. *Arist.* 13). The names and demotics of these two are given: there are no other literary references to them, but it has been noticed that if Plutarch has the demotics the wrong way round there are nineteen ostraca against one of them, Agasias of Agryle.[20] Even if not all of Plutarch's details are correct, there could be truth behind this story, though the conspirators were perhaps more interested in coming to terms with Persia and obtaining a leading position in Athens with Persian support than in replacing an explicitly democratic regime with an explicitly oligarchic one.[21] It is harder to salvage anything from Plutarch's other story, that after the war Aristeides 'saw that the Athenians were seeking to acquire democracy' (ζητοῦντας τὴν δημοκρατίαν ἀπολαβεῖν), and, thinking that the dēmos deserved it and would not easily be forced out, 'he proposed a decree that the constitution should be common and that the officials[22] should be chosen from all Athenians' (Plut. *Arist.* 22. 1). No such decree was enacted; we cannot tell what the basis of the story is.

The 470s and 460s are in *Ath. Pol.* a period when the state was dominated by the Areopagus, but the only concrete detail we are offered is the

[16] They are identified with the council of the Areopagus by Sealey (1960: 160 n. 35 = 1967: 35–6 n. 35; cf. 1976: 149–50).

[17] *Ath. Pol.* 22. 2 with Rhodes (1981*a*) ad loc., cf. (1972*a*) 190–3.

[18] Solon's practice: *Ath. Pol.* 8. 1.

[19] Those who think they can say include Buck (1965), Badian (1971).

[20] Harvey (1984). For the latest count of ostraca see Willemsen and Brenne (1991) 148.

[21] That they wanted an oligarchy is accepted, with the story in general, by Burn (1962) 525–7; Barron (1988) 603–4. Among those who reject the whole story are Hignett (1963) 320–1; Lazenby (1993) 229.

[22] Or specifically the nine archons? The Greek word *archontes* could have either meaning.

story that the Areopagus provided money for the citizens leaving Athens before the battle of Salamis.[23] I have suggested that this dominance of the Areopagus may be simply a product of fourth-century rationalizing: Ephialtes' removal of the Areopagus' 'additional powers' was a democratic reform; the last major constitutional change had been that of Cleisthenes, also a democratic reform; so if the Areopagus needed to have additional powers removed by Ephialtes it must have acquired them later than the time of Cleisthenes.[24] An alternative explanation for Ephialtes' reform can be constructed: the dēmos had been drawn into political activity through the participatory machinery of Cleisthenes; a powerful council of ex-archons came to appear anachronistic when the archons were no longer Athens' leading officials; and judicial decisions of the Areopagus which favoured Cimon were seen as provocative by Cimon's opponents (Rhodes 1992: 72–3).

This was perhaps the time when a conscious belief in democracy first emerged and the word *dēmokratia* ('people power') was coined.[25] The first sign of what was to be the common Greek division of constitutions into monarchies, oligarchies, and democracies is found in Pindar's second *Pythian*, possibly of 468 (where oligarchy appears as the rule of the wise and democracy as the rule of the boisterous army);[26] Aeschylus in the *Supplices*, possibly of 463, refers to the 'powerful hand of the people' (δήμου κρατοῦσα χείρ: 604) in the Argive assembly; the earliest known Athenian to be given the name Democrates, which was to become a reasonably common name in Athens, was born about this time.[27] (Earlier, a king of Argos was called Damocratidas, and one of the legendary heroes of Plataea was called Damocrates.[28])

Kratos had been used in conjunction with *dēmos* earlier, in the Great Rhetra at Sparta,[29] but nothing seems to have developed from that. Herodotus knows the word *dēmokratia*: he glosses it as the rule of the *dēmos*, *plēthos* ('mass'), or *homilos* ('crowd') and as *isonomia* (3. 80. 6–82. 4), but when he uses it with reference to the Asiatic Greeks under Persian rule he seems to mean no more than constitutional government as opposed to

[23] *Ath. Pol.* 23. 1–2 (contrast the version of Cleid. *FGrH* 323 F 21, in which the credit is given to Themistocles—who as archon in 493/2 will have been a member of the Areopagus), 25. 1.   [24] Rhodes (1981a: 287; 1992: 64–5).

[25] Hansen (1986), refuting the arguments for a later date, is reluctant to believe that the word was not already used by Cleisthenes (cf. 1994: 27–8, 33). Some scholars have been reluctant to accept a doctrinaire belief in democracy at this time, or indeed at any time: see e.g. Sealey (1964) 11–22 =(1967) 42–58; (1981); Ruschenbusch (1966; 1979).

[26] Pind. *Pyth.* 2. 86–8 (for Hieron of Syracuse); date: Bowra (1964) 410.

[27] Davies (1971) 359–60. For his son's gravestone see Stroud (1984).

[28] Damocratidas, Paus. 4. 35. 2; Damocrates, Plut. *Arist.* 11. 3.

[29] Plut. *Lyc.* 6. 2; cf. Tyrt. fr. 4. 9 West.

tyranny.[30] He knows the word *oligarchia* ('few-rule'), and glosses that as the *kratos* ('power') of the *aristoi* ('best') (3. 81. 3), but he does not put the two elements together to make *aristokratia*. Thucydides, of course, knows the word *dēmokratia*:[31] what he normally opposes to it is *oligarchia* and its cognates;[32] he uses *aristokratia* twice, as a fine-sounding word employed by supporters of oligarchy, and, again ironically, as a term for the regime imposed on Thasos by the Athenian oligarchs in 411.[33] Aristophanes uses *dēmokratia* and its cognates (e.g. *Ach.* 618), and he uses a personification of the Athenian dēmos; but apart from one use of the verb *aristokrateisthai* (*Birds* 125) he does not mention *aristokratia* or *oligarchia*—and indeed in the fragments of comedy I have found no use of those words except one contrast between *aristokratia* and *dēmokratia*, almost certainly of the fourth century.[34]

Not more than one Athenian—and to my knowledge hardly any other Greek—was ever given a name from the *olig-* root.[35] Aristocrates is a widespread name: the earliest instances I know are a ruler of Arcadian Orchomenus in the seventh century[36] and an Aeginetan in the sixth;[37] in Athens it is possible that there was an Aristocrates son of Scellias who was *chorēgos* in the first half of the fifth century;[38] the well-known Aristocrates son of Scellias (who would be his grandson) and two other men of this name were born about the second quarter of the century and held office during the Peloponnesian War;[39] and the name was popular for men who were born towards the end of the fifth century and active in the first half of the fourth.

[30] Hdt. 4. 137. 2; 6. 43. 3. For this interpretation of the Asiatic 'democracies' cf. M. M. Austin (1990) 306.   [31] Esp. Thuc. 2. 37. 1, 65. 9; 6. 39. 1.

[32] e.g. Thuc. 6. 38–9; 8. 63–8; and notice especially 3. 62. 3.

[33] Thuc. 3. 82. 8; 8. 64. 3. The Thasian regime is referred to as oligarchy in an inscription, *SEG* xxxviii. 851.

[34] Heniochus fr. 5 KA = fr. 5 Edmonds. Heniochus is said to be a writer of the middle comedy (*Suda* [H 392] Ἡνίοχος), and a 4th-cent. date for him is generally accepted, but Edmonds ad loc. suggested that the passage made best sense in the context of 411.

[35] Olianthides at Athens in the 3rd cent.: Wuensch (1897) no. 37, *a* 1, cf. Fraser and Matthews (1987–) ii s.n. Oligus at Elis (possibly a Boeotian) in the late 6th cent.: Gauer (1991) 224–5, no. Le 446 = *SEG* xlii. 382. J, cf. Fraser and Matthews (1987–), iiiA s.n. Oligeidas at Thespiae in the early 5th cent. (*IG* vii. 1880 = *SEG* xv. 325 = *CEG* i. 113). There was a phratry at Corinth called *Oligaithidai*: Pind. *Ol.* 13. 97 with schol. (137), cf. Fraser and Matthews (1987–) iiiA s.n. Ὀλίγαιθος. I thank Mrs Matthews for her help here.

[36] Polyb. 4. 33. 6 (Callisth. *FGrH* 124 F 33); Str. 362. 8. 4. 10 (Tyrt. fr. 8 West; Apollod. *FGrH* 244 F 334); Paus. 4. 17. 2–3; D.L. 1. 94. Paus. 8. 5. 11–13, cf. 13. 5, made him the grandson of an earlier Aristocrates. Cf. Fraser and Matthews (1987–) iiiA s.n. nos. 38–9.

[37] Hdt. 6. 73. 2, cf. Fraser and Matthews (1987–), iiiA s.n. no. 6.

[38] *IG* i³. 964 (i². 772). The stone has been rediscovered, and should be accepted as part of the dedication of the well-known Aristocrates, mentioned in Plato *Gorg.* 472 A–B; but the inscription has archaic features, and Raubitschek suggests that it is a copy of a dedication by a homonymous grandfather. See Davies (1971) 56; Shear (1973) 173–5 no. 1; Raubitschek (1982); Barron (1983) 1–2 no. 6. In *IG* i³ the inscription is dated *c.*440–430 (?).

[39] *PA* nos. 1904, 1911, 1925 = Develin (1989) nos. 426, 423, 420; cf. Fraser and Matthews (1987–) s.n. nos. 99–100.

If Ephialtes and his supporters were the first Athenians consciously working for a constitution which they regarded as democratic, Cimon was the
first Athenian consciously opposed to democracy. Plutarch uses in connection with him the term *misodēmos* ('people-hating') and the charge of
'arousing the aristocracy of Cleisthenes' time' (τὴν ἐπὶ Κλεισθένους ἐγείρειν
ἀριστοκρατίαν);[40] also the words *lakōnismos* ('Spartanizing') and *philolakōn*
('Sparta-loving')[41]—and for good measure the charge of incest with his sister. *Misodēmos* is used by Aristophanes;[42] *lakōnismos* first appears in this
sense in Xenophon, but the verb *lakōnizein* is found in fragments of Aristophanes and Eupolis;[43] as it happens, the only attestation of *philolakōn* earlier
than Dio Chrysostom and Plutarch is the title of a fourth- or third-century
comedy by Stephanus,[44] but the word *philathēnaios* ('Athens-loving') was
used by Aristophanes.[45] Certainly Plutarch was capable of misrepresenting
classical Athens, and material found only in Plutarch must be used with caution, but the charges which he reports here could be contemporary charges,
and the atypical characterization of Cleisthenes' constitution as aristocracy
encourages faith in that.

Ephialtes' reform aroused strong feelings. Not only was Cimon ostracized:
Ephialtes was murdered;[46] Aeschylus featured the Areopagus and its position in Athens, however problematically for us, in the *Eumenides* (esp. 681–
710); and there is the story of a plot at the time of the battle of Tanagra,
reported not only by Plutarch but also by Thucydides. Thucydides refers
to 'men of Athens . . . who hoped to put a stop to the dēmos (δῆμον . . .
καταπαύσειν) and to the building of the long walls' (1. 107. 4). Plutarch
twice tells the story of Cimon's attempting to return to the Athenian lines
(*Cim.* 17; *Per.* 10): in both versions he refers again to *lakōnismos*; and in the
Cimon he names one of Cimon's supporters, Euthippus—who may be the
archon of 461/0[47] but who otherwise has not turned up on an ostracon or
anywhere else. All the evidence suggests that foreign policy and the government of Athens were both live issues at the time, and that Cimon stood both
for friendship with Sparta and for a non-democratic form of government:

---

[40] Plut. *Per.* 9. 5, *Cim.* 15. 3.
[41] Plut. *Cim.* 15. 3 (cf. 17. 3: participle of the verb *lakōnizein*); 16. 1.
[42] Ar. *Wasps* 474; fr. 110 KA; cf. *Wasps* 471 (*misopolis*, 'city-hating').
[43] e.g. Xen. *Hell.* 4. 4. 15; Ar. fr. 358 KA; Eup. fr. 385 KA; also *lakedaimoniazein* Ar. fr.
97 KA.
[44] Pages vii. 614–15 KA. If an attractive emendation may be accepted, Dio Chrysostom uses
philolakōn in 37. 17 (by opposing Sparta on one occasion the Corinthians showed that they
were not simply *philolakones*); Plutarch uses it of Cimon (n. 41 above), of Ctesias (*Artox.* 13.
7), and in a saying implausibly attributed to the early Spartan king Theopompus (*Lyc.* 20. 3;
Apophth. Lac. 221 D, cf. fr. 86 Sandbach).   [45] Ar. *Ach.* 142; *Wasps* 282.
[46] Ant. 5. 68; *Ath. Pol.* 25. 4; Plut. *Per.* 10. 7–8.
[47] Cf. Develin (1989), *sub anno*. 'Straight-horse' is a suitably aristocratic name for an opponent of the new democracy.

the *patria nomima* ('traditional institutions') which we find in Diodorus and Plutarch[48] may well indicate Cimon's perception of the regime which Ephialtes had attacked.

After Ephialtes, *Ath. Pol.* gives us a matter-of-fact account of democratic laws of the 450s (26. 2–4), and a further attack on the Areopagus, by Pericles, which is probably Ephialtes' reform misunderstood (27. 1). For anecdotal material we again turn to Plutarch. Cimon was succeeded as leader of the opposition to Pericles by his relative Thucydides son of Melesias, who was less a military man and more *agoraios* ('a man of the town square') and *politikos* ('a man of the city', or perhaps 'a politician'): he produced a polarization of Athenian politics, in which men rallied to the banners of democracy and oligarchy, and he brought the *kaloi k'agathoi* (the 'fine gentlemen') physically together (Plut. *Per.* 11. 1–3). Plutarch then continues with Pericles' pursuing policies to gratify the lower classes, and being charged with squandering the money collected from the allies on the adornment of Athens rather than war against Persia, but successfully defending himself on that count (*Per.* 11. 6–14. 2), until in the end Thucydides was ostracized and the *hetaireia* (the upper-class 'association') opposed to Pericles was broken up (*Per.* 14. 3). Andrewes was severe on the whole of this, even the opening section on Thucydides' opposition to Pericles,[49] but I think he went too far. Though Thucydides is unlikely to have had no military career, it is not implausible that he should have been remembered for his political rather than his military activity. It is clear from the historian Thucydides (esp. 3. 82. 8) that by the 420s men in various states were rallying to the banners of democracy and oligarchy, and from the middle of the century the Athenians were setting up democracies in the member states of the Delian League,[50] so it is not impossible that, less than twenty years after the controversial reforms of Ephialtes, there should have been something of a polarization in Athens; and there are other indications that groups of like-minded men could sit together in the council, assembly, and jury-courts.[51]

In the end, says Plutarch, Thucydides was ostracized, and the *hetaireia* opposed to Pericles was broken up. The ostracism need not be doubted: we have 67 ostraca against Thucydides and 4 against Pericles.[52] I do not want to become involved in arguments about what groups of men are *hetaireiai* and what are not, but I can believe that after the ostracism of Thucydides—and

---

[48] D.S. 11. 77. 6; Plut. *Cim.* 15. 2.   [49] Andrewes (1978) esp. 1–2.

[50] e.g. Erythrae in the late 450s (*IG* i³. 14=ML 40); Miletus by the 430s (inscription published by Herrmann 1970). Welwei (1986) has argued that it was not until later in the 5th cent. that the Athenians adopted this as a conscious policy, but I think he is mistaken.

[51] Philoch. *FGrH* 328 F 140; Ar. *Eccl.* 298–9; *Ath. Pol.* 63–5 (with Boegehold 1960: 400–1 on 65. 2).

[52] *Agora* xxv, pp. 132–3 with nos. 1050–1, 98 with nos. 651–2; Willemsen and Brenne (1991) 151, 155.

perhaps of one or two others, including Pericles' teacher Damon (*Ath. Pol.* 27. 4)—whatever cohesiveness Thucydides had achieved was lost, and the oligarchic opposition which had continued intermittently since the time of Ephialtes did for a time die down. Certainly we should not see a further sign of this oligarchic opposition in the stories of attacks on Pericles and his friends later in Plutarch's *Pericles* (31–2): I am among those who have been persuaded by Frost (1964*a*, *b*) that these attacks are to be dated to the early 430s, while Thucydides was away from Athens, and are the work not of upper-class oligarchs but of men like Cleon.

That brings us to the time of the Peloponnesian War. Thucydides the historian wants his readers to believe that Pericles was in practice an un-challenged ruler, who led the people rather than letting them lead him, whereas his successors were men who competed to win the favour of the people in the short term.[53] His first hint of opposition to democracy in Athens is his report of a fear that the religious offences of 415 were products of a revolutionary plot against the *dēmos*;[54] this leads him to a digression on the Peisistratid tyranny, which he ends by saying that the Athenians thought the offences had been committed 'with a view to an oligarchic and tyrannic conspiracy' (ἐπὶ ξυνωμοσίᾳ ὀλιγαρχικῇ καὶ τυραννικῇ).[55] Although in his history as a whole he sets oligarchy against democracy, and although here he does mention oligarchy, it is clear from the digression that Thucydides is thinking more of tyranny as the alternative to democracy in Athens—and that may reflect current thinking in Athens, since we shall see references to tyranny in Euripides and Aristophanes too (cf. below).

I believe firmly that the pamphlet of the Old Oligarch is to be dated 431–424,[56] and that it shows that in the early years of the Peloponnesian War it was possible to present a theoretical case against Athenian democracy, while conceding that the democracy was appropriate for Athens as a naval power and would not be easily overthrown. In this work it is oligarchy that is contrasted with democracy,[57] and tyranny is not mentioned. What argu-ments does the author offer against democracy?[58] First of all, it promotes the interests of the wrong people, the poor, the *ponēroi* ('wretched'), and the dēmos rather than the rich, the *gennaioi* ('well-born'), and the *chrēstoi* ('valuable') ([Xen.] *Ath. Pol.* 1. 2–4): in every land what is best is opposed to democracy, because the best men (*beltistoi*) are educated and disciplined

---

[53] Thuc. 2. 65. 8–10. Pericles could be compared with the tyrant Peisistratus: cf. Plut. *Per.* 7. 1; 16. 1 (the latter citing an unknown comedian: *Adespota* fr. 703 KA).

[54] Thuc. 6. 27. 3, 28. 2.

[55] Thuc. 6. (53. 2–)60. 1. Nicias' 'city plotting against us through oligarchy' (πόλιν δι᾿ ὀλιγ-αρχίας ἐπιβουλεύουσαν) in 6. 11. 7 is taken by Dover ad loc. to refer to Sparta as oligarchic itself, not as seeking to impose an oligarchy on Athens.   [56] e.g. Forrest (1970).

[57] The participle *oligarchoumenos* is used in [Xen.] *Ath. Pol.* 2. 17, 20 (*bis*).

[58] For a general review of arguments for and against democracy to be found in 5th-cent. sources see Raaflaub (1989) 33–70 = Connor *et al.* (1990) 33–70.

but the poor are ignorant and dissolute (1. 5). Other points made are that democracy allows every man to take part in political debate and to serve in the council (1. 6–9); that oligarchic states have to keep to agreements, because those responsible for making the agreements are few and identifiable, but in a democracy ordinary citizens can blame the proposer or the presiding official and deny their share in the responsibility (2. 17);[59] but the transference of lawsuits from the allied states benefits the Athenians (1. 16–18), and the great busy-ness of Athens cannot be significantly changed without abolishing the democracy (3. 1–9). The idea that the lower classes prefer democracy because it serves their own interests is a product of the sophists' distinction between *physis* ('nature') and *nomos* (human 'convention'): the form of government belongs to the realm of *nomos*; there is no absolutely right form; but each man will prefer the form from which he stands to benefit, and this is in accordance with *physis*.[60]

How far we can and should establish the political views of Aristophanes is a question which need not concern us here; but I assume that the points made against democracy in his plays, whether or not Aristophanes himself thought them cogent, are points which other Athenians of his time could have made; and I also assume that his representation of Cleon is not a total fantasy but would have been recognized by members of the audience as a caricature of the Cleon whom they knew. What do we find there? The Athenian *dēmos* may be a mighty tyrant, but it can easily be fooled and induced to change its mind.[61] The politicians who pretend to serve the *dēmos* are in fact manipulating the *dēmos* in pursuit of their own interests;[62] and they are not gentlemanly and cultivated men but vulgar and ignorant,[63] or at any rate ignorant in the areas which matter, since one of the features of modern Athens is a nasty, new cleverness with which old-fashioned respectability cannot cope.[64] As in democratic Athens all sorts and conditions of men can make speeches in the assembly, it is a democratic feature of Euripides' plays that all kinds of characters make speeches in them (*Frogs* 948–52). In the *Frogs* Aristophanes complains directly that Athens rejects the 'fine gentlemen' (*kaloi k'agathoi*) and relies on worthless men.[65] Nevertheless, we have noticed that, although democracy and the *dēmos* appear frequently

[59] On this point notice the different attitudes expressed in Thuc. 2. 59. 2 and, in Pericles' speech, 60. 4.
[60] Lys. 25. 7–11 is most explicit. In Arist. *Pol.* 1279ᵃ28–31 the criterion by which the perverted forms of each kind of constitution are to be distinguished from the correct forms is whether the rulers rule in their own interest or in the whole community's interest. In Xen. *Mem.* 1. 2. 40–6 Alcibiades pursues a line of argument to show that what the *plēthos* ('mass') enacts without persuading the rich is not law but violence.
[61] Ar. *Ach.* 632–42; *Knights* 1111–20; *Wasps* 281–5.
[62] Ar. *Knights* 40–72; *Wasps* 655–724.   [63] Ar. *Knights* 128–222 and *passim*.
[64] Ar. *Ach.* 676–718; *Clouds passim*.
[65] Ar. *Frogs* 718–37, cf. 1454–60; and see Arnott (1991). For the same idea see Eupolis fr. 384 KA.

in Aristophanes, aristocracy is found only once and oligarchy not at all. As in Thucydides' account of 415, the obvious alternative to democracy is tyranny; tyranny (*tyrannis*), conspiracy (*xynōmosia*), rejection of the city's laws, and hatred of the dēmos go together (note *Wasps* 463–507); Cleon in the *Knights* repeatedly denounces his opponents as conspirators;[66] and in Cloudcuckooland there are birds condemned to death for rising up against the democratic (*dēmotikoi*) birds (*Birds* 1583–5). In the *Lysistrata* what the women do is seize the Acropolis (e.g. 176), like Cylon in the seventh century and Peisistratus in the sixth.

In Euripides' *Supplices* the Theban herald wants to deliver Creon's message to the tyrant (*tyrannos*) of Athens (399–402); but Athens is a free city, where the dēmos rules by a system of rotation and the poor man has equal shares with the rich (403–8). In Thebes with its single ruler there is no chance for a demagogue to turn the people this way and that, and to give short-term gratification, for his own advantage; time brings understanding; a poor peasant, even if he is not ignorant, is distracted by his toil from the public interest (409–25).[67] Theseus in reply criticizes tyranny for its rejection of law, and praises democracy for its freedom and equality, and as being better than tyranny for all the people (426–56).

Thucydides, who admired the restraint and orderliness (*sōphronein, kosmos*) of Chios and the compromise of Athens' intermediate regime of 411/0,[68] remarks several times on the volatility of democratic assemblies.[69] Twice a Thucydidean speaker champions democracy, but each time what is championed is less egalitarian than Athenian practice. In Pericles' funeral speech advancement depends on merit as it cannot have done when most appointments were made by lot.[70] Athenagoras in Syracuse, replying to the allegation that democracy is neither intelligent nor fair and the owners of property are the best rulers, says that the rich are best at guarding property, the intelligent are best at deliberating, the many are best at listening and deciding—and in a democracy all these are given their fair share (6. 39. 1).

There is a reasonable degree of convergence between our sources. Democracy could be represented as unfair, because it served the interests of the worse members of the community, because those members were not good at formulating and deciding policy but their assemblies were fickle and easily led astray by self-seeking demagogues. Men who preferred oligarchy could claim that there was no naturally right form of government, but what was natural was that the lower classes preferred democracy out of self-interest, while their own self-interest favoured oligarchy. Opponents of the democracy of post-Periclean Athens who did not merely grouse with their

---

[66] Ar. *Knights* 236, 257, 452, 476, 628, 862.
[67] On short-term gratification by the demagogues cf. Thuc. 2. 65. 10.
[68] Thuc. 8. 24. 4, 97. 2. [69] Thuc. 2. 65. 4; 4. 28. 3; 6. 63. 2; 8. 1. 4.
[70] Thuc. 2. 37. 1 (where in taking ἀπὸ μέρους to refer to rotation I have the agreement of Gomme, Rusten, and Hornblower).

friends but were active in politics probably talked not so much of aristocracy or oligarchy as of 'not the same form of democracy' (μὴ τὸν αὐτὸν τρόπον δημοκρατουμένοις), like Peisander on his first visit to Athens in 411 (Thuc. 8. 53. 1), and probably talked more of what was wrong with contemporary democracy than of what they would put in its place. In spite of the polarization between pro-Athenian democrats and pro-Spartan oligarchs of which we tend to think in the late fifth century, and in spite of the fact that there were men prepared to champion oligarchy, the bogey which the Athenian demagogues conjured up to frighten their supporters was not oligarchy but tyranny: possibly there were those who accused Cleon of trying to make himself tyrant,[71] and he chose to respond in the same vein.

Down to the time of Thucydides son of Melesias, men who have appeared as oligarchs have been men from aristocratic backgrounds, resisting democratic reform, men who resemble their predecessors of the archaic period; but we shall see that the oligarchs of the later fifth century were men of a different kind, from the same backgrounds as those of their contemporaries who became democratic leaders. I have been asked how far Athens is likely to have differed from other cities in these respects. The evidence does not allow certainty, but we can at least point to differences in circumstances which are likely to have produced different results. Athens will have had not only an unusually large number of citizens in total but an unusually large number of poorer citizens; and because of Athens' position in the Delian League it will probably have had an unusually high proportion of men other than agricultural workers among those poorer citizens, and also an unusually high proportion of rich men whose families had not been rich, landowning families for generations. In other words, the social mixture in the late fifth century will probably have differed more from the social mixture in earlier centuries in Athens than in other states. Democracy in other states will not have been quite the same thing as democracy in Athens, and I should guess that oligarchic opposition to democracy in other states will more probably have been a continuation of the older kind of aristocratic opposition than the new kind which I shall try to demonstrate for Athens.

Names of non-democrats, for the 420s and early 410s, totally elude us. Anybody who opposed Cleon, whatever his own position, could be denounced as a conspirator. Nicias, opposed to Cleon in *Ath. Pol.*'s schematic list of political leaders (28. 3), came from the same kind of background as Cleon but adopted a traditional style of leadership in contrast to Cleon's ostentatiously populist style. He was certainly opposed to Cleon's kind of democracy; there is no sign that he himself was opposed to democracy as

---

[71] In Ar. *Knights* 843–59 the Sausage-seller suggests in the course of his contest with the Paphlagonian that shields brought as spoils from Pylos are being kept ready for serious use, and 'if you were to start fuming and to look to the ostracon-game', i.e. if the people were to try to ostracize Cleon, his supporters might use them.

such; his son Niceratus was killed by the Thirty; on the other hand, his brothers Diognetus and Eucrates were of doubtful loyalty at the end of the century, though Eucrates finally took the democratic side and was killed by the Thirty.[72] Alcibiades is represented as saying in Sparta that democracy is acknowledged folly: he had been inclined to the dēmos because democracy was something that had to be accepted, but the word *dēmokratia* can cover everything opposed to tyranny, and he had tried to moderate the licence of the extremists (Thuc. 6. 89. 3–6). The truth seems to be that Alcibiades was interested primarily in his own advancement, and that in the early part of his career this aristocrat had tried to beat the demagogues at their own game.

We know nothing about most of the men accused of involvement in the religious scandals of 415; but some of them, perhaps many, were rich men who would not necessarily be loyal to the democracy in a crisis. Andocides was to try to return from exile to the Athens of the Four Hundred (And. 2. 10–16), though he eventually returned to and held office under the restored democracy of 403, and if he was oligarchically inclined the other members of his *hetaireia* may have shared that inclination. Alcibiades was as willing to live with oligarchy as with democracy. On the other hand, in Adeimantus[73] we do seem to have one man who was a loyal servant of the democracy as well as a friend of Alcibiades. Of the prosecutors and investigators (And. 1. 27, 36), Cleonymus had been an associate of Cleon in the 420s,[74] and Androcles was a democrat in 411 (Thuc. 8. 65. 2); but Peisander and Charicles, who 'seemed to be most well disposed towards the dēmos', appear later as oligarchs.[75] We do not know the position of Cimon's son Thessalus.[76]

It is important to stress that we do not know the political position of Thessalus, since he is one of the few members of the old aristocracy to make a political appearance in the late fifth century. Most of the oligarchs whom we shall encounter were, like the new democratic leaders, members of families which had risen to prominence during the fifth century. Alcibiades was of the old aristocracy; so were Critias and his cousin Charmides; and it is possible but not certain that the Melesias who was a member of the Four Hundred was the son of Pericles' opponent Thucydides.[77] In general, however, the division between democrats and oligarchs at the end of the

---

[72] Niceratus: Lys. 18. 6; Eucrates: ibid. 4–5; Diognetus: ibid. 9–11. See Davies (1971) 404–5.

[73] *PA* no. 202 = Fraser and Matthews (1987–) ii s.n. no. 19.

[74] See Meiggs and Lewis (1969), p. 188.

[75] Peisander: Thuc. 8. 49 etc.; Charicles: Davies (1971) 502–3.

[76] Plut. *Alc.* 19. 3; 22. 4.

[77] Identification accepted by Davies (1971) 232–3; doubted by A. Andrewes in Gomme, Andrewes, and Dover (1945–81) v. 289. Melesias the son of Thucydides was an uninvolved man (*apragmōn*) under the democracy (Plato *Lach.* 179 C, *Meno* 94 C–D). Of the other men to be mentioned below, Aristocrates (Davies 1971: 56–7, cf. above, p. 125) and Cephisophon (Davies 1971: 145 with 148) have better pedigrees than most.

century is not a division between the new ruling class and the old but a division within the new ruling class.[78]

By 411 there were complicating factors. It could be claimed that the democracy had squandered Athens' resources and was not making a success of the war: a change of regime might save public money, allow Alcibiades to return, and enable Athens to obtain Persian support and fight the war more effectively—or alternatively to make peace with Sparta and end the war. Peisander and Charicles are not the only men now found on the oligarchic side who had appeared to be loyal democratic citizens earlier.[79] Antiphon and Phrynichus both figure in a list of politicians in the *Wasps*,[80] and Phrynichus was a general in 412/1.[81] Aristocrates was one of the tribal representatives among those who in 421 swore to the Peace of Nicias and to Athens' alliance with Sparta;[82] he is mentioned in the *Birds* simply for his name (Ar. *Birds* 126), and that passage tells us nothing about his politics. The Callaeschrus who was a member of the Four Hundred was probably not the father of Critias but a man who had been treasurer of Athena in 412/1.[83] Altogether, of the twenty-one men listed by Develin as holding office under the regime of the Four Hundred, eight are known to have held office earlier, under the democracy;[84] the other thirteen are not, but our evidence is so thin that we cannot assert that none of them did hold office under the democracy. Some of the oligarchs of 411 may have been opportunists, simply pursuing their own advantage; others may genuinely have been persuaded that a change of regime was Athens' best chance in difficult circumstances; some seem to have been interested in the institutions of other Greek states;[85] but by no means all were doctrinaire lovers of oligarchy and haters of democracy.

In 410, probably after the battle of Cyzicus, the democracy was restored. But there was tension between men who had been on the oligarchic side and

---

[78] Cf. Mossé (1995) 71–2. This is the best point at which to note that lavish burials of those whose families could afford them disappeared *c.*500 except in a few families, but started again *c.*425—but that that is not just an Athenian but a general Greek phenomenon: see Morris (1994).

[79] Lys. 25. 8–9 (cf. p. 129 with n. 60 above) claims that in the late 5th cent. many men were not consistent supporters of democracy or oligarchy but changed sides to suit their immediate interests, and mentions as examples the 'demagogues' Phrynichus and Peisander.

[80] Ar. *Wasps* 1301–2. MacDowell regards these as a social group of men who, although some of them were oligarchs later, were not necessarily linked by a desire for oligarchy in 422 (1971 ad loc.; 1995: 173).

[81] For the record of office-holding see Develin (1989).

[82] Thuc. 5. 19. 2, 24. 1, with Andrewes and Lewis (1957).

[83] Davies (1971) 327; cf. Fraser and Matthews (1987–) ii s.n. no. 12 (treasurer and member of Four Hundred), 32 (father of Critias).

[84] The others are Dieitrephes, Aristoteles (not since the 420s: it may be the same man who was general in 431/0, general (I should say) in 426/5 and *hellēnotamias* in 421/0), Antiphon (*PA* no. 1283 = Fraser and Matthews (1987–) ii s.n. no. 5), Polystratus, Laespodias, and Onomacles.

[85] Notice the echo of oligarchic Boeotia in the 'future constitution' of 411 (*Ath. Pol.* 30. 3 with Rhodes 1981a: 393), and the echo of Sparta in 404 (n. 89 below).

men who had been on the democratic in 411/0;[86] and, although for a time victory over Sparta seemed possible, the democratic regime refused to make peace when peace with Sparta might have been to Athens' advantage,[87] and the trial of the generals after the battle of Arginusae[88] did not show the democracy at its best.

In 404 the democracy had lost the war, and the navy and the citizens who had served in it were not going to be important to Athens for the foreseeable future. There were recent memories, both of the unpleasant regime of the Four Hundred, and of the intermediate regime of the Five Thousand which men like Thucydides could admire; and these memories may have filled some men with a determination not to risk oligarchy again but others with the confidence that another overthrow of the democracy could not lead to another regime like that of the Four Hundred. Thrasybulus, a friend of Alcibiades rather than a staunch democrat in 411 (Andrewes 1953: 3–4), seems to belong to the first category, and Theramenes to the second. There were also men like Critias, who had no qualms about another regime like that of the Four Hundred.[89] Even if we are properly cautious about identifying bearers of the same name, there are seven members of the Thirty who are among the few men known to have been members of the Four Hundred or closely involved with them.[90] If we look for men who had held office under the democracy: Theramenes served as a general from 410 to 407 but probably was not regularly elected; he was regularly elected for 405/4 but was rejected at the *dokimasia* (the vetting of officials before they took up their appointments; Lys. 13. 10). Chremon was a member of the council of 405/4, which according to Lysias was 'corrupted and enthusiastic for oligarchy' (Lys. 13. 20). Only five other members of the Thirty are known to have held office under the democracy: they include the Sophocles who was exiled after agreeing to the treaty of Gela in 424 (Thuc. 4. 65. 3), and the Aristoteles who is found in no democratic office after the 420s but who was an active oligarch in 411.[91]

---

[86] See esp. Andrewes (1953).

[87] After Cyzicus: Philoch. *FGrH* 328 F 139, D.S. 13. 52–3. After Arginusae (but this is probably the post-Cyzicus peace offer misplaced): *Ath. Pol.* 34. 1, schol. Ar. *Frogs* 1532. A peace offer in 408 which resulted in an exchange of prisoners: Androt. *FGrH* 324 F 44. Cleophon opposed to peace after Aegospotami: Lys. 13. 5–12; 30. 10–13.

[88] Xen. *Hell.* 1. 7; D.S. 13. 101–103. 2.

[89] His funeral monument is said to have depicted Oligarchia setting light to Demokratia, and to have had an inscription referring to the brief stopping of the *hybris* ('insolence') of the accursed *dēmos* (schol. Aeschin. 1. 39 (82 Dilts) = 88 A 13 DK)—but the story is doubted by Stupperich (1994) 99. The regime of the Thirty was, of course, an oligarchy: the term 'thirty tyrants' seems to have been popularized by Ephorus (cf. Krentz 1982: 16 n. 2). There was some conscious emulation of Sparta among the oligarchs of 404, e.g. the use of the title 'ephor' for the political agents who prepared the way for the revolution (Lys. 12. 43); for further suggestions see Krentz (1982) 63–8; Whitehead (1982–3).

[90] Critias, Melobius, Mnasilochus, Eratosthenes, Charicles, Onomacles, and Aristoteles.

[91] Cf. above, p. 133 with n. 84. The other three are Anaetius (*hellēnotamias* 410/9), Charicles

Obviously, when so little of the iceberg is visible above the water, we must be extremely cautious. We are told that the rule of the Thirty began moderately and respectably.[92] If there was only one board of Ten after the overthrow of the Thirty,[93] that board included Rhinon, who had held office in 417/6, who stayed in Athens under the Thirty and was sufficiently trusted by his fellows to be elected to the Ten, but who then worked for reconciliation and held office under the restored democracy. Cephisophon, who first appears as one of the envoys sent to Sparta, with the encouragement of Pausanias, by the citizens who had remained in Athens under the Thirty,[94] is another man who lived through the regime of the Thirty but held office under the restored democracy. There is the case of the financier Chariades, *epistatēs* of the Erechtheum in 409/8 and *hellēnotamias* in 406/5, who stayed in Athens under the Thirty to serve as treasurer of Athena in 404/3. Clearly there were some men who could live with the democracy, who could even make themselves acceptable to the restored democracy, who nevertheless stayed in Athens and kept a fairly high profile under the oligarchy.

Against them we must set the men who did go into exile, and who joined in the fight against the oligarchs. There is Thrasybulus, the friend of Alcibiades; Archinus, who worked for a moderate settlement after the restoration of the democracy, was with Thrasybulus at Phyle;[95] even Phormisius, who proposed a property qualification for citizenship in the restored democracy, was one of the exiles.[96] We cannot quantify, but it looks as if more men were alienated by this second oligarchy than by the first, and that the men at the centre of the second oligarchy were a more uniform set of extremists than the men at the centre of the first.

After that, oligarchy and 'better forms of democracy' could be discussed in an academic way, but they could not be contemplated openly as options for Athens, though by the middle of the fourth century changes in constitutional detail could be made which were not democratic as democracy was understood in the late fifth century.[97] But I have no space in this paper to look at the fourth century in detail. I will end by repeating some of the points made above. First, it is not unrealistic to think of the ruling families of early Athens as an aristocracy, not ennobled by some fount of honour,

(investigator 415, general 414/3, member of the Four Hundred), and Onomacles (general 412/1, envoy under the Four Hundred).

[92] *Ath. Pol.* 35. 2–3, with other texts cited by Rhodes (1981*a*) ad loc.

[93] Contrast *Ath. Pol.* 38. 3, which has two boards of Ten, under the second of which the reconciliation was arranged.

[94] Xen. *Hell.* 2. 4. 36. His colleague was a man called Meletus, but identifying bearers of that name is difficult. [95] See Rhodes (1981*a*) 431.

[96] See Rhodes (1981*a*) 432.

[97] See Rhodes (1979–80; 1995*b*).

but regarding themselves as the best families and reluctant to share power with men from other families who were equally rich but outside the privileged circle. In the fifth century Ephialtes and his supporters campaigned openly for democracy; they were opposed by aristocrats who disapproved of democracy, and this opposition persisted into the 440s and was more serious than is sometimes allowed. After that our next trace of oligarchy is in the pamphlet of the Old Oligarch, but what the new-style demagogues claimed to be keeping at bay was not oligarchy but tyranny. At the end of the century, when the democracy was challenged by oligarchy, the oligarchic leaders were not aristocrats fighting back but, no less than the demagogues, were from families new to active politics; and we must remember that in this turbulent period men were moved by a mixture of ideas and objectives. Men with respectable democratic careers behind them were caught up in the regime of the Four Hundred; and, though the Thirty were a less variegated set of men than the Four Hundred, even under their regime there were men who cannot fairly be labelled oligarchs without qualification. 'Hard' oligarchs were few; men who could live with some kind of oligarchy were more numerous.

8

Syracusan Democracy: 'Most Like the Athenian'?[1]

N. K. RUTTER

THE nature of the government of Syracuse in the second half of the fifth century BC has been controversial. H. Wentker (1956) saw the constitution of the later fifth century as an aristocracy, but Peter Brunt (1957: 244) rejected that interpretation, stating flatly that 'Syracuse was not from 466 to 406 an oligarchy, but as Diodorus xi. 68. 6 and, more important, the contemporary Thucydides say, a democracy.' Who is right? Is either right? At the outset, there are obvious problems of definition, which it is one of the purposes of this volume to clarify: for example, what sort of democracy are we talking about? Wentker wrote of Syracuse: 'Für eine syrakusische Demokratie nach attischem Muster spricht nichts' ('Nothing speaks for a Syracusan democracy on the Athenian model': 1956: 163 n. 237). That 'nach attischem Muster' is an important qualification. Then, regarding the detail of the Syracusan political arrangements during our period, there is a substantial variety of evidence, each element with its own problems of interpretation, and each with its own view of the subject. My main tasks in this paper will be to introduce this evidence, and to provide a short overview of the problems associated with each part of it; I shall conclude with some assessment of where it leaves us with regard to the questions of interpretation and definition posed above.

The evidence

What, then, is the evidence? There are four main parts to it. First of all, the general development of Syracuse, town and territory, before the later fifth century; second, a number of notes by Aristotle, mainly in the fifth book of his *Politics*; third, extended accounts of Syracusan affairs in books 11 and 12 of Diodorus' *Bibliothēkē*; and finally, Thucydides' description of the intervention of the Athenians in Sicilian affairs, particularly in books 6 and 7. The evidence for Syracusan history at this period may not be all that full—certainly nowhere near as full as that for Athens—but it is good to have four separate and distinctive viewpoints. One obvious question will be: do they fit together?

[1] The expression derives from Thucydides' comparison of Syracuse with Athens at 8. 96. 5.

The development of Syracuse

I begin with the Syracusans and their polis in the archaic period (Figure 8.1).[2] In the second half of the eighth century the Corinthian founders of Syracuse ejected the native inhabitants of the peninsula of Ortygia and settled there themselves (Thuc. 6. 3. 2). From a very early date the immediately adjacent mainland was included in the urban nucleus, whence Syracusan control was rapidly extended westwards and southwards over a rich coastal plain which was to be the key factor in the prosperity of Syracuse and one of the constants in the history of the city. At Polichne, close to the confluence of the Anapus and Ciane rivers, a sanctuary of Olympian Zeus was established, the first traces of which date from the beginning of the seventh century at the latest. I shall be referring to this cult again later; in the fifth century it was the place where the roll of Syracusan citizens was kept (Plut. *Nic.* 14. 6), and as such was of obvious importance in the definition of citizenship of the polis.

The southern limit of the earliest phase of Syracusan expansion is marked by the settlement of Helorus, where small, one-roomed houses have been excavated dating to the late eighth/early seventh centuries (Voza 1978: 134–5). Further Syracusan expansion in south-east Sicily took place in the course of the seventh century. Strong-points were established at Akrai and Kasmenai, and in 599/8 the colony of Kamarina was founded on the south coast. By the beginning of the sixth century, therefore, Syracuse controlled a territory of approximately 1,500 square miles, which, as Dunbabin pointed out (1948: 63), was more extensive than that of any state of metropolitan Greece except Lakonia.

We know very little of the social structure and institutions of Syracuse in the archaic period. At the opening of the fifth century Syracuse was governed by a group of landed aristocrats known in the sources as *gamoroi*, 'sharers of the earth'. The type of a racing chariot on their coinage, which began at the end of the sixth century, is an indication of their interests: they were a horse-rearing aristocracy familiar not only in Sicily but in other parts of the Greek world too. They were the top layer of Syracusan society. At the bottom were the *killyrioi*, the 'slaves' of the *gamoroi*, as Herodotus calls them.[3] At the time I have referred to, the opening of the fifth century, the power of the *gamoroi* was weakening, and we hear of a free dēmos which made common cause with the *killyrioi* against their masters, who were forced to withdraw from Syracuse. This event probably took place around 490, and Aristotle cites it as an example of a democracy that collapsed

[2] Good accounts of the early development of Syracuse can be found in Dunbabin (1948) and Sjöqvist (1973).

[3] Hdt. 7. 155. 2. Aristotle (*Constitution of Syracuse*, fr. 586 Rose) compared these *killyrioi* with the helots of Sparta, the *penestai* of Thessaly, and the *clarōtai* of Crete. If the analogy is sound, then they were of an intermediate status between free men and chattel slaves.

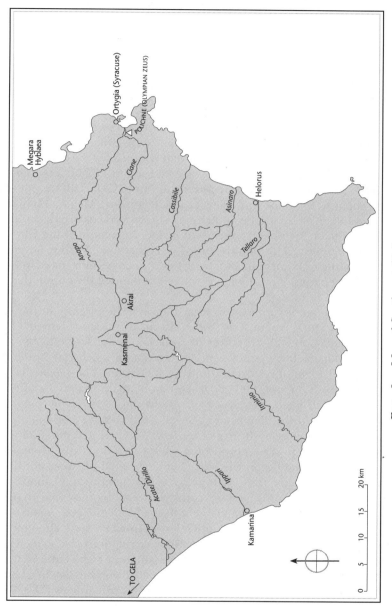

Fig. 8.1. Map of South-east Sicily.

through contempt caused by misgovernment (*Pol.* 1302^{b}27–32). I shall have more to say later about Aristotle's characterizations of constitutions. For the moment, it is interesting to observe here the reference to a dēmos, opposed to the *gamoroi*. There are, however, no grounds for thinking that they were not themselves for the most part farmers, even if composed of later arrivals in Syracuse in the seventh and sixth centuries.

In 485 the *gamoroi* were restored to Syracuse by Gelon, the tyrant of Gela, who proceeded to transfer his own capital to Syracuse, inaugurating a period of tyranny there that lasted until 466—the tyranny of the Deinomenids, so named after their ancestor Deinomenes. These years were a period of change and upheaval which as far as the Syracusans were concerned amounted to a refoundation of their city, with all that that entailed for the distribution and ownership of land.[4] Kamarina was evacuated and its inhabitants transferred to Syracuse and given Syracusan citizenship; from Gela, half the population was brought to Syracuse and likewise made citizens; Megara Hyblaea was besieged and taken, its wealthy inhabitants made Syracusan citizens, its poor enslaved; similar treatment was meted out to the people of the Chalcidian colony of Euboea. The population of Syracuse was further augmented, after the battle of Himera in 480, by the enrolment as citizens of more than 10,000 mercenaries. Thus Gelon ruthlessly expanded the population of his power-base of Syracuse.[5]

With an eye on our interest in what followed the tyranny in the second half of the century, we must ask what effects all these movements had on the social and political structures of Syracuse. I subscribe to the widely held view that Gelon's policy represented not so much revolution, but a substantial element of restoration and consolidation. The *gamoroi* returned with Gelon to Syracuse. Gelon's treatment of the populations of Megara and Euboea had been selective: he brought the *pacheis*, the 'fat cats', to Syracuse, but sold the dēmos into slavery. So it was the well-off who were restored at the expense of the free citizens who had created the situation that had helped Gelon to seize power (and who would normally be considered supporters of a tyrant). On the other hand, the well-off were not the only class to prosper under the tyranny. Economic activity was stimulated by temple-building and other public works, above all by the construction and servicing of a fleet. Even supposing a fleet of half the size mentioned by Herodotus (the figures in his list of Gelon's armaments are all in multiples of two: 7. 158. 4), 100 triremes would still have required 20,000 men to man them, leaving aside all those employed in maintaining and equipping them. In 474, a few years after Gelon's death, this fleet won the day in a battle off Cumae against the experienced Etruscans and Carthaginians (D.S. 11. 51).

---

[4] The fullest single source for these events is Hdt. 7. 154–6.

[5] For an account of the Syracusan tyranny of the early 5th cent., and a very useful collection of the sources on which it is based, see Berve (1967) i. 142–54; ii. 599–607.

What we do not know, however, is who precisely manned this fleet, whether Syracusans or others.[6]

These, briefly, are the antecedents of 'democracy' at Syracuse—power in the hands of a landowning group, power which seems if anything to have been restored rather than undermined by the tyrants. No Solon here, and certainly no Cleisthenes, but to the extent that the tyrants' power was based on personal loyalty to themselves, there may have been a blurring of the old divisions of the kind that took place under the Peisistratid tyrants in Athens, and from this time also dates the creation of a naval capacity.

The social and political legacy of the Deinomenid tyranny was very confused, and it was a decade or more after the end of the tyranny in 466 before the numerous problems were addressed and solutions to them began to be worked out. On the social side, I summarize very substantially by remarking that the problems revolved round a sorting out of rights and property between what Diodorus (11. 72. 3) calls the 'old citizens' and the very mixed 'new' population drawn from the elements I outlined above. Some of the incomers were repatriated, like the half of the Geloans brought to Syracuse by Gelon; others were eventually forced to depart, like the 7,000 surviving mercenaries of the tyrants.

Politically, we come to a more detailed examination of the problem I outlined at the beginning of this paper: what sort of constitution replaced the tyranny? Let us look at some problems in the interpretation of what Aristotle, Diodorus, and Thucydides have to say.

Aristotle

There are abundant and varied references to Syracusan history in Aristotle's *Politics*, eighteen in all, fifteen of them in book 5; of those fifteen, four refer to the period between 466 and 406.

(1) 1304ª27–9: 'At Syracuse the people were responsible for the victory in the war against the Athenians [415–413] and turned the existing *politeia* into a democracy.'

This comment is part of Aristotle's discussion of the reasons why constitutions change. One of the reasons is the growth in reputation and power of some office, or of some element in the state. I leave aside for a moment the problem of what Aristotle means here by *politeia*, and comment simply that this remark can be linked to what Diodorus says of events in 412, when one of the constitutional reforms of a certain Diocles was the introduction of the lot into the process of choosing magistrates (13. 34. 6).

(2) 1305ᵇ39–1306ª2: 'Changes in oligarchy also take place when its members waste their substance in riotous living; men who have done that want

---

[6] Only much later, with reference to events in 411, do we hear (Thuc. 8. 84. 2) of 'a majority of free men' manning a small Syracusan and Thurian fleet.

to create a revolution, and they either attempt to be tyrants themselves or set up some other person (as Hipparinus set up Dionysius in Syracuse . . .)'

As part of a discussion about how changes are brought about in oligarchies, Aristotle characterizes the constitution that preceded the tyranny of Dionysius I (i.e. before 406) as an oligarchy.

(3) 1312^{b}6–9:

This opposition of constitutions may take different forms. Democracy quarrels with tyranny in the same sort of way as, in Hesiod's phrase, 'potter quarrels with potter . . .'; kingship and aristocracy quarrel with tyranny because of the opposite nature of their constitutional structure. That was the reason why the Spartans [ruled as they were by kings] suppressed a great many tyrannies, and why the Syracusans did the same during the period when they enjoyed a good constitution.

Here Aristotle is discussing ways in which tyranny may be destroyed: one of the ways is by external causes; another is by conflict of ideologies. The aristocratic 'good government' referred to is that characterized in (1) above as *politeia*, between 466 and 412.

(4) 1316^{a}32–3: '[Tyranny] may also turn into a democracy, like that of the family of Gelon at Syracuse.'

As part of his discussion of Plato's failure to explain the cause of change in tyrannies, Aristotle gives this example from Syracuse of a change from tyranny to democracy.

I want to make two points about the interpretation of these illustrations taken by Aristotle from the fifth-century political history of Syracuse. First, briefly, context is always important: in passage (4), for example, the mention of change from tyranny to democracy is part of a passage where Aristotle is trying to demonstrate a variety of possible changes from tyranny; he needs an example of change from tyranny to democracy, and Syracuse comes to mind in a general way. In an equally general way, the same period was characterized in passage (1) as a *politeia*. Similarly, the Syracusan constitution between 412 and 406 is in passage (1) a democracy, and in passage (2) an oligarchy.

A second point is that there are problems with nomenclature, in particular with the term just mentioned, *politeia*, meaning not just a constitution in general, but a specific type of constitution, called by Aristotle 'polity'.[7] Initially, in book 3 of the *Politics* (1279^{a}22–^{b}10), *politeia* is defined in the context of a sixfold model of types of constitution. There is the rule of the one, the rule of the few, and the rule of the many, and each of these has a positive and a negative variant: monarchy and tyranny, aristocracy and oligarchy, *politeia* and democracy. So in this classification *politeia* is the good form of the rule of the many, democracy the bad. Later on, though, in

---

[7] This issue is discussed in greater detail by Andrew Lintott in the next chapter of this volume.

books 4 and 6, Aristotle often abandons this sixfold model and operates in practice with only two basic types, oligarchy and democracy (described in 1290ᵃ13–19; cf. 1289ᵃ8–11, 1291ᵇ15–18). Each of these can be subdivided, typically into four variants, from most positive to most negative. In this scheme the best form of democracy is very nearly identical with *politeia* in the earlier scheme, but Aristotle introduces a complication when he allows that a constitution can include elements of both democracy and oligarchy (1316ᵇ39–1317ᵃ10). In that case the term *politeia* may be used to refer either to a 'golden mean' between democracy and oligarchy (1295ᵃ25–1296ᵇ12) or, 'to put it simply', to a mixture of the two (1293ᵇ31–4). As a general principle, then, *politeia* according to Aristotle should provide a combination of oligarchic and democratic features: there may be a popular assembly, but its powers will be limited; some officials may be appointed oligarchically, others democratically, depending, for example, on the role of the lot in the appointment; some juries may be taken from all classes, some from certain classes only. Aristotle allows that there is a variety of ways in which oligarchic and democratic elements can be combined to construct a *politeia*, so that it can tend towards aristocracy or democracy, but he also regards it as 'manifest' that aristocracies and 'polities' are not far removed from one another (1294ᵃ28–9). He has no analysis of the position of Syracuse on the spectrum.

The conclusion of the discussion so far seems somewhat negative—that nothing definite about Syracusan constitutional arrangements after the Deinomenid tyranny can be inferred from Aristotle's elliptical comments. On the other hand, his classification of the varieties of democracy is wide-ranging and suggestive. He refers in his discussion (1292ᵇ21 ff.) to a situation in which the 'farming class and the class possessed of moderate means' are the sovereign power in the constitution; 'able to live by their work, but unable to enjoy any leisure, they make the law supreme, and confine the meetings of the assembly to a minimum'. We may not be too far here from Syracuse after 466 (but perhaps before 412), and we must not try to match the Syracusan experience of democracy with a democracy of the radical Athenian type, or even of the type current in 466, before the reforms of Ephialtes.

Diodorus

Diodorus was as far from the fifth century as we are from Henry VIII, and he relies for his information on the source that he is using at any particular time. On the other hand, his account of the fifth century is much fuller than that of Aristotle (as a Sicilian he had a personal interest in Sicilian affairs) and, an important point I think, he is the only authority to preserve some reasonably detailed evidence about what happened in the years immediately following the fall of the Deinomenid tyranny.[8]

First, a general point. I mentioned just now that Diodorus' material is derivative, and a lot of effort in Diodoran scholarship has gone into attempts to identify his sources. For what it is worth, it is likely that his source for the Syracusan affairs we are interested in was Timaeus, a native of Tauromenium (Taormina) in Sicily, who died aged over 90 around 250 BC.[9] However, the results of such investigations into sources do not get us very far in this period, since they are not secure. Arguments often become circular: this or that passage in Diodorus derives from X, so X has such and such characteristics as a historian, and these characteristics can be detected in further passages of Diodorus, and so on. What I have come to regard as more interesting, and more productive, is to look at Diodorus himself, his language and his own context in hellenistic historiography, to investigate in fact what is Diodoran in Diodorus, and see what we can get out of that.

For example, Diodorus uses the word *dēmokratia* to characterize the post-Deinomenid constitution. What does the word mean to him, and in what contexts does he use it? To judge from the fifty-seven appearances of *dēmokrat-* words in his work, the majority (forty-six) using the noun, he refers to the concept of democracy in a very generalized way. I highlight one aspect of his usage, his frequent references to the introduction of 'democracy' after the fall of a tyranny, to an extent that I think justifies the use of the word 'formula'.[10] Several different sources lie behind these references, and the elements of standardization (in both content and vocabulary) must

---

[8] The passages in which Diodorus describes or refers to constitutional procedures in Syracuse between 466 and 406 are (with his own dates): 11. 72. 2–3 (463/2), deliberations of an assembly after the overthrow of Thrasybulus, the last Deinomenid; 11. 86. 4–87 (454/3), attempt of Tyndarides to set up a tyranny; introduction of petalism (akin to ostracism), and its rapid repeal after a period of increasing faction; 11. 88. 4–5 (453/2) and 91. 2 (451/0), appointment of generals, and their subsequent exile or death for supposed misconduct; 11. 92 (451/0), decision on the fate of the Sicel rebel Ducetius; 13. 19. 4–33, (413/12), stormy assembly to consider the treatment of Athenian captives; 13. 34. 6 (412/11), reform of Diocles, who persuaded the people to change their constitution so that the administration would be conducted by magistrates chosen by lot; 13. 91. 3–92. 1 (406/5, as also the remaining references), another stormy meeting of the assembly; Dionysius accuses the generals of bribe-taking, and denounces 'the rest of the most renowned citizens', presenting them as friends of oligarchy; 13. 92. 3, opposition between the 'most respectable citizens' and 'the common crowd' in their attitudes to Dionysius; 13. 92. 4–7, frequent assemblies to discuss preparations for war; Dionysius persuades the Syracusans to recall exiles; 13. 94. 4–95. 1, the assembly appoints Dionysius general with full powers.   [9] See Pearson (1987).

[10] The list of such occasions is as follows: 2. 38. 6, Dionysus passed on rule over India to his sons and their descendants; later, when their rule was dissolved, the cities received a democratic government; 2. 39. 4, a similar situation after the rule of Heracles and his descendants; 11. 53. 5, the people of Akragas gained their democracy after the expulsion of the tyrant Thrasydaeus; 11. 68. 5, the Syracusans liberated cities of Sicily from tyrants and restored democracies to them; 16. 70. 5, Timoleon introduced democratic laws to Syracuse after the tyrannies of Dionysius I and II; 20. 32. 2, Xenodicus recovered Echetla from Agathocles and restored democracy there; 21. 16. 6. the Syracusans recovered democracy after the fall of Agathocles; 33. 5a. 1, in Pisidia the fall of a tyranny was followed by democracy.

be the responsibility of Diodorus himself. That would suggest that as far as his terminology is concerned we should not lay too much stress on the fact that he calls the post-466 constitution of Syracuse a democracy. There is also the fact that Diodorus was writing in the late hellenistic period, at a time when the word 'democracy' would have lost in the Greek cities all internal political and social significance, and would signify simply a republican regime, contrasting with a home-grown tyrant or a foreign monarch.[11]

So much for nomenclature. Now let us consider how Diodorus describes his Syracusan democracy in action. I make some general points, and conclude with short discussions of two passages: 11. 72. 2–3 and 11. 87. 1–2.

The fundamental institutional expression of Diodorus' Syracusan democracy is an assembly which deliberates and makes decisions. It was convened (on what authority Diodorus does not tell us) after the overthrow of Thrasybulus, the last tyrant, and proceeded to deliberate on its 'own form of democracy'. Diodorus is silent too on the membership of this assembly (apart from a vague *dēmos*, 11. 86. 5, 92. 4), and there is only one allusion to any form of *probouleusis*, that is, provision for the preparation of agenda for the sovereign assembly by another body such as the boulē at Athens: at 92. 2 'the magistrates convened an assembly and laid before it the question of what should be done about Ducetius'. It is a feature of Diodorus' accounts of Syracusan politics that moralizing generalities overlie and obscure the social and structural realities. For example, under the year 454/3 he describes the activities of a would-be tyrant Tyndarides (11. 86. 4), but he does not tell us who the poor were who rallied to him, nor who were the 'most respectable' citizens who killed him (11. 86. 5). Subsequently, 'powerful' (87. 1) and 'influential' (87. 4) men are driven into exile, and the lead in politics is taken by 'citizens of the baser sort and who excelled in boldness': they encourage the masses to disorder and revolution. Demagogues and informers appear, and the young practise clever oratory, forsaking the sober training of former days (87. 5).

Does all this add up to 'democracy', even in a Cleisthenic sense? There are reasons for adopting a cautious approach to this question, and for illustration I offer some analysis of the two passages referred to above: the accounts (1) of the decisions of the assembly convened after the departure of Thrasybulus, and (2) of petalism, the Syracusan form of ostracism.

(1) 11. 72. 2–3. 2:

After they [the Syracusans] had overthrown the tyranny of Thrasybulus they convened an assembly, and after deliberating on their own form of democracy they all voted unanimously to make a huge statue of Zeus the Liberator, and to celebrate each year with sacrifices the Festival of Liberation and hold games of distinction on the anniversary of the overthrow of the tyrant and the liberation of their native city;

---

[11] For discussion of the evolution of the term *dēmokratia* in the hellenistic period, see Gauthier (1993) esp. 217–25.

they also voted to sacrifice to the gods at the games four hundred and fifty bulls and to use them for the citizens' feast. [3] As for all the magistracies, they proposed to assign them to the old citizens; but the mercenaries who had been enrolled as citizens in the time of Gelon they did not see fit to allow a share in this dignity, whether because they judged them to be unworthy or because they were suspicious that men who had been nurtured in tyranny and had served in war under a monarch might attempt a revolution. And that is what actually happened. For Gelon had enrolled as citizens more than ten thousand foreign mercenaries, of whom there were left at the time in question more than seven thousand.

The first of the assembly's decisions, described in 72. 2, amounted to the reinforcement of a cult, that of Zeus Olympios, which as I mentioned earlier had been at the heart of Syracusan religion from the earliest days of the colony. The appearances of this cult in history demonstrate its strong association with the ruling group at Syracuse. When Hippocrates, the tyrant of Gela before Gelon, attacked Syracuse in the 490s, he tried to drive a wedge between the commons and the priest of Zeus and his associates, equated with 'those in charge of affairs in Syracuse'; the latter were removing gold dedications in the temple, in particular the robe of the statue of Zeus in which a large amount of gold had been worked, and Hippocrates was able to rebuke them as despoilers (D.S. 10. 28. 1–2). In the later fourth century Timoleon's measures of restoration at Syracuse included the institution of the 'amphipoly' of Zeus Olympios, an annual eponymous office. The names of the first priest, Kallimenes the son of Alkidas (D.S. 16. 70. 6), and of others known, Theomnastos and Heraklios (Cic. *Verr.* 4. 61. 137), are all Dorian names from the Peloponnese, and suggest descent from the oldest families in Syracuse.

I referred earlier to the holding of the list of Syracusan citizens in the temple of Olympian Zeus, a fact which lends significance to the second measure of the post-tyrant assembly recorded by Diodorus, that confining all offices in the new constitution to 'the old citizens'.[12] The religious and constitutional spheres are closely intertwined here, and the traditional ruling group of Syracuse is reasserting its authority in both. Many incomers were disadvantaged by the second measure, in particular the mercenaries enfranchised by Gelon, and it is difficult to imagine how such a measure could have been passed by an assembly of *all* the adult males in Syracuse. This in turn suggests that originally at least a broad oligarchy based on the revolutionary forces seized power.

(2) 11. 87. 1–2

[1] Among the Athenians each citizen had to write on a potsherd the name of the

---

[12] Aristotle (*Pol.* 1275^{b}32–9) noted the problem posed by 'those who come to share in a *politeia* after a revolution'; he illustrated his point with reference to Athens after the expulsion of the Peisistratids, when Cleisthenes is said to have enrolled in the tribes many foreigners and slave immigrants.

man who in his opinion had the most power to tyrannize over his fellow citizens, but among the Syracusans the name of the most powerful citizen had to be written on an olive leaf: when the leaves were counted, the recipient of the most leaves had to go into exile for five years. [2] In this way they thought they would humble the arrogance of the most powerful men in the respective cities; for in general they were not exacting a punishment for wrongdoing from those who transgressed the law, but were effecting a humbling of the power and growing influence of the men in question.

According to Diodorus, petalism at Syracuse possessed many of the features of ostracism at Athens, which he describes in closely similar terms earlier in book 11 (55. 1–3). In Athens each citizen had to write on a potsherd (*ostrakon*) the name of 'the man who in his opinion had the greatest power to destroy democracy'; the man who received the largest number of *ostraka* was exiled for five[13] years. The purpose of the law was not the punishment of wrongdoing but the diminution through exile of the presumption of men who had risen too high. In his account of petalism at Syracuse Diodorus repeats the notion that it was not instituted as a punishment for a crime committed, but to diminish the influence and growing power of the men in question. However, the background to the introduction of petalism at Syracuse is more clearly defined as a series of attempts to set up tyranny (such as that of Tyndarides referred to earlier), and the 'power to destroy democracy' mentioned as the danger in the account of Athens has become at Syracuse the 'power to tyrannize over the citizens'. If the original idea for petalism came from Athens (and there was a background of tyranny there too), its operation at Syracuse seems to have been less well regulated. According to Diodorus the exile of many influential men caused others among the *chariestatoi* ('most refined', a common Diodoran term of approval) to withdraw from public life, leaving the field open to the 'worst elements'. Factional quarrels and disorder increased until the Syracusans thought better of their innovation and repealed the law of petalism.

Why was petalism introduced, and why was it relatively quickly abolished? In line with his thinking about the nature of the government of Syracuse at this time, Wentker (1956: 56–8) thought of it as a measure introduced by the nobility to protect themselves against the poor and their champions. Brunt (1957: 244) expressed himself baffled by the thought of petalism as an aristocratic measure. But Diodorus is clear about the background to the introduction of the institution: frequent attempts at tyranny by people like Tyndarides, who gathered about him many of the poor. This time, in contrast to the period of Deinomenid rule, the potential beneficiaries of tyranny were the poor, and it is equally hard to understand why a vote on potential tyrants should be put in their hands. We have to assume either that the law was passed and operated on a severely restricted fran-

---

[13] A slip on Diodorus' part for 'ten'.

chise, which would tend to favour Wentker's point of view, or that it was designed to favour the factional interests of those who thought they had popular support. The first of these alternatives seems preferable, since if we look at the other end of the law's brief life, its repeal, it is difficult to imagine how that came about unless the *chariestatoi* controlled decision-making.

Thucydides

How do the points made so far on the basis of other sources of information look in the light of Thucydides?[14] In many ways he presents Syracusan decision-making as comparable with that of Athens. He says that Sicilian cities including Syracuse were democratic (7. 55. 2), and his accounts of public meetings there share features with those he describes as taking place in Athens. There is free debate in an assembly which passes laws, instructs ambassadors, appoints and deposes generals, addresses the military situation, and discusses terms of peace. Athenagoras is a champion of the Syracusan people, as Cleon is in Athens, and the overconfidence of the dēmos of both cities is characterized in the same dismissive phrase. Athenagoras' defence of democracy against oligarchic intriguers is a rare thing among surviving Greek writers. Yet Athenagoras' allusions to intrigue and party strife at Syracuse share many elements with Diodorus' picture: attempts at oligarchy or tyranny, the role of the young—this last feature reminding us once again of Athens, in particular the contrast between young and old introduced in Thucydides' report of the debate between Nicias and Alcibiades.[15]

So much for the three accounts of Syracusan politics in the fifth century. To what extent are they compatible with each other? Is Thucydides somewhat on his own in presenting what seems to be a more democratic picture than Aristotle and Diodorus? Before I attempt to draw the discussion together, I make two points.

First, there is the question of the perspectives of the three sources. They

[14] Evidence in Thucydides on the working of the Syracusan constitution between 415 and 413: 6. 32. 3–41, an assembly (*ekklēsia*, 32. 3; *xullogos*, 41. 4) freely debates reports of an Athenian attack; 6. 36–40, Athenagoras is introduced (35. 2) in terms that recall Thucydides' introduction to the Athenian Cleon (3. 36. 6), and his speech includes (38) allusions to intrigue and party strife at Syracuse; he attacks would-be oligarchs, and defends democracy as a form of government; the debate ends (41) when one of the generals refuses to allow any more speeches; 6. 63. 2, the confident Syracusans urge their generals to lead them to Katana, 'as the crowd likes to do' (Thucydides uses the same phrase of the Athenians, 4. 28. 3); 6. 72–3, an assembly is encouraged by Hermocrates (a private individual) and votes in favour of a reduction in the number of generals and the election of new ones, and the dispatch of ambassadors to Corinth and Sparta; 6. 103. 3–4, (possibly) formal discussion of peace terms; 7. 2. 1, Gongylus finds the Syracusans on the point of holding an assembly about ending the war; 7. 21. 2, Gylippus calls together the Syracusans, and his plea that they should man ships is strongly supported by Hermocrates; 7. 73. 1, to thwart an Athenian retreat Hermocrates approaches 'the authorities' (later (73. 3) 'the magistrates'). [15] 6. 12. 2, 17. 1.

report on the same subject, the Syracusan constitution, from different points of view and under the influence of different historiographical traditions. Some of these perspectives have been traced in the course of this paper. Here I make a further point about Thucydides.[16] In his accounts of the decision-making of states Thucydides distinguishes not between oligarchy and democracy but between those two on the one hand and arbitrary government on the other: when he describes the decisions and decision-making of free cities his language, in particular his use of the collective ethnic, is the same, whether the cities are oligarchic or democratic. The citizens of both oligarchies and democracies are responsible for their public actions, and both forms of government are from that point of view distinguished not from each other but from tyranny. Distinctions between the forms of independent government are blurred.

A second point concerns chronology, not the chronology of the three authors, but that of events in the fifth century itself. Diodorus' most detailed accounts of Syracusan political life refer to the 460s and 450s, while Thucydides concentrates on the years 415–413. Was there a development over time? The Athenian form of democracy certainly developed in the course of the fifth century, and at Syracuse we know that there were experiments, even failed ones like petalism. Not long after the defeat of the Athenians we hear from Diodorus (13. 34. 6) of a change in the Syracusan constitution to the effect that the administration would be conducted by magistrates chosen by lot.

Yet in spite of general probabilities and specific hints, it will not do methodologically to rely on unrecorded constitutional changes as an explanation of what appears to be a contrast between Thucydides and Diodorus. We have to return first of all to Aristotle's point discussed above about the fluidity of the concept, and the term, *dēmokratia*. Aristotle's theorizing is useful, in that he shows us the different ways in which governments could operate in ancient Greece, and in particular the varied ways in which institutional arrangements could be mixed, so varied indeed that they might well admit of apparently conflicting analysis.

Furthermore, in practical real-life terms Robin Osborne (1987: 123–32) has compared the cases of Thasos, Elis, and Athens, all with constitutions that are described as democratic, yet each functioning in different ways, e.g. in the manner in which they did or did not integrate the urban with the country areas. In Thasos the city dominated the countryside and exploited it when it did not ignore it. Elis was united as a single city in 471, but without the desertion of other major settlements: the loose political organization left the villages with a strong degree of independence and community identity. In Athens the political reorganization of the late sixth century both

---

[16] The point derives from a reference I owe to Stephen Hodkinson: Pope (1988).

recognized the independent existence of local communities and gave them a direct role in running the whole city. In the case of Syracuse it would be worth exploring further the implications of Dunbabin's picture of settlement patterns in the area of south-eastern Sicily controlled by Syracuse (1948: 112). He refers to its patchwork appearance: military colonies at Akrai and Kasmenai, probably with Sicel villages to work their land; Greek farmers in a walled town at Helorus and other little country towns; Greek farmers dotting the countryside in the more fertile parts; Sicel serfs scattered on big estates over the same area; Sicels in some parts who kept their nationality and appear to have been free peasants; one free Sicel town with a Greek trading-post.

I began this paper by referring to the sharp distinction that has sometimes been drawn between a 'democratic' and an 'oligarchic' view of Syracuse in the second half of the fifth century. The subsequent discussion has shown that it is by no means easy to make a clear decision in favour of one view or the other. On the one hand, all three sources use the word *dēmokratia* to characterize Syracuse at that time. Diodorus describes the operation of an assembly which passes laws (11. 72, 86–7), makes arrangements for 'petalism' (11. 87), and decides on the treatment of prisoners (11. 92). Thucydides' picture is along similar lines, but with more detail: for him a sovereign Syracusan assembly makes decisions in ways comparable with the democratic Athenians.

Yet such comparisons ought not to be pushed too far. Although sovereign power in Syracuse seems to be in the hands of the *plēthos* (the multitude/'commons'; Thuc. 6. 38. 1), a probouleutic council (boulē) of Athenian type seems to be crucially absent. Control seems to be in the hands of magistrates or powerful individuals, and on one occasion (Thuc. 6. 41) a general put a stop to the proceedings of the assembly. If our knowledge of the processes of political decision-making is incomplete, we are totally ignorant of other important areas of government such as the election and competence of magistrates and the judiciary power. Furthermore, such other information as we have about the social and political development of Syracuse does not encourage us to accept without reservations Thucydides' comparison of the city with Athens. Up to the beginning of the fifth century Syracuse was an agriculturally based land power which made no military use, as far as we can see, of its magnificent natural harbours. Far from inaugurating revolution, the Deinomenid tyrants between 485 and 466 consolidated the old élite. After the expulsion of the tyrant family there was no Cleisthenic reform; on the contrary the traditional ruling group seems to have resumed control.

Aristotle's theoretical analysis showed us that many different mixes of oligarchy and democracy were possible. In practical terms we have seen how different ways of organizing a state, involving different balances between its constituent parts as well as differences in the details of its constitutional arrangements, could be referred to under the umbrella of *dēmokratia*. The term was an elastic one, and we should not be mesmerized by our image of the 'radical' Athenian democracy when looking at other states with 'democratic' credentials. Aristotle describes the Syracusan constitution between 466 and 406 as a *politeia* (1304ᵃ27–9) which changed only in 412 into a democracy; but elsewhere he refers to the sixty-year period as an oligarchy (1305ᵇ39–1306ᵃ2) and as a democracy (1316ᵃ2–3). We should respect Aristotle's difficulty, and his judgement. In the sixty years after the fall of the Deinomenid tyranny Syracuse does seem to have developed a key feature of ancient Greek democracy by putting sovereign power into the hands of a popular assembly, but beyond that the evidence does not allow us to go. Not only do we lack information about significant details of the assembly's operation—What did a 'popular' assembly mean in Syracusan terms? Who convened it? Who prepared its business? Did it meet regularly? If so, how often?—but there is no information either about other important areas of government. What we know of the history of Syracuse suggests that oligarchic traditions remained strong there.

9
Aristotle and the Mixed Constitution

ANDREW LINTOTT

IN the *Politics* Aristotle appears in more than one guise—as an analyst of the nature of the polis and political activity and as the proponent of an ideal polis (in books 7–8, according to the numeration of W. D. Ross in the Oxford Classical Text). The detailed examination of existing constitutions in books 2–6 mixes analysis with recommendations to lawgivers and statesmen in the various types of city. Aristotle here acts as a sort of political consultant and indeed proffers advice to political leaders in cities of whose constitutions he does not approve. However, he also manifests preferences of his own for constitutions that in his view are correct: his touchstone is that they should be oriented towards the exercise of virtue and the common interest. The most problematic and intriguing of these is the so-called *politeia*, which is the correct form of democracy. As expounded by him, it is a mixed or blended constitution. Although this was a rarity in actual fact, both then and later, the notion of the mixed constitution was to play an important part in political theory both in the ancient world and more recently, from about AD 1500 to the time of the American Revolution. I have discussed its significance at Rome elsewhere (Lintott 1997). Here I want to look more closely at its Greek origins.

The background to Aristotle's discussion

Any constitution is likely in practice to be a mixture of elements which are not entirely consistent. Even Athens, which in the classical era was an example of pure, or extreme, democracy by Aristotle's canons (1298^b28 ff.),[1] possessed by tradition the aristocratic or oligarchic institution of the Areopagus. What ancient writers mean by a mixed constitution, and what it has come to mean in more recent times,[2] is a constitution where features whose political direction would normally have been thought to have been different, which had different aims and served the interests of different classes, have been blended or combined with the effect of neutralizing their undesirable effects and enhancing their desirable ones. This blending was assumed in

[1] See Lintott (1992) esp. 115, 119–26.

[2] The major relevant modern works are Aalders (1968); von Fritz (1954); Nippel (1980) (with an important survey of the influence of the theory in early modern times). On Aristotle in this context, apart from the still fundamental commentary of Newman (1887–1902), see Mulgan (1977) esp. 53–77; Keyt and Miller (1991).

the classical Greek world to be the deliberate policy of a lawgiver: only with Polybius' description in Book 6 of the Roman constitution (and also with that of Carthage) do we find it suggested that the mixture can arise from a process of natural growth.[3]

By the mid-fifth century or a little later, to judge from the famous triangular debate between the three Persians in Herodotus (3. 80–2), the Greeks had come to distinguish clearly and contrast the elemental constitutions of monarchy, oligarchy, and democracy. It seems to me that this is a prerequisite for talking meaningfully about mixture. One might wish to see the origins of a theory of a balanced constitution when Solon was reforming Athens in the early sixth century but, once one has allowed that Solon was on his own admission a mediator (frr. 5; 36 West), the interpretation of Solon in our sources owes so much to fourth-century theory that it would be unwise to impute a conscious intention of mixing to him.[4] A fragment of the Pythagorean disciple Alcmaeon of Croton, which should belong to the early fifth century, refers to an *isonomia* of powers (*dunameis*), such as the wet and the dry or the hot and the cold, as constitutive of health in the body (24 B 4 DK). The use of *isonomia* to describe a balance of power as well as an equality may well have implications for the use of the term as a political slogan, but this falls well short of indicating any theory of mixing constitutional elements.[5] For this we have to wait until Thucydides.

Thucydidean speakers on more than one occasion are found arguing for some kind of balance or blending in political operations. Brasidas at Akanthos declares that it is undesirable either to subject the few to the many or the many to the few (4. 86. 4). Alcibiades in the Sicilian debate at Athens argues against Nicias' attempt to divide the young from the old, saying that youth and age are useless without one another and similarly that the humble, the average, and the really excellent would have the greatest strength when blended together (*xunkrathen*)—a statement more about abilities than political orientations (6. 18. 6). Athenagoras at Syracuse is more concerned with political systems when he talks about different sections of society having different functions but an equal share in their community (6. 39. 1). Yet he does not talk about mixture and indeed is not advocating a mixed constitution, but a democracy, albeit (in my view) one of a moderate pre-Periclean kind (Lintott 1982: 189–93). Democracy of course has a natural claim to

---

[3] *Pol.* 6. 4–9, 51, 57. On this see now Lintott (1997).

[4] A division of constitutions into monarchies, aristocracies, and hoplite democracies is also to be found in Pind. *Pyth.* 2. 86 ff., written about 470 BC and thus antedating Herodotus' writing. For Solon being regarded as a *mesos*, a man in the middle or a moderate man, see also *Ath. Pol.* 5. 2–3 with Solon frr. 4a–c West. On 4th-cent. sources on Solon see Rhodes (1981a) 15–25; on theoretical interpretations of his work see Hansen (1989b).

[5] On *isonomia* see Ostwald (1969) 149–58; Vlastos (1964); Hansen (1991) 65–71. The attempt of Ryffel (1949) 24 ff. to interpret Hippodamus' constitution (Arist. *Pol.* 1267^{b}23 ff.) as mixed seems forced.

be inclusive, and this may be easily mistaken at first glance as a claim to be balanced.

By contrast to these statements advocating various forms of blending or balance, the first reference to an actual mixed form of government is Thucydides' well-known description of the installation of the 5,000 in power at Athens in the autumn of 411 (8. 97. 1). What was produced then was, in his words, a blend (*xunkrasis*) which was moderate in the direction of both the many and the few. I should say here that I accept that there was indeed a fusion of oligarchic and democratic elements. Even if the restriction of the assembly to possessors of hoplite weapons and armour was more theoretical than real and the Council of 500 had been restored, I assume that there would have been property qualifications both for membership of this council and for tenure of magistracies, which in any case we know to have been unpaid.[6] The blend is praised by Thucydides as *metria* (moderate), and its espousal of moderation and those in the middle forms part of a political tradition which goes back to Solon—and to Phocylides (Arist. *Pol.* 1295[b]33–4). In the same vein, Alcibiades at Sparta is portrayed by Thucydides claiming (not very plausibly) that he tried to be more moderate in politics than the prevailing lawlessness (6. 89. 3), while in Euripides' *Supplices* (238 ff.) the wealthy are said to be useless, the poor dangerous, but it is those in the middle who save cities.

The 5,000 did not last a year, and we have no direct evidence of talk of mixture at Athens in the period of political conflict which ended with the restoration of democracy in 403. However, the mixed constitution cannot have disappeared down a black hole at the end of the fifth and in the early fourth century. If we trust Aristotle, at some point before he wrote the *Politics* the term *politeia* came to be used to describe a form of government which lay between oligarchy and democracy, based, like the 5,000, on a property qualification, where the mass of the people governed in the common interest (*Pol.* 1265[b]26–9; 1279[a]37–[b]4; *NE* 1160[a]30 ff.). It is tantalizing that we know so little about this stage in the development of Greek political thought, although conjecture can suggest contexts where this idea might have arisen. One source may have been the posthumous rehabilitation of Theramenes as a man who was no turncoat but believed in principle in a constitution based on the warriors. This is how he finally is made to present himself in Xenophon's history, produced in the middle of the fourth century (*Hell.* 2. 3. 48), and the Theramenes papyrus suggests that this sort of point was likely to have been made earlier in a political post-mortem

---

[6] See Lintott (1982) 153–4, and for full and judicious surveys of the problem Rhodes (1972*b*); Gomme, Andrewes, and Dover (1945–81) v, 323 ff. Swain (1994) 308 is inclined to play down the sense of blending constitutions in favour of the notion of blending humours (by analogy with medicine) and hence of creating moderation, but Thucydides' phraseology here (ἐς τοὺς ὀλίγους καὶ τοὺς πολλούς) recalls that used by him for constitutional revolutions (4. 81. 2; 8. 53. 3, 89. 2).

after the overthrow of the oligarchy of the Thirty.[7] Another occasion in this same period may have been the discussion of Phormisius' proposal to limit Athenian citizenship to those possessing land (Lys. 34). More theoretically, the concept of the mixed constitution seems to have been used in appreciations of Solon's work. In Aristotle's discussion of Solon as a lawgiver (1273[b]35 ff.: see below) it is stated that for some his constitution was a good example of mixing (although others criticized it for introducing democracy in some form). M. H. Hansen (1989*b*) has shown how Solon was the great exemplar in fourth-century Athens, acting as a charter both for the current democracy and for a more moderate democracy, that is in effect a *politeia*, in accordance with the interpretation placed on his legislation. We also find in Isocrates' *Panathenaicus* (153) a reference to *politeia* as democracy mixed with aristocracy, which may well have come later than Aristotle's drafting of the *Politics* as lectures, but nevertheless illustrates a climate of thought.

However, a context equally or more important for the discussion of *politeia* must have been the Spartan constitution, especially as it lent itself easily to explanation as a mixture. This may well have begun in the heyday of Spartan power in the early fourth century. According to Aristotle, some people claimed that the mixed constitution was the best and for this reason praised that of Sparta, on the ground that it was composed of monarchy, oligarchy, and democracy, the kingship being monarchic, the gerousia being oligarchic, and the magistracy of the ephors being democratic (*Pol.* 1265[b]33 ff.). A somewhat different interpretation had been given by Plato in the *Laws* (691 E–692 A), who talked of *to metrion* created by god at Sparta, in particular the kingship which had become a blend (*summeiktos*) of essential ingredients and had a limit (*metron*).[8] Plato himself in this work advocated a form of government based on a limited citizen body of soldiers, with a central function being given to a representative council: he claimed this to be a mean between a monarchy and democracy, the ideal mean point for a constitution (756 E–757 A).[9]

A further possibility is that the concepts of the *politeia* and the *miktē* were mooted in discussions of the Boeotian federation and its constituent cities. In these only citizens with a property qualification could participate in the councils, and the whole system of representation of the sections of Boeotia in the central assembly was linked with the provision of military contingents, each *meros* providing one boeotarch, sixty councillors, about 1,000 hoplites, and 100 cavalry (*Hell. Oxy.* 16). In short, there is no reason

---

[7] Merkelbach and Youtie (1968); cf. Henrichs (1968); Andrewes (1970).

[8] He went on to argue (693 D ff.) that constitutions in general were a mixture of Persian monarchy and Athenian democracy.

[9] Cf. the letter to Dion (8, 355 D ff.) recommending a combination of freedom with a royal power which was subject to account. Plutarch's view (*Dion* 53) that Dion actually wished to create a constitution on the Laconian or Cretan model may be an unsafe deduction from this letter.

to doubt Aristotle when he takes the *politeia* as an established concept in fourth-century political thought and one which had come to be associated with mixture. Blending institutions and pursuing moderation would have been linked with military efficiency, as well as with the creation of harmony and avoidance of *stasis*, from the creation of the 5,000 onwards—or at least from the time of Thucydides' appreciation of it.

Aristotle's criticism of earlier theories

Aristotle's first reference to a mixed or median constitution in the *Politics* comes in a passage in book 2 (1265^b26 ff.), to which I have already briefly referred. He argues that the system described in Plato's *Laws* 'aims to be neither democracy nor oligarchy but a mean between them which they call *politeia*: for it is formed from the hoplites'. He comments that it is perhaps well designed as something containing more features common in existing cities than did other constitutions (sc. theoretical ones), but it is not the best constitution after that of the *Republic*. For the Spartan constitution might be preferable or one more aristocratic than that. He then puts forward the view of some devotees of Sparta, that the best constitution should be one mixed from all the constitutions. Here, then, Aristotle isolates two distinct, though similar, notions—that of a hoplite constitution, which is a halfway house between oligarchy and democracy, and that of a constitution which positively mixes features of pure constitutions (Sparta being a spectacular example, because it is a mixture of all three main pure types). He goes on to dismiss Plato's suggestion (*Laws* 756 E) that the best constitution is a mixture of democracy and tyranny (Plato had in fact talked of monarchy and democracy), arguing that these are either the worst constitutions or not constitutions at all. It is a better idea to mix more types. As for the constitution in the *Laws*, it is effectively oligarchic.

At the end of the book—after his review of some other theoretical constitutions and those of Sparta, Crete, and Carthage—Aristotle turns to the subject of writers about constitutions, some of whom had lived their lives as private citizens, while others had actually been lawgivers, like Lycurgus, assumed to have been the creator of the Spartan mixed constitution, and Solon (1273^b27 ff.). He has not mentioned Solon before and the account of him that follows has in part the function of comparing him with Lycurgus. 'Some people', says Aristotle, 'think that Solon was a good lawgiver, for he both overthrew an oligarchy that was too undiluted (*akraton*) and stopped the dēmos being slaves and established the ancestral democracy, by mixing the constitution well; for the Areopagus council was oligarchic, the fact that the magistrates were elective was aristocratic, and the lawcourts were popular (*dēmotikon*)' ($1273^b35–41$).[10]

---

[10] At 1294^b8 Aristotle says that elective offices are *thought* to be oligarchic, but goes on

Aristotle corrects this view of 'some people' by remarking that the Areopagus and elected magistracies seem to have existed beforehand and were
left alone by Solon, but that his innovation was the creation of democracy
through establishing universal citizen membership of the lawcourts. Thus
he accepts that Solon's was a mixed constitution but points out that two of
the three main elements he mixed had already been created. He goes on to
record the objection of 'some people' that the democratic lawcourt, selected
by lot, in due course led to greater concessions to the dēmos by Ephialtes,
Pericles, and other demagogues down to his own time of writing. This,
he argues, was not Solon's intention, but the result of later circumstances,
such as the surge in the confidence of the dēmos as a result of the naval
supremacy in the Persian Wars and its acceptance of inferior demagogues
who opposed the decent people. Solon only wanted to give the dēmos the
minimum possible power, that of electing magistrates and holding them to
account—otherwise it would be a slave and enemy of decent people—and
based the magistracies themselves on a property qualification (1274^a15–21,
cf. 1281^b28–34).

The treatment of Solon's constitution provides a contrast with that of
Lycurgus earlier in the book (1269^a29 ff.)—though this was more a critique of the present Spartan constitution than of Lycurgus himself. Earlier
thinkers had recommended Solon's constitution as an example of good
blending (it is very likely that this idea started about the time of the oligarchic revolution of 411); others had criticized it as being essentially unbal-
anced, since, the argument seems to have been, any concession to democracy
was to go for a ride on a tiger.[11] Aristotle himself endorses Solon's system,
especially as one which introduced a democratic element but not to excess.
However, whereas Lycurgus' constitution still existed in Aristotle's day,
Solon's, or so it is implied here, was beyond recall—for reasons the lawgiver
himself could not have foreseen. Aristotle does not specifically describe
Solon's constitution as a *politeia*, but it was both a mixed constitution and,
if not a hoplite democracy through a legally restricted franchise, nevertheless a political form in which the hoplites would have played a dominant
role (later at 1297^b12–15 he points out that what were called *politeiai* in
his day were called *dēmokratiai* in the archaic period). The notions of *politeia* and mixed constitution are perhaps not absolutely coextensive, but

immediately to argue that election without property qualification is part of an aristocratic
miktē. So, what is puzzling is not so much that election is aristocratic, since oligarchic and
aristocratic features overlap in Aristotle's thought, but that the Areopagus is at the same time
treated as oligarchic and not aristocratic. Aristotle perhaps does not regard the Areopagus here
as composed of former elected archons, but as a repository of the old nobility, which is in
his view based not only on excellence (*aretē*) but on long-standing wealth and in this respect
oligarchic (cf. 1294^a19–22).

[11] 1274^a3 ff.; cf. 1281^a14 ff. for Aristotle's treatment of the problems raised by the principle
of majority rule.

the overlap between them is still such as to justify our treating them as twin concepts.

Aristotle's theory of the politeia

The *politeia* as a particular form finds its place in the taxonomy of three correct and three deviant constitutions given in both *Nicomachean Ethics* and *Politics*, being the third of the correct trio, following kingship and aristocracy. 'Whenever the many manage their city in the common interest, it is called by the name common to all constitutions, constitution (*politeia*)'[12] (Aristotle puns here not only on the word *politeia*, but also on *koinon*). 'There is a good reason for this,' he goes on. 'For, while it is easy for one man or a few to be outstanding in virtue, it is immediately difficult for any greater number to be perfect in every virtue, but this is most likely with military virtue. And it is for this reason that in this constitution (*politeia*) the most powerful class is that which defends it and those who share in it (i.e. are citizens) are those who possess hoplite arms' (*Pol.* 1279ª37 ff.). In the *Nicomachean Ethics* (1160ª33–4, cf. ᵇ17) he remarks that *politeia* is the common term for what he would prefer to call timocratic, since it is a constitution based on a *timēma* (property qualification), which aims to have a mass citizenship. *Politeia* was already an established term for a hoplite constitution (cf. 1265ᵇ26 ff.), and Aristotle equates this in the *Politics* with an ideal type of constitution based on a mass of citizens which pursues the common interest.

The emphasis on *politeia* as an existing term for a hoplite democracy or one based on a property qualification is made more tantalizing in the more detailed review of constitutions in book 4. Aristotle there first considers the various forms of oligarchy and democracy. He then points out the existence of aristocracy and monarchy (the rule of one or a few virtuous men respectively), and adds that there also exists *politeia*, which passes unnoticed by those drawing up lists of constitutions, because it rarely occurs and so philosophers like Plato use only the four basic constitutions (1293ª35–ᵇ1). He next distinguishes aristocracy (when it is not the absolute, perfect type, in which a city is ruled by a few virtuous men) from oligarchy and *politeia* by the fact that the magistrates in an aristocracy are chosen according to wealth and excellence (*ploutindēn, aristindēn*).[13] Taking Carthage and Sparta as illustrations, he says that the former looks towards wealth, virtue, and the people, the latter only to virtue and the people and is a mixture of these

---

[12] To my knowledge there is no earlier surviving example of the use of the term *politeia* in this sense, but there is no reason to disbelieve Aristotle's claim that it was established terminology (see also 1297ᵇ24–5). One may see in the appropriation of the term a sign of the supreme confidence of the 4th-cent. proponents of this form of constitution. On the importance of the notion of *koinōnia* in the thought of the *Politics* at this point see Lintott (1992) 115–16.

[13] As in the picture of the pre-Solonian constitution in the *Athēnaiōn Politeia* (3. 1, 6) and in the portrayal of Carthage earlier in the *Politics* (1273ª23 ff.).

two things, democracy and virtue (1293^{b}10–17).[14] So Sparta is treated as an aristocracy on account of its cultivation of excellence, even if it is also by Aristotle's standards a *politeia*.

The definitions of *politeia* and aristocracy are then elaborated. *Politeia* is described as a mixture of oligarchy and democracy, of which those tending towards democracy are usually called *politeia* and those tending to oligarchy are called aristocracy. Aristocracy assigns superiority to the best citizens. These are usually the rich, because it is the rich who possess *paideia* and noble birth and also the possessions in pursuit of which the poor do wrong (1293^{b}33–40). When the discussion returns to *politeia*, it does so in a baffling sentence: 'In the majority of cities the form of *politeia* is called (*kaleitai*); for only the mixture aims at the rich and poor, wealth and freedom' (1294^{a}15–16). If *kaleitai* means simply 'has a name', 'exists', as W. L. Newman thought, then Aristotle is contradicting his previous remark on the rarity of the constitution (1293^{a}41). Ross has supplied *kakōs*, so that the sentence means 'the term *politeia* is wrongly used in most cities, because they are not genuine mixtures'.[15] Such a mixture must set its sights on the objects of both oligarchy and democracy. Given that there are three elements disputing equal rights in the city—freedom, wealth, and virtue—*politeia* is a mixture of the first two, that is, the wealthy and the poor, while a mixture of all three elements is aristocracy. It cannot be said that this last passage has clarified Aristotle's view of the *politeia*: indeed, he seems to have contradicted the definition he gave in his original taxonomy (1279^{a}37–^{b}6) and reinforced earlier in this current discussion (1293^{b}14–18), whereby virtue is an essential feature of a *politeia*. I do not think he has in fact abandoned his original position, but he has become distracted in his effort to present the *politeia* as a balance between classes, which takes no account of a traditional aristocracy based on wealth and virtue. Mixed constitutions and virtuous hoplite democracies had, in his view, coincided in fact. It was not so easy to reconcile their definitions theoretically. The essential features of his concept of the *politeia* are nevertheless clear: democracy, virtue, the pursuit of the common interest, and the reconciliation of the claims of the wealthy and the poor.

Mixture as the mean

Aristotle's next question is how such a mixed constitution can be created. In answering it, he intends also to illuminate the distinctive features of

---

[14] This of course neglects the fact that Spartan citizenship was in effect based on a property qualification, since the ability to contribute food to the common messes was necessary for membership of the *homoioi*.

[15] Aalders (1968) 65 n. 25 has argued that we should supply either *kalōs* or nothing, thus understanding the phrase as 'the term *politeia* is (properly) used'—a view which may be defended on the supposition that Aristotle is talking of the prevalence of the terminology, rather than the constitution itself. This goes far beyond Aristotle's references to 'some people' in 1265^{b}33 and 1273^{b}35, but note 1297^{b}24–5—'what we now call *politeiai*'.

oligarchy and democracy (1294ª30 ff.), for it is a matter of separating these and then putting together one from each side as in a tally. One technique is illustrated by jury service. Oligarchies fine the wealthy for non-attendance but do not pay the poor who serve, while democracies pay the poor but do not fine the wealthy absentees. Aristotle seems to suggest that what is common and a mean is a combination of both the positive features, namely both fines for the wealthy and pay for the poor (1294ª36–ᵇ1). This is made clearer in a later passage discussing how a lawgiver may preserve this constitution (1297ª38–40): a just mixture there involves pay for assembly and jury service and fines for failure by the rich to attend. A second technique is to take a mean point between the regulations of each pure constitution—for example, not no property qualification for assembly membership nor a large one but a moderate property qualification (1294ᵇ1–6). A third technique is to combine a constitutional provision from each constitution. So, in so far as it is (1) democratic to have magistrates selected by lot but oligarchic to have them elected, (2) democratic to have no property qualification but oligarchic to have one, it is characteristic of an aristocracy and a *politeia* to take one of the two features from each side, thus election without property qualification (1294ᵇ6–13). Aristotle does not suggest here allotment *with* a property qualification, perhaps because he knows well that this is a feature of the appointment of archons and *tamiai* in democratic Athens.[16]

It is a sign of a good mixture that you can call the same constitution oligarchy and democracy, and it is a feature of the mean that both the extremes are visible in it (1294ᵇ13 ff.). Many people, says Aristotle, treat the Spartan constitution as democratic because of its democratic elements— equality between rich and poor both in their education and, when adult, in their diet in the *syssitia* (the men's common eating-houses) and their dress, the election of the gerousia (council of elders), and popular participation in the election of the ephors. Others treat the constitution as oligarchic, because its magistrates are all elected, none chosen by lot, and, among many other things of this kind, capital penalties are decided by a few (1294ᵇ18–34). Aristotle is not abandoning his own view of Sparta as a *politeia*, but stressing that it fulfils the characteristics of a mixed constitution.

The mean (*to meson*) has inevitably formed part of the discussion of mixture but has played a subordinate role. It returns to the foreground when Aristotle asks what is the best constitution and way of life for most men and most cities (1295ª25 ff.), that is, with no Utopian assumptions but on the basis of normal human capacities and conditions of life. In this discussion aristocracy and *politeia* are assimilated, since the aristocracies which are not Utopian (outside the normal range of cities) are close to *politeiai* (1295ª31–4). As far as the way of life is concerned, Aristotle applies here the doctrine of the *Ethics* (*NE* 1100ᵇ8 ff.; 1153ᵇ9 ff.; cf. 1106ᵇ36 ff.),

---

[16] *Ath. Pol.* 8. 1; 47. 1; 55. 1.

that, in so far as the happy life is one lived without impediment according to excellence, and excellence is a mean, it follows that the best life is the attainment of the mean available to individuals. This principle, he believes, should then also apply to the virtues and vices of a city and constitution, for a constitution is the way of life of a city (1295^a35-^b1).

Given that what is moderate and a mean is best, this is also, in Aristotle's view, true of the possession of property. Men of moderate possessions are ready to obey reason, while those who are excessively handsome, strong, well-born, or wealthy on the one hand and those who are excessively poor, weak, or degraded do not. The rich and noble tend to become despotic and the poor slavish, something completely removed from friendship and political partnership (community—*koinōnia*) (1295^b3-24). It is a city of *mesoi* (that is, men of moderate wealth and attitudes), which is a city of equals, where men do not want others' riches nor possess riches that others covet. A large middle class makes a city stable, unlikely to fall victim to oligarchy, tyranny, or faction, and this is why large cities are less prone to faction and small cities more prone ($1295^b34-1296^a13$).

Democracies, he continues, are also more secure and lasting than oligarchies because of the *mesoi*, since there are more of them and they have a greater share of privileges in democracies than oligarchies. The best law-givers belong to the *mesoi*—Solon (this is clear from his poems), Lycurgus, Charondas, and pretty well the majority of the rest (1296^a13-21). Nevertheless, Aristotle points out, *stasis* (civil strife) between the dēmos and the wealthy is the rule in most cities, because the middle class is small and whichever side conquers its opponents takes supremacy in the constitution as its prize.[17] Hence the middle constitution (*mesē politeia*) occurs rarely and among few peoples. One man alone of those formerly in power, according to Aristotle, was persuaded to deliver this form of constitution (1296^a22-40). Here one immediately thinks of Theramenes, but I have tried to argue elsewhere that Solon is a more likely candidate, in so far as Theramenes is associated in partnership with Aristocrates by both Thucydides and the *Athēnaiōn Politieia*. Moreover, Aristotle is advising lawgivers here and he may not reckon Theramenes among this number, since the 5,000 were produced by a series of resolutions in the Athenian assembly, whose proposers may not have been known to Aristotle.[18]

Aristotle takes a final look at the *politeia* when answering the question what sort of constitutions suit what sort of people (1296^b13 ff.). In his view, the lawgiver should always direct his aim at the *mesoi* or try to win their support as a source of stability ($1296^b34-1297^a7$). More specifically, when, after reviewing oligarchic and democratic devices and how they should be

---

[17] So previously Thucydides in his digression on *stasis* (3. 82. 8).
[18] See Lintott (1992) 126 n. 25; Aalders (1968) 66 n. 26.

mixed,[19] he turns to the *politeia*, he states baldly that it must be constituted only from the hoplites (1297^b1 ff.): it is impossible to lay down simple rules for property qualifications, but one must be found which is as broadly based as possible to ensure that more people are members of the *politeia* (that is, politically qualified members of the citizen body) than not; the poor will accept this, if they are not subject to violent harassment or stripped of their property (1297^b1–12—interestingly, Aristotle assumes that the poor may be called up in war).[20] He also mentions constitutions, such as that of Malis, which are based on those who have formerly borne arms as well as the current hoplites but where the magistrates are chosen from those who currently do military service. And there is a look back to Greek political history in the archaic period, in which he argues that after the fall of the kings the earliest constitutions were based on warriors, at first on cavalry and then on hoplites; the later constitutions involved an expansion of the membership of the full citizen body: for this reason, 'what we now call *politeiai*, those in former times called *dēmokratiai*' (1297^b12–25).[21]

Problems in Aristotle's concept of the *politeia*

At the end Aristotle has returned to his starting-point, since the *politeia* was first described as a mean and a warrior democracy (2, 1265^b26ff.). If the hoplite basis is for Aristotle a fundamental feature of a *politeia* and if the hoplites are *mesoi*, men of middling property and moderate, a mean between rich and poor, the question arises whether the notion of mixing elements really is important for Aristotle. We may also wonder how far he has a clearly defined position for the *politeia* in his own thought.

In the taxonomy of constitutions in book 3 (1279^a37 ff.) it is a constitution where the many rule in the light of the common interest, which involves acting according to virtue (*aretē*). Indeed *aretē*, according to Aristotelian theory, is a necessary element in the operation of any correct constitution which produces *koinōnia* and the good life. However, this definition is overlapped by that of *aristokratia*. In the taxonomy of six constitutions aristocracy is the rule of a few best men in the light of what is best for the city (1279^a34–6) and it seems to retain this sense later in book 3 (1286^b3 ff.). But in book 4 Aristotle distinguishes between the ideal aristocracy, which is the rule of the best men and really deserves the name, and what are called aristocracies, which differ from oligarchies and the so-called *politeia* in choosing

---

[19] On the devices (*sophismata*) in 1297^a14 ff. see Saunders (1993).

[20] Aristotle points out that the poor will be reluctant to fight unless paid. This neatly distinguishes them from the full members of the citizen body, for whom fighting will be a duty (and a right) without their necessarily receiving any financial compensation. Aristotle probably visualizes the poor serving as light-armed troops or in the navy.

[21] If true, this would of course imply that the term *dēmokratia* was established at Athens by Solon's time.

their magistracies both according to wealth (*ploutindēn*) and according to worth (*aristindēn*). For even in cities that do not make the pursuit of virtue a universal concern, there are those of good repute and thought to be of good character. So a constitution such as the Carthaginian, which sets its sights on wealth, virtue, and the dēmos, is an aristocracy.

The confusion arises from the combination of two definitions of aristocracy (a strong form and a weak form, the latter being a constitution designed to allow some scope for the pursuit of virtue), with two definitions of *politeia*. Of the latter the first is a received and practical definition, which amounts to a hoplite democracy ($1279^{b}2$ ff., $1297^{b}1$ff.) and is related to a property qualification. Hence Aristotle would prefer to call it timocratic (*NE* $1160^{a}33-5$). The other is Aristotle's own classification of the *politeia* as a correct constitution, one that pursues the common interest of the citizens and is related to virtue. This last feature leads him at times to reclassify what we would take on his premises to be a *politeia* as an aristocracy. At one point he suggests that, where elections are according to excellence and wealth, this is an aristocracy ($1293^{b}10$ ff.). There is an obvious connection with the chapter in the *Athenaiōn Politeia* where the primitive constitution before Draco and Solon is said to have elected its magistrates according to excellence and wealth (*aristindēn kai ploutindēn*: *Ath. Pol.* 3. 1, 6).[22] Aristotle may well have had a historical progression in his mind, whereby Athens moved from monarchy in pre-Solonian times to aristocracy and then through Solon's legislation to what was a *politeia* or timocracy. However, the nature of elections cannot be the appropriate criterion for distinguishing between aristocracy and *politeia* as two correct constitutions, according to the taxonomy of $1279^{a}21-^{b}19$, but rather the size of the body of full citizens. Moreover, to classify the Carthaginian constitution, which had a broad electorate, as an aristocracy, even if this term had been used of it before, blurs a useful distinction made in his six types.

If we take the *politeia* as a timocracy with full membership of the citizen body dependent on wealth and the carrying of hoplite arms, is the concept of mixing essential to it or is this a piece of analytic over-elaboration of secondary features? If we are thinking of the *politeia* as combining aristocratic (or oligarchic) and democratic elements, then it is worth comparing passages where Aristotle handles the phenomenon in a different way. In the list of the various types of democracy and oligarchy ($1291^{b}30$ ff.) Aristotle says that the first type of democracy is that which gets its name especially in respect of equality (in Lintott 1992: 118–19 I discuss whether he is referring here to the term *isonomia*). This equality consists in a balance of power between the rich and the poor, but the dēmos is the decisive factor, because

---

[22] P. J. Rhodes' translation of *aristindēn* as 'based on good birth' seems automatic, if one simply thinks of the historical context, but does not reflect the connections of *Ath. Pol.* with Aristotelian philosophy.

it is more numerous. In so far as the second democracy in the descending scale towards extreme democracy involves property qualifications, it can be assumed that this first type does so as well. In fact it does not seem far removed from the (vaguely defined) first and most moderate type of oligarchy (1293ᵃ10 ff.), nor from the *politeia*.

Again, there is a section which follows shortly after the discussion of archaic hoplite democracies, where Aristotle has moved from the question of what constitution suits what type of people to considering what forms of the three main constitutional elements—deliberative body, magistracy, and judicial body—suit the varying types of constitution (1297ᵇ41 ff.). The deliberative body (*to bouleuomenon*) has charge over war, peace, and the making and breaking of alliances; over legislation, over death, banishment, and confiscations, and over elections and holding officials to account (*euthunai*). There are in theory three possible forms of assigning these powers of decision: either all of them must be given to all citizens (that is, a total democracy) or all to some citizens (that is, a total oligarchy) or some to all citizens and some to some citizens.

The democratic principle is that everyone should deliberate about everything, and Aristotle considers various methods by which this might be articulated, that is, in effect, ways in which all decisions are not taken by full assemblies as in the ultimate democracy (1298ᵃ9 ff.). The oligarchic principle is that some people should deliberate about everything: when a considerable number of people are elected from more moderate property qualifications and do not change what the law forbids them to change, this is what Aristotle calls *oligarchia politikē* (this seems to mean an oligarchy which is almost a *politeia*). When there is a small elected group that governs according to law, this is oligarchy; when the deliberative body elects itself and children replace fathers, this is extreme oligarchy. When all control matters like peace, war, and the holding of magistrates to account (*euthunai*), but elected (not allotted) magistrates control other matters, this is aristocracy. Finally, when some matters are in the hands of elected magistrates, others of allotted magistrates (whether this occurs through simple allotment or is based on a preselected list or they are both elected and allotted), these are characteristics either of an aristocratic *politeia* or of a *politeia* (1298ᵃ35–ᵇ10). It should be noted that this is only marginally distinguishable from the second type of moderate democratic organization, discussed earlier in this section of the text (1298ᵃ19 ff.). The *politeia* here has become part of a spectrum including various types of oligarchy and democracy, which changes its colour according to the levels of participation of the citizen body and the stability of the law—one in which the distinctions are often fine. The discussion is not about compounding a constitution out of elements, but making alterations to the fundamental constitutional organs, which redefine the ensemble they comprise.

Why is Aristotle interested in a mixed constitution?

The notion of a mixed constitution, that differs from other constitutions significantly because it is mixed, does not seem so important to Aristotle as that of one which is moderate, possessing a broad base of *mesoi*, and thus able to pursue virtue rather than being obsessed with wealth or poverty (cf. 1295^{b}3 ff.). Yet Aristotle does lay stress on mixing.[23] Why is this?

One major reason, I would suggest, is that the mixed constitution had already become an important part of Greek political thought. The constitution of the 5,000 established at Athens in 411, even if it did not last long itself, seems to have had a considerable impact on political theory. I have already looked at the unfortunately sparse evidence that we have for this in surviving sources. Aristotle knew of people who had praised Sparta as a mixed constitution (2, 1265^{b}33 ff.). It is likely that this occurred at the time of Sparta's great successes at the end of the fifth and the beginning of the fourth century. He also knew of people who had praised Solon's constitution for similar reasons (1273^{b}36 ff.). This seems naturally to be associated with the importance of Solon in the conceptual field of the Athenian orators and philosophers of the fourth century, some of whom treated Solon's legislation as a charter for the existing democracy, while others, notably Isocrates, regarded them as representative of a more moderate constitution.[24]

Another possible explanation is that he was giving advice to legislators about how to create and preserve a constitution. If you are seeking to create something moderate, then mixing is an obvious technique. Even if the essence of the *politeia* is to be a democracy of the warriors with full citizen rights dependent on a modest property qualification, the efficiency and stability of this constitution will depend on the nature of its particular institutions. These will inevitably have features in common with constitutions at other points on the spectrum. The lawgiver's task is to make sure that these are not drawn purely from the oligarchic or the democratic end of the spectrum.

However, a more theoretical solution is possible. Aristotle is in favour of a *politeia* for two main reasons: first, because it pursues common, not sectional, interests and is thus one of the correct constitutions; second, because it is more proof against *stasis* and subversion than pure constitutions. The techniques he describes of amalgamating and mediating elements of pure constitutions are not ends in themselves but serve to ensure that neither of the ideologies of the two pure constitutions with which he is most concerned, oligarchy and democracy, prevails. The *politeia* aims at both the rich and the poor, and (the priorities of these two classes) wealth and freedom (1294^{a}15–17). It therefore does not commit itself to either of the two partisan beliefs of the rich and the poor—that all men should be unequal in

---

[23] 1265^{b}33–4, 1273^{b}39; 1293^{b}17, 1294^{a}23, 1294^{a}35 ff.   [24] Isoc. 7 *Areop.* 22–7, 36–57.

every respect, that is, both in property and political rights (the oligarchic view), or that all men should be equal in every respect (the democratic view) (1280ᵃ23–5). By rejecting these two beliefs in favour of a compromise, it would promote harmony and avoid *stasis*.²⁵ It may be argued that the attraction of the mixed constitution for Aristotle was more that it blended ideologies than that it blended institutions. This was the spirit of Solon, who freed the people but did not allow the poor to be equal with the rich (fr. 5 West).

The later notion of the mixed constitution as something which gains strength from combining into a harmonious whole political elements which tend in opposite directions and so conflict is not essential to Aristotle's concept. The idea of checks and balances only occurs in passing in his later discussion of the democracy based on farmers (1318ᵇ6–1319ᵃ4)—the most moderate form of democracy related to equality, which in effect also corresponds to the Solonian constitution. At one point (1318ᵇ38–9), where he is arguing for the assignment of office to those of wealth and ability and of the right to judge in *euthunai* to the dēmos, he says that being interdependent and not being able to do everything one wants are expedient. From a more social point of view, although he regards the *mesoi* as in themselves an element that creates balance by reacting against extremes and preventing *stasis*, he envisages them doing so only when they are actually stronger than the rich or the poor or both. Where the moderate element is small, it is likely to be simply swamped in the conflicts of the oligarchs and democrats (1295ᵇ34–1296ᵃ21). Hence the principle of a hoplite democracy, where the moderate men are dominant, is more fundamental than the balancing of constitutional elements.

Mixture, then, has an important, but subordinate, role in both the *politeia* and aristocracy. A final problem is why Aristotle takes such pains to separate the *politeia* from democracy in his taxonomy, when it seems to differ little, if at all, from his most moderate form of democracy, based on farmers. Here he does seem to be influenced by those who had given democracy a bad name, and so cannot assign something called democracy a place among correct constitutions. The earlier existence of the term *politeia* suggests that he was not the first to have this difficulty. Whereas some oligarchic revolutionaries in 411 seem to have wanted something called democracy which was not too democratic (*Ath. Pol.* 29. 3), Aristotle wanted a not too democratic democracy, which was called something else.

²⁵ See by contrast 1295ᵇ18 ff., 1296ᵇ22 ff. For the two partisan beliefs see also 1301ᵃ25 ff.

10

The Polis in Italy: Ethnicity, Colonization, and Citizenship in the Western Mediterranean

KATHRYN LOMAS

THE fundamental problem faced by anyone who attempts to get to grips with the history of Greek colonization in the west, and particularly that of colonization in Italy, is that the Greeks of southern Italy and Sicily are typically treated as peripheral to both Greek and Roman history, occupying an uncomfortable no man's land between the two disciplines. The effect of this is potentially to create major problems of interpretation; to examine the history of these colonies on the same terms as the Greek poleis of the mainland runs the risk of oversimplification and of denying the impact on them of the non-Greeks with whom they were forced to interact. On the other hand, the fact that the power of the western Greeks was in decline by the time that Roman domination of Italy was securely established means that they are frequently treated as peripheral to the history of Italy, along with most of the Italic peoples of the south. Nor is the process helped by the Hellenocentrism of many of the literary sources, which tend to play down any non-Greek involvement in the history of the western poleis, and the pro-Roman agenda of most of these authors, many of whom were writing after the Roman conquest. Recently, however, growing interest in the phenomenon of colonization and the growing body of analyses from a post-colonial perspective[1] have raised the profile of this region and highlighted the need to look at these communities in the context of their colonial situation and the wider history of the area.

The concept of the democratic polis is one which is very much based on studies of the way the polis developed in mainland Greece, and in particular on examination of Athens—not surprisingly, given that there is far more detailed evidence available for the constitutional development and political life of Athens than there is for other cities in the Greek world. However, there are significant differences in the way in which the polis developed in the western Mediterranean. One of the most noticeable is the relative weakness of democratic government in the western colonies. There is no doubt that

---

[1] For discussion and further bibliography on post-imperialist and post-colonial approaches to the ancient world see Webster (1996) 1–18; Mattingley (1997) 7–20.

the main form of statehood in the colonial world was the polis but in most cases it was considerably less democratic in nature. The political history of the archaic and classical periods is dominated to a much greater extent by tyrannies, and by the interplay of oligarchic factions (Sartori 1953). On a more fundamental level, there are divergences in the ways in which the basic forms of definition and identity within the state were constructed. This paper will explore these differences in the Greek colonies of southern Italy and examine the implications for the ways in which these states developed.

The presence of a wide variety of non-Greek neighbours inevitably raises some profound questions. The colonies, particularly those founded in the earliest wave of colonization in the eighth and seventh centuries BC, were subject to external cultural influences of an immediacy not experienced by many other cities of the Aegean or of mainland Greece. The close physical proximity of the Italians of the interior—the Messapians of Adriatic Italy, the Osco-Sabellic groups which came to dominate the rest of southern Italy by the end of the fifth century, the Etruscans, and later, the Romans—was the cause both of intense stress and competition for land and resources, and of constant contact resulting in transference of both cultural influences and of population, factors which inevitably affected the ways in which these states developed.[2] Perhaps the most central of these questions is the impact of this proximity on forms of self-definition adopted by the Greeks. There are signs that basic rules for inclusion and exclusion within the city were defined rather differently from the practice of the poleis of the Greek mainland, and that the ways in which these were modified owed much to contact with the non-Greek populations of the region. Legal forms of acceptance and integration—in other words, citizenship—are central to this theme, but more importantly, it merges with the wider question of mobility of population and extent of integration across state and ethnic boundaries, and ultimately with the nature of ethnic identity in the west.

The sources

The literary sources for the western Greeks are distinctly fragmentary, either for reasons of survival or because the Italiote cities are not the principal subject of the work. Diodorus, for instance, includes a considerable amount of Italiote history as part of his wider history of the Greeks, but only in a very confused and fragmented form. There is also much less epigraphy of pre-hellenistic date, as compared with some of the cities of the Greek mainland. As a result, there are limitations on how accurately the colonial view of citizenship can be reconstructed, but there are, nevertheless, enough pieces of evidence to gain some insights into citizenship and

---

[2] Argued persuasively for south-east Italy by Herring (1991). See also Whitehouse and Wilkins (1989); Lomas (1993*b*).

who could hold it, and a wealth of archaeological material which can provide some indications of movement across ethnic and state boundaries.

The constraints imposed by the literary source material are not just due to the relatively small quantity. It is also problematic in nature. Unlike the sources for the polis in Greece, many of which are contemporary with its classical heyday, most of the extant authors who write about the history of southern Italy lived long after the events they describe. There is also an ongoing debate over the extent to which most, if not all, references to Italiote history in later authors can be traced to one historian—Timaeus of Tauromenion—who wrote in the fourth/third centuries BC.[3] Very little is known about his work, as it survives only in isolated fragments and quotations, but these snippets, together with known facts about his life, suggest that he left Sicily in fraught circumstances and spent most of his life as an exile in Athens, embittered against virtually everything and everyone outside his own circle of extreme oligarchs. He was, however, a firm supporter of Rome. His work was both widely admired among the Roman aristocracy and appears to have been profoundly anti-democratic in its sentiments and, more importantly, deeply hostile to the Greeks of Italy (Momigliano 1959: 529–56). While he was undoubtedly influential in the development of Roman historiography, this seems insufficient reason to dismiss all references to Italiote history as Timaean in origin and therefore irrevocably biased. Nevertheless, both the late and fragmentary nature of the evidence and our uncertain understanding of its provenance limit, to some extent, the possibilities for reconstructing the development of the polis in southern Italy prior to the Roman conquest.[4] Apart from the period of war and Roman conquest, from *c.*350 to 270 BC, and the Greek revolt during the Second Punic war, coverage is patchy, to say the least. These deficiencies can be made good to some extent by using epigraphic and archaeological evidence, but inevitably this necessitates a different approach and limits our ability to answer certain questions.

Settlement, colonization, and polis formation

The polis in the west, although recognizably the same entity as the polis in Greece, nevertheless developed in a distinctive manner.[5] The colonization process itself must have been partly responsible for this divergence: the western colonies were very diverse in their chronology, in place of origin, in demographic composition, and in their circumstances of foundation.

[3] Pearson (1987); Musti (1988) 78–94.

[4] The problems of the source tradition for Magna Graecia are discussed further by De Sensi Sestito (1987) 85–113; Musti (1988) 11–60; Maddoli (1982) 9–30; Lomas (1993*a*) 13–17; (1997).

[5] This divergence has been the focus of a number of recent works, notably C. J. Smith and Serrati (2000).

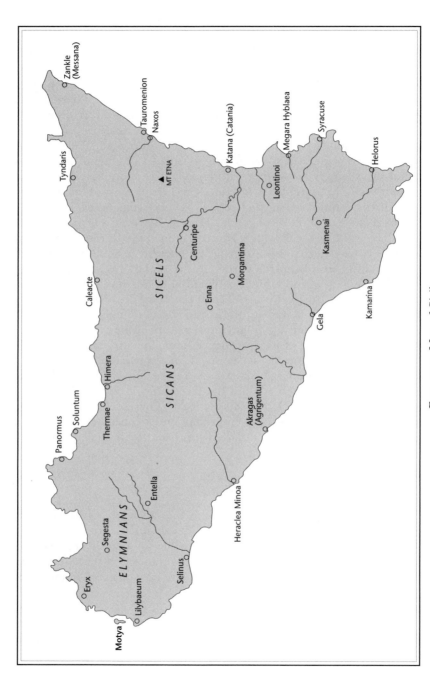

Fig. 10.1. Map of Sicily.

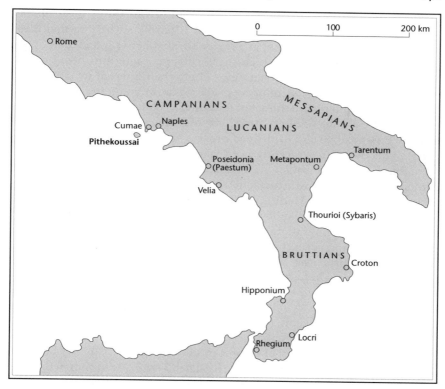

FIG. 10.2. Map of southern Italy.

Some—such as Thurii—were founded as late as the fifth century BC, but most were the product of a much earlier phase of settlement in the eighth and seventh centuries. The vast range of myths and historical traditions about founders and the processes of settlement and foundation is indicative of the similarly vast range of possible motivations for Greek migration and settlement. The migrants themselves also came from many different areas of Greece. Importantly, the earliest Greek contacts with Italy and Sicily and the first wave of colonization (*c.*750–*c.*650 BC on traditional dating) took place either before the development of the polis or very early in its history. The debate over whether the concept of the polis had developed before the foundation of the earliest colonies (Snodgrass 1994: 7–9), or whether its evolution coincided with the colonizations of the eighth century BC,[6] is still far from resolved; but whatever the case, it is clear that the polis was a very

---

[6] Argued by from a Greek perspective by Morris (1991), and from an Italian one by Herring (1991). De Polignac (1995) postulates colonization as an essential mechanism of consolidation of polis structures, while Malkin (1994*b*) goes further and suggests that the process of colonial foundation was one of the factors which triggered the development of the polis.

new, and still developing, form of statehood at the time the earliest colonies were founded. Against this background, it is hardly surprising that these cities show signs of developing in a regionally distinctive manner.

In addition, the ways in which these colonies came into being are an important factor in our understanding of both their internal structures and their relations with outside influences. There is an ongoing and lively debate between those who regard the act of founding a colony as a structured event sponsored by a polis or alternative form of state, and those who regard it as a much more open and ill-defined process of private enterprise (Graham 1964). This debate has recently been taken one stage further by the argument that what was at work in the eighth century BC was a process of general demographic mobility which resulted in groups of Greek settlers being disseminated all over the Mediterranean, rather than a structured colonizing movement, and that we should think in terms of Greek settlement—some of it within existing communities—rather than colonial foundation.[7] Clearly, if this model is accepted, then it has profound implications for our understanding of the processes of urban, and particularly polis, development in the Greek west and in particular for the study of citizenship and ethnic interaction. Despite the increasing recognition of the problems surrounding the terms 'colony' and 'foundation', they will be used in this paper—in the absence of a widely accepted alternative—to denote Greek settlement and the processes by which it took place, but they should not be understood as implying the 'statist' model of colonization criticized by Robin Osborne.

Despite these considerations, there has been a strong tradition in modern scholarship of studying the constitutional and administrative history of the western colonies primarily in relation to outside forces—in the first instance their Greek founders, and later, in the context of Roman domination.[8] One of the strengths of the recent re-evaluation of models of the colonization process has been to relocate the debate away from consideration of the founding states and towards study of the colonies in their own right.[9] Further to this, it is also important to take local context and contact with non-Greeks into consideration. While the connection with the wider Greek world was clearly an important factor in the history of the colonies, there are points of divergence which are more effectively studied in the context of the regional background. This paper does not aim to provide a definitive

---

[7] Purcell (1990); R. Osborne (1998). Osborne argues strongly for the replacement of the term 'colonization' with something less prescriptive, but in default of a widely accepted alternative, I shall continue to use it although with the qualifier that it should be taken to refer to a loose and ill-defined process, not an act of state. Despite his well-founded misgivings about the dangers of oversimplifying the colonization/settlement process and taking later sources too much at face value, there are still major problems to be solved about the ill-defined relationship between urbanization, polis formation, and ethnic mobility.

[8] Exemplified by the seminal work of Franco Sartori (1953), whose collection of data of the constitutional history of the west focused on tracing development back to these two elements.

[9] C. J. Smith and Serrati (2000); Shepherd (1995) 51–82.

answer to the question of why the democratic tradition was less strong in the western colonies, but will consider the evolution of some of the essential underpinnings of this tradition—the ways in which citizenship and ethnic identity were used to include or exclude sections of the population.

The best-documented, but possibly most extreme, example of the democratic polis, fifth-century Athens, had few status differentiations within the citizen body but eventually imposed strong barriers between citizens and non-citizens. The emphasis was on equal participation by citizens in the life of the community, through the various subdivisions of the citizen body.[10] By the middle of the fifth century, however, the boundaries between citizens and non-citizens had become rigid and strictly defined, and were based to a large degree on genealogy and ethnicity.[11] This was central to Pericles' citizenship law of 451–450 BC, which restricted citizenship to those with both an Athenian father and an Athenian mother.[12] This close link between citizenship and descent, accompanied by an increasing unwillingness to admit non-Athenians (and particularly non-Greeks) to citizenship, placed issues of ethnic definition at the centre of Athenian identity and of the democratic polis, and marginalized other inhabitants of the city. Despite the fact that Athens may be an extreme example of the link between ethnicity, kinship, and citizenship, other mainland and Aegean Greek states seem to have had similar restrictions on admission of non-Greeks to the citizen body. At this point we encounter the difficult question of Greek perceptions of non-Greeks, and the 'barbarian' problem. The division of the world, in Greek eyes, into Greeks and barbarians was widespread, but as Edith Hall (1989) has demonstrated, it did not crystallize and attach pejorative connotations to the term *barbaros* until the period after the Persian Wars, and when it did, it did so most sharply at Athens.

The western poleis in the archaic period

In contrast, these issues of inclusion and exclusion were defined very differently in parts of the western Mediterranean. The foundation process of the earliest settlements, those of the eighth and seventh centuries BC, must have been a contributory factor. Whether the concept of a polis had fully evolved or not at the time of the earliest colonizations, it was clearly at a very early stage of its history, and was subject to a number of modifying factors. It is highly likely that the population of these settlements was originally mixed even in respect of the Greek population, arising from the fact that the foundation of a colony was not necessarily a single decisive act. The multiplicity of foundation legends attached to some cities seem to have had at least some

[10] Hdt. 3. 80. 6; 5. 78; Dem. 15. 18; Thuc. 2. 37. 2; Arist. *Pol.* 1317ª40–ᵇ17; Gauthier (1981) 166–79. On changing concepts of the citizen in archaic Greece see Davies (1997) 32–3.
[11] Fowler (1998) discusses the role of genealogies in forging identities and legitimating claims to power and control.　　　　[12] *Ath. Pol.* 26. 4; Patterson (1981).

basis in historical reality. Some have traditions of foundation by a cohesive group, but many suggest a more complex process. The Spartan *Parthenioi* who colonized Tarentum[13] fall into the former category, for instance, but Zankle (Messana) was initially colonized by Chalcidians, then at a later date by Messenians, changing its name from Zankle to Messana in the process.[14] Naples provides another, spectacularly confusing, example, and there is still no absolute consensus about how to conflate the various literary traditions and archaeological evidence. The original foundation, known as Palaepolis, was a settlement of Euboeans from Cumae, at some date in the seventh century. Syracuse tried to develop interests in Campania (*c*.510–474) and added some settlers as part of this, and there was a further foundation made by Athens in the fifth century.[15] The date of this is unknown and has been variously placed at *c*.470, *c*.450, and 415/14 BC, although numismatic evidence points most strongly to *c*.450 BC and virtually rules out the obvious choice of 415/14 (Rutter 1979: 4–5, 44–6). The circumstance was a visit to Naples by an Athenian fleet, known only from Lycophron and a fragment of Timaeus.[16] Strabo also refers to a tradition that the first city founded at Naples was a Rhodian colony called Parthenope. Archaeologically, traces of an early settlement, including some very early Rhodian and Mycenaean material and more substantial seventh-century structures, have been found on Pizzofalcone, which has been tentatively identified with Parthenope/ Palaepolis, and also on the Vomero.[17] This led to a most peculiar pattern of urban development. As late as 327 BC, according to Livy (8. 22. 5, 26. 6), Palaepolis and Neapolis were two physically separate communities located side by side. They apparently formed a single political entity but the exact nature of the relationship is obscure. Naples was not unified as a single city until the end of the war with Rome in 325 BC, when the pro-Roman faction which gained power in the city transferred all the functions of government to Neapolis.

It is possible that this multiplicity of influences in the earliest colonies militated against the development of a strictly exclusive and descent-based view of citizenship. As in many archaic societies, the initial emphasis was on setting up boundaries between different groups within the state and on restricting access to power, resources, and influence by manipulating these, not on the boundaries between citizen and non-citizen. Many accounts of the early history of the colonies centre on the activities and eventual expul-

---

[13] Antiochus, *FGrH* 555 F 12; Strabo 6. 3. 2–3; Paus. 10. 10. 6; D.S. 8. 21; D.H. *Ant. Rom.* 19. 1. 2. On the foundation myths of Tarentum see Malkin (1994*a*) 115–42.

[14] Strabo 6. 1. 6, 2. 3; Thuc. 6. 4. 5.

[15] Strabo 5. 4. 7; 14. 2. 10; ps.-Scymnus 251; Livy 8. 22. 5; Vell. Pat. 1. 4. 1; Lutat. Daph. ap. Serv. *Georg.* 4. 563.

[16] Lycophr. *Alex.* 732–7; Timaeus, *FGrH* 566 F 98.

[17] Strabo 14. 2. 10; Frederiksen (1984) 86–7.

sion of closed hereditary élites such as the *gamoroi* at Syracuse.[18] However, the most striking feature of the western Mediterranean is the way in which definitions of citizenship interface with issues of ethnic identity. Mobility between Greek and non-Greek communities was a highly charged issue, and an extremely significant one as it raises important questions of cultural definition. In particular, it challenges the view that all Greeks predicated their view of the world on the dichotomy between Greek and non-Greek.

The problem with the vast majority of the evidence for mobility across ethnic boundaries is that it is often impossible to judge what the status of migrants was in their adopted communities. There is an ample (and growing) body of archaeological evidence from Italy for the cultural influence of Greeks on indigenous communities, and for the presence of non-Greeks in Greek poleis, but separating evidence for migration of groups or individuals from that for grants of citizenship is impossible in most cases. For the late fifth century onwards, however, there is literary and epigraphic evidence which throws more light on the phenomena of both ethnic mobility and citizenship.

From the very earliest stages of occupation at some colonies on the Italian mainland, there are indications that these settlements contained both Greek and indigenous inhabitants. At Metapontum, for instance, there is little spatial differentiation between Greek and indigenous burials in the early years of the city's history, and some evidence for the coexistence of Greek and indigenous ceramic production.[19] A similar pattern is found at nearby Policoro, site of Siris and later of Heracklea. The broad pattern is of replacement of this pattern of ethnic and cultural mixture by a more purely Greek occupation in the seventh century, but it does establish that there was little formal division of either territory or culture in the very early stages of colonial development (La Genière 1979). The earlier settlement of Pithekoussai, off the coast of Campania, has also yielded substantial quantities of Italic grave goods, as well as evidence of Phoenician residents, possibly pointing to an ethnically mixed population.[20] In addition to the archaeological material, there is epigraphic evidence in the form of an early Greek inscription, a curse scratched on to a proto-Corinthian aryballos from Cumae dating to *c.*675 BC, stating that it was the property of Tataia.[21] Although the origin of this female name is not certain and it has been variously claimed as Italic and Etruscan, it is definitely not Greek and is derived from one or other of the languages spoken in Italy (Morel 1983: 133–5).

---

[18] Hdt. 7. 155–6 and Rutter (this volume). Cf. Polyb. 12. 5. 4–11 on the 'Hundred Houses' at Locri.

[19] Adamesteanu and Vatin (1976) 114; Adamesteanu (1976) 643–51; Morel (1983) 133–5; J. C. Carter (1990) 405–41; (1993) 342–67.   [20] Morel (1983) 133–5; Wilson (2000).

[21] *IG* xiv. 865; Jeffery (1990) no. 240.

The problem with this archaeological evidence is that it is impossible
to establish from it what the social and legal status of the Italic inhabitants in the early colonies was. It may also have varied from city to city,
according to the nature and circumstance of each individual foundation
process and relations between the Greeks and their various neighbours. It
is likely that many colonies were founded by groups which were largely,
if not entirely, male and that many of the female inhabitants during the
early years of a colony's history would have been women of indigenous origin who had intermarried with the Greek settlers, with a greater or lesser
degree of willingness.[22] Italic burials within a Greek colony may therefore represent evidence of intermarriage or of voluntary coexistence of the
different ethnic groups in some instances, but in others they may represent enslavement of the local population. Some cities were undoubtedly
more aggressive and expansionist than others, and enslavement of existing
populations almost certainly happened in some instances, but by no means
all or even the majority. The contrasting cases of Syracuse and Megara
Hyblaea show how relations between Greeks and indigenous populations
could differ even within a relatively small geographical area. According
to Thucydides, Syracuse adopted an aggressive policy towards the Sicels
from the outset, driving some out of its territory and enslaving those who
remained.[23] In contrast, there is a strong tradition in the sources that neighbouring Megara was founded on land donated by the Sicels to a group of
landless Greeks, and accordingly maintained good relations with them.[24]
In Italy, the source tradition for the foundation of Tarentum purports to
preserve an oracle which invited the colonists to 'be a plague to the Iapy-
gians', putting it firmly in the Syracusan rather than the Megarian model
of inter-state relations.[25] Malkin argues that the consistent history of hostility between the Tarentines and their Iapygian neighbours, taken together
with this oracle, supports the notion that Tarentum was aggressive towards the Italic population from an early date. Despite this undoubted
evidence for aggression on the part of some colonies, Italic burials cannot simply be explained away as representing a slave population. Most of
these tombs are by no means significantly wealthy, but possession of an
archaeologically visible burial, with a number of grave goods, argues that

[22] The complexities of the issue are illustrated by Polybius, who cites two contrasting traditions for the foundation of Locri. One of these ascribes the foundation to exactly this type of
group of fugitive slaves, bandits, etc. (12. 8. 2), while the other—unusually—places a group of
female dedicants at the centre of the foundation story (12. 5. 4–11) and asserts that because of
this membership of the Locrian élite was passed through the female line.
[23] Thuc. 6. 3. 1–3; Di Vita (1956). The problems of interpretation are discussed by Morel
(1983) 124–35.
[24] Thuc. 6. 4. 1–2. For discussion of Greek–native interactions in the hinterland of Megara
see Vallet and Voza (1984) 56–8; De Angelis (1994) 97–9.
[25] Antiochus, *FGrH* 555 F 13, quoted by Strabo 6. 3. 4; Malkin (1994a) 117–27.

these were people with at least a modicum of social status and economic means.[26]

Classical and hellenistic evidence

From the late fifth century onwards, however, the evidence for Italians absorbed into Greek communities is stronger, and also more informative, since it gives some indication of status. The fullest evidence relates to Naples. Unlike the inland Italic states of Campania and the neighbouring Greek city of Cumae, it was not overrun by the Oscan incursions of the late fifth century. Instead, it absorbed some of the Oscans into the city and apparently offered them citizenship and access to the political life of the city. Strabo says (5. 4. 7) that lists of *dēmarchoi*, the chief magistrates of Naples, which were still extant in his own day, were originally composed only of Greeks, but included the names of both Oscans and Greeks from the early fourth century onwards. His explanation is that this admission of non-Greeks to citizenship and to the magistracies of the city was forced on Naples after the sack of Cumae, and that it was the price paid by Naples to avoid the same fate. This interpretation, however, appears to be more a part of his constructed scheme of Greek versus barbarian than a reflection of historical reality. The same notion of the Greeks being led astray as a result of pressure from the Oscan Campanians also occurs in Livy's account of Naples' war with Rome in 327–325 BC (8. 22. 5–26. 7), but is clearly not the whole story. The narrative is explicitly structured around a combination of ethnic and political polarities in which pro-Roman factions are equated with Greek and oligarchic elements, while the people who opposed Rome are characterized both as democrats and as ethnically Oscan. In fact, it is clear from Livy's own narrative that the dissent is not between ethnic groups but between political factions. The group of Roman supporters who seize power and negotiate peace in 326/5 cut across the ethnic divide and are led by Charilaus, a Greek, and the Oscan Nymphius, probably a Hellenized form of Nympsius (Livy 8. 25. 9). The only known political programme of this group seems to be to establish the dominance of Neapolis over Palaepolis. Significantly, Dionysius of Halicarnassus, who may well have been using a Greek, possibly even Neapolitan, source, omits ethnicity as a factor in these events.[27] The implication of both sources is that by the late fourth century BC, a significant proportion of Oscans had obtained Neapolitan citi-

---

[26] Morris (1987) makes a persuasive case for regarding variations in burials and funerary practice as a reflection of social status and cultural norms. He stresses that there were significant variations between different Greek states and different chronological periods (and even more so between entirely different cultures) in the number and status of the people who were able to secure a properly marked burial.

[27] D.H. *Ant. Rom.* 15. 5–9. 2, discussed by Frederiksen (1984) 208–12.

zenship, had held political office, and had become part of the city's social
and political élite.

The tension between Greek tendencies to view the history of the western colonies as a polarization between Greeks and non-Greeks and the
evidence of epigraphy and archaeology is also evident in other cases. At
Cumae—conquered by the Oscan invaders in 421 BC—there are signs of
extensive Oscanization. Oscan replaces Greek as the best-attested language
in inscriptions, Oscan names are vastly more frequent than Greek ones,
and the cults, civic government, and material culture of the city all reflect
those of the Italian invaders. Much of the Greek population migrated to
Naples, where they apparently formed a distinct group within the city as
late as 327 BC.[28] Elsewhere the picture is more complicated. Aristoxenus[29]
comments that at Paestum the Greek population was enslaved by the Lucanians and Greek culture, rites, and language were suppressed on all except
one day each year. The archaeological evidence, in contrast, indicates that
many aspects of Greek culture persisted until well into the third century,
and there is certainly no sign of destruction in the archaeological record, as
would be expected if the city had been subjected to violence. The Oscan
language is epigraphically attested, as at Cumae, but there are also Greek
inscriptions and Greek names continue to occur. Production of Greek cultural artefacts—red-figure pottery in particular—also continues, and Greek
cults and burial practices coexisted with those of the Lucanians throughout
the fourth century (Pedley 1990: 97–124). The Lucanians certainly had an
impact on Paestum, but not to the extent that Aristoxenus would have us
believe.

The Greek Table of Heraclea,[30] dating to the fourth century BC, also
provides evidence for mixed ethnicity and high social status. This is a long
and highly complex Greek inscription describing the divisions and usage of
the sacred territories of the sanctuaries of Dionysus and Athena. It includes
several names of non-Greek origin in the lists of magistrates which forms
part of the rubric at the beginning of each of the two tables. Table I lists
among the *horistai* empowered to undertake the division of the territories
of the sanctuary of Dionysus the name Dazimos Pyrrhou (Dazimos, son of
Pyrrhos). Table II, concerning the division of the territory of the sanctuary
of Athena, likewise includes Dazimos Pyrrhou among the list of *horistai* but
also includes another Dazimos as ephor. The significant thing about these
names is their non-Greek origin and the status of their owners. Dazimos is
well authenticated as a Messapic name,[31] and thus the individuals named

[28] D.H. *Ant. Rom.* 15. 6. 4. A phratry of the Kumaioi is attested in an inscription of the 2nd
cent. AD (*IG* xiv. 721; Miranda 1990). The complexity of the issue is indicated by Strabo's
description of Cumae (5. 4. 7) as a city where Hellenism was sufficiently marked to attract
philhellenic Roman notables of his own day.   [29] Quoted in Athen. 14. 632 A–B.
[30] *IG* xiv. 645; Uguzzoni and Ghinatti (1968).   [31] Parlangeli (1960); Santoro (1982).

in the Table of Heraclea, or their ancestors, are likely to have been of non-Greek origin. Both examples are Hellenized in form, but the name of the father, Pyrrhos, although ostensibly more Greek, is also ambiguous. It has strong connections with western Greece and Epirus, thus originating in a region closely related to the Illyrian-speaking area of the Dalmatian coast, ultimately the origin of the Messapic language of south-east Italy. While it is dangerous to argue for too immediate a connection between onomastics and ethnicity, given that names may have persisted in migrating families for generations after the event, it does give some insight into the key question of migration and citizenship. Both Dazimoi were demonstrably citizens with full political rights, because in this case they occupy elected magistracies at Heraclea. The ephorate is recognized as the chief executive magistracy of Heraclea, and Dazimos is named as the eponymous magistrate in whose name the legislation is enacted.[32] The role of the *horistai* is less clear-cut, but they were clearly in large measure responsible for enacting the survey and distribution authorized in the tables. The texts themselves, and comparison with *horistai* known from elsewhere in the Greek world, suggest that they were panels of elected magistrates (three in each case) nominated to oversee the legality of the occupation of the lands concerned, rather than being directly in charge of the survey and division.[33] Whatever the details, the basic point behind this is that individuals who were of sufficiently non-Greek origin to maintain Messapic names were sufficiently embedded in the fabric of the state of Heraclea to be elected to senior positions in the state, and had thus made an important transition across both an ethnic and a legal boundary.

There is also considerable onomastic evidence of the intertwining of Greek and Italic populations both here and elsewhere in Magna Graecia. Inscriptions from the Aegean which record the names of Greeks from Italy indicate that mixed Graeco-Italic names were not uncommon. The second-century Tarentines Demetrios Dazou (Demetrios, son of Dazos) and Parmenion Dazimou (Parmenion, son of Dazimos)[34] both have Messapic patronymics. At Oropus *c*.80 BC a victory list features a Cumaean ephebe, Attinius Herakleidou (Attinius, son of Herakleides), and at Velia there are a number of families which mix Greek and Oscan elements, notably Tertia Pakkia, daughter of Dionysius.[35] At Naples the greater depth of epigraphic evidence permits some detailed studies of individual families. A series of family mausolea—mostly rock-cut chamber tombs which show influences from the hellenistic east in their construction and decoration, and date to the fourth–second centuries BC (although one example was still in use in the Augustan period)—contain Greek funerary texts which show a

---

[32] *IG* xiv. 645; *SEG* xxx. 1162–70; Sartori (1953) 84–99; Uguzzoni and Ghinatti (1968) 125–30, 153–7. [33] On this problem see Uguzzoni and Ghinatti (1968) 155.
[34] Hatzfeld (1912) nos. 33, 65. [35] *IG* vii. 417; xiv. 660.

mixture of Greek and Oscan names, alternating between generations (Leiwo 1995: 61–5). The pattern here is therefore similar to that found at Heraclea, although on a larger scale and with both greater diversity and chronological depth of evidence. All of these communities clearly admitted non-Greek citizens, some of whom rose to hold high political office, and the Greek and non-Greek populations coexisted, and even intermarried with little obvious signs of tension.

Ethnicity and citizenship in Magna Graecia

The central question that this evidence raises is whether definitions of citizenship were significantly different in the western colonies, as compared with the cities of mainland and Aegean Greece. If this is the case, it also raises the problem of where the impetus for this difference comes from, how it modifies concepts of cultural and ethnic identity, and how it modifies polis identity in the west.

One view of Greek citizenship is that as the primacy of the polis as a form of political organization declines in the hellenistic period, citizenship becomes less exclusive. Instances of *isopoliteia*—exchange of citizenship and grants of citizenship by more than one city to an individual—become more common, and the active duties of the citizen in respect of the state decrease. The ease of changing or acquiring citizenship increases as the active participation of the citizen in the political life of the polis declines (Gauthier 1981: 166–79). This approach would suggest that the opening up of citizenship to outsiders in the western colonies is simply a chronological development, reflecting a wider trend in the hellenistic world as a whole. However, the issue is by no means clear-cut, or explicable simply as a result of chronological change and evolution. There is much debate about whether a comparatively relaxed approach to citizenship in the hellenistic world was universal. In Alexandria citizenship was defined so as to exclude one particular ethnic group, the Jews; and the status of new citizens, and in particular of non-Greeks, in the Graeco-Macedonian colonies of the hellenistic east is still debated.[36] In the western colonies the ability of Greeks to move between poleis and to change their status is demonstrable from a much earlier date, and is not at all a purely hellenistic phenomenon. There is a telling comment relating to 415 BC[37] in which the cities of Greek Sicily are described as having mixed populations, with ease of migration and change of citizenship. This is selected by Alcibiades (and therefore also by the author, Thucydides) as evidence of the potential weakness and instability of the western poleis. His argument is that a mobile population without a strong connection to ancestral lands is lacking in military strength, social cohesion, and a strong

---

[36] Briant (1982); Sherwin-White (1987).

[37] Thuc. 6. 17. 2. Herodotus, however, comments rather more approvingly on the nomadic life of the Scythians (4. 46).

state identity. There are also hints at the topos of barbarization, and an implied difference between Aegean Greece and the western colonies. This occurs, admittedly, in a highly partial context—Alcibiades' speech advocating the expedition against Syracuse. The central feature, however, is that demographic mobility and permeability of legal boundaries were presented by Thucydides as being a different (and peculiar) feature of the western poleis. Centuries later, the same phenomenon is commented on by Cicero in the *Pro Archia* (7, 10). Archias was granted citizenship by many of the Greek cities of southern Italy, and in explanation of this Cicero comments that the Greek cities of Italy were notably liberal with such grants, also adding a pejorative spin by the suggestion that they were not particular about the character of people who were granted citizenship. Although there is evidence of mobility across legal and ethnic boundaries in both Italy and Sicily, the processes underlying this appear to be very different. In Sicily the ease of demographic movement and of changing citizenship which was noted by Thucydides was the product of specific political circumstances. There was a long tradition of large-scale migration and manipulation of the citizen body, usually generated by tyrants. In the 480s BC Gelon destroyed Kamarina and absorbed the population into Syracuse; at Megara Hyblaea he was more selective, enslaving the poorer citizens and granting Syracusan citizenship to the élite. According to Diodorus, he also enfranchised up to 10,000 mercenaries.[38] Nor was the democratic regime of 466–405 at Syracuse averse to demographic manœuvring to consolidate territorial interests and settle old scores.[39] The big upheavals, however, occur under Dionysius I and his successors.[40] At Syracuse in 405–404 BC there were major redistributions of land to favour Dionysius' supporters and reward his mercenaries, and also major changes to the composition of the citizen body (D.S. 14. 7. 1–5). Land was allotted not just to existing citizens, but also non-Syracusan inhabitants (*xenoi*) and freed slaves, whom he enfranchised and termed *neopolitai*. In 403 BC Enna, Naxos, Katana, and Leontinoi all fell under the control of Dionysios. Katane and Naxos were acquired after he suborned members of their élites but suffered widespread enslavement or displacement of their populations; Leontinoi surrendered and the population was ordered to move to Syracuse, where it was absorbed into the citizen body (D.S. 14. 14. 4–15. 4). Further major realignments occurred after the Carthaginian defeat of 396 BC (D.S. 14. 77. 5–78. 6). Leontinoi was resettled with discharged mercenaries and population displaced from Locri and Medma in southern Italy was settled at Messana. A group of exiles from the Peloponnese were also placed there but later moved to Tyndaris,

---

[38] Hdt. 7. 156; D.S. 11. 72. 3; note also Rutter (this volume).
[39] D.S. 11. 72. 3–73. 3; 11. 76. 4–6.
[40] McKechnie (1989) 34–43; Krasilnikoff (1995) 174–82.

after protest from Sparta. Further demographic movement was occasioned by the activities of Dionysius' successors in the fourth century.

This process—the use of itinerant populations to subvert and undermine the status of the polis—is common to many tyrants and hellenistic monarchs throughout the Greek world (McKechnie 1989: 34–43), despite the fact that Thucydides indicates that it was a particular issue in Sicily. It also primarily concerns movement of groups of Greeks from one polis to another, and thus reflects the ability of cities to absorb new population of the same ethnic group into citizenship. There was a certain amount of absorption of non-Greeks—there were Campanians among Dionysius' mercenaries, for instance—but Greeks accounted for most of the demographic movement which took place.[41] In Italy, however, there is much stronger evidence for migration across ethnic as well as legal boundaries. The mechanisms underlying the process are also strikingly different. Apart from the disruption caused in Calabria by the imperial ambitions of Syracuse and its tyrants in the fourth century, the causes do not lie in direct political and military action. The impetus seems to lie in the greater diversity of ethnic groups with which the Greeks had to interact, and the influence of a different concept of citizenship among the peoples of Italy on that of the Greeks.

One of the distinguishing characteristics of ethnic interaction in ancient Italy is the extent to which both ethnic and legal boundaries were permeable. Movement between communities of different ethnic background and absorption into the citizen body of a different state were not by any means a rare or infrequent occurrence, either for groups or for individuals. This could happen for a whole spectrum of reasons—war, political exile, economic motivation, or kinship connections—but there seems to have been little barrier to adopting the citizenship of a different, or even ethnically dissimilar, state. The definition of citizenship as a transferable (and revocable) legal status became a central feature of Roman expansion and the ultimate integration of Roman Italy. In archaic Italy it was less systematized, but examples of groups and individuals who had crossed ethnic barriers and state boundaries are well documented in central and southern Italy.

The famous example is, of course, Demaratus of Corinth, who fled the tyranny of Cypselos and migrated to Tarquinii in Etruria,[42] marrying into the local population and producing a son, Tarquinius, who himself mi-

---

[41] The extent of exchange of population between Greek and indigenous Sicilian communities is difficult to judge. It is entirely possible that mobility between Greek and Elymnian, or Greek and Sicel, communities did take place, but there is no conclusive literary evidence. Paradoxically, the question is obscured further by the fact that the archaeological evidence from cities such as Segesta and Morgantina is so heavily Hellenized that it is almost impossible to distinguish between Greek and non-Greek populations.

[42] Livy 1. 34; D.H. *Ant. Rom.* 3. 46–7; Val. Max. 3. 4. 2; Plut. *Rom.* 16. 8; Pliny *NH* 35. 152; Ampolo (1976–7).

grated to Rome and eventually became king.[43] The tradition concerning an even earlier episode in the history of Rome ascribes a central role in the new state to a group of migrant Sabines led by Attus Clausus. Even if these examples are to be dismissed as insufficiently historical,[44] there are numerous attestations of later migrations and epigraphic evidence for individual mobility. An inscription from a rich burial of the late seventh century at Tarquinii names *Rutile Hipukrates* (Rutilus Hippokrates), whose name is composed of Latin and Greek elements, and whose burial indicates a high socio-economic status (*TLE²* 49). At Caere there is evidence of more Latin migrants, *Ate Peticina* (Attus Peticius), *Tita Vendia*, and *Kalatur Phapena* (Kalator Fabius) (*TLE²* 65, 865), and from Veii there is *Tite Latine* (Titus Latinius). Slightly later, dating from the sixth century, there is a further example from Caere—*Ati Cventinasa* (Attius, son of Quintus)—who also appears to be of Latin origin (*TLE²* 50). Apart from their obvious interest in the context of citizenship, these individuals, and the evidence for mobility which they represent, have recently been interpreted as a potential answer to the vexed question of the transmission of Etruscan culture throughout archaic Latium and Etruria, and thus central to the development of the history of the region.[45] Nor was this primarily an archaic phenomenon which declined and died out. Livy (8. 19. 4–20. 8) cites examples of individuals such as Vitruvius Vaccus, a citizen of Fundi but resident at Privernum (and commander of the city's army) during the war with Rome in 330/329 BC. Vaccus is also said by Livy to have been influential in Rome, where he owned a house, and by inference had kinship ties with the Roman élite. Again, we are faced with an example of an individual of high status who migrated between states on the strength of social connections and kinship ties with the élites of neighbouring cities.

The whole issue of mobility across boundaries of citizenship and ethnicity was, therefore, a more open question in the western colonies than it was in some other areas of the Greek world, indicating a rather different approach both to citizenship and to non-Greeks. There are, however, major differences in this respect between the Italian and Sicilian colonies, a factor which is in itself an important indicator of the ways in which colonial poleis could develop along different lines even within a relatively small area of the western Mediterranean.[46] In Sicily, as noted above, a similar pattern of demographic mobility and ethnic diversity was in fact the product of

---

[43] Cic. *Rep.* 2. 34; *Pol.* 6. 11a. 7.

[44] The reliability of the source tradition is discussed at length in Cornell (1995) 122–40.

[45] Ampolo (1976–7) 333–45; Cornell (1995) 163–5; (1997) 9–19.

[46] Cf. R. Osborne (1998) 262. The argument that processes of Greek settlement must have been similar in Italy and Sicily must surely be correct for the 8th cent. BC, but the Greek states of the two regions develop along very different lines thereafter. See C. J. Smith and Serrati (2000).

very specific political circumstances. The vast majority of known examples concern action by tyrants, or aggressive behaviour on the part of Syracuse.

In Italy the motivation for mobility and ethnic diversity seems to have been very different. The greater proximity of several distinct ethnic groups—Etruscans, Messapians, Campanians, Lucanians, and Bruttians—which demonstrably had very different ideas about citizenship created a fluid situation, encouraging migration not just between different states but also across ethnic boundaries. The archaeological evidence for intermingling of Greek and non-Greek population within the colonies, particularly in the early years of their history, is becoming increasingly strong, but little is known about the status of the non-Greek inhabitants or their role in the life of the polis until the fifth century BC. If Osborne's conjecture that the early process of Greek settlement was not necessarily linked to that of state formation (or more specifically polis formation) is correct, then the need to examine citizenship and ideas about ethnicity in the context of the Italian population becomes even more pressing. Recent research is starting to point very firmly towards the need to consider colonies in the context of their surrounding environment, as well as (or possibly even more than) in relation to developments in mainland Greece and the Aegean. Archaeologists have long been aware of the need to look at colonies and the non-Greek hinterland as part of a cultural *koinē* in which both cultures participate and interact.[47] This should now perhaps be extended beyond the field of material culture and into that of urban history more generally. Incontrovertible material evidence establishes that there was an ongoing process of interaction between Greeks and Italians from the time of the earliest Greek settlement, with movement of population as well as artefacts across legal and ethnic boundaries. Other, more circumstantial, evidence suggests that in the fifth and fourth centuries some of this non-Greek population was absorbed into the citizen body of the Greek cities in a manner which has closer parallels from Latium, Etruria, and Campania than from the poleis of Greece itself.

If this was the case, it clearly has important implications for notions of Hellenism and identity in the west, and in particular in Italy. All the signs are that the Greeks of Italy, while continuing to define themselves as Greek and maintain connections with the rest of the Greek world, evolved a definition of citizenship and an approach to ethnic difference which owes much to the inclusive ethos of their Italian neighbours. It is a point which usefully underlines in yet another field of civic life that Greek culture was not some homogeneous monolith but developed important regional variations. This may well not be a specifically western phenomenon, but may be equally true of other areas on the margins of the Greek world. These are clearly beyond the scope of this paper, but the same issues of distance from mainland Greece

---

[47] Herring (1991); Lomas (1993*b*). For an archaeological study of regional identities in Sicily see Shepherd (1995).

and extensive contact with non-Greek peoples also apply to the Greek cities of Asia Minor and to those of the Black Sea. It would be surprising if contact with Lycians, Carians, Cimmerians, and a myriad of other ethnic groups had not had an impact on constructions of ethnicity and Greek identity in these regions.[48] It is clear that the norms of mainland Greece and the Aegean can no longer be simply extrapolated to the fringes of the Greek world. In these regions identity was defined as much by interaction with non-Greek neighbours as with the Greeks of the homeland.

[48] e.g. at Kedrai, which was described by Xenophon (*Hell.* 2. 1. 16) as having a mixed population, to cite only one example. Clearly a full discussion of this topic is well beyond the scope of this paper. It should also be noted, however, that proximity to a different ethnic group does not always guarantee an erosion of difference. It appears to have had this effect in some areas of civic life in Italy, but in other circumstances proximity to an external group can have the opposite effect of hardening boundaries and sharpening a sense of ethnic difference.

COMMUNITIES
BEYOND THE POLIS

ETHNĒ

11

Politics without the Polis: Cities and the Achaean Ethnos, *c*.800–500 BC

CATHERINE MORGAN

CITIES have long been perceived as ideal contexts for the development and conduct of complex political relations. Perhaps inevitably, therefore, the study of early Greek urban development has become closely entwined with the origins of the polis.[1] Some have seen a direct or even causal connection, although with certain (chiefly colonial) exceptions, this presents chronological difficulties—and from an archaic and classical perspective, the development of big sites in poleis continued largely independent of whether they served the political role of polis towns at any given time.[2] None the less, the basic notion of community of place (Arist. *Pol.* 1326^{b}25–1327^{a}10) underlies much of our understanding of the relationship between residence and the political needs and solutions of emerging poleis. This is indeed an important area of study, but it should not be confined to the polis as traditionally understood. The issues are equally relevant to the study of ethnē.[3] That archaeological discoveries over the last decade or so preclude simple distinctions between big sites in poleis and ethnē during the Early Iron Age and archaic period (from the eleventh to the sixth century BC) should surprise only those rooted in a classical historical perspective. The existence of prehistoric sites which fit abstract models of urbanism has long been noted,[4] along with the need to assess the Greek

I thank Roger Brock and Stephen Hodkinson for their patience and encouragement, and Zosia Archibald, Emmanuele Curti, Chris Hayward, and Annette Rathje and her students at the Institute of Archaeology, University of Copenhagen, for valuable comment on an earlier version of the text. I gratefully acknowledge the financial support of the British Academy Research Leave Scheme during the preliminary stages of my research.

References to *BCH* without author or title are to the archaeological reports published annually in *Bulletin de correspondance hellénique.*

[1] C. Lloyd (1983); Wheatley (1972). For a critical view see Humphreys (1978); Snodgrass (1980) 28–33. Equally, Morris's (1991) separation of the social phenomenon of polis evolution from the monumental development of urban centres has unexplored implications for ethnē.

[2] Morris (1991); Morgan and Coulton (1997).

[3] The distinction between poleis and ethnē, and especially definition of the latter during our period, are complex issues which, while of considerable importance to the present argument, demand fuller discussion than this paper allows. The reader is therefore referred to the comments of the editors in their introductory chapter and especially to the framework of different planes of organization outlined by Archibald (this volume), which closely reflects my own views. The problem will be treated more fully in my book *Ethnē: Early Greek States beyond the Polis* (in preparation).

[4] For a review see Effenterre (1990).

evidence within the broadest comparative perspective (as exemplified by Zosia Archibald's comparison of Iron Age Thracian, Macedonian, and Thessalian sites in this volume). A rounded understanding of any region must balance comparative and particularist observations, and it is with this in mind that I shall consider the implications of big site development in ethnē from both a local (specifically Achaean) and a broader Greek stand-point.

Fɪɢ. 11.1. Map of Greece and Asia Minor: principal sites mentioned in the text.

Early Iron Age and archaic evidence from big sites in ethnē takes many forms. Most commonly, we have as yet slight traces from what were later to become major cities, as continued excavation in modern centres reaches deep layers. Larissa, for example, has produced geometric graves and also evidence of construction on the eastern slopes of the acropolis, the 'Frourio' hill (Tziaphalias 1994: 154–6), and at Patras, finds around the acropolis are reportedly early, and sixth-century pottery has been found in deep sections in Psila Alonia square (see Figure 11.1 for the location of these sites).[5] These glimpses highlight the chronological depth of activity, but are rarely sufficient for detailed reconstruction. Elsewhere, fuller pictures emerge from survey (e.g. in Boeotia, tracing the development of Askra, Haliartos, or Thespiae)[6] or from the combined results of (chiefly rescue) excavations over many decades. These reveal striking comparisons across ostensible geographical and political divides; the spatial organization of Thessalian Pherai,[7] for example, is similar to that of Argos[8] or Megara (Travlos 1988: 258–76). Alternatively, one or two major excavations may focus understanding of otherwise scattered traces. This is especially true in Macedonia, where urban excavation has proceeded apace in recent years. Toumba (probably ancient Kissos, Gareskos, or Therme), a table-like elevation preserved within modern Thessaloniki, has produced the deep sections characteristic of northern Greek and Balkan tells[9] (Figure 11.2). Settlement here began in the Early Bronze Age, and from the ninth century onwards was concentrated immediately on and around the hill. This is but one of a series of such mounds around the densely wooded and well-watered head of the Thermaic Gulf. Here, in addition to internal complexities arising from population concentration, activities such as herding, hunting, and woodland management (evidenced at Toumba by environmental data and tools) carry implications for territorial relations between centres. Historically, Thessaloniki's origins lie in a synoikism of local centres enforced by Cassander in c.315 (Strabo 7, frr. 21, 24–5). Yet while the built form of the new city may well have embodied current polis ideals, it must also be considered in the context of an established settlement network which did not disappear entirely with the synoikism.[10]

Clearly, evidence from different sites varies greatly in quantity and nature. We know enough to recognize the inadequacy of simplistic settlement categories based on state form or geographical area and the dangers of generalizing from a few well-documented cases, yet too little to reconstruct

---

[5] T. Papadopoulos (1979) 28 (but cf. Petropoulos 1990: 495 and n. 5); Petropoulos and Rizakis (1994) 197 n. 23.   [6] Snodgrass (1995); Bintliff and Snodgrass (1988).

[7] Apostolopoulou Kakavoyianni (1992); Dougleri Intzesiloglou (1994).

[8] Hägg (1982); Foley (1988) 29–30, figs. 7, 8.

[9] Soueref (1997). Cf. Archibald's discussion of northern tell sites in this volume.

[10] Papakonstantinou-Diamantorou (1990), noting more recent excavation reports in *AEMTh*.

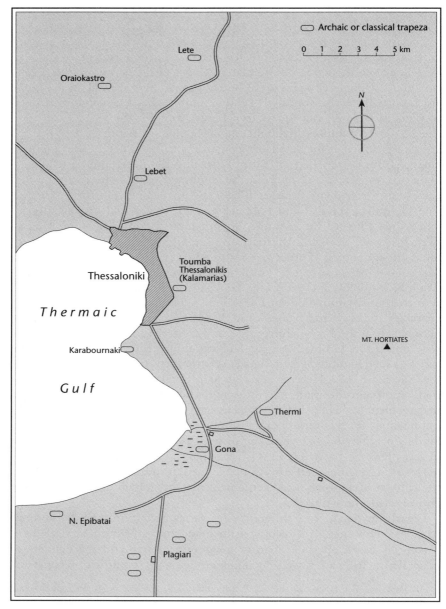

F IG. 11.2. Map of the Thermaic Gulf.

most sites with the detail possible at Athens or Corinth, for example, or to
advance alternative general models of the nature and role of early cities. The

challenge is therefore to find an approach which admits the widest range of evidence, yet does not strain the limitations of lesser-known cases, and it is for this reason that I shall focus on basic issues of scale as outlined below. A further, rarely considered, issue concerns the 'negative' cases, those regions or parts of regions which lack major settlement centres. Were they somehow backward, or did they maintain forms of organization which could operate in parallel with regional systems (or subsystems within wider political entities) which operated around big sites? This gives rise to a number of questions, including the problems surrounding particular environments such as closed valleys, and the applicability of models of synoikism. But because of the regional fragmentation implicit in them, such situations are more often found in areas traditionally regarded as ethnē.

Achaea offers ample scope to explore all of these issues, since its regional structure during the eighth century and archaic period encompassed great variation, with big sites of different types in close proximity to other forms of settlement organization. On the basis of topography, site groupings, and the spread of particular artefact types, four major subzones may be identified (Figure 11.3).[11] Along the north coast from Aigeira to Neos Erineos, a series of small headlands and narrow plains was punctuated by the outfall of rivers. Secondly, the *chōra* of Patras, from Drepanon probably to Tsoukaleika, comprised a broader area of plain with fewer natural divisions. Thirdly, the broad plains and gentle uplands of Dyme lay west of the Peiros; and finally, inland lay the Pharai valley, an increasingly narrow route through the mountains, punctuated by small, well-watered plains. That these areas were further subdivided is evident from the earliest record of the region's political structure, Herodotus' statement (1. 145) that it comprised twelve *merē* (or portions—the term is not further explained), which he names but does not locate or otherwise discuss. The passage is problematic: Herodotus is primarily concerned to explain that the number of Ionian poleis in Asia Minor reflected the twelve divisions in which the Ionians had previously lived when they had occupied Achaea, so contemporary Achaea *per se* is of secondary interest (Morgan and Hall 1996: 167–9). This may help to explain the apparent contrast between such parallel divisions of a whole and the more explicit strategy of describing peoples in some kind of geographical relationship to each other (ethno-geography) which Herodotus deploys elsewhere, most strikingly in neighbouring Arcadia (Nielsen 1996*d*: 29–36). The term *meros* is itself curious; it might just be a convenient alternative to *polis* for the protohistoric ancestors of the Ionian cities. But since the term carries no strong organizational connotations, it may have served to gloss over local divergences irrelevant to Herodotus' argument.[12] Yet the *meros* names themselves are interesting: toponyms lie along the north coast

[11] Morgan and Hall (1996) 166–93; Rizakis (1995).
[12] Morgan and Hall (1996) 217 n. 25; *contra*, Helly (1997).

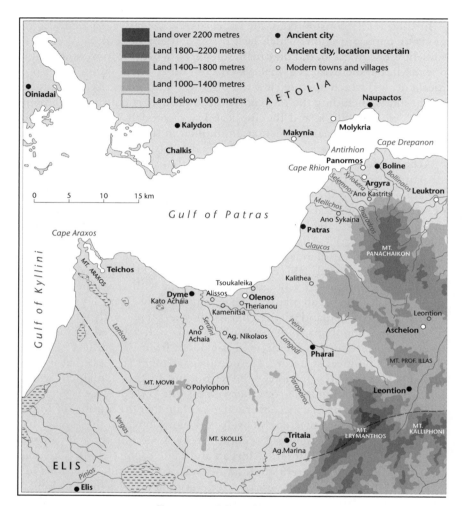

Oiniadai

A E T O L I A

Naupactos

Kalydon

Makynia   Molykria

Chalkis   Antirhion   Cape Drepanon
Panormos
Cape Rhion   ● Boline
Argyra   Leuktron
Ano Kastritsi
Meilichos
Ano Sykaina
Patras

Gulf of Patras   Glaucos   MT. PANACHAIKON

Cape Araxos

Gulf of Kyllini

MT. ARAXOS   Teichos   Kalithea
Tsoukaleika   Leontion
Dyme ●   Alissos   ○ Olenos   Ascheion ○
Kato Achaia   ○ Therianou
Kamenitsa   Peiros
Larisos   Serdini   ○ Ag. Nikolaos   Langadi   Pharai   MT. PROF. ILLAS
Ano Achaia
Paraperios
MT. MOVRI   ○ Polylophon   Leontion ●
Vergas
MT. SKOLLIS   MT. ERYMANTHOS   MT. KALLIPHONI
Tritaia
Ag. Marina
ELIS
Pinios
● Elis

0   5   10   15 km

Selemnos   Kylokera   Bollinatos   Charadros

FIG. 11.3. Map of Achaea.

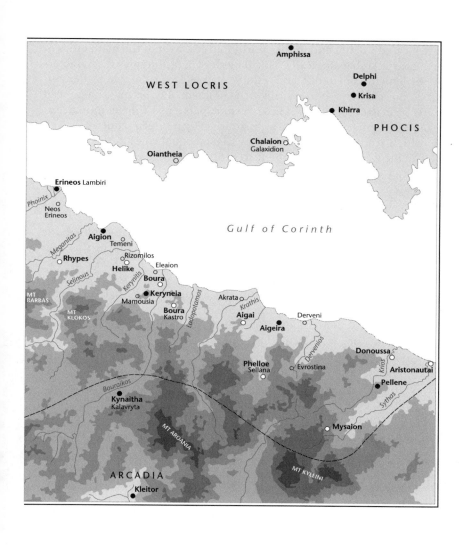

WEST LOCRIS

Amphissa

Delphi
Krisa
Khirra

PHOCIS

Oiantheia

Chalaion
Galaxidion

Erineos Lambiri

Phoinix

Neos
Erineos

Meganitas

Aigion
Temeni

Rhypes

Rizomilos

Helike

Eleaion

Selinous

Boura

Keryneia

Kerynitis

Mamousia

MT
BARBAS

Boura
Kastro

MT
KLOKOS

Akrata

Aigai

Ladopotamos

Krathis

Derveni

Aigeira

Gulf of Corinth

Donoussa

Krios

Aristonautai

Derwenios

Phelloe
Sellana

Evrostina

Pellene

Sythas

Bouraikos

Kynaitha
Kalavryta

MT AROANIA

MT KYLLINI

Mysaion

ARCADIA

Kleitor

and west of the Peiros (Olenos); the name Dyme, with its etymological connection with terms for 'west', may reflect the area's geographical position in relation to the rest of Achaea (Strabo 8. 7. 5); and ethnic plurals (Pharees and Tritaiees), presumably referring to the perceived identity of the inhabitants, are located inland, and in the case of Patrees, west of the main cities of the north coast. Archaeologically, as will be shown, toponyms are characterized by settlement continuity, and 'ethnic' names by less stable settlement structures, possibly involving forms of synoikism. Dyme may have been settled via internal migration. These various patterns of development include examples which may be seen as 'primitive' by modern scholars, as well as some which seem 'advanced', yet they played equal roles in the regional system which emerged through the fifth century at the latest (Morgan and Hall 1996: 193–9).

Clearly, such complexities offer promising ground for analysis, but before moving to review the Achaean evidence in detail, it is necessary to consider certain issues of terminology. Whether or not big sites should be called cities is largely a matter of opinion. Urbanism, however, is a more problematic concept and may generate anachronistic expectations. The term was first coined by Ildefonso Cerdá in his 1868–71 study of Barcelona, *Teoría general de la urbanización*, a work concerned with wider issues of town planning which marks a striking departure from the comparatively narrow architectural, Vitruvian, perspectives dominant since antiquity, and one which addressed a variety of contemporary concerns, including public health and efficiency of transport and circulation. Plainly, at least some of these concerns existed in early Greece (water provision, for example), and we are entitled to take an outsider perspective in studying them.[13] The anachronism lies in the moral connotations of social health and progress.[14] It seems probable that a distinction between *architectura* (building forms, materials, and locations) and *geometria* (land apportionment, usually for different social, fiscal, or military purposes), while most explicit in Roman work, was present in Greek thought by the fourth century (and probably earlier at least in the colonial world: Fischer-Hansen 1996). But even though Hippodamus (according to Arist. *Pol.* 2. 8) sought to embody social and political concerns in town planning, and a conceptual link between social morality and residence pattern dates back much earlier (see e.g. Homer's description of the Cyclopes, *Od.* 9. 105–15), it remains unclear whether (at least on the Greek mainland) this interest was regularly translated into practical design much before the fourth century.[15] So both the nature of the social concerns

[13] Morgan and Coulton (1997) 96–9; Wheatley (1972). On the Hippocratic *Airs, Waters, Places* see recently Ginouvès *et al.* (1994).

[14] Cf. Watkin (1977) on architectural scholarship.

[15] Arguments in the old Greek world usually centre on Crete and the islands: see e.g. R. Martin (1974) pt. II ch. 1; (1980); Lang (1996) 181–92.

in ancient and modern thought and the extent of their physical correlates differ. Modern urbanism certainly overlaps with ancient concerns in that it has something of the architectural focus of Vitruvius, of Frontinus' concern with land surveying, and of Hippocrates' interest in public health, but it does not fully correspond to any of these and covers aspects beyond all three. It embodies moral philosophies of progress which sit ill with the mainland Greek archaeological record—a point well illustrated by the difficulty (if not fallacy) of relating western colonial planning to the evolution of mother cities (see below). This seems particularly dangerous when considering this early period, since what tends to be sought, explicitly or implicitly, is evidence of progress towards a polis ideal. I shall therefore prefer more neutral terminology in referring to big-site problems whenever and wherever they occur.

Big sites, whether identified via excavation or survey, have usually been viewed from the perspective of cities.[16] There are two basic approaches to defining ancient cities (Morgan and Coulton 1997: 88–91). One can treat a site in isolation and look for evidence fitting predetermined criteria (perhaps the best known being the ten proposed by Gordon Childe).[17] This has the value of clarity, but is rarely sensitive to diachronic variation, and, inevitably, is only as reliable as the choice of criteria (Childe's list, for example, fits a number of classical cases, but causes difficulties in earlier periods: Morgan and Coulton 1997: 129). It may be that cities thus defined did not exist during the archaic period, but this still leaves the problem of describing such site variation as we do have. For the Early Iron Age and Archaic periods, the alternative approach of considering how sites fit into their local context seems more fruitful, and it is in this sense that big sites are here defined.[18]

The essential nature of the ancient city has been extensively debated in the works of Fustel de Coulanges, Marx, Weber, Finley, and many others. Their scholarship has been frequently reviewed,[19] and here I merely note three issues emphasized in the majority of studies and of particular relevance to discussions of big sites. First, a true city is more than just an agglomeration of population.[20] Sheer settlement density cannot be an issue in the early Greek mainland, since so many big sites incorporated open areas and the true extent of the majority remains unknown.[21] None the less, settle-

---

[16] e.g. Morris (1991); Owens (1991) ch. 2.
[17] Childe (1950); Wheatley (1972). For an alternative formulation see Trigger (1972).
[18] See e.g. Mersch (1997) on Attica.
[19] For a recent review with full bibliography see Hansen (1997*b*).
[20] See e.g. Grove (1972).
[21] Nucleated settlement is chiefly an island phenomenon: Wagstaff and Cherry (1982); Schallin (1997). Topography occasionally forces compaction on the mainland, e.g. at Delphi: Jacquemin (1993); Morgan (1990) 107–13; *BCH* 116 (1992) 694–8; 117 (1993) 619–31. Site size: Morgan and Coulton (1997) 91–4.

ment size has important demographic implications: expansion rests on, and
gives rise to, a complex of social and material issues, including access to
land and water, subsistence scheduling, proximity to kin or social equals,
management of waste, and the impact of new building on notions of privacy
and access.[22] At Corinth, for example, where, during the eighth century
at least, regional settlement was strongly concentrated, the distribution of
wells and graves suggests that households clustered around water sources.[23]
Most evidence comes from the general area of the Roman forum, which in
our period was a deep road valley behind the limestone ridge of Temple
Hill. The location of the Greek agora is unknown, although a site north or
east of the forum seems likely (Williams 1970: 32–8). In a settlement located
on a south–north trending limestone terrace, focused on the conjunction of
two valleys and cut by a major limestone ridge, a lack of formal, let alone
orthogonal, planning is hardly surprising. Discussion of the comparative
status or potential impact of colonial town planning therefore seems irrelevant.[24] Certainly, there is no reason to dismiss Corinth as a primitive
or random agglomeration. Significant issues of communal decision-making
must have surrounded such matters as residence rights and access to water,
and these should be set alongside evidence for communal action such as the
development of sanctuaries across the region (Morgan 1994). In short, even
if population size cannot be established, it is possible to raise in general
terms problems of scale and to consider the social dynamics of a growing
settlement, under circumstances where decisions about proximal residence
(who is a desirable neighbour, for example) and access to amenities can have
a substantial impact on spatial development.[25]

Discussion of services and functions comes close to the concerns of
modern urbanism. Organic growth rests on face-to-face connections, but
it also creates overarching needs, and thus eventually a whole greater than
the sum of its parts. Yet it is important to stress the novelty of the process
by which fresh needs were created and answered through our period. Insti-
tutionalized provision of services was therefore later, although its date and
form vary greatly. Plutarch (*Themistocles* 31. 1) describes Themistocles as
having once been water commissioner in Athens, and major public works
date back earlier still. Eupalinos' tunnel on Samos is an unusually elaborate
sixth-century example (H. Kienast 1995); somewhat more modest is the
near contemporary public provision on the south hill at Olynthos. Alongside some twenty pre-Persian War cisterns found here (those with cement
linings at least probably for water), Crouch has suggested that an aqueduct

[22] Fletcher (1995) ch. 1; M. G. Smith (1972).

[23] Morgan and Coulton (1997) 94–5; J. B. Salmon (1984) 40–1; Williams (1982).

[24] Williams (1995) 31–41; *contra* e.g. Malkin (1994*b*) 1–2. Danner (1997) for analogous
conclusions *re* Megara.

[25] Compare, for example, complaints on curse tablets from the 5th cent. onwards: e.g. Gager
(1992) 159, 163, 202–3.

should be dated to the sixth century (rather than the fourth as originally assumed), and if she is correct, public provision of drinkable water would seem to have been a priority of the new community.[26]

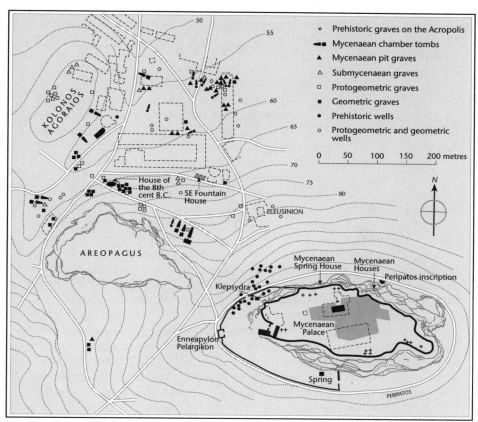

FIG. 11.4. Early Iron Age and archaic Athens.

The second issue is the economic base of the city, especially in relation to agricultural production. With certain possible exceptions, the *preferential* location of specialist craft activities within or beside large settlements seems to be largely a phenomenon of the sixth century. There is no evidence that economic functions (of production or consumption) were particularly concentrated at big sites in earlier times, and that these sites should therefore be primary units of economic analysis.[27] If this seems surprising, it is worth considering whether the circumstances of potential exceptions were in any way unusual, or whether they represent forms of organization that might

[26] Crouch (1993) 171–6; Morgan and Coulton (1997) 96–9 for review and bibliography.
[27] Morris (1991) 38–9; Morgan and Coulton (1997) 99–103.

be considered 'advanced'. In Athens (Figure 11.4), the location of an early Potters' Quarter in the later, Greek agora is reflected in the imprecise ancient usage of the toponyms Kerameikos and agora.[28] A well-watered site, beside a main road and just outside the main settlement, fits what was to become an ideal for craftsmen, being easy of access but with space to work and a tolerance of pollution from kilns which might not have been available in an ordinary residential area. Indeed, the majority of archaic and classical Athenian kiln sites lay outside the walls, especially on roads to the north-west and south-west of the city—and in the case of the early agora, the sheer quantity of potters' and metalworkers' debris in the 35 or so sub-Mycenaean to late geometric well and pit deposits here leaves little room for regular settlement (Baziotopoulou-Valavani 1994). J. K. Papadopoulos relates the rise of the agora as a political centre to the increased importance of the road which ran through it, reflecting strengthened ties to Eleusis from the sixth century and the development of Piraeus from the early fifth. This fits the date of *c*.550–500 proposed for the canalization of the Eridanos and the landscaping of the northern part of the agora.[29] Whether the agora was a Peisistratid or a Cleisthenic creation is largely irrelevant here; the *horos* (boundary-marker) inscriptions of *c*.500–480 serve as a benchmark for the change. There may have been an earlier political centre elsewhere; to judge by the Aglaureion inscription, certain major institutions lay closer to Late Bronze Age habitation areas north and east of the Acropolis,[30] but their sites have not been located or excavated and their relative dates remain unknown. The earliest evidence of pottery production so far discovered in the area now called Kerameikos dates from the mid-fifth century onwards,[31] but since the area between this and the agora lies beneath modern roads, evidence of the pace and nature of the potters' move is lacking. In short, there is evidence here for an early concentration of potters beside a large settlement. Yet when one considers the likely number of rural Attic workshops which probably served settlements in their immediate areas,[32] it is questionable whether, at least at this stage, the Athenian Kerameikos should be seen as a craft centre of regional importance, fulfilling a role in Attica significantly disproportionate to the needs of the neighbouring settlement. It is also important to stress that physical concentration does not automatically imply full-time specialization and the exchange relationships which that entails. Without wishing to enter into the complex debate about pottery production

[28] J. K. Papadopoulos (1996); Wycherley (1957) 221–4.

[29] Ammerman (1996). Cf. Argos: Courtils (1992); *BCH* 93 (1969) 994–1003; 98 (1974) 761; Bommelaer and Grandjean (1972) 168–77; *BCH* 111 (1987) 591; 106 (1982) 640; 102 (1978) 783; 91 (1967) 802–8.

[30] See most recently Shear (1994) 225–8; S. G. Miller (1995*b*) (with earlier bibliography).

[31] Baziotopoulou-Valavani (1994) 47; Knigge (1990) 39, 163. See also Oakley (1992) for a workshop of the last quarter of the 5th cent. in the Thission area.

[32] Mainly identified by style: see e.g. Rombos (1988), e.g. app. c–d.

and the subsistence organization of different regions, I merely note that the scale of early settlement and the inclusion of cultivable land within big sites make the combination of different activities (including craft production and agriculture) a practical proposition. Dependence on imported staple foods (notably grain) in a way that would free a significant part of the population from food production was a rare and generally much later phenomenon.[33]

A further, possibly exceptional, case is Oropos (ancient Graia), located on the northern Attic coast but culturally Euboean (*Ergon* 1996: 27–38). Settlement here extended over a wide area; our evidence comes from one of two small quarters to be excavated (on School Board (*OΣK*) property), next to a river whose flooding finally caused the area's abandonment at the end of the seventh century. The majority of houses in this densely settled area have produced evidence of bronze- and ironworking from the mid-eighth century onwards, here too accompanied by potters' kilns (reflecting the symbiotic needs of these crafts). There are no native metals in this area, unlike, for example, the Lavritike to the south (J. E. Jones 1982), and in this respect Graia shows notable similarities with Lefkandi, Eretria, and Pithekoussai (and architectural, technical, and stylistic comparisons between these sites form part of the continuing research programme).[34] Euboeans may therefore have preferred to locate metalworking in settlement centres, and this in turn raises a number of questions about the long-term impact of proximity, for example upon the development of craft specializations (noting the suggestion that both bronze and iron were worked by the same people at Graia). It is, however, interesting that at least on present evidence, the polis centres of Eretria or Chalkis do not seem to have been especially favoured in this respect, and so there is no close relationship between the location of political power and centralization of craft production.

Elsewhere, large-scale exploitation of resources reflects chances of distribution, although this can have a major impact on big settlements as well as regional economies. Corinthian building stone is a case in point. Limestone and conglomerate, especially the oolitic limestone used for the majority of public buildings in the Corinthia and widely exported,[35] were quarried at a number of sites in the countryside (notably Mavrospilies, Kenchreai, and Examilia).[36] There was also a major outcrop of oolite in the heart of the city, extending from the centre west towards the Potters' Quarter, although there is no evidence to suggest that its exploitation pre-dates the eighth-

---

[33] See e.g. Arafat and Morgan (1989).

[34] Themelis (1983); Popham *et al.* (1979–80) 93–7; Ridgway (1992) 91–6, 99–100. I am grateful to Roger Doonan for information about his continuing study of metallurgical evidence from the site.

[35] One type of limestone extensively used at Delphi (e.g. D. Laroche and Nenna 1993) does not occur locally, and the Corinthia is the most likely source (for later testimony see the inscriptions *FdD* iii/5. 19. 98, 23. 27); C. Hayward (pers.comm.).

[36] Hayward (forthcoming; 1996) (Examilia).

century expansion of settlement discussed above. A conservative estimate of the total volume of stone extracted across the region from the sixth century BC to the fourth century AD is at least 3 million cubic metres (Hayward forthcoming). The implications of this in terms of the impact on daily life, manpower and profits must have been considerable, and the question of who owned the quarries and/or had the right to exploit them is important, if currently unanswerable.[37] Certainly, if quarrymen preferred to work stone they knew, locals may have been employed for cutting and transport, and the development of support services, notably roads, which have a public dimension, is a major issue in its own right.[38]

In short, with the exception of activities governed by resource location, which may or may not affect big sites, production evidence from the countryside, from sanctuaries, and from smaller settlements is plentiful, and activities such as pottery production or metalworking were located to satisfy a diversity of local permanent and occasional markets. There is no evidence for any absolute perception of big sites as *the* places for craft production, but rather varying patterns of attraction reflecting such factors as population concentration, functional need, and supply-points for raw materials.

The final area of discussion concerns the extent to which cities served as statements of community identity in terms of the location of government or ideological institutions such as communal cults. This problem has perhaps received the greatest attention, and numerous examples could be cited—the debate about the nature and date of the first public building in the Athenian agora,[39] for example, as well as controversies about the precise function of specific buildings (such as the Old Bouleuterion in Athens).[40] Yet here too alternative approaches are possible. From an archaeological viewpoint, Max Weber's characterization of state organization and political discourse as centred upon cities and separate from the traditional skills of community life[41] would seem to demand evidence that distinct activities were actually performed there—in other words, that we identify specific homes for them. By contrast, Émile Durkheim's view that the political institutions of the ancient city should be understood in terms of the totality of forms of social interaction[42] would permit a broader interpretation, admitting evidence for the existence of institutions such as magistracies without knowing their scope or location. This in turn encourages consideration of a wide range of epigraphical evidence in particular, stressing the choice of place for the

[37] Hayward (forthcoming); Burford (1969) 168–75 argues that Corinthian quarries were exploited from the first for public works and so may have been publicly owned. Yet Corinthian stoneworking has a longer history (Brookes 1981), and whether individuals could profit from stone on private land, or provide it for public building as a liturgy, remains an open question.

[38] Pikoulas (1995); Wiseman (1978) *passim*.   [39] Shear (1994); Camp (1994) 9–11.

[40] S. G. Miller (1995a); Shear (1995).

[41] Weber (1992) 122–67; Hansen (1997b) 32–4.

[42] Durkheim (1984) i, ch. 5, esp. 136–9; ii, ch. 3, esp. 233–42.

erection of inscriptions as much as their content (Thomas 1992: 65–72).
Here too, without wishing to imply an evolutionary perspective, different
emphases may better describe different periods. The lack of evidence from
the Greek mainland for significant collections of non-religious public buildings, or for cities as consumer centres much before the fourth century, has
long been noted.[43] However, two sites may prove to be exceptions. At Pallantion, the construction of four temples on the acropolis, probably in the
first half of the sixth century, is notable in its own right, but if Temple A is
indeed a rare instance of a mainland building which served the dual function of both temple and bouleutērion (or political meeting-place of some
form), then it embodies a complex of functions rare at this late date.[44] And
at Tegea unpublished column capitals dating from the late seventh century
onwards are reported from the area of the settlement, although as yet we
cannot identify the structures to which they belonged.[45] In both cases we
can merely note the presence of something potentially interesting, and also
that both sites are in Arcadia—yet another case of important evidence from
a region sometimes regarded as ethnos territory or at least marginal to the
world of the polis as conceived in modern scholarship from the nineteenth
century onwards.[46] Elsewhere, the earliest evidence concerns management
of space, as in the case of Athens, although it is still hard to identify the earliest agora on the mainland. In Athens the problem of dating an 'old agora'
remains, Corinth and Sparta have not been excavated, and sixth-century
Argos is perhaps best (if still partially) understood. But again caution is
needed; what should we expect of an agora during our period?[47] Lato on
Crete is often cited as an important case of early planning, yet many of
the structures surrounding the open space interpreted as an agora date to
the fourth century and later.[48] The space itself is created by a change of
terrace angle, and identification of function rests partly on inference from
later use, and partly on the proximity of 'theatral' rock-cut steps and what
was probably an open-air cult place. The identification may be correct, but
the assumptions on which it rests should be recognized. Evidence from
the colonies and islands is often clearer, but the best mainland evidence for
civic political institutions tends to be epigraphical, with magistracies widely
attested.[49]

In short, the view that Early Iron Age and archaic settlement concentrations are not really cities may seem attractive, although it should be
applied to the full range of mainland evidence without prior assumptions

[43] See most recently Hansen and Fischer Hansen (1994); Morris (1991) 34–6.
[44] Østby (1995a) 54–63; (1995b) 289, fig. 171.
[45] Østby (1995b) 306 n. 467; Spyropoulos (1993) 258.
[46] See the introduction to this volume.
[47] S. G. Miller (1995b) 216, 219–23; Baziotopoulou-Valavani (1994).
[48] R. Martin (1951) 42–62, 224–48; (1971) 81–4; Lang (1996) 63–8.
[49] For a review see Effenterre and Ruzé (1994; 1995).

about location or political type. Yet the relevance of the argument is debatable, since the meaning of the term 'city' probably changed over time, and what constitutes a city in earlier times is not self-evident. Early evidence suggests a punctuated process whereby changes within existing settlement concentrations accumulated to the point where key decisions about the site's physical form, provision of services and resources, and local role became inevitable. While the solutions adopted varied greatly and require excavation data to determine, the range of evidence currently available permits the general inference that basic issues of scale were confronted in a number of regions during our period.

One further issue worthy of brief note concerns the economic logic of settlement concentration. Nucleation, to whatever extent, is sometimes seen as an enforced departure from a 'natural' state of dispersal close to resources.[50] From here it is easy to slip into socio-political explanations, for example by arguing that population concentration is caused by some escalation in local power hierarchies, with resulting negative (and circular) judgement upon continuing dispersed settlement.[51] Yet the assumption that there is an automatic subsistence advantage in rural settlement is questionable. Ensuring food supplies during bad years via a combination of diversification and exchange is attested throughout the Bronze Age, and here we may note the advantages of central points for exchange (not least as the domains of those who profited from it).[52] Equally, a consistent feature of survey data throughout our period from a wide variety of regions (from Boeotia to Methana and the Langadas basin) is the scarcity of rural settlement.[53] This is a striking situation if it was so desirable; and while geometric surface evidence *can* be hard to detect, this is not always the case (and is certainly not so with archaic), whereas the overall trend seems very consistent. Eighth- and seventh-century evidence generally indicates a high degree of centralization, with movement from long-established nuclei as a lasting trend being a feature of the sixth century and later. In Boeotia this case has been made by John Bintliff and Anthony Snodgrass, and the same is true of, for example, much of eastern and southern Arcadia.[54] It has long been observed that in most cases where political development is linked with synoikism in (usually later) literary sources, this does not correspond to changes on the ground, and big-site and rural expansion tend to occur together.[55] Megalopolis may be an exception, but even here earlier rural settlements did not altogether disappear.[56] There are a number of striking

---

[50] See most recently Schallin (1997) 18–19.
[51] See e.g. Lohmann (1992), with discussion (58–60).
[52] See e.g. Halstead (1992) among extensive literature.
[53] Foxhall (1997) 123–7, noting also Wright *et al.* (1990) 610; Davis *et al.* (1997) 452, 455–74; Gill and Foxhall (1997); Ekroth (1996) 179–227; Andreou and Kotsakis (1994).
[54] Bintliff and Snodgrass (1989); Morgan (1999).   [55] e.g. Cavanagh (1991) 105–10.
[56] J. A. Lloyd, Owens, and Roy (1988); Pikoulas (1988); Nielsen (1996*d*) 286–34.

early cases of what may be termed internal colonization, whereby areas were settled via population movement from other parts of the same region (in Attica,[57] for example, and also Achaean Dyme), but there is no evidence that these were undertaken to preserve any idea of scattered, rural settlement. Instead, movement occurs in the context of one settlement hierarchy and contributes to the formation or development of another.

This point is worth emphasizing simply because the perception that population concentration has socio-political consequences which are somehow inimical to ideal subsistence conditions may in turn support particular views of the kind of complex societies to which big sites properly belong. It is thence a small step to the idea that the values expressed in the institutions located in towns are contrary to those of the tribal ethnos, which is often, but erroneously, characterized as unurbanized.[58] In part this stems from a very literal reading of Thucydides' highly schematized and philosophical account of social evolution (1. 2–18). But it also reflects the fact that the ethnos has not become an ideal scholarly type in the same way as the polis, but tends to be defined by largely negative comparison.[59] Clearly, this embodies a series of unhelpful preconceptions, but more importantly, it does not fit the evidence.

The case of Achaea

It is against this background that I wish to consider eighth-century and archaic Achaea, a region where, as noted, big sites of different types operated alongside other forms of settlement organization in a very varied regional structure (Figure 11.3). Evidence for concentrated settlement in big sites is primarily focused on the north coast.[60] Many of these sites (Akrata, possibly ancient Aigai, for example) have produced only fragmentary surface evidence,[61] sufficient to suggest a string of centres along a physically punctuated coast, but not to reconstruct it in detail. Only two sites, Aegeira and Aigion, have been substantially excavated, and these show significant differences in internal organization.

At Aegeira, a settlement split between a lower port town and an acropolis, excavation has focused on the acropolis, a plateau some 750 square metres in area. Settlement here dates back to LH IIIB, with architectural evidence

---

[57] D'Onofrio (1997); Mersch (1997).

[58] Ehrenberg (1969) 3–25; Larsen (1968) 3–8, 11; Daviero Rocchi (1993) 113–14; Snodgrass (1980) 42. Sakellariou (1989) 86–92 rightly rejects the negative connotations for ethnē of a link between urban centres and poleis, but does so on the negative grounds that certain archaic poleis and *merē* (citing Achaea) lack urban centres, rather than noting the positive presence of big sites in ethnē. In part, the discrepancy hinges on definitions of urbanism, however.

[59] For a review of scholarly idealization of the polis see Sakellariou (1989), noting also the general comparative way in which ethnē enter into his discussion.

[60] For summary and bibliography see Morgan and Hall (1996) 169–81.

[61] *AD* 17/2 (1961–2) 130; Rizakis (1995) 213–14.

from *c*.1200 and a substantial settlement layer of the tenth to eighth centuries.[62] Perhaps the most striking eighth-century construction has been identified (albeit controversially) as the first of a series of cult buildings on the plateau. The area is heavily eroded, the building sequence complex, and artefacts few, but there appears at this stage to have been settlement around the building (Mazarakis Ainian 1997: 164–6, 272, 275). However, by *c*.650 and the construction of Temple B the acropolis had become primarily, if not exclusively, a sacred precinct.[63] This may imply greater separation of public and private activities, but at present we can only speculate that settlement moved down to the port area. According to Pausanias (7. 26. 1–2), the site's original name, Hyperesia, was changed to Aigeira during the Ionian occupation, and the 'dockyard', like the city, was thenceforth called Aegeira. It is therefore tempting to speculate that the acropolis was originally called Hyperesia, and the name of the port was adopted for the whole complex when settlement shifted.[64] Clearly, however, further research is required. It is, though, interesting that with the exception of one late-eighth-century and archaic rural site (ancient Phelloe, modern Seliana),[65] activity seems to have been centred on this site.

At Aigion, by contrast, where evidence comes mainly from rescue excavation in the modern city, eighth-century burials and traces of a late-eighth or seventh-century apsidal building are concentrated on a low plateau over the harbour.[66] Archaic evidence is as yet very slight, but this may be a matter of chance given the circumstances of excavation, and there is no reason to infer any significant change in settlement organization until classical times (a development beyond the scope of this paper). Here too, Strabo (8. 7. 5) attributes city formation to synoikism, but as yet, we lack evidence of the rural settlements that might have contributed to this; one late eighth-century rural burial site has been found (at Kato Mavriki),[67] but there is no firm archaic evidence. However, Aigion's establishment of a major sanctuary at Ano Mazaraki (Rakita) in the Meganeitas valley, close to the border with Arcadian Azania, may have been intended to mark her boundary beside a much-frequented road, and if so, reflects an approach to territorial definition unique at this date in Achaea.[68] The shrine, with its mid-eighth-century hecatompedon (construction 100 feet in length) and votive deposit containing a wealth of small finds, including weapons, scarabs, and jewellery,

---

[62] Alzinger (1976–7; 1981–2; 1983); Alzinger, Deger-Jalkotzy, and Alram-Stern (1985; 1986); Alzinger and Mitsopoulou-Leon (1972–5); Deger-Jalkotzy (1991).

[63] For a summary see Gogos (1986–7) 119–27.

[64] Morgan and Hall (1996) 173. Ikaros of Hyperesia won the stade race in the 23rd Olympiad, 685 BC (Pausanias 4. 15. 1).

[65] Alzinger, Deger-Jalkotzy, and Alram-Stern (1986) 319–26; Dekoulakou (1982) 229–31.

[66] Papakosta (1991); Morgan and Hall (1996) 176–7 for bibliography.

[67] *AD* 33/2 (1978) 97–8, 100–2; 43/2 (1988) 166, 168; Kourou (1980).

[68] Petropoulos (1987–8; 1992–3); Morgan (1997) 189–91.

shows strong links with Aigion (which has the finest natural harbour along the gulf) as well as with the central and eastern Peloponnese. In short, while there are similarities between Aegeira and Aigion, there are also significant differences in their spatial organization (including location of cults), extent of access to imports, and territorial perceptions. Clearly, much remains to be investigated, but even this evidence is sufficient to tempt speculation about the extent of variety within the string of north-coast settlements.

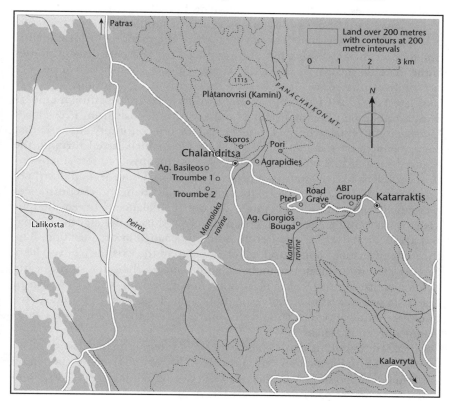

FIG. 11.5. Geometric and archaic sites in the Pharai valley.

A very different picture emerges in the Pharai valley (Figure 11.5), which contained the *merē* of Tritaiees and Pharees. In general, valleys are crudely divisible into 'penetrative' systems (such as the Nemea or Enipeus valleys)[69] without constant populations and open to outside interests, and 'closed' systems (such as the Pharai valley), which are often environmentally circumscribed and have at least some element of constant residence. During the eighth century evidence from the Pharai valley comprises graves of

[69] Wright *et al.* (1990); Decourt (1990).

many forms (cists, pithoi, a reused Mycenaean tholos, etc.), many of which
are grouped in different ways (beneath tumuli, for example, or surrounded
by a peribolos wall). Most graves are robbed, but it is interesting to note
the presence of a distinctive and apparently very local ceramic iconography yet an absence of imports.[70] Such deliberate material differentiation is
suggestive of highly structured relations between neighbours, and this in
turn raises many (as yet unanswerable) questions about the circumstances of
local boundaries in a confined environment. For all that there is no big site
at this stage, we cannot dismiss this as an area of simple, low-level relations.

It is surely no accident that the area where the marking of local identities appears most complex has also produced the sharpest discontinuities
in the material record. At present, archaic evidence comprises two cases of
late-sixth-century reuse of earlier tombs, sherds at Ag. Giorgios and (perhaps later) Ai-Lias Chalandritsas, and further west, architectural members
from a public building at Vasiliko, and a votive deposit from Prevedos.[71]
Investigation remains limited, but the lack of site continuity suggests that
there was at least a major shift in site location which lasted through the
classical period. It is tempting to suggest that this involved settlement nucleation, but this must await systematic exploration. I have argued elsewhere
(Morgan and Hall 1996: 191–3) that only a small change in circumstances
(perhaps in population level) might disrupt the balance between the mu-
tually self-aware neighbouring groups inferred during the eighth century,
and act as a catalyst for apparently dramatic change in organization. The
chronology of such change and its relationship to the existence of two *merē*
here by Herodotus' time are more difficult issues, although a shift as early
as the seventh century would be striking in comparison with other parts of
Achaea. Clearly, systematic investigation is much needed, but even such a
brief, preliminary review should dispel the notion that complex relations
belong only in big sites.

Consideration of the pattern and process of integration in this area raises
the issue of synoikism, a recurring theme in literary sources for the region
as a whole, and an important factor in the two remaining areas, Patras and
Dyme. Strabo (8. 7. 5) notes that each Achaean *meros* was formed from
seven or eight dēmoi. Yet the lateness of the source, a suspicious numerical
regularity, and a lack of earlier epigraphical evidence[72] may combine to suggest that these dēmoi were a hellenistic invention to enhance the pedigree

[70] Morgan and Hall (1996) 189–93 for bibliography; P. Zapheiropoulos (1952) 409–12; N.
Zapheiropoulos (1956) 197–201; Morgan (1988) 323–9.
[71] Burials: *AD* 44/2 (1989) 134, 136; P. Zapheiropoulos (1952) 403–4. *AD* 44/2 (1989) 132–3
(Vasiliko), 133 (Prevedos); 46/2 (1991) 156 (Prevedos), 157 (Ai-Lias).
[72] *Syll.*[3] 531, listing three phylai at Dyme in the 3rd cent. BC. Whether this reflects earlier
subdivisions is debatable (especially given the shortage of pre-hellenistic Achaean inscriptions
of any kind): N. F. Jones (1987) 130–2; Morgan and Hall (1996) 170. *Contra* the hypotheses of
Helly (1997) 220–35.

of the members of the Achaean League. If they existed during our period, we cannot trace them on the ground, and their nature remains a matter of speculation. In the case of Patras, there is a significant mismatch between the complex traditions of synoikism and dioikism recounted by Pausanias (7. 18. 2–6) and Strabo (8. 3. 2), and the archaeological record.[73] This may be partially explained by the cultural disjunction exacerbated by Roman colonization and the very different kind of land division resulting from cadastration (Arafat 1996: 134–8), but as survey data show, the problem cannot wholly be explained thus. Pausanias reports a first synoikism from the poleis of Aroe, Antheia, and Mesatis, then a dioikism imposed in 279 when the population was dispersed among the towns (*polismata*) of Mesatis, Antheia, Boline, Argyra, and Arva as well as at Patras, and finally, a further synoikism imposed by Augustus. Yet although groups of sites equated with areas later of importance to synoikized Patras existed as early as the eighth century, there is strikingly little sign of activity during the archaic period.[74] Archaeologically, it is difficult to recognize the kind of change which *could* be explained by synoikism before classical times, when Patras seemingly expanded[75] and large rural installations gradually appear in the *chōra*.[76] At Patras itself there is continuity from the geometric period onwards, but insufficient evidence to assess the site's place within local settlement structures. How the physical rhythms and practical interrelations of settlement should be distinguished from the ebb and flow of regional political ties is therefore an open question, as is the political role of any big site at Patras.

At Dyme, by contrast, the main settlement dates from the sixth century,[77] and although there is some evidence for eighth-century activity in the surrounding countryside, the area is exceptional for being internally colonized.[78] Settlement in both town and country expanded steadily thereafter (Lakakis 1991). A temple was built at Santameri close to the Elean border,[79] but there is as yet no other evidence of public building. On the basis of the accounts of Strabo (8. 3. 2, 11), Pausanias (7. 17. 6–7), and Stephanus of Byzantium (s.v. Δύμη), it has been suggested that the name Dyme was adopted after a synoikism,[80] and since it appears as the home of the Olympic victor Pataikos in 496 (Moretti 1957: no. 171), this would seem to be a *terminus ante quem*. None the less, dispersed settlement lasted well into the classical period, and while it is impossible to reconstruct relationships between sites, nothing in the present record indicates that local or regional centres pre-dated the town of Dyme.

---

[73] Petropoulos (1991); Petropoulos and Rizakis (1994); Morgan and Hall (1996) 181–6.
[74] Petropoulos (1991); Petropoulos and Rizakis (1994) 197–8.
[75] Papapostolou (1990); Petropoulos (1994*b*) 43.
[76] Petropoulos (1994*a*); Petropoulos and Rizakis (1994) 198–9.
[77] Rizakis (1992) ch. IV; *AD* 39/2 (1984) 101.
[78] Morgan and Hall (1996) 186–9 for bibliography.   [79] *AD* 22/2 (1967) 216.
[80] Koerner (1974) 469; Moggi (1976) 123; Morgan and Hall (1996) 186–7.

Despite problems with the concept of synoikism as treated in ancient literary sources, it is often cited as a key process in early city/state development.[81] Explicitly archaeological models for the development of big sites in their regional contexts are, however, rare, and Boeotia is one of the few cases where intensive survey data have been employed in this way. Two model trajectories have been reconstructed by Bintliff and Snodgrass.[82] The first involves the growth of a single centre through the geometric and archaic periods, resulting in a small, compact principal settlement or *astu* (often within an abandoned Mycenaean settlement) and a move into the countryside, often relatively early, accompanied by a modest climax in rural settlement. In Achaea, this broadly describes both Aigeira and Aigion. Overall, however, Achaea echoes Boeotia in producing relatively few sites between *c.*900 and 600, with movement away from acropoleis being an essentially sixth-century and later phenomenon. The second trajectory involves the sudden appearance in the fifth or fourth centuries of larger, more dispersed cities, in most cases coinciding with substantial rural installations indicating intensive farming. The fact that intensive activity in the countryside generally coincides with the maximum population and expansion of the city centre indicates overall growth rather than a move away from the country. In Achaea this may fit Patras and perhaps Dyme too.

In reviewing Early Iron Age and archaic Achaea, it is therefore clear that the region held a variety of localized, but probably interacting, settlement strategies, and that big sites may have functioned differently in different areas. Settlement nuclei existed along the north coast by the eighth century, and where investigated, they appear similar in nature and development to those in regions conventionally regarded as poleis in the sense of city-states. Yet evidence from the Pharai valley belies the notion that 'city' development is a true measure of social and political dynamism. The diversity of the Achaean record in comparison with uniform historical models raises significant problems. By the fifth century at the latest, Achaean regional identity had real political meaning,[83] but those who regarded themselves as Achaean would have had very different experiences of local settlement. How may we trace in the archaeological record the developing interplay between a region across which material traits are shared and individual communities within it? Were big sites, or cities, really perceived as a social ideal, and if so, how did individuals in different settlement systems compare their experiences?

Achaea is hardly an exceptional case. The dynamic process of construction of local and regional communities is well attested in other ethnē (Thessaly and Arcadia, for example), whereas the politicization of tribal, or

---

[81] For a review see Cavanagh (1991); Moggi (1976) for literary evidence; see also Moggi (1975).

[82] Bintliff and Snodgrass (1988; 1989). For a broader review see Bintliff (1994).

[83] Morgan and Hall (1996) 193–9.

regional-ethnic, identity (that which delineates our expectations of tribal structures) is increasingly being recognized as a later phenomenon.[84] The idea that the development of cities effected a transformation in tribal structures relatively late in the classical period is quite wrong. Big sites were a feature of the social and political landscape right across the early Greek world, and far from being marginal territory for city development, areas like Achaea contained a diversity of settlement orderings.

In choosing Achaea as a case study, I have deliberately strayed from, or even precluded, the detailed discussion of site development which has characterized approaches to cities and urbanism in the early Greek world. Clearly, the attention long devoted to centres like Athens or Corinth has produced a level of information rarely available elsewhere, and it would be wrong not to make the fullest possible use of it. None the less, it is disappointing to find the same limited range of case studies cited in discussions of urbanism, feeding rather than challenging modern preconceptions. Both our rapidly expanding database and changing conceptions of the nature and ubiquity of the polis force us to take a broader view, and there is much to be said for focusing on the most basic implications of settlement scale as a means of comparing evidence of different kinds from different systems. The challenge is surely to understand the way in which big sites fitted into the complex spectrum of socio-political orderings which we now see with greater clarity across the Greek world.

[84] Archibald (this volume); Nielsen (1997; 1999); Morgan (1999).

12

Space, Hierarchy, and Community in Archaic and Classical Macedonia, Thessaly, and Thrace

ZOSIA HALINA ARCHIBALD

Defining the subject and search for models

ANCIENT Macedonia, Thessaly, and Thrace are often described in ways which suggest that they had a good deal in common. Each possessed areas of extensive plain and well-watered river valleys, suitable for cattle- and horse-rearing; each was famed for its cavalry—well represented on coins, monumental paintings, and sculpture; each was capable of producing a more than adequate food supply for its population. Each had an enviable reputation for wealth, epitomized by racehorses and an aristocratic lifestyle.[1] The prominence of cattle- and horse-rearing in ancient descriptions of these states does not mean simply that the aristocratic élites liked to put on a good show. Livestock constituted a vital asset, both for traction and transport, and a strategic card of perennial attraction to other states lacking such resources.

Greek writers and poets were evidently impressed by the display which Macedonian, Thessalian, or Thracian aristocrats could afford and evidently enjoyed putting on. They were less interested in the detailed political work-ings of these states. Part of the attraction of these three regions for ancient writers was their wealth—wealth of a kind many Greeks could not even dream of. Not surprisingly, perhaps, the unfamiliar proved of much greater interest to writers and poets than the familiar. My intention in this paper is to illuminate those political and institutional features which these re-gions nevertheless shared with the cities of central, southern, and eastern Greece as well as those which rendered them different. Although Thessaly is usually treated as a 'federal' Greek region, such as Achaea or Aetolia,

I am grateful to Roger Brock and Steve Hodkinson for helping to clarify some of my gnomic utterances, and to the anonymous reviewers of the volume for constructive comments.

[1] Horses: Kraay (1976) 115 and figs. 375–96 (Thessaly), 139–48 and figs. 481–513, 526–7 (Macedonia and Thrace); Spence (1993) 23–5 (Thessaly), 26–7 (Macedonia), 176–8 (social implications of a cavalry preponderance over hoplites); key texts: Thuc. 2. 98. 3–4; 2. 100; Plato, *Meno* 70 A–B; Dem. 23. 199 (another Menon); Isoc. 8. 117; Xen. *Hell.* 6. 1. 3 (Polydamas of Pharsalus); 7. 1. 11; 3. 2. 5 (Thracian horseracing); Zhivkova (1973) pls. 1, 11–12, 22–3 (Thracian chariots); T. R. Martin (1985) 34–75 (Thessalian land and mobile resources); Prestianni-Giallombardo and Tripodi (1996) (image of the horse in Macedonia); Archibald (1998) chs. 4, 6, 10–12 (emergence of the Odrysian kingdom and Thracian warrior élite).

composed of many cities or large sites (see Morgan in this volume) with certain common institutions, I shall argue that, during the archaic and classical periods, Thessaly was organized in a very similar way to Macedonia and Thrace, even though it lacked a central authority similar to the hereditary monarchies of the latter two kingdoms. This is not to suggest that Thessaly was like a kingdom; one of the region's weaknesses was the absence of institutional structures which could counteract initiatives taken by strong individual leaders with a very particular power-base against the interests of other communities. The similarities lie, I would suggest, in the way strong dynasties put into effect power structures beyond the local and territorial level. By fostering a regional organization of land and resources, leading Thessalian families created the means by which numerous disparate communities could be organized for common purposes, even if the main practical function of this organization was war. It is therefore in the organization of space that the greatest similarities can be seen between Thessaly, Macedonia, and Thrace. The particular institutional mechanisms adopted in each of the three areas for administrative purposes were, as far as current evidence allows an evaluation, particular to each.

What distinguished these three states from others in the Aegean, excluding Persia, was their size and range of resources. But it is not clear what roles geography and population dynamics respectively may have played in their political structures. In the best-documented ancient city, Athens, the relationship between city and countryside, in both social and political terms, was intimate and tightly knit (R. Osborne 1985). Although elsewhere relations between territory and administration may have been less closely interconnected, politics was everywhere concerned with the appropriation, allocation, administration, and exploitation of land. The organization and use of space deserve special consideration in the case of three states which had exceptional land resources. These were three of the largest regions of the Aegean area which have been designated by historians, ancient and modern, as inhabited by ethnē (variously translated as 'peoples' or 'tribes') in the archaic and classical periods. Regions dominated by ethnē are often assumed to have had a political organization different from that of the polis. Anthony Snodgrass (1980: 46) identified a general correlation between the presence of poleis and democratic institutions on the one hand and of oligarchic systems in the ethnos on the other. Reassessing pre-classical Greece, Robin Osborne emphasizes that in many parts of Greece 'the sense of belonging to a people (ethnos) who inhabited a whole region was, throughout the archaic period, stronger than the sense of belonging to a particular community, determined to be distinguished from its neighbours' (R. Osborne 1996: 286). He adds that this strategy should not be seen as the polis *manquée*, 'but as an alternative mode of social organization, consciously chosen in areas where there was only a need for a rather limited range of functions to be performed collectively' (ibid.). Whereas Osborne's first statement is worth investigating, the second betrays a misunderstanding, also detectable in Snodgrass's analysis, of how various communities were integrated, either in the ethnos or in a different supra-local entity, the kingdom or state. Precisely what the distinction between ethnē and poleis meant in the fifth century BC, when prose writers began to use these terms frequently, is not clear. *Ethnos* can be translated in various ways according to context: it can mean community as well as people, Greek and non-Greek (C. P. Jones 1996). Polis and ethnos were not juxtaposed as political systems before Aristotle, whose comparisons do not in any case refer like to like, with cities and kingdoms featuring indiscriminately like stamps in an album.[2] Little wonder, then, that modern historians have sometimes over-generalized the true state of affairs, adopting an adversarial scheme in which ethnos and polis are juxtaposed. But ethnos and polis should not be juxtaposed, since they do not represent *alternative* modes but rather *different levels* of social organization. In all three of our 'ethnic' territories there were large centres of population which can be described as cities (see Morgan in this volume for further discussion). Some of these have long been known, others are only just becoming known through archaeological investigation. The question which needs to be answered, therefore, is not whether there were any 'cities' but what the relationship was between cities and other types of settlement on the one hand and broader regional powers on the other.

Politics and administration are still viewed by ancient historians primarily as the outcome of institutions. Recent attempts to systematize our knowledge of Greek political institutions, using specific terms as markers or symptoms of political structures, have been less successful in the case of general categories, such as the polis,[3] rather more successful with technical terms, such as the subdivisions of the polis, which had, by comparison, a far more precise usage and function (N. F. Jones 1987). It is as yet far from clear whether and in what capacity 'polis' is a defining term, particularly when confronting non-Greek or peripheral regions with the institutions of central, southern, and eastern Greece, together with their various colonial offshoots. John Davies has suggested that 'micro-state' is to be preferred, not least because it is inclusive rather than exclusive, positively inviting comparison with other European and Mediterranean polities (Davies 1997: 27–36). Such an approach also avoids the potential confusion inherent in the term 'polis' between state and city. In Thessaly, Macedonia, and Thrace the 'state' entity was a complex web of social groups, cities, and other settlements. Unfortunately, the analysis of political machinery in the three states under consideration is hampered by a shortage of appro-

---

[2] See e.g. Arist. *Pol.* 1269^{a}36–^{b}12 (Thessalians *tout court*); 1305^{b}28–30 (Pharsalus); Roussel (1976) 161–7; Morgan (1991) 132–3.

[3] Esp. Hansen (1993; 1997b; 1997c); see Davies (1997) 24–7.

priate written sources. Before the fourth century BC, inscriptions are rare in Thessaly, virtually non-existent in Macedonia and Thrace, while ancient narrative discussions of these communities (to which the authors did not belong and had limited access), are inconsistent and imprecise. Our most detailed narratives, from Herodotus and Thucydides, do not set out to compare and contrast different political systems. Judgement takes precedence over analysis (cf. Roussel 1976: 167; Hatzopoulos 1996: i. 149–53, 219–30, 463–86). So a modern reassessment of the north-eastern states bordering on central Greece should try to redress this imbalance in favour of a more empirical approach.

What is most apparent in our three regions is that the political and geographical fragmentation characteristic of many parts of Greece did not occur in any of them. Even in Thessaly, where individuals and groups of Pharsalians, Larissaeans, or others are sometimes referred to, it is the collective voice that is most often heard,[4] although the spotlight falls on individual leaders such as Lycophron and Jason of Pherai in the fourth century BC (Xen. *Hell.* 2. 3. 2; 6. 1. 4–19; 6. 4. 20–37). This collective approach, represented by a caste of leaders with bases in different cities, closely resembles the ruling groups of the manifestly monarchical Macedon and Thrace. We might therefore expect a more complex relationship between territory and power than in autonomous, nucleated communities.

Modern historians often assume that civic identity developed comparatively late in our three regions and was largely the result of ideas and attitudes penetrating from the coastal colonies of Chalkidike and the Thermaic Gulf in the case of Macedon and Thrace, and more generally from central and southern Greece.[5] This perception is based on an assumed relationship of active models and passive recipients (as between poleis of the Aegean coast on the one hand and inland civic communities of Thessaly, Macedonia and Thrace on the other). In view of my earlier remarks about categories and definitions, these assumptions may need to be re-examined. The development of urban life in Macedonia presents a peculiar problem. On the one hand this is seen as part of a controlled central strategy on the part of Argead rulers in the fourth century BC, with movements of population to new, planned city centres. Yet, on the other, Hecataeus and Herodotus describe native poleis—Macedonian, Paeonian, and Thracian—already in existence during the second half of the sixth and beginning of the fifth century BC.[6] Ps.-Scylax refers to *poleis hellēnides* and *poleis* (by implication

---

[4] Hdt. 8. 27; 9. 1; Thuc. 1. 102. 4; 2. 22. 3; 3. 93. 2; 4. 78; 132. 2–3; 5. 5; Sordi (1958) 109–234, 329–40; T. R. Martin (1985) 60–7; Hatzopoulos (1996) i. 219–20, 491–2; *IG* ii². 116 = Harding no. 59, cf. nos. 49, 62, 87.

[5] Westlake (1935) 24, 32; Sordi (1958) 313–17; Hammond, Griffith, and Walbank (1972–88) i. 65–6, 145–7, 192, 203; iii. 54 (Thrace); Hammond (1989) 9–19.

[6] Hecat. *FGrH* I F 1, 152, 161, 166, 169; Hdt. 7. 123. 3; ps.-Scyl. 66; Siganidou (1993) 29–31; Hatzopoulos (1996) i. 37–123, 463–86.

non-Greek, or simply 'other', including inland—not coastal, i.e. colonial—foundations). Should we take them to be analogous to poleis elsewhere? If so, what implications does this have for civic structures and institutions? Macedon was an ethnos led by a dynasty of kings, the Argeads. How could autonomous civic structures develop in such a context? The same argument can be applied to Thrace. During the fifth century BC the southern part (between the Balkan range and the Black and Aegean Seas) of the overall region occupied by Thracian tribes (stretching as far as the Carpathian mountains), was united under a princely dynasty, from the Odrysian tribe (see Figure 12.3 below). Thucydides describes the various tribal communities under Odrysian authority in his account of king Sitalces' invasion of Chalkidike in 429 BC (2. 96. 1–97. 2). The historian does not discuss cities in the interior; but the existence of urban centres can be surmised from archaeological evidence, and one of these, identified from a new inscription as Pistiros, in the central (Thracian) plain north-west of Pazardjik, is in process of excavation.[7]

As far as Thessaly is concerned, there is unambiguous evidence for civic or community centres of some kind, if not actual cities, as early as anywhere else in the Greek peninsula. A plethora of sites (status uncertain) is mentioned by Homer, but a preliminary conspectus of their successors shows that only some of these names (albeit a significant minority) continued to represent major cities and centres of population in the classical period (Helly 1995: 89–95 and figs. 1–2). Epigraphic discoveries over recent decades have almost tripled the number of inscriptions known from Thessaly and published in *Inscriptiones Graecae* (volume ix/2). These latest finds have increased our knowledge of Thessalian political institutions, not only in the better-represented hellenistic and imperial ages but for pre-hellenistic times too. There was an extraordinary range of civic centres in Thessaly, hitherto hardly known even by name, and whose documentation has barely begun.[8]

It seems clear, therefore, that there is a great deal of potential information still to be derived from more concentrated study of local landscapes, the degree of interaction between different communities, and the intensity of land use. It is clear too that this kind of information is highly relevant to historians. In central and southern Greece the emergence of historical poleis or 'micro-states' often coincided with two material trends: towards distinct settlement nucleations within a given territory (though leading centres might vary over time) and, parallel with this, the extension of a given community's influence to include remote parts of an emerging

---

[7] Bouzek, Domaradzki, and Archibald (1996); Archibald (1998) 107–12, 135–45.

[8] See the annual bulletins in *RÉG* and *SEG*, esp. *RÉG* 106 (1993) 505–13; 108 (1995) 475–88; *SEG* 40 (1990) 149–59; 41 (1991) 182–5; 42 (1992) 133–45; A. Tsiaphalias publishes 80 inscriptions, many previously unknown, in *AD* 43/2 (1988) 276–84; Decourt (1995).

political terrain.⁹ This process was very slow; the intensification of activity documented by archaeological surveys often took several hundred years at least. The time perspective is a very long one compared with the much shorter scale of historical chronologies. But it is the large timescale which sets out the fundamental perspective for 'historical' time. The emergence of historically attested institutions must be set somewhere into this. In the northern and north-eastern Aegean both the pattern of subsistence and the size of coastal and inland plains, together with the distribution of natural resources within them, militated against the kind of land division which was more likely to occur around small harbours ringed by hills and rocky coasts. It is worth looking at community development in the light of such practical constraints.

The expansion of archaeological surveys which document changes in spatial as well as temporal relations has presented archaeologists and historians with issues which are not addressed by traditional studies of institutional development. What is the relationship between 'sites' on the ground, large and small, and the machinery of government? Can we detect the results on the ground of deliberate political actions? These kinds of questions have been asked of other archaeological material in Europe and the Near East. We might consider in this connection how they have been approached with regard to other emerging European states or kingdoms. The European Iron Age (approximately eight centuries from c.800 BC) for the most part lacks the historical scaffolding afforded by ancient sources. Archaeologists have made a virtue of necessity, developing new methods of analysis with some surprisingly sophisticated results. Study of different types of settlement has shown that craft or industrial activities took place on most sites, so it is hard to isolate controlling settlement types, a role which has been suggested for hillforts, on the grounds that specialist activities were concentrated there.¹⁰ The role of larger settlements can best be understood by investigating the wider context, social, political, and geographical, to which they belonged.¹¹ Such approaches explicitly embed political considerations within a wider socio-economic framework.¹² Moreover, many scholars now believe that kinship links, of the type traditionally considered fundamental to 'clan' or 'tribal' societies, were less significant than *local* community structures.¹³

Empirical studies of the kind referred to, which analyse settlement characteristics in a much more systematic way and in far more detail than is the case for Greek sites, demonstrate the huge inadequacies of such theoretical models as have been adopted to date for these 'prehistoric' Euro-

⁹ De Polignac (1995); Jameson, Runnels, and van Andel (1994) 372–81; Morgan and Whitelaw (1991); J. M. Hall (1995).
¹⁰ J. D. Hill (1995) 48–9 with further refs.; Cumberpatch (1995) 69–84.
¹¹ Woolf (1993); Cumberpatch (1995); Gebhard (1995); Ferrell (1995); J. D. Hill (1995).
¹² Cf. Morgan (1991) 149 with reference to Achaean social structures.
¹³ Gosden (1989); Kristiansen (1991); J. D. Hill (1995) 51.

pean societies (concepts such as 'central place', 'chiefdom', and the like: cf. Büchsenschütz 1995: 63). This is where the absence of documents referring to the mechanisms of social organization is felt most keenly. The supposed 'tribal' origins and structures of some continental European societies in the pre-Roman period are beginning to look just as artificial as Greek and Macedonian 'tribes' were, in historical times at least.[14] The inference of socio-political networks from a painstaking reconstruction of detailed interactions between different sites is a difficult process. The symbolic way in which such networks were cemented (through agreements, the use of designated officials, development of administrative functions) may be near impossible to recover. But the very fact that complex interactions were so highly developed presupposes the existence of equally complex enabling mechanisms. Field studies in northern Europe thus complement in spatial terms what can be inferred from rare epigraphic documents in Macedonia (Hatzopoulos 1996) and the Molossian kingdom of Epirus (see Davies in this volume) about the potential levels of organization in an ethnos-dominated region and the ways in which they might fluctuate over time.

The use of space over time should in principle provide some objective indication of the intensity of social interaction. Ferrell has applied 'rank size analysis' (a statistical technique used successfully by modern geographers to determine a site's relative importance within a region) to four areas of the north-east of England (Ferrell 1995). Her study shows that in three of the areas examined there is no evidence of a marked settlement hierarchy, in contrast to assumptions previously made about 'hillforts' forming control points within the region. Only in north-east Durham, the area connected with the rise of Stanwick as a centre of political power in the first century BC, does her analysis show a hierarchical correlation (Ferrell 1995: 133–4). It seems, therefore, that different patterns of settlement coexisted within north-east Britain and that larger sites of 'hillfort' type do not necessarily tell us very much about the overall pattern of settlement or ranking of other sites. The importance of this method of investigation rests on the fact that it does not depend on postulates about a site's impact on the surrounding landscape; the 'rank size rule' is a phenomenon discovered empirically.[15] There is a power law (logarithmic) relationship between settlement size and position within a regional hierarchy: the nature of the hierarchy depends on the kinds of interactions enjoyed by settlements within the group. This in turn depends on the degree to which the regional group is itself open to other, external interactions, as well as to those of its members. Where sites are relatively isolated, from each other as well as from outside, there is little

---

[14] Bourriot (1976); Roussel (1976); Hatzopoulos (1996) i. 45, 49, 102–3, 118–122, 220, 245–56.
[15] Zipf (1949); Stewart (1958) 222; Ferrell (1995) 130; for other applications see Bak (1997) 24–6.

evidence of hierarchy. The higher the interdependence between sites, the greater the likelihood of ranking among them. If more sites are connected up to external contacts, this tends to flatten the degree of hierarchical ranking.[16]

Rihll and Wilson (1991) have used a slightly different route to argue that a settlement's size is proportional to its importance within a region, but their methods are also based on the principle that dynamic interactions have a direct effect on a settlement's growth. Like Ferrell's study, their model is based on deductive reasoning, not on a theoretical proposition, and can be applied elsewhere. The emphasis in both of these studies on dynamic inter-actions at the expense of static institutions reflects a growing trend in the kinds of models which archaeologists and geographers are coming to pre-fer.[17] At the same time, 'urbanization'—the material symptoms of the kinds of interactions here posited—is now recognized as a Mediterranean-wide phenomenon in the first half of the first millennium BC (*Urbanization*) and, by the same definition, was widespread in Europe as a whole in the second half (Audouze and Büchsenschütz 1991: 212–43). Perhaps we should con-sider such phenomena as different stages in the development of increasingly more complex and more closely integrated social and political networks.

Before considering our three regions more closely, let me summarize the value of these comparative studies to the topics explored in this chapter. Detailed spatial exploration and analysis have been successfully applied by archaeologists in parts of north-west Europe, providing a great deal of infor-mation about the nature of socio-economic interaction within and between given regions, information which can also be used to infer socio-political relationships. The analysis of spatial relations has rarely been used by clas-sical archaeologists as a method of understanding intercommunity contacts of a socio-economic or political kind, despite the successful application of such methods by geographers. Yet such methods are particularly appro-priate in the study of ethnos-dominated regions. What follows will explore how we might begin to examine the interplay of spatial with other factors in Thessaly, Macedonia, and Thrace.

Space

Thessaly has the clearest geographical definition of the three areas under consideration (Figure 12.1). It is limited to the west by the Pindus range, with its very different ecological patterns, to the north by the massif of Olympus, and to the south by the eastern extension of the Pindus which culminates in the Othrys mountains and the Malian Gulf. The valley of the Spercheius river forms a bridge to Boeotia. The chains of hills which cut across this lozenge-shaped expanse separated off the principal plains

---

[16] Vapnarsky (1969), cited by Ferrell (1995) 130.
[17] Van der Leeuw (1981); Hodges (1987); Cherry (1987) 149–52.

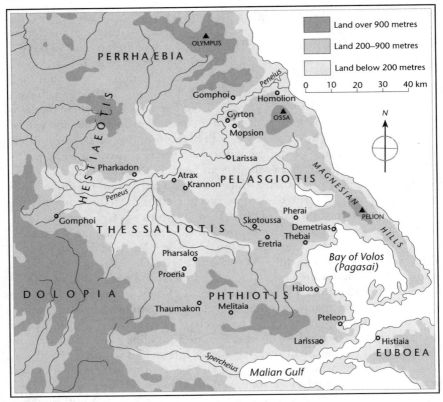

FIG. 12.1. Principal geographical features and sites
of Thessaly in the archaic and classical periods.

that constituted its four historical divisions (tetrads): Hestiaeotis in the
upper Peneius basin in the far west, broader Thessaliotis in the south-west,
drained by the southern tributaries of the Peneius, Phthiotis in the hill-
locked south-eastern corner, and Pelasgiotis in the widest eastern slice of
the plain, from the Vale of Tempe to the Bay of Volos (Pagasai). Around the
four tetrads lay the 'Perioecis', literally, the ring of territory surrounding
these inner provinces: Perrhaebia in the far north, Dolopia in the west,
Achaea and Magnesia in the drier, hillier far south and east. The very
concept of an 'inner' territory and an 'outer' one emphasizes a distinctly
landward focus, which is underscored by the consistent avoidance, both in
prehistoric and in early historic times, of the coastal fringe.

Macedonia is much more difficult to encompass because it had no clearly
defined boundaries. The historical focus of the people of Macedonia, the
Makednoi, according to classical and later sources, was on either side of the
lower Haliacmon river, particularly the regions of Bottiaea, Emathia, and

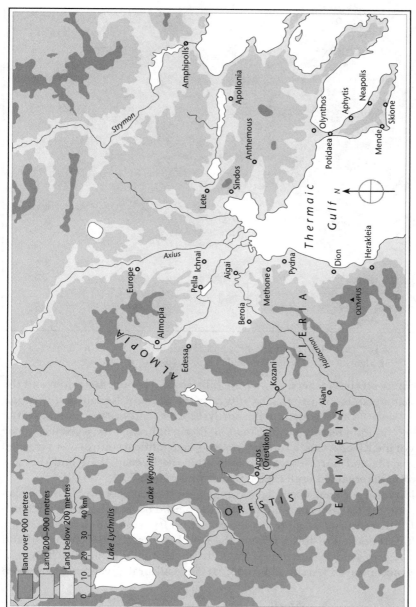

Fig. 12.2. Principal geographical features and sites of Macedonia in the archaic and classical periods.

Land over 900 metres
Land 200–900 metres
Land below 200 metres

0 10 20 30 40 km

Lake Lychnitis

Lake Vegoritis

ORESTIS

ELIMEIA

Argos (Orestikon)

Aiani

Kozani

Edessa

Almopia

ALMOPIA

Europe

Beroia

Pella Ichnai

Aigai

Axius

Methone

Pydna

PIERIA

OLYMPUS

Haliacmon

Dion

Herakleia

N

Thermaic Gulf

Potidaea

Olynthos

Aphytis

Neapolis

Skione

Mende

Lete

Sindos

Anthemous

Apollonia

Amphipolis

Strymon

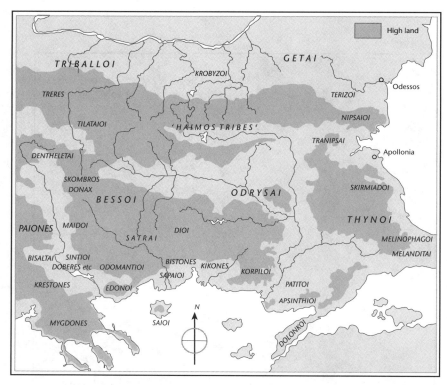

FIG. 12.3. Thrace in the fifth and fourth centuries BC: (*a*) tribes
as identified by Herodotus and Thucydides [for (*b*) see opposite].

Pieria, protected respectively by the hills around Mount Bermium and the
Pierian uplands (Figure 12.2). Culturally the adjacent Kozani and Kastoria
plains and the hilly regions to the north (Florina) and west (Grevena) shared
many common features with Emathia–Pieria in prehistory, as well as those
east of the River Axius, although Macedonian political control was extended
westwards and north-eastwards only after the Persian Wars and the new
territories remained under separate administration.[18]

Thracian speakers occupied a vast geographical area between the Aegean
Sea and the Carpathian mountains in the period broadly between the tenth
and fifth centuries BC. Thrace for present purposes is understood as the
southern portion of this territory, the land between the Balkan massif and
the Aegean, which constituted the Odrysian kingdom from the fifth century BC onwards (Archibald 1998: 93 ff.). Cultural divergences between

---

[18] Hatzopoulos (1996) i. 167–216; he applies the term 'new lands' to areas east of the River
Axius.

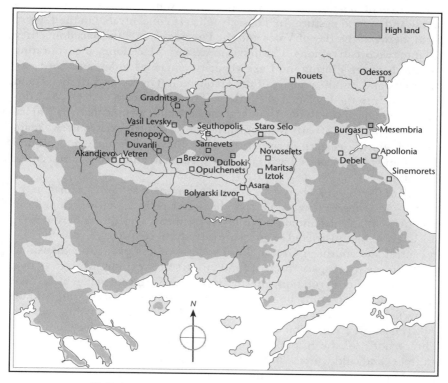

(*b*) Principal geographical features and sites; many
significant sites which can be connected with the Odrysian
princes lie well inland and north of the Rhodope range.

the northern and southern provinces of Thrace (i.e. north and south of the
Balkan range) in the early first millennium BC were enhanced by the creation
of a multi-tribal kingdom under the command of a dynasty drawn from the
Odrysian tribe, based on the central (Thracian) plain and the valleys of the
Hebros (Maritsa) and Tonzos (Tundja) rivers (Figure 12.3).

Tell settlements

The most visible, though by no means the only, kinds of settlement from
the prehistoric age in Macedonia, Thrace, and Thessaly are the conical or
flat-topped tells or table mounds (*toumba* or *magula* in Greece), which accumulated over centuries of habitation. They were usually built in plains with
easy access to water supplies. In early Neolithic times they might actually
be located on river flood plains, thereafter more usually just above them,
so as to exploit natural irrigation (van Andel and Runnels 1995), and well

placed to exploit a range of different resources: water meadow, well-drained
arable and upland pasture. In Thessaly tells are concentrated in the Larissa
plain, between the Bay of Volos and the Peneius river.[19] In Macedonia they
fall into two broad regions. The first is in western Macedonia, incorporating
the area between Florina and Lake Vegoritis (ancient Lynkos and Eordaea),
the upper and middle reaches of the Haliacmon (Orestis and Elimeia), and
extending into the lowlands of Bottiaea. The second is in eastern Macedonia, either side of the River Axius and the Chalcidic peninsula.[20] In Thrace
analogous patterns of early prehistoric tell development existed in two main
areas: along the eastern peripheries of the Strymon estuary and around
the Drama plain,[21] as well as in northern, eastern, and throughout central
Bulgaria.[22]

Each of the regions where tells became a dominant settlement form in the
Balkan–Aegean area (Figure 12.4) is characterized by a well-developed soil
structure with a substantial humus layer. Primitive agriculture here was far
less likely to be constricted by pressure on natural resources, as was the case
in central and southern Greece; local soils were less prone to exhaustion,
there was plenty of space to spread and virgin soil to exploit. Moreover, by a
simple form of crop rotation, alternating cereals with root vegetables, small
herds could successfully be reared on the stubble after harvesting and on
fallow fields, providing manure which would help to regenerate the existing
soils (Halstead 1989). The western parts of Thessaly and Macedonia, like
Thrace north of the Rhodopes, have a continental climate with hot, dry
summers and cold winters and high levels of rainfall in spring and autumn.
The climate and vegetation of the coastal regions are much more similar to
those of central and southern Greece (with cool, wet winters and hot, very
dry summers), but large parts of the Thermaic Gulf, the lower Strymon,
and Nestos estuaries were marshy in the pre-Roman period and known
sites are situated on foothills rather than in the lowlands,[23] while the barren
Magnesian hills made the coast of Thessaly unattractive for settlement
except around the Bay of Volos.

The significance of tell locations for later periods lies in what they can
tell us about preferential economic strategies. Additional factors, strategic
or otherwise, would have strengthened the attraction of particular locations
as these economies became more diversified. Some of the finest Thessalian
sites (Pharsalos, Krannon, Pherai) best exemplify the early association of
some cities with fortresses.[24] Many of the economic considerations relevant

[19] Gallis (1992); van Andel and Runnels (1995) 488, fig. 6.
[20] Heurtley (1939) xxii–xxiii; Kokkinou and Trantalidou (1991); Andreou and Kotsakis
(1987).
[21] In the modern *Ephoreia* of Eastern Macedonia: Koukouli-Chrysanthaki (1982); Renfrew
and Gimbutas (1986).   [22] Dennell (1978); Detev (1982).
[23] Rapp and Kraft (1994); Hatzopoulos (1996) 111.
[24] Hansen (1993) 9; Katakouta and Toufexis (1994): Pharsalus.

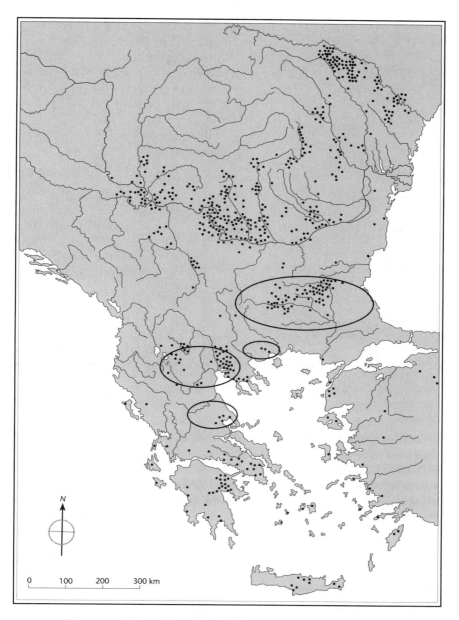

FIG. 12.4. General location of Bronze Age settlement in the
Balkans. Principal concentrations of tell sites referred to in
the text are encircled; clockwise from bottom: Larissa plain;
central and eastern Macedonia; Drama plain; Thracian plain.

in prehistory continued to be highly relevant in later centuries. But environmental factors have rarely played a crucial part in determining settlement patterns (B. K. Roberts 1996: 145). With the exception of three intensive field surveys which are still in progress, two of which are in Macedonia— one in the environs of Grevena, south-west of Kozani,[25] the other in the Langada Basin[26]—the third in Bulgaria,[27] little detailed survey work on site distribution has yet been carried out in the regions under consideration. Investigation of all three areas is still largely confined to primary data collection (site registration and the accession of finds). In Thessaly an extensive programme mounted by the French School at Athens since 1975 in association with the Greek Archaeological Service has made considerable progress towards the creation of successive site maps for the region.[28] No comparable maps have yet been created for the whole region of Macedonia in successive phases, though site registers have been published for certain localities (Karamitrou-Mendesidi 1993). The same is true of Thrace. There is clearly a great deal more to be learnt, not least because the current focus of published settlement studies is, with a few notable exceptions, largely confined to periods before the first millennium BC.

The existence of tells has created a problem, in so far as researchers have been preoccupied with the discontinuity of such sites. In practice, settlement and activities were more fluid in the past than distribution maps suggest.[29] The beginnings of new settlement networks, beyond but not excluding older tell sites, were already apparent in the Late Bronze Age (second half of the second millennium BC).

Thessaly

Recent investigations at Krannon, Larissa, Velestino (Pherai), Halai, and elsewhere have shown that many classical Thessalian centres had lengthy settlement histories, reaching back to the early second millennium BC.[30] The change is best exemplified around the Bay of Volos (Pagasai). The older tells of Dimini and Sesklo still show signs of significant activity in Late Bronze Age times. Communal tombs with protogeometric and geometric pottery

---

[25] Wilkie (1988) 241; Wilkie *et al.* (1990) 309.

[26] Andreou and Kotsakis (1987; 1994).

[27] The survey, begun in 1996, is jointly sponsored by the Institute of Archaeology, Sofia, on behalf of the Bulgarian Academy, and the École Française d'Athènes, under the direction of Alexei Gotsev and Véronique Chankowski respectively. A preliminary report will appear in *BCH*.　　　　　　　　　　　　　　　　　　　　　　[28] Decourt (1990); Gallis (1992).

[29] B. K. Roberts (1996) 120–45; Bailey (1997).

[30] Krannon: *AD* 38/2 (1983) 204–5; Larissa: *AD* 32/2 (1977) 119–26; 35/2 (1980) 287–8 (Phrourion hill); 42/2 (1987) 274–8 (Ag. Giorgios Larissis); Velestino: *AAA* 16 (1983) 95–106 (Magoula); *AD* 38/2 (1983) 193; 39/2 (1984) 144–6; 40/2 (1985) 191–3; 42/2 (1987) 255–61, 270–1; 43/2 (1988) 243–9; 44/2 (1989) 219–24; 45/2 (1990) 201–3; 207. Volos: *AD* 37/2 (1982) 225–6; 38/2 (1983) 197; 39/2 (1984) 141–2; 42/2 (1987) 254–5; 43/2 (1988) 240–1; 44/2 (1989) 218–19.

(tenth to eighth centuries BC) were built close by, indicating the close proximity of Early Iron Age communities.[31] It now looks as though the emerging pattern of archaic settlement, while including new sites in remoter locations, was not divorced from older ones. The degree of continuity between older, Bronze Age sites and those of the first millennium BC has not been hitherto suspected. But what kind of continuity do these activities represent? In Thessaly the trend away from tell sites to naturally defended hilltops preceded rather than succeeded changes at the end of the Bronze Age (late second millennium BC). What characterized this period is greatly enhanced diversification in the economic sphere and a more visible social hierarchy. During the first half of the first millennium BC some sites began to emerge with greater prominence than others. These include the places connected with illustrious heroes in the Homeric poems. Halstead has suggested that at this time access to food resources and raw materials may have depended on the ability to accumulate private capital resources (the control of stored grain, woollen textiles, draught animals: Halstead 1989: 77). The existence of a site hierarchy, while plausible in terms of current evidence, will need to be demonstrated not just by extensive mapping of site locations but also by statistical measurements of the kind carried out by Ferrell in north-east Britain.

Macedonia

Thessaly is usually included within the sphere of Mycenaean polities. Current investigations in Macedonia, however, indicate that the caesura so often drawn between the palace-based economies of central and southern Greece and the tribal areas of the north is neither as simple nor as great as is usually depicted. Features such as extensive storage capacity and the development of full-time crafts beyond the domestic or village level, indicative of controlling élites, which evidently had direct contact with Mycenaean centres in the form of imported pottery and even a local linear script, demonstrate a sophisticated level of community organization.[32]

Archaeological investigations in Macedonia have accelerated enormously since M. Andronikos' spectacular tomb finds at Vergina. But little has been added to our knowledge of pre-hellenistic settlements. No large-scale topographic studies comparable to those in Thessaly have yet been initiated. But there is some evidence that, as in Thessaly, older centres of habitation, with their origins in the second millennium BC if not earlier, continued to

---

[31] Dimini: *AD* 35/2 (1980) 272; 39/2 (1984) 138–40; 42/2 (1987) 245–6; 44/2 (1989) 225–7; Milojčić and Theocharis (1976); Marzolff (1980) on the area survey incorporating the Volos Bay area; Snodgrass (1971) 155, 180, 205–6 on proto- and full geometric pottery and tombs. Halai: J. E. Coleman (Cornell Univ.) in *Arch. Rep.* (1992–3), 49–50.

[32] Hänsel (1979); Wardle (1980); id., *Arch. Rep.* (1987–8) 42–5; linear script on a pithos rim, Megali Rachi, Aiani: Panayotou (1986).

act as nuclei. New excavations at the 'Mesimeriane Toumba' at Trilophos, near Thessaloniki, the 'Double Trapeza' at Anchialos, at burials close to unexcavated sites at Gynaikokastro, Kilkis, and elsewhere,[33] show that such locations continued to be inhabited for many centuries, and in the case of the 'Toumba' now engulfed by the city of Thessaloniki, continuously, it seems, from the second millennium BC onwards.[34]

Thrace

In Thrace there seems to have been a more widespread move to lowland locations, within the vicinity of tells, around the beginning of the first millennium BC, sometimes, as in the area of Nova Zagora, east central Bulgaria, in very close proximity. There is also growing evidence that upland positions were utilized in a more systematic way. But the relationship between these different changes has not been examined in detail. Excavation, even of the most limited kind, has been conducted only at a tiny proportion of these sites. But impressions of disparate and chaotic movement have given way to an emerging pattern of small, longer- and shorter-lived, sites (Gotsev 1997).

Such small village-type sites were superseded in certain locations by completely new kinds of urban settlement in the period between the fifth and first half of the fourth century BC. At Vasil Levsky, near Karlovo, in a well-watered river basin below the Sredna Gora, there are signs of dressed masonry structures, imported Greek painted roof tiles, Attic figured and black-glazed pottery, as well as local 'greyware', also turned on the fast wheel.[35] Both the relative volume of different finds, native as well as imported, and the distance of this site from any waterway, indeed from any Aegean centre, indicate that this was a planned native foundation, organized by a local ruler collaborating with Greek merchants who supplied building materials and probably experienced masons for the stonework. Whatever its precise character, however, this site did not outlive the fifth century BC.

At Vetren, north-west of Pazardjik, and only one kilometre from the modern bed of the River Maritsa, a much more ambitious settlement was

[33] Trilophos: D. Grammenos and K. Skourtopoulou, *AEMTh* 6 (1992) 1995, 339–48; Anchialos/Sindos: M. Tiverios, *AEMTh* 5 (1991) 1994, 235–46; 6 (1992) 1995, 357–68; Gynaikokastro: Th. Savopoulou, *AEMTh* 2 (1988) 1991, 219–29; Giannitsa: A. Chrysostomou, *AEMTh* 5 (1991) 1994, 127–36; Aik. Papaeuthymiou-Papanthimou and A. Pilali-Papasteriou, *AEMTh* 6 (1992) 1995, 151–62; ibid., A. Chrysostomou, P. Chrysostomou, 163–76.

[34] K. Soueref, *AEMTh* 2 (1988) 1991, 243–55; 3 (1989) 1992, 215–26; 5 (1991) 1994, 191–208 (Early Iron Age to 4th-cent.-BC levels); 6 (1992) 1995, 273–94; S. Andreou-K. Kotsakis, 5 (1991) 1994, 209–20 (Late Bronze Age/Early Iron Age levels, resemblances with Assiros and Kastanas); Kotsakis and Andreou (1992) 259–72; Th. Stephanidou-Tiveriou, 6 (1992) 1995, 295–304.

[35] K. Kisyov, *Archeologicheski razkopki i prouchvaniya, 1989* (Archaeological Reports and Discoveries: Kyustendil 1990, in Bulgarian), 41–2; I am most grateful to Kostadin Kisyov, Director of the Archaeological Museum at Plovdiv, for allowing me to see his excavation and finds in 1989.

founded in the second half of the fifth century BC. Traces of the easternmost section of a large, planned city are in the process of excavation on a terrace above a former river bed. These include sections of a powerful circuit wall, over two metres thick, whose construction began in the fifth century with a remodelling early in the fourth (Domaradzki 1996). The size of this site is hard to establish because of dramatic geo-morphological changes to the local environment. But the known direction of the northern and eastern circuit walls provides grounds for believing that the area enclosed would originally, on a conservative estimate, have covered at least 50 hectares. The large numbers of coins discovered (more than 800 to date), including rare Thracian regal issues of the late fifth and fourth centuries BC, as well as inscriptions, one of which is a royal or princely decree, show that this was an important administrative and commercial centre, with a river port in the vicinity.[36]

Hierarchy and community

In both Thrace and Macedonia much of the initiative and capital resources required for planning new sites came from rulers and their immediate circles: Perdiccas (454–413 BC) engineered the synoikism (refoundation on one site of multiple communities) of Olynthos in 432 BC (Thuc. 1. 58. 2); his son Archelaos (413–399 BC) built roads and forts and reorganized the training and equipment of infantry and cavalrymen (2. 100. 1–2). Archelaos' new capital at Pella can hardly have been conceived on more modest lines than Olynthos, even if it had far fewer inhabitants to begin with. In Thrace the Odrysian Sitalces (c.450–424 BC) built roads, while both he and his nephew Seuthes (424–c.410 BC) kept a very close managerial hand on the organization of fiscal matters (2. 98. 1, 97. 3–5). In both regions major decisions of public concern were expressed, and continued to be expressed well into the hellenistic age, as royal decisions.[37] The role of kings as founders of cities is comparable to that of *oikistēs*—the nominal founder of a Greek colony. But unlike the leaders of the socially sanctioned Greek colonies, Macedonian and Thracian rulers had the power to initiate projects and concentrate resources. Historians like Herodotus, Thucydides, and their successors of the fourth century BC highlight such personal initiatives.[38] What such accounts fail to illuminate is that 'royal' foundations were exceptions, not the rule, and were rarely created in a vacuum. They usually involved a *rearrangement* of existing communities, which might subsequently be re-engineered along different lines (well

[36] Velkov and Domaradzka (1994); Bouzek, Domaradzki, and Archibald (1996); Archibald (1998) 138–42, 226–30.

[37] Badian (1982) 35–6; Hatzopoulos (1996) i. 337–8, 368, 371–2; Velkov and Domaradzka (1994); Archibald (1998) 226–8, 310–11.

[38] Just. 8. 6. 1; Arr. *Anab.* 7. 9. 2 (Philip II); cf. Hatzopoulos (1996) i. 179–209, 473–4.

illustrated at Olynthos, both in Thucydides' narrative and in the excavated city).[39]

Such foundations tell us nothing about the general state of community development. For that we are dependent on investigations of the settlements themselves, their location in space, and their institutions. I have briefly outlined the apparent longevity of some major and lesser sites in Thessaly and Macedonia. It is hard to believe that the mechanisms and political practices in place during the fourth and third centuries BC should in all cases have been entirely different from those pertaining two centuries earlier, planned changes notwithstanding. Two new studies, one on Thessaly (Helly 1995), the other on Macedonia (Hatzopoulos 1996), have attempted to discern the evolution of political and administrative processes during the classical period. Helly has reconsidered two fragments of Aristotle's lost *Constitution of the Thessalians* which refer to the division of Thessaly into μοῖραι under Aleuas the Red (frr. 497–8 Rose; or a Skopas: Xen. *Hell.* 6. 1. 19). Land division is linked here with the introduction of a new military organization, with each unit of land providing forty cavalrymen and eighty hoplites. Aleuas cannot be dated at all precisely. Helly dates both him and the land reorganization to the late seventh or early sixth century BC (1995: 95–6, 175–99). The details of military recruitment on which the reform was based are provided by the pedantic writer Asclepiodotus of the late first century BC, so the neat scheme which Helly resurrects may well represent a late sophistication lacking in the original arrangement. What is significant about the reform is that it was intended to be a *regional* plan, applied in theory to all Thessalian communities. We do not know how different types of settlement—urban centres, rural villages, hamlets—were integrated or how extensive the original scheme was. Nevertheless, the 'tetrads', which underpinned the subdivision into *klēroi*, were artificial units, which logically came into existence as part of the same scheme.[40] The dynamic force behind the implementation of the reform and its administration was the leading families, variously referred to as *basileis* (nobles) or the 'leading men', among whom the Aleuadai of Larissa, the Skopadai of Krannon, and the Echekratidai of Pharsalos were simply the best known outside Thessaly (Helly 1995: 101–30). The 'leading men' provided candidates for civic magistracies, whose responsibilities are slowly being delineated in recently discovered inscriptions. But the integration of civic and regional officials still presents many unresolved problems, a matter to which I shall return below.[41]

Hatzopoulos argues that the regional institutions of Macedonia were simi-

---

[39] D. M. Robinson (1929–52); Hatzopoulos (1996) i. 195–201.

[40] Gschnitzer (1954) 451–64; Sordi (1958) 313–20.

[41] Helly (1995) 19–58; *contra*: Hatzopoulos (1996) i. 477 n. 2; Sordi (1997), with additional comment by Ducat (1997), Mulliez (1997); Lévêque (1998).

lar to those of Thessaly, with a similar concept of community (ethnos) law
and mechanisms for community representation. But unlike the 'federal'
states of central Greece, which began to develop truly representative bodies
in the fifth and fourth centuries BC (in the form of federal assemblies with
statutory elected members of the constituent cities or members), Macedonia and Thessaly retained an overarching regional hierarchy which in either
case did not properly integrate its constituent parts with the mechanisms of
government (Hatzopoulos 1996: i. 219–20, 427–9, 477–96). In both states
the smallest political units, while having full responsibility for local, internal
affairs, did not negotiate with bodies outside the ethnos or kingdom, but always through an intermediary, regional authority. There was no deliberative
assembly. This is why, to the outside world, it was the king or his officials
(or in the case of Thessaly, a body of distinguished worthies) who acted,
not individual communities (ibid. 81, 261 ff., 324–59). It is possible that a
similar system existed in Thrace under the Odrysian kings. Current evidence does not show what criteria and limitations applied to office-holders,
whether local or regional. Indeed, were it not for Hatzopoulos' indefatigable
persistence, the existence of Macedonian *civic* magistrates called *epistatai*
(as distinct from royal appointees) would not have been recognized at all
(ibid. 381–429).

These huge gaps in our knowledge of local administrative practice make
the occasional detailed document very hard to evaluate. This is aptly illustrated in an inscription found near Metropolis, Hestiaeotis, which seems
to show the persistent determination of a lineage (?) group (*syngeneia*),
called the 'Basaidai', to retain strict control over the office of *tagos* as late
as the second half of the third century BC.[42] The culture of exclusivity
nurtured by Thessalian, Macedonian, and Thracian aristocrats made such
élite groups open to criticism from contemporary circles which fostered a
more egalitarian ethos. But all Greek communities restricted citizenship
in order to manipulate access to power. Documents such as this do not
provide the means to judge the degree to which Thessalian communities
had less 'open government' because eligibility for office was restricted to
a named group (whose membership and numbers are unknown). It is also
possible to find self-organizing units which show precisely the opposite tendency, namely towards the empowerment of relatively insignificant groups
living in close proximity. In the partly urbanized, still largely rural, territories of the middle and lower Strymon valley and the Drama plain, as
well as Orestis in western Macedonia, 'sympolities' (collective community
organizations) were mechanisms designed to cope with a dispersed civic
membership which was not restricted by ethnic considerations.[43] Common
resources and decision-making could thus be pooled between one or more

---

[42] Helly (1970); Moretti (1976) no. 97; *SEG* xxxvi. 548; Davies (1996) 646–9.
[43] Hatzopoulos (1996) i. 63–104; 65 n. 2: Thessalian parallel.

'urban' units and various villages. Although most of the epigraphic evidence is hellenistic or later, there are strong grounds for believing that these kinds of mechanisms were much older. There is no need, then, to see urban sites as populated exclusively by Greeks or Macedonians at the expense of underprivileged 'natives'.

It might prove helpful to pursue the different levels by which communities were integrated within the ethnos and beyond it. Integration might be charted in two ways—economic and institutional. The first cannot be done until settlements are better documented. They could then be analysed spatially for different periods in the way Ferrell has described for north-east England. This leaves the institutional approach. Apart from the evidence for public magistracies, various 'second-order' bodies (intermediate between state or community and individual) provide clues about how social and political integration worked. In a new reassessment of 'second-order' entities John Davies has identified two alternative mechanisms operating in the Greek world, one based on assimilation, with the creation of quasi-kin groups from amongst neighbouring communities; the other on segregation, with certain social groups being subordinated to a landowning élite (Davies 1996: 609–10). These twin strategies, the one based on physical proximity, the other on shared values, evidently represent more widespread social phenomena; Ferrell has identified a similar pattern in her spatial analyses and suggests that economic independence or mutual reliance would tend to reinforce one or other strategy.[44] The three polities under discussion seem outwardly to have adopted the second mechanism as the means of establishing extensive power relations. 'Seem', because the process itself and its results are more complex than the allegedly simple origins attributed by historians allow—the appearance of a ruling dynasty (the Argeadae in Macedonia, the Odrysians in Thrace) or a once-for-all solution (the reforms of an Aleuas or Skopas). What we can document epigraphically is a mature stage of political development, frequently reflecting Hellenistic cross-fertilization of institutional styles and titles.[45] How far were these processes of social and political integration consciously initiated by groups of people?

In his *Archaeologia* Thucydides states that many of the peripheral, barely Greek, fringe areas of the peninsula pursued an archaic lifestyle, carrying arms even in the fifth century BC. By linking the bearing of arms with piracy, the historian casts such societies into a category of political primitivism which had long since been thrown off by the more advanced poleis of central and southern Greece (1. 5. 3–6. 2). I have argued, on the basis of archaeological research outside the Mediterranean, that Iron Age urban centres emerged as a function of wider socio-political developments within

---

[44] Ferrell (1995) 134–5, citing Durkheim (1984).
[45] N. F. Jones (1987) 79–81, 266–81; Hatzopoulos (1996) i. 103, 118–21.

European regions. We are not obliged to believe that urban centres developed in our three regions in spite of royal or aristocratic fiat, or that ethnos identity was somehow at variance with civic identity;[46] on the contrary, these broader regional entities provided innovating opportunities which contributed to the creation of 'nation' states.

---

[46] Westlake (1935) 31–2; cf. Hatzopoulos (1996) i. 480.

13
A Wholly Non-Aristotelian Universe: The Molossians as Ethnos, State, and Monarchy

J. K. DAVIES

KING PYRRHUS apart, the history of the Molossians features all too rarely in the textbooks. Yet the increase in relevant epigraphic documentation, and the quality of loving scholarly attention which it has recently been receiving, have combined to shed such extra light on the region's affairs and political articulation that it is becoming possible to recognize that it provides a valuable case study of the themes and preoccupations of the present volume. The purpose of this paper is therefore to bring the evidence before a wider audience which may not be fully aware of recent and current work, especially that of Nicholas Hammond and Pierre Cabanes.[1] I shall focus mainly on the fourth century BC rather than on Epirus in Pyrrhus' time or on its third-century vicissitudes and the shift to republic c.232, since it seems to have been in the late fifth and the fourth centuries that the main work of political creativity in the region was being carried forward.

Readers to whom the Molossians may be little more than a name may find it helpful to orient themselves in the light of Figures 13.1 and 13.2. The Molossian homeland lay within Epirus, that area of present-day Greece and Albania which lies between the Adriatic Sea and the watershed formed by the north–south Pindus mountain chain. In its original meaning ('mainland' as seen from the Greek coastal colonies, especially Corcyra) Epirus was no more than a geographical expression for an area inhabited by various peoples who had settled in the fertile but inaccessible upland plains. Severe constraints of physical geography caused their cultural and linguistic links to be more with the Macedonians to the east and the Illyrians to the north than with the coast, for at least in summer the Zygos pass above Metsovo made Macedon and Thessaly accessible, while the low watershed north-

The comments and suggestions of the two editors have much improved this paper. To them both, and to Zosia Archibald, my grateful thanks. Once again, I gladly acknowledge with gratitude the generosity of the Leverhulme Trust in making possible the dedication of my time to these and other connected scholarly endeavours. Thanks are also due to Susie White for her help with the maps.

[1] The most useful, in chronological order of publication, are Cross (1932); Franke (1955); Lévêque (1957b); Franke (1961); Hammond (1967); Cabanes (1976a); and Cabanes (1981) (with *SEG* xxxi. 590 as a summary of inscriptions there used).

FIG. 13.1. Mainland Greece and the Adriatic.

west of present-day Ioannina allowed movement into the upper valleys of
the Aous and the Drin. In contrast, the water-flow (from a high rainfall area)
has caused all the rivers of the region to carve such precipitous gorges on
their descent from the uplands to the coast as to present near-impenetrable
obstacles to their use as routes of communication. As a result the region
long seems to have interacted comparatively little with the Greeks to the
south and west, so that such 'history' as can be written is largely an archaeo-

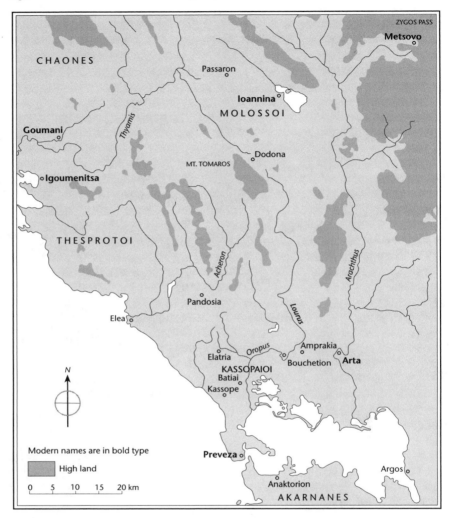

FIG. 13.2. Epirus in the fourth century BC.

logically based survey of culture and settlement[2] until contemporary Greek descriptions began with Hecataeus in the late sixth century. By then the sanctuary and oracle of Zeus at Dodona had long been visited, the names of the various peoples of Epirus were known, the three predominant peoples— Chaones, Thesprotoi, and Molossoi—and some others were approximately localizable as on Figure 13.2 (though boundaries were clearly very fluid),

[2] For which see above all Hammond (1967).

and political relationships between the ruling families and Greek powers were beginning to take some sort of shape.

Aristotelian and other universes

None the less, as will become clear below, Greek visitors in the early fifth century clearly found the region, its culture, and its polity alien, and erected a mental boundary between it and their own Greekness which took a century or more to dismantle. In fact it was not Greek needs, ambitions, or curiosity which eventually eliminated the barriers so much as a calculated effort by the ruling dynasty of one Epeirote people, the Molossoi, to manœuvre themselves into a position of predominance within the region. Based as they seem to have been in the fertile plain round Ioannina, they were better placed to do so than their neighbours, and one can even dimly detect what would now be called a twin-track policy. One track was cultural—to present themselves as Greek (with a Trojan War ancestry—(5) below), to take from Greek culture what could be turned to political use, and to manipulate the Greek political process in their own interest as best they could. The other track was power politics. Visible components, described in more detail below, are a dispute with Corcyra in the 470s (6), collaboration with neighbours in exerting pressure on Akarnania in 429 (6), *rapprochements* with Athens in the 420s and later (7), a push westwards over the Tomaros range by *c*.400 to take over Dodona from the Thesprotoi,[3] involvement with Syracuse and the Illyrians in the 380s, and an opportunistic alliance with Athens in the 370s (7). The parallel in both respects with Macedonian activity in the same period is obvious, and will recur throughout this paper.

However, the 'alienness' alluded to above, and flagged in the phraseology of the title of this paper, needs closer notice. Though originally devised as a rhetorical trope, the title has proved to be an accurate summary of the Molossian situation, in three ways. First, as set out below (p. 253), we are dealing with what it became customary to refer to as a *koinon*, a 'common thing'. It is a matter of observation that the ways in which the Molossoi/ Epeirotes ran their *koinon* were so far removed from the centralized polis systems on which Aristotle concentrated overwhelmingly in his *Politics* as to require recognition as a different sort of polity. Secondly, psychologically, Aristotle does really seem to have been unable to get his mind round the so-called *koina*. Granted, among the 158 *Constitutions* there was a *Constitution of the Epeirōtai*, though its only surviving fragment (fr. 494 Rose, from Stephanus of Byzantium) merely reports the name *Amyntai* as that of an *ethnos Thesprōtikon*. Granted, also, Aristotle does occasionally glance in *Politics* at the Molossian monarchy of his own day, once as one of a string of examples of how the benefactors of communities can become kings (1310^b34 ff.:

---

[3] See nn. 28 and 74 below.

Kodros, Cyrus, kings of Lakedaimonioi and Makedones and Molottoi), and once as an illustration, along with the Lakedaimonian monarchy, of the principle that the less direct power monarchs have, the less they are envied by their subjects and therefore the less despotic they are, so the longer they endure (1313ª23 ff.): but that is all. There is no trace of any reflection of the developments which (as will be set out below) the epigraphical documentation reveals: not, surely, out of specific prejudice against the Molossians, but as an aspect of the fact that those polities which were peoples rather than singleton or synoikized poleis—Achaeans, Aetolians, Akarnanians, Arcadians, Lycians, Malians, Phocians, Thessalians—are barely studied or alluded to by Aristotle. Weil surmised that their absence was because Aristotle had not finished the study of such polities at the time of compiling the *Politics* (1960: 309, 383), but that is hard to accept in the light of the use made of the *Politeiai* in the four central books of the *Politics*. More plausibly, such polities were for him *symmachiai* ('alliances') of the kind which he belittles at 1280ª25 ff., rather than integrated polities, and were therefore not strictly the business of *Politics*.

Moreover, there is a third aspect, to do with Aristotle's teleological approach. Conscious as he plainly was of the Greek lawgiver tradition, throughout the *Politics* he tends to regard a polity as something created by a political engineer and applied to a society in order to achieve certain objectives. He has little time for the alternative view of a governmental system as something which is secondary to, derives its shape from, and is a gradual, organic, and unplanned outgrowth of, the essential components of the society which evolves it and is 'administered' by it (I choose that word, rather than 'governed' or 'controlled', in order not to imply a greater gulf between society and a state apparatus than it is prudent to predicate in most Greek polities). Yet, when we inspect a 'constitution' or a system within which certain components interlock in certain sorts of ways, the primary challenge, no matter whether such a system is 'organic' or the product of conscious creation, is always that of identifying the power-bases, entrenched interests, prejudices, or feared contingencies to which the system is a 'best fit' response. I have no doubt, as will appear, that such an approach illuminates the arrangements visible among the Molossoi/Epeirotai, but it goes directly against Aristotelian assumptions. Perhaps the clearest example of the latter is his criticism of Lycophron the sophist at 1280ᵇ6–10: driven by the view that 'any polis which is really so called, not just nominally, must concern itself with virtue', he argues that if it does not it is simply an 'alliance', differing only spatially from other 'alliances', and in such a context 'law is an agreement, and, as Lycophron said, a guarantor to each other of just things, but quite unable to make the citizens good and just'. For any observer so relentlessly opposed to Lycophron's pragmatic analysis, Epeirote arrangements were bound to appear pre- or non-moral, as it were, and therefore to fall outside the circle of polities which deserved to be taken seriously.

That Aristotelian mental frameworks have influenced the directions of study within classical scholarship, and still do, is undeniable. It is a great pity, since they obscure the study of some very important socio-political evolutions. Epirus, like Lycia (see Keen, this volume), is one of the areas where the nature and scale of such evolution has become more visible in the last twenty-five years as more documents have come to light. The shape of what follows will therefore be first to sketch what was previously known, and then to show how the epigraphic documentation has filled out, and in some respects subverted, the older picture. As Hatzopoulos has written:

> even in the Hellenistic age one may read exhaustively the literary sources concerning Pyrrhos without even suspecting the existence of the elaborate institutions of the *ethnos* revealed to us by contemporary inscriptions. . . . It is probably by mere chance that half a dozen inscriptions from pre-republican Epirus have preserved for us the memory not only of local governing bodies, but also of a body of magistrates at the central level called either *damiorgoi* or *hieromnemones* and headed by a *prostatas* and a secretary.[4]

More recent work has brought out the existence of comparable institutions in Macedon itself.[5]

The older external evidence

First, then, to sketch what we would know without the newer epigraphical evidence. This makes no pretence of adding to currently available surveys and analyses, and provides only a set of very basic guideposts. It is convenient to identify twelve sets of evidence, of very various kinds. (1) From the Greek outsider's point of view (but hardly from that of the Molossians themselves), the first must be the creation of the coastal settlement map by colonization[6] (see Figures 13.1–2). If we leave on one side those settlements reputedly founded in mythical time, after the Trojan War,[7] the defining steps were the eighth- to sixth-century Corinthian foundations of (in approximate chronological order) Corcyra, Epidamnos, Amprakia, Anaktorion, Herakleia, Apollonia, and the undatable Elea,[8] the Elean colonies at Bouchetion, Elatria and Pandosia in the river valleys north-west of Arta,[9]

[4] Hatzopoulos (1994) 165–6, citing Cabanes (1976a) 151–95.
[5] See Hatzopoulos (1996); Cabanes (1996); Archibald (1998).
[6] Hammond (1982) 266–73; Sueref (1993).
[7] Viz. Bylliake, Orikos, Bouthrotos, and Amphilochian Argos, for which see Thuc. 2. 68. 3 and the Hecataean tradition as set out by Hammond (1967) 419, 451 ff.
[8] Hammond (1967) 414 ff., 425–43; J. B. Salmon (1984) 95–100, 209–17; Cabanes (1988a) 51–61. For Elea see Franke (1961) 40–1; and Hammond (1967) 542.
[9] For their Elean origin cf. [Dem.] 7. 32, with Strabo 7. 7. 5 (324 C.), and Hammond (1956); Franke (1961) 52; Hammond (1967) 427, 477–8, 481, 498; Dakaris (1971b). Batiai, mentioned

and the parentless Orikos.[10] Of these, only Pandosia represents any substantial advance beyond the coastal fringe. The contrast with item (2), the remote inland oracle site of Dodona, is therefore all the sharper, for not only was the oracle frequented by Greeks from the eighth century onwards,[11] but the institution was always seen as Greek, whatever the ethnic origins of the priestly *Selloi* may have been and whatever may have been meant by calling Zeus at Dodona 'Pelasgian'.[12] Item (3) is the description of the area and its inhabitants in ancient ethnographic sources. The basic surviving account is that of Strabo, as he journeys southwards down the East coast of the Adriatic. The core of his account has been plausibly argued by Hammond to derive from Hecataeus via Theopompus.[13] As it has reached us, the material comprises a seemingly endless set of fairly outlandish names of ethnē, which are presented either as being all on one level (thus Theopompus, allegedly naming fourteen, though we do not know which ones), or as being grouped in some way round the three major names Chaones, Thesprotoi, and Molossoi, which can be more or less safely located geographically (see Figure 13.2).

Item (4), closely linked with (3), comprises the cultural characteristics of the region, especially its land-use, population, and settlement patterns.[14] Transhumant pastoralism is widely assumed to have been a prime pattern of land use, from Upper Palaeolithic through the archaic and classical periods to recent observation,[15] though current warnings of the interdependence between pastoralism and agriculture and of the preconditions required for long-distance transhumance enjoin caution.[16] The ethnic mix of the region is being studied, with all appropriate reserve, both via the personal names attested epigraphically[17] and via the mapping of the movements of peoples and crystallizations of polities within the southern Balkan

by Strabo loc. cit. but not by Demosthenes, which may have been a fourth Elean colony, is located by Hammond (1967) 55–6, 478 at Kastro.

[10] Hammond (1967) 127 ff., 416. Statements that Orikos was a Euboean foundation of 730 BC. (Boardman 1980: 226; Sueref 1993: 33) seem to stem from a conjecture of Beaumont based on Schol. A.R. 4. 1174–5a–b (Hammond 1967: 416 n. 2).

[11] Cf. Hesiod fr. 319 MW, and *Il.* 2. 748–51, 16. 231 ff., with Hammond (1967) 371 ff.

[12] Parke (1967) 1–163, esp. 3–4; Hammond (1967) 367 ff.; Sueref (1993) 36–7; De Simone (1993), with copious bibliography.

[13] Strabo 7. 5. 6–12 (315 ff. C.), with Hammond (1967) 454–5; Theopompus, *FGrH* 115 F 382.   [14] Useful synoptic sketch in Cabanes (1989) 152–5.

[15] Respectively Kourtessi-Philippakis (1993); Cabanes (1979) 192–3; Vokotopoulou (1986) i. 340, 374–5, and Hammond (1991); and Campbell (1957).

[16] Cf. the discussions by Cherry (1988); Hodkinson (1988) 51–8; Halstead (1990); Morley (1996) 143–58; with the summary by Whittaker (1988) 3–4 of the messages conveyed by the papers in Whittaker (1988): however, note also the cumulative evidence for the Early Iron Age assembled by Snodgrass (1987) 188 ff. L. Nixon and S. Price, 'The Diachronic Analysis of Pastoralism through Comparative Variables' (*ABSA*, forthcoming), provides a more complex diachronic analysis of the factors involved in transhumance.

[17] Cf. especially the papers collected in Cabanes (1993b).

zone.[18] In particular, the post-Homeric emergence of the Molossians themselves, and their intrusion into previously Thesprotian territory, is being seen within a context of movement to and fro across the Pindus chain.[19] Fundamental to the political developments to be sketched below is the entire absence of poleis from the inland region, whether in the human geographers' sense of 'functionally differentiated nucleated settlement plus agricultural/pastoral hinterland' or in the Aristotelian sense of polity. True, Stephanus of Byzantium quotes Hecataeus for some polis names in the region, and there is a case for thinking that the well-preserved and excavated urban site of Kassope may go back to the fourth century,[20] but settlement in 'villages' is explicitly attested for the whole region in the mid-fourth century by [Skylax] 28 (Chaones) and 30–2 (Thesprotoi, Kassopoi, Molottia). In this way the region illustrates the fundamental perception that there is no necessary correlation between the process of urbanization and the process of crystallization into a large effective polity, whether an Aristotelian polis or not. In one direction, as comparative evidence makes increasingly clear (Morgan, this volume), big nucleated sites could and did develop in landscapes not conventionally deemed to be part of the patchwork of poleis: in another, as here in Epirus, polities could become geographically extended and politically effective entities long before urbanization developed.[21]

(5) A fifth item is the story of the origin and history of the Molossian royal family. Its developed version, set out by Justin 17. 3. 1–22, traces the family back to Pyrrhus son of Achilles and his rape of Heracles' granddaughter Lanassa at Dodona, while also creating a Trojan pedigree for the Chaones through Priam's son Helenus and Hector's widow Andromache. The version probably owes much to the third-century historian Proxenus (*FGrH* 703), but since an encomium of Alexandros I is attributed to the

---

[18] Cf. Papazoglou (1978); Hammond (1994); Archibald (1998) 93 ff.

[19] Strabo 7. 7. 11 (328 C.) for the explicit statement. Cf. Lepore (1962) 58; Hammond (1967) 365 ff.; Sueref (1993) 36; De Simone (1993) 53. Cf. also Dakaris ap. Cabanes (1979) 187 for the identification of a north–south line of forts, on the western edge of the Ioannina basin, defining the 5th-cent. frontier between Molossoi and Thesprotoi. The installations will have become otiose in the 4th cent. once Molossia had expanded over the Tomaros range to take in Dodona and the headwaters of the Acheron.

[20] Oidantion (*FGrH* 1 F 98—but the polis-title may be Theopompus', not Hecataeus'), Sesarethos (F 99), Baiake (F 104: but Hammond (1967) 451 identifies with Strabo's Bylliake, 7. 5. 8), and possibly Dodona (F 108). For Stephanus' accuracy on these matters cf. Whitehead (1994). For the site of Kassope cf. Dakaris (1971b) and especially Hoepfner and Schwandner (1986) 75–140. The latter infer from the entry for 'Kassopa' in D3, line 25, that a synoikized city was already in being by the mid-4th cent. (1986: 77 and 280 n. 142), but the absence of a comparable entry in D5 should give pause, while [Demosthenes]' terminology in 7. 32 would be a serious *suggestio falsi* if Kassope already existed as a *polis*.

[21] Cabanes (1988a) 213–33; (1989) 153–4. This is not the occasion to join the argument about the degree of precision with which the words *polis* and *kōmē* were used in ancient sources: see Rhodes (1993). For a brief dogmatic sketch of the necessity of separating the various processes alluded to in this paragraph see Davies (1997) 29–30.

younger Theodektes in the third quarter of the fourth century (*FGrH* 113 T 1), while substantial components of the story of the family's Thessalian origins were already known to Pindar, it would be unwise to assume that the story was wholly a third-century construct.[22] Its similarity to Herodotus' *logos* of the origins of the Argead kings of Macedon suggests that the two *logoi* were related in some way (though we have no means of telling which was primary), and that the Molossian one had a comparable purpose, that of creating a cultural passport as Greeks for the royal family.

With item (6) we enter the fifth century via two vignettes of Epeirote affairs, one placed in the 470s–460s (Thuc. 1. 136–137. 2), the other in 429 (Thuc. 2. 80–2), which between them put some flesh on to the bones of Hecataeus' ethnography.[23] The first is Thucydides' uncharacteristically Herodotean[24] account of Themistocles, on the run from Argos and refused entry to Corcyra, turning perforce to Admetus, the king of the Molossians, 'who was not friendly to him' (1. 136. 2, with ibid. 4 for a partial explanation) but none the less accepted his suppliant status, protected it against an Athenian and Spartan posse, and helped him on his way to Pydna and Persia. The second, more politically meaty, describes the attempt of the Amprakiotai and Chaones and their allies to overrun Akarnania in summer 429, meeting defeat in an attack on the city of Stratos. For Thucydides the Chaones and the other Epeirotes are barbarians, then without kings but led 'by annual leadership' by Photius and Nikanor 'from the ruling lineage'.[25] The Thesprotians are also 'kingless' (2. 80. 5), while the Molossians and Atintanes were led by Sabulinthos as guardian of the boy-king Tharyps. Oroidos as king led the Parauaioi, 1,000 Orestai being entrusted to him by their king Antiochus (2. 80. 6). The prospect of Macedonian assistance (2. 80. 7) helps to emphasize the permeability of the Pindus watershed and the distances over which alliances could be contracted.[26] Since Thucydides has already reported that though the citizens of Amphilochian Argos had brought in and Hellenized some of the neighbouring Amprakiotai, 'the

[22] The crystallization of the story is analysed by Cross (1932) 7 ff. and Dakaris (1964) 14–49. Carlier (1984) does not cover the Molossian–Epeirote kingship.

[23] The brief sketch of the topography of the coast opposite Corcyra at Thuc. 1. 46. 4 shows an unselfconscious use of the term '*Thesprōtis (gē)*' for the area but is otherwise ethnographically uninformative. Likewise, the Greek word '*ēpeiros*' at Thuc. 1. 136. 1 clearly means 'mainland' and is not for Thucydides the name of a polity.

[24] The motif of *hiketeia* ('supplication': Gould 1973) clearly derives from the narrative of Odysseus at the Phaeacian court (*Od.* 7. 139 ff.) and was itself copied by Proxenos (?) for young Pyrrhus (Plut. *Pyrrhus* 3.2).

[25] 2. 68. 9; 80. 5; 81. 3; 81. 4; 81. 6; 81. 8; 82. Quoted phrases from 2. 80. 5.

[26] Cabanes (1979) 192 used Plut. *Pyrrhus* 11. 9, Polyb. 9. 37. 7, and Livy 31. 29. 15 as evidence that forms of speech in north-west Greece, westwards and southwards from Macedon, varied little. Within the general framework of north-west Greek that may be true, but the passages in Polybius and Livy are focused on the contrast between Greek and Roman/Latin, and therefore provide no relevant evidence. Plutarch's evidence, implying that some of Pyrrhos' (Epeirote) soldiers could pretend to be Macedonians, is perhaps more substantial.

other Amphilochoi are barbarians' (2. 68. 5), we are meant to be left in no doubt that the Greek–barbarian boundary is real and close: the contrast with Aetolia, whose inhabitants Thucydides cannot quite bring himself at 3. 94. 5 to describe as barbarians,[27] should tell us something about contemporary Athenian perceptions.

Item (7) is a scattered set of documents and references which link the Molossian royal family to various Greek powers from the 420s onwards. It begins with the tradition that a certain Tharybas[28] was sent to Athens for education and on his return instituted 'laws and a senate and annual magistrates and the structure of a state'.[29] Consistently, the Athenians who honoured an exile named Arybbas in the 340s thought they knew that his father and grandfather (viz. Alketas I and Tharybas/Tharyps) had previously received the honour of [*polit*]*eia*.[30] The trail then goes cold until 385/4, under which year Diodorus narrates Dionysius' attempt to establish his influence on the eastern shore of the Adriatic by allying himself to the Illyrians through Alketas I, then in exile in Syracuse, and by providing military resources to help them restore Alketas to power.[31] The story has its oddities, for Dionysius' ulterior motive is implausibly said to have been to pillage Delphi,[32] while the alleged loss of 15,000 Molossian lives at the hands of the Illyrians will hardly have endeared Alketas to his subjects. However, the coda to the story, the despatch of a Spartan force to assist the Epeirotes, is plausible enough in view of Spartan willingness a couple of years later to commit substantial effort and resources to besieging Olynthos and breaking up her confederation, while the tension between Illyrians and Epeirotes implied by the story is confirmed by a report in Frontinus of a further Illyrian attack on Epirus c.360.[33] Moreover, the implication of

---

[27] Cf. also Hdt. 8. 47, clearly reflecting a sense that Thesprotia, the Acheron river, and Amprakia formed a cultural boundary; Eur. *Phoen.* 138 (Tydeus the Aetolian is *meixobarbaros* ['half-barbarian'] in his weaponry); and [Skylax] 33 ('Thenceforward [sc. from Ambrakia] Greece begins to be continuous as far as the Peneius river'). Brief discussion in Cabanes (1979) 190–1.

[28] *Sic*, by emendation of a confused manuscript tradition, on the assumption that the spellings Arybbas (*IG* ii². 226), Tharrypas (Plut. *Pyrrhus* 1. 3), and Tharyps (Thuc. 2. 80. 6) represent the same dynastic name. See Dakaris (1964) 50–63.

[29] Justin 17. 3. 10 and 12 ('leges et senatum annuosque magistratus et rei publicae formam'): Plut. *Pyrrhus* 1. 3 reflects a subtly different tradition by emphasizing how he 'adorned the cities [*sic*] with Greek habits and letters and humane laws'. The embassies to, *inter alia*, Molossia and Thesprotia claimed by the putative speaker of [And.] 4. 41 ('Phaiax'?), could, if historical, belong in this context.

[30] *IG* ii². 226 (see n. 36 below), lines 2–5. All editions restore [*polit*]*eian* ('citizenship'), but [*atel*]*eian* is formally possible. However, Arybbas is invited to *deipnon* in the prytaneion, as are citizens, not to *xenia*, as his companions are (lines 28–33), so the presumption of citizenship must stand.   [31] D.S. 15. 13. 1–4. Biographical sketch in Dakaris (1964) 63–7.

[32] Ibid. 1. Dodona would make more sense, as my former pupil Nick Beeson suggested to me before 1977 (thus too Caven 1990: 149), but the single treasury there in the early 4th cent. (Dakaris 1971a: 42, fig. 9, whence Hammond 1994: 432, fig. 19) cannot have held much.

[33] Xen. *Hell.* 5. 2. 11 ff. and 37; 5. 3 *passim* (Spartans and Olynthus): Front. *Strat.* 2. 5. 19,

Diodorus' narrative, that Epirus was being drawn into the general concert
of Greek powers, is confirmed by Alketas' appearance in the next decade as
the (perhaps subordinate) ally of Jason of Pherai in south-eastern Thessaly,
as confederate ally (with his son Neoptolemus I) of Athens, and as a supportive witness for the Athenian general Timotheus at the latter's trial in
November 373.[34]

Other components of the picture can be sketched more briefly. (8) The
coinage of the region, limited in comparison with that of the Damastinoi
to the north (May 1939), starts in the early fourth century and is relevant
in the present context mainly for showing the ethnic names which were
and were not in use. Names used are ΜΟΛΟΣΣΩΝ ('of Molossians') on an
early fourth-century issue, an ethnic ΕΛΕΑΙ or ΕΛΕΑΤΑΝ ('of Eleatai') on
an issue of the third quarter of the century (which probably denotes the
ethnos 'Elaioi' known as a Thesprotian constituent ethnos in the late fourth
century), issues of the ΚΑΣΣΩΠΑΙΟΙ ('Kassopaians') in the same period,
and a series labelled ΑΠΕΙΡΩΤΑΝ ('of Apeirotai'), the start of which is
dated to the 320s by Franke and Hammond on (it seems) historical evidence
rather than numismatic criteria.[35]

(9) The Athenian decree mentioned above, which offered the exiled Arybbas some help and protection but was carefully vague about his requests,
is commonly dated *c*.343/2 on somewhat shaky grounds.[36] Its value in the
present context is partly that his hosts made a point of emphasizing his
Greekness by recording, at top and bottom of the huge stele, his three Panhellenic chariot victories,[37] but mainly that it shows how ancestral links

involving the Dardanian king Bardylis (on whose kingdom and expansion see Hammond 1994:
428–9) and 'Harrybas' the Molossian.

[34] Xen. *Hell*. 5. 2. 7; *IG* ii². 43 = Tod ii. 123, lines 109–10, with (1) D.S. 15. 36. 5 for
Timotheus' diplomacy of 376/5, (2) Xen. *Hell*. 6. 2. 10 for action as ally, (3) Nepos, *Tim*. 2. 2
for 'Epirotas, Athamanas, Chaonas' as allies, and (4) *IG* ii². 101 = *Syll*.³ 154 for the prescript of
an Athenian decree of 373/2 honouring 'Alketas son of Leptines, Syracusan', i.e., presumably,
Alketas of Epirus as adoptive son of Dionysius' brother; [Dem.] 49. 22–4.

[35] Respectively Franke (1961) 85–106, group I; Franke (1961) 40 ff.; Hammond (1967) 548;
and Franke (1961) 116 ff. with Hammond (1967) 537, 560, arguing that since Aristotle wrote
a *Constitution of the Epeirotai*, the Epeirote alliance was in being by 326/5, so that the coinage
so labelled can be placed in that decade.

[36] *IG* ii². 226 (= *Syll*.³ 228 = Tod ii. 173), much studied in recent years: cf. *SEG* xxviii. 51;
M. J. Osborne (1981–3) i. 56, D14; ii. 81, D14; iii. 29, T6, and 50, T37; Heskel (1988); Lawton
(1992) 241; (1995) 134 no. 122: see also n. 30 above. He had been extruded from his throne
by Philip (Justin 8. 6. 4–7) in favour of Alexandros I by the date of [Dem.] 7. 32 in 343/2,
but the *terminus post quem non* which Diodorus ostensibly provides by recording his death as
his first entry for 342/1 (16. 72. 1) is subverted by Justin's statement (7. 6. 12) that he 'in
exilio consenuit': to the point indeed where he has been thought to be the 'Aryptaios' who
took his Molossians into the anti-Macedonian alliance of 323 but covertly collaborated with
the Macedonians (D.S. 18. 11. 1). For the problems see Beloch and Reuss quoted by Cross
(1932) 39 n. 2, 43 n. 2, but also Errington (1975) and Heskel (1988).

[37] At Olympia and P[yth]ia τελέωι, which here probably means 'four-horse chariot' because
of the reliefs atop the decree (thus Moretti 1957: 125 no. 450, with discussion, and Lawton

and contemporary axis-building combined to lock Epirus (as we may now begin to call the region) inescapably into the power struggles of Balkan Greece. (10) The career of Alexandros I reflects the same picture even more clearly.[38] Born c.362, client king for Philip from early 342 in place of the deposed Arybbas, and active in the Macedonian interest in northern Greece until his crossing to Italy in spring 334 and his death in battle in winter 331/0, he took Epirus irreversibly into the mainstream of Greek, and indeed of Mediterranean, politics. The same is true for the sequel, item (11), the interlocking histories of the Molossian and Macedonian royal families thereafter. The key link here was Olympias, daughter of Neoptolemus I of the Molossians, taken in 357 as wife by Philip II of Macedon and mother of Alexander the Great. Both actively and symbolically she was a major figure in Balkan politics thereafter until 317, when King Aiakides of Epirus supported her in Macedon once too often and was promptly deposed by a 'common decree of the Epeirotai'.[39] Even more is it true for the last item, (12), the detailed portrayal by Plutarch of King Pyrrhus I (reigned 307–302 and again 296–272). For present purposes his main contribution is his description of how 'the kings were accustomed to offer sacrifice to Zeus Areios at Passaron, a place of the Molossian land, and to make oaths with the Epeirotai, the kings swearing that they would rule according to the laws, the Epeirotai that they would preserve the kingship according to the laws'.[40] The similarity of the ceremony to the monthly exchange of oaths between Spartan kings and 'the ephors on behalf of the city' has long been noticed,[41] with 'the agreements which Lycurgus made for the king with the city' echoing (or pre-echoing) the formal structures within Epirus whose creation Justin attributed to 'Tharybas'.[42]

The newer epigraphical evidence

The literary and numismatic evidence, then, takes us far enough into the social and political structures of what became Epirus to be tantalizing, but not far enough to elucidate their articulation. It is here that the new, or newly restudied, epigraphic evidence from the fourth century fills out the picture. For the sake of the Greekless reader I present it here in the form of translated documents, with some attempt at approximate chronological

---

1995: 135): the third crown is lost. Conjectural dates in Heskel (1988) 193–4, without reference to Moretti.

[38] Basic data best still in Berve (1926) ii. 19–21 s.v. 38 Alexandros. He does not figure in Heckel (1992).

[39] D.S. 19. 36. 4. For her judicial execution soon afterwards see Will (1979) 51–2.

[40] Plut. *Pyrrhus* 5. 2.

[41] Most recently by Carlier (1984) 276, who notes, however, that the Epeirote ceremony was not periodic, as it was at Sparta.

[42] Justin 17. 3. 10–12, quoted above, n. 29.

order.[43] Their sequence in time has long been a subject of debate, but for present purposes it is the overall impression and the general direction of development which matter most. It would of course be wholly impractical to present the whole of the third-century material here, and in any case it is the documents which certainly, probably, or possibly date from the fourth century which show the development most clearly.

D1. *Dodona, sanctuary of Zeus: citizenship decree, c.370–368*
Franke (1955) 89; Evangelidis (1956) 1–13, whence *SEG* xv. 384; Murakawa (1957) 393–4, whence *SEG* xviii. 264; Hammond (1967) 525 ff.; Larsen (1964); (1967); (1968) 276–8; Harvey (1969); Cabanes (1976*a*) 534 no. 1; Hannick (1976) 139–41, whence *SEG* xxvi. 696; Cabanes (1981) 33 no. 1, with further references. The date is approximate, representing a presumed period of sole kingship after the death of Alketas, perhaps *c.*370, but before the joint kingship of Neoptolemus (I) and Arybbas attested by Paus. 1. 11. 3. The words underlined were written *in rasura*, i.e. as a replacement for words originally cut but then chiselled out (Evangelidis 1956: 2).

> By good fortune. While Neoptolemos the (son) of Alketas was king, to <u>Philista</u> <u>the wife of Antimachos</u> from Arrhonos was given citizenship, to herself and descendants, when Eidummas Arktan was *prostatas*, when Amphikorios Arktan was secretary, when *damiorgoi* were Androkades Arktan of Eurumenaioi,[44] Laphurgas of Tripolitai, Eustratos of Kelaithoi, Amunandros of Peiales, Sabon of Geno(i)aioi, Deinon of Ethnēstai, Agelaos of Triphylai, Thoinos of Omphales, Kartomos of Onopernoi, Damoitas of Amymnoi, of (month) Datuios.

D2. *Dodona, sanctuary of Zeus: citizenship decree, c.370–368*
Same stele and same references as D1. However, differences of orthography (Evangelidis 1956: 4) prove that D1 and D2 were cut by different masons, perhaps therefore at different times in the same year. The last two names are written in the nominative case, not (as with the others) in the genitive, for no obvious reason.

> By good fortune. When Neoptolemos the (son) of Alketas was king, to the family of Phinto of Arrhonos was given citizenship, to herself and descendants, when Eidumas Arktan was *prostatas* of Molossoi, when Amphikorios Arkt[a]n was

---

[43] Professional epigraphists may take exception to the format of the lemmata which follow. The objective has been purely to allow the Greekless reader to follow the sequence of basic study and debate, not to attempt a proper republication. Names have been given in strict transcription, with no attempt to harmonize or to Romanize, since inconsistent spellings in the documents are themselves relevant historical evidence. Round brackets ( ) enclose editorial corrections, additions, and explanations. Square brackets [ ] enclose letters now lost or illegible, which can sometimes be restored. The number of dots indicates the approximate number of lost letters. Dashes within square brackets [- - -] indicate gaps of uncertain length: the more the dashes, the longer the gap. The brace { } in D6 encloses a letter cut onto the stone in error.

[44] Or 'of Eurumenai' if Hammond (1967) 526–7 is correct in identifying it with the polis Eurumenai named by D.S. 19. 88. 4 in 312, but since the form 'Eurumenaioi' here appears to denote a constituency rather than a personal ethnic, it is safer to transcribe as literally as possible.

secretary, when *damiorgoi* were Androkade[s] Arktan of Eurumenaioi, Laphurgas of Tripolitai, Eustratos of Kelaithoi, Amunandros of Peiales, Sabon of Genwaioi, Deinon.

D3. *Epidaurus, Asklepieion: list of* thearodokoi, *c.360*
IG iv²/1. 95, with *SEG* xxvi. 189; Daux (1971) 355–7 for the name 'Phorbadas' (not 'Korradas') in line 32; Cabanes (1976*a*) 116–20, 144–5, 173–85, whence *SEG* xxvi. 427 and 447; Hammond (1980*a*) 473, whence *SEG* xxx. 361; Hammond (1980*b*) 9 ff.; Cabanes (1981) 38 no. 7 (lines 20–32 only), whence *SEG* xxxi. 590; Cabanes (1983) 107; *SEG* xlii. 291.

The document, too long to quote in full, comprises a list of *thearodokoi*. These 'sacred-envoy-receivers' were appointed in each city or polity by major temples and sanctuaries to act as hosts for the envoys who were sent out periodically by each temple to announce the dates of festivals, etc. This list is of those appointed by those in charge of the sanctuary of Asclepius at Epidaurus, and like other such lists is arranged geographically in the order of the itinerary followed by the envoys. Since the *thearodokos* for Macedonia was Perdiccas (*IG* iv²/1. 94. 9: king 365–359) and for Syracuse Dion and Herakleidas (ibid. 95. 39–40), the date of the list's initial creation must be *c.360*. Names added later are denoted here by smaller type, those added *in rasura* (see D1 above for the term) by underlining. The relevant portion is headed 'Thearodokoi to Akarnania' and moves west from Corinth along the Corinthian Gulf to list, first, communities in Akarnania (lines 8–19), and then communities further to the north-west. The latter section runs:

20 Leukas: Timophrades
    Palairos: Leontios
    Anaktorion: Aristion Periandrou
    Apeiros: Geron Aristodamou[45]
    Pandosia: Dioszotos
25 Kassopa: Skepas, Aristodamos
    Thesprotoi: Petoas, Simakos
    Poionos: Admatos
    Korkyra: Mnasalkidas, Antiredas
    Chaonia: Dorupsos
30 Artichia: Schidas
    Molossoi: Tharups
    Ambrakia: Phorbadas, Timogenes
73 Apeiros: of Kasopa[46]

D4. *Dodona, sanctuary of Zeus: citizenship decree, 350s–340s?*
Evangelidis (1957) 247–55, whence *SEG* xxiii. 471; Hammond (1967) 528–31 (restoring the first lines as '[By good fortune. While king was Neoptolemos, when *prostatas* was]' and thereby dating the document in the reign of Neoptolemus I, but

---

[45] The assumption is that 'Apeiros' in line 23 was a geographical heading, like 'Akarnania' in line 8 or 'on Sicily' in line 60, but that the name 'Geron Aristodamou' was later added, with line 73, in order to record the replacement of Aristodamos as *thearodokos* at Kassopa by his son.
[46] See preceding note.

the restoration has not found subsequent favour. He also suggested, less precisely, a date before *c*.343, on the ground that an Orestas cannot have been an official of the polity after Philip II's annexation of Parauaia 'and presumably (of) Orestis at the same time' (p. 529)), whence *SEG* xxiv. 446; Cabanes (1976*a*) 536–9 no. 2, whence *SEG* xxvi. 697; Cabanes (1981) 34 no. 2, with further references; Chaniotis (1986), for the meaning of *enteleia* in line 10, whence *SEG* xxxvi. 1600; *SEG* xxxvii. 515.

[. . . .]*INOUMOL* [when there was *prostatas*] Droatos of Kelaith[oi, sec]retary was Paus[anias of Trip]olitai, *synarchon*[*tes* were Theari]das Kelaithos, Alk[on Pei]alas, Menephulos [. . .], Antikkas Ethnēstes, M[. . . . . T]riphulas, Gennadas O[noperno]s, Hektor Onphalas, D[amoitas] Amumnos, Airopos Ge[noaios, A]neroitas Arktan, N[ikon] Phullatas, Anereias Tr[ipolit]as, Phrunos Orestas, Ar[chidamo]s Paroros, Omostak[ios Kues]tos, the commonalty of t[he Mo]lossoi gave citizenship to [Arist]okles, Mondai[os - - - sons of Ant]igenes, N[au]pa[ktians], to be [bene]factors of the [Molos]soi, both to th[e]mselves and d[escendants as] to every Molo[ss]os, a[nd exemption from tax]es and tax liability as for citizens [and, of land, right] to ownership, and such [all other honours as pertain] to the other b[enefactors who] enjoy citizenship.

D5. *Argos: list of* thearodokoi, *c.330*
Charneux (1966), whence *SEG* xxiii. 189; Hammond (1980*a*) 472; Hammond (1980*b*) 14 ff.; Cabanes (1981) 38 no. 8 (lines 8–16 only); Cabanes (1983) 106–7; S. G. Miller (1988) 157 n. 41, 161, whence *SEG* xxxvi. 337; *SEG* xxxvii. 278.

This list of *thearodokoi* was set up by Argos, perhaps in respect of the sanctuary of Zeus at Nemea and probably *c*.330 BC (S. G. Miller 1988: 161). The relevant extant portion begins with the names of *thearodokoi* at [Medi]on, [Anak]torion, [Thurreio]n, [Palair]os, [Aluze]a, [Tur]beion, [Leu]kas, and (Amphilochian) [Argo]s, and then continues:

```
    10  [Ambr]akia: [Ph]orbadas
        [Ape]iros: Kleopatra
        [Phoin]ika: Saturinos, Puladas, Karchax
        [Kema?]ra: [Mnasalk?]idas, Aischrion son of Teuthras⁴⁷
    15  [Apo]l[l]onia: Do . . theos
        [Kork]ura: Nai[- -]
```

D6. *Dodona, sanctuary of Zeus: copper plaque bearing a Molossian proxeny decree, 330s?*
Evangelidis (1935) 245–7; Hammond (1967) 564 f. (restoring 'tou Alexandrou' in the last two lines as '[king Neoptole]mos (son of) Alexandros' and dating the document in 317–312 or 302–297); Cabanes (1976*a*) 539 no. 3; (1981) 35 no. 3 (offering a date 'in the years preceding 330'). No republication in *SEG* to date.

God. To Lagetas son of Lagetas, Thessalian Pheraian, as a benefactor Molossoi gave, to himself and descendants, *proxenos* status, citizenship, right of owning land, exemption from taxes and full fiscal rights and freedom from seizure and security,

⁴⁷ For the restoration of this line cf. Cabanes (1976*a*) 144 n. 74 and Hammond (1980*b*) 14–15.

to them and (their) properties, in war and peace. When the *prostates* was Lusa-
nias Omphalas, secretary was [Do]kimos Omphales, sacred remembrancers were
[. . . . .]ri[. . .Ompha]llas, Philippos Genoa[io]s, [. . . . .] Onopernes, Simos
L[. . . . . . . .Ar]ktan, Anaxan[dros . . . .], Lukkaortas {i}Tale[an, ...
. . ., M]enedamos Peial[es, ...]tou Alexandrou.

D7. *Goumani: Thesprotian manumission record, mid-fourth-century?*
Dakaris (1972) 86 no. 252; Cabanes (1976a) 576–7 no. 49, whence *SEG* xxvi. 717;
SEG xxxvii. 515.

With good fortune. When *prostatas* of Thesprotoi was Alexandros, priest (was)
Phustaios, in month Gamilion, Xenus son of Nikanor, Ikadotos, released Pha-
lakros as free and dedicated him to Themis, with the joint approval of Andron
son of Nikanor, [So]s[- -] Antigon[- - -]

D8. *Dodona, sanctuary of Zeus: lead tablet recording consultation by Chaones,*
c.330–320?
Evangelidis (1952) 297–8 no. 1; Evangelidis (1953–4) 99–103; *SEG* xv. 397; Parke
(1967) 261 no. 5; *SEG* xxxii. 615; *SEG* xliii. 337.

Good fortune. The city of the Chaones requests Zeus Naios and Dione to answer
whether it is better and more good and more expedient that they transfer the
building of the temple of Athena the Citadel-Goddess. (trans. Parke, adapted)

D9. *Dodona, sanctuary of Zeus: stone stele with decree of Molossians, before 330?*
Cabanes (1976a) 541 no. 6; *SEG* xxvi. 699.

[Gods. When king was Al]exa[ndros, when *p*]*rosta*[*tas* of Molos]sians was Ar[isto-
ma]chos Om[phalas, and when] secr[etary was Me]neda[mos Laru]os, [Molossoi]
ga[ve] exe[mption from taxes - - - -]

D10. *Dodona, sanctuary of Zeus: bronze plaque recording an offering by Zakynthi-*
ans, late 330s?
Egger (1877) 254 ff.; Carapanos (1878) i. 39–40; Franke (1955) 38, suggesting a date
soon after 334; Dakaris (1964) pl. 4; Hammond (1967) 534; (no reference in Parke
1967); Cabanes (1981) 26, 36 no. 4.

God. Fortune. Zeus, ruler of Dodona, the gift to you I send from me: Agathon
son of Echephulos and descent line, *proxenoi* of Molossians and allies in thirty
generations, descent line from Kassandra of Troy, Zakynthians.

D11. *Dodona, sanctuary of Zeus: bronze plaque, 343–331?*
Carapanos (1878) i. 32. 5; *SGDI* 1337; Fraser (1954) 57 n. 13 (attributing to the
fourth century and to Alexandros I); Hammond (1967) 536. Restorations are very
uncertain. For the word-end restored as '?allie]s?' a restoration as '?[commonal]ty?'
is equally possible.

[When king wa]s Alex[andros, when *prostatas* of Molos]soi was Bakch[- -, and
secret]ary was Sun[- - - of Molossoi and ?allie]s? of the Mol[ossoi - - - -] citizenship.

D12. *Dodona, sanctuary of Zeus: bronze plaque, 343–331?*
SGDI 1334; Fraser (1954) 57 n. 13 (attributing to the fourth century and to Alexandros I); Hammond (1967) 535–6.

> With good fortune. While king was Alexandros, when *prostates* of Molossoi was Aristoma[ch]os Omphalas and secretary was Menedamos Omphalas, they the commonalty of Molossoi gave equivalence-of-citizenship to Simias of Apollonia, resident in Theptinon, to himself and to descent line and to desc[ent from] descent line.

D13. *Dodona, sanctuary of Zeus: bronze plaque, 343–331?*
Carapanos (1878) i. 27. 3; *SGDI* 1335; Fraser (1954) 57 n. 13 (attributing to the fourth century and to Alexandros I); Hammond (1967) 535–6 (restoring 'of the [Molossians]' rather than 'of the [Epeirotai]'); Cabanes (1976a) 541 no. 5.

> [While king] was [Al]exandros, when o[f] Molossoi [*prostatas*] was Aris[to]machos Ompha[las, secr]etar[y] was Menedamos [Omphalas, re]solved by t[h]e assembly of the [Molossoi]: Kteson i[s] benefactor, [hence to give] citizenship to Ktes[on and] descent line.

D14. *Dodona, sanctuary of Zeus: limestone stele, 343–331?*
Cabanes (1976a) 588–9 no. 74; *SEG* xxvi. 700.

> [God], Fortune. While king was [Alex]andros, when *prostatas* of Molossoi was Theudotos Koroneiatas, when secretary was Menedamo[s] Larruos, Pheideta son of Inon released Kleanor as free, both remaining and running away wherever he may choose. Witnesses: Mega[s] son of Sinon, Amunandros son of Eruxi[s], Dokimos son of Eruxis, Amunandros son of Inon, Nikanor son of Alipon.

D15. *Dodona, sanctuary of Zeus: bronze plaque, c.330?*
Carapanos (1878) i. 27. 2; *SGDI* 1351; Cabanes (1976a) 580 no. 55; Cabanes (1981) 27, 36 no. 5 (assigning a date near to 330).

> Released Grupon from slavery the following, by foreigners' manumission, Theodotos, Aleximachos, So[m]utha, Galaithos, Xenus. Witnesses: of Mollossoi [*sic*] Androkkas Dodonaios, Philipos Dodonaios, Philoxenos Dodonaios, Draipos Dodonaios, Agilaios Dodonaios, Krainus Phoinatos, Amunandros Dodonaios. Of Threspotoi [*sic*] Dokimos Larisaios, Peiandros Eleaios, Menandros Tiaios, Alexandros Tiaios, Deinon son of Thoxouchares, Philippo[s], Philon Onopernos. When *prostatas* was Philoxenos Onopern[os. Of Zeus] Naios (and) Diona.

D16. *Dodona, sanctuary of Zeus: bronze plaque, late fourth century?*
Carapanos (1878) i. 27. 1; *SGDI* 1336; Michel, *Recueil* 317; Franke (1955) 35–6 (construing the phrase 'the allies of the Apeirotai' as a partitive genitive and as denoting 'those within the Epeirote alliance'); Hammond (1967) 559–60 (dating it to 317–312 or 302–297); Cabanes (1976a) 545 no. 12; (1981) 28, 37 no. 6.

> God. Fortu[ne. To K]leomachos Atintan the allies of the Apeirotai gave within Apeiros tax exemption, when king was Neoptolemos son of Alexandros, when *prostatas* was Derkas of Molossoi—and full fiscal rights.

Such documents reveal some of the components of this non-Aristotelian society. With so much work recently done, and with more to come,[48] it would be absurd to attempt a new synthesis here. Probably more helpful, especially to those exploring Epeirote politics for the first time, will be a brief overview of some salient aspects, structured so as to bring out the points of similarity with, and difference from, the norms of that fourth-century Greece into which Epirus and its constituents were being increasingly drawn.

The main components of the Epeirote polity

Inevitably, the monarchy has to come first. Even if we decline to accept as historical the details of the developed story of its origins (item (5) above),[49] the Aeacid dynasty was clearly well rooted in Molossian society in the archaic period, and provided military leadership while also serving as a unifying focus and as 'the government' (items (6) and (7) above). Its similarity to the Macedonian monarchy on the other side of Pindus (and probably also, did we but have adequate information, to the Illyrian and Thracian monarchies) would be obvious enough even without Aristotle's own juxtaposition of them at *Politics* 1310^{b}34 ff. We may even think tentatively of Balkan Iron Age monarchy as a specific type of polity with its own uniformities and patterns of interaction. However, there are qualifications to be made. One is to note the evidence, inconclusive but far from negligible, which led scholars of an earlier generation to postulate the custom of joint kingship.[50] A second is to follow the logic of Aristotle's other juxtaposition, with the Lakedaimonian kingship, which reminds us that monarchy cannot exist without its acceptance by a people, and to recall that the annual ceremony at Passaron described by Plutarch comprised a periodically renewable contract between a people, as the primary entity, and the reigning dynast (item (12) above). On this evidence the focus of comparison should rather be with the fully Greek societies which developed such 'contracts' or understandings between ruler and people: viz., with archaic and classical Laconia; with Thessaly, its elective *tagia*, and its four artificially created 'ridings' or *tetrarchiai* (see Archibald, this volume);[51] or with Thucydides' generalizing reference to the 'hereditary kingships with stated prerogatives' of archaic Greece, as illustrated by Cyrene after the 'New Deal' of Demonax

---

[48] A presentation by Dr V. Kontorini at the Rome Epigraphical Congress in Sept. 1997 made it clear both that there was much new material and that its full publication would take some time.

[49] But cf. the echo of the myth in DIO.

[50] Beloch (1927) 143–53; Accame (1934); Evangelidis (1956) 5. The theme is not explored by Errington (1975) or Hammond (1991).

[51] Harpocration s.v. *Tetrarchia*, quoting Hellanicus, *FGrH* 4 F 52, and Aristotle fr. 497 Rose: Schol. Eur. *Rhes.* 307, quoting Aristotle fr. 498 Rose.

in the 530s (see Mitchell, this volume).[52] However, though the comparison is helpful, caution is in order on both sides. Just as the 'contract' between Spartan kings and Spartan people cannot have predated the débâcle at Eleusis in 506, so, too, it is unsafe to suppose that the Passaron ceremony was necessarily any older than the reforms of 'Tharybas' in the late fifth century. Even that ascription of date assumes that Plutarch, in reporting the 'people' concerned as being 'the Epeirotai', not 'the Molossians', was reproducing a reformulation of the 320s or later rather than a primary, late-fifth-century formulation. On the other hand, Thucydides' evidence of practice among the other peoples of Epirus suggests that as early as 429 a more than merely monarchical system of political leadership was in place. Indeed, it may be more than chance that his terminology, using the word *prostateia*[53] for the 'annual leadership [of the Chaones] from the ruling lineage', foreshadows the use of the word *prostatas* in the Molossian documents.

Secondly, there is the Molossian polity itself, as revealed by those documents. It is best to start from documents D1 and D2, since the citation of King Neoptolemus (I) places them in the early 360s. They are dated by the names of the king and of a (presumably annual) *prostatas* ('chairman', 'president', 'leader'), cite the names of an (also presumably annual) *grammateus* ('secretary'), and list a number of *damiorgoi* ('public workers' *vel sim.*), each identified (as are the *prostatas* and the *grammateus*) by an 'ethnic'. Later documents diverge from the format of D1 and D2 in various ways: D4 by listing *synarchontes* ('co-rulers') in place of *damiorgoi*, D6 by listing *hieromnamoneuontes* ('sacred remembrancers') in their place, D7, D9, D11, D12, D13, D14, and D16 by identifying explicitly of which people the *prostatas* was *prostatas*, D6 and D7 by not citing the king's name, D12 and D13 by replacing the list of *damiorgoi* with a reference to a public body ('the commonalty [*koinon*] of Molossoi' (D12) or 'the assembly of the [Molossians]' (D13)) as the validator of decisions, and D16 by referring instead to 'the allies of the Apeirotai' as the validating body.

On the one hand, we are clearly dealing with a polity whose public formalities were still very fluid in the fourth century, and whose shape and relationship with its neighbours were in rapid evolution. On the other hand, the polity already comprised far more than a court and courtiers, and showed a range of office-holders whose titles may well have had deep regional roots. *Basileus* ('king'), indeed, and *grammateus* are pan-Greek, though the prominence of the *grammateus* as the third-highest official in

---

[52] Thuc. 1. 13. 1, with Hdt. 4. 161. 3 (Cyrene) and 6. 56–60 (Laconia), with Carlier (1984) 240–324 and Hodkinson (1997) 92.
[53] Thus CG, while ABEFM give *prostasia*. The superiority of the CG tradition is thereby reflected, for there seems to be a difference of nuance between the two words: Thucydides uses *prostasia* to denote political leadership (2. 65. 11; 6. 89. 4), while Xenophon uses *prostateia* in a military context (*Mem.* 3. 6. 10).

later Aetolia[54] may be a significant parallel. Equally pan-Greek is *koinon* in the sense of 'the common thing', 'the state', 'the commonwealth', *vel sim.*, for though commentators have tended to associate the word especially with non-polis polities, it was in fact in general fifth-century use to denote polities of every kind, both 'sovereign' and constituent.[55] However, other terms used in these documents are more helpful. Even the rare term *synarchontes* is not quite as colourless as it seems, for apart from its use in fifth-century Attic accounts,[56] its main use was to denote the officers of the later Achaean League.[57] Likewise, though the term *prostatas*, as the title of an office-holder, is far from unknown in the Ionian Aegean, it is noticeably more common in Arcadia, in the Dorian Aegean, and in areas colonized or influenced by Corinth.[58] Hence its application to the Chaones by Thucydides, and its use by the Molossians, have a certain regional appropriateness. Even more is that true for the terms *damiorgoi* and *hieromnamoneuontes*. The latter at once recalls the *hieromnēmones* of the Delphi–Anthela Amphiktyony,[59] and perhaps even hints that the Molossians were at one stage minded to use their new possession of Dodona as the centre of a new regional cultic grouping. As for *damiorgoi*, the known distribution of the term is eloquent: Elis, the Achaean colonies, West Locris, Delphi, Thessaly (possibly), Argos, Mycenae, Corinth, Thera, Cyrene, and Arcadia.[60] It would be fair, I think, to see the public vocabulary of fourth-century Molossia/Epirus as having been drawn partly from the common Greek stock, partly from the terminology of the neighbouring colonial foundations (Corinthian, Elean, Achaean), and partly from terms current in Dorian–North-west Greek regional speech. In itself, such a conclusion, with all that it may be taken to imply for actual influences as well as for terminological influences, is in no way surprising. It does, however, serve to point more towards indigenous development than to imposition from outside, and in particular to expose as eccentric the tradition which Plutarch and Justin preserve of strong fifth-

---

[54] Cf. Busolt and Swoboda (1920–6) ii. 1525 n. 2, and Larsen (1968) 208.

[55] Tod ii. 137 (Aetolia, 367/6 BC) and other northern Greek examples are usefully collected by Hammond (1991), but the usage is general not only in Herodotus and Thucydides (indices, s.v.) but also in epigraphic Attic, with references to the *koinon* of Athens (*IG* i³. 34, lines 63–4), Chalkis (ibid. 40, line 11), Selymbria (ibid. 118, line 12), or of the deme of Sypalettos (ibid. 235, line 10). Cf. also *SEG* xxxiv. 1755, and for some later examples of the usage in Asia Minor, Hornblower (1982) 52 ff. and M. Wörrle (1991).

[56] Cf. *IG* i², p. 371, s.v. ξυνάρχων. A full list is impracticable here.

[57] Polyb. 23. 16. 6, with Walbank ad loc. and Walbank's note on Polyb. 2. 37. 10–11, sect. (*e*).

[58] Cf. Schaefer (1962) 1289–92, replacing and amplifying the scattered citations in Busolt and Swoboda (1920–6).

[59] Cf. *CID* i. 10 (Amphiktyonic law of 380) etc., but also the more recent appearance of the term as the title for a magistracy in 7th-cent. Tiryns (*SEG* xxx. 380). The use of the term to denote the administrators of Delos (*I. de Délos* 89: 104. 33 etc.) is probably not counter-evidence, for the term is not attested in a Delian context until 410/9 (*I. de Délos* 93: but ibid. 92 might be earlier) and is probably an Athenian imposition, modelled on Delphi.

[60] Murakawa (1957) 389–94; Jeffery (1973–4); Veligianni-Terzi (1977) 46–9 and *passim*.

century Athenian influence on the introduction of 'laws and a senate and annual magistrates and the structure of a state'.[61] Whether that tradition reflected an embryonic Greek idea of the diffusion of cultures or (more crudely) a piece of Athenian cultural bombast is impossible to decide in the absence of a clearly identifiable primary source for the relevant section of Justin's narrative,[62] but in any case it will be as well not to take it too seriously.

If we turn from terminology to actuality, there are equally informative shifts in the modes of recording public decisions and of identifying the validating body. Here it will be wise to start from D4, D6, D9, and D11–13. All these documents unmistakably cast the 'Molossians' or 'the commonalty of Molossians' in the same role of authoritative corporate body as is implied by the Passaron ceremony or by the deposition of Aeacids. (The shift in designation to 'allies of the Apeirotai' visible in D16 does not vary that particular aspect.) However, the two earlier documents D1 and D2 present a different picture. The 'Molossians' as such are absent, the decision is recorded in the passive voice, and it is the office-holders who predominate. The question must arise, therefore, whether the 'Molossians' corporately took those decisions, or a much smaller body of representatives or royal counsellors. One thinks of the nine Homeric *aisumnētai* of Phaeacia, whose role in managing contests and displays was simultaneously public and royal,[63] or, better still, of the '*kosmos* and the *damioi* and the twenty of the *pol*[*is*]' who were the 'swearers' of the first extant decree from Dreros on Crete, or, even closer yet, of the way in which the Cretan decree of *c*.500 for Spensithios 'seemed good to Dataleis, and we the polis pledged, from tribes five from each'.[64] Granted, we should perhaps not build too much on the format of D1 and D2, but the problem of where 'sovereignty' lay among the fourth-century Molossoi must have been a real one.[65] If so, the parallel with the political tensions which Greek communities further south had experienced in earlier centuries may be a close one: not just with Cretan poleis, either, but with Sparta throughout her history, early sixth-century Corinth, or late sixth-century Athens. It could be, therefore, that through the shifts in Molossian/Epeirote public practices and terminology in the fourth century we are seeing an evolution which unfolds later than the processes imputed to

---

[61] See n. 29 above.

[62] Cf. Hammond (1967) 507–8.

[63] *Od.* 8. 258–9, significantly called *dēmioi* in a way which prefigures the *damiorgoi* of D1 and D2.

[64] Jeffery (1990) 315 no. 1a = ML 2, with *SEG* xxvii. 620 and xl. 770; *SEG* xxvii. 631. Cf. also the role of the three tribes of Mylasa in Caria in 'validating' an assembly decision (*Syll.*[3] 167, dated to 367/6, with Ruzé 1983).

[65] This is not the place to broach the controversy whether *damiorgos* denotes a status or an office; see Jeffery (1973–4).

Greek poleis of the archaic period but is not essentially different in nature from them.

A third aspect comprises the 'ethnic' identifiers attached to each office-holder's name in D1, D2, D4, and D6. Most disappointingly, none of them can be located precisely on a map, though some of them are known from Stephanus of Byzantium or elsewhere as constituent communities of one or other of the three main ethnē.[66] Even so, however, they both shed light on the Molossian polity and pose problems. For example, the presence on these lists of 'ethnics' known to be Thesprotian (e.g. *Kelaithoi, Onopernoi*), Chaonian (e.g. (in one tradition) *Omphales*), or even Thessalian (*Peiales*) forces us to ask how non-Molossians had come to be permitted to hold high office within the fourth-century Molossian polity. Merely to imagine what a parallel situation would be further south—Megarians, Aeginetans, and Phleiousians, say, holding office in Corinth—is enough to point up the (for Greece) exceptional nature of what was going on. Hammond has called it the Molossians' 'genius for incorporation',[67] but there was more to it than unilateral finesse. Behind it, as behind the comparable techniques of expansion by incorporation later pursued by Philip II of Macedon or the Aetolian League, lay the threat of effective force. Perhaps more important is the inference which we are entitled to draw from the limited range of topics which these documents deal with, viz. that since the 'Molossians' were nowhere near being a participatory democracy on an Athenian or an Argive model, the physical or conceptual boundaries of the polity did not have to be as rigid as they had become in the synoikized *poleis*. It may therefore be just to credit the cantonal populations of north-west Greece with a significantly greater willingness to merge identities within a larger *koinon* than can be attributed to the more rigidly articulated *poleis* of the south.

However, two unsolved problems remain. One is anthropological, that of determining what such 'ethnic' identifiers meant in practice. To call them 'tribal' begs too many questions, while later evidence shows that one such ethnos, the Prasaiboi, itself comprising subgroups and subsubgroups (Cabanes 1985–9), has to be seen as a construct, not a primordial entity. That is germane to the second problem, that of determining whether, for the purposes of the political-administrative processes reflected in these documents, the identifiers served as quasi-surnames or as labels for constituencies. In favour of the latter is the absence of any 'double representation' from the same groups within the colleges listed on D1–2, D4, or D6, even though 'Arktanes' and 'Omphales' perhaps have more than their fair share of executive office. Against it are perhaps the variation in the size of the colleges (10 in D1–2, 15 in D4, 9+ in D6), though explanations for that variation can be devised, and the fact that there are more attested ethnic identifiers

---

[66] See Evangelidis (1956) 8 ff.; Hammond (1967) 525–40, 564–6; Cabanes (1976a) *passim*.
[67] Hammond (1967) 539, also citing Philip II.

than there are places in the colleges. A tentative presumption in favour of constituencies is not unreasonable, providing that we are prepared to accept what is implied thereby. Constituencies, however 'natural' their geographical or ethnic boundaries as communities, do not form themselves: rather, via one or more absolutely fundamental creative political acts, they have to be delineated and defined as segments of a larger polity. Though it might be rash to infer from the tradition about 'Tharybas' (item (7) above) that he, as the Molossian equivalent of Cleisthenes of Athens, was the person responsible, some such formal process of state formation has to be assumed. The obvious immediate comparison is with the military and political functions performed by the 'parts' (*merē, moirai*) of Aetolia, Phocis, Malis, Thessaly, or Boeotia, though the roles performed by the 'tribes' (*phylai*) of the southern *poleis* were not dissimilar. It will be wise not to underestimate the political engineering skills of the north-west Greeks.

A fourth aspect takes us into Molossian society, for the publication of DI–2 in 1956 provoked a flurry of comment on their content, viz. the bestowal of citizenship upon women.[68] Two aspects need to be distinguished. The first is the question of whether marriage between a male citizen and a female non-citizen yielded legitimate offspring. As Hannick showed in 1976, Greek states took varying views; but while the requirement among the Molossoi was evidently (as in post-451 Athens) for bilateral citizen descent, we do not need to assume that the particular norm which the two decrees reflect was one of the 'Greek habits . . . and humane laws' which 'Tharybas' putatively brought back from Athens. Indeed, the relevant parallel (nowhere yet cited in this context, to my knowledge) comes from much closer to hand, in the form of Attalus' drunken injunction in 337 that 'the Macedonians should ask of the gods that from Philip and Cleopatra there should be born a legitimate heir to the kingdom'.[69] The chances are that in Molossia, as in Macedon, it was not so much a matter of law as of social pressures and expectations: the son of a foreign woman was vulnerable to exclusion from an inheritance. However, it is the second aspect of DI and D2 which has the more far-reaching implications. Whatever snooty outsiders may have thought of their level of culture and political development, the Molossians saw themselves by 370 as having a polity, membership of which could properly be denoted by the word *politeia*. Citizenship and monarchy were not incompatible concepts.

Fifth, a summary glance at the shift of nomenclature from 'Molossians' to the wider term 'Epeirotai'. This had probably been formalized by the 320s, if the Aristotelian *Constitution of the Epeirotai* known from one citation (fr. 494 Rose) was compiled in his lifetime and if the coinage labelled ΑΠΕΙΡΩΤΑΝ ('of Apeirotai') is correctly dated in the 320s (see n. 35 above). It

[68] Full references in Harvey (1969) 226 n. 1 and in Hannick (1976) 139 ff.
[69] Plut. *Alex.* 9. 7, with Hamilton ad loc.

is in any case unambiguous on the third-century documentation (of which D16 may be the earliest example). The term 'Epeiros' must have begun as a purely geographical term for 'mainland', as seen above all from Corcyra, and it probably retained that meaning for Hecateus in the first half of the fifth century.[70] By the late fifth century it was being used as an ethnic identifier both by outside observers and by individuals from the region,[71] so that its appearance on the two fourth-century lists of *thearodokoi* (D3, line 23, and D5, line 11) is at least comprehensible. However, since D3 carries entries for 'Thesprotoi', 'Chaonia', and 'Molossoi' under the general heading 'Apeiros', it is safer to assume that, as seen from Epidaurus *c.*360, the latter denoted an area, not a specific polity, though the lack of a clear end for the 'Apeiros' section enjoins caution. It is not until D5, some thirty years later, that Queen Cleopatra's presence as the representative of Epirus combines with the real absence of its constituent peoples to provide some certainty that 'Apeiros' has taken on the status of a name for a recognized polity. Whether the presence of [Phoin]ika as a separate entity on D5 (line 12) indicates that the Chaones were not yet part of the larger polity may have to be left open;[72] but at least, however dimly, we begin to see the processes of state formation at work, and perhaps even to suspect that the impulse was neither wholly 'top–down' nor wholly 'bottom–up', but a complex mixture of the two.

Lastly, the shrine of Dodona and its documentation. With the exception of D8, included above for its striking evidence that the Chaones could formally term themselves a polis, I am not here concerned with the surviving oracle texts or dedications[73] so much as with the role which the sanctuary came to have (or, perhaps, had had imposed upon it) within the Molossian polity. That role stemmed from conquest, or at least from takeover, for the evidence is clear and unambiguous that at least until Herodotus' time Dodona was seen by the Greek world as being within Thesprotian rather than Molossian territory.[74] If, as is plausible, Molossian westward encroachment over the Tomaros range is a late-fifth-century development, it is attractive to see the first treasury, and with it the start of monumental architecture at the sanctuary *c.*400, as a deliberate (royal?) Molossian investment in prestige. Similarly, the Molossians' use of Dodona as a noticeboard for the display of public decisions from (on present evidence) the 360s onwards will have been both an imitation of practice elsewhere (Delphi, Olympia, Ptoion, etc.) and a sign that they had in mind an audience of regional and national readers.

[70] Hecateus, *FGrH* 1 F 27 and 106, with Hammond (1967) 476.
[71] Hammond (1980*b*) 15–16; note also *SEG* xxxvi. 1514.
[72] Hellanicus, *FGrH* 4 F 83 and *IG* v/1. 1231, with Hammond (1967) 506.
[73] For which see *pro tem.* Parke (1967) 259–79 and *SEG* xliii. 318–41.
[74] See n. 19 above, and also *Od.* 14. 327 ff.=19. 296 ff. (not quite conclusive), Aesch. *PV* 657 ff. (Zeus as Thesprotian), Hdt. 2. 56. 1, and Pindar fr. 59 Maehler.

It is unlikely to be chance, either, that the decisions set up there concerned individuals, whether by manumission (D7, D14, D15) or by conferment of status as citizen or *proxenos* (D1, D2, D4, D6, D9, D11, D12, D13, D16), but not (again, on present evidence) treaties, decrees of public policy, or accounts. Though the contrast in these respects with, say, early Argive or Athenian public documentation should not be pushed too far, it helps to remind us that for most purposes royal policies were not subject to public confirmation.

In one sense, then, this was a very non-Aristotelian world: fringe-Greek at best, monarchically governed, with fluid geographical and ethnic boundaries, no significant urban agglomerations, no clearly developed civic life, and managed by custom rather than law. Yet for two fundamental reasons we ignore such polities at our peril. First, it was they—whether Epirus, or neighbouring Aetolia and Macedon, or the Anatolian hinterland to the east—which were the crucible of Greek political creativity in the fourth and third centuries BC, rather than the established and stable poleis, which found it so difficult to merge their sovereignties in any way which was at once militarily effective and politically acceptable. The basis of the effectiveness of the ethnē, and of their political and military trajectories, has therefore to be traced and understood. Secondly, so far from being un-Greek, as supercilious southerners thought, their world shows clear signs of similarity to that of the communities of southern, Aegean, and proto-urban Greece in the archaic period. Whether Thucydides or Skylax or Aristotle liked it or not, in describing these (to us) dimly accessible polities of the north-west, they were describing aspects of their own past. We might do well to follow the same trail.

ADDENDUM (2002)

The evidence of Skylax (p. 241) is also discussed by Didier Marcotte, 'Le Périple dit de Scylax: Esquisse d'un commentaire épigraphique et archéologique', *Boll. Class.* 7 (1986) 166–82 (summarized in *SEG* xxxvi. 1514). Documents D3 (p. 247) and D5 (p. 248) are now republished and discussed in detail by Paula Perlman, *City and Sanctuary in Ancient Greece: The* Theorodokia *in the Peloponnese* (Göttingen: Vandenhoeck & Ruprecht, 2000), D3 at 68–81 and 180–4 as no. E2, and D5 at 100–4 and 205–7 as no. A1.

14
Homeric and Macedonian Kingship

PIERRE CARLIER

IT is quite commonplace to say that Homeric and Macedonian institutions resemble each other. According to many historians,[1] they are both examples of the traditional Greek kingship, the *basileia*, of heroic times described by Aristotle.[2] Some scholars go further: they compare Homeric and Macedonian kings to the kings of the Germanic tribes, and suggest that the Homeric and Macedonian kingships belong to the typically Indo-European form of 'military kingship', or *Heerkönigtum*.[3]

All these assimilations are very flimsy. Yet most historians assert them in a few sentences, as if they were obvious. Surprisingly, a systematic comparison between Homeric and Macedonian kingship has never been attempted. In this paper I shall not undertake an exhaustive comparison, but shall outline a few observations and hypotheses which are suggested by a comparative examination of the Homeric and Macedonian evidence.

Macedonian kingship before Alexander the Great is very obscure: the main pieces of evidence are brief allusions in historians like Herodotus and Thucydides and polemic statements in the Attic orators. Modern pictures of Macedonian kingship are mainly retrospective constructions built on the accounts of the Alexander historians of the first and second centuries AD, or on the accounts of the last Antigonids by Polybius and Livy.[4] In comparison, we have much more detail on Homeric kingship, but as everyone knows, the Homeric poems are not constitutional descriptions, but poetic creations ('Die Ilias ist kein Geschichtsbuch'—'the *Iliad* is no history book'—is the famous title Franz Hampl gave to one of his studies: Hampl 1962). The extent of reality and fiction in the world of Homer is hotly debated, and historical interpretation of the Homeric account is the subject of widely

---

[1] For instance, among many others, Costanzi (1915) 4–7; Granier (1931); Adcock (1953); Aymard (1950); Edson (1970) 22–3.

[2] *Pol.* 1285ᵇ4–5 τέταρτον δ᾽ εἶδος μοναρχίας βασιλικῆς αἱ κατὰ τοὺς ἡρωϊκοὺς χρόνους ἑκούσιαί τε καὶ πάτριαι γιγνόμεναι κατὰ νόμον. The view, expressed e.g. by Hammond (Hammond, Griffith, and Walbank 1972–88: ii. 158), that, according to Aristotle, Macedonian kingship belongs to this type of kingship, is rightly criticized by Lévy (1978) 210–13.

[3] That is one of the leitmotivs of Granier (1931: 1–3, 13–15, and *passim*). Hampl (1934) uses the notion of *Heerkönigtum* but does not insist on the parallel with the ancient Germans.

[4] For a detailed up-to-date bibliography see Hatzopoulos (1996) 17–33. Among the most influential studies which have not been already quoted in nn. 1–3, one may mention Francisci (1946) ii. 345–435; Briant (1973) 237–350; Errington (1978); Goukowsky (1978) 9–15; Hammond (1989) 16–29, 49–70; Borza (1990) 231–52.

divergent theories. I do not want to discuss the Homeric question here, and shall content myself with a minimalist statement which everyone may accept: that the Homeric kings behave as the poet wants his audience to believe these kings behaved. In other words, even if the poet does not exactly picture any real institution, his description is realistic.[5]

Similarities

Let us first consider whether the Homeric evidence cannot suggest hypotheses for solving some problems about the Macedonian political system.

(1) One of the main results of archaeological and epigraphical investigations in Macedonia has been to prove the existence of many Macedonian poleis whose institutions were very similar to those of southern Greece and also the rise of regional districts, *merides*, during the Antigonid period, if not earlier.[6] Some historians have felt surprise in face of this evidence; for them, a strong king should not have tolerated the emergence of poleis inside his kingdom. Such a superimposition of local, regional, and royal power was quite well known in the Achaemenid and Seleucid kingdoms,[7] but those kingdoms were empires including heterogeneous populations, while Macedonia has normally been considered as a national kingdom. For a reader of the *Catalogue of Ships* in *Iliad* 2, however, the Macedonian situation looks quite familiar. The map of the Achaean world described in the *Catalogue* mentions three political levels : (1) the boroughs—sometimes called poleis—and the small ethnē enumerated within each contingent, more than 300 in all; (2) the 29 political entities corresponding to the military contingents, mostly (but not always) kingdoms ruled by one king and very often named by a global ethnic such as 'Phocians' or 'Arcadians'; (3) the pan-Achaean community whose supreme leader was Agamemnon. At each of these three levels there are similar political institutions which work in a similar way. It is worth pointing out that this Iliadic superimposition of communities has no confederate character: not all the kings leading a contingent belong to the pan-Achaean council, but only those who are acknowledged as the most powerful, the bravest, or the wisest by the whole pan-Achaean community. In Macedonia it is probable that some evolution towards confederacy[8] began during the Antigonid period, but the phenomenon is much later than in Thessaly and in Epirus. A non-federal coexistence of several levels of political entities, analogous to the situation described by Homer, may have prevailed for a long time in Macedonia.

---

[5] For more details see Carlier (1984); for second thoughts, Carlier (1996a).

[6] For a full discussion of the evidence see Hatzopoulos (1996) 51–216.

[7] The most illuminating study remains Bikerman (1938).

[8] The most detailed book on 'Greek federalism' is Larsen (1968)—though see the comments in the Introduction to this volume (pp. 22–3 and 27–30 with nn. 57, 62). For a good concise analysis see Cabanes (1976b); see also, most recently, Beck (1997).

(2) One of the most vexed questions in Macedonian studies is the composition of the assembly. F. Granier (1931: 49–52) has dogmatically asserted that the Macedonians, like the ancient Germans, had an assembly of the army (*Heeresversammlung*) but no civil assembly of the people (*Volksversammlung*). P. Briant (1973: 279–96) has rightly criticized Granier's theory for contradicting the clearest ancient text (Curt. 6. 8. 25: 'exercitus—in pace erat vulgi'), but he suggests a sharp distinction between the assembly of the army and the assembly of the people which is not convincing.[9] In the Homeric poems the agora ('convening of the people') is one of the main institutions of every civilized community (only savage people like the Cyclopes have no assembly: *Od.* 9. 112–15), and the agora takes place in the same way, at home and abroad, in times of peace and in times of war; in both cases, all the members of the community who happen to be nearby are convened. One may wonder whether such a rule did not prevail in Macedonia: it is the simplest way of taking account of the evidence.

(3) The meaning of the title *hetairos* in Macedonian society is a very complex problem. According to Theopompus (*FGrH* 115 F 224, 225), there were in Philip's reign about 800 *hetairoi* who received lands from the king, some of them being Greeks; these *hetairoi* probably fought as horsemen in the 'cavalry of the *hetairoi*'. It is probable, however, that when the ancient texts say that a dignitary is 'one of the *hetairoi*', they refer to a much narrower group, those who can take part in the royal council, who can serve as ambassadors, who receive the high military commands and the satrapies in Alexander's empire: according to H. Berve's prosopographical studies (1926: i. 30–7), these high dignitaries called *hetairoi* were about 80 in number. *Hetairos* can also designate the closest friend of a king (Hephaestion, for instance). But in addition the title was somehow extended to the whole army: when a certain Alexander—perhaps Alexander the Great—reorganized the Macedonian phalanx, he gave to the infantrymen the name of *pezetairoi*.[10] Some historians have tried to explain the various meanings of the word in terms of historical evolution: they suppose, for instance, that the title originally belonged to the companions who lived in the house of the king (his *Hausgefolgschaft*), and that with the rise of Macedonian power, the name was inherited on the one hand by those who advised the king and helped him to govern, and on the other by those who fought with the king.[11] Such reconstructions are not necessary. In the Homeric poems *hetairos* already has several meanings: (1) the closest friend of a hero (Patroclus for Achilles); (2) the noble young men who serve a king or an important warrior by preparing his meals, driving his chariot, taking back the booty he has won, and protecting his corpse (most of them have their own inde-

---

[9] Briant is rightly criticized by Lévy (1978) 20–2 and by Tréheux (1987) 46.
[10] Anaximenes of Lampsacus (*FGrH* 72 F 4) quoted by Harpocration, s.v.
[11] On the Macedonian *hetairoi*, one of the most balanced studies remains Plaumann (1913).

pendent household and do not live in the king's house in time of peace); and (3) sometimes all the *laoi*, i.e. all the subjects of a king who fight or travel with him.[12] The word *hetairos* always conveys the idea of a close link of friendship and loyalty, but it can be used in various contexts for smaller or wider groups.

Contrasts

It cannot be denied that Homeric and Macedonian kings have in some ways similar functions: they have religious duties, they lead the army, and they act as judges in some circumstances. A closer examination, however, reveals important differences.

(1) The Homeric kings have to see that all the traditional sacrifices of the religious calendar are celebrated, they may decide to hold exceptional sacrifices to gain the favour of a divinity, they normally preside over the ceremonies, and they deliver the ritual prayers.[13] The Macedonian kings also play a very important part in the religious rites of their kingdom, in the cult of Zeus Olympios at Aigai, of the Muses at Dion, and in the cults of Heracles, the ancestor of the dynasty.[14] In one of his ill-inspired predictions Demosthenes even maintained that young Alexander would not move from Pella and that his only activity would be to accomplish the traditional sacrifices and look at the victims' livers (Aeschines 3. 160). It is worth noting, however, that the Homeric kings, while sacrificing, are generally surrounded by the elders, who pray with them and throw barley on the victims. Ancient texts do not tell us about a Macedonian group playing a similar role in religious rites. Such an *argumentum ex silentio* is weak, but it is tempting to suggest that the religious pre-eminence of the king is stronger in the Temenid kingdom of Macedonia than in the Homeric communities.

(2) Macedonian kings, like Homeric kings, lead the army, inspect the troops before battle and harshly punish anyone who does not fight with enough energy. If we believe the historians of Philip and Alexander, the Macedonian kings at least used to fight in front of their warriors and to win battles thanks to their own personal bravery. They are much better warriors than Agamemnon, leader of the Greek forces at Troy and the 'most kingly' of the Achaeans in the *Iliad*, who does not very often appear in the thick of battle;[15] it is well known that Alexander's own model of a fighter

---

[12] For a brief analysis of the Homeric *hetairoi* see Carlier (1984) 178–82; among the more detailed studies see Kakridis (1963); Stagakis (1975).

[13] For more details see Carlier (1984) 162–5. The typical scene of sacrifice in the Homeric poems has been studied by Arend (1933).

[14] On the religious functions of the Macedonian kings see e.g. Hammond (1989) 22–4. We lack a systematic study of Macedonian religion to replace Baege (1913).

[15] On the character of Agamemnon and the ideology of royal imperfection in the *Iliad* see Carlier (1984) 195–204.

was Achilles rather than Agamemnon, and the Conqueror's life is often described as a permanent *aristeia*. At least partially, these narratives reflect the propaganda of the kings themselves: they show that the monarch's virtues and his victories are more magnified in Philip's and Alexander's Macedonia than in the Homeric poems.

(3) In the Homeric world the decision to make war, to conclude a peace agreement or a truce, and the main strategic choices are prerogatives of the king; but before the royal decision there are lively discussions among the elders, usually in front of the assembled people. When the Trojan herald Idaeus comes to the Achaean camp, he transmits the Trojan proposals of peace—restitution of Menelaus' treasures, but without Helen—to the assembled Achaeans. Diomedes energetically protests and asks the Achaeans to continue war until they win. The Achaeans loudly approve Diomedes. Agamemnon asks the Trojan messenger to listen to the popular opinion, but emphasizes that the final decision rests with himself: ἐμοὶ δ' ἐπιανδάνει οὕτως, 'that is also my good pleasure' (*Il.* 7. 407).

Macedonian practice in military and diplomatic affairs varies according to the situation. After the death of Alexander, Perdiccas had the last plans of the Conqueror cancelled by the assembly (D.S. 18. 4. 1): this does not mean that the Macedonian people is sovereign in military and diplomatic affairs, but only that at this moment the '*epimelētēs* [guardian] of the kings' preferred to share with the Macedonians the responsibility for abandoning Alexander's projects; the only obvious conclusion one can draw from this event is that the weight of the assembly grows when there is no strong king. On the banks of the Hyphasis in India Alexander himself experienced the opposition of his army: the soldiers refused to go further east. This refusal is not proof of any constitutional power of the assembly; Alexander had to give up, but it was only the acknowledgement of a necessity. Even the most absolute monarchs, even the most hard-hearted tyrants, cannot force soldiers to campaign against their will. Alexander tried to conceal his loss of face by pretending to obey oracles which ordered a return towards the west (D.S. 17. 94; Arrian 5. 25–8); it is more honourable for a Macedonian king to make concessions to the gods than to the dēmos. During the expedition in Asia Alexander tried to obtain the approval of most members of his council: to convince his Companions more easily, he was even suspected of having falsified a letter from Darius (D.S. 17. 39. 1). Such an attitude proves that Alexander wanted to get the support of the dignitaries of his army, not that there was any vote in the council meetings and still less that Alexander considered the opinion of the council as binding upon him. We are very well informed about the negotiations before the Peace of Philocrates of 346: neither Aeschines nor Demosthenes mentions any Macedonian institution besides the king. Both Philip's admirers (like Isocrates) and his opponents assume that the Macedonian monarch is free to do whatever he wants in foreign affairs. Greek authors in Philip's time had perhaps little precise information about Macedonian institutions, but their silence about the royal council and the assembly would be very surprising if those institutions played a decisive official role in foreign affairs: sudden, unexpected decisions of the king alone are frequently contrasted with the collective decisions of the Greek cities, prepared by long public discussions.[16] The comparison of Macedonian institutions with Homeric ones already reveals part of the same contrast. In Macedonia foreign affairs are often discussed secretly by the king and some of his *philoi*. The king and the dignitaries sometimes ask for the people's approval, but the Homeric rule of free discussion of the elders in front of the assembly does not exist among the Macedonians.

(4) The Homeric poems twice mention the possibility of direct actions by the dēmos against those who bring misfortune to the whole community. Hector once regrets that the Trojans did not dare to stone Paris to death (*Il.* 3. 56–7). After a private expedition of Eupeithes, Antinous' father, against the Thesprotians, the people of Ithaca wanted to kill him and to confiscate his property, but King Odysseus managed to save him (*Od.* 16. 424–30).[17] These popular interventions are not trials: they look like lynching. Judging is one of the main duties and privileges of the elders (one of their titles is δικασπόλοι, 'judges'), but also of the king: when Sarpedon dies, Glaucus says that he has protected Lycia 'by his judgements and by his strength', Λυκίην εἴρυτο δίκῃσί τε καὶ σθένεϊ ᾧ (*Il.* 16. 542). The only indications we have about judicial procedure come from the famous trial scene on Achilles' shield (*Il.* 18. 497–508). The interpretation of this unique text is notoriously difficult, and I shall merely summarize the analyses I have developed elsewhere.[18] Three institutions are mentioned in this trial. The *laoi* ('people') listen to the discussion and shout loudly in favour of the litigant they support; the *gerontes* ('elders') give their opinion one after another; the *histōr* says which of the elders has given the best advice, and consequently which of the litigants is right. The text does not say that the *histōr* is a king, but we may note that his role is exactly parallel to that of the king in political discussions. In both cases the decision is reached in the same way: after listening to the elders, in front of the assembled people, one man finally decides.

In Macedonia it seems that most trials were judged by judges appointed by the king, but that all free Macedonians had a right to appeal to the king.[19] In capital affairs, according to some ancient authors, a traditional Macedonian custom ordered that the accused should be introduced before

---

[16] e.g. Dem. 1. 4; 4. 17.

[17] It is interesting to note that one of these popular executions exists only as a wish, and that the other was not carried out.

[18] Carlier (1984) 172–7. van Wees (1992) 34 agrees with my interpretation. Among other recent analyses see Westbrook (1992) and Scheid-Tissinier (1994).

[19] Griffith in Hammond, Griffith, and Walbank (1972–88) ii. 393–5.

the assembly: 'De capitalibus rebus vetusto Macedonum modo inquirebat exercitus—in pace erat vulgi—et nihil potestas regum valebat nisi prius valuisset auctoritas' (Curt. 6. 8. 25).[20] The exact role of the assembly is not easy to determine, and it may have varied according to the circumstances. Sometimes, perhaps, the end of the investigation took place before the assembly, the king managed to convince the people that the accused was guilty, and the Macedonians immediately stoned to death the so-called traitor, acting as a collective executioner. In other cases, however, Diodorus says that the Macedonians condemned (κατέγνωσαν) a defendant, which suggests that some sort of vote—probably by acclamation—took place.[21]

Very often Macedonian kings chose to kill rivals or opponents without any trial. This suggests that strong kings held trials before the people only when they thought it convenient for their propaganda, to share with the Macedonians responsibility for the elimination of a powerful opponent. Some Macedonians, however, influenced by the Greek way of thinking, probably maintained that the right of life and death lay with the Macedonian dēmos, and that each accused man should have the right to defend himself in conditions which were fair. Both attitudes can be taken by the same persons in different circumstances: Olympias, who had Cleopatra and her child assassinated without any trial in 336, protests against Cassander's unfairness in 317 because she was not given the opportunity of defending herself before the Macedonians (D.S. 19. 51. 1–4).

It is undeniable that in judicial matters the Macedonian assembly some-times has much more power than the Homeric *laoi*, but it would be exces-sive to speak of a democratic evolution: the riotous lynching has become a pseudo-trial manipulated by the king. There is no trace in Macedonian judicial practice of a debate between elders, and the procedural rules es-tablished in many Greek cities in order to make trials fair are not common practice in Macedonia.[22]

As the Homeric poems do not relate any accession of a new king, we have no description of the ceremonies on such an occasion, and we cannot say whether the new king was acclaimed by his people. What is certain is that the poet justifies the power of the kings by the possession of an inherited sceptre. It is true that in the *Odyssey* the suitors refuse to acknowledge Telemachus as the successor of his father, but the victory of Odysseus is

---

[20] In his 1867 edition of Curtius E. Hedicke added two words to the text of the manuscripts: 'inqirebat ⟨rex, judicabat⟩ exercitus'. This correction, which has been accepted by Granier, Briant, and many other historians, clarifies the respective roles of the king and the assembly, but precisely for that reason it arouses suspicion. Such a 'palaeographical' correction reflects a modern historical hypothesis.

[21] D.S. 17. 79 (Philotas); 18. 36. 4 (Perdiccas); 18. 37 (Eumenes); 19. 51. 12 (Olympias). It is inexact to say that Philotas' friend Amyntas was *acquitted*: the assembly asked Alexander to spare the young man, which is not the same thing (Curt. 7. 1. 18).

[22] For more details see Lévy (1978) 213–18.

the triumph of dynastic legitimacy (Carlier 1996a: 11–15). The idea that primitive Indo-European kings all had to be elected is without foundation. Macedonian kings had to be acclaimed by the assembly, but in normal conditions the Macedonians merely acknowledged by their acclamation the dynastic legitimacy of the king and his ability to reign[23]—and especially to lead the army. Of course, many usurpers tried to gain the kingship by being acclaimed, but such phenomena are quite common in all monarchies. It is only when the royal family of the Temenids became extinct that the Macedonians acclaimed kings outside the royal house, and they acclaimed those who had already gained power by themselves and won great victories. The Macedonians did not *elect* their kings, and there is nothing even remotely democratic in the acclamation of the new king.[24]

Homeric kings and Macedonian kings were both hereditary, claiming a divine origin. They both have very wide powers, and the ultimate decision stays with them. Neither the Macedonian nor the Homeric kings can be considered as absolute monarchs,[25] because they are not the only institutions of the community. In both cases there is also a popular assembly. The Macedonian assembly sometimes takes decisions by acclamation, which the Homeric *agora* never does, but the pressure of the king on the dēmos is much stronger in Macedonia, and free discussion is much rarer (the common people have no right to speak in the Homeric poems, but they can listen to very straightforward discussions between the elders). Moreover, Homeric kingship is often called *geras*, which suggests that this honourable privilege is given by the people, or at least acknowledged by the dēmos.

Both in Macedonia and in the Homeric poems there are institutions called 'councils' in modern languages, but the two 'councils' have different names in Greek (while *synedrion* is the usual term for the Macedonian council, the Homeric elders are called *gerontes*, *boulēphoroi*, or *basileis*—this last term underlining that as a group, the elders are narrowly associated with the royal functions); their composition, their functions, and above all their political significations are quite different. The members of the Macedonian council are all chosen by the king to advise and help him; a young king cannot immediately get rid of the most powerful aristocrats or the highest dignitaries named by his father, but he can promote to his council whomever he wants, even foreigners: the members of the council are

---

[23] The two required qualities do not always coincide, and that is why the Macedonians sometimes prefer the adult brother of the late king to his infant son.

[24] For a more detailed discussion see Briant (1973) 303–25; Errington (1978) 92–9.

[25] Momigliano (1935) and Lévy (1978) have rightly reacted against the 'democratic' interpretations of Granier and Briant, but they have gone too far in calling Macedonian kingship an 'absolutism'. If traditionally there had been the same gap between the king and the Macedonians as between the Achaemenid monarch and his subjects, no Macedonian would have protested against the orientalizing despotism of Alexander. Moreover, even the barbarian kingship of the Persian king is not considered as a *pambasileia* by Aristotle (*Pol.* 3. 14), because even Persian kingship is somehow κατὰ νόμον ('legally established').

the *philoi*, the *hetairoi* of the king. On the other hand, the Homeric elders, even if they hold a hereditary position, are considered—like the king—as having received their *geras*, their honourable privilege, from the dēmos. The Macedonian council advises the king in his palace or tent, but does not play any role as such in the assemblies. In contrast to this, the Homeric *gerontes* take part in all the meetings of the assembly, they sit in the middle of the agora, and they speak in front of the common people, who may express their opinion by shouting. Here is probably the main difference: in Macedonia, under normal circumstances, there is no link between the popular assembly and the royal council.[26]

Macedonian political evolution

We have no direct information on the Macedonian kingship of the seventh century, when a group of Macedonians was beginning the conquest of the higher Haliacmon valley under the direction of kings who claimed to be Temenids from Argos, but it is a reasonable hypothesis to suggest that it was not completely different from the kingships of early archaic Greece. Homeric kingships are probably amalgams of traditional images about heroic kings and—principally—of political practices familiar to the poet and his audience. It is not absurd to suppose that the first Temenids resembled the Homeric kings. Some similarities were retained later.

If we accept this hypothesis, we have also to admit that Macedonians and southern Greeks had quite divergent political evolutions during the archaic and classical periods. While in Greece collective decision by vote was replacing monarchic decision,[27] and at least in the democracies the council was becoming a committee preparing the projects to be voted on by the assembly, the power of the Macedonian king was growing, and the council becoming more and more dependent on the king. Those who suppose that the political evolution of all communities should take the same direction are surprised by the strength of the Macedonian kings. For A. Aymard (1950 = 1967: 162) there were many seeds of democracy in Macedonia, but the Macedonian assembly did not try to use its potential powers because the Macedonians had to fight frequent wars, and the anxiety of self-preservation created among them a strong loyalty towards the family of the war leaders. This military factor was important, but there were others as well.

The control of the Thracian mines gave great wealth to the Temenid kings, and money increases power. As Thucydides observes, tyrannies appeared in Greece with the increase of monetary wealth; previously, there were only traditional kingships with limited prerogatives (1. 13. 3 πρότερον δὲ

[26] Historians of Macedonia familiar with archaic and classical Greek history have strongly asserted that there was not in Macedonia anything similar to the boulē or the gerousia of Greek cities (Hammond, Griffith, and Walbank 1972–88: ii. 395–7; Hammond 1989: 53).
[27] For more details see Carlier (1991).

ἦσαν ἐπὶ ῥητοῖς γέρασι πατρικαὶ βασιλεῖαι). Similarly, the considerable wealth
of the Macedonian kings allowed them to build roads and fortifications, to
pay mercenaries, to give magnificent gifts to many people, and to live in a
brilliant court: it strengthened their hold on their subjects.

Macedonian society before Alexander is little known, but it seems that
the Macedonian upper class was too heterogeneous—petty kings of upper
Macedonia, landlords of the newly conquered territories, Greek *hetairoi*—
to constitute a united group facing the king; moreover, the gap between
the aristocracy and the common people of peasants and shepherds was
apparently so wide that any co-ordinated action of the aristocratic royal
council and the dēmos was impossible. To these factors we should add the
geographical scale of the Macedonian kingdom. The comparatively large
distances and considerable time involved in travel will have slowed communications and inhibited the emergence of collective discussion, thereby
making monarchic decision-making a more viable practice.

Last, but not least, the influence of the Persian model, during the period
of Persian domination of Macedon from 510 to 479 BC and afterwards, must
not be underestimated.[28] For every king in the Mediterranean world, the
Great King was a fascinating example.

At least from the reign of Alexander, some upper-class Macedonians
adopted certain Greek political ideas: *nomos* (law) as opposed to *bia* (might),
freedom of speech, hatred of tyranny. This Greek influence compelled the
Antigonids to pretend to be constitutional kings reigning with moderation
over free citizens. During the reigns of the Temenids, however, the main
trend of evolution seems to have been towards autocracy. This evolution
was completed in the oriental hellenistic kingdoms. Hence Macedonian
kingship is not only a case of non-democratic politics, but also of non-
democratic evolution.

---

[28] On the imitation of the Achaemenids by the Temenids, which did not, however, lead to
a complete assimilation of the two types of kingship, see Goukowsky (1978) 9–12; D. Kienast
(1973).

15
The 'Kings' of Lycia in the Achaemenid Period

ANTONY G. KEEN

THE communities of Lycia sit on the periphery of the Greek world. A now lost *Constitution of the Lycians* was produced under the aegis of Aristotle (fr. 548*bis* Rose), the existence of which implies something about the Aristotelian attitude towards the Lycians, for Hansen points out (1996*b*: 204) that wholly barbarian communities were not treated amongst the *politeiai*.[1]

None the less, many Greeks considered the citizens of Lycia to be 'barbarians' (e.g. Hdt. 1. 173. 1; Men. *Aspis* 25), and they spoke a language, related to Luwian and Hittite,[2] which points to their being a native Anatolian people. However, in the classical period the Lycians were becoming highly Hellenized (Bryce 1986: 203), and beginning to be perceived as such by Greeks, a process which developed to the point where Cicero was able to describe them as 'a Greek people' (*Verr.* 4. 21).

The surviving sources (literary and non-literary) about Lycia are slight and often confusing and contradictory. Two main points emerge clearly, however: the existence of cities, and that of coin-issuing dynasts.

The cities

Lycia seems to have become urbanized rather earlier than its neighbours, Caria and Pamphylia. More than eighty classical-period settlements of various sizes are known, either in literary sources or in the archaeological record, of which at least thirty may have been urban nucleated settlements of sufficient size to warrant the description 'polis' (Keen forthcoming (*b*)). The term is certainly found in some classical Greek authors. Hecataeus (*FGrH* 1 F 255–7) lists three poleis in Lycia, Xanthos, Patara, and Sindia (= Isinda);[3]

This paper is in part a revised and edited form of the fuller treatment found in Keen (1998) 34–56. I should like to thank the publishers, E. J. Brill, for permission to reuse the material and to make use of the map printed in that volume (p. xii).

Note the following abbreviations: M = Mørkholm and Neumann (1978), catalogue; N = Neumann (1979), catalogue; *TAM* = *Tituli Asiae Minoris*.

[1] This would be contradicted if a *Politeia* of the Carthaginians existed, but this is postulated solely on the basis of the discussion in *Politics* book 2 (1272^{b}24–1273^{b}20); above, p. 1 n. 4.

[2] Pedersen (1945); Tritsch (1950); E. Laroche (1957–8; 1960; 1967); Gusmani (1960); Houwink ten Cate (1961) 51–86; Neumann (1990).

[3] French (1994) 86. One should qualify this statement to say that at least Stephanus indicates

he also lists (F 258–9) as Pamphylian two, Phellos and Melanippe, that would usually be considered Lycian. Pseudo-Skylax (100) lists seven (disregarding those he includes in Lycia which belong in Pamphylia; see Keen 1998: 18–19). Arrian (*Anab.* 1. 24. 4) uses *polisma*, a term cognate with *polis* in the physical sense and largely used of marginal areas, for the majority of western Lycian settlements.[4] Menander (*Aspis* 30–2), however, speaks of Lycia being comprised of *kōmai*. Since these are external classifications, made by Greeks filtering their view of Lycian cities through their own assumptions, they tell us little about the political system. One of the major problems of interpreting Lycian history is the application by Greeks of terms such as *polis* or *basileus*, and one cannot necessarily assume that a Lycian polis is the same as one in mainland Greece.

There are documents from fourth-century Xanthos in which Xanthos and other cities are described as *poleis*, both in the topographical sense (*SEG* 39. 1414. 24) and, in the latter half of the century, the political (N 320. *b.* 12, 18), that is as, to use Aristotle's phrase (*Pol.* 1276^{b}1–2), a *koinōnia politōn politeias*, an 'association of citizens in a constitution' (trans. Sinclair). So by the late fourth century there are indications that the city was seen as some form of political entity. However, one must be wary in taking such a 'polis system' back further.[5]

The dynasts

If one were to approach Lycia from a viewpoint informed by other indigenous areas of Asia Minor, such as Phrygia, Lydia, or Cilicia, rather than a Greek perception, evidence of monarchical tendencies should be expected. Lycian coinage gives evidence for a number of individuals with the right to mint. The earliest coins, from the early fifth century, are usually uninscribed,[6] and so it is difficult to draw conclusions from this material. In the fifth and fourth centuries (*c.*500–360), however, it is clear that a mixture of 'dynasts' minted contemporaneously, and at a number of different cities right across Lycia; in all, more than thirty dynasts are known.

Many in the fifth century seem to have minted on both the light coinage standard found in western Lycia and the heavier central and east Lycian standard.[7] Possibly the right to mint was personal and did not derive from rule of any one city. It has been suggested[8] that city mints used by dynasts

that Hecataeus called them *poleis*; Stephanus is not necessarily to be relied upon, but his accuracy with site classification as regards Hecataeus may be fairly reliable. See Whitehead (1994) esp. 119 for Hecataeus.

[4] For *polisma* see Flensted-Jensen (1995) 129–31.
[5] Further on the political identity of cities in Lycia, see Keen (forthcoming (*a*)).
[6] G. F. Hill (1897) xxvi–xxviii; Mørkholm (1964) 68.
[7] Childs (1981) 58 n. 22. For the coinage division see Mørkholm (1964); Zahle (1989).
[8] e.g. Mørkholm and Zahle (1972) 112; Borchhardt (1976) 108.

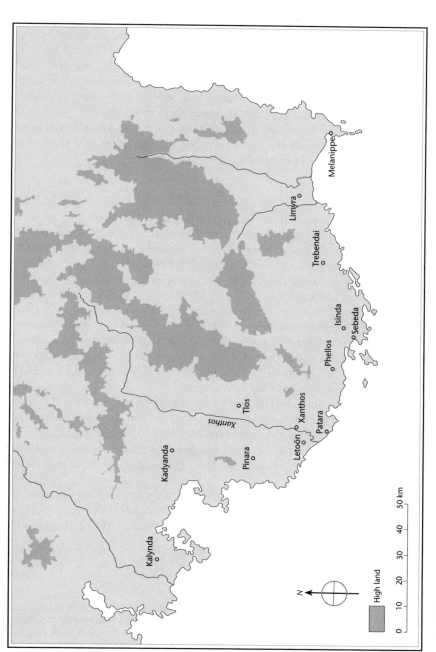

The light west Lycian coin standard was used as far as the cities on the eastern Xanthos valley (Tlos, Patara, etc.); the heavier standard was used to the east. Pillar tombs were spread from Kadyanda in the north-west as far as Trebendai in central Lycia. The term χñtawati was used between Pinara and Limyra.

Fig. 15.1. Lycia.

represented only their private estates; however, the coinage record does not present a very clear picture of Lycia's political system.

The existence of two coin-issuing dynasts named Wekhssere, one dated to *c.*450 and one to the early fourth century,[9] might suggest that the right of minting could be passed on through the generations (cf. Bryce 1986: 162). It also seems likely that the distinctive pillar tombs to be found across western and central Lycia are another manifestation of the dynastic system.[10] Thirty-five are known, ranging in date from *c.*540 to *c.*390.[11]

In the mid-fifth century numismatic evidence provides a number of links between these dynasts (see below). From this it is apparent that there was some form of association between individual leaders.

Lycian unity

We cannot deduce merely from the Aristotelian treatment of Lycia as a single constitution that Lycia formed a unified state. Such a state was treated in the *Politeia* of the Thessalians or of the Arcadians (cf. Harpocration s.v. μύριοι), and probably also the Bottiaeans (Flensted-Jensen 1995: 126–7), but almost certainly not in that of the Cyprians, as there is no evidence for common political structures in Cyprus (Mørkholm and Zahle 1972: 113), nor of the Cretans. It may be (as a referee has suggested) that Lycia, Cyprus, and Crete were all marginal areas as far as an Athenian-based scholar was concerned (even one born in Chalkidike and who had worked in Macedon), and so warranted no more than a general treatment. Lycia's appearance as an undifferentiated mass in Herodotus' list (3. 90) of Darius I's tribute districts is also weak evidence for Lycian unity.[12]

In Homer's account of the Lycians he names only Lycia and the Xanthos river (Bryce 1986: 13), and seems to be equating the two. In the fifth century there is a single entry on the Athenian tribute lists, 'Lycians' (*IG* i[3]. 261. 1. 29–30; 262. v. 32–3; 266. iii. 34).[13] The Athenians may have been treating Lycia as a polis, similar to Xenophon's description of the Persian empire as a polis.[14]

Internal documentary evidence might also support the case for unity. The use of the Lycians' name for themselves, *Trm̃mili*,[15] outweighs other documentary uses of ethnics. Excluding coins, a Lycian city-ethnic appears

---

[9] For the existence of two Wekhsseres see Jenkins (1959) 33.
[10] Zahle (1980) 38; (1983) 32–3, 64–5, 107–11; Keen (1992) 53.
[11] Deltour-Levie (1982); Zahle (1983) 142–3.
[12] Though used as such by Bryce (1983) 33.
[13] Two of these, however, are restorations.
[14] *Cyr.* 1. 3. 18; 1. 4. 25; 1. 5. 7. See Hansen (1993) 20 and n. 142. One of the editors has suggested that the Athenians might simply have adopted the Persian tribute system. This is possible, but does not affect the general point, as it would then raise the question of why the Persians treated Lycia as such a unit.
[15] All references to *Trm̃mili* and other derived words: Melchert (1993) 78–9.

only fourteen times in Lycian inscriptions; *Trm̃mili* is used twenty-one times (of course not every occasion may refer to an individual). It is also extremely rare that a Greek or Roman literary source identifies a Lycian as anything other than a 'Lycian'.

The evidence would seem to point towards a unified Lycia, in which a number of dynasts operated. It is now necessary to see whether it was an area merely of co-operating fiefdoms,[16] or whether there was a more central monarchy.

Lycian 'kings'

Homer (*Il.* 6. 172–3) speaks of an *anax* of Lycia, and describes Sarpedon and Glaucus as *basileis* of Lycia (*Il.* 12. 318–20). Few later Greek sources mention Lycian rulers. None is attested on the Athenian tribute lists, in marked contrast to regular appearances of Carian dynasts.[17] The reason may be that Caria was not quite so organized or urbanized, and the Carian dynasts ruled without any formal constitutional mechanisms or strong geographical centre; thus, Athens' relations were specific to individuals, rather than with geo-political entities, as may be the case with Lycia. Theopompus mentions a Lycian *basileus* Pericles (*FGrH* 115 F 103. 17), but Herodotus speaks solely of 'the Lycians' in his account of the fall of Xanthos *c.*540, Thucydides (2. 69), describing the invasion of Lycia by Melesandros in 430/29, mentions no leaders on the other side, and Diodorus (15. 90. 3) mentions Lycian participation in the 'Satraps' Revolt' only as an *ethnos*. In the last two cases this is not too surprising; Diodorus is generally being too concise, and Thucydides not sufficiently interested, to include the names of local leaders. The 'Inscribed Pillar' of Xanthos, the tomb of the dynast Kheriga,[18] records the Athenian defeat of 430/29 (*TAM* i. 44. *a.* 45), indicating that Kheriga was a leader involved in this action (on which see Keen 1993: 153–5).

The absence of Lycian leaders from Herodotus' account is more perplexing, as he came from Halicarnassus, not far away, and might be expected to know some names. The only pre-Persian ruler of Lycia whom he mentions is the legendary Sarpedon.[19] It is, however, difficult to draw conclusions one way or the other in the light of Herodotus' rather anecdotal evidence about Lycia, and he may simply be conceiving of Xanthos in terms of being

[16] So Hornblower (1994*b*) 218: 'Classical Lycia was highly balkanized under a plethora of local dynasts.'

[17] *IG* i³. 71. I. 112–13, I. 155–6, II. 96–7; 259. II. 27, V. 16; 261. V. 12; 263. I. 14–15; 267. III. 25; 270. V. 10; 271. I. 84; 272. II. 79; 280. I. 66–7; 282. IV. 48–9; 284. 7–8.

[18] Identification of Kheriga as owner: Bousquet (1975) 141–2; (1992) 168–9; Keen (1992) 59; *contra* Childs (1979).

[19] The story of Lykon son of Pandion, from whom the Lycians supposedly got their name, might imply that Lykon was a ruler of Lycia, but Sarpedon is the only one explicitly named as ruling (1. 173. 3).

a Greek-style polis (as Hecataeus describes it). Also, Herodotus records the only other classical-period Lycian leader apart from Perikles to be mentioned in a Greek source.[20] This is Kybernis, son of Kossikas, according to Herodotus (7. 98) one of the best-known individuals with Xerxes' fleet, and probably Lycian ruler at the time. It may be that this man was a relative of the later fifth-century coin-issuing dynasts Kuprlli and Kheriga, since his name may be a Greek form of Kuprlli; he is unlikely, however, to have been the same man as the Kuprlli who minted coins.[21]

Better evidence comes from Lycian epigraphy. A number of inscriptions from the late fifth and fourth centuries contain the formula *ẽnẽ . . . χñtawata*.[22] *χñtawata* was once believed to be a rank in itself,[23] but the consensus now is that the phrase means 'under the authority/command of'.[24] The rank is probably expressed in the related term *χñtawati*, found on a trilingual inscription from the Letoön sanctuary (N 320. *a*. 7–8).[25] There it is used in a religious context, to name the deity for whom the inscription establishes cultic practices, the *Xñtawati Xbidẽñni*. This is equated with the Greek *Basileus Kaunios* (N 320. *b*. 7). Can *ẽnẽ . . . χñtawata* be translated as 'under the kingship of'? Support comes from a study of individuals connected with this formula (or minor variations thereof).

The most obvious is the Alakhssañtra attested at Tlos (*TAM* i. 29. 9), almost certainly Alexander the Great (Bryce 1986: 49). Alexander was certainly a *basileus*, and is named as such on an inscription from the Letoön (*SEG* xxx. 1533). An undated inscription from Kadyanda names one Pttule as *χñtawati* (*TAM* i. 35. 1). He has been identified as one of the Ptolemies,[26] who first seized Lycia in 309 and had firm possession by the early third century.[27] Bryce is doubtful (1986: 49), as there appear to be no securely dated Lycian-language inscriptions after Alexander, but *pttule* does seem a personal name (Melchert 1993: 107). There is no other evidence for a Pttule from within Lycia who might be a *χñtawati*; the name appears on no coins (except possibly abbreviated (M 212) on coins usually thought to be giving a form of Patara: Mørkholm and Neumann 1978: 23), and occurs only in one other document (*TAM* i. 65. 7, 8), from Isinda, usually dated to the fifth or fourth century (Friedrich 1932: 73), in an obscure context. If, however, Pttule is a Ptolemy (more probably I than II), here too the individual was a *basileus*.

[20] Omitting the Kalyndan *basileus* Damasithymos (Hdt. 7. 98; 8. 87. 2) since Kalynda was Carian (Hdt. 1. 132) (and see Keen 1998: 95 on problems of the identification of this 'Kalynda').

[21] Bryce (1982) 331; Keen (1992) 56–9; (1998) 88–90.

[22] *TAM* i. 11. 2–3; 43. 2; 61. 2; 64. 2; 67. 2; 77. 2*b*; 83. 5–6; 103. 3; 131. 1–2; N 310. 4; 314. 7–8.

[23] So Treuber (1887) 104 n. 2; E. Laroche (1957–8) 182 (but see 1974: 134); and Houwink ten Cate (1961) 9, 92.   [24] Gusmani (1963) 284–9; Bryce (1986) 133.

[25] On this inscription generally see Metzger *et al.* (1979) *passim*.

[26] E. Laroche (1979) 56; supported by Frei (1981) 364.

[27] D.S. 20. 27. 1; Frei (1990) 12; Kolb and Kupke (1992) 21–2.

More important is the application of the term to native Lycians. The most instructive inscriptions (*TAM* i. 67. 2; 83. 5–6; 103. 3; 132. 1–2; N 314. 7–8) relate to Pericles (in Lycian 'Perikle'), a coin-issuer of the early fourth century (M 148–50). This is one of the few Lycian individuals to appear in the Greek historical record, in the Theopompus passage already mentioned, where he is called *basileus* of the Lycians.[28] In a recently discovered inscription from Limyra (Wörrle 1991: 203–17) Pericles describes himself as '*basileus* of [all] Lycia'. Hornblower comments (1994*b*: 214) that this is 'perhaps a hit at the pretensions of the Xanthian dynasts'; Wörrle is certain that this is a claim to a title held in western Lycia. Another coin-issuer in the east (M 138–9), Mithrapata, is named in connection with the formula (*TAM* i. 64. 2). Mithrapata may also have described himself as a 'king' (Wörrle 1991: 208–9).

Of the western coin-issuers, two, Kheriga in the late fifth century and Arttumpara in the fourth, are identified with the formula.[29] Kheriga provides other evidence. On his tomb, the 'Inscribed Pillar', the Greek epigram speaks of his *basileia* (*SEG* xlii. 1245. 8). His son Erbbina had a statue-base erected for himself on which he is described as *tyrannos* (*SEG* ix. 1414. 7),[30] often a synonym for *basileus* (Andrewes 1956: 20–30). In the same inscription Erbbina is described as the man 'who ruled over the Lycians' (*SEG* xxxix. 1414. 4).[31] Kheriga and his son both have close associations with the city of Xanthos.

There are two seeming aberrations. One is a Lycian called Arppakhu (Greek Harpagos), despite the name almost certainly not a male-line descendant of the sixth-century Persian general.[32] Arppakhu is linked with the formula in an inscription from the vicinity of Phellos (*TAM* i. 77. 2*b*; N 310. 4), but his name appears nowhere on coinage. He was, however, the son-in-law of one coin-issuer, Kuprlli (M 124–6, 204–5), and the father of another, Kheriga,[33] already noted as a *xñtawati*. It is notable that Kuprlli minted coinage over a long period, *c*.480–440 (Mørkholm and Zahle 1972: 75–6). Perhaps Arppakhu was 'regent' in Kuprlli's final days, but not entitled to mint in his own name.

The other oddity is the Persian Autophradates, attested from Sebeda with *ẽnẽ* . . . *xñtawata* (*TAM* i. 61. 2). Autophradates was Lydian satrap, holding overall responsibility for Lycia, in the early fourth century, spanning the period of the 'Satraps' Revolt'.[34] On the side of the Pajawa tomb from

---

[28] He is also mentioned at Polyaen. 5. 42, but without comment on his status.

[29] Kheriga: *TAM* i. 43. 2; coinage: M 129–30, 222; Arttumpara: *TAM* i. 11. 2–3; coinage: M 231, 302.

[30] Now on this inscription: Savalli (1988) 113. Statue-base: Bourgarel and Metzger (1992); Bousquet (1992).   [31] As restored by Bousquet (1992) 156.

[32] Keen (1992) 56–60; (1998) 76–9; *contra* Jacobs (1987) 27–9.

[33] Genealogy reconstructed from *TAM* i. 44. *a*. 1–2, 30.

[34] Theopomp. F 103. 4; D.S. 15. 90. 3; Nep. *Dat.* 2. 1.

Xanthos he is named only as 'Persian satrap' (*TAM* i. 40. *d*. 1–2). I have suggested elsewhere (Keen 1998: 149–53) that Arttuṁpara and Mithrapata were also Persian officials placed in Lycia. This would suggest that χñtawati, while clearly the closest translation of *basileus* available to the Lycians, may have a wider meaning than simply 'king', being applicable to anyone in overall authority. However, here I shall continue to use the term 'king' for non-Persians who used the formula, to distinguish them from the other dynasts.

As Bryce observes (1986: 133), *ẽnẽ . . . χñtawata* was probably a quasi-dating formula;[35] the Pttule inscription (*TAM* i. 35. 1) may even give a regnal year (E. Laroche 1979: 56). Since this formula is found from Pinara in the west to Limyra in the east, this area was probably politically linked, under the authority of individuals to whom the formula was applied.

It is not likely that all coin-issuers who can be identified described them-selves as 'kings'; if they did, one would expect more occurrences of the formula on inscriptions. Rather, the use of the term, and the claim to 'king-ship', seems to have been restricted to a select few, who in the fifth century seem to be closely connected with one another: Arppakhu and Kheriga were father and son (*SEG* xlii. 1245. 5).

Kheriga, his son Erbbina, and his maternal grandfather (Keen 1998: 78) Kuprlli probably constituted part of a dynasty based on Xanthos.[36] When their line petered out with Erbbina (Keen 1998: 145–6), the two Persians, Arttuṁpara and Mithrapata, took over control in western and eastern Ly-cia respectively, before in the east Pericles claimed the role of 'king'. After Alexander's conquests, Macedonian rulers were acknowledged as being in command. Numismatic evidence provides a number of links between the fifth-century dynast Kuprlli and other coin-issuers, both through the in-clusion of his coins and those of others in the same hoards, and through die-links.[37] Six dynasts are known to have been associated with the later Xanthian dynasts Kherẽi, an associate—indeed, probably a relative—of Kheriga's, and Erbbina, Kheriga's son.[38]

It is also relevant to note that Kheriga claimed in the Greek epigram on his tomb to have distributed part of his kingdom to his relatives (*SEG* xlii. 1245. 8). As Savalli suggests (1988: 111), this does not suggest that Lycia was divided, but that Kheriga had closely involved his family in the administration of the country. It has already been noted that Arppakhu, father of Kheriga, though identified as a χñtawati and connected with the

---

[35] Zahle (1983) 30 argues that the formula was used only by close associates of the individual named.

[36] For this dynasty see Bousquet (1992) 172–4; Keen (1998) *passim*.

[37] For the evidence see Six (1887) 47; Jenkins (1959) 33 and n. 1; Mørkholm (1964) 69 and n. 11; Mørkholm and Zahle (1972) 75–6; M. Thompson, Mørkholm, and Kraay (1973) no. 1251; Mørkholm and Zahle (1976) 59; *Coin Hoards*, 2 (1976) no. 27; Spier (1987) 33, 35, 36; Zahle (1989) 173.   [38] Mørkholm and Zahle (1976) 56–7.

dynasty, probably by marriage, never coined under his own name, and is perhaps an example of this.

This suggests that there was a hierarchical structure, with a central 'king', probably based at Xanthos,[39] who dominated over a number of lesser dynasts who each none the less had rights of minting coinage (perhaps originally granted by the king), and therefore some degree of autonomy.[40] A. H. M. Jones (1971: 96) described this as a 'federation of princes', but the term 'federal' is anachronistic. Frei (1990: 8) describes the system as an 'adelige Schicht'. The implication is of a feudal monarchy and 'nobility' along medieval lines, but there is no evidence to prove such a model.

The cities and the kings

Not all of the cities in Lycia were closely tied in with the monarchy at Xanthos. A number of coins are known on the heavier standard carrying only a city name and no dynast name.[41] Some of these cities cannot be located, but most of those which can were in central Lycia, and the others probably were. This area mainly consists of a great number of small valleys separated by mountainous ridges. The geography contributed to the rise of a large number of cities in antiquity (Zahle 1980: 46–8), which may have expressed their independence through issuing coinage.

To clarify the relationship of the monarchy to such cities one might note the entry on the Athenian tribute list of 446/5, 'the Lycians and their dependencies' (Λύκιοι καὶ συν[τελ(εῖς)]: *IG* i³. 266. III. 34). This entry may be acknowledging that there were Lycian dynasts and cities which possessed the right to mint their own coinage, semi-independent of any central authority, or alternatively suggesting that there were fringe areas whose attachment to the central monarchy was tenuous.[42]

The phenomenon of quasi-independent cities does not seem to have occurred in western Lycia. Though there are coins of western Lycian cities that carry only a city name, most belong to a group carrying the helmeted head of Athena on the obverse (M 240–7). In this case, the head of Athena was probably standing as a badge representing a dynast (in all likelihood the ruler of Xanthos). Bryce (1986: 51), however, places these coins in the period of Carian domination of Lycia, in which case the promotion of western cities minting their own coinage is part of the Carian plan to promote a polis identity to supplant a regional identity (see below). The only example of a coin on the western standard outside of this group that carries a city name alone is an example that carries the legend *ptt*, which

---

[39] For the evidence for Xanthos as Lycia's capital see Keen (1998) 56–60.

[40] Childs (1981) 58; Frei (1990) 8–9.

[41] Aperlai: M 112–14; Zagaba: M 14, 109, 134–6. For Zagaba as a city rather than, as sometimes assumed, a dynast, see Carruba (1993) 12–13.

[42] For a fuller discussion of the *synteleis* see Keen (1998) 41–2.

may be an abbreviation of the Lycian name for Patara (M 212)—but it may, as noted above, be the abbreviation for Pttule.[43]

Carian rule

Lycian participation in the 'Satraps' Revolt' (D.S. 15. 90. 3) brought very significant changes to the nature of Lycian government. The dynastic system seems to have been swept away—coin-issuing within Lycia ceases (unless Bryce is correct about the date of the Athena-head coinage). The territory came under the authority of the Hekatomnids, certainly by the reign of Pixodaros in the 330s, for whose rule there is documentary evidence (*TAM* i. 45; N 320. *b*. 1–2; *SEG* xxxvi. 1216). Lycia became almost an occupied country, and little power was exercised locally. It is in this context that we should view local attestations of Xanthos as a polis *qua* political community. The Hekatomnids perhaps attempted to undermine Lycian unity by dealing directly with individual cities rather than with any national structure (see further Keen forthcoming (*a*)). This presumably promoted a sense of civic identity, so that decrees could be passed by the polis of the Xanthians (*SEG* xxvii. 942. 12 with 5).

On the other hand, the Lycian dynastic system in some ways foreshadows the personal kingships of the Successors of Alexander the Great. If, as Hornblower has argued (1982: 353), Mausolus was the first proper hellenistic ruler, and his ideas influenced the Macedonians who followed, there is a case for saying that Mausolus was influenced by the Lycian 'kings' in many aspects of his rule. For instance, the Mausoleum is surely a deliberate imitation of the Lycian 'Nereid Monument',[44] and the Lycian rulers were his predecessors in the blending of Greek and oriental in a monarchic establishment.

Conclusion

To come to any firm conclusions about political structures in Lycia would be foolish; the evidence is not solid enough. However, we can make educated guesses, and if those are near the mark, then Lycia underwent some remarkable changes. At the beginning of the fifth century there seems to be a political structure based on a number of leaders, whose relations with each other may have been feudal in nature, but may also have been along the informal lines sketched out by van Wees in his study of Homeric leaders and society.[45] Particularly noteworthy is that there was not a simple 'vertical' relationship between cities and dynasts, where one dynast had

---

[43] Schweyer (1996) 29 prints the abbreviation as 'Ptta', which would have to be Pttara rather than Pttule.
[44] Cf. Coupel and Demargne (1969) 159; Wörrle (1991) 215; Hornblower (1994*b*) 215.
[45] Van Wees (1992) *passim*; (1995*a*).

responsibility for his own city or cities. Instead, there seems to be a more flexible relationship between cities and dynasts, which probably encouraged the development of political infrastructure within the cities.

Subsequently a number of factors came into play; the Persian desire for a stable vassal state may have led to them supporting the central Xanthian monarchy, which probably curbed the independence of bordering cities. No doubt Greek political ideas filtered into the area, and may have promoted the city as a political unity, thus moving Lycia further towards the Greek 'norm' of a polis-based structure. The Hekatomnid desire to break potential sources of resistance played its part.

The dynamic that we see in Lycia is in many ways parallel to that of the 'non-polis' communities in Greece, as discussed elsewhere in this volume. Lycia seems to have been confronting many of the same questions of the relationship between the city and larger regional political bodies. The Lycians certainly arrived at the same solution, the ultimate emergence in the hellenistic period of a representative confederacy, one that persisted into the Roman period,[46] as the best means of reconciling traditional Lycian nationhood with their new identity as citizens of poleis.

APPENDIX

Major Lycian Dynasts of the Fifth and Fourth Centuries with their Probable Bases of Power

Kybernis, c.525–480, Xanthos
Kuprlli, c.480–440, Xanthos, nephew of Kybernis?
Arppakhu, c.440?, Xanthos, son-in-law of Kuprlli
Kheriga, c.440–410, Xanthos, son of Arppakhu
Kherẽi, c.410–390, Xanthos, brother of Kheriga?
Erbbina, c.390–380, Xanthos, son of Kheriga
Arttuṁpara, c.380–370, western Lycia, Persian official?
Mithrapata, c.380–370, eastern Lycia, Persian official?
Pericles, c.380–360, Limyra

[46] The latest reference is *IGR* iii. 473, *c.* AD 200; see *SEG* xli. 1358.

16

The Pre-polis Polis

†W. G. FORREST

IN a café in Marseilles in 1949 an itinerant newsboy approached Jacques Duclos, then leader of the French Communist Party. '*Le Figaro*, monsieur?' Duclos's eyebrows were memorable. 'Faire ça à moi? Va-t-en.' An invitation to give an alternative-to-democracy paper brought similar shock to me but provoked evasion rather than dismissal. So I ask what was going on three hundred years before there was any democracy to which there might have been an alternative.

Solon was not a democrat; he believed in common decency. Cleisthenes was not a democrat; he believed that he could exploit popular discontent to his own political advantage. It is impossible to measure or define that discontent but it is not until March 463 that we have any serious evidence that the word *dēmokratia* was in the air or before 462 that any action was taken under that slogan.[1]

Three hundred years before. What were things like in 762? Fourteen years earlier it had been as if Blackpool had agreed to play Blackburn Rovers for some sort of trophy. They had attracted Preston North End and some other Lancastrians, perhaps even Leeds United from across the border, to join the competition and they had appointed a local referee or referees to cope with disputes. So, in 776, the people of Elis, 'Pisa', and Achaea chose Iphitos and some others to supervise their new Olympic Games. But who were the judges and whence came the teams?

To the judges we shall return. Whence the competitors? Not precisely 'whence?' We must not get involved in the early history of Elis, still less of 'Pisa'. Rather 'from what sort of communities did they come?' I advance no new thesis, only an inflation of a suggestion made in the *Oxford History of the Classical World* (Boardman, Griffin, and Murray 1986: 13–17).

Over the last twenty or thirty years the archaeologist has been doing what he did in the 1930s, providing material for a completely new look at the history of early Greece. Then Payne and others dug at Perachora so that Blakeway could destroy the travelling potter and Andrewes invent

George Forrest left the text of this article almost completed at the time of his death in Oct. 1997. The editors have supplied a conclusion (beginning at n. 18) based on manuscript hints of the author's intentions and notes taken from the original seminar, together with references, footnotes, and bibliography; the maps are taken from originals drawn by Alan Greaves.

[1] Aesch. *Supp.* 604; Rhodes (1992) 62–77, esp. 74 and n. 40; *contra*, Hansen (1994) 27–8, 33.

the tyrant. Now Popham and others have dug at Lefkandi so that . . .? Some might think it premature to play historical games. My defence is that Vincent Desborough had pointed the way as early as 1952 (Desborough 1952: *passim*).

Desborough thought that he could detect some archaeological *koina* ('groupings'); one of them, the Ionian Islands with the west Peloponnese; another, our immediate concern, south-east Thessaly, north-east Boeotia, north Euboea, and the Sporades. His was purely archaeological observation. Lefkandi, which turns out to be very much a part of the latter grouping, tempts the historian. Very crudely: did the political map coincide with the archaeological map? Was the stunningly rich settlement at Lefkandi[2] the political centre of a *koinon*? There is, we all know, no evidence. But is the idea of a political *koinon* absurd? If not, what sort of thing might it have been?

Let us pause to look at a few stories that have been dismissed or passed over by historians less credulous than I.

According to Herodotus (1. 144), there had once existed some sort of association comprising six Dorian communities of south-west Asia Minor. He calls them *poleis* and such, in a technical sense, later they became; the three cities of Rhodes with Cos, Cnidos and Herodotus' own Halicarnassus. They met regularly at the sanctuary of Triopian Apollo by Cnidos for a religious, athletic, and, no doubt, bibulous festival. A Halicarnassian victor, Agasikles, broke the rules and Halicarnassus was expelled from the community. The Hexapolis became a Pentapolis.

But there was more to it than just the National Anthem, a football match, and a drunken binge. Another citizen of Halicarnassus, Dionysius, at *Roman Antiquities* 4. 25, records that a great Roman reformer, Servius Tullius, sought inspiration for his new order in, among other places, the Hex- or Pentapolis. The morning after their jamboree (I assume that it was the morning after) they met to discuss foreign policy and to settle internal disputes. So, we have an association of communities around a sanctuary, capable of taking decisions, political decisions, on behalf of all, an amphiktyony, and we have an errant member. Where do we place the break-up? The date of Tullius does not help. Herodotus does not write as if Agasiklogate were yesterday but does not help within a century or so. By the middle of the fifth century Halicarnassus was linguistically Ionicized (*Syll.*[3] 45, 46), but we must ask linguists how long it takes to turn Dorians into Ionians in official language. I can only conclude that there is nothing against the idea that the Hexapolis found itself in trouble about 700.

There was another break-up a bit to the north. Twelve Ionian cities met regularly at the sanctuary of Poseidon at Mykale. They too had their celebrations and their games. They too talked concerted politics. Thales

---

[2] On which see Popham, Sackett, and Themelis (1979–80).

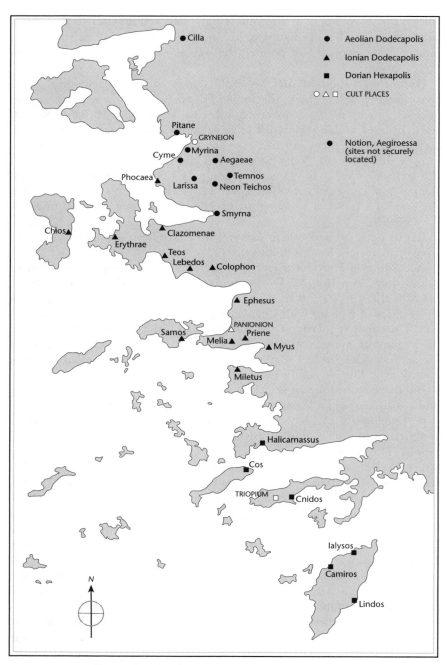

● Aeolian Dodecapolis
▲ Ionian Dodecapolis
■ Dorian Hexapolis
○ △ □ CULT PLACES

● Notion, Aegiroessa
(sites not securely
located)

Cilla

Pitane
GRYNEION
Cyme ● Myrina
● Aegaeae
Phocaea ● Temnos
Larissa ● Neon Teichos

● Smyrna

Chios ▲
Clazomenae
Erythrae
Teos
Lebedos
▲ Colophon

▲ Ephesus

PANIONION
Priene
Samos ●
Melia ▲
▲ Myus

▲ Miletus

■ Halicarnassus

Cos

TRIOPIUM □ ■ Cnidos

Ialysos

Camiros

Lindos

N

FIG. 16.1. Confederacies in archaic Asia Minor.

offered them political advice together, no doubt, with a weather forecast (Hdt. 1. 70) and, a little later, Bias of Priene advocated a proto-*Mayflower* enterprise (Hdt. 1. 170). These stories may be dismissed but the Ionians did, a little later, organize joint political action, something that we call the Ionian Revolt.

Move back. Again one city had caused trouble. Melia had been, if not in control of the sanctuary of Poseidon, at least close enough to it to give offence to the others. We have only one source for the Meliac War, Vitruvius (4. 1. 4). 'Because of the arrogance of the people of Melia the city was destroyed by the other communities, *communi consilio.*' Now we have an authority which not only bans Agasikles and expels his city but destroys it. The date? Keil (*RE* s.v. Melia) wrote 'um spätestens um 700' ('around 700 at the latest'). There are archaeological hints in the neighbourhood of Melia which point towards Keil's lowest date.[3]

Further north there was the Aeolian *koinon*, thought to have been centred at Gryneion.[4] Its story is obscure but Herodotus (1. 149) seems to think of it as some sort of unity, and one of its members, Smyrna, was forced by Ionian Colophon into the Ionian grouping. Mimnermus would put the transition before about 640,[5] Pausanias (5. 8. 7) before 688.

All this is cloudy. So too is our passage to the mainland via Crete. Here historians have concentrated their interest on the hellenistic *koinon*. Some have muttered about the possibility of an earlier association, none, so far as I know, with reference to a solid event. But when, in 480, the Greeks appealed for help against the Persians (Hdt. 7. 145), the Cretans sought guidance from Delphi jointly (7. 169 κοινῇ). To what body had the Greeks made their appeal and what body with what authority decided to turn to Apollo?

To pass to the mainland. Entities which are more than *poleis* abound. Most of them raise problems which it is impossible to discuss here. How did the villages of Sparta come together, absorb Amyklai, grow to dominate Geronthrai and Pharis, occupy Aigytis, destroy Helos? Was there a Thessalian *tagos* only in time of war or regularly or never? What did the distribution of the tripods at the Ptoion mean in the story of Theban expansion in Boeotia? Did the Aetolians get together and celebrate every year to any political purpose in Kalydon or Thermon or wherever?[6]

---

[3] P. Hommel in Kleiner, Hommel, and Müller-Wiener (1967) 91–3; Shipley (1987) 29–31.

[4] Or Gryneia, where there was a temple of Apollo: Strabo 13. 3. 5; Paus. 1. 21. 7.

[5] 'We settled at lovely Colophon . . . Setting forth from there . . . by the will of the gods we captured Aeolian Smyrna' (fr. 9 West, from Strabo 14. 1. 4). Mimnermus' traditional floruit is 632–629, but these dates may be significantly too late: Cook (1958–9) 13 says 'it seems clear that Smyrna had become a thoroughly Ionic city at latest by the beginning of the eighth century'.

[6] On Sparta see Forrest (1980) ch. 3; on the Thessalian *tagos*, *OCD*³ s.v., with further bibliography; on the Ptoion, Schachter (1981); on Aetolia, Bommeljé and Doorn (1987).

We could play games with any of these but I concentrate on three cases which are a trifle more arguable. First, the Calaurian amphiktyony. Its centre was the sanctuary of Poseidon on the island which we now call Poros. Its members were communities around the Saronic Gulf: Hermione, Aegina, Epidaurus, Athens with three others, Nauplion and Prasiae to the south and Boeotian Orchomenus, inland, to the north.[7] The southern limit is easily explained. Today the *Flying Dolphin* hydrofoil calls at all these points and only in high summer ventures further to Monemvasia. Prasiae (modern Leonidhi) is a natural frontier. For obvious reasons the *Dolphin* does not call at Orchomenus. So, why Orchomenus?

Orchomenus was not an integral part of Boeotia. When, towards the end of the sixth century, Boeotian cities began to issue coins, they did so with a common type. But not for Orchomenus the Boeotian shield; instead an ear of corn and, more interestingly, an incuse of Aeginetan pattern, Calaurian Aegina.[8] Earlier, towards 900, Attic influence in Orchomenian pottery is so strong that Professor Coldstream has been tempted to suggest an Attic presence, Calaurian Athens (Coldstream 1968: 341–3 with 196–8). But the problem of Orchomenus is more entertaining than important. For significance we return to the Gulf.

At 5. 82 ff. Herodotus sets out to explain an 'ancient' hostility between Athens and Aegina. Epidaurus had acquired olive-wood from Athens to fashion statues of Damia and Auxesia and, together with the wood, took on a religious obligation to Athena and Erechtheus. Later, in expansive mood, the Aeginetans attacked Epidaurus, seized the statues, but refused to admit that they had thereby taken over the obligation. Angry Athenians reacted with force; hence the hostility. Evidence and argument would seem to point to a date early in the seventh century for the quarrel.[9] If that is right, at or around the time at which Halicarnassus conceivably, and Smyrna and Melia very probably, were leaving or were being forced to leave their associations, Aegina too was in trouble with some of her Calaurian friends.

Associations there were. Quarrels there were, real or imagined by me, within a short generation of 700 BC; too many not to invite a general expla-nation. Before moving towards that explanation, we note another common feature. The associations all had a religious centre which was not attached to anything that we might be tempted to regard as a dominant political centre. Triopian Apollo by Cnidus for the Dorians, Poseidon by Melia for the Ionians, Apollo (perhaps) for the Aeolians by Gryneion, for Calaurians Poseidon on Poros, Itonian Athena for Boeotians at Alalkomenai and, in the same form, Athena near, not at, Pharsalos for Thessalians. Where are the 'cities' which we should single out as politically important; where are

---

[7] Strabo 8. 6. 14; T. Kelly (1966); Tausend (1992) 12–19.
[8] Head (1911) 346; Kraay (1976) pl. 19, no. 345.
[9] Hdt. 5. 82–6; Dunbabin (1936–7).

Rhodes, Miletus, Kyme or Mytilene, Aegina or Pharsalos itself or Thebes? That may turn out to be an interesting question.

In the early years of the sixth century there was a Sacred War. As a result of that war a body known as the Amphiktyones took control of the sanctuary of Apollo at Delphi. Whether this was an incursion or merely a reassertion of some sort of existing influence we cannot tell. The concluding lines of the *Homeric Hymn to Apollo* seem to me to dictate incursion; hints of earlier Argive or Corinthian ambitions towards the north might move us towards reassertion. But no matter.[10]

Two things are firm: that there was a force in the north that was pressing southwards; that our evidence does not permit any coherent story of its encounters with another southern force which was, at least, resistant. Sir John Boardman explains the story of the mythographer Antoninus Liberalis 4 about the anti-Delphic hero Kragaleus and his troubles with various divinities.[11] I cannot. But troubles there were. What was this northern Amphiktyony? Yet another association of states with a religious focus but some political gumption, using as its centre the sanctuary of Demeter at Anthela by Thermopylae. The members of this group were indeed the Amphiktyones, 'those living around': Thessalians, Ionians (of Euboea), the Dorians (of Doris), the Malians, Locrians, Phocians, and so on. But there is no major city at Anthela—or, to be fair, no major city has yet been discovered or is likely to be discovered in that neighbourhood.

Bereft of a city, of a polis backbone, Demeter has no more physical support than Poseidon had at Poros or at Mykale, Apollo at Gryneion or Cnidus. No more physical support. So whence the *authority* for Apollo or Poseidon or Athena or Demeter?

Before we try to approach that question—to which the answer is, of course, 'somewhere in the collectivity'—we must look at those who dwelt around Anthela. In the period on which I am increasingly concentrating, the second half of the eighth century, we have Pherae, of no great note, Pharsalos, which could produce Cleomachus and a troop of 'Thessalian' cavalry for battle in Euboea (Plut. *Mor.* 760 E–761 B); in northern Boeotia, Malis, Doris, the Sporades, nothing of note or just nothing. In Euboea, Chalcis, hidden under the present town. Then there is Eretria, New Eretria, where things keep turning up to surprise and still may.[12] The general picture as we have it is that Eretria, New Eretria, started to come to life shortly before 700 BC. Came to life and prospered. But then there is Lefkandi. Lefkandi petered out around 700 BC. I find it impossible not to believe that Lefkandi was Old Eretria. I find it very difficult to believe that the move

---

[10] On the historiography of the First Sacred War see now Davies (1994*b*).

[11] Boardman (1978) 228, 231, following Parke and Boardman (1957).

[12] The Swiss excavations at Eretria are published in *Eretria*, i–ix. *Fouilles et Recherches* (1968–93).

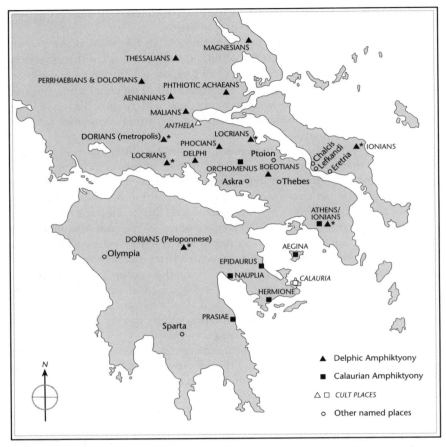

Note. In the Delphic Amphiktyony each ethnic group held two seats and two votes: those of the Locrians were divided between the Western (Ozolian) and Eastern (Epicnemidian and Opuntian) Locrians, those of the Ionians between Athens and the Euboean Ionians, and those of the Dorians beween the Dorians of the metropolis (i.e. the region called Doris) and the Dorians of the Peloponnese (who did not include Sparta: Roux 1979: 4–9).

FIG. 16.2. Amphiktyonies in archaic Greece.

from Lefkandi to New Eretria was not the result of defeat in or readjustment after the Lelantine War.[13] That war can only be understood if we assume that Eretria, like Halicarnassus, like Melia, like Smyrna, like Aegina, had found itself uncomfortable or unwelcome inside the association to which it had belonged and broke with it or was broken from it.

There are two interesting questions. Why the break? and what was the set-up before the break? To the latter I have no answer whatsoever, only

[13] For this war see V. Parker (1997) or, briefly, Boardman (1982) 760–3.

more questions. The excavations at Lefkandi have revealed, from just after 1000 BC, the tomb of a *basileus* who had his horses and his wife laid out beside him in death, a great man (Popham, Touloupa, and Sackett 1982). I call him *basileus*—'king'—not just out of courtesy. The splendour merits the title. But was he the only *basileus* of Lefkandi or was he just a particularly big one among a gaggle? Look from another angle. Hesiod, once more about the same date, the date of the break, writes not of the *basileus*, but of *basileis* in the plural. How many *basileis* could you see from Hesiod's Askra? Was there anyone in Askra itself who would rate the title or was the nearest one available at Thespiae? And, if so, was there more than one in Thespiae? Who *were* Hesiod's *basileis*? Strictly local? or did they hail also from Haliartos, Onchestos, Eutresis, etc.? We might be even more adventurous. Western Boeotia was not at the heart of the Anthelan amphiktyony, and Hesiod thought that it was a long way to Chalcis. Moreover, the just and noble lords of Euboea who gave him his prize tripod (if, that is, it was the Euboeans who gave it for the *Theogony*) do not much resemble the bribe-guzzlers of the *Works and Days* (*WD* 38–9, 263–4). But (1) prize-winning inspires different language from litigation; (2) Hesiod's views on distance were somewhat idiosyncratic; and (3) there is at least some Euboean archaeological contact with his neighbourhood. I should not have the nerve to propose, but I should not rule out the possibility, that Hesiod appeared twice before the same body of judges—or at least committees of the same body.

So where are we in all this? In the dark is the answer. But at this moment, it seems to me that the most likely story is that, in principle, *basileus* was essentially singular;[14] that there was one Knopos in Erythrae, one Agamemnon in Cyme, one Hector in Chios town, one Amphikrates at Tigani in Samos, one father of Pheidon at Argos, but not one for the whole of Chios or Samos or the Argolid, and so on down the line to one Amphidamas at Chalcis and one unknown at Lefkandi; that the collective *basileis* does not reflect a weakened form of *basileus* but describes what I earlier called the collectivity which could give political force to the sanctuary around which as representatives of their own towns or villages they congregated. Of course, according to personal talent or fluctuating fortune, one *basileus* might from time to time or even over a period become more of a *basileus* than the rest; indeed, short of passing disaster, Bacchis, the *basileus* of Corinth, would always matter more than the *basileus* of, say, Tenea; Pheidon's father at Argos more than whoever it was at, say, Tiryns; X at Thespiae less than Y at Thebes. But the principle was one unit, one *basileus*; a *koinon* of units, a *koinon* of *basileis*, equipollent in theory if not in practice.

Let no one think that I am proposing a standard pattern. No, only a notional pattern which might help us to disentangle the differences. Let

---

[14] On Homeric *basileis* see van Wees (1992) 31–6 with nn. 20, 23–4, 274–6, 281–94, who argues for monarchy within a wider circle of 'princes'.

me add in passing that the process of disentanglement is not helped by the importation of the word *tyrannos* by seventh-century Greeks and its exploitation by later Greek political philosophers. On my very crude analysis a 'tyrant' was simply a *basileus* who ceased to observe traditional decencies, who overrode other *basileis* who may or may not have been *de facto* inferiors and asserted his own superiority too publicly. Cypselus in Corinth was, in his own words *basileus kleitoio Korinthou* (Hdt. 5. 92 ε 2) but is widely called 'tyrant', Pheidon of Argos was a *basileus* who became a 'tyrant' (Arist. *Pol.* 1310^b26–8). This is more a linguistic than a factual puzzle.

Our question, before moving on to the break-up of the system, is to ask whether there are any signs of trouble inside the units of the system before the break-up, anything more than the docile discontent of Hesiod's 'them-and-us' which might lead towards a redefinition of the 'them' or the 'us'.

There are, but it is very difficult to separate them off from the reasons for the overall disintegration. I suggest only two. First, we have the appearance of two or even more *basileis* inside a monarchic unit—the largest number I know of is five at Erythrae, but these can be explained away in various ways. Less easy to explain away is the replacement of the life archon at Athens by the decennial archon and later, in 683, the appearance of the annual archon or, in Corinth, the removal of Bacchis in favour of a body of 200, one family we are told—but quite a large family.

Secondly, we have the possibility of physical evidence. In Dreros and perhaps in Lyttos in Crete assembly-places were constructed, just before 700, usually called *agorai*, but these were not *agorai* 'markets', they were *agorai* 'speaking-places', 'assembly-places'. Dreros is the firm one, Dreros whence came the earliest known record on stone of a 'popular' decision (ML 2). There, about or a bit before 700, was prepared a little area with benches along one side, a formal meeting-place. Not much to start with but something: that is, there is a debate going on, with a plurality of opinion expressed on a regular basis.

So, having recorded these traces or suggestions of movement inside a monarchic unit, let us move to possible reasons for the disintegration of the conglomerations.

Almost all of us, at some point, have explained the general political upheavals of the seventh century by invoking what we somewhat airily describe as the expansion of the Greek world in the eighth. And, of course, we are right—so long as we don't think that we are saying very much. It would be nice to be more precise.

We all now accept something like Sir John Boardman's view that we can distinguish an earlier stage of 'colonization' (with 'colonization' very firmly in inverted commas) to the west, to Al Mina, probably into the Black Sea and

Sinope from the main wave starting with Syracuse.[15] There can be many differences of emphasis but, roughly, this early stage will be perhaps less casual (and more competently organized) than the adventures of Hesiod's father, or, for that matter, of Odysseus, but certainly less systematic and with a purpose different from that of Syracuse and its successors. I do not wish to impose too rigid a distinction between the pursuers of metal in Elba, Al Mina, or Sinope and those who simply wanted enough to eat at Syracuse, but the Argonauts were not the same as the farmers of Tenea or the Megarians who founded the City of the Blind at Chalcedon. A distinction can be made.

Indeed the glimmers of light that we are beginning to see in what we used to dismiss as the Dark Ages might tempt us to ask just how we should be softening the rigid distinction which has usually been drawn between the chaos of the Dorian, Ionian, or Aeolian migrations to Asia Minor and these late ninth- or early eighth-century adventures. What were the differences between the rag-bag that had assembled in Chios, say, by about 900 (Cretans, Euboeans, Boeotians, even a Cypriot) and the Argonauts, except that the *Argo* was one ship, went much further, and came back again? Of these the important one is that it went *much* further.

So, what were the results? I mention four. The first would be the simple widening of experience. Greeks were seeing cities, artefacts, societies the like of which they had never seen before. Look at the effect that Egypt had on Herodotos, then try to imagine the effect on the first Greeks to reach the Delta 250 years earlier around 720. Diodorus sings the praises of wise and wealthy King Bocchoris. *We* know that Bocchoris was an insignificant princelet in about 720; I am sure that Diodorus, probably through Hecataeus of Abdera, merely reflects the astonishment of these first visitors. How else does a tinpot little nobody become praised in song (D.S. 1. 45, 65, *et al.*)? Experiences like that make people think.

The second was increase in prosperity. Greece was getting richer. It was a period of ups and downs, drought here, another kind of disaster there, revolution here, riot there; a killing here and another kind of killing somewhere else. But, by and large, things were improving. I have argued elsewhere (Forrest 1966: ch. 3, esp. 74–5) that we should not look within the cities primarily for the appearance of a new wealthy class to supplant the aristocracy to explain the seventh-century upheavals, but rather for confusions, for new balances. The same, I suggest was true within my associations, the *koina*. Aegina moves up, Athens down, Eretria up, and Chalcis down (or the other way round), and such readjustment causes tensions.

The third has been noted elsewhere but has not, I think, had the emphasis it deserves. The people of Aegina, say, might feel an urge for self-assertion

---

[15] See e.g. the papers by Snodgrass, Popham, Ridgway, and Coldstream in Tsetskhladze and De Angelis (1994); but cf., *contra*, R. Osborne (1998).

at the expense of Epidaurus, but for the people of Epidaurus, by the same token, the old *koinon* could seem to offer security. The sense of a shared past, the survival of established machinery, established practices, could cement the unity so that when Melia or Halicarnassus misbehaved the other Ionians or Dorians could get together and punish them. And so on.

But the colonial world had no *koina*; the new arrivals at Syracuse had nowhere to turn. They did not have neighbours. They had a lot of natives who hadn't the faintest idea what an amphiktyony was. The Syracusan may have left Corinth because he disliked the system. In that case he had to sit down and devise something new; but even if he had liked the system and only left because he was hungry, even if he only wanted to reproduce what he had known back home, he still had to sit down and ask himself what it *was* that he had known back home. It is no accident that the first lawgivers, Zaleukos and Charondas, appear in the outback.[16] It is no good arguing for the rule of law unless you can define 'law' and its rule.

So, new experience to absorb, a new economy to enjoy, and a new impulse to define. To the fourth consequence, stemming from and playing upon all three. This takes us abroad and to a specific experience; to Cyprus and Phoenicia.

By the end of the ninth century there was a firm Greek presence in the Levant, at Al Mina if nowhere else. There, I believe, Greeks may have picked up more than wealth, some artistic motifs, and the alphabet—the idea of that political organization which we call the city-state—and they may even have remarked signs of movement inside that organization such as were to manifest themselves somewhat later back home.[17]

In the city of Tyre there was a serious quarrel inside the ruling house which ended in the flight of Princess Dido and the triumph of her brother Pygmalion (Justin 18. 4). This was about 820 BC. But the quarrel, though told in personal terms, was not a purely family affair: the supporters of each contestant were bound together by something more than personal loyalty.

Similarly, at the same time, in Jerusalem the Princess Athaliah found herself at odds with the priest Jehoiada and others, and similarly, there too each of the parties appears to have had some common interest (2 Kgs. 11; 2 Chron. 22–3). I know—perhaps *we* know—too little of Phoenician and Judaean history to offer any definition of those interests, still less an explanation of their origins, but it is difficult to resist the temptation to see some sort of link with the earlier commercial expansion of the cities.

Dido and her companions escaped to Kition, the Phoenician toehold in south-east Cyprus, thence to Crete and ultimately to the site of Carthage,[18]

---

[16] Arist. *Pol.* 1274ª22–5. On early lawgivers see now R. Osborne (1997).

[17] For the details of what follows see Drews (1979); cf. Snodgrass (1980) 32–4 and Demand (1996) 9–10.

[18] *Editors' note.* The original text ends at this point. The part of W.G.F.'s abstract referring to

the foundation of which is traditionally dated to 814 BC. The route will strike the reader of Aristotle as significant: in book 2 of the *Politics* (2. 10–11, 1271^{b}20–1273^{b}26) he remarks on a number of resemblances between the Spartan, Cretan and Carthaginian constitutions. This link has been suggestively explored by R. Drews. Noting in particular that the Carthaginians have a plurality of kings and a board of elders, he argues that the latter may well have numbered thirty, like the Spartan gerousia; the kings—suffetes, technically—numbered two, and were quite probably based on the system which had obtained at Tyre (Drewes 1979: 47–51, 53–6). What was true of Carthage could equally well have been true of Kition, and the success of both will have looked attractive to Cretans admiring the ever increasing number of Phoenicians passing through or taking up residence to work metals, trade, and the like.[19] The Spartans believed that Lycurgus had brought their constitution from Crete (Hdt. 1. 65. 4); the tendency today is to disbelieve this, but why should they not have been right, at least regarding certain features, even if they got the date wrong? We have already noted agorai springing up at Lyttos and Dreros in the late eighth century, just a generation ahead of the likely date of the Lycurgan reforms. And Sparta was a constitutional pioneer in mainland Greece.

If this seems speculative, it need not be the only thread by which the case hangs. Cyprus is often shuffled to one side in discussions of the development of the polis as a specimen tainted by the influence of 'oriental despotism'. Nancy Demand has recently raised cogent objections to such attitudes: viewed objectively, the early kings of Cyprus look very like contemporary *basileis* in mainland Greece, and there are striking parallels between the royal tombs at Salamis and the burial of the *basileus* of Lefkandi a couple of centuries earlier (Demand 1996: esp. 11–14). Cyprus lay right on the natural route to the El Dorado of Al Mina and the Levant and, before the end of the eighth century, the dominant external influence in ceramics is Euboian (Reyes 1994: 1323, 139–40). The Euboeans certainly brought home plenty from their eastern travels: metalworking techniques, artistic motifs, perhaps the alphabet too, if that did not come by the other route, via a *poinikastas* (scribe; lit. 'Phoenicianizer') in Crete. This might simply have been a matter of observation, although since the resurgent Assyrian empire was putting pressure on its neighbours in the later eighth century, it may be that some Greek residents of Cyprus chose to migrate westwards like the Phoenicians

his conclusion read: 'Whence the idea of the *polis* as an independent unit? From Tyre through Kypros and thence by one route through Krete to Karthage (with a side-line to Sparta), by another directly to Euboia.'

[19] Some degree of uniformity in the constitutions of poleis on both islands may have been apparent to outsiders, to judge by the fact that the Aristotelian school produced *Constitutions* of the Cretans and the Cyprians *en bloc*, rather than of individual cities.

before them.[20] Once again, we find that the route leads to political upheavals: not constitutional reform this time, but a falling out within one of the old *koina* in the Lelantine War. We have far too little evidence even to speculate what Eretria's offence was, although there is no indication of any religious aspect, as there is in many of the other cases. An offence connected with the consequences of the eastern experience seems more likely: the position of the representative *basileis* in Thessaly or Malis or Doris will not have been touched by influences from the east, but the Euboean Ionians in Eretria and elsewhere can hardly have failed to be affected. Change came from the east, and they (or their friends or their subjects) had been there and seen a different way of organizing themselves. In particular, the position of the *basileus* had to change: he would become far more tied up with his community and its location. Authority was exercised (and restricted) in an agora like the ones we saw springing up in Crete, not carried with him like a briefcase to meetings of the *koinon*. One can at least speculate that tension between the gravitational pull of the *koinon* on the one hand and the nascent polis on the other led to a falling out within the amphiktyony.

This time, Eretria must have lost, since Old Eretria was destroyed. Eretria, however, remained within the amphiktyony (Aeschines 2. 116); but then the Delphic Amphiktyony held a trump card—Apollo and his oracle. Other *koina* had less to offer. Meanwhile, evidence from poleis planted overseas was proving that, just as you could succeed without monarchy, so you could get on without groups of *basileis* congregating at out-of-the-way cult places. The model of the polis did not always win the tug-of-war—the continuing role of ethnē in many parts of Greece is tribute to the continuing attractions of keeping in with your neighbours—but the pre-polis polis had had its day.[21]

[20] For pressure from the Mesopotamian powers as the ultimate driving force in this process see Purcell (1990) 38–44.

[21] W.G.F. left a note: 'I assure the reader that the flimsiness of this account and lack of documentation does not mark idleness or arrogance; rather, as I explained to a very tolerant audience at Leeds, [it is due] to a desire to emphasise how tentative/speculative the case remains.'

17
Argead and Aetolian Relations with the Delphic Polis in the Late Fourth Century BC

MICHAEL ARNUSH

THIS paper addresses the position of the Delphic polis in Greek affairs of the fourth century BC, specifically in the years of Alexander of Macedon's sovereignty over the Greeks and during the uncertainty that arose just after his death. When we think of the sanctuary of Apollo at Delphi the local polis does not immediately come to mind. The oracular seat was a devotional magnet for pilgrims and politicians, both Greek and barbarian, who sought answers to problems domestic and foreign and who compensated the god with lavish gifts. These treasures, together with the presence of the oracle, were both a blessing and a curse for the sanctuary and the polis, for Delphi not only served as a 'clearing-house' for divination and diplomacy, it also represented an economic jewel in the crown of whatever group controlled her. How did schizophrenic Delphi—the polis, the oracular seat, and as well the site of the *synedrion* of the amphiktyony[1]—function synchronously? To what extent was the polis subsumed by greater forces at work, reducing its impact and influence to local administrative matters? Did the character of the polis ever express itself in a tangible way, and where among the bits of testimonia can we discern the personality and even independence of the Delphic polis?

The rich epigraphic corpus unearthed at Delphi over the last century by French, Greek, and German archaeologists has provided the basis for numerous investigations into the complex organizations at work there during the fourth century BC. The dossiers of amphiktyonic finances, of the

I wish to thank Stephen Hodkinson and Roger Brock for their encouragements and comments, and John Davies, who together provided me the opportunity to deliver a version of this paper at the Universities of Manchester and Liverpool.

The following non-standard abbreviations are used: *CD*=Daux (1943); *ÉCD*=Bousquet (1988).

[1] The Delphic Amphiktyony, consisting of twenty-four representatives of a dozen Greek ethnē, served in an administrative capacity at the sanctuary, overseeing the maintenance of the Temple of Apollo and other structures within the temenos, levying of fines for religious transgressions, and waging sacred wars against those who threatened the sanctuary of Apollo. The amphiktyonic *synedrion* or council met biannually, at the sanctuary of Demeter at Anthela near Thermopylae and at Delphi. On the amphiktyony see Roux (1979) 1–59; Davies (1998) 3–4, 10–14.

receipts and expenses of the *naopoioi* or temple stewards, and of the roster of participants in the Delphic Amphiktyony are just a few examples of the aspects of local and international governance that the inscriptions from the excavations at the sanctuary have brought to light. Since the earliest days of the involvement of the École Française d'Athènes in the temenos of Apollo a reconstruction of the basic chronological framework—the eponymous archon list—has received considerable attention, particularly for the fourth and third centuries BC. Robert Flacelière (1937) and then Georges Daux, in his extra fascicle to the epigraphic third volume of *Fouilles de Delphes* published six years later (Daux 1943 = *CD*), represent the pioneers in Delphic chronological studies. The epigraphic corpus collected in *Fouilles de Delphes* and the annual publications of Delphic inscriptions in *BCH* have received careful scrutiny by Jean Bousquet, whose *Études sur les comptes de Delphes* of 1988 (*ÉCD*) and second volume in the new series *Corpus des inscriptions de Delphes* of the following year (*CID* ii) reflect a lifetime of improving upon the treatments of Flacelière and Daux.

The primary source for the workings of the polis derives from this epigraphic record. Aristotle's account of the Delphic *politeia*[2] has not outlasted the institutions which the Macedonian philosopher described and so a reconstruction of its inner workings depends wholly on glimpses provided by inscriptions scattered over nearly a millennium. The evidence from the fourth and third centuries brings to light some fundamental particulars: the city was governed by an ekklēsia or assembly, a boulē or council of fifteen members for each half of the year, a college of eight *prytaneis*, and the eponymous archon (Roux 1979: 61). The assembly was responsible for issuing the decrees of the polis, manifested particularly in honorific decrees. As for the boulē, every year thirty men were elected to serve as *bouleutai*, or councillors, and each half of this body served for six months (Daux 1936: 427–30), together with a *grammateus* or secretary (Daux 1936: 428–9; Roux 1979: 74). Both Argos and Rhodes also elected individuals to local councils for six-month terms (Busolt and Swoboda 1920–6: i. 419 n. 4). The boulē's responsibilities included both financial and judicial affairs, and in surviving inscriptions the *bouleutai* are typically named along with, and after, the eponymous archon; in most honorific decrees that mention the archon, however, only three[3] to five *bouleutai*[4] are usually named, suggesting either that the boulē appointed standing committees for local bureaucratic business, or that some of the bouleutic names in honorific decrees served as eponymous officials, so that any reader of the text would associate their names along with that of the archon with the specific year.[5]

The eight *prytaneis* held the primary responsibility for the administration

---

[2] *NE* 1181[b]15–24, a reference to the overall collection of *politeiai*; Rhodes (1981a) 1–2.
[3] e.g. *FdD* iii/1. 356.   [4] e.g. *FdD* iii/4. 399.
[5] Roux (1979) 71–7; cf. Tréheux (1980) 519–24; (1989) 241–2.

of the sanctuary of Apollo. Elected annually and eligible to hold office more than once, they were also the chief civic magistrates of the Delphic polis (Roux 1979: 81–2). Pausanias adds the eponymous archon to these *prytaneis* when he equates the Delphic *prytanis* with the Athenian chief magistrate.[6] The eight *prytaneis*, then, together with the archon were also the local administrators of the money received by the Delphic Amphiktyony and served as the liaison between this body and the Delphic polis (Roux 1979: 89–92). The role of the archon *per se* is never defined in Delphic inscriptions, but since when he does appear in the same document as the *prytaneis* their names are usually side by side, it suggests that their responsibilities were analogous if not identical.

The amphiktyony, a regional and religious organization, was composed of twelve constituent groups of Greeks operating out of Delphi and Thermopylae. Each of twelve ethnē sent two sacred ambassadors, or *hieromnēmones*, to the meetings of the amphiktyonic *synedrion* to administer the sanctuary and oversee the quadrennial Pythian Games.[7] The Delphians, the citizens of the polis of Delphi, counted as one of these ethnē, an aspect of the Apollonian temenos which created a situation unique in the amphiktyony, for no other city-state held two permanent seats on the *synedrion*.[8] The Delphic polis also had *prytaneis* elected annually who worked with the amphiktyony on behalf of the polis, contributing financially to and contracting out the work done on the temple after the earthquake of 373/2.[9] Delphi issued decrees, awarded grants of citizenship, and had in place such political structures as a boulē and ekklēsia, all suggesting that Delphi was indeed a polis.[10] Delphi also meets the criteria for a polis outlined by M. H. Hansen in his investigation of Boeotian poleis: independence and autonomy, territorial integrity, and representation in a federal amphiktyony.[11]

[6] 10. 2. 3 Ἡρακλείδου μὲν πρυτανεύοντος ἐν Δελφοῖς καὶ Ἀγαθοκλέους Ἀθήνῃσιν.

[7] Roux (1979) 14 ff.; Daux (1957) 95–120; Londey (1984) 25–6. The ethnē of the mid-4th cent., before the Third Sacred War, included two representatives each from the Thessalians, the Phocians, the Delphians, the Dorians, the Ionians, the Perrhaebian-Dolopians, the Boeotians, the Locrians, the Phthiotic Achaeans, the Magnesians, the Aenianians, and the Malians. Philip II's reorganization of the amphiktyony at the conclusion of the war in 346, in part to punish the defeated Phocians and in part to seize control of the *synedrion*, resulted in two Macedonian *hieromnēmones* replacing the Phocian representatives, termed first 'representatives from Philip' and later 'representatives from Alexander'. On the selection, role, and tenure of amphiktyonic *hieromnēmones* see Davies (1998) 3 ff.

[8] Some poleis, notably Athens, did dominate the representation of ethnē, but Delphi is the only polis permanently assigned seats on the *synedrion*.

[9] *ÉCD* 19 and nn. 4–5; Roux (1979) 98; Davies (1998) 3 calls them 'stewards of the Sacred Monies of Apollo', an apt name.

[10] *CID* ii. 31. 1, an account of the *naopoioi* from 358 BC, refers to Delphi as a polis in the political sense (Hansen 1996a: 44); cf. Hdt. 8. 36. 2, the earliest attestation of the Delphic polis.

[11] Hansen (1995b) 34 ff. Like other poleis, Delphi also has sufficient sovereignty to make decisions about citizenship (e.g. *FdD* iii/1. 199) and external affairs, which P. J. Rhodes considers the other necessary criteria for a polis (1995a: 109). Another critical element was temple-

Although the amphiktyonic *hieromnēmones* were originally limited to oversight of the sanctuary, by the fifth century they and their subordinates—secretaries, sacred heralds, and the like—entered into foreign policy, intervening in local affairs, arbitrating in interstate disputes, and imposing sanctions on poleis that acted against the interests of the members of the league.[12] As the amphiktyony began to find its voice in political disputes, the members tried to utilize it to impose their own political will on others and influence the direction of panhellenic growth or entrenchment. The amphiktyony crossed virtually all political and military boundaries, since it encompassed virtually all of the Aegean world. The panhellenic nature of this league suggests that this political oddity should have survived the petty demands of individual interests and served instead as a model for a wider, truly panhellenic world—an Isocratean *kosmos*. But Thebes, Thessaly, Philip and Alexander of Macedon, and the Aetolian *koinon* or League all managed to wrest control of the amphiktyony temporarily from its members, assisted by the acquisition of seats on the *synedrion*. With this lever, they would convert the amphiktyony into a forum to issue mandates to the rest of the Greek world. This placed Delphi in a delicate position: she had to co-operate with a host of occupying powers, each with its own agenda; she had, we must assume, some desire to maintain and even assert her independence, however grateful she might have been for efforts extended on her behalf by outside powers; she had to work with the amphiktyony, which at times reflected the fractious nature of the Greeks and at other times served as little more than a mouthpiece for external forces. John Davies (1998: 2) postulates a 'bifocal management' of the sanctuary of Apollo, where the amphiktyony and the Delphic polis together handle the affairs of the temenos. Aspects of this mutual arrangement are the focus of this study, in which we shall see Delphic and amphiktyonic responses to external factors resulting in a fairly standard practice of one political body underscoring the efforts of the other.

The amphiktyony of the fourth century was a remarkably prolific bureaucracy, issuing decrees in particular with reference to two events central to the history of Delphi that occurred within thirty years of each other: the restoration of the Temple of Apollo after the devastating earthquake that struck Delphi in 373 (Roux 1979: 98), and the payment, beginning in 346, of indemnifications incurred by Phocis after it had seized and pillaged the

building (Snodgrass 1980: 33–4, 58–62), for which Delphi was internationally renowned. Alcock (1995) 326–44 rightly argues that Pausanias' well-known description of what the Phocian city of Panopeus lacks to earn the designation of polis (10. 4. 1–2) should not be taken as a 'trait list'; nevertheless, Delphi possesses government offices, a gymnasium, a theatre, an agora, fountains, boundaries, and representatives at an assembly (i.e. the amphiktyony), all of which fall within Pausanias' scheme.

[12] Roux (1979) 20 ff.; Davies (1998) 10 ff.

sanctuary during the Third Sacred War.[13] From Alexander's death in 323/2 until the Gallic invasion of central Greece in 279/8 very few amphiktyonic decrees survive, and those that do are extremely fragmentary, so we need turn to other portions of the immense epigraphic corpus. Among this vast array of texts (dedications, manumissions, temple accounts, boundary disputes, etc.) resides a seemingly mundane and banal collection of documents—proxeny decrees[14] issued by the Delphic polis—which have been critical for reconstructing the archon list but have received virtually no attention otherwise. A typical Delphic proxeny decree[15] begins with the stock phrase Δελφοὶ ἔδωκαν—'the Delphians [presumably the ekklēsia and the boulē] bestowed'—and then proceeds to name the recipient of the decree together with his patronymic and ethnic (father's name and place of origin) in the genitive case, the award of proxenic status to both the recipient and his descendants, and then the honours accorded this foreign dignitary, with some variation in the order and package of honours provided. Typically, the honours include *proxenia*—the status and privileges granted to a representative of Delphic interests abroad; *promanteia*—the right to consult the oracle first; *proedria*—the privilege of a front-row seat in the theatre and stadium; *prodikia*—the right to priority in a trial if one were needed; *asylia*—a general inviolability or right of sanctuary; and *ateleia pantōn*—an exemption from all taxes exacted by the Delphic sanctuary from visitors. Then the decree terminates with a formulaic reference to the eponymous archon and typically three, sometimes five, of the fifteen *bouleutai*.[16]

There are thousands of such decrees dating from the sixth century BC until well into the Roman imperial period and, except for slight variations in the formulaic presentation of the awards, the proxeny decrees remain remarkably consistent in tone for centuries. Since formulae are no guide to an absolute date, we can situate these documents chronologically only via other references to the recipients or magistrates named. Letter-forms and styles do not help us much either: as with the body of late classical and early Hellenistic texts from Athens, the trends in letter-forms are broad and not particularly instructive. For much of the fourth century Attic and Delphic inscriptions alike appeared in large well-written letters and in the *stoichēdon* style. Line-breaks usually coincided with syllabic divisions, and the well-cut letters were even in shape and carefully situated within their *stoichoi*. This degenerated by the end of the fourth century to shallow and ugly letters, with tapering *hastae*, in the 'deteriorated style'.[17]

[13] D.S. 16. 56. 6; Roux (1979) 166; *FdD* iii/5. 19–20.

[14] Proxeny decrees originally recognized the role played by a *proxenos*, who was a citizen of one state but represented at home the interests of another; by the 4th cent. proxeny decrees naming the *proxenos* (and benefactor) were largely honorary and reflected less political responsibility.   [15] e.g. *FdD* iii/4. 6.

[16] For variations on this theme see e.g. *FdD* iii/1. 356.

[17] Dow (1975) xv–xvi. The *hastae*, or strokes, of an inscribed letter fit neatly within *stoichoi*

So, the formulaic nature of proxeny decrees, the endless droning on and on of awards accorded to foreign dignitaries otherwise generally unknown to historians, and the limited usefulness of these documents for establishing relative and absolute dates for Delphic magistrates have nearly reduced them to the slag-heap of epigraphic ejecta. J. K. Davies, while noting that 'the endless proxeny decrees of . . . Delphi . . . will often have been purely ritual actions', has warned that 'to dismiss all assembly business thus would be foolish . . . because decisions whom to honour, and how, could carry major diplomatic consequences' (Davies 1984: 306–7). Few efforts, however, have been made to collate and assess the data gleaned from the recipients of these decrees. In fact, with the exception of the occasional prosopographic identification scattered throughout *FdD* and *BCH*, and an article to which I shall return by Marchetti, only Bouvier has examined the formulae and frequency of specific types of honorific grants from the fourth century BC onwards and has identified ninety-three men of letters who received such decrees during the same period.[18]

Other honorific grants at Delphi connoted more than a ritual action. The Delphic grant of *promanteia* to Philip II *c.*346 signified the pre-eminence of the Macedonian over the other members of the amphiktyony and amounted to an expression of gratitude for his role in ending the recently concluded Third Sacred War.[19] In fact, as Demosthenes protested in his Third Philippic, Philip's *promanteia* was a privilege which took precedence over the rest of the Greek world.[20] A similar award to the Thebans *c.*360 suggests that in both instances Delphi was acknowledging the considerable influence each had on Greek politics.

Gerolymatos' work on intelligence-gathering (1986) has revealed that Boeotia and Athens both employed *proxenia* as a useful diplomatic tool in relations with individuals and poleis, modifying the institution to accommodate their specific needs. This runs counter to the positions of Wilhelm and Klaffenbach, that the sheer number of awards of *proxenia* granted by Delphi suggested instead the minimal importance of these honours.[21] This was the question addressed by Davies, and a few specific studies on *proxenia* have emerged, such as Buckler's work (1989) on the position of Phocis in

(rows, sometimes outlined on the stone) both horizontally and vertically, and in what R. P. Austin called the 'perfect stoichedon inscription' (1938: introduction) each row of text contained the same number of letters spaced similarly.

[18] Bouvier (1978) 101–18; (1985) 119–35. See also C. Marek, *Die Proxenie* (Frankfurt a.M. and New York: P. Lang, 1984).

[19] On the peace of 346 see Buckler (1989) 114–42.

[20] Dem. 9. 32. For a discussion of the significance of this award and whether it should be classified as 'la promantie ordinaire conçue comme un tour de faveur' or 'la promantie amphictionique conçue comme le droit de consulter l'oracle' see Pouilloux (1952) 504–6. Pouilloux argues for the latter and sees the award to the Thebans *c.*360 (*Syll.*³ 176) as a precedent for the award to Philip.

[21] Wilhelm (1942) 11–86; Klaffenbach (1966) 80–5; see more recently Gawantka (1975) 52 ff.

the aftermath of the Third Sacred War, or Roesch's examination (1985) of Boeotia in the second half of the fourth century. These studies have utilized proxeny decrees to expound quite successfully on the political fortunes of Delphi *vis-à-vis* other controlling states and have pointed to a growing realization that Delphi did occasionally demonstrate a degree of independence in her foreign policy. In fact, Marchetti (1977: 133–45) zeroed in on possible Delphic resistance to Macedonia in 324/3 just before the outbreak of the Lamian War, arguing that the Delphic Amphiktyony was the focal point for hostility against Macedon. Here I propose to consider Delphic honorary decrees issued between 336/5 and 321/0, during and immediately after the reign of Alexander the Great (336–323), and ask whether the proxeny decrees not only in 324/3, but in fact throughout the period, reflected a particular political pose struck by the Delphic polis. I shall suggest that Delphic foreign policy took on the most subtle form of expression during this period and that the sanctuary used the grant of *proxenia* first to equivocate in her relations between Aetolia and Macedonia and then to maintain and extend the anti-Macedonian sentiment prevalent in Greece leading up to and after the Lamian War. Some evidence points towards the influence of the Aetolians on Delphic policy, which may reflect the nascent stages of a Delphic–Aetolian relationship which resulted in Aetolian protection of the sanctuary in 279 BC when it was nearly sacked by the Gauls.[22]

Early evidence for Delphic overtures to Aetolia

Discontent with Macedonian rule had been brewing among the Greeks from the time of Philip's death. Sparta had remained aloof from the League of Corinth and she, together with Athens and Thebes, had made overtures to King Darius of Persia in 333 before the Battle of Issos, with the expectation that Alexander would be crushed in Cilicia. Sparta played her hand in 331/0 at Megalopolis, where she had rallied nearly all of the Peloponnese in a revolt which Antipater crushed. Lycurgan Athens, which had stood on the sidelines during the Spartan-led revolt, had a militant anti-Macedonian faction which was extremely vocal but whose policy had already failed. Demosthenes' stirring but futile speech *On the Crown* in 330/29 reflects an Athenian populace proud of past resistance and anticipating a renewal of action against Macedonia some time in the future.

During the archonship of Sarpadon at Delphi in 335/4,[23] Delphi extended

[22] A recent expression of this theory comes from Bousquet (*CID* ii. 233–4), who asked whether 'L'Étolie n'en a pas profité pour prendre sa place à Delphes, sans actes violents qui auraient frappé les témoins, mais progressivement, après une première mainmise contemporaine de la Guerre Lamiaque et des premiers conflits entre les Diadoques qui occupent le devant de l'histoire'.

[23] I have argued elsewhere (Arnush 1995: 95–104) for this date *contra* Bousquet (*ÉCD* 58 n. 50), who notes that in 335/4 when Alexander destroyed Thebes the Aetolians' relationship

a grant of collective *promanteia* to the Aetolian people. In a separate proxeny decree issued in Sarpadon's archonship the name of the recipient is only partially preserved.[24] The honoured individual should be identified with Polyperchon son of Simmias, one of Alexander's commanders at Gaugamela in 331. Every indication suggests that Polyperchon departed for the war against Darius when Alexander did, in the spring of 334; it is likely that recipients of proxeny decrees were present at Delphi when the honour was conferred. This provides a *terminus ante quem* of spring 334 for the proxeny decree and the beginning of Sarpadon's archonship. The award of collective *promanteia* has international ramifications, for it represents the first tangible evidence for any relationship between Delphi and the Aetolians. If Delphi could strike a political pose independent of Philip II in 335/4 and make a gesture towards the Aetolians, at a time when Aetolia sided with Thebes against Macedon, Alexander crushed Thebes, and relations between Aetolia and Macedon had grown ever worse (Bosworth 1976: 170–3), then Macedon's political and diplomatic influence over the sanctuary was in fact limited.[25]

The award of *promanteia* by Delphi to the Aetolians may well have been the result of nothing more than a temporary or internationally inconsequential relationship which the sources have not preserved; an analogy may be found in a fragmentary inscription dating to 323/2, which seems to record an award of collective *promanteia* to the Cyreneans for their earlier humanitarian assistance to Delphi during a famine.[26] On the other hand, the grant of *promanteia* to the Aetolians might have marked the onset of a formalized relationship of co-operation between the two. Aetolia had supported Philip at Chaeronea in 338, as, probably, had Delphi. Hence, they found themselves on the same allied side against the Greeks in the last desperate attempt by the latter to resist the Macedonian juggernaut. But as tensions rose between the Macedonians and the Greeks after Philip's death, the tenuous relationship between the Macedonians and the Aetolians underwent considerable strain as well. Perhaps Delphi made a tentative gesture to the Aetolians in the light of the unsettled atmosphere in Greece in the first year

with Macedonia had deteriorated so severely that they could not have received *promanteia*, *proedria*, and *ateleia* from a Delphi that had fallen under Macedonian control after the Third Sacred War in 346. For the collective *promanteia* see Inv. 7088A, B = *FdD* iii/4. 399 = Bousquet (1957) 485 ff. = *SEG* 17. 228.

[24] Inv. 4181 = *SEG* 17. 230; Bousquet (1957) 487–9.

[25] Evidence for Delphic stirrings of independent action under Macedonian 'control' appears when Alexander is unable to prevent the polis from honouring individual Aetolians with proxeny decrees in two other years: 329/8, and, more telling, 334/3, the year after Thebes was razed. See Bourguet (1899) 357; *FdD* iii/1. 147–8. See Davies (1998) 13–14, who argues that the evidence from the financial records of the sanctuary just before and after Chaeronea suggests that the creation of the *tamiai* or treasurers was an attempt to increase Macedonian control over the amphiktyony and hence the sanctuary.

[26] Bousquet (1952) 70 and pl. LI. 6; (1985) 249.

of Alexander's reign and did so to test the political waters, so to speak, and seek possible alliances with ethnē and leagues that might offer an alternative to the Macedonian yoke. The award of *promanteia*, the one tangible bit of evidence we have for this relationship by 335/4, may not be the first gesture, of course, but instead the first overt sign of an emerging alliance that would endure long beyond Alexander's reign.

The years that followed witnessed a series of revealing Delphic proxeny decrees. In 335/4, 330/29, and in 329/8 three different Thessalians were honoured with *proxenia*. In addition, in 334/3 and 329/8 Delphi honoured two Aetolians and in 333/2 a family of Macedonians received honours.[27] Any or all of these awards may have been motivated by non-political bene-factions extended to the sanctuary of Apollo, and the only other award from this period—to the dithyrambic poet Aristonoos of Corinth in 334/3 (*FdD* iii/2. 190)—was in fact probably in honour of the hymns he composed to mark the completion of the renovations to the Temple of Apollo (*FdD* iii/2. 191). But the other decrees, I maintain, indicate attempts by the Delphic polis to hedge its bets. The Aetolians and Thessalians had been allied in the past, particularly at Chaeronea, and represented two of the most potent military forces on the mainland. The decision by Alexander not to cede Naupactos to the Aetolians—a prize promised by Philip and one critical for control of the Corinthian Gulf and the north-west—led to a rapid deteri-oration of relations between the Aetolians and the Macedonian monarch. The proxeny decrees to the Aetolians and the Thessalians would then have represented a subtle attempt by Delphi to ingratiate itself with these al-lies. But surely Delphi was also mindful of Alexander's presence on—if not control of—the Delphic Amphiktyonic Council, where his delegates, like those of his father before him, held two of twenty-four seats and probably outstripped whatever voice the Thessalians and others had had before the Macedonians' forcible inclusion.[28] Accordingly, overtures to Aetolia and Thessaly were counterbalanced with gestures of *proxenia*—and hence good will—to a Macedonian family from Pella during the same period, as well as perhaps to Polyperchon, the Macedonian commander, just before the war against the Persian empire.[29] Delphi might have been interested in testing

---

[27] Thessalians: Bousquet (1940–1) 93; Bourguet (1899) 354, 359; *FdD* iii/1. 401; Aetolians: Bourguet (1899) 357; *FdD* iii/1. 147–8; Macedonians: Bousquet (1956) 558–62; (1959) 158–64.

[28] The exclusion of Alexander's representatives to the amphiktyony in 324/3, if intentional, suggests that the *synedrion* sought to distance itself from the Macedonians. For the Thessalian influence on the amphiktyony, especially in the 330s, see Davies (1998) 11; Roux (1979) 46 ff.; *CID* ii. 152.

[29] See above, p. 300. Of course, it is possible that any award to an individual could be motivated not by Delphic desires to appeal to his state's interests but to appeal to the honorand himself, for example, if the individual is in exile, as in the case of the Theban honorands in 324/3, for which see below, n. 32. Unfortunately, the documentary evidence for the honorands is usually too tenuous to determine which if any were disassociated from their homelands.

the waters, but she was not willing to provoke outright hostilities with the Macedonian king.

Resistance to Macedonia

The possibility of serious opposition to Alexander took a dramatic turn when the king proclaimed in 324/3 that the Greeks must recall thousands of their exiles.[30] This antagonized the Corinthian League and particularly the Athenians, who nearly went to war with Alexander. Tempers also flared among the Aetolians, whose occupancy of Oiniadai in the north-west would be severely compromised by such an amnesty. As both Bousquet and Marchetti have argued, a clear expression of anti-Macedonian sentiment appeared in the amphiktyony first in the autumn of 324 and then again in the spring of 323, when the representatives of Alexander to the Delphic Amphiktyony were not seated—οὐκ ἐνεκάθηντο—on the council.[31] Equally fascinating are two other bits of evidence: the first is the one extant proxeny decree issued by Delphi in this year, which records the renewal of *proxenia* for members of a prominent Theban family.[32] How ironic that in the same year that Alexander was noticeably unrepresented on the amphiktyonic council—presumably at the urging of the loudest voices among the amphiktyons, the Spartans and the Athenians—the Delphic polis extended honours to the homeless citizens of a city, Thebes, which had opposed and then fallen victim to Alexander in 335.

The other evidence for Delphic resistance to Alexander was a none too subtle insult directed at the queen mother, Olympias. Three years earlier, in 327/6, the Delphic Amphiktyony had decreed that money be set aside to purchase crowns of gold to honour the mother of the king—an honour worthy of the mother of a god.[33] Yet in 324/3, during the same year when

---

[30] Mendels (1984) 143–9. The main ancient sources are D.S. 17. 109; 18. 8. 1–5; Curt. 10. 2. 4; Just. 13. 5. 2–4; Mendels provides a full bibliography (1984: 143 n. 87).

[31] Inv. 7112+ =*CID* ii. 102 =*FdD* iii/5. 61+, col. I; Marchetti (1977) 144–5. The restored text for the autumn meeting of 324, which contains the formulaic list (as in the order outlined in n. 7 above) of twenty-two of the twenty-four *hieromnēmones* and their ethnicities, lists first the Thessalians, and then, before the Delphians, it notes (col. I a, lines 4–17, esp. 5–6) π]αρ' Ἀλ[ε]|ξάνδρ[ο]υ οὐκ ἐνεκάθ[ηντο . . . In the subsequent spring of 323 (col. II a, lines 24–33), twenty-one representatives are named; the Thessalians sent only one and no reference is made at all to Alexander's ambassadors. In previous years the Macedonian representatives were regularly named (for example, as recently as 325/4 at the autumn meeting: *CID* ii. 100, lines 2–3). Either the representatives of Alexander were prevented from sitting with the council at the meeting or they were not invited at all; what was notable in the autumn seems to have become codified by the spring, as if the initial snub was succeeded by an intentional omission. Cf. Aeschines 3. 116, where in 343 BC the *hieromnēmones* συνεκάθηντο—that is, they took their seats and conducted business.

[32] Inv. 1140 =*FdD* iii/1. 356. Daux (1943) 16 notes the difficulty of assigning this text to either the autumn or the following spring (as Bourguet argued in *FdD* iii) of the year 324/3, but since the first action taken by Delphi in this regard may well be the slight in the autumn at the meeting of the council, a subsequent award to Thebans would reflect Delphic strengthening resolve.   [33] *FdD* iii/5. 58, p. 223, lines 4–8; Marchetti (1977) 145 ff.

Alexander is not represented on the council, the money that had been set aside for the crowns made its way into the hands of the temple treasurers and the crowns were never purchased,[34] an obvious insult to the Macedonian queen.

These two declarations of independence by the amphiktyony—not seating the Macedonian representatives and back-pedalling on gifts for the queen mother—mirror the growing discomfort and rebellious spirit expressed by Delphi. It may even be that Delphi's efforts to maintain some autonomy and to rid herself of Macedonian domination, begun in 335/4, had such a profound impact on the *hieromnēmones* that they took the dramatic step of insulting both mother and son in one year. If, as Davies asserts (1998: 10), the amphiktyony's voice in all matters pertaining to the sanctuary was of paramount importance, then the actions of the polis are probably inseparable from those of the *synedrion*. The impetus for an anti-Macedonian stance may have been generated first by either body; in either case, the sympathetic stance of the polis *vis-à-vis* the amphiktyony indicates the relative lack of autonomy of Delphi when it came to interstate politics.

Alexander died in the summer of 323, just before the archonship of Megakles at Delphi (*ÉCD* 16, 68). As soon as word reached the Greek mainland of the death of the Macedonian king, Athens and Aetolia rallied most of Greece to the national cause and waged war against Antipater and the Macedonians.[35] The recipients of Delphic proxeny decrees in 323/2 include a Megarian and two Messenians, one of whom belonged to one of the most influential and wealthiest of Messenian families.[36] Besieged in Lamia in Thessaly in the war's early stages, Antipater snatched victory from the jaws of defeat with the help of Craterus at the battle of Krannon in the winter of 322 and brought the war to a close by the late summer of 322/1— except for the continuing hostility between Aetolia and Macedonia. In this year those honoured included citizens again of Megara and Messene, as well as some from Corinth and Boeotian Orchomenus.[37] With the exception of Orchomenus, we know from Diodorus Siculus (18. 11) that these cities lent their support to the Hellenic cause, and if we can read a political agenda behind Delphi's granting of *proxenia*, then she may well have been rewarding individuals from cities whose efforts in the war were particularly laudable. Diodorus notes Boeotia as problematic in its opposition and in fact supportive of the Macedonian cause, on account of Athenian support of the exiled Thebans, Boeotia's claims to Theban territory in the aftermath of Alexander's destruction of the polis, and Boeotia's fear that Athens would wrest away control of the profitable Theban land at the conclusion of the war. Of the Peloponnesian states that rallied to the Greek standard, the

---

[34] Inv. 3859+6745+6744 =*CID* ii. 97 lines 5–6.
[35] D.S. 18. 11 lists the Greeks involved.   [36] *FdD* iii/1. 177; iii/4. 7, 8.
[37] *FdD* iii/1. 161, 178, 179, 185; *SGDI* 2661 (archon Diokles).

Messenians are singled out by Diodorus and so might be particularly worthy of an expression of gratitude by Delphi. In addition, Delphic financial accounts from the next year—321/0—refer to reimbursements issued to heralds who had travelled to Boeotia, Corinth, Athens, Thermopylae, and Euboea (*ÉCD* 71 ff.). Although the heralds could have been on temple business, they might instead have been conveying messages of political import to strategically essential city-states during the war against Antipater.

Delphic efforts to extend diplomatic gestures to co-operative poleis continued after Antipater's settlement of Greece in 322, and so I turn finally to the Delphic archonship of Archetimos, 321/0. Five proxeny decrees were issued during this year, in honour of Patron son of Eupalinos of Elateia in Phocis,[38] Philinos son of Rhinon of Skotoussa in Thessaly,[39] Deinippos son of Deinylos the Messenian from Ithome,[40] Laodamas son of Stra[t]ios of Ambrakia,[41] and Telemachos the son of Hieron of Thespiae.[42] I propose that these honorific decrees were also intended as a gesture of good will at a time when, with the Macedonian civil war looming, the Greeks led by the Aetolians were attempting to revive the Hellenic coalition.

The proxeny decree granted to Patron of Elateia is particularly illuminating, in part because it represents the first extant decree for a Phocian from Delphi. Delphic acknowledgement of a Phocian can probably be traced to the approaching termination of the indemnity paid by the Phocians since their exploitation of the sanctuary during the Third Sacred War that ended in 346. In the archonship of Megakles in 323/2, two years before Patron received his grant, epigraphic evidence from Delphi indicates that the amount of annual indemnity paid decreased substantially, perhaps because of Phokian difficulties before the Battle of Krannon (*ÉCD* 68). A Delphic grant of *proxenia* on the heels of this change in the financial arrangement may in fact indicate the beginning of a *rapprochement* resulting in the termination of the Phocian payments, the last of which seems to have been made two years after the archonship of Archetimos, during Eribas' archonship in 319/8 (*ÉCD* 68). The award would have represented a sea change in Delphi's attitude towards Phocis, for Phocis' participation in a continuing anti-Macedonian resistance would be critical on account of its geographic location.

The next individual honoured in 321/0 is Philinos of Skotoussa in Thessaly, and his award can be viewed in terms of the Aetolian campaign against Macedon (D.S. 18. 38. 3). Although the Lamian War ended in 322, the Aetolians continued offensive sorties against the Macedonians even though Antipater and Craterus were occupied with the opposition to Perdiccas, chiliarch and guardian of Alexander's heirs. The Aetolians invaded Thes-

---

[38] Inv. 4343 = Daux (1933) 69–70.   [39] Inv. 3407 + 4499 + 6062 = Bousquet (1958) 62–4.
[40] *FdD* iii/4. 6.   [41] Empéreur (1981) 419–20 no. 2.
[42] Inv. 1315 = *FdD* iii/1. 96 and p. 389.

saly in 321/o, persuading most of the Thessalians to join them in the war against the Macedonians. The Thessalians were powerful allies for the Aetolians, as they had been at Chaeronea and again upon the news of Alexander's death, but the 4,000 Thessalian troops were no match for the Macedonian army. The decree honouring this Thessalian could be interpreted as an expression of gratitude either by Delphi alone, or perhaps prompted by the Aetolians for the Thessalian efforts against Macedon.

The third recipient of *proxenia* from Delphi was Deinippos son of Deinylos, a citizen of Ithome in Messenia. The presence of a Messenian among those honoured by Delphi in the years leading up to the Lamian War has already been addressed, and Delphic gratitude towards Messenian leadership in the anti-Macedonian movement need not have ended with the defeat at Krannon.

The significance of the homeland of the next Delphic honorand, Laodamas Stra[t]iou of Ambrakia, may lie in Ambrakia's role in the Lamian War, though it remains somewhat elusive. Diodorus does not specifically mention the role of the Ambrakians in the revolt of 323, although presumably they are included among the Leukadians, Athamanians, and Molossians from north-west Greece who provided support. And when the Aetolians fighting in central Greece were diverted from the war by an Akarnanian invasion of Aetolia, Ambrakia's significance arguably might be found instead in her geographic importance. Ideally situated at the crossroads linking Epirus, Thessaly, Amphilochia, and Aetolia, the Ambrakians should have supported Aetolia against the Akarnanians. If so, then a Delphic gesture of appreciation would be appropriate if Ambrakia's efforts had allowed Aetolia to resume the war against Macedon.

The last of the five decrees issued during the archonship of Archetimos, in honour of Telemachos Hieronos of Thespiae, is at once the easiest and most difficult to contextualize. Since Telemachos had served as a *naopoios* ('temple-builder') at Delphi some five or six years previously,[43] the decree granting him proxeny status might have been accorded for his prior service to the sanctuary. If, on the other hand, the gesture by Delphi was politically motivated, how can this be reconciled with Boeotia's opposition to the Greek revolt in the Lamian War?

The destruction of Thebes in 335 brought freedom and autonomy to the citizens of Thespiae, who had been under Theban control for thirty-five years. Thespiae soon reclaimed its territory, including the port of Kreusis, which controlled access to Plataea, central Boeotia, and northern Attica from the Corinthian Gulf. Delphi, the Aetolians, and other Greeks interested in continuing the war with Macedon might have envisaged a growing relationship with erstwhile opponents such as Thespiae to provide crucial access to central Greece south of Thermopylae.

[43] *CID* ii. 119 (=*FdD* iii/5. 91), line 49.

There remain two last tantalizing bits of evidence: the first comes from the unusual shift in dialects used in a document issued at Delphi in 321/0. In an amphiktyonic decree detailing the operations of treasurers who oversaw the expenditure of league revenues at Delphi, Thermopylae, and elsewhere, dialect features not typical of the customary Attic *koinē* but instead of the patois of north-west Greece appear—and this is the dialect of both Phocis and Aetolia.[44] Why should there suddenly be a dramatic change from a dialect familiar to most foreign visitors to the sanctuary, to one commonly used only by the local inhabitants and their neighbours immediately east and west? This phenomenon occurs only from 322/1 to 321/0 and it may be completely anomalous, but it might reflect one of two political trends: either a nearly silent declaration of independence, and influence upon the amphiktyony, by Delphi, or a subtle shift in Delphic attitudes towards her Aetolian or Phocian neighbours. The abrupt cessation of the use of a north-western dialect may be equally anomalous or it might reflect the Macedonian success in routing the Greek coalition at Krannon, suggesting that Aetolia's influence at Delphi diminished somewhat although her opposition to Macedonia continued beyond the end of the war.

The last, suggestive piece of evidence comes from the appearance of a particular amphiktyonic *hieromnēmōn*, or representative, in 322/1 and 321/0. During the archonships of Diokles and Archetimos, respectively, in four different decrees addressing the construction of a *hoplothēkē*, or armoury, as well as other financial considerations, the names of five *hieromnēmones* appear without ethnic adjectives.[45] One of the five is named Pleistainos. The name appears again in the Delphic epigraphic corpus in the third century, as the donor of a monumental column and gilded statue to Apollo. The benefactor Pleistainos in this latter instance is an Aetolian, and he hails from a powerful and influential Aetolian family.[46] The traditional view is that the Aetolians joined the amphiktyony as *hieromnēmones* just after the war against Brennus and the Gauls in 279, when the Aetolian *koinon* had saved the sanctuary from destruction and won two seats on the amphiktyony.[47] If the Pleistainos of 322/1–321/0 is an ancestor of the hellenistic benefactor, his presence on the amphiktyonic *synedrion*, specifically as an Aetolian representative, would precede the accepted date of formal Aetolian participation

---

[44] Inv. 7202 = *ÉCD* 71–5 (text 72). As Bousquet notes (1988: 74–5 n. 65, 139), these variations of dialect (e.g., -ττ- for -σσ- in Θετταλῶν, τέτταρες, τετταράκοντα) first appear in 322/1, the previous year, and may suggest Aetolian influence upon the sanctuary of Apollo.

[45] *FdD* iii/5. 78, 79, 81 and Inv. 7202 + 10061.

[46] *ÉCD* 75 and nn. 68–9. An Aetolian Pleistainos appears again in a decree under the archon Athambos (*SGDI* 2595) in 269/8 and in Aetolia in the 2nd cent. (*ÉCD* 75). Bourguet (at *FdD* iii/5. 78) tentatively offers the ethnicity of the 4th-cent. Pleistainos as Thessalian, while Bousquet (*ÉCD*) leaves the issue unresolved.

[47] The earliest appearance of Aetolian *hieromnēmones* occurs in the archonship of Aristagoras (*CD* 33 no. G2). See Flacelière (1937) 40–91.

in the amphiktyony by forty years. No amphiktyonic formulaic preambles of *hieromnēmones* survive from this period, so the evidence is too tenuous to argue for Aetolia joining the amphiktyony before 279, although it would be in keeping with the pattern we have established of increasing Aetolian interest in Delphi. Pleistainos' presence in the Delphic epigraphic corpus is tantalizing, but unless more complete amphiktyonic decrees from 321–279 are discovered this issue will remain unresolved.

Conclusions

What has emerged, then, is a pattern of Delphi extending diplomatic gestures to a seemingly disparate amalgamation of poleis and ethnē during the age of Alexander, all of which were linked to opposition to Macedonian control, to the nearly united front against Antipater fashioned by Athens and Aetolia in the wake of Alexander's death, or to the future of the Hellenic cause after the end of the Lamian War. Further, Delphi's growing relationship with Aetolia, first articulated in 335, may have led to Aetolian efforts to nudge, prod, and support Delphic foreign policy through the granting of proxenic status to further the anti-Macedonian cause. The corpus of Delphic proxeny decrees from the 330s and 320s supports the notion that the polis took a rebellious political stance and should continue the debate on the relative importance of these seemingly banal documents.

The more complicated issue lies with the relationship between the Delphic polis and the amphiktyony. These texts also suggest that the polis of Delphi found a means—albeit a subtle one—to express a degree of autonomy coincidentally with amphiktyonic assertions of independence. The harmony of attitudes from both the league and the city-state by the late 320s speaks as well to a concerted effort by all who had Delphi's interests at heart to break free of Macedonian control, even at the expense of Aetolian influence. Delphi was a polis, with all of the necessary trappings of a Greek city-state of the fourth century. Yet the amphiktyony, though only intermittently active, had such a profound influence on Delphic behaviour (Davies 1998: 10–11) that the actions of the two on the international stage are inseparable. Whoever took action first, the other was sure to follow, and together Delphi and her amphiktyony presented a united front to the other Greeks in a period of considerable turmoil and uncertainty. Delphi the polis was dependent upon the amphiktyony for matters financial, administrative, and political, and took a political stance wholly in concert with the amphiktyons, sacrificing some autonomy for enduring protection and clout.

18

Problems of Democracy in the Arcadian Confederacy 370–362 BC

JAMES ROY

THIS paper is an attempt to examine a case study of a democratic regime operating not in a single polis but in a confederacy, that formed by the several communities which shared a common Arcadian identity but were themselves independent states. The effective life of the democratic Arcadian confederacy as a major political force was no more than a few years, from 370 until internal disagreement split the Arcadians into two blocs c.363. One or both of the Arcadian groupings continued to claim to be the Arcadian League until at least the later fourth century;[1] it is not clear whether the groupings ever reunited.

The main evidence for the confederacy as a major political force is in Xenophon's *Hellenica* and Diodorus Siculus. Xenophon's account is generally fuller, though he notoriously omits much (e.g. the founding of Megalopolis) and is clearly biased in favour of Sparta and against democratic tendencies.[2] Xenophon is reasonably well informed about the Arcadian League, though he reports the league's affairs (like much else) in terms of his notion—which he does not define—of opposition between democrats and oligarchs.

The foundation of the Arcadian League[3]

The league emerged, according to Xenophon, from political developments at Mantinea and Tegea in the aftermath of the Spartan defeat at Leuctra in 371. In both cities a democratic, anti-Spartan tendency developed, and gave the new confederacy a similar disposition. In 384 Mantinea had been dioikized by the Spartans, who destroyed the fortifications and forced the

I am grateful for comments made when this paper was discussed at a seminar in the University of Leeds, and particularly for helpful criticism and suggestions offered then and later by the editors of this volume. I also wish to thank T. H. Nielsen for helpful suggestions. Responsibility for the views expressed, and for any deficiencies, remains entirely my own.

[1] See Charneux (1983) 256–62 on *IG* iv. 616, an Argive inscription of the later 4th cent. with references to an Arcadian *koinon*.

[2] Xenophon's bias, though obviously present, is not simple: see Tuplin (1993).

[3] There is a valuable survey of the Arcadian League in Trampedach (1994) 21–37, with sections on its foundation, its constitution, the *eparitoi*, and its foreign policy. There is also a useful summary in Beck (1997) 67–83.

population to resettle in four or five separate settlements; thereafter government at Mantinea was an *aristokratia* which pleased the wealthy landowners
of Mantinea.[4] Xenophon (*Hell.* 6. 5. 3–5) describes how in 370 the Mantineans rebuilt their city, and three points emerge from his account. First,
Sparta strongly opposed the rebuilding of the city, but could find no effective argument against it; second, Xenophon makes no mention of any
violent disagreement over the issue within Mantinea, though somehow the
pro-Spartan regime set up after the dioikism had given way to magistrates
unsympathetic to Sparta's case; and, third, the new synoikism was undertaken, as the Mantinean magistrates claimed, according to a 'decree adopted
by the whole polis'. Thus, though there is no direct evidence of a change
of constitution at Mantinea after Leuctra,[5] political dominance had passed,
peacefully as it seems, to an anti-Spartan group of presumably democratic
tendency which could claim to be supported by the whole polis.

In Tegea at the same time there was a violent political struggle (*Hell.*
6. 5. 6–10). One party advocated 'that the whole *Arkadikon* should unite,
and that whatever prevailed in the *koinon* should be binding also on the
poleis'; this party believed that the majority of the Tegean *dēmos* would

[4] On the dioikism see Moggi (1976) 140–56, quoting the ancient sources. Xen. *Hell.* 5. 2. 1–7
mentions four villages after the dioikism (and *aristokratia*), while D.S. 15. 12. 1–2 mentions
five, and Paus. 8. 8. 9 writes generally of villages but with a small residual settlement where
the town had been.

[5] Whether there was significant constitutional change at Mantinea after Leuctra depends at
least partly on the political arrangements imposed by the Spartans under the dioikism. While
Xenophon, Diodorus, and Pausanias describe the settlements under the dioikism as villages
(previous note), it is notable that the Arcadian Polybius (4. 27. 6) writes of dioikism not into
villages but from one polis into several. (I am grateful to T. H. Nielsen for drawing this passage
to my attention.) Polybius' phrase suggests that the Mantineans were dioikized into several
separate political units, and that interpretation is supported by the report in Xen. *Hell.* 5. 2.
7 that after the dioikism, when the Spartans required military support from the Mantineans,
they sent not a single *xenagos* to all Mantineans but one to each of the villages (and so the
Mantineans presumably fought as several separate military contingents). Moggi (1976) 156
n. 65 takes this view, arguing that the Spartans divided the Mantineans into 'distretti . . .
politicamente autonomi e indipendenti gli uni dagli altri': see also Nielsen (1996*a*), especially
p. 131 on the possibility that Nestane was a dependent polis of Mantinea. Hansen (1995*c*)
76–7, on the other hand, argues that Mantinea, though dioikized, remained a single political
community, but the texts he cites (Xen. *Hell.* 6. 4. 18 and D.S. 15. 5. 4, 15. 12. 2) do not seem
decisive: in particular, Xenophon's phrase 'The Mantineans joined strongly in the campaign,
for they were then under aristocratic government [*aristokratoumenoi*]', while using—naturally
enough—the collective term 'Mantineans', refers to military service, for which we know that
they were levied separately, and speaks of aristocratic government in terms which could apply
equally to a unitary Mantinean state or to a series of separate but similarly run statelets. On
the resynoikism of Mantinea after Leuctra (on which see Moggi 1976: 251–6), Xen. *Hell.* 6. 5.
3 reports that 'the Mantineans . . . all came together and voted to make Mantinea one polis and
fortify the polis': since the last phrase certainly refers to fortifying a rebuilt urban centre, the
repetition of the word 'polis' suggests that 'to make Mantinea one polis' similarly has reference
to recreating the urban centre, but the same phrase could also refer to political reunification,
i.e. reuniting the several poleis of Polybius into a single polis. Clearly, if there was political
reunification in 370, it would involve constitutional change and revision of the appointments to
official posts, and the time of change would offer an opportunity for different political leaders
to come to the fore in Mantinea.

support them. Their opponents dominated the magistrates (*thearoi*).[6] The federalists got help from Mantinea, and secured control after bloody fighting in which some of their opponents were killed and about 800 fled into exile at Sparta. There was thus in effect a political purge at Tegea, leaving the democratic federalists with no strong opposition, but we hear of no such purge at Mantinea. Diodorus (15. 59) has a somewhat different account of these events: he does not specifically refer to Mantinea, though he refers to 'Lycomedes of Tegea', clearly meaning the Mantinean politician Lycomedes: Diodorus also allows more success to Sparta's countermeasures than subsequent events make plausible. The confusion in Diodorus' account makes it difficult to use him to correct that of Xenophon.[7]

In response to these developments Sparta campaigned against Mantinea (*Hell.* 6. 5. 10–22). Many Arcadian states supported Mantinea, but Orchomenus and Heraea supported Sparta, and both were attacked by other Arcadians. Of Orchomenus and Heraea Xenophon says that they refused to join the *Arkadikon* (*Hell.* 6. 5. 11, 22): his wording shows that some form of Arcadian union was emerging.

Arcadia, Argos, and Elis presumably allied among themselves: Elis had helped the rebuilding of Mantinea (*Hell.* 6. 5. 5), and Argos' hostility to Sparta is well known. At any rate the three states together sought an alliance with Athens, which was refused, but then secured an alliance with Boeotia.[8] That alliance led to the famous invasion of Laconia and Messenia by Boeotia and its Peloponnesian allies in winter 370/69. After that invasion no more is heard of any Arcadian state opposing confederacy for some years. Presumably most, or all, Arcadian states had joined the confederacy by 369 (as is already implied by *Hell.* 6. 5. 11, mentioned above).[9]

Confederate Arcadian constitution

There are very serious gaps in our knowledge of the Arcadian confederacy's constitution, and it is therefore impossible to use the constitution as evidence of the kind of democracy practised in Arcadia in the 360s. None the less, what is known of the constitution is broadly consistent with the view that the League was democratic.

For the constitution of the new confederacy there is—with one notable exception, to be discussed below—no epigraphic evidence. In addition, there is no epigraphic evidence for the contemporary constitutions of the

---

[6] How well balanced support for the two sides actually was depends on whether or not one follows Dobree in deleting a negative in *Hell.* 6. 5. 7: '[the opponents] were (not) fewer in number'.

[7] See Roy (1974) on arguments of Dušanić (1970) 284, 291–2, derived from this passage of Diodorus.   [8] Xen. *Hell.* 6. 5. 19; D.S. 15. 62. 3; 16. 12. 19–20.

[9] When, probably in 363, the Arcadians gathered at Tegea to swear to the peace with Elis, there were present Arcadians 'from all the poleis' (*Hell.* 7. 4. 36).

member states of the confederacy. It is a great pity that in particular there
is no such evidence for the constitution of the newly founded Megalopolis,
since the framework chosen by the confederacy for its new creation might
have revealed something of the league's thinking. It is in fact impossible to
compare the constitutional forms in use in the various member states to see
whether they had adopted any such standardization as can be seen in the
Boeotian constitutions reported in *Hell. Oxy.* 16; there is at any rate no sign
of anything of the kind in Arcadia, and events of 363–2 make it unlikely.

It has been suggested that the Arcadian confederate constitution drew
on the model of the Boeotian equivalent,[10] but there is in fact little reason
to think that the Arcadian constitution was heavily influenced by Boeotia.
Hell. 6. 5. 10–22 suggests that the *Arkadikon* was coming together before
it formed an alliance with Boeotia, and the negotiations for alliance show
that the confederacy would have preferred Athens to Boeotia as an ally.
Also, the role of the sole *stratēgos*, or general, in the Arcadian confederacy
is unlike that of the Boeotian commanders, the Boeotarchs, or of the fairly
weak archon, in the contemporary Boeotian League.[11]

There is also the question whether Plato influenced the new Arcadian
constitution, because of two separate reports of Platonic involvement.[12]
According to one report, found in both D.L. 3. 23 and Aelian *VH* 2. 42,
when (as the sources put it) the Arcadians and Thebans were founding
Megalopolis, they invited Plato to come and act as lawgiver (*nomothetēs*),
but he refused when he discovered that the Arcadians did not want to
'have equality' (*ison echein*, in both sources). Since an Arcadian democrat
could well have understood *isonomia* (if that is what is meant) differently
from Plato,[13] this report presents no obstacle to the belief that the new
confederacy was democratic. If true, the report would suggest that the
Arcadians were willing to seek expert advice on a suitable constitution for
Megalopolis, but only within certain guidelines which they already had in
mind. The other report, in Plut. *Mor.* 1126 c (=*Adv. Colotem* 32), says that
Plato sent one of his associates, Aristonymus, to Arcadia to organize, or
reorganize, the constitution (διακοσμήσοντα τὴν πολιτείαν). The ambiguity
of the verb leaves it unclear whether Aristonymus drew up the original
confederate constitution, or instituted some later reform. Nothing else is
known of Aristonymus' work for Arcadia, and his career is not otherwise
known. If he drew up the initial constitution, that would strengthen the
view that it was not modelled on that of the Boeotian League; but, if he did
so as a Platonist, it would make a subsequent misunderstanding between

---

[10] e.g. by P. Salmon (1978) 5, 104–6; see the criticisms of Trampedach (1994) 28.

[11] On the Boeotian League see most recently Rhodes (1994) 582; Beck (1997) 83–106.

[12] On both incidents see Trampedach (1994) 21–41, replacing Wörle (1981) 103–5.

[13] See Trampedach (1994) 37–41: he notes both that the supposed incident may well be
unhistorical, and that, if it is historical, *ison echein* may refer to property division (so Gehrke
1985: 156 n. 23). On Platonic *isonomia* in general see Vlastos (1973) 164–203.

the Arcadians and Plato at the time of the founding of Megalopolis harder to understand.[14]

Some elements of the confederacy's constitution are known from literary sources.[15] There was a single *stratēgos*, apparently of considerable influence; there were magistrates, referred to by Xenophon (*Hell.* 7. 4. 33–40) simply as *archontes*; and there was a meeting of citizens known as the *Myrioi* ('Ten Thousand'). Further elements are shown by the one decree of the confederacy surviving complete, preserved on an inscription found at Tegea.[16] The decree is brief: 'God. Fortune. It was resolved by the council [*boulē*] of the Arcadians and the *Myrioi* that Phylarchus son of Lysicrates Athenian be *proxenos* and benefactor of all Arcadians, himself and his descendants. The following were *damiorgoi* . . .', and there follow the names of fifty *damiorgoi* grouped by their place of origin. While the *Myrioi* are known from elsewhere, both the confederate council and the officials called *damiorgoi* are attested only in this text. The council is not surprising, but the *damiorgoi*, as they appear here, are a puzzle (to be discussed below).

It is agreed that the lettering of the inscription belongs to the fourth century, but otherwise the date of the decree is obscure. The text must obviously be later than the foundation of Megalopolis and the adhesion of Heraea and Orchomenus to the confederacy, since there are *damiorgoi* from all three. Honours for an Athenian are more likely after Athens and Arcadia agreed on a mutual defence pact in 366 (and the fact that above the text is sculpted an image of Fortune touching a trophy suggests that the decree was associated with a military victory). The presence of both Mantinean and Tegean *damiorgoi* means that the text must be either before the split in the league *c*.363, or after a reunion. A scholiast on Aeschines 3. 83, listing separately 'the Arcadians with Mantinea' and 'the Megalopolitans', suggests that the split still persisted in 343/2, and in fact no reunion of the separate blocs is known.[17] Another problem is to understand the list of *damiorgoi*. Fifty are listed: 10 from Megalopolis; 5 each from Tegea, Mantinea, Cynuria, Orchomenus, Cleitor, Heraea, and Thelpusa; 3 from Maenalia; and 2 from Lepreum. Fifty is a fine round number, and so it is tempting to suppose

[14] Trampedach (1994) 41 envisages the possibility that Plato, having refused to go to Megalopolis himself, sent Aristonymus instead to draw up its constitution.

[15] What is known is set out in Larsen (1968) 186–9; Rhodes (1994) 582–4; Trampedach (1994) 27–35. See also Roy (1971; 1974; 1994) and Gehrke (1985) 154–8. Korchagin (1981) offers an implausible reconstruction of the origins of the league.

[16] Tod 132 (listed in Rhodes with Lewis 1997: 91). See Dušanić (1979) 120–2; *SEG*. xxix. 405, xxxii. 411 (listed in Rhodes with Lewis 1997: 91), for a very fragmentary text which is probably also a confederate decree, but of no help in reconstructing the confederate constitution.

[17] I am now much less confident about the dating of this text than I was in 1971 (Roy 1971: 571). If the text were to be dated after 343/2 on the assumption that the different groups in Arcadia eventually reunited, then it would lose much of its weight as evidence for the confederate constitution in the 360s, given the possibility of constitutional change as time went on.

that the list is complete; on the other hand many Arcadian communities are missing (Phigalia, Psophis, Cynaetha, Caphyae, Lusi, Stymphalus, Alea, Torthyneum; Pallantion, also missing, may be included among the Maenalians). The missing states are almost all in northern Arcadia; but Cleitor, from the north, is present, and Phigalia, from the south-west, is missing. The varying numbers of *damiorgoi* suggest some very rough form of proportional representation:[18] Lepreum was small,[19] and Maenalia would be small after losing communities to Megalopolis,[20] but it not clear why Megalopolis had twice as many *damiorgoi* as any other community. Dušanić (1978*a*: 350 n. 14) suggests that the number of Megalopolitan *damiorgoi* reflects the greater importance of Megalopolis, and that the text therefore does not belong in the 360s, when Megalopolis was still weak; but possibly the large Megalopolitan quota was an act of propaganda like the very name of Megalopolis itself (*Megalē Polis*, 'Great City'). The distribution does, however, ensure that none of the older Arcadian communities, and in particular neither Mantinea nor Tegea, enjoys a dominant position. P. Salmon (1978: 5, 104–6) suggests that the list of *damiorgoi* represents a division into districts modelled on the Boeotian League: he has, however, no convincing solution for the obvious problems posed by the list, suggesting without evidence that some missing communities (e.g. Caphyae and Alea) were subjects of other Arcadian poleis and that others (e.g. Stymphalus, Phigalia, and Pheneos) were not members of the league. It is theoretically possible that the fifty *damiorgoi* were drawn from different Arcadian communities in turn; but it is very hard to imagine a reasonable system of rotation which at the same time would exclude almost all of northern Arcadia but include all the major states of the rest of Arcadia. Given the major, and unsolved, problems posed by this text, it is very dangerous to use it as evidence of Boeotian influence, when that is on other grounds unlikely.

Despite all the uncertainties about the list of *damiorgoi* in this text, one point about them is clear, namely that they were associated with their respective home poleis. While some may have taken a confederate rather than a local view of current politics, it is easy to see that views held in individual poleis could readily be channelled into confederate politics. The events of 363–2 do indeed suggest that individual Arcadian poleis remained a major focus of political activity alongside the confederate political process.

The *Myrioi* have also been much discussed, in an effort to ascertain whether they formed a primary assembly of all citizens of the confederacy

---

[18] Xen. *Hell.* 7. 4. 33 shows that confederate member states paid a contribution towards the upkeep of the *eparitoi*, but his text does not make clear to what extent, if at all, the contribution was proportional.

[19] If Lepreum in some sense represented all the Triphylian communities within the Arcadian confederacy, then it is surprising that it was allocated only two *damiorgoi*. On Lepreum and Triphylia in this period see Nielsen (1997) 151–4.

[20] Cf. Paus. 8. 27. 3; D.S. 15. 72. 4.

(i.e. presumably all citizens of all constituent states), or whether they were a more limited body and, if so, to any extent oligarchic. There is no clear evidence beyond what can be deduced from the name (and, of course, the need to ensure that any conclusions about the *Myrioi* are broadly in accord with what is known about other aspects of the league). As previous modern discussions of the *Myrioi* have pointed out, the number of Arcadian citizens must have exceeded ten thousand, and even the number of Arcadian hoplites—if one were to think of membership of the primary assembly as limited to hoplites—was probably greater than ten thousand. If the name *Myrioi* represented a real and precise numerical limit on membership of the assembly, it would suggest a major restriction of political rights within the Arcadian citizen body. Schaefer, however, presented strong arguments for seeing *myrioi* as an ideal number, not a real and exclusive number, making it possible to regard the *Myrioi* as a primary confederate assembly open to all citizens (Schaefer 1961: 311–14). More recently Trampedach, after a full reconsideration of earlier views, has accepted Schaefer's argument that the word *myrioi* represented for classical Greeks the border between the countable and the uncountable, and has suggested that it was applied to the Arcadian confederate primary assembly to evoke the power of the united and democratic Arcadia.[21] Since it is unlikely that, even if the assembly was open to all, as many as 10,000 would make their way across Arcadia to attend it, the name can well be interpreted as a grandiose attempt to elevate the standing of the assembly, just as the name *Megalē Polis* sought to elevate the importance of the new city.

It is often said that Megalopolis was the confederacy's capital. It was certainly created by a confederate board of ten Arcadian oikists, whatever part the Theban leader Epaminondas played (Paus. 8. 27. 2). The date of the foundation remains uncertain, between 371/0 and 368/7:[22] it may have been at a time when friendship between Arcadia and Thebes was strong enough for Epaminondas to play a significant role, but it is equally possible that his role was exaggerated. Megalopolis was not founded purely—if at all—as a confederate capital; there is no reason to doubt that it was intended to function as a polis, as its name suggests and as it undoubtedly did. Moreover, there were strategic reasons for creating a strong community in south-western Arcadia, since that area was crossed by major routes for the Spartan army marching towards Messenia or Tegea.[23] The new founda-

---

[21] Trampedach (1994) 27–33, with extensive references to and discussion of earlier work. Recently Rhodes (1994: 583) also accepted the *Myrioi* as 'probably an assembly open to all citizens', and Beck (1997: 80–1) saw the *Myrioi* as a 'direkte Volksversammlung' of all Arcadian citizens.

[22] Hornblower (1990) (with valid criticism of the arguments for dating in Roy 1971); Roy (1994) 193.

[23] Pikoulas (1988) 198–227. It was easier for the Spartans to march up the valley of the River Eurotas and across the relatively low watershed into the Megalopolitan basin, and on

tion's name was a declaration of Arcadian pride (and a hostage to fortune). But the only reason for seeing Megalopolis as a confederate capital is Pausanias' statement that the building at Megalopolis called the Thersilion was constructed as a meeting-place for the *Myrioi* (Paus. 8. 32. 1). The building has been excavated, and identified from Pausanias' description of it and its location. It is not clear when the Thersilion was built: it is usually dated to the 360s, but there does not seem to be a compelling reason to put it then rather than in, say, the 350s.[24] The only meeting of the *Myrioi* certainly dated before 362 and clearly located took place at Tegea, probably in 363 (Xen. *Hell.* 7. 4. 36): the inscription Tod 132 was set up at Tegea as a record of a confederate decree, which might suggest that the meeting at which the decree was voted also took place at Tegea, but—as stated above—the text is difficult to date. (It is of course possible that Xenophon's refusal to mention Megalopolis during most of his narrative of the 360s has deprived us of evidence of confederate assemblies held there.) In the original excavation report on Megalopolis Schultz argued that the Thersilion had a superficial area of *c*.35,000 square feet, and could therefore have seated nearly 6,000 men if they had about 6 square feet each: he then goes on, 'Standing room might have been found for 10,000.'[25] Such an estimate seems optimistic, and in any case supposes that as many as 10,000 were likely to turn up to a meeting. There is no difficulty about accepting the report that the Thersilion was built for the *Myrioi*, even if it could not accommodate 10,000 people, but there is no need to assume that it was built at the earliest possible opportunity after the foundation of Megalopolis, or that it was intended only for meetings of the *Myrioi*, or that the provision of confederate accommodation was a major element in the layout of Megalopolis. (There is no reason to accept the suggestion of Bury (1898) that in Megalopolis the area north of the River Helisson served the needs of the polis itself while the area south of the river served the confederacy's purposes.[26])

What little we know of the confederate constitution can be summed up as broadly consistent with the view that the Arcadian League operated

from there either south-west to Messenia or eastwards towards Tegea, than to march directly westwards to Messenia or northwards to Tegea.

[24] See Petronotis (1973) 228–32 (with references to earlier work) and figs. 9–14; also Gneisz (1990) 89–92. It is often assumed that the Thersilion must have been built before the league split *c*.363, but the *Myrioi* continued to exist until at least 348/7 (Dem. 19. 11; Aeschines 2. 79). [25] R. W. Schultz, in Gardner *et al.* (1892) 23.

[26] It is certain that the theatre, situated beside the Thersilion in the south part of the city, eventually served purely Megalopolitan purposes: the seating was inscribed, for the first time in the 3rd or 2nd century BC and again around the Hadrianic period, according to subdivisions of the citizen body of Megalopolis, and a token of the 4th or 3rd century BC suggests that the seating arrangements were instituted before the inscriptions on the seats: see N. F. Jones (1987) 135–8. See Tsiolis (1995) for a discussion of the nature and purpose of the Thersilion, with good arguments that the building served various purely Megalopolitan purposes as well as originally providing a meeting-place for the *Myrioi*.

as a democracy until *c*.363. Though there may have been advice from outside Arcadia, the constitution of the league seems to have been determined mainly by the Arcadians themselves. There are hints, however, that alongside the democratic politics of the confederacy there was scope for more varied political tendencies within the individual member states of the league.

The eparitoi

Within the confederate political process an extremely important force for democracy was—until *c*.363—the confederate military force known as the *eparitoi*.[27] There are problems in reconciling what Diodorus and Xenophon say about a confederate Arcadian élite force. D.S. 15. 62. 2 (reporting 370) says that Lycomedes, as confederate *stratēgos*, attacked Orchomenus with 'the so-called *epilektoi*, 5,000 in number'; Xenophon, however, gives a fairly detailed account of the same expedition (*Hell.* 6. 5. 10–15), reporting it as a purely Mantinean attack on Orchomenus. In the circumstances it is doubtful that Diodorus' report can be trusted; it may be, as W. E. Thompson suggests (1983: 155), a doublet of Diodorus' other reference to élite confederate troops, where the wording is very similar. D.S. 15. 67. 2 (on 369) says that Lycomedes, as confederate *stratēgos*, attacked Pellana in Laconia with 'the so-called *epilektoi*, 5,000 in number'; Xenophon does not report this incident. Xenophon first mentions a confederate élite force in *Hell.* 7. 4. 33–4 (referring to *c*.363), where he calls them *eparitoi*, and this passage, crucial to understanding their importance, will be considered in detail shortly. Xenophon then refers to *eparitoi* again in 7. 4. 36 and 7. 5. 3. There is also a reference to the *eparitoi* in Hesychius (s.v.), who glosses them as 'public guards among the Arcadians', but he may be offering no more than an interpretation of their role in *Hell.* 7. 4. 33, where the confederate magistrates sent *eparitoi* to arrest political opponents.

Other groups of élite troops elsewhere in Greece may have led the Arcadians to consider the formation of such a force. The Theban Sacred Band is famous, though nothing suggests that there were among the *eparitoi* the homosexual linkings found in the Sacred Band. Some of the other cases would have been seen by the Arcadians rather as examples to avoid. The Thousand at Argos seem to have subverted the democratic constitution in 418 (according to D.S. 12. 80. 2–3 and Paus. 2. 20. 2, though they are not mentioned by Thuc. 5. 81. 2). In the 360s Elis also had an élite force of 300, which sided with the oligarchs during *stasis*: it is not known when the force was set up.[28]

The crucial passage for understanding the role of the *eparitoi* is *Hell.* 7.

---

[27] On the *eparitoi* see Pritchett (1974) 223; Dušanić (1970) 342; Trampedach (1994) 34–5.
[28] See Pritchett (1974) 222–3 on all these forces.

4. 33–4. The Arcadian confederate officials had been using funds[29] from the sanctuary at Olympia to pay the *eparitoi*, but the Mantineans then objected, and instead paid their share of the cost themselves. Despite an attempt by the confederate officials to arrest the chief Mantineans, other Arcadians began to agree with the Mantineans, and a decree was passed in the *Myrioi* that the sacred funds should not be used. Xenophon (*Hell.* 7. 4. 33–4) does not explicitly say that no Arcadian state other than Mantinea then resumed payment of its contribution to confederate funds, but his narrative implies that none, or at most very few, did so. The *eparitoi* were evidently then not paid, and those who could not afford to serve without pay fell away, being replaced by those who could, who joined the *eparitoi*, as Xenophon says, 'in order that they themselves should no longer be in the power of those men, but those men should be in their power'. The officials who had handled the sacred funds then realized that, in the event of *euthynai* (formal scrutiny at the end of their term of office), they would be at great risk, and appealed for help to Thebes. Later Xenophon refers to those of the *eparitoi* who still sympathized with the confederate officials (*Hell.* 7. 4. 36), but he makes clear that the new *eparitoi* had generally very different views, and as a body sent ambassadors to Sparta to seek help (*Hell.* 7. 5. 3). Several conclusions can be drawn from what Xenophon says. First, the *eparitoi* were a permanent force, paid by the confederacy till the system of payment broke down. Second, since the Mantineans knew how much to contribute, before the confederacy began to pay the *eparitoi* from Olympic funds there must already have been *eparitoi* and a system whereby confederate member states paid their respective contributions towards the cost of the force. Third, Xenophon presents the change in the membership of the *eparitoi* as a major stage in the break-up of the confederacy; clearly, in his view, the *eparitoi* as previously constituted had been of major political importance within the confederacy.

W. E. Thompson (1983: 156–8) argues for a different view of the *eparitoi*, but his arguments do not take sufficient account of Xenophon's words. The *eparitoi* cannot have been, as he suggests, a new body paid from Olympic funds: the Mantineans already knew how much they were due to pay. There is no evidence that the confederate magistrates used the Olympic funds, as he also suggests, to transform the nature of the *eparitoi*: Xenophon, who detests the confederate officials and happily reports criticism of their use of Olympic funds as sacrilegious, does not charge them with that. (The question is discussed further below.) Thompson asks why, if the rich needed only

[29] Xenophon consistently speaks of the Arcadians using sacred funds: the phrase *ta hiera chrēmata* occurs five times in *Hell.* 7. 4. 33–4. There is no mention of selling off dedications, though funds could have been raised in that way. Money or bullion may have been held at Olympia: in 312 Antigonus' treacherous admiral Telesphorus took 50 talents of silver from Olympia and—apparently—used some of the silver to hire mercenaries, but this amount (*ta chrēmata*) was then restored to Olympia by Antigonus' general Ptolemaeus (D.S. 19. 87.2–3).

to join the *eparitoi* in order to use the body's political influence, they waited
so long to do so: the answer is presumably that, so long as the confederate
officials could find the funds to maintain a body of *eparitoi* politically sympathetic to themselves, they would not allow political opponents to join the
corps, but that, when the funds dried up and the previous members of the
corps fell away (and, one might add, when at the same time the political
authority of the confederate officials within the confederacy was slipping),
then the opponents could not be kept out. Xenophon (*Hell.* 7. 4. 34) tells us
that the change in the personnel of the *eparitoi* took place quickly, but we
need not believe that it was done, in Thompson's phrase, 'in the twinkling
of an eye'; *Hell.* 7. 4. 36 shows us a transitional phase when there were both
old and new members in the force.[30] Thompson adds that if the *eparitoi* had
previously been paid from taxes, they must have been ultimately responsible
to the taxpayers, i.e. the wealthier citizens, not the magistrates: that is not a
persuasive argument, since it does not take account of the authority of the
state (polis or confederacy) in classical Greece.

There remains the question of whether the *epilektoi* of D.S. 15. 67. 2 (if
not also 15. 62. 2) are the same as the *eparitoi* of Xenophon. The difficulty
in identifying the two bodies is firstly the difference of name, and secondly
the difficulty of believing that as many as 5,000 men were maintained as a
permanent force from confederate funds.[31] The difference of name is no real
problem, since any élite corps could reasonably be called *epilektoi* ('select'),
even if they had a more precise name; and, if we do not regard the two
bodies as the same, we have to believe that the confederacy had two different élite corps, which seems unlikely. (Thompson 1983: 154–6 stresses
the likelihood that Diodorus' *epilektoi* and Xenophon's *eparitoi* were different, and suggests that the *epilektoi* were peltasts: there is no evidence for
that view.) The difficulty about payment is more serious, as has often been
realized, and so it has been supposed that Diodorus was wrong in believing
that there were as many as 5,000 men in the corps. We do not, however,
know when or how confederate payment began, and it is possible that a
larger élite group was maintained for a time early in the league's history:
in 369 it might have been funded wholly or partly from booty taken in
Laconia in the great invasion of 370/69. The most economical resolution of
the different reports seems to be the supposition that the confederacy had
an élite corps from at least 369, though the corps may at first have been
bigger than was subsequently the case, and possibly financed differently;
but that well before the events of *Hell.* 7. 4. 33–4 (and possibly from the
corps's inception) a system of pay through contributions by member states

---

[30] It should be noted that *Hell.* 7. 4. 33–4 is Xenophon's entire account of events not only in
Arcadia but in Greece as a whole for the period of rather more than a year from summer 364
to (roughly) autumn 363.

[31] The number 5,000 is given by D.S. 15. 67. 2. Xenophon does not say how many *eparitoi*
there were. Beck (1997) 82 accepts the number of 5,000 for the *eparitoi* without discussion.

had been instituted, and the *eparitoi* had become a source of support for those holding office in the confederacy.

The developments affecting the *eparitoi* are the first evidence for political tensions within the Arcadian confederacy after the early difficulties when the confederacy was being set up. In the early years there was conflict between supporters and opponents of confederation, and between democrats and oligarchs. These early differences were linked to attitudes to Sparta: confederalist democrats were hostile to Sparta, and oligarchic anti-confederalists were pro-Spartan.[32] Similar issues re-emerged once Mantinea challenged the use of Olympic funds *c.*363: once more there was dispute between democrats, still anti-Spartan, and oligarchs, who challenged the power of the confederate officials and turned to Sparta for help. These same divisive issues had probably always been present in the confederacy's politics, even between *c.*369 and *c.*363, when we hear nothing of them. Given the stress of more or less constant warfare, and given Xenophon's propensity for omission, it would obviously be dangerous to deduce from his silence that there was no internal tension in the Arcadian confederacy *c.*369–*c.*363. None the less, Xenophon presents Mantinean opposition *c.*363 to the use of Olympic funds, and the consequent change in the composition and political allegiance of the *eparitoi*, as major new developments, bringing tensions and conflicts much more intense than those of the preceding years.[33] That consideration is important when one tries to reconstruct how the *eparitoi* had developed before the use of Olympic funds was ended in *c.*363.

The Arcadians did not have access to Olympic funds before Elis and Arcadia went to war in 365.[34] As indicated above, before Olympic funds were used the *eparitoi* had been maintained by contributions from the member states of the confederacy. There is no direct evidence on why the confederacy began to use Olympic funds for the *eparitoi*, and so no way of telling whether, because the élite corps was expensive, some Arcadian states had started to oppose the system of contributions for the *eparitoi* or even to oppose the continued existence of the corps. None the less, two points are obvious: switching from members' contributions to Olympic funds would relieve the member states of a serious financial burden, and the change would give the confederate officials more secure control of the funding for the *eparitoi*, and so of the *eparitoi* themselves. Until then contributions from member states will have provided the confederate officials with the necessary funds to pay the *eparitoi*, and so will already have allowed them to recruit men

---

[32] There were no doubt also tensions between individual member states: see Roy (1972) for the suggestion that Cleitor used its influence within the confederacy against Orchomenus.

[33] Pausanias (8. 8. 10) actually reports that the Mantineans were discovered to be negotiating for peace with Sparta on their own, without reference to the Arcadian confederacy (which he calls *koinon*): Xenophon does not mention such an incident, but reports (*Hell.* 7. 5. 3) that, after the change in membership of the *eparitoi*, ambassadors from the *eparitoi* negotiated with Sparta. [34] Xen. *Hell.* 7. 4. 12–14; cf. D.S. 15. 77. 1–4.

politically sympathetic to themselves: there is no reason to suppose that Olympic funds were used to change the political allegiance of the corps. None the less, once the confederate officials began to draw on the Olympic treasury, they may well have been glad to have direct control of funds for the *eparitoi*, increasing their own power and diminishing that of the member states.

Xenophon (*Hell.* 7. 4. 34) reports the views of those Arcadians who came to see the use of Olympic funds as a sacrilege that would be bequeathed to their children. Yet using Olympic funds need not always have been so controversial. Before the Peloponnesian War the Corinthians had suggested that the Spartans and their allies might draw on the treasury at Olympia.[35] Furthermore, the change to using Olympic funds need not have been sudden and complete: a 'loan' from Olympia might, for instance, have been used initially to cover a deficit arising from late payment of some contributions. Of course, once opposition to drawing on the Olympic treasury began to develop, arguments of moral censure were readily available.

While the switch to using Olympic funds for the *eparitoi* need not have marked any major change in the confederacy, in *c*.363 the decision to stop drawing on the Olympic treasury was clearly linked to the emergence of major political disagreements within the Arcadian League. Mantinea's opposition to the use of Olympic funds provoked a crisis, and it is hard to believe that the Mantineans were not aware of the likely consequences of what they were doing. Certainly when they opposed drawing on Olympia they began to pay once more their own contribution towards the upkeep of the *eparitoi*, avoiding any charge of improper conduct; but, predictably enough, other states which also expressed their opposition to using Olympic funds did not contribute their share of funding. As noted above, the lack of funds precipitated a crisis in the confederacy. Some of the existing *eparitoi* dropped out, and new men joined who challenged the authority of the confederate officials and looked for support to Sparta (which reveals their political sympathies). At the same time conflict developed (*Hell.* 7. 4. 33, 36–8) between confederate officials and individual member states, at first Mantinea but soon numerous others. When the Arcadians gathered at Tegea, probably still in 363, to swear to peace with Elis, confederate officials used *eparitoi* still loyal to them to arrest men from many member states (though many of those arrested quickly escaped). The crisis finally split the confederacy into two blocs, one (including Megalopolis and Tegea) still linked to Boeotia and the other (including Mantinea) looking to Sparta and Athens.

It is clear that the *eparitoi* were an important focus of political opinion within the confederacy. Until *c*.363 they were democratic in outlook, and loyal to the democratic officials of the confederacy. They may well have

---

[35] Thuc. 1. 121. 3: the point is taken up by Pericles at Thuc. 1. 143. 1. Cf. *Dissoi Logoi* 3. 8. See R. Parker (1983) 170–5 on the use of wealth from sanctuaries to finance warfare.

served on occasion as an instrument for maintaining democratic control, though we have no direct evidence of such use of the corps until the crisis of *c*.363. However, when that crisis gave the opponents of democratic confederation the opportunity to join the *eparitoi* and change the political tendency of the corps, Xenophon (*Hell.* 7. 4. 34) shows that they profited by that opportunity in full awareness of what they were doing: evidently the role of the *eparitoi* in buttressing democratic confederation was well known. Without more evidence of the internal politics of the confederacy in the period *c*.369–*c*.363 it is impossible to tell how far the democratic nature of the league depended on its democratic constitution and political processes and how far it depended—as Xenophon's account of *c*.363–2 would suggest—on the presence of a permanent military force committed to democracy.

Foreign relations

The foreign relations of the league also suggest its democratic tendency. In the very complex interstate relations of central and southern Greece in the 360s any state's policy was sometimes driven by force of circumstances; but Arcadia consistently supported democrats whenever it could (except perhaps in overthrowing Euphron of Sicyon, of whom more below).

1. In 369 Arcadia, Argos, and Elis helped Phliasian democratic exiles in an attempt to take control of Phlius (Xen. *Hell.* 7. 2. 5–9). (The political tendencies among Phliasians at this time have to be deduced from a series of events rather than from a single passage.[36])

2. After Epaminondas came to terms with the oligarchs in Sicyon in 369,[37] in 368[38] Arcadia and Argos helped Euphron to install a democratic regime in Sicyon (though the regime then rapidly deteriorated, and Arcadia deposed Euphron in 366: Xen. *Hell.* 7. 3. 1).[39] It is notable that Xenophon puts into the mouth of Euphron the view that democracy in Sicyon will appeal to Arcadia and Argos (*Hell.* 7. 1. 44).

3. In 366 Epaminondas came to terms with the ruling oligarchs in Achaea;

---

[36] See Gehrke (1985) 130–1; Cartledge (1987) 262–6; and Legon (1967); W. E. Thompson (1970) corrects some points of Legon's analysis, but does not give compelling grounds for denying that a split between oligarchs and democrats was a significant factor in Phliasian politics of this period. Piccirilli (1974) denies the likelihood of a democratic *coup d'état* in Phlius during the Corinthian War; cf. Gehrke (1985) 127–8.

[37] Xen. *Hell.* 7. 1. 18, 1. 22, 1. 44–6, 2. 2–3, 2. 11, 3. 2–4.

[38] Xen. *Hell.* 7. 1. 44–6; cf. D.S. 15. 70. 3.

[39] On the chronology of events in Sicyon see Meloni (1951), though he interprets events very differently from the present paper, reversing Xenophon's judgement about the relative importance of internal and external policies for Euphron. See also Griffin (1982). Gehrke (1985) 370–2 re-examines the chronology in detail and argues strongly for a chronology based on Xenophon, as opposed to Meloni's chronology based on Diodorus (retained here). Gehrke's dating puts the beginning of Euphron's tyranny early in 366, and consequently makes its duration very brief.

the Arcadians and other opponents (whether Achaean or Boeotian) protested vigorously to Thebes about the arrangement, and persuaded the
Boeotians to expel the oligarchs and set up democracies in Achaea, with
Boeotian harmosts. The Arcadian intervention proved disastrous, for the
oligarchs soon regained control and became firmly pro-Spartan.[40]

4. In 365 Elis broke off its alliance with Arcadia,[41] but Elean democrats
remained friendly to Arcadia, and, after a failed democratic coup, Arcadia
established them in the place called Pylos east of the city of Elis.[42]

5. In 365 or 364 the Arcadians provoked a democratic uprising in Pellene,
and established the Pellenean democrats in Olurus, which the Pellenean
oligarchs then besieged and recaptured.[43]

This is not a record of success, but it is a record of support for democracy.
There is no comparable record of Arcadian support for oligarchs.

Two arguments have been brought forward by Thompson to challenge
the view that confederate Arcadia's foreign policy was consistently democratic. One concerns the episode in Achaea in 366, when Epaminondas came
to terms with the Achaean oligarchs, but Thebes overturned his settlement
after protests from the Arcadians and other opponents. Thompson argues
that, since the Thebans were moved to accept the protest at a time when
Arcadia was unpopular in Thebes for having walked out of the peace conference sponsored by the Thebans in 366, the protests must have come not
from the Arcadian faction which repudiated the peace conference but from
a pro-Theban group in Arcadia; and, Thompson also argues, it is unlikely
that Lycomedes, who led the walkout from the conference, would ever have
asked the Thebans to send harmosts to the Peloponnese.[44] Xenophon reports Epaminondas' negotiations with the Achaean oligarchs as an attempt
to present the Arcadians and other Peloponnesian allies with a *fait accompli*
which would increase Theban influence over them; while Xenophon relates
that the Peloponnesian allies marched against Achaea with Epaminondas,
he gives the allies no part in the negotiations but stresses Epaminondas' personal role in them. If Xenophon is right (and we have no better evidence),[45]
Epaminondas did indeed present Arcadia and the other Peloponnesian allies with a *fait accompli*, which they understandably resented. For Arcadia
the available choices were: to acquiesce in Epaminondas' settlement and
accept an Achaea run by oligarchs; or to try, without Theban approval and
at the obvious risk of seriously offending Thebes, to overthrow the Achaean
oligarchs and install a different regime in Achaea; or to persuade Thebes

[40] Xen. *Hell.* 7. 1. 41–3; cf. D.S. 15. 75. 2. See Gehrke (1985) 14–15.
[41] Xen. *Hell.* 7. 4. 12; cf. D.S. 15. 77. 1–2.
[42] Xen. *Hell.* 7. 4. 12–16; D.S. 15. 77. 1–4. See Gehrke (1985) 54–6.
[43] Xen. *Hell.* 7. 4. 16–18. See Gehrke (1985) 14–15.
[44] W. E. Thompson (1983) 152–4; also Buckler (1980) 185–93.
[45] D.S. 15. 75. 2 attributes the entire operation to Epaminondas, mentioning no allies of
Thebes.

to change Epaminondas' settlement. Arcadia chose the last of the three, and must have known that Theban agreement, if given at all, would have its price; and, if the price of the change was Theban harmosts in Achaea, that price may have seemed preferable to a secure oligarchic regime there. There is, however, nothing to suggest that Lycomedes or any other Arcadian asked Thebes to send harmosts to Achaea (as Thompson contemplates); it is much easier to believe that the harmosts were imposed by Thebans who were willing to change Epaminondas' Achaean settlement but none the less wanted to retain Theban control in Achaea. In sum, Arcadia's protest against Epaminondas' Achaean settlement can be taken as a pro-democratic Arcadian response to Epaminondas' agreement with Achaean oligarchs.

Thompson also argues (1983: 150–2) that the deposition of Euphron was not a pro-democratic measure, and here his arguments cannot so immediately be refuted. In 368 Arcadia and Argos helped Euphron establish a democratic regime in Sicyon. Euphron, however, rapidly made himself tyrant, using mercenaries commanded by his son; and, besides exiling pro-Spartan Sicyonians and expropriating their wealth, he also killed some of his own political sympathizers and exiled others (Xen. *Hell.* 7. 1. 44–6). In 366 the confederate Arcadian general Aeneas of Stymphalus led Arcadian forces into Sicyon and overthrew Euphron 'because he thought the situation in Sicyon intolerable' (Xen. *Hell.* 7. 3. 1–3). Aeneas then summoned the *kratistoi* ('best') of the Sicyonians in Sicyon and recalled the Sicyonians banished without decree (ibid. 2): those recalled presumably included both pro-Spartans and democrats, since Euphron had exiled both. (Xenophon in fact reports a claim of Euphron to have banished all Sicyonians who had removed Sicyon from alliance with Sparta (*Hell.* 7. 3. 3), though Xenophon clearly doubted the claim.) In summoning the *kratistoi* Aeneas presumably meant to give them a role in the running of Sicyon, but Xenophon does not report either what Aeneas intended or what the *kratistoi* did. Euphron fled, but first handed over the harbour at Sicyon to the Spartans (*Hell.* 7. 3. 2–3). The Arcadians and 'the citizens themselves' of Sicyon recovered the harbour, presumably shortly afterwards (*Hell.* 7. 4. 1). *Stasis* followed in Sicyon between the *beltistoi* ('best') and the dēmos (*Hell.* 7. 3. 4). Euphron returned with mercenaries from Athens and took control of the town with the help of the dēmos, but could not secure complete control because the acropolis was held by a Theban harmost: Euphron therefore went to Thebes to persuade the Thebans to expel the *beltistoi* and hand the polis back to him (*Hell.* 7. 3. 4). The former exiles also went to Thebes to block his plans, and some of them killed Euphron in Thebes (*Hell.* 7. 3. 5). Euphron's fellow citizens took his body back to Sicyon and buried it in the agora, and honoured him as founder of the city (*archēgetēs*) (*Hell.* 7. 3. 12). This typically incomplete Xenophontic narrative poses several problems.

It is not difficult to understand why the Arcadians would have turned against Euphron: he seems to have become thoroughly tyrannical;[46] the Arcadians may also have reproached him with military failure (Griffin 1982: 73–4); and there was also a concern, expressed in contemporary alliances, to prevent breaches of constitution (Roy 1971: 598–9). There were thus motives enough for deposing Euphron. It is, however, clear that the dēmos in Sicyon continued to support Euphron, so that their support could not be used by the Arcadians in an attempt to overthrow him. That goes some way to explaining why Aeneas, unable to rely on the dēmos against Euphron, summoned the *kratistoi* in Sicyon. Questions remain, however: how much control the *kratistoi* enjoyed in Sicyon after Euphron was deposed; which Sicyonians recovered the harbour with the Arcadians, and how they related to the dēmos which supported Euphron on his return; and what political circumstances allowed the citizens to bury Euphron with such great honour. Thompson's interpretation is that there were two factions in Arcadia, one supporting the dēmos in Sicyon and one (including Aeneas) supporting the *kratistoi*; this allows him to argue that Aeneas restored the *kratistoi* to power in Sicyon and helped them to recover the harbour, while the other Arcadian faction on other occasions supported the Sicyonian dēmos, which itself consistently supported Euphron. This interpretation does not, however, take account of the fact that Xenophon emphasizes the pro-Spartan sympathies of the Sicyonian *kratistoi* (*Hell.* 7. 1. 44), making it hard to believe that any confederate Arcadian politician could give them wholehearted support, or that these *kratistoi* would have wanted Arcadian support to deprive the Spartans of control of the harbour at Sicyon;[47] nor does it give much weight to the *stasis* which followed the deposition of Euphron, and which suggests that the dēmos was still powerful. It is reasonable to suppose that Aeneas used the *kratistoi* to remove Euphron and get government going again without giving the *kratistoi* lasting control; and that 'the citizens' whom the Arcadians helped to recover the harbour simply represented the Sicyonians as a whole rather than any particular faction. These suppositions amount to believing that in Sicyon a rather messy political situation followed Euphron's deposition, and that the Arcadians made the best of a bad job, unable to support wholeheartedly either the pro-Spartan *kratistoi* or the pro-Euphron dēmos.

The deposition of Euphron and the use of the *kratistoi* in Sicyon would be the only evidence of Arcadian support for oligarchs, if so interpreted. If, on the other hand, it is accepted that the episode need not be taken in that

---

[46] See Whitehead (1980) and Cartledge (1980) on Euphron's granting of freedom to slaves, or an unfree labour force, as a measure to promote his tyranny.

[47] See Griffin (1982) 71–3 on the possibility that there were also pro-Theban oligarchs at Sicyon. Such a group would presumably have wanted to recover the harbour at Sicyon from Spartan control, but it is hard to believe that the Arcadians would have wanted to help them do so.

way, then there is no obstacle to believing that in its foreign policy from 370 to 363 confederate Arcadia supported democrats whenever the opportunity arose, and opposed oligarchs so far as possible.

Conclusion

The main evidence for democratic tendencies in confederate Arcadia in the 360s is in three elements: the situation in Mantinea and Tegea in 370, when the movement to confederation was launched; the use of the *eparitoi* to secure democracy; and foreign policy. We do not know enough about the confederate constitution to draw conclusions from it alone; but, if the *Myrioi* are accepted as a primary assembly, the form of the confederate constitution suits democracy well enough. The decline of Spartan power after Leuctra, however, made the 360s a difficult time for Peloponnesian states, and the new circumstances which allowed the Arcadian confederacy to emerge and to play a leading role in interstate politics also brought with them tensions, uncertainties, and even threats as new political alignments were developed in the Peloponnese. These vicissitudes must have made the political life of the confederacy more difficult. In the face of such difficulties it cannot have been easy to develop within Arcadia confederate political processes which were securely democratic, and indeed it appears that the confederacy did not entirely succeed in shifting the balance of political activity from the individual polis to the confederacy. There is no sign that efforts were made to secure democratic constitutions or even democratic regimes in all the member states; and the movement that split the league from *c*.363 is reported by Xenophon as starting from a political reaction in Mantinea. Confederate democracy thus appears to have rested on a rather insecure internal base, and was eventually thrown into crisis by challenges from within member states. None the less, while opposition to confederation developed within member states, leading men from these states also had a motive to maintain the confederacy, because confederation offered opportunities to men from smaller Arcadian states which otherwise they would never have had. For a few years such men could exercise major influence on the complex interstate politics of southern and central Greece: the confederate general Aeneas of Stymphalus is the prime example because Xenophon chose to name him, but others will have enjoyed brief power. Some, no doubt, were convinced confederalists, like Lycomedes of Mantinea (Xen. *Hell.* 7. 1. 23–4), while others may have been more self-serving: evidence on the conduct of politics within the confederacy is very limited until the crisis of *c*.363, by which time the confederate officials were struggling to retain power. The confederate standing army clearly helped to maintain a democratic confederate regime, until it was overtaken by political forces emerging from individual poleis. So long as the democratic tendency of the confederacy could be maintained internally, it pursued democratic aims in its external policy, supporting democrats in neighbouring states, though not with much lasting success. The Arcadian democratic confederacy was a major political force for only a few years, and even in these years it suffered a number of setbacks, though admittedly our information is patchy and often comes from the hostile reporter Xenophon. None the less, we know enough to see an interesting and original attempt to transplant democracy from the polis to a supra-polis structure.

19
Land-use, Ethnicity, and Federalism in West Crete

N. V. SEKUNDA

Two groups of evidence survive concerning federalism in west Crete. First, a number of references to the 'Polichnitai'. It will be suggested that this term is used of an alliance of small communities (*polichnai*), and is not an 'ethnic', i.e. a name given to the citizens of a polis. Second, we have evidence concerning a League of the Oreioi, the inhabitants of the White Mountains in south-west Crete.

This paper attempts to identify the centripetal and centrifugal forces leading to the establishment and collapse of these alliance systems. In the case of the 'Polichnitai' it seems possible to suggest that the principal factors leading to the establishment of the league were a common Kydonian ethnicity which existed in the states of west Crete, and the presence of a common neighbour in the form of the Aeginetan colony of Kydonia. The League of the Polichnitai broke up in the fourth century as a result of the growth of the polis in the area. However, federal structures survived in one area of west Crete, in the heart of the White Mountains, in the form of the League of the Oreioi. Here the common factor was probably terrain: a shared knowledge of the mountain passes made individual action hazardous and promoted common political and military activity. Comparative material will be used from the Turkish period, when the Christian mountain communities united against the Muslim Cretans of Chaniá and the lowlands.

PART I: THE POLICHNITAI

According to a legend reported by Herodotus (7. 170), the Cretan king Minos died a violent death at Kamikos in Sicily. 'After a time' (ἀνὰ δὲ χρόνον), Herodotus tells us, all the Cretans, except the Polichnitai and Praisians, joined an expedition to Sicily and unsuccessfully besieged Kamikos. The date of this Cretan expedition is unclear, but it would be reasonable to assume that it took place during the initial period of Greek colonization of Sicily in the early seventh century. Therefore this passage seemingly preserves a native Cretan tradition that Praisian and Polichnitan particularism existed in the early archaic period. We know that the Praisians were the remaining community of Eteocretans living in the territory of Praisos, but who were the Polichnitai?

The term 'Polichnitai' occurs a second time in Thucydides (2. 85. 5–6), who mentions that in 429 an Athenian fleet raided west Crete, attacking Kydonia with the help of the Polichnitai, 'who are neighbours of the Kydoniatai'. Thus the Polichnitai are localized in west Crete. Finally, Stephanus tells us that there is a polis in Crete called Polichne, and that the ethnic given to one of its inhabitants is Polichnites (the singular of Polichnitai).[1]

Modern scholars have tried to identify and locate a city in west Crete called Polichne. When the great Delphic *theōrodokoi* list was published in 1921, one of the city names in the section of the stone dealing with west Crete was illegible. Plassart, the original editor, read ἐν . . . . αις, which Guarducci proposed to restore as ἐν [Πολίχν]αις. Faure, however, rejected the restoration. On his behalf Bousquet made an improved reading, which Faure restored as ἐν Κεραίαις. On the basis of other evidence, including coins of Keraia recovered in the region of the modern town of Mesklá, Faure located the ancient community of the Keraitai at the modern sites of Mesklá, Zourva, and Lakkous. This identification accords with the position of the missing city in the list, for it lay between Anopolis and Kydonia. Faure accordingly suggested that Polichne must be located at another site.[2]

The search for a polis called Polichne is, I believe, based on a misunderstanding of the ancient texts by Stephanus. Stephanus, who lived long after Herodotus and Thucydides, was neither a historian nor a geographer, but a grammarian concerned with the derivation of ethnics. I suggest that a city called Polichne never existed; it is rather a creation of Stephanus to explain the ethnic Polichnitai in Herodotus and Thucydides. A recent study has demonstrated Stephanus' tendency to read between the lines of earlier writers and generate polis site classifications not intended by his original sources (Whitehead 1994: 109–20). 'Polichnitai' literally means 'those who live in small poleis', or *polichnai*.[3] We should interpret Herodotus' and Thucydides' use of this term as matching their definition of an ethnos, that is, as a people living in small communities where the fully formed polis structure had not emerged (Hansen 1997a: 11–12). We might usefully compare Thucydides' description (3. 94) of the contemporary Aetolians, whom he describes as 'a large ethnos living in unwalled villages'. Can we identify the community to which the Polichnitai belonged?

---

[1] Steph. Byz. s.v. Πολίχνα, . . . ἔστι καὶ Κρήτης Πολίχνη πόλις, ἧς ὁ πολίτης Πολιχνίτης.

[2] Plassart (1921) 19, III. 112; Guarducci (1936) 153–8; Faure (1962) 52–4.

[3] For *polichnē* or *polichē* in this sense cf. D.S. 13. 7. 5; 14. 72. 3; Thuc. 7. 4. 6; Plut. *Timoleon* 11. 3; 12. 3; 24. 2.

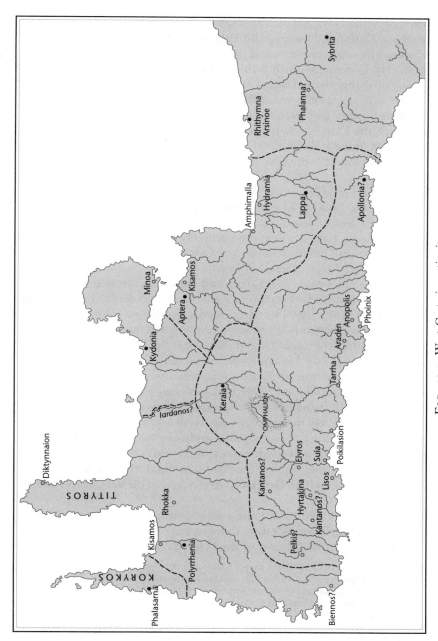

FIG. 19.1. West Crete in antiquity.

Diktynnaion
TITYROS
Rhokka
Kisamos
KORYKOS
Phalasarna
Polyrrhenia
Pelkis?
Kantanos?
Hyrtakina
Lisos
Biennos?
Kantanos?
Suia
Elyros
Poikilasion
Tarrha
Araden
Anopolis
Phoinix
OMPHALION
Keraia
Iardanos?
Kydonia
Minoa
Aptera
Kisamos
Amphimalla
Hydramia
Lappa
Apollonia?
Rhithymna
Arsinoe
Phalanna?
Sybrita

The Kydones

We are told in the *Odyssey* (19. 175) that Crete was inhabited by Achaeans, Eteocretans, Kydones, Dorians, and Pelasgians, and (*Od*. 3. 276–300) that the Kydones live 'by the waters of the Iardanos', generally assumed to be one of the rivers running north from the White Mountains into the Cretan Sea, most probably the perennial Keritis, whose source lies near Mesklá. Strabo (10. 4. 6; 5. 2. 4) informs us that, according to Staphylus of Naukratis, the Dorians occupy that part of Crete towards the east, the Kydones the western part, the Eteocretans the southern. Thus the geographical location of the League of the Polichnitai and of the tribe of the Kydones coincides, which suggests that it is possible to identify the 'Polichnitai' as a league of Kydones.

We know very little about the Kydones, not even the basic fact whether they were Greek or not. There is no evidence for a distinct Kydonian language in the first millennium BC: inscriptions are in West Cretan dialect. However, the Kydones may be survivors of a pre-Greek population group.[4] One group of personal names used exclusively in the area comprises the names Τάσκος, Τάσκις, Τάσκυς, Τάσσκις, Τασκύδας, Τασκάδας, Τασκιάδας, Τασκαννάδας, Τασκαιννάδας, Τασκομένης, and Τασκομένη attested at Polyrrhenia, Keraia, Anopolis, and Hyrtakina. Stray examples occur in Sparta and Magnesia on the Maeander. The Magnesian is probably a colonist of Cretan origin, while the Spartan has probably received his name through guest-friendship.[5] In the opinion of Olivier Masson it is difficult to see any root in *Task(o)-* which could be explicable in Greek. This may suggest that at least an element of the Kydonian population was derived from a pre-Hellenic substrate population.[6] The root has been connected to the *Tašk-* root found in the Hittite names *Taškuili-* and *Taškuwani-*. Another group of names found exclusively in west Crete, at Kydonia, Keraia, and Polyrrhenia, comprises the names Ορύας, Ορούας, and Ορυάδης.[7] These names have been connected with the Pisidian names 'Ορας and 'Ουραμμοας, which are believed to be of Luwian origin.[8] On the other hand, this second group of names could equally well be Greek and derived from the verb ὀρούω 'to rise and rush violently on'.

There is further evidence for the survival of an originally non-Greek substrate population in west Crete in more recent times. In the early modern period the most inaccessible area of the White Mountains, the Sfakiá, was

---

[4] On the Kydones see Willetts (1962) 133–5; Guarducci in *ICret* ii. 107 ff.

[5] Note also the existence of a sanctuary of Diktynna in Sparta (Paus. 3. 12. 8), which may have been founded by a Spartan with close connections with west Crete.

[6] Masson (1985) 195–7. See also Guarducci in *ICret*. ii. 138.

[7] Guarducci (1935) 69–73, esp. 70; Zucker (1952) 25; see also L. Robert in *BÉ* (1953) no. 36 and Guarducci in *ICret*. i. 35; ii. 235–6, 247. Cf. the name "Ορυσσος in Plut. *Pyrr*. 30. 4, and see Guarducci in *ICret*. ii. 11.

[8] Huxley (1961) 29–30; cf. 43: 'the Kydonians are the Luwians of western Crete'.

inhabited by a community called Sfakiots, who also had their own dialect. They were particularly proud of their particularism and heritage. 'The Sfacioti are a healthy, strong and stout people, they pretend to be of a very ancient Stock.'[9] Many visitors have remarked that the Sfakiots are very tall, many over six feet tall, with blond hair and blue eyes.[10] These striking features, which differentiate them from other Cretans, can still be found among the people of the area. Given the particularism of the Kydones in antiquity and the Sfakiots in modern times, together with their geographical isolation, it could be argued that the Sfakiots may be vestigial survivors of the Kydones. A concept of ethnic 'otherness' may have been one of the factors leading to political co-operation among the ancient Kydones.

Another element promoting Kydonian co-operation may have been religious association. This would be in line with other early examples of Greek leagues/amphiktyonies: for example, the Ionian League arose between the Ionian communities participating in the Panionia held at the Panionion.[11] On Crete evidence for the worship of the goddess Diktynna is found only in the cities in the west of the island, at Phalasarna, Polyrrhenia, Kydonia, Aptera, and Lisos. Thus it would be reasonable to assume that Diktynna was originally a Kydonian deity. Her worship is also attested at Las and Sparta in Laconia, Astypalaia, Phocis, Athens, and Marseilles, but this was presumably due to a later spread in her cult.[12] The main shrine of the goddess lay on the peninsula called Mt. Tityros in antiquity and Rhodope in modern times. In the first half of the first millennium the shrine may have originated as a pan-Kydonian sanctuary.

Thus the Kydones may have thought of themselves as a distinct ethnos. Hesychius (s.v.), it should be noted, describes them as an ethnos. Ethnicity was therefore one factor promoting local political co-operation, manifested in the League of the Polichnitai. A more decisive one which arose in the late sixth century was, however, the existence of an outside threat.

The Aeginetan conquest of Kydonia

The ancient city of Kydonia lay on the site of the modern city of Chaniá, 'probably the oldest extant city in Europe' (Rackham and Moody 1996: 94). The historical city was founded by Samians in 524 BC. An earlier settlement lay on the same site in the Late Bronze Age. However, we have no archaeological evidence for any intervening occupation of the site—in other words, that a 'Kydonian' city of Kydonia existed before the Samian settlement. According to one ancient tradition, Minos is said to have founded

---

[9] Randolph (1687) 87.   [10] Perrot (1867) 261; Doren (1974) 104, 147, 168.
[11] Roebuck (1955); cf. Shipley (1987) 30 on the origin of the Panionion. See also Forrest (this volume).
[12] Cf. Willetts (1962) 184 ff. Huxley (1961) 24 argues that Diktynna may also be Luwian in origin.

'Kydonia'.[13] Pausanias (8. 53. 4) and Stephanus (s.v. Κυδωνία) preserve a more interesting version, making Kydonia the foundation of one Kydon. Given the name of the oikist, it seems reasonable to assume that the city of Kydonia was originally a Kydonian settlement. Florus (1. 42. 4=3. 7. 4), a Roman historian of the second century AD, informs us that the Greeks usually refer to Kydonia as 'mother of cities' ('urbium matrem'). This is unintelligible in the context within which such a statement would normally be understood, namely that Kydonia had sent out numerous colonies, for Kydonia, like most other Cretan cities, had no reputation as a colonizer. We have no knowledge of what Florus' Greek sources actually stated, but one way in which it could be interpreted might be to assume that originally Kydonia had been the mother city of all the dispersed Kydonian *polichnai* of west Crete.

In the last quarter of the sixth century, however, the ethnic and political complexion of the city changed dramatically, when west Crete was drawn into an internal struggle between the Samian tyrant Polycrates and his political opponents. The rebels failed to oust Polycrates in a coup in 524, and afterwards—according to the account of Herodotus—'settled in Kydonia in Crete, though their intent in sailing there had not been this but to drive out the Zakynthians who were in the island. They stayed there for five years and grew so prosperous that all those temples that are now in Kydonia were built by those Samians. In the sixth year, however, the Aeginetans beat them in a sea battle, with the help of the Cretans, and made them slaves' (Hdt. 3. 59; cf. 3. 44).

Thus the Aeginetans captured the city of Kydonia in 519 BC, and reinforced the city with colonists from their homeland (Strabo 8. 6. 16) who continued to use the Aeginetan dialect and alphabet. The latest inscription recovered from Kydonia using the Aeginetan script is the tombstone of Melissis dating to the early fifth century.[14] The Aeginetan settlers in Kydonia, however, assumed a new ethnic based on the name of the city. The result is a plethora of different preserved ethnics for the Kydones and the inhabitants of the city of Kydonia. Stephanus Byzantinus (s.v.) lists the following: Κυδωνία . . . ὁ πολίτης Κυδωνιάτης καὶ Κύδων καὶ Κυδώνιος, καὶ Κυδωνία θηλυκῶς καὶ Κυδωνίς, καὶ Κυδωνικὸς ἀνήρ. Spyridakis (1970: 25) has suggested that 'the ancient Kydones are confused with the Kydonians' in Stephanus and that 'the same mistake is common among modern historians': thus we should distinguish between the ethnic Kydones for the autochthonous community and the ethnic Kydoniatai for the Aeginetan colonists. This proposal, though not certain, seems most plausible.

---

[13] D.S. 5. 78. 2; *IG* xii/5. 444. 21 ff. (Marmor Parium).
[14] Chaniá Museum E 49; *ICret.* ii. 122 no. 13; Jeffery (1990) 316 no. 29c.

The Aeginetan presence in Crete

The degree of Aeginetan penetration into Crete before 519 is disputable. According to some scholars, the Aeginetans already had traditionally close relations with Cretans; hence they joined the Cretans to expel the Samian intruders.[15] Any attempt to assess the extent of existing Aeginetan influence in Crete in the last quarter of the sixth century is hampered by uncertainty over the chronology of early Aeginetan coinage. It is certain, though, that the establishment of a colony at Kydonia led to a rise in Aeginetan influence throughout the island. Aeginetan trading acumen and early use of coinage may have led to the early prosperity and growth of the colony.[16] A dedication to Apollo offered by an Aeginetan has been recovered in the region of Ayia Pelagia. This site, lying 14 kilometres to the north-west of Iraklion, has been identified as the site of Apollonia. According to Polybius (28. 14), Apollonia was destroyed by the Kydonians in 171 BC, despite an alliance and an agreement on reciprocal civic rights (*sympoliteia*) existing between the two cities. This has led Alan Johnston (1989) to suggest that this city of Apollonia was a further Aeginetan colony on the island.

The first coins to circulate on Crete were Aeginetan staters, and the Aeginetic standard was adopted throughout the island, as is attested in the fines set in the early inscribed law codes. E. S. G. Robinson (1928) has suggested that some of these early coins previously attributed to Aegina—principally hemidrachms both of the sea-turtle and land-tortoise types, peculiar in style and fabric, and mostly marked with a crescent symbol (which he attributed to Artemis-Diktynna)—were mostly struck in Kydonia. The growth in the power of Kydonia and the initiation of minting in the city might, he suggested, be connected with a partial expulsion of the population of the island of Aegina, Kydonia's mother city, by the Athenians in 457–6, which was followed by a total expulsion in 431 (Thuc. 1. 108. 4; 2. 27). Aeginetan refugees fled to Kydonia and swelled the size of the population (Robinson 1928: 194). One individual involved in these events may have been Alkimidas of Aegina, celebrated in Pindar's sixth Nemean Ode, dating to the 460s, for the scholia to the poem also identify Alkimidas as being a Cretan, citing one Asklepiades. Figueira (1988: 539–40) has suggested that Alkimidas may have emigrated to Kydonia after the fall of Aegina to Athens in 457–6. During the period 457–431 BC the number of Aeginetan staters fell to nothing, and at this time the first mints in Crete outside Kydonia also started up, first at Gortyn and then at Phaistos (Le Rider 1966: 160–75).

Thus an Aeginetan colony, growing steadily in power, now existed in the

---

[15] e.g. How and Wells (1912) 272.

[16] E. S. G. Robinson (1928) 196. Robinson later expressed doubts about his previous suggestion in *NC* (1961) 113.

midst of Kydonian territory, on a site which had once perhaps constituted the *mētropolis* of the Kydonian community. This seems to have been the external stimulus which forced the disparate communities of Kydones to unite into the 'League of the Polichnitai'. The Polichnitai are first mentioned in 429, when they are at war with the Kydoniates.

The Peloponnesian War

Following his naval victory at Naupactos in 429 BC, the Athenian admiral Phormio requested reinforcements. Thucydides (2. 85. 5–6) describes the subsequent Athenian actions:

So they sent him twenty ships, but gave the commander in charge of them special orders to sail first to Crete. For Nicias, a Cretan of Gortyn who was also a *proxenos* of theirs, persuaded them to sail against Kydonia, a hostile town, promising to bring it over to the Athenians; but he was really asking them to intervene to gratify the Polichnitai who are neighbours of the Kydoniatai, so he took the ships, went to Crete, and with the Polichnitai ravaged the lands of the Kydoniatai, and because of the winds and bad sailing conditions passed not a little time there.[17]

Kydonia's Aeginetan connections explain her hostility to Athens (How and Wells 1912: 272), but do not explain why the Athenians diverted precious resources to the island in 429. Figueira (1988: 538–42) has suggested some possible reasons: principally to secure their communications by attacking an anti-Athenian base in the Cretan Sea, a base which had recently been reinforced by an influx of Aeginetan refugees hostile to Athens.

The text, however, tells us that the principal reason for the intervention of Nicias of Gortyn with the Athenians was to gratify the Polichnitai. It is probable that the states of the island were divided into a pro-Lakedaimonian camp, which would certainly have included Kydonia, and a pro-Athenian camp, presumably including the Polichnitai. Finally, let us note that Thucydides does not give the impression that the Polichnitai in this passage were a small and insignificant community. Rather they were powerful enough to lend military assistance to the Athenians in ravaging Kydoniate territory. This is, I believe, further evidence that the Polichnitai are to be identified as a league rather than as a small and as yet unlocated polis. At this point we might turn to examine the name Polichnitai itself.

---

[17] This passage has given rise to a considerable amount of comment, principally concerning the identity of Nicias of Gortyn. Connor (1976) 61–2 suggested that the text of Thucydides had originally stated that the ships were sent upon the instigation of the Athenian Nicias son of Niceratus who was Gortynian *proxenos* at Athens, but this interpretation has been rejected first by M. B. Walbank (1978) 175–6 and then by Gerolymatos (1987) 81. The same suggestion had already been made by Kirsten, and then rejected by van Effenterre (1948: 118 n. 2).

The term 'Polichnitai'

The term 'Polichnitai' used of this league of Kydonian states is quite an unusual title for a league. *Polichnē* means 'small town' in ancient Greek, and thus the Polichnitai are 'small towners'. Why would the Kydones have chosen to call themselves such? One would have expected them to term themselves the 'League of the Kydones' or something similar. Perhaps this term was not adopted because not all the Kydonian communities were members, and perhaps some non-Kydonian communities were. A further possibility is that the term may have originated as a contemptuous description of the Kydones given to them originally by their Samian or Aeginetan opponents, which later stuck.

I believe a more probable reason why the name was adopted was that the Polichnitai wished to distinguish themselves from 'the polis' (or even *mētropolis* in local parlance) which the city of Kydonia represented. More specifically, the Kydones wished to distinguish themselves from the Kydoniates, their principal adversaries. Thus we may have a curious example of conquerors gradually adopting a variant form of the name of the conquered, forcing the conquered to adopt a new name in order to distinguish themselves from their conquerors.

There were a number of ancient towns in the Greek world called Polichne,[18] and the term *polichne* is sometimes used to describe a small or subsidiary town.[19] We might fruitfully compare the way in which Strabo, writing at the beginning of our era, uses the term *polichnē* for a subsidiary town belonging to a wider confederate structure but lacking a single nodal polis. Two examples can be given. In describing the synoikism of the city of Demetrias by Demetrios Poliorketes (9. 5. 15) he terms the nearby communities from which the inhabitants of the new polis were drawn as *polichnai*. In a second case he uses the term *polichnai* of the small towns of Laconia which constituted the 'Laconian League'. During the classical and most of the hellenistic period Laconia had existed as a unitary state, with Sparta as the nodal polis. Following the defeat of Nabis of Sparta by Rome, the subsidiary towns of Laconia, detached from Sparta, were organized into a separate political entity. The exact date at which this happened is disputed. The 'Laconian League' seems to have been created either in 195 or in 146. Later on this community was reconstituted as the Free Laconians or 'Eleutherolaconians'.[20] In his geographical description of Laconia Strabo states that outside Sparta there are about thirty *polichnai* (8. 4. 11). He seems to be contrasting the unitary polis of Sparta with the separate structure of the many *polichnai* which made

---

[18] Hdt. 6. 26 (Chios); Thuc. 8. 14. 3 (Ionia); the Athenian tribute list for 453/2 BC mentions the Πολιχνῖται in Asia (*IG* i². 193 (=*IG* i³. 225) VIII vs. 17).
[19] e.g. Plut. *Timoleon* 11. 3 (the *polichnē* of the Tauromenians).
[20] Cartledge and Spawforth (1989) 77, 100–1.

up the 'Eleutherolaconians', a structure which lacked a central and controlling polis.

The passage of Thucydides discussed in the previous section is the last we hear of the 'Polichnitai': it would be reasonable to deduce from this fact that the capacity of the Kydones for corporate action disintegrated in the fourth century. Why?

The emergence of the polis in west Crete

Although evidence for the history of west Crete during this period is extremely sparse, it seems that during the fourth and third centuries BC the city-states of Phalasarna, Polyrrhenia, Keraia, and Aptera emerged and started to pursue independent policies. It must be stated that we have no firm idea which of these states were ethnically Kydonian and which lay in the territory of the 'Polichnitai'. I shall follow the assumption that all west Cretan states outside Kydonia were Kydonian and had at one time belonged to the League of the Polichnitai. The only real support for this is that Diktynna was worshipped as far east as Aptera.

Polyrrhenia seems to have had an economy which relied heavily on pasturage of the foothills of the White Mountains. Its very name ('many sheep') implies an economy heavily reliant on animal husbandry.[21] Strabo (10. 4. 13) tells us that the Polyrrhenians used to live in villages until the Achaeans and Laconians synoikized them, building a wall round a craggy place facing south. The date cannot be pinned down with any certainty. By the middle of the fourth century, however, the date of the ancient source called pseudo-Skylax, the territory of Polyrrhenia had spread from the north coast to the south, from the Diktynnaion to the north, which lay within the territory of Pergamia, to Hyrtakina in the south.[22] Thus it had expanded to absorb a number of communities which were presumably originally autonomous members of the Polichnitai, such as Kisamos and Rhokka (see Figure 19.1). A third-century funerary inscription from Rome records the ethnic of the deceased as 'a Cretan, a Polyrrhenian, and a Kisamian'.[23] We may take this to indicate that at some time prior to the third century Kisamos had voluntarily associated herself with the Polyrrhenian state by a legal agreement. Pergamia may have been incorporated in some similar way, for a third-century funerary inscription of Hyrtakina preserves the ethnic Pergamia, presumably referring to the Cretan city Pergamia rather than the Asian city of Pergamon.[24] The status of the city of Kantanos, ly-

---

[21] Steph. Byz. s.v.; cf. Chaniotis (1995) 40 n. 8.

[22] Pseudo-Skylax 47; for the date see *OCD*[3] s.v. 'Scylax'; F. Gisinger, 'Scylax (2)', *RE* ii/5 (1927) 643. The site of Pergamia has not been identified with any certainty, and is therefore not included in Fig. 19.1, but it lay between Polyrrhenia and Kydonia (cf. *Arch. Rep.* (1995–6) 47).   [23] *IG* xiv. 1575; cf. Guarducci in *ICret.* ii. 96.

[24] *ICret.* ii. 15. 3 (pp. 187–8).

ing between Polyrrhenia and Hyrtakina, is uncertain. It was probably not independent, but rather lay within the territory of one state or the other. Towards the west, however, Phalasarna had emerged as an entirely independent state, for an inscription dating to shortly before 275 records an alliance between that state and Polyrrhenia.²⁵ Towards the east Aptera also seemingly emerges as a normal polis in the fourth century. The ethnic is first mentioned in an inscription from Epidaurus dating to c.370, which mentions that Tychamenes of Aptera was paid for delivering cypress-wood for the new temple of Asclepius at Epidaurus.²⁶

Thus it seems that during the period from 429 to c.350 BC the imperatives dictating corporate action among the 'Polichnitai' had become outweighed by a much more powerful social force, the emergence in west Crete of the polis as a form of political organization in general, and the emergence of the polis of Polyrrhenia in particular. In one area of west Crete, however, it seems that the centripetal forces retained the upper hand over the centrifugal ones.

PART II: THE LEAGUE OF THE OREIOI

An area existed in Crete termed the 'Oreia'. Theophrastus records the name and gives its location (*Hist. Plant.* 2. 2. 2). 'The cypress in most regions grows from seed, but in Crete from the trunk also, for instance in the Oreia [τῆς ὀρείας] about Tarrha' (Loeb translation). Thus the Oreia corresponded to the White Mountains. The latter term was also used in antiquity, as Strabo confirms: 'The island is mountainous and thickly wooded, but it has fruitful glens. Of the mountains, those towards the west are called Leuka [=white]' (10. 4. 4). A number of other references to the term Oreia exist in the ancient sources.²⁷

During the first half of the third century BC the communities living in the Oreia joined together in a league, issuing their own confederate coinage. The date of this coinage is uncertain, but it was preceded by coins of Hyrtakina and Lisos bearing blazons which imitate coins of Sicyon. A date of c.260–250 BC has been suggested for the latter (Le Rider 1966: 183, 191 n. 4). *IG* v/1. 723 (=*GVI* 2075) is a metrical funerary epigram of an Oreian buried at Sparta, dating to the early third century. The deceased states that [πατ]ρὶς δέ μοί ἐστιν 'Ορειοί. He may have died at the Battle of Corinth in 265 BC at which King Areus of Sparta also died, as was first suggested by Wilamowitz

---

²⁵ *ICret.* ii. 11. 1 (pp. 131–3).   ²⁶ *IG* iv/1². 102. 26.

²⁷ 1: *IG* v/1. 725. 2: *IG* ii². 1130. 12 (=*ICret.* ii, p. 313 =4). 3: Callimachus 36=*AP* 7. 518. Legrand (1894) suggested that the fictitious Astakides is to be identified with Leonidas of Tarentum, who may ultimately have been of Cretan origin. See also Gow and Page (1965: commentary, 193); Wilhelm (1950) 72–5. 4: See also Ch. Kritzas, *Kret. Khron.* (1990) 7–17 no. 9.

(*IG* ad loc.). If Wilamowitz's suggestion is correct, a *terminus ante quem* of 265 BC is given for the foundation of the league.

An inscription has been found at the site of the ancient city of Lisos recording a treaty of alliance between Magas of Cyrene and the League of the Oreioi. The regnal dates of Magas are 274–259 BC, thus giving a similar *terminus ante quem* for the foundation of the league. The text of the inscription can be translated thus:[28]

> - - - - - to make an alliance] with King M[a
> gas] on the same terms as that made with the Gortynians,
> in the pr[esenc
> 5 e] of the Gortynians and the alli
> es, and to inscrib[e] and erect a stele
> in the Diktynna[io]
> n in Lisos, to consider as ours his friend
> and enemy, and if someone happens
> 10 to make war against the eparchy of Magas
> the Oreioi are to help, a[nd]
> in the same way if someone happens
> to make war against the Oreia
> Magas is to help. Oath:
> 15 'I swear by Diktynna and by those
> living in the same temenos of Diktynna
> and by the gods in Poikilasion and
> by Zeus Kretagenes and by
> all gods and goddesses to be well-inclined
> 20 to King Magas; if they keep their oath ma
> ny and good rewards, if they break it then
> the opposite.'

The extent of the League

Henri van Effenterre (1948: 125) has suggested that Lisos, the findspot of this inscription, was the capital of the league; however, it need not have had a capital at all. Other 'cities' (or perhaps more properly 'communities') belonging to the league can be identified from the federal coinage which they struck. This coinage bears the devices of a male wild goat's head, usually accompanied by an arrowhead, on the obverse, with a bee on the reverse. The distinguished Greek numismatist Svoronos (1888: 380–7) first noted the common blazons and suggested that an 'Alliance monétaire entre les quatre villes, Elyros, Hyrtakos, Lisos et Tarra' had once existed.

Other communities which did not issue coins may have belonged to the league. Guarducci noted a passage in Stephanus mentioning that Kantanos

---

[28] *ICret.* ii. 17. 1 (p. 211) = *SEG* xxv. 1028a; Schmitt (1969) 109–11, no. 468; cf. van Effenterre (1948) 119 ff.; Willetts (1955) 226.

also lay in the 'periorion'.[29] So the League of the Oreioi seems to have included Hyrtakina, Lisos, Elyros, Poikilasion, and Tarrha at the very least, perhaps also Kantanos, and perhaps considerably more communities too. It is impossible to decide how far the league extended to the east.

The War of Lyttos

Polybius (4. 53. 5) tells us that in 221 BC, during the so-called 'War of Lyttos', the Cretans united against Lyttos under the leadership of Knossos, but the Polyrrhenians, the Keraians, the Lappaioi, the Oreioi, and the Arcadians abandoned the alliance and took the part of the Lyttians. Eleutherna, Aptera, and Kydonia later joined the Polyrrhenian alliance in what van Effenterre (1948: 126) calls this 'grand mouvement insurrectionnel de la Crète Sud-occidentale contre l'hégémonie cnossienne' ('large movement of insurrection in south-west Crete against the hegemony of Knossos').[30]

The west Cretan states listed by Polybius do not include Phalasarna, Araden, Anopolis, or Phoinix. Phalasarna may already have fallen under the domination of Polyrrhenia,[31] or may have stayed out through fear of Polyrrhenian power. The states of the eastern White Mountains, Araden, Anopolis, and Phoinix, may not appear in the list given by Polybius because they belonged to the League of the Oreioi, though this does not necessarily follow. The putative state borders in Figure 19.1 are based on these assumptions. Polyrrhenia was definitely the senior partner in this alliance, for Polybius twice refers to the heterogeneous alliance as 'the Polyrrhenians and their allies' (4. 55. 3; cf. 4. 61. 2). Bronze coins of Polyrrhenia exist bearing the device of a Boeotian shield on the obverse, and the League of the Oreioi's devices of a goat's head and arrowhead on the reverse.[32] It is possible that the Polyrrhenians struck these coins at some date when they were in alliance with the League of the Oreioi, such as the circumstances in 221 described by Polybius.

Thus it seems that, although federalist tendencies had become weakened among the Kydonian communities in west Crete in general, they still re-

[29] Steph. Byz. s.v. Κάντανος· πόλις Κρήτης. ὡς Ξενίων, ἐν περιορίου Κρητικοῦ τόπου; Guarducci (1938).

[30] The manuscripts of Polybius read 'Horioi' (῟Οριοι), preserving a rough breathing. As we know practically nothing of Cretan pronunciation, a point justly emphasized by Willetts (1967) 7, this could reflect genuine local usage. Modern authorities tend to the view that psilosis (the disappearance of the aspirate) is general in most Cretan dialect groups, so that the correct pronunciation is without the rough breathing. Thus the general view is that we should read Oreioi for 'Horioi' in this passage (e.g. F. W. Walbank (1957–79) i. 509).

[31] Cf. *ICret.* ii. 19. 2 (p. 221), mentioning Ptolemy III Euergetes (246–221 BC) and Berenike at Phalasarna, presumably when still independent, and Polyb. 22. 15, which mentions civil strife and a Kydoniate garrison in occupation of Phalasarna, in either 185 or 184 BC (cf. F. W. Walbank (1957–79) iii. 200). The latter incident is presumably a last-ditch attempt by Phalasarnan separatists to secure independence from Polyrrhenia with Kydoniate help.

[32] Svoronos (1890) 277–8, nos. 9–10, pl. xxv. 33–4.

mained strong in the heart of the White Mountains. A League of the Oreioi was in place throughout most of the third century, and at times neighbouring communities, such as the Polyrrhenians and Keraitai, chose to ally themselves with the Oreioi rather than join in on different sides in the hope of territorial gain. Why, one may ask, were the circumstances different in this particular area? If we turn to the early modern period, interesting parallels become available. We first need to describe the physical characteristics and economic system existing there at that time.

The Sfakiá in the early modern period

The uppermost heights of the White Mountains, together with the deeply cut ravines and rocky outcrops lying to the south and east, are known in modern times as the Sfakiá, which roughly corresponds to the area of the ancient Oreia. The name Sfakiá is derived from the ancient Greek *σφάξ (*sphax*), a word normally found only in compounds, but in this context meaning 'ravine'. *Sphax* seems to be derived from the verb σφάζω 'to cut', usually found in the sense 'to cut the throat of', or 'to slaughter'.[33] The name also gives some impression of the precipitous nature of the landscape.

The landscape of the Sfakiá conditioned its economy. Buondelmonti stated that during the Venetian period the Sfakiots lived on goats' milk and cypress-logs (Perrot 1867: 181). Raulin (1869: i. 252) mentions that yogurt was exported even as far as Istanbul. The cheeses of Sfakiá and Ayio-Vasili were highly thought of in the Orient. The forests of Crete were heavily utilized for timbers for the Venetian fleet (Thiriet 1959: 322, 416). This was presumably before the destructive forest fire of 1612.

Within the peaks of the White Mountains lie a number of upland plains, the highest of them being the Plain of Omalo (1,100 metres). These plains have been formed by deposition into upland lakes and so the soil is very fertile. Their extreme altitude means that the growing cycles of the plains are well behind those enjoyed on the coast. Omalo is a month behind; the north-facing plateaux lying at about 500–600 metres are a fortnight behind; but not the south-facing ones such as Aradena or Anopolis (Raulin 1869: i. 86, 215). Furthermore, they can be exploited for agriculture only in the spring, summer, and autumn, for they lie under snow for four or five months of the year (ibid. 225).

Because of these conditions a system of transhumant agriculture existed in the early modern period. Flocks had to be driven down from the mountains to the plains lying near the coast, or to the east or the foothills, when the first rains fell in November. No winter pens existed for the flocks in the mountains, and so the sheep provided milk for the towns throughout the winter. Therefore most of the inhabitants of the mountains lived in the

---

[33] Doren (1974) 149; Chantraine (1968–80) iv/1. 1073.

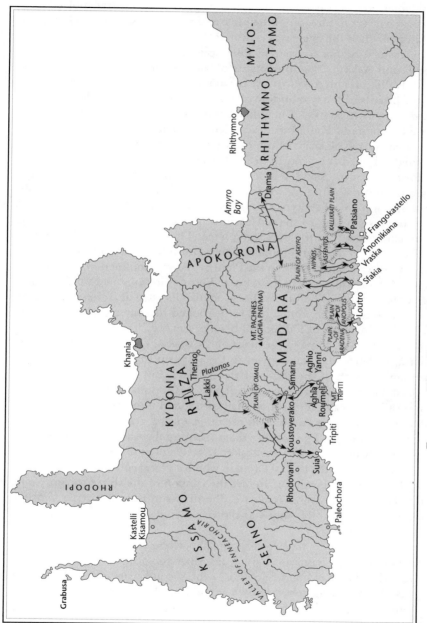

FIG. 19.2. West Crete in the early modern period.

plains from November to March. In October grain was set in the coastal plain which was harvested in May. In May seed corn was transported from the coast harvest to be reset in the hills, and this crop was in turn harvested in October, when the cycle was repeated (Raulin 1869: i. 85, 225, 251).

The eastern Sfakiá consists of four upland plains, Kallikrati, Asfentos, Nipros, and Askyfo. The inhabitants of the easternmost and westernmost plains, Kallikrati and Askyfo, were for most of the time in a state of war with the inhabitants of the two middle plains. It would be reasonable to suppose that the ultimate source of hostility lay in disputes over pasturage rights. The inhabitants of Kallikrati descended to Patsiano, those of Asfentos to Anomikiana or Kolokasia, those of Nipros to Vraska. The inhabitants of Askyfo descended either north to the coast near Dhramia, or south through the gorge known as 'Askyfou to farangi' to the village now known as Khora Sfakion. All these winter residences lay on the south coast; only the inhabitants of the plain of Askyfo also descended to the north coast. This was solely because, owing to the lawlessness of the times, they had been able to buy land cheaply in the northern plains. They descended to the coast in October or November and remained there until the following April. Some people would remain behind in the Plain of Askyfo, confined to their houses by snow for several weeks in the winter. Those who remained would lay in a stock of food and fuel before the heavy snowfalls, 'just as if they were going to sea for some weeks'. Snow had to be melted for water, and all livestock would die if insufficient fodder had been preserved.[34]

Moving west, we come to the heart of the Sfakiá, lying to the south of the Madará, which is the name given to the uppermost reaches of the White Mountains. South of the peaks of the Madará, but still lying high above the coastal strip, are found the two plains of Anopolis and Aradena. What Raulin calls the 'canton' of Anopolis was divided into two feuding groups, who would frequently come to an exchange of fire, centred on the hamlets of Gyro and Kampi. The winter village of Anopolis was Lutró (the ancient Phoinix), to which the flocks were taken from October to April. Loutró is the only port on the south coast of Crete in which a vessel could anchor securely throughout the whole winter. In fact the captain of the ship carrying Saint Paul to Rome was trying to make for Phoinix from Kaloi Limenes in order to winter there when the ship was blown off course, eventually ending up in Malta (Acts 27: 12).[35]

Finally, we move to the western Sfakiá, where the principal residence of the Sfakiots was Samaria. Perrot describes the gorge connecting Ayia-Roumeli (by the coast) and Samaria as the second principal valley of the Sfakiots. A continuing gorge, known as the Xyloskala, linked Samaria with the Plain of Omalo. The Samaria gorge is impassable when it snows or

[34] Raulin (1869) i. 74 n. 1, 84–5, 158; Perrot (1867) 67–8, 189; Pashley (1837) i. 73.
[35] Raulin (1869) i. 74 n. 1, 85; Perrot (1867) 189; Pashley (1837) ii. 243.

rains. Consequently, during the days when the narrow ravine is blocked by flooding river water, and the inhabitants of Samaria are unable to descend to Ayia-Roumeli and the sea, they say that 'The door is closed.' (Perrot 1867: 71–3).

On maps of the Venetian period Omalo is marked as a lake, the swallow-hole of the plain not being active enough to drain it (Rackham and Moody 1996: 28). In more recent times the swallow-hole has become more active. We know that Omalo was a plain in antiquity too. Diodorus (5. 70. 4; cf. Callim. *Jov. I* 41) tells us that when Zeus was being carried away by the Kouretes, after having been suckled by the goat Amaltheia, 'they say that the umbilical cord fell from him near the river Triton, and that this spot has been made sacred and has been called Omphalon after that incident, while in like manner the plain round it is called Omphaleion'. The ancient name Omphaleion has become normalized to Omalo, which means 'level, flat' in modern Greek. The western Sfakiots living in the Samaria gorge would not winter at Omalo, but rather in Samaria or Ayia-Roumeli.[36]

The foothills of the White Mountains lying to the north of the Omalo, and thus lying outside the Sfakiá, are known as the Rhíza. Láki and Thériso, lying four miles to the east, are the principal villages of the Rhíza. The Lakhiots were a different people from the Sfakiots, sharing neither their physical characteristics nor dialect. Nevertheless, Raulin informs us that the Sfakiots of Samaria shared the eastern half of the Omalo with the Lákhiots. When Raulin visited, he noted that in the south-east portion of the plain, presumably in that part which belonged to Samaria, a large number of the small houses were already shut up for the winter.[37] The inhabitants of the district of Selino made use of the western part of the Omalo. Like the Lakhiots, the Selinountes were distinct from the Sfakiots.

Common pasturage and common ownership of the upland plain of Omalo were the principal factors which helped to bind the mountain peoples together in resistance to the Cretan Muslims of Chaniá, acting on behalf of the Ottoman government. Spratt, speaking of the eastern flank of the White Mountains, informs us that 'the mountain pasturage is common to all the villages on this side, and therefore free (within agreed limits) to the Sfakian shepherds also' (Spratt 1856: ii. 157–8). Thus the Rhiziotes would share the pasturage with the Sfakiots. During the wars for independence of the late eighteenth and early nineteenth centuries the Rhiziotes, the inhabitants of the neighbouring villages of Láki and Thériso, banded together and greatly distinguished themselves (Spratt 1856: ii. 168). Spratt furthermore informs us (ii. 183) that the Selinontes, Therisotes, Lakhiotes, and Sfakiots fought together as allies 'as they possessed communication with each other by the

---

[36] Raulin (1869) i. 105–6, 125; Perrot (1867) 71–3; Doren (1974) 125.
[37] Pashley (1837) ii. 156; Raulin (1869) i. 105–6.

secret passes through the Omalo, besides having a common right to some portion of its territory, or to the mountains that surrounded it'.

Squabbling and disagreement could be fatal. During the 1770 revolt of Daskaloyiannis, a merchant of Anopolis, the Sfakiots disagreed over whether to support the revolt or not. While they were discussing whether to surrender or resist, the Turks took the passes. The fall of the passes made defeat inevitable, and the consequences could be disastrous. In 1824 the Muslims took Askyfo and advanced through Loutró to Anopolis, which was devastated. In seventeen days in March nearly 2,000 olive-trees were burnt. Before 1821 there were 12,000 Sfakiots, but in 1834 their number had fallen to 4,000.[38]

Therefore in the early modern period the different communities living in the White Mountains adopted a federal policy as their transhumant economic systems, dictated by the terrain they shared, made individual action risky. We shall now turn back to the ancient evidence to see if similar economic factors may have been at work.

The White Mountains in antiquity

The economic system practised in the White Mountains in the early modern period was highly specific, for the movement of herdsmen with their flocks to mountain pasture was accompanied by other sectors of the population moving simultaneously to exploit the agricultural possibilities offered by the upland plains. So here animal husbandry and cultivation operated in co-operation rather than opposition.[39] How similar, we must ask ourselves, might the system have been in antiquity? Caution must be exercised, for modern scholars studying ancient pastoralism converge towards the view that pastoral or part-pastoral economies are extremely specific to different conditions obtaining in different periods.[40]

Literary sources suggest that Crete was as heavily forested in antiquity as in the early modern period, perhaps even more so, though the evidence is scant.[41] The mountains of Crete in general, and the Oreia in particular, were principally populated by cypress forests. Thus Theophrastus states that

The cypress in most regions grows from seed, but in Crete from the trunk also, for instance in the Oreia about Tarrha; for there grows the cypress which they clip, and when cut it shoots in every possible way, from the part which has been cut, from the ground, from the middle, and from the upper parts; and occasionally, but rarely, it shoots from the roots also. (*Hist. Plant.* 2. 2. 2, Loeb translation)

Similarly Pliny gives Crete as the native country of the cypress and adds:

[38] Perrot (1867) 193; Raulin (1869) i. 74; Doren (1974) 148.
[39] Cf. Forbes (1995) esp. 331.   [40] e.g. Hodkinson (1988); Skydsgaard (1988).
[41] Cf. Rackham and Moody (1996) 128–31.

in Crete this tree is produced by spontaneous generation wherever anybody stirs the earth, and shoots out at once, in this case without any demand being made of the soil and of its own accord, and especially in the Mountains of Ida and those called the White Mountains, and in the greatest number on the summits of the peaks that are never free from snow, which may well surprise us, as the tree does not occur elsewhere except in a warm climate and has a great dislike for snow. (*NH* 16. 141, Loeb translation)

Strabo states 'The island is mountainous and wooded, but it has fruitful glens' (10. 4. 4). Solinus adds 'trees growing in abundance: for in part of this island the cypresses which have been cut down sprout again to a great extent' (11. 11–12).[42] Large cypress trunks were exported to provide building timbers for temple construction.[43] It has been suggested that King Magas may have wanted to procure building timbers for his fleet through his alliance with the League of the Oreioi (van Effenterre 1948: 125).

It could be argued that if Crete was more heavily forested in antiquity then the available mountain pasture would be less. However, Athenaeus (658 D) mentions Cretan cheeses, which at least implies the existence of pastoralism in Crete as a whole. In an important article Chaniotis (1995) has examined a series of hellenistic inscriptions from Hierapytna in east Crete concerning grazing rights with neighbouring and more distant states. He suggests that these inscriptions and the transhumant system they attest are the result of specific social and demographic problems in east Crete. The transhumant pastoral system attested was one strategy adopted to cope with an expanded landless populace; as were mercenary service, piracy, and ultimately territorial expansion. These ideas are most convincing.

Chaniotis also draws attention to evidence relevant to west Crete. First, he notes (1995: 68) that Plutarch (*Lyc.* 31. 7) states that the tomb of Lycurgus lay on a ξενικὴ ὁδός ('route of the aliens') near Pergamia, between Polyrrhenia and Kydonia. Chaniotis demonstrates that these 'routes of the aliens' were most probably used by transhumant shepherds. We have already mentioned that the name Polyrrhenia, 'many sheep', implies the existence of pastoralism. Chaniotis further notes (ibid. 72) the existence of the name Eumelos, 'owner of good sheep', at Polyrrhenia, and the 'goat' names Aigedas at Keraia and Aigeidas and Aigylos at Polyrrhenia. Finally, he notes (ibid. 69) the existence of a board of officials named συνευνομιῶται ('magistrates responsible for orderly grazing'?) at Polyrrhenia (*ICret.* ii. 23. 9). Elsewhere in Crete these officials are responsible, among their other duties, for supervision of the 'routes of the aliens'. The recent discovery of an important sanctuary of Pan in Hyrtakina also implies the importance of pastoralism in the area. While one should not make too much of this evidence, it indicates

---

[42] I would like to thank Simon Northwood for his help with this passage and translation.
[43] Athen. 27 D–F; *IG* iv/1². 102. 26; Plato, *Laws* 625 B; cf. Burford (1969) 176; Meiggs (1982) 99, 200–1, 424.

that mountain pasturage was exploited in the White Mountains in the hellenistic period, possibly transhumantly.

The debate as to whether we can project early modern transhumant systems into antiquity is, as already mentioned, a contentious one, into which I would not wish to be too deeply drawn. It is worth noting, however, that a forthcoming study emphasizes that for transhumant systems to be successful they need an export market for their produce.[44] It could be argued that the opening up of new markets in the early hellenistic period created conditions stimulating the growth of transhumance in the White Mountains, and hence the need for political as well as economic co-operation between previously separate political communities in the area. The White Mountains may have exported cheeses to Alexandria, Byzantium, and Antioch in antiquity, as they did to Alexandria, Istanbul, and northern Syria in the early modern period.

As regards the Oreia itself, one factor, communication, must have been the same in antiquity as in the early modern period. Movement of animals, herdsmen, and cultivators towards upland pastures and plains and then back to the coast, and indeed easy movement of individuals in any direction, is only practicable by the narrow mountain gorges. Many of these passes were originally occupied by more than one autonomous community. We might expect to see such communities living in the same mountain pass converge both economically and politically. Stephanus tells us that Suia, which does not appear in the ancient epigraphic record as an independent state, was a small Cretan city, the *epineion* of Elyros.[45] The next port city to the west, Lisos, was similarly linked to upland Hyrtakina. However, remains of an ancient road system have been recovered linking Lisos with both Elyros and Hyrtakina, so both communities may have used Lisos as their port.[46] We have already noted that both communities minted coins c.260–250 BC bearing blazons imitating coins of Sicyon. Svoronos (1890: 372) took these coins to be evidence for an original alliance of Hyrtakina and Lisos which was an initial step in the foundation of the League of the Oreioi, which later expanded to include other cities. This suggestion is highly plausible. The league may have emerged in an accelerating process of coalescence. The different political communities shared knowledge of the passes through the Oreia, they may have shared ports, and they may also have shared rights to upland grazing or to cultivate the upland plains. Shared common knowledge of the terrain will have made individual defence impractical, and will have supplied the impetus which eventually led to the formation of the League of the Oreioi.

[44] L. Nixon and S. Price, 'The Diachronic Analysis of Pastoralism through Comparative Variables' (*ABSA*, forthcoming).

[45] Steph. Byz. s.v. Συία, πόλις μικρὰ Κρήτης, ἐπίνειον οὖσα τῆς Ἐλύρου.

[46] Cf. Niniou-Kindele (1990) (which I have not seen).

An inscription from Gortyn, dated to 183 BC, records an agreement between King Eumenes II and the Cretan League.[47] The names of thirty-one Cretan states are recorded, including Elyros, Hyrtakina, Tarrha, and perhaps Lisos, plus Anopolis and Araden: all listed separately without any reference to the League of the Oreioi. We may therefore assume that the league broke up some time between 221 and 183, perhaps in 217 BC when Philip V became *prostatēs* of the Cretan League.[48] A pan-Cretan solution to inter-city strife was adopted instead of local confederate or alliance systems.

Conclusion

In the archaic period common ethnicity seems to have been the principal factor promoting federalism in west Crete. The alliance of the Polichnitai seems to have been based upon their Kydonian identity. This assumption must remain to some degree speculative, however, as we have no precise knowledge of either the extent of the alliance of the Polichnitai or of the Kydonian ethnic area. From the end of the sixth century down through the fifth the presence of a common enemy in the form of the Aeginetan colony of Kydonia was a further factor promoting political co-operation. Subsequently the emergence of particularist poleis broke up the alliance. Polyrrhenia especially took on the character of an expansive state, so much so that by the middle of the fourth century its borders stretched from coast to coast. Within the White Mountains, however, a further dynamic existed which promoted confederacy: the terrain. Common knowledge of the mountain passes made particularist defence strategies dangerous and promoted alliance. We see this exhibited not only in the emergence of the League of the Oreioi, but also in the alliance which Polybius terms 'the Polyrrhenians and their allies' during the War of Lyttos, as the Oreioi, Keraitai, and Polyrrhenians probably all shared knowledge of the northern passes through the White Mountains. The situation can be compared with the Turkish period, when the existence of a common external threat, and common knowledge of the upland passes, resulted in a military alliance of the Sfakiots, Lakhiots, Therisotes, and Selinontes.

[47] *ICret.* iv. 179 (p. 251).
[48] Polyb. 7. 11. 9; Guarducci (1938) 53–4; Ager (1994) 1 n. 2.

Bibliography

[Anon.] (1991). *A Man of Respect: The True Story of a Mafia Assassin*. London: Pan.

AALDERS, G. J. D. (1968). *Die Theorie der gemischten Verfassung im Altertum*. Amsterdam: Hakkert.

ACCAME, S. (1934). 'La diarchia dei Molossi'. *RFIC* 62: 522–34.

ADAMESTEANU, D. (1976). 'Greci e indigeni nell'agro di Heraklea (Policoro)'. *Rendiconti dei Lincei* 26: 643–51.

—— and VATIN, C. (1976). 'L'arrières-pays de Métaponte'. *CRAI*: 110–15.

ADCOCK, F. E. (1953). 'Greek and Macedonian Kingship'. *PBA* 39: 163–80.

ADKINS, A. W. H. (1960). *Merit and Responsibility*. Oxford: Clarendon Press.

—— (1972). *Moral Values and Political Behaviour in Ancient Greece*. London: Chatto and Windus.

AGER, S. L. (1994). 'Hellenistic Crete and κοινοδίκιον'. *JHS* 114: 1–18.

ALCOCK, S. E. (1995). 'Pausanias and the Polis: Use and Abuse', in *CPC Acts* 2: 326–44.

ALZINGER, W. (1976–7). 'Grabungen Aegeira'. *ÖJh* 51: 30–4.

—— (1981–2). 'Aegeira'. *ÖJh* 53: Grab., 8–15.

—— (1982). 'Pausanias und der Tempel von Aigeira'. *Tagung Innsbruck* 13–18.

—— (1983). 'Aegeira'. *ÖJh* 54: Grab., 35–40.

—— (1984). 'Aegeira-Hyperesia'. *ÖJh* 55: Grab., 13–18.

—— and MITSOPOULOU-LEON, V. (1972–5). 'Aegeira'. *ÖJh* 50: Grab., 9–31.

—— DEGER-JALKOTZY, S., and ALRAM-STERN, E. (1985). 'Aegeira-Hyperesia und die Siedlung Phelloe in Achaia I'. *Klio* 67: 389–451.

—— —— —— (1986). 'Aegira-Hyperesia und die Siedlung Phelloe in Achaia II, III'. *Klio* 68: 6–62, 309–47.

AMIT, M. (1973). *Great and Small Poleis*. Brussels: Latomus.

AMMERMAN, A. J. (1996). 'The Eridanos Valley and the Athenian Agora'. *AJA* 100: 699–715.

AMPOLO, C. (1976–7). 'Demarato: Osservazioni sulla mobilità sociale arcaia'. *DdA* 9–10: 333–45.

ANDERSON, J. K. (1958–9). 'Old Smyrna: The Corinthian Pottery'. *ABSA* 53–4: 138–51.

ANDREOU, S., and KOTSAKIS, K. (1987). 'Διαστάσεις του Χώρου στην Κεντρική Μακεδονία', in: Αμητός: Τιμητικός τόμος για τον καθ. Μ. Ανδρόνικο, i. 57–86. 2 vols.; Thessaloniki: Aristotelian University.

—— —— (1994). 'Prehistoric Rural Communities in Perspective: The Langadas Survey Project', in *Structures rurales*, 17–25.

ANDREWES, A. (1953). 'The Generals in the Hellespont, 410–407 B.C.'. *JHS* 73: 2–9.

—— (1956). *The Greek Tyrants*. London: Hutchinson.

—— (1966). 'The Government of Classical Sparta', in E. Badian (ed.), *Ancient*

Society and Institutions: Studies Presented to Victor Ehrenberg on his 75th Birthday, 1–20. Oxford: Blackwell.

—— (1970). 'Lysias and the Theramenes Papyrus'. *ZPE* 6: 35–8.

—— (1978). 'The Opposition to Perikles'. *JHS* 98: 1–8.

—— and LEWIS, D. M. (1957). 'Note on the Peace of Nikias'. *JHS* 77: 177–80.

APOSTOLOPOULOU KAKAVOYIANNI, O. (1992). 'Εὑρήματα τῆς Πρωτογεωμετρικῆς καὶ Γεωμετρικῆς Περιόδου ἀπό τις Φέρες', in *Praktika*, 312–20.

APPLEBAUM, S. (1979). *Jews and Greeks in Cyrene*. Leiden: Brill.

ARAFAT, K. (1996). *Pausanias' Greece: Ancient Artists and Roman Rulers*. Cambridge: Cambridge University Press.

—— and MORGAN, C. (1989). 'Pots and Potters in Classical Athens and Corinth: A Review'. *OJA* 8: 311–46.

ARCHIBALD, Z. H. (1998). *The Odrysian Kingdom of Thrace: Orpheus Unmasked*. Oxford: Clarendon Press.

AREND, W. (1933). *Die typischen Szenen bei Homer*. Berlin: Weidmann.

ARLACCHI, P. (1986). *Mafia Business*. London: Verso.

ARNOTT, W. G. (1991). 'A Lesson from the *Frogs*'. *G&R* NS 38: 18–23.

ARNUSH, M. (1995). 'The Archonship of Sarpadon at Delphi'. *ZPE* 105: 95–104.

ASHERI, D. (1996). 'L'ideale monarchico di Dario: Erodoto III 80–82 e DNb, Kent'. *Annali di archeologia e storia antica* NS 3: 99–106.

AUDOUZE, F., and BÜCHSENSCHÜTZ, O. (1991). *Towns, Villages and Countryside of Celtic Europe*. London: Batsford (English trans. of French edn., Hachette, 1989).

AURENCHE, O. (1974). *Les Groupes d'Alcibiade, de Léogoras et de Teucros: Remarques sur la vie politique athénienne en 415 avant J.C.* Paris: Les Belles Lettres.

AUSTIN, M. M. (1981). *The Hellenistic World from Alexander to the Roman Conquest: A Selection of Ancient Sources in Translation*. Cambridge: Cambridge University Press.

—— (1990). 'Greek Tyrants and the Persians, 546–479 B.C.'. *CQ* NS 40: 289–306.

AUSTIN, R. P. (1938). *The Stoichedon Style in Greek Inscriptions*. London: Oxford University Press.

AXIOTIS, M. (1992). *Περπατώντας τη Λέσβο*. 2 vols.; Mytilene: Gutenberg.

AYMARD, A. (1950). 'Sur l'assemblée macédonienne'. *RÉA* 52: 115–37 = *Études d'histoire ancienne* (Paris: Presses Universitaires de France; 1967), 143–63.

BACCHIELLI, L. (1981). 'La formazione della "Grande Agora"', in *L'Agora di Cirene* ii/1. 25–50. Rome: L'Erma di Bretschneider.

—— (1985). 'Modelli architectonichi a Cyrene durante il regime democratico', in G. Barker, J. A. Lloyd, and J. M. Reynolds (eds.), *Cyrene in Antiquity* (BAR int. series 236), 1–14. Oxford: British Archaeological Reports.

BADIAN, E. (1971). 'Archons and *Strategoi*'. *Antichthon* 5: 1–34.

—— (1982). 'Greeks and Macedonians', in B. Barr-Sharrar and E. N. Borza (eds.), *Macedonia and Greece in Late Classical and Early Hellenistic Times* (Studies in the History of Art, 10), 33–51. Washington: National Gallery of Art.

—— (1993). *From Plataea to Potidaea*. Baltimore: Johns Hopkins University Press.

BAEGE, W. (1913). *De Macedonum Sacris* (diss. Phil., Halle). Halle: Niemeyer.

BAILEY, D. W. (1997). 'Impermanence and Flux in the Landscape of Early Agricultural South Eastern Europe', in J. Chapman and P. Dolukhanov (eds.), *Landscapes in Flux: Central and Eastern Europe in Antiquity* (Colloquia Pontica, 3), 41–58. Oxford: Oxbow.

BAK, P. (1997). *How Nature Works*. Oxford: Clarendon Press.

BARCELÓ, P. (1993). *Basileia, Monarchia, Tyrannis* (Historia Einzelschriften 79). Stuttgart: Steiner.

BARRON, J. P. (1961). 'The History of Samos to 439 B.C.' (D.Phil. thesis, Oxford).

—— (1983). 'The Fifth-century *horoi* of Aigina'. *JHS* 103: 1–12.

—— (1988). 'The Liberation of Greece', in J. Boardman, N. G. L. Hammond, D. M. Lewis, and M. Ostwald (eds.), *The Cambridge Ancient History*, 2nd edn., iv. 592–622. Cambridge: Cambridge University Press.

BAZIOTOPOULOU-VALAVANI, E. (1994). ᾿Ανασκαφές σε Αθηναϊκά κεραμικά εργαστήρια των αρχαϊκών και κλασσικών χρόνων', in Coulson *et al.*, *Archaeology*, 45–54.

BECK, H. (1997). *Polis und Koinon: Untersuchungen zur Geschichte und Struktur der griechischen Bundesstaaten im 4. Jahrhundert v. Chr.* (Historia Einzelschriften 114). Stuttgart: Steiner.

BELOCH, K. J. (1927). *Griechische Geschichte*, iv/2, 2nd edn. Berlin and Leipzig: De Gruyter.

BERVE, H. (1926). *Das Alexanderreich auf prosopographische Grundlage*. 2 vols.; Munich: Beck.

—— (1967). *Die Tyrannis bei den Griechen*. Munich: Beck.

BICKERMAN, E. (1938). *Institutions des Séleucides*. Paris: Geuthner.

BINTLIFF, J. (1994). 'The History of the Greek Countryside: As the Wave Breaks. Prospects for Future Research', in *Structures rurales*, 7–15.

—— and SNODGRASS, A. M. (1988). 'Mediterranean Survey and the City'. *Antiquity* 62: 57–71.

—— —— (1989). 'From Polis to Chorion in South-west Boiotia', in H. Beister and J. Buckler (eds.), *Boiotika: Vorträge vom 5. internationalen Böoten Kolloquium zu Ehren von Professor Dr. Siegfried Lauffer*, 285–99. Munich: Maris.

BLOK, A. (1974). *The Mafia of a Sicilian Village 1860–1960*. New York: Blackwell.

BLUM, I., DARMEZIN, L., DECOURT, J.-C., HELLY, B., and LUCAS, G. (1992). *Topographie antique et géographie historique en pays grec*. Paris: CNRS.

BLUNDELL, M. W. (1989). *Helping Friends and Harming Enemies: A Study in Sophocles and Greek Ethics*. Cambridge: Cambridge University Press.

BOARDMAN, J. (1966). 'Evidence for the Dating of Greek Settlements in Cyrenaica'. *ABSA* 61: 149–56.

—— (1978). 'Herakles, Delphi and Kleisthenes of Sikyon'. *RA*: 227–34.

—— (1980). *The Greeks Overseas*, 3rd edn., London: Thames and Hudson.

—— (1982). 'The Islands: Euboea', in J. Boardman and N. G. L. Hammond (eds.), *The Cambridge Ancient History*, 2nd edn., iii/3. 754–65. Cambridge: Cambridge University Press.

—— GRIFFIN, J., and MURRAY, O. (eds.) (1986). *The Oxford History of the Classical World*. Oxford: Clarendon Press.

—— and HAYES, J. (1966). *Excavations at Tokra 1963–5*, vol. i. Oxford: Alden.

BOEGEHOLD, A. L. (1960). 'Aristotle's *Athenaion Politeia*, 65. 2: the "Official Token"'. *Hesperia* 29: 393–401.

BOHRINGER, F. (1980). 'Mégare: Traditions mythiques, espace sacré et naissance de la cité'. *AC* 49: 5–22.

BOMMELAER, J.-F., and GRANDJEAN, Y. (1972). 'Recherches dans le quartier sud d'Argos'. *BCH* 96: 155–228.

BOMMELJÉ, S., and DOORN, P. K. (1987). *Aetolia and the Aetolians: Towards the Interdisciplinary Study of a Greek Region.* Utrecht: Parnassus.

BONANNO, J. (1983). *A Man of Honour.* London: Deutsch.

BORCHHARDT, J. (1976). *Die Bauskulptur des Heroons von Limyra.* Berlin: Gebr. Mann.

BORZA, E. N. (1990). *In the Shadow of Olympus: The Emergence of Macedon.* Princeton: Princeton University Press.

BOSWORTH, A. B. (1976). 'Early Relations between Aetolia and Macedon'. *AJAH* 1: 164–81.

BOUND, M. (1991). *The Giglio Wreck: A Wreck of the Archaic Period (c. 600 BC) off the Tuscan Island of Giglio. An Account of its Discovery and Excavation. A Review of the Main Finds* (Enalia supp. 1). Athens: HIMA.

BOURGAREL, A., and METZGER, H. (1992). 'Les deux bases d'Arbinas', in H. Metzger (ed.), *Fouilles de Xanthos,* ix. *La Région nord du Létôon: Les sculptures. Les inscriptions gréco-lyciennes,* 149–54. Paris: Klincksieck.

BOURGUET, E. (1899). 'Inscriptions de Delphes'. *BCH* 23: 353–69.

BOURRIOT, F. (1976). *Recherches sur la nature du génos: Étude d'histoire sociale athénienne. Périodes archaïque et classique.* Lille: Université de Lille III.

BOUSQUET, J. (1940–1). 'Inscriptions de Delphes'. *BCH* 64–5: 76–120.

——(1952). *Fouilles de Delphes,* ii/7. *Le Trésor de Cyrène.* Paris: De Boccard.

——(1956). 'Inscriptions de Delphes'. *BCH* 80: 547–97.

——(1957). 'Inscriptions de Delphes: Les Aitoliens à Delphes au IVᵉ siècle'. *BCH* 81: 485–95.

——(1958). 'Inscriptions de Delphes'. *BCH* 82: 61–91.

——(1959). 'Inscriptions de Delphes'. *BCH* 83: 146–92.

——(1975). 'Arbinas'. *CRAI*: 138–48.

——(1985). 'Inscriptions de Delphes'. *BCH* 109: 222–53.

——(1988). *Études sur les comptes de Delphes* (Bibliothèque des Écoles Françaises d'Athènes et de Rome, 267). Athens and Paris.

——(1992). 'Les inscriptions du Létôon en l'honneur d'Arbinas et l'épigramme grecque de la stèle de Xanthos', in H. Metzger (ed.), *Fouilles de Xanthos,* ix. *La Région nord du Létôon: Les sculptures. Les inscriptions gréco-lyciennes,* 155–87. Paris: Klincksieck.

BOUVIER, H. (1978). 'Honneurs et récompenses à Delphes'. *ZPE* 30: 101–18.

——(1985). 'Hommes de lettres dans les inscriptions delphiques'. *ZPE* 58: 119–35.

BOUZEK, J., DOMARADZKI, M., and ARCHIBALD, Z. H. (eds.) (1996). *Pistiros,* i. *Excavations and Studies.* Prague: Charles University.

BOWIE, E. L. (1997). 'The Theognidea: A Step Towards a Collection of Fragments?', in G. W. Most (ed.), *Collecting Fragments,* 53–66. Göttingen: Vandenhoeck and Ruprecht.

BOWRA, C. M. (1941). 'Xenophanes, Fragment 3'. *CQ* 35: 119–26.

——(1964). *Pindar.* Oxford: Clarendon Press.

BRAUND, D. (1994a). *Georgia in Antiquity.* Oxford: Clarendon Press.

——(1994b). 'The Luxuries of Athenian Democracy'. *G&R* NS 41: 41–8.

——(1998). 'Herodotus on the Problematics of Reciprocity', in C. Gill, N. Postlethwaite, and R. Seaford (eds.), *Reciprocity in Ancient Greece*, 159–80. Oxford: Clarendon Press.

BRAUNERT, H., and PETERSEN, T. (1972). 'Megalopolis: Anspruch und Wirklichkeit'. *Chiron* 2: 57–90.

BREMMER, J. N. (1990). 'Adolescents, Symposion, and Pederasty' in Murray (ed.) (1990), 135–48.

BRIANT, P. (1973). *Antigone le Borgne*. Besançon-Paris: Les Belles Lettres.

—— (1982). *Rois, tributs et paysans*. Paris: Les Belles Lettres.

BROCK, R. (1989). 'Athenian Oligarchs: The Numbers Game'. *JHS* 109: 160–4.

—— (1991). 'The Emergence of Democratic Ideology'. *Historia* 40: 160–9.

BROOKES, A. C. (1981). 'Stoneworking in the Geometric Period at Corinth'. *Hesperia* 50: 185–90.

BRUNT, P. A. (1957). Review of Wentker (1956). *CR* ns 7: 243–5.

BRYCE, T. R. (1982). 'A Ruling Dynasty in Lycia'. *Klio* 74: 329–37.

—— (1983). 'Political Unity in Lycia during the "Dynastic" Period'. *JNES* 42: 31–42.

—— (1986). *The Lycians*. Copenhagen: Museum Tusculanum.

BÜCHSENSCHÜTZ, O. (1995). 'The Significance of Major Settlements in European Iron Age Society', in B. Arnold and D. Blair Gibson (eds.), *Celtic Chiefdom, Celtic State*, 53–63. Cambridge: Cambridge University Press.

BUCK, R. J. (1965). 'The Reforms of 487 B.C. in the Selection of Archons'. *CPh* 60: 96–101.

—— (1979). *A History of Boeotia*. Edmonton: University of Alberta Press.

—— (1994). *Boeotia and the Boeotian League 423–371 BC*. Edmonton: University of Alberta Press.

BUCKLER, J. (1980). *The Theban Hegemony, 371–362 BC*. Cambridge, Mass.: Harvard University Press.

—— (1989). *Philip II and the Sacred War* (Mnemosyne suppl. 109). Leiden: Brill.

BUCKLEY, T. (1996). *Aspects of Greek History 750–323 BC: A Source-based Approach*. London and New York: Routledge.

BURFORD, A. (1969). *The Greek Temple Builders at Epidaurus*. Liverpool: Liverpool University Press.

BURN, A. R. (1960). *The Lyric Age of Greece*. London: Arnold.

—— (1962). *Persia and the Greeks*. London: Arnold.

BURSTEIN, S. M. (1976). *Outpost of Hellenism: The Emergence of Heraclea on the Black Sea* (University of California Classical Studies 14). Berkeley, Calif.: University of California Press.

BURY, J. B. (1898). 'The Double City of Megalopolis'. *JHS* 18: 15–22.

BUSOLT, G., and SWOBODA, H. (1920–6). *Griechische Staatskunde*. 2 vols.; Munich: Beck.

BUZAIAN, A., and LLOYD, J. A. (1996). 'Early Urbanism in Cyrenaica: New Evidence from Euesperides (Benghazi)'. *Libyan Studies* 27: 129–52.

CABANES, P. (1974). 'Les inscriptions du théâtre de Bouthrôtos', in *Actes du colloque 1972 sur l'esclavage*, 105–209. Paris and Besançon: Les Belles Lettres.

—— (1976a). *L'Épire de la mort de Pyrrhos à la conquête romaine (272–167)*. Paris: Les Belles Lettres.

—— (1976b). 'Recherches sur les états fédéraux en Grèce'. *CH* 21: 391–407.

CABANES, P. (1979). 'Frontière et rencontre de civilisations dans la Grèce du nord-ouest'. *Ktéma* 4: 183–99.

—— (1980). 'Societé et institutions dans les monarchies de Grèce septentrionale au IVᵉ siècle'. *RÉG* 93: 324–51.

—— (1981). 'Problèmes de géographie administrative et politique dans l'Épire du IVᵉ siècle avant J.-C.', in *La Géographie administrative et politique d'Alexandre à Mahomet. Actes du Colloque de Strasbourg, 14–16 Juin 1979*, 19–38. Leiden: Brill.

—— (1982). 'La recherche épigraphique en Épire'. *AncW* 8: 3–12.

—— (1983). 'Les états fédéraux de Grèce du nord-ouest: Pouvoirs locaux et pouvoir fédéral', in P. Dimakis (ed.), *Symposia 1979: Vorträge zur griechischen und hellenistischen Rechtsgeschichte (Ägina, 3–7 Sept. 1979)*, 99–111. Cologne and Vienna: Böhlau Verlag.

—— (1985–9). 'Le koinon des Prasaiboi: Institutions et société d'après les inscriptions de Bouthrôtos', in F. J. Fernàndez Nieto (ed.), *Symposion 1982: Actas de la sociedad de historia del derecho griego y hellenistico, Santander, Sept. 1982*, 147–183. Valencia; also in A. Biscardi, J. Mélèze-Modrzejewski, and G. Thür (eds.), *Symposion 1982: Vorträge zur griechischen und hellenistischen Rechtsgeschichte*, 147–83. Cologne-Vienna: Böhlau Verlag.

—— (1986). 'Nouvelles inscriptions d'Albanie méridionale'. *ZPE* 63: 137–55.

—— (ed.) (1987). *L'Illyrie méridionale et l'Épire dans l'Antiquité: Actes du colloque international de Clermont-Ferrand, 22–25 octobre 1984*. Clermont-Ferrand: Adosa.

—— (1988a). *Les Illyriens, de Bardylis à Genthios (IVᵉ–IIᵉ siècles avant J.-C.)*. Paris: Sedes.

—— (1988b). 'Les politarques en Épire et en Illyrie méridionale'. *Historia* 37: 480–7.

—— (1989). 'L'Épire et l'Illyrie méridionale'. *RÉG* 102: 146–59.

—— (ed.) (1993a). *L'Illyrie méridionale et l'Épire dans l'Antiquité, ii. Actes du IIᵉ colloque international de Clermont-Ferrand, 25–27 octobre 1990*. Paris: De Boccard.

—— (ed.) (1993b). *Grecs et Illyriens dans les inscriptions en langue grecque d'Épidamne-Dyrrachion et d'Apollonie d'Illyrie: Actes de la Table ronde internationale, Clermont-Ferrand, 19–21 octobre 1989*. Paris: Éditions Recherche sur les Civilisations.

—— (1996). 'La Grèce du nord (Épire, Macédoine) en plein développement au IVᵉ siècle avant J.-C.', in Carlier 1996b: 195–204.

CAIRNS, D. L. (1996). '*Hybris*, Dishonour, and Thinking Big'. *JHS* 116: 1–32.

CAMERON, A. (1995). *Callimachus and his Critics*. Princeton: Princeton University Press.

CAMERON, G. G. (1943). 'Darius, Egypt and the "Lands beyond the Sea"'. *JNES* 2: 307–14.

CAMP, J. McK. (1994). 'Before Democracy: Alkmaionidai and Peisistratidai', in Coulson *et al.*, *Archaeology*, 7–12.

CAMPBELL, J. K. (1957). *Honour, Family, and Patronage: A Study of Institutions and Moral Values in a Greek Mountain Community*. Oxford: Clarendon Press.

CARAPANOS, C. (1878). *Dodone et ses ruines*. 2 vols.; Paris: Hachette.

CARLIER, P. (1984). *La Royauté en Grèce avant Alexandre*. Strasbourg: AECR.

—— (1991). 'La procédure de décision politique du monde mycénien à l'époque archaïque', in D. Musti (ed.), *Dal palazzo alla città*. Rome: CNR, 85–95.

—— (1996a). 'Les *basileis* homériques sont-ils des rois?'. *Ktéma* 21: 5–22.

——(ed.) (1996*b*). *Le IV*ᵉ *siècle av. J.-C.: Approches historiographiques*. Nancy: ADRA/ Paris: De Boccard.

CARRIÈRE, J. (1975). *Théognis: Poèmes élégiaques*. Paris: Les Belles Lettres.

CARRUBA, O. (1993). 'Dynasten und Städte', in J. Borchhardt and G. Dobesch (eds.), *Akten des II. Internationalen Lykien-Symposions*, i. 11–25. Vienna: Österreichischen Akademie der Wissenschaften.

CARTER, J. C. (1990). 'Metapontum: Land, Wealth and Population', in J. P. Descœudres (ed.), *Greek Colonists and Native Populations*, 405–44. Oxford: Clarendon Press.

——(1993). 'Taking Possession of the Land: Early Greek Colonisation in Southern Italy', in A. R. and R. T. Scott (eds.), *Eius Virtutis Studiosi: Classical and Post-classical Studies in Memory of Frank Edward Brown*, 342–67. Washington: National Gallery of Art.

CARTER, L. B. (1986). *The Quiet Athenian*. Oxford: Clarendon Press.

CARTLEDGE, P. (1980). 'Euphron and the δοῦλοι again'. *LCM* 5: 209–11.

——(1983). '"Trade and Politics" Revisited: Archaic Greece', in P. Garnsey, K. Hopkins, and C. R. Whittaker (eds.), *Trade in the Ancient Economy*, 6–15. London: Chatto and Windus.

——(1987). *Agesilaos and the Crisis of Sparta*. London: Duckworth.

——(1990). 'Fowl Play: A Curious Lawsuit in Classical Athens', in P. Cartledge, P. Millett, and S. Todd (eds.), *Nomos: Essays in Athenian Law, Politics and Society*, 41–61. Cambridge: Cambridge University Press.

——(2000). 'Boiotian Swine F(or)ever? The Boiotian Superstate 395 BC', in P. Flensted-Jensen, T. H. Nielsen, and L. Rubinstein (eds.), *Polis and Politics: Studies in Ancient Greek History Presented to Mogens Herman Hansen on his Sixtieth Birthday, August 20, 2000* (Copenhagen; Museum Tusculanum).

——and Spawforth, A. (1989). *Hellenistic and Roman Sparta: A Tale of Two Cities*. London: Routledge.

CAVANAGH, W. G. (1991). 'Surveys, Cities and Synoecism', in J. Rich and A. Wallace-Hadrill (eds.), *City and Country in the Ancient World*, 97–118. London: Routledge.

CAVEN, B. (1990). *Dionysius I, War-lord of Sicily*. New Haven and London: Yale University Press.

CAWKWELL, G. L. (1992). 'Early Colonisation'. *CQ* NS 42: 289–303.

CHAMOUX, F. (1953). *Cyrène sous la monarchie des Battiades*. Paris: De Boccard.

——(1985). 'Du silphion', in G. Barker, J. A. Lloyd, and J. Reynolds (eds.), *Cyrene in Antiquity* (BAR int. series 236), 165–72. Oxford: British Archaeological Reports.

CHANIOTIS, A. (1986). '*Entéleia*: Zu Inhalt und Begriff eines Vorrechtes'. *ZPE* 64: 159–62.

——(1995). 'Problems of "Pastoralism" and "Transhumance" in Classical and Hellenistic Crete'. *Orbis Terrarum* 1: 39–89.

CHANTRAINE, P. (1968–80). *Dictionnaire étymologique de la langue grecque: Histoire des mots*. Paris: Les Belles Lettres.

CHARNEUX, P. (1966). 'Liste argienne de théarodoques'. *BCH* 90: 156–239.

——(1983). 'Sur quelques inscriptions d'Argos'. *BCH* 107: 251–67.

CHERRY, J. (1987). 'Power in Space: Studies of the State', in J. M. Wagstaff (ed.), *Landscape and Culture: Geographical and Archaeological Perspectives*, 146–72. Oxford: Blackwell.

CHERRY, J. (1988). 'Pastoralism and the Role of Animals in the Pre- and Protohistoric Economies of the Aegean', in C. R. Whittaker (ed.), *Pastoral Economies in Classical Antiquity* (Cambridge Philological Society, suppl. 14), 6–34. Cambridge.

—— DAVIS, J. L., and MANTZOURANI, E. (1991). *Landscape Archaeology as Long-term History: Northern Keos in the Cycladic Islands from Earliest Settlement until Modern Times*. Los Angeles: UCLA Institute of Archaeology.

CHILDE, V. G. (1950). 'The Urban Revolution'. *Town Planning Review* 21: 9–16.

CHILDS, W. A. P. (1979). 'The Authorship of the Inscribed Pillar of Xanthos'. *AS* 29: 97–102.

—— (1981). 'Lycian Relations with Persians and Greeks'. *AS* 31: 55–80.

CLINKENBEARD, B. (1982). 'Lesbian Wine and Storage Amphorae: A Progress Report on Identification'. *Hesperia* 51: 248–68.

COLDSTREAM, J. N. (1968). *Greek Geometric Pottery*. London: Methuen.

CONNOR, W. R. (1976). 'Nicias the Cretan?'. *AJAH* 1: 61–4.

—— HANSEN, M. H., RAAFLAUB, K. A., and STRAUSS, B. S. (1990). *Aspects of Athenian Democracy* (*C&M* dissertationes, 11). Copenhagen: Museum Tusculanum.

COOK, J. M. (1958–9). 'Old Smyrna 1948–1951'. *ABSA* 53–4: 1–34.

—— (1961). 'The Problem of Classical Ionia'. *PCPhS* NS 7: 9–18.

—— (1973). *The Troad*. Oxford: Clarendon Press.

—— (1983). *The Persian Empire*. London: Dent.

CORNELL, T. J. (1995). *The Beginnings of Rome: Italy and Rome from the Bronze Age to the Punic Wars*. London: Routledge.

—— (1997). 'Ethnicity as a Factor in Early Roman History', in T. J. Cornell and K. Lomas (eds.), *Gender and Ethnicity in Ancient Italy* (Accordia Specialist Studies on Italy 6), 9–21. London: Accordia Research Centre.

COSTANZI, V. (1915). *Studi di storia macedonica fino a Filippo*. Pisa: Stabilmento tipografico toscano.

COUPEL, P., and DEMARGNE, P. (1969). *Fouilles de Xanthos*, iii. *Le Monument des Néréides*. Paris: Klincksieck.

COURTILS, J. DES (1992). 'L'architecture et l'histoire d'Argos dans la première moitié du Ve siècle avant J.C.', in M. Pièrart (ed.), *Polydipsion Argos* (*BCH* supp. 22), 241–51. Paris and Athens: De Boccard.

CROSS, A. G. N. (1932). *Epirus: A Study in Greek Constitutional Development*. Cambridge: Cambridge University Press.

CROUCH, D. (1993). *Water Management in Ancient Greek Cities*. Oxford: Clarendon Press.

CUMBERPATCH, C. G. (1995). 'Production and Society in the Later Iron Age of Bohemia and Moravia', in J. D. Hill and C. G. Cumberpatch (eds.), *Different Iron Ages: Studies on the Iron Age in Temperate Europe* (BAR int. series 602), 67–93. Oxford: British Archaeological Reports.

DAKARIS, S. I. (1964). *Οι γενεαλογικοί μύθοι των Μολοσσών*. Athens: Bibl. Ath. Arch. Etaireias 53.

—— (1971a). *Archaeological Guide to Dodona*. Athens: The Ancient Dodona Cultural Society.

—— (1971b). *Cassopaia and the Elean Colonies* (Archaies Ellenikes Poleis 4). Athens: Athens Center of Ekistics.

—— (1972). *Thesprotia* (Archaies Ellenikes Poleis 15). Athens: Athens Center of Ekistics.

DANNER, P. (1997). 'Megara, Megara Hyblaea and Selinus: The Relationship between the Town Planning of a Mother City, a Colony and Sub-colony in the Archaic Period', in *Urbanization*, 143–65.

DAUX, G. (1933). 'Notes de chronologie delphique'. *BCH* 57: 68–97.

—— (1936). *Delphes au IIe et au Ier siècle depuis l'abaissement de l'Étolie jusqu'à la paix romaine.* Paris: De Boccard.

—— (1943). *Fouilles de Delphes*, iii. *Épigraphie, Chronologie delphique* (fasc. hors série). Paris: De Boccard.

—— (1957). 'Remarques sur la composition du conseil amphictionique'. *BCH* 81: 95–120.

—— (1959). 'Inscriptions de Delphes'. *BCH* 83: 466–95.

—— (1971). 'Sur quelques inscriptions (anthroponymes, concours à Pergame, serment éphébique)'. *RÉG* 84: 350–83.

DAVIDSON, J. (1993). 'Fish, Sex and Revolution at Athens'. *CQ* NS 43: 53–66.

—— (1997). *Courtesans and Fishcakes: The Consuming Passions of Classical Athens.* London: Harper Collins.

DAVIERO ROCCHI, G. (1993). *Città-stato e stati federali della Grecia classica: Lineamenti di storia delle istituzioni politiche.* Milan: LED.

DAVIES, J. K. (1971). *Athenian Propertied Families, 600–300 BC.* Oxford: Clarendon Press.

—— (1984). 'Cultural, Social and Economic Features of the Hellenistic World', in F. W. Walbank, A. E. Astin, M. W. Frederiksen. and R M. Ogilvie (eds.), *The Cambridge Ancient History*, 2nd edn., vii/1. 257–320. Cambridge: Cambridge University Press.

—— (1993). *Democracy and Classical Greece*, 2nd edn. London: Fontana.

—— (1994a). 'On the Non-usability of the Concept of "Sovereignty" in an Ancient Greek Context', in L. A. Foresti, A. Barzanò, C. Bearzot, L. Prandi, and G. Zecchini (eds.), *Federazioni e federalismo nell'Europa antica*, i. 51–65. Milan: Università Cattolica del Sacro Cuore.

—— (1994b). 'The Tradition about the First Sacred War', in S. Hornblower (ed.), *Greek Historiography*, 193–212. Oxford: Clarendon Press.

—— (1996). 'Strutture e suddivisioni delle "*poleis*" arcaiche: Le repartizioni minori', in S. Settis (ed.), *I greci: Storia, cultura, arte, società*, 599–652. Rome: Einaudi.

—— (1997). 'The "Origins of the Greek *Polis*": Where Should We Be Looking?', in Mitchell and Rhodes, *Development*, 24–38.

—— (1998). 'Finance, Administration and *Realpolitik*: The Case of Fourth-century Delphi', in M. Austin, J. Harries, and C. Smith (eds.), *Modus Operandi: Essays in Honour of Geoffrey Rickman* (BICS supp. 71), 1–14. London: Institute of Classical Studies.

DAVIS, J. L., ALCOCK, S. E., BENNET, J., LOLOS, Y. G., and SHELMERDINE, C. W. (1997). 'The Pylos Regional Archaeological Project, Part I: Overview and the Archaeological Survey'. *Hesperia* 66: 391–494.

DE ANGELIS, F. (1994). 'The Foundation of Selinous', in F. De Angelis and G. Tsetskhladze (eds.), *The Archaeology of Greek Colonisation: Essays Dedicated to Sir John Boardman*, 87–110. Oxford: Oxford University Committee for Archaeology.

DECOURT, J.-C. (1990). *La Vallée de l'Énipeus en Thessalie: Études de topographie et de géographie antique* (*BCH* supp. 21). Athens: EFA/Paris: De Boccard.

——(1995). *Inscriptions de Thessalie*, i. *Les Cités de la vallée de l'Énipeus* (Études épigraphiques 3). Paris.

DEGER-JALKOTZY, S. (1991). 'Zum Verlauf der Periode SH IIIC in Achaia', in *Achaia und Elis*, 19–29.

DEKOULAKOU, I. (1982). 'Κεραμεική 8ου και 7ου αι. Π.Χ. από Τάφους της Αχαίας και της Αιτωλίας'. *AS Atene* 60: 219–35.

DELTOUR-LEVIE, C. (1982). *Les Piliers funéraires de Lycie*. Louvain-la-Neuve: Institut Supérieur d'Archéologie et d'Histoire de l'Art.

DEMAND, N. (1996). '*Poleis* on Cyprus and Oriental Despotism', in *CPC Papers* 3: 7–15.

DENNELL, R. (1978). *Early Farming in South Bulgaria from the Fifth to the Third Millennium BC*. (BAR int. series 45). Oxford: British Archaeological Reports.

DE POLIGNAC, F. (1984). *La Naissance de la cité grecque*. Paris: La Découverte.

——(1995). *Cults, Territory and the Origins of the Greek City-state*. Chicago: University of Chicago Press.

DESBOROUGH, V. R. D'A. (1952). *Protogeometric Pottery*. Oxford: Clarendon Press.

DE SENSI SESTITO, G. (1987). 'Taranto post-architea nel giudizio di Timeo: Nota a Strabo 6. 3. 4 C280'. *11ᵃ Miscellenea greca e romana* (Rome), 84–113.

DE SIMONE, C. (1993). 'Il santuario di Dodona e la mantica greca più antica: considerazioni linguistico-culturali', in P. Cabanes (ed.), *L'Illyrie méridionale et l'Épire dans l'antiquité*, ii. *Actes du IIᵉ colloque international de Clermont-Ferrand, 25–27 Octobre 1990*, 51–4. Paris: De Boccard.

DETEV, P. (1982). 'Le systéme d'agglomérations préhistoriques dans le bassin de la Maritsa', in *Thracia Praehistorica* (supp. Pulpudeva 3). Sofia: Bulgarian Academy of Sciences.

DEVELIN, R. (1989). *Athenian Officials, 684–321 B.C.* Cambridge: Cambridge University Press.

DI VITA, A. (1956). 'La penetrazione siracusana nella Sicilia sud-orientale alla luce delle più recenti scoperte archeologiche'. *Kokalos* 2: 177–205.

DOMARADZKI, M. (1996). 'An Interim Report on Archaeological Investigations at Vetren-Pistiros, 1988–1994', in J. Bouzek, M. Domaradzki, and Z. H. Archibald (eds.), *Pistiros*, i. *Excavations and Studies*, 13–34. Prague: Charles University.

DONLAN, W. (1980). *The Aristocratic Ideal in Ancient Greece*. Lawrence, Kan.: Coronado.

——(1985). '*Pistos Philos Hetairos*', in Figueira and Nagy, *Theognis*, 223–44.

——(1997). 'The Relations of Power in the Pre-state and Early State Polities', in Mitchell and Rhodes, *Development*, 39–48.

D'ONOFRIO, A.-M. (1997). 'The 7th Century BC in Attica: The Basis of Political Organisation', in *Urbanization*, 63–88.

DOREN, D. McN. (1974). *Winds of Crete*. London: John Murray.

DOUGHERTY, C. (1993). *The Poetics of Colonization: From City to Text in Archaic Greece*. Oxford: Clarendon Press.

DOUGLERI INTZESILOGLOU, A. (1994). 'Οι νεώτερες αρχαιολογικές έρευνες στην περιοχή των αρχαίων Φερών', in *Thessalia*, 71–92.

DOW, S. (1975). 'The Study of Lettering', in S. V. Tracy (ed.), *The Lettering of an*

Athenian Mason (*Hesperia* supp. 15), pp. xiii–xxiii. Princeton: American School of Classical Studies at Athens.

DREHER, M. (1995). 'Poleis und Nicht-Poleis im Zweiten Athenischen Seebund', in *CPC Acts* 2: 171–200.

DREWS, R. (1979). 'Phoenicians, Carthage and the Spartan *eunomia*'. *AJP* 100: 45–58.

——(1983). *Basileus: The Evidence for Kingship in Geometric Greece*. New Haven: Yale University Press.

DUBOIS, P. (1988). *Sowing the Body*. Chicago and London: University of Chicago Press.

DUCAT, P. (1997). 'Bruno Helly et les Pénestes', *Topoi* 7: 183–9.

DUNBABIN, T. J. (1936–7). '"Ἔχθρη παλαίη'. *ABSA* 37: 83–91.

——(1948). *The Western Greeks*. Oxford: Clarendon Press.

DUNN, J. (1992). *Democracy: The Unfinished Journey. 508 BC to AD 1993*. Oxford: Clarendon Press.

DUPONT, P. (1982). 'Amphores commerciales archaïques de la Grèce de l'Est'. *PdP* 37: 193–208.

DURKHEIM, É. (1984). *The Division of Labour in Society*, 2nd edn. (trans. W. D. Halls). Basingstoke: Macmillan.

DUŠANIĆ, S. (1970). *Arkadski savez IV veka* [Arcadian League of the IVth Century], in Serbian with English summary (281–345). Belgrade: Beogradski univerzitet, Filosofski fakultet.

——(1978*a*). 'Notes épigraphiques sur l'histoire arcadienne du IVᵉ siècle'. *BCH* 102: 333–58.

——(1978*b*). 'The Ὅρκον τῶν οἰκιστήρων'. *Chiron* 8: 55–76.

——(1979). 'Arkadika'. *Ath Mitt.* 94: 117–35.

EDER, W. (1995). 'Monarchie und Demokratie im 4. Jhdt. v. Chr.: Die Rolle des Fürstenspiegels in der athenischen Demokratie', in W. Eder (ed.), *Die athenische Demokratie im 4. Jhdt. v. Chr.*, 153–74. Stuttgart: Steiner.

EDMUNDS, L. (1997). 'The Seal of Theognis', in L. Edmunds and R. W. Wallace (eds.), *Poet, Public and Performance in Ancient Greece*, 29–48. Baltimore: Johns Hopkins University Press.

EDSON, C. F. (1970). 'Early Macedonia', in *Ancient Macedonia*, i. 17–44. Thessaloniki: Society for Macedonian Studies.

EFFENTERRE, H. VAN (1948). *La Crète et le monde grec de Platon à Polybe*. (BÉFAR 163). Paris: De Boccard.

——(1990). 'La notion de "ville" dans la préhistoire égéenne', in P. Darcque and R. Treuil (eds.), *L'Habitat égéen préhistorique* (*BCH* supp. 19), 485–91. Paris: De Boccard.

——and RUZÉ, F. (1994). *Nomima: Recueil d'inscriptions politiques et juridiques de l'archaïsme grec*, vol. i. Rome: EFR.

————(1995). *Nomima: Recueil d'inscriptions politiques et juridiques de l'archaïsme grec*, vol. ii. Rome: EFR.

EGGER, E. (1877). 'Inscription inédite de Dodone'. *BCH* 1: 254–8.

EHRENBERG, V. (1940). 'Isonomia'. *RE* supp. vii. 293–301.

——(1950). 'Origins of Democracy'. *Historia* 1: 515–48.

——(1956). 'Das Harmodioslied'. *WS* 69: 57–69.

EHRENBERG, V. (1960). *The Greek State*. Oxford: Blackwell.
—— (1965). *Polis und Imperium*. Zurich: Artemis.
—— (1969). *The Greek State*, 2nd edn. London: Methuen.
EKROTH, G. (1996). 'The Berbati-Limnes Archaeological Survey: The Late Geometric and Archaic Periods', in B. Wells with C. Runnels (eds.), *The Berbati-Limnes Archaeological Survey 1988–1990*, 179–227. Stockholm: Åström.
EMPÉREUR, J.-Y. (1981). 'Inscriptions de Delphes'. *BCH* 105: 417–27.
ERBSE, H. (1998). 'Theognidea'. *Hermes* 126: 238–41.
ERRINGTON, M. (1975). 'Arybbas the Molossian'. *GRBS* 16: 41–50.
—— (1978). 'The Nature of the Macedonian State under the Monarchy'. *Chiron* 8: 77–133.
EVANGELIDIS, D. E. (1935). 'Ἠπειρωτικαί ἔρευναι, Ι'. *Epeirotika Chronika* 1: 192–264.
—— (1952). 'Ἡ ἀνασκαφή τῆς Δοδώνης'. *PAE* [1955]: 279–325.
—— (1953–4). 'Ἐπιγραφή ἐκ Δοδώνης'. *AE* 92–3 [1955]: 99–103.
—— (1956). 'Ψήφισμα του βασιλέως Νεοπτολέμου ἐκ Δοδώνης'. *AE* 95: 1–13.
—— (1957). 'Τιμητικόν ψήφισμα των Μολοσσών ἐκ Δοδώνης'. *Hellenika* 15: 247–55.
FABBRICOTTI, E. (1981). 'Divinità greche e divinità libie in rilievi di età ellenistica'. *QAL* 12: 221–44.
FARRAR, C. (1988). *The Origins of Democratic Thinking*. Cambridge: Cambridge University Press.
FAURE, P. (1962). 'Cavernes et sites aux deux extrémités de Crète'. *BCH* 86: 36–56.
FERRELL, G. (1995). 'Space and Society: New Perspectives on the Iron Age of North-east England', in J. D. Hill and C. G. Cumberpatch (eds.), *Different Iron Ages: Studies on the Iron Age in Temperate Europe* (BAR int. series 602), 129–47. Oxford: British Archaeological Reports.
FIGUEIRA, T. J. (1981). *Aegina*. New York: Arno.
—— (1984). 'The Ten *Archontes* of 579/8 at Athens'. *Hesperia* 53: 447–73.
—— (1985). 'The Theognidea and Megarian Society' and 'Chronological table' in Figueira and Nagy, *Theognis*, 112–58; 261–303.
—— (1988). 'Four Notes on the Aeginetans in Exile'. *Athenaeum* 66: 523–51.
FINER, S. E. (1997). *The History of Government*. 3 vols.; Oxford: Clarendon Press.
FINLEY, M. I. (1959), 'Was Greek Civilisation Based on Slave Labour?'. *Historia* 8: 145–64; repr. in Finley (1968) 53–72 and (1981) 97–116.
—— (ed.) (1968). *Slavery in Classical Antiquity*, 2nd edn. Cambridge: Heffers.
—— (1973). *Democracy Ancient and Modern*. London: Chatto and Windus.
—— (1978). *The World of Odysseus*, 2nd rev. edn. London: Chatto and Windus.
—— (1981). *Economy and Society in Ancient Greece*, ed. B. D. Shaw and R. P. Saller. London: Chatto and Windus.
—— (1983). *Politics in the Ancient World*. Cambridge: Cambridge University Press.
—— (1985). 'Athenian Demagogues', in M. I. Finley (ed.), *Democracy Ancient and Modern*, rev. edn., 38–75. London: Hogarth Press (revised version of *P&P* 21 (1962) 3–24.
—— (1987), *Ancient Sicily*, 2nd edn. London: Chatto and Windus.
FISCHER-HANSEN, T. (1996). 'The Earliest Town-planning of the Western Greek Colonies with Special Regard to Sicily', in *CPC Acts* 3: 317–73.
FISHER, N. R. E. (1992). *Hybris*. Warminster: Aris and Phillips.
—— (1998). 'Gymnasia and the Democratic Values of Leisure', in P. Cartledge, P.

Millett, and S. Von Reden (eds.), *Kosmos: Essays in Order, Conflict and Community in Classical Athens*, 84–104. Cambridge: Cambridge University Press.

FLACELIÈRE, R. (1937). *Les Aitoliens à Delphes*. Paris: De Boccard.

FLENSTED-JENSEN, P. (1995). 'The Bottiaians and their *poleis*', in *CPC Papers* 2: 103–32.

FLETCHER, R. (1995). *The Limits of Settlement Growth*. Cambridge: Cambridge University Press.

FOLEY, A. (1988). *The Argolid 800–600 B.C.* Göteborg: Åström.

FOLLAIN, J. (1995). *A Dishonoured Society*. London: Little, Brown.

FORBES, H. (1995). 'The Identification of Pastoralist Sites within the Context of Estate-based Agriculture in Ancient Greece: Beyond the "Transhumance versus Agro-pastoralism" Debate'. *ABSA* 90: 325–38.

FORD, A. L. (1985). 'The Seal of Theognis: The Politics of Authorship in Archaic Greece', in Figueira and Nagy, *Theognis*, 82–95.

FORESTI, L. A., BARZANÒ, A., BEARZOT, C., PRANDI, L., and ZECCHINI, G. (eds.) (1994). *Federazioni e federalismo nell'Europa antica*. Milan: Università Cattolica del Sacro Cuore.

FORREST, W. G. (1960). 'Themistokles and Argos'. *CQ* NS 10: 221–41.

—— (1966). *The Emergence of Greek Democracy*. London: Weidenfeld and Nicolson.

—— (1970). 'The Date of the Pseudo-Xenophontic *Athenaion Politeia*'. *Klio* 52: 107–16.

—— (1975). 'An Athenian Generation Gap'. *YCS* 24: 37–52.

—— (1980). *A History of Sparta*, 2nd edn. London: Duckworth.

—— (1983). 'Democracy and Oligarchy in Sparta and Athens'. *EMC* 27: 285–96.

FOWLER, R. L. (1998). 'Genealogical Thinking, Hesiod's *Catalogue* and the Creation of the Hellenes'. *PCPhS* 44: 1–19.

FOXHALL, L. (1997). 'A View from the Top: Evaluating the Solonian Property Classes', in Mitchell and Rhodes, *Development*, 113–36.

—— (1998). 'The Politics of Affection: Emotional Attachments in Athenian Society', in P. Cartledge, P. Millett, and S. Von Reden (eds.), *Kosmos: Essays in Order, Conflict and Community in Classical Athens*, 52–67. Cambridge: Cambridge University Press.

FRANCISCI, P. DE (1946). *Arcana Imperii*. Milan: Giuffre.

FRANKE, P. R. (1955). *Alt-Epirus und das Königtum der Molosser*. Kallmünz: Verlag Michael Lassleben.

—— (1961). *Die antiken Münzen von Epirus*, vol. i. Wiesbaden: Steiner.

FRASER, P. M. (1954). 'A Bronze from Dodona'. *JHS* 74: 56–8.

—— and MATTHEWS, E. (1987–). *A Lexicon of Greek Personal Names*. Oxford: Clarendon Press.

FREDERIKSEN, M. W. (1984). *Campania*. London: British School at Rome.

FREI, P. (1981). Review of Metzger, Laroche, Dupont-Sommer, and Mayrhofer (1979). *BO* 38: 354–71.

—— (1990). 'Geschichte Lykiens im Altertum', in R. Jacobek and A. Dinstl (eds.), *Götter, Heroen, Herrscher in Lykien*, 7–17. Vienna: Schroll.

FRENCH, D. H. (1994). 'Isinda and Lagbe', in D. H. French (ed.), *Studies in the History and Topography of Lycia and Pisidia*, 53–92. London: BIAA.

FRIEDRICH, J. (1932). *Kleinasiatische Sprachdenkmäler*. Berlin: de Gruyter.

FROST, F. J. (1964*a*). 'Pericles and Dracontides'. *JHS* 84: 69–72.

—— (1964*b*). 'Pericles, Thucydides the Son of Melesias, and Athenian Politics before the War'. *Historia* 13: 385–99.

FUKUYAMA, F. (1992). *The End of History and the Last Man*. Harmondsworth: Penguin.

GAGER, J. G. (ed.) (1992). *Curse Tablets and Binding Spells from the Ancient World*. Oxford: Clarendon Press.

GALLIS, K. (1992). *Ἄτλας προϊστορικῶν οἰκισμῶν τῆς ἀνατολικῆς Θεσσαλικῆς πεδιάδας*. Larissa: Etairia Istorikon Erevnon Thessalia.

GARDNER, E. A. (1888). *Naukratis*, vol. ii. London: Trübner and Co.

—— LORING, W., RICHARDS, G. C., and WOODHOUSE, W. J. (1892). *Excavations at Megalopolis*. London: Society for the Promotion of Hellenic Studies.

GARNSEY, P. (1996). *Ideas of Slavery from Aristotle to Augustine*. Cambridge: Cambridge University Press.

GAUER, W. (1991). *Die Bronzegefäße von Olympia*, vol. i (Olympische Forschungen 20). Berlin: De Gruyter.

GAUTHIER, P. (1981). 'La citoyenneté en Grèce et à Rome: Participation et intégration'. *Ktéma* 6: 166–79.

—— (1985). *Les Cités grecques et leurs bienfaiteurs* (*BCH* supp. 12). Paris: De Boccard.

—— (1993). 'Les cités hellénistiques', in *CPC Acts* 1: 211–31.

GAWANTKA, W. (1975). *Isopolitie: Ein Beitrag zur Geschichte der zwischenstaatlichen Beziehungen in der griechischen Antike* (Vestigia 22). Munich: Beck.

GEBHARD, R. (1995). 'The "Celtic" *Oppidum* of Manching and its Exchange System', in J. D. Hill and C. G. Cumberpatch (eds.), *Different Iron Ages: Studies on the Iron Age in Temperate Europe* (BAR int. series 602), 111–20. Oxford: British Archaeological Reports.

GEHRKE, H.-J. (1985). *Stasis: Untersuchungen zu den inneren Kriegen in den griechischen Staaten des 5. und 4. Jahrhunderts v. Chr.* Munich: Beck.

—— (1986) *Jenseits von Athen und Sparta*. Munich: Beck.

GEORGINI, G. (1993). *La città e il tiranno*. Milan: Giuffre.

GERBER, D. E. (1991). 'Early Greek Elegy and Iambus 1921–1989'. *Lustrum* 33: 186–214.

GEROLYMATOS, A. (1986). *Espionage and Treason: A Study of the Proxenia in Political and Military Intelligence Gathering in Classical Greece*. Amsterdam: Gieben.

—— (1987). 'Nicias of Gortyn'. *Chiron* 17: 81–5.

GIGON, O. (1987). *Aristotelis Opera*, iii. *Librorum Deperditorum Fragmenta*. Berlin: De Gruyter.

GILL, D., and FOXHALL, L. (1997). 'Early Iron Age and Archaic Methana', in H. Forbes and C. Mee (eds.), *A Rough and Rocky Place*, 57–61. Liverpool: Liverpool University Press.

GINOUVÈS, R., GUIMIER-SORBETS, A.-M., JOUANNA, J., and VILLARD, L. (eds.) (1994). *L'Eau, la santé et la maladie dans le monde grec*. Paris: De Boccard.

GLIDDEN, D. K. (1981). 'The *Lysis* on Loving One's Own'. *CQ* NS 31: 39–59.

GNEISZ, D. (1990). *Das antike Rathaus: Das griechische Bouleuterion und die frührömische Curia* (doctoral dissertation, Vienna). Vienna: Verband der Wiss. Ges. Österreichs.

GOGOS, S. (1986–7). 'Kult und Heiligtümer der Artemis von Aegeira'. *ÖJh* 57: 108–39.

GOLDHILL, S. (1987). 'The Great Dionysia and Civic Ideology'. *JHS* 107: 58–78.

GOMME, A. W., ANDREWES, A., and DOVER, K. J. (1945–81). *A Historical Commentary on Thucydides*. 5 vols.; Oxford: Clarendon Press.

GOSDEN, C. (1989). 'Debt, Production and Prehistory'. *Journal of Anthropological Archaeology* 8: 355–7.

GOTSEV, A. (1997). 'Characteristics of the Settlement system during the Early Iron Age in Ancient Thrace', in *Urbanization*, 407–21.

The Gotti Tapes [Tape transcripts, no author]. London: Arrow, 1992.

GOUKOWSKY, P. (1978). *Essai sur les origines du mythe d'Alexandre*. Nancy: Université de Nancy II.

GOULD, J. P. (1973). 'Hiketeia'. *JHS* 93: 74–103.

——(1989). *Herodotus*. London: Weidenfeld and Nicolson.

GOW, A. S. F., and PAGE, D. L. (1965). *The Greek Anthology: Hellenistic Epigrams*. Cambridge: Cambridge University Press.

GRAF, D. F. (1985). 'Greek Tyrants and Achaemenid Politics', in J. W. Eadie and J. Ober (eds.), *The Craft of the Ancient Historian: Essays in Honor of Chester G. Starr*, 79–123. Lanham, Md.: University Press of America.

GRAHAM, A. J. (1964). *Colony and Mother City in Ancient Greece*. Manchester: Manchester University Press.

GRANIER, F. (1931). *Die makedonische Heeresversammlung*. Munich: Beck.

GRANT, M. (1988). 'Alternative Paths: Greek Monarchy and Federalism', in M. Grant and R. Kitzinger (eds.), *Civilization of the Ancient Mediterranean*, i. 487–494. New York: Scribner.

GREENHALGH, P. A. L. (1972). 'Aristocracy and its Advocates in Archaic Greece'. *G&R* 19: 190–207.

GREENSTEIN MILLENDER, E. (1996). ' "The Teacher of Hellas": Athenian Democratic Ideology and the "Barbarization" of Sparta in Fifth-century Greek Thought'. (Ph.D. thesis, Pennsylvania).

GRIFFIN, A. (1982). *Sikyon*. Oxford: Clarendon Press.

GROVE, D. (1972). 'The Function and Future of Urban Centres', in P. J. Ucko, R. Tringham, and G. W. Dimbleby (eds.), *Man, Settlement and Urbanism*, 559–65. London: Duckworth.

GRUEN, E. S. (1993). 'The Polis in the Hellenistic World', in R. M. Rosen and J. Farrell (eds.), *Nomodeiktes: Greek Studies in Honor of Martin Ostwald*, 339–54. Ann Arbor, MI: University of Michigan Press.

GSCHNITZER, F. (1954). 'Namen und Wesen der thessalischen Tetraden'. *Hermes* 82: 451–64.

GUARDUCCI, M. (1935). 'Un catalogo di Cretesi in una iscrizione dell'Argolide'. *Historia* (Milan) 13: 69–73.

——(1936). 'Contributi alla topografia della Creta occidentale'. *RFIC* 64 (NS 14): 153–62.

——(1938). 'Una nuova confederazione cretese, gli Orii'. *Riv Fil.* 16: 50–5.

GUSMANI, R. (1960). 'Concordanze e discordanze nella flessione nominale del licio e del luvio'. *RIL* 94: 497–512.

——(1963). 'Kleinasiatische Miszellen'. *IF* 68: 284–94.

HÄGG, R. (1982). 'Zur Stadtwerdung des dorischen Argos', in D. Papenfuss and V. M. Strocka (eds.), *Palast und Hütte*, 297–307. Mainz: von Zabern.

HALL, E. (1989). *Inventing the Barbarian: Greek Self-definition through Tragedy.* Oxford: Clarendon Press.

HALL, J. M. (1995). 'How Argive was the "Argive" Heraion? The Political and Cultic Geography of the Argive Plain, 900–400 BC'. *AJA* 99: 577–613.

—— (1997). *Ethnic Identity in Greek Antiquity.* Cambridge: Cambridge University Press.

HALSTEAD, P. (1989). 'The Economy has a Normal Surplus: Economic Stability and Social Change among Early Farming Communities of Thessaly, Greece', in P. Halstead and J. O'Shea (eds.), *Bad Year Economics: Cultural Responses to Risk and Uncertainty*, 68–80. Cambridge: Cambridge University Press.

—— (1990). 'Present to Past in the Pindhos: Diversification and Specialization in Mountain Economies'. *Rivista di studi liguri* 56: 61–80.

—— (1992). 'Agriculture in the Bronze Age: Towards a Model of Palatial Economy', in B. Wells (ed.), *Agriculture in Ancient Greece*, 105–16. Stockholm: Svenska Institutet i Athen.

HAMMOND, N. G. L. (1956). 'The Colonies of Elis in Cassopaea', in Ἀφιέρωμα εἰς τὴν Ἤπειρον, εἰς μνήμην Χρίστου Σούλη, 26–36. Athens.

—— (1967). *Epirus: The Geography, the Ancient Remains, the History and the Topography of Epirus and Adjacent Areas.* Oxford: Clarendon Press.

—— (1980a). 'Some Passages in Arrian concerning Alexander'. *CQ* NS 30: 455–76.

—— (1980b). 'The Hosts of Sacred Envoys Travelling through Epirus'. *Epeirotika Chronika* 22: 9–20.

—— (1982). 'Illyris, Epirus and Macedonia', in J. Boardman and N. G. L. Hammond (eds.), *The Cambridge Ancient History*, 2nd edn., iii/3. 261–85. Cambridge: Cambridge University Press.

—— (1989). *The Macedonian State: Origins, Institutions and History.* Oxford: Clarendon Press.

—— (1991). 'The *koina* of Epirus and Macedonia'. *ICS* 16: 183–92.

—— (1994). 'Illyrians and North-west Greeks', in D. M. Lewis, J. Boardman, S. Hornblower, and M. Ostwald (eds.), *The Cambridge Ancient History*, 2nd edn., vi. 433–43. Cambridge: Cambridge University Press.

—— GRIFFITH, G. T., and WALBANK, F. W. (1972–88). *A History of Macedonia.* 3 vols.; Oxford: Clarendon Press.

HAMPL, F. (1934). *Der König der Makedonen* (diss. phil., Leipzig). Weida: Thür.

—— (1962). 'Die Ilias ist kein Geschichtsbuch'. *Serta Philologica Aenipontana*, 37–63. Innsbruck.

HANNICK, J.-M. (1976). 'Droit et cité et mariages mixtes dans la Grèce classique'. *AC* 45: 133–48.

HÄNSEL, B. (1979). 'Ergebnisse der Grabungen bei Kastanas in Zentralmakedonien, 1975–78'. *JRGZM* 26: 167–202.

HANSEN, M. H. (1985). *Demography and Democracy.* Herning: Systime.

—— (1986). 'The Origins of the Term *Demokratia*'. *LCM* 11: 35–6.

—— (1989a). *Was Athens a Democracy? Popular Rule, Liberty and Equality in Ancient and Modern Political Thought.* Copenhagen: Royal Danish Academy of Sciences and Letters.

—— (1989*b*). 'Solonian Democracy in Fourth-century Athens'. *C&M* 40: 71–99 = W. R. Connor, M. H. Hansen, K. A. Raaflaub, and B. S. Strauss (eds.), *Aspects of Athenian Democracy* (*C&M* dissertationes 11), 71–99. Copenhagen: Museum Tusculanum.

—— (1991). *The Athenian Democracy in the Age of Demosthenes*. Oxford: Blackwell.

—— (1992). 'The Tradition of the Athenian Democracy A.D. 1750–1990'. *G&R* 39: 14–30.

—— (1993). 'The *Polis* as a Citizen-state', in *CPC Acts* 1: 7–29.

—— (1994). 'The 2500th Anniversary of Cleisthenes' Reforms and the Tradition of Athenian Democracy', in R. Osborne and S. Hornblower (eds.), *Ritual, Finance, Politics: Athenian Democratic Accounts Presented to David Lewis*, 25–37. Oxford: Clarendon Press.

—— (1995*a*). 'The "Autonomous City-state": Ancient Fact or Modern Fiction?', in *CPC Papers* 2: 21–43.

—— (1995*b*). 'Boiotian Poleis: A Test Case', in *CPC Acts* 2: 13–63.

—— (1995*c*). '*Kome*: A study in How the Greeks Designated and Classified Settlements Which were Not *Poleis*', in *CPC Papers* 2: 45–81.

—— (1996*a*). '*Πολλαχῶς πόλις λέγεται* (Arist. *Pol.* 1276ᵃ23): The Copenhagen Inventory of Poleis and the Lex Hafniensis de Civitate', in *CPC Acts* 3: 7–72.

—— (1996*b*). 'Aristotle's Two Complementary Views of the Greek Polis', in R. Wallace and E. Harris (eds.), *Transitions to Empire*, 195–210. Norman, Okla.: University of Oklahoma Press.

—— (1997*a*). '*Πόλις* as the Generic Term for State', in *CPC Papers* 4: 9–15.

—— (1997*b*). 'The Polis as an Urban Centre: The Literary and Epigraphical Evidence', in *CPC Acts* 4: 9–86.

—— (1997*c*). 'The Copenhagen Inventory of *Poleis* and the *Lex Hafniensis de Civitate*', in Mitchell and Rhodes, *Development*, 9–23.

—— and FISCHER HANSEN, T. (1994). 'Monumental Political Architecture in Archaic and Classical Greek *Poleis*: Evidence and Historical Significance', in *CPC Papers* 1: 23–90.

HANSON, V. D. (1995). *The Other Greeks*. New York: The Free Press.

HARDER, A. (1985). *Euripides' Kresphontes and Archelaos*. Leiden: Brill.

HARVEY, F. D. (1965–6). 'Two Kinds of Equality'. *C&M* 26: 101–46; 27: 99–100.

—— (1969). 'Those Epirote Women Again (*SEG*, XV, 384)'. *CPh* 64: 226–9.

—— (1984). 'The Conspiracy of Agasias and Aischines (Pl. *Arist.* 13)'. *Klio* 66: 58–73.

HATZFELD, J. (1912). 'Les Italiens résidents à Delos'. *BCH* 36: 5–218.

HATZOPOULOS, M. B. (1994). 'State and Government in Classical and Hellenistic Greece', in K. Buraselis (ed.), *Ενότητα και ενότητες της αρχαιότητας/Unity and units of antiquity*, 161–8. Athens: Nea Synora-Livani.

—— (1996). *Macedonian Institutions under the Kings: A Historical and Epigraphic Study* (Meletemata 22). 2 vols.; Athens: National Hellenic Research Foundation.

HAYWARD, C. L. (1996). 'High-resolution Provenance Determination of Construction-stone: A Preliminary Study of Corinthian Oolitic Limestone Quarries at Examilia'. *Geoarchaeology* 11: 215–34.

—— (forthcoming). 'Geology of Corinth: Study of a Basic Resource'. *Proceedings of a Conference to Mark the Centennial of the Corinth Excavations* (*Athens, December 1996*). Princeton: ASCSA.

HEAD, B. V. (1911). *Historia Numorum*, 2nd edn. Oxford: Clarendon Press.

HECKEL, W. (1992). *The Marshals of Alexander's Empire*. London: Routledge.

HELLY, B. (1970). 'La convention des Basaidai'. *BCH* 94: 161–89.

—— (1995). *L'État thessalien: Aleuas le Roux, les Tétrades et les Tagoi* (Collection de la maison de l'Orient Mediterranéen 25, série épigraphique 2). Lyons.

—— (1997). 'Arithmétique et histoire. L'organisation militaire et politique des Ioniens en Achaïe à l'époque archaïque'. *Topoi Orient–Occident* 7: 207–62.

HENRICHS, A. (1968). 'Zur Interpretation des Michigan-Papyrus über Theramenes'. *ZPE* 3: 101–8.

HERMAN, G. (1987). *Ritualised Friendship and the Greek City*. Cambridge: Cambridge University Press.

—— (1994). 'How Violent was Athenian Society?', in R. Osborne and S. Hornblower (eds.), *Ritual, Finance, Politics: Athenian Democratic Accounts Presented to David Lewis*, 99–117. Oxford: Clarendon Press.

HERRING, E. (1991). 'Sociopolitical Change in the South Italian Iron Age and Classical Periods: An Application of the Peer Polity Interaction Model'. *Accordia Research Papers* 2: 33–54.

HERRMANN, P. (1970). 'Zu den Beziehungen zwischen Athen und Milet im 5. Jahrhundert'. *Klio* 2: 163–73.

HESKEL, J. (1988). 'The Political Background of the Arybbas Decree'. *GRBS* 29: 185–96.

HEURTLEY, W. G. (1939). *Prehistoric Macedonia*. Cambridge: Cambridge University Press.

HIGNETT, C. (1963). *Xerxes' Invasion of Greece*. Oxford: Clarendon Press.

HILL, G. F. (1897). *Catalogue of the Greek Coins of Lycia, Pamphylia and Pisidia*. London: Trustees of the British Museum.

—— MEIGGS, R., and ANDREWES, A. (1951). *Sources for Greek History between the Persian and Peloponnesian Wars*, 2nd edn. Oxford: Clarendon Press.

HILL, J. D. (1995). 'How Should We Understand Iron Age Societies and Hillforts? A Contextual Study from Southern Britain', in Hill and Cumberpatch (1995), 45–66.

—— and CUMBERPATCH, C. G. (eds.) (1995). *Different Iron Ages: Studies on the Iron Age in Temperate Europe* (BAR int. series 602). Oxford: British Archaeological Reports.

HODGES, R. (1987). 'Spatial Models, Anthropology and Archaeology', in J. M. Wagstaff (ed.), *Landscape and Culture: Geographical and Archaeological Perspectives*, 118–33. Oxford: Blackwell.

HODKINSON, S. (1986). 'Land Tenure and Inheritance in Classical Sparta'. *CQ* NS 36: 378–406.

—— (1988). 'Animal Husbandry in the Greek Polis', in C. R. Whittaker (ed.), *Pastoral Economies in Classical Antiquity* (Cambridge Philological Society, supp. 14), 35–74. Cambridge.

—— (1989). 'Inheritance, Marriage and Demography', in A. Powell (ed.), *Classical Sparta: Techniques behind her Success*, 79–121. London: Routledge.

—— (1997). 'The Development of Spartan Society and Institutions in the Archaic Period', in Mitchell and Rhodes, *Development*, 83–102.

HOEPFNER, W., and SCHWANDNER, E.-L. (1986). *Haus und Stadt im klassischen Griechenland*. Munich: Deutscher Kunstverlag.

HORNBLOWER, S. (1982). *Mausolus*. Oxford: Clarendon Press.

—— (1983). *The Greek World 479–323 BC*. London: Methuen.

—— (1990). 'When was Megalopolis Founded?' *ABSA* 85: 71–7.

—— (1991). *A Commentary on Thucydides*, vol. i. Oxford: Clarendon Press.

—— (1994a). 'Persia', in D. M. Lewis, J. Boardman, S. Hornblower, and M. Ostwald (eds.), *The Cambridge Ancient History*, 2nd edn., vi. 45–96. Cambridge: Cambridge University Press.

—— (1994b). 'Asia Minor', in D. M. Lewis, J. Boardman, S. Hornblower, and M. Ostwald (eds.), *The Cambridge Ancient History*, 2nd edn., vi. 209–33. Cambridge: Cambridge University Press.

HOUWINK TEN CATE, P. (1961). *The Luwian Population Groups of Lycia and Cilicia Aspera*. Leiden: Brill.

HOW, W. W., and WELLS, J. (1912). *A Commentary on Herodotus*, vol. i. Oxford: Clarendon Press.

HOWGEGO, C. (1990). 'Why did Ancient States Strike Coins?' *NC* 150: 1–25.

HUDSON-WILLIAMS, T. (1910). *The Elegies of Theognis*. London: Bell.

HUMPHREYS, S. C. (1978). 'Town and Country in Ancient Greece', in S. C. Humphreys (ed.), *Anthropology and the Greeks*, 130–5. London: Routledge.

HÜTTL, W. (1929). *Verfassungsgeschichte von Syrakus*. Prague: Franz Kraus.

HUXLEY, G. L. (1961). *Crete and the Luwians*. Oxford: 126a High Street.

—— (1966). *The Early Ionians*. London: Faber.

JACOBS, B. (1987). *Griechische und persische Elemente in der Grabkunst Lykiens zur Zeit der Achämenidenherrschaft*. Jonsered: P. Åström.

JACOBY, F. (1931). 'Theognis'. *SÖAW* 10: 90–180.

JACQUEMIN, A. (1993). 'Répercussions de l'éntrée de Delphes dans l'amphictionie sur la construction à Delphes à l'époque archaïque', in J. des Courtils and J.-C. Moretti (eds.), *Les Grands Ateliers d'architecture dans le monde egéen du vi^e siècle av. J.C.* (*Actes du colloque d'Istanbul, 23–25 mai 1991*), 217–25. Paris: De Boccard.

JAEGER, W. (1939). *Paedeia: The Ideals of Greek Culture* (trans. G. Highet). Oxford: Clarendon Press.

JAMESON, M. H., RUNNELS, C. N., and VAN ANDEL, TJ. (1994). *A Greek Countryside: The Southern Argolid from Prehistory to the Present Day*. Stanford, Calif.: Stanford University Press.

JEFFERY, L. H. (1973–4). 'Demiourgoi in the Archaic Period'. *ArchClass* 25–6: 319–30.

—— (1976). *Archaic Greece: The City-states c. 700–500 B.C.* London: Methuen.

—— (1990). *The Local Scripts of Archaic Greece*, 2nd edn., ed. A. W. Johnston. Oxford: Clarendon Press.

JENKINS, G. K. (1959). 'Recent Acquisitions of Greek Coins by the British Museum'. *NC* 19: 23–45.

JOHNSON, D. L. (1973). *Jabal-al-Akhdar, Cyrenaica: An Historical Geography of Settlement and Livelihood*. Chicago: University of Chicago, Department of Geography.

368   *Bibliography*

JOHNSTON, A. W. (1989). 'Aeginetans Abroad'. *Horos* 7: 131–5.

JONES, A. H. M. (1971). *The Cities of the Eastern Roman Provinces*, 2nd edn. Oxford: Clarendon Press.

JONES, C. P. (1996). '"Eθνος and γένος in Herodotus'. *CQ* NS 46: 315–20.

JONES, J. E. (1982). 'The Laurion Silver Mines: A Review of Recent Researches and Results'. *G&R* 29: 169–83.

JONES, N. F. (1987). *Public Organization in Ancient Greece: A Documentary Study*. Philadelphia: American Philosophical Society.

KAKRIDIS, H. I. (1963). 'La notion de l'amitié et de l'hospitalité chez Homère' (doctoral dissertation, Paris). Thessaloniki: Bibliotheke tou Philosophou.

KARAMITROU-MENDESIDI, G. (1993). *Kozani, City of Elimiotis: Archaeological Guide*. Thessaloniki.

KARDULIAS, P. N. (ed.) (1994). *Beyond the Site: Regional Studies in the Aegean Area*. Lanham, Md.: University Press of America.

KATAKOUTA, S., and TOUFEXIS, G. (1994). 'Τα τείχη της Φαρσάλου', in *Thessalia*, 189–200.

KEEN, A. G. (1992). 'Dynastic tombs of Xanthos'. *AS* 42: 53–63.

——(1993). 'Athenian Campaigns in Karia and Lykia during the Peloponnesian War'. *JHS* 113: 152–7.

——(1998). *Dynastic Lycia: A Political History of the Lycians and their Relations with Foreign Powers, c. 545–362 BC*. Leiden: Brill.

——(forthcoming (*a*)). 'The Poleis of the Southern Anatolian coast and their Civic Identity', in A. M. Snodgrass and G. R. Tsetskhladze (eds.), *Greek Settlements in the Eastern Mediterranean and the Black Sea*. Oxford: British Archaeological Reports.

——(forthcoming (*b*)). 'An Inventory of Lykian *Poleis* in the Archaic and Classical Periods', in M. H. Hansen and S. Hornblower (eds.), *Inventory of Archaic and Classical Greek Poleis*. Oxford: Clarendon Press.

KELLY, D. H. (1981). 'Policy-making in the Spartan Assembly'. *Antichthon* 15: 47–61.

KELLY, T. (1966). 'The Calaurian Amphictyony'. *AJA* 70: 113–21.

KENT, R. G. (1943). 'Old Persian Texts IV'. *JNES* 2: 302–6.

KEULS, E. C. (1993). *The Reign of the Phallus: Sexual Politics in Ancient Athens*, 2nd edn. Berkeley: University of California Press.

KEYT, D., and MILLER, F. D., Jr. (eds.) (1991). *A Companion to Aristotle's Politics*. Oxford: Blackwell.

KIENAST, D. (1973). *Philipp II. von Makedonien und das Reich der Achaimeniden*. Munich: Fink.

KIENAST, H. (1995). *Die Wasserleitung des Eupalinos auf Samos*. Bonn: Habelt.

KLAFFENBACH, G. (1966). *Griechische Epigraphik*, 2nd edn. Göttingen: Vandenhoeck and Ruprecht.

KLEINER, G., HOMMEL, P., and MÜLLER-WIENER, W. (1967). *Panionion und Melie* (*JDAI* supp. 23). Berlin: de Gruyter.

KNIGGE, U. (1990). *The Athenian Kerameikos*. Athens: Krene.

KOERNER, R. (1974). 'Die staatliche Entwicklung in Alt-Achaia'. *Klio* 56: 457–95.

KOKKINOU, D., and TRANTALIDOU, K. (1991). 'Neolithic and Bronze Age Settlement in Western Macedonia'. *ABSA* 86: 93–106.

KOLB, F., and KUPKE, B. (1992). *Lykien*. Mainz: Philipp von Zabern.

KOLDEWEY, R. (1890). *Die antiken Baureste der Insel Lesbos*. Berlin: Reimer.

KONSTAN, D. (1997). *Friendship in the Ancient World*. Cambridge: Cambridge University Press.

KONTIS, G. D. (1978). *Λέσβος και η μικρασιατική της περιοχή*. Athens: AGC.

KORCHAGIN, YU. V. (1981). 'The Formation of the Arcadian League' (in Russian with brief English summary). *Vestnik Leningradskogo Universiteta* 20: 84–7.

KOTSAKIS, K., and ANDREOU, S. (1992). *'Επιφανειακή έρευνα Λαγκαδά· Περίοδος 1992'*. *AEMTh* 6 (1995): 349–56.

KOUKOULI-CHRYSANTHAKI, C. (1982). 'Late Bronze Age in Eastern Macedonia', in *Thracia Praehistorica* (supp. Pulpudeva 3), 1978: 231–58. Sofia.

KOUROU, N. (1980). *'Ταφικό σύνολο από την περιοχή Αιγίου'*, in *Στήλη· Τόμος εις μνήμην Νικόλαου Κοντολέοντος*, 313–17. Athens: *Σωματείο οι Φίλοι του Νικολάου Κοντολέοντος*.

KOURTESSI-PHILIPPAKIS, G. (1993). 'Les plus anciennes occupations humaines dans le territoire épirote et aux confins de l'Illyrie méridionale', in P. Cabanes (ed.), *L'Illyrie méridionale et l'Épire dans l'antiquité*, ii. *Actes du IIᵉ colloque international de Clermont-Ferrand, 25–27 octobre 1990*, 11–16. Paris: De Boccard.

KRAAY, C. M. (1964). 'Hoards, Small Change, and the Origins of Coinage'. *JHS* 84: 76–91.

——(1976). *Archaic and Classical Greek Coins*. London: Methuen.

KRASILNIKOFF, J. A. (1995). 'The Power Base of Sicilian Tyrants', in T. Fischer-Hansen (ed.), *Ancient Sicily* (Acta Hyberborea 6), 171–84. Copenhagen: Museum Tusculanum.

KRENTZ, P. (1982). *The Thirty at Athens*. Ithaca, NY: Cornell University Press.

KRISTIANSEN, K. (1991). 'Chiefdoms, States and Systems of Social Evolution', in T. Earle (ed.), *Chiefdoms: Power, Economy and Ideology*, 111–16. Cambridge: Cambridge University Press.

KURKE, L. (1991). *The Traffic in Praise: Pindar and the Poetics of Social Economy*. London and Ithaca, NY: Cornell University Press.

——(1992). 'The Politics of *ἁβροσύνη* in Archaic Greece', *ClAnt* 11: 91–120.

——(1994). 'Crisis and Decorum in Sixth-century Lesbos: Reading Alkaios Otherwise'. *QUCC* ns 47: 67–92.

LA GENIÈRE, J. DE (1979). 'The Iron Age in Southern Italy', in D. Ridgway and F. R. Ridgway (eds.), *Italy before the Romans*, 59–94. Edinburgh: Edinburgh University Press.

LAKAKIS, M. (1991). *'Αγροτικοί οικισμοί στη Δυμαία χώρα· η περίπτωση του Πετροχωρίου'*, in *Achaia und Elis*, 241–6.

LANG, F. (1996). *Archaische Siedlungen in Griechenland*. Berlin: Akademie Verlag.

LANZA, D. (1977). *Il tiranno e il suo pubblico*. Turin: Einaudi.

LAROCHE, D., and NENNA, M.-D. (1993). 'Études sur les trésors en Poros à Delphes', in J. des Courtils and J.-C. Moretti (eds.), *Les Grands Ateliers d'architecture dans le monde égéen du VIᵉ siècle av. J.C. (Actes du colloque d'Istanbul, 23–25 mai 1991)*, 227–45. Paris: De Boccard.

LAROCHE, E. (1957–8). 'Comparaison du louvite et du lycien'. *BSL* 53: 159–97.

——(1960). 'Comparaison du louvite et du lycien'. *BSL* 55: 155–85.

——(1967). 'Comparaison du louvite et du lycien'. *BSL* 62: 46–94.

LAROCHE, E. (1974). 'Les épitaphes lyciennes', in P. Demargne, *Fouilles de Xanthos*, v. *Tombes-maisons, tombes rupestres et sarcophages*, 123–48. Paris: Klincksieck.

—— (1979). 'L'inscription lycienne', in H. Metzger, E. Laroche, A. Dupont-Sommer, and M. Mayrhofer, *Fouilles de Xanthos*, vi. *La Stèle trilingue du Létôon*, 49–127. Paris: Klincksieck.

LARONDE, A. (1987). *Cyrène et la Libye hellénistique: Libykai Historiai*. Paris: CNRS.

—— (1988). 'Cyrène sous les derniers Battiades', in B. Gentili (ed.), *Cirene: Storia, mito, letteratura*, 35–50. Urbino: QuattroVenti.

—— (1990). 'Greeks and Libyans in Cyrenaica', in J. P. Descœudres (ed.), *Greek Colonists and Native Populations*, 169–80. Oxford: Clarendon Press.

LARSEN, J. A. O. (1955). *Representative Government in Greek and Roman History*. Berkeley: University of California Press.

—— (1964). 'Epirote Grants of Citizenship to Women'. *CPh* 58: 106–7.

—— (1967). 'Epirote Grants of Citizenship to Women Once More'. *CPh* 62: 255–6.

—— (1968). *Greek Federal States: Their Institutions and History*. Oxford: Clarendon Press.

LAWTON, C. L. (1992). 'Sculptural and Epigraphical Restorations to Attic Documents'. *Hesperia* 61: 239–51.

—— (1995). *Attic Document Reliefs*. Oxford: Clarendon Press.

LAZENBY, J. F. (1993). *The Defence of Greece, 490–479 B.C.* Warminster: Aris and Phillips.

LEGON, R. P. (1967). 'Phliasian Politics and Policy in the Early Fourth Century B.C.' *Historia* 16: 324–37.

—— (1981). *Megara: The Political History of a Greek City-state to 336 B.C.* Cornell, NY: Cornell University Press.

LEGRAND, P. E. (1894). 'Léonidas de Crète?' *RÉG* 7: 192–5.

LEIWO, M. (1995). *Neapolitana: A Study of Population and Language in Graeco-Roman Naples*. Helsinki: Societas Scientarum Fennica.

LEPORE, E. (1962). *Ricerche sull'antico Epiro: Le origini storiche e gli interessi greci*. Naples: Libreria Scientifica Editrice.

LE RIDER, G. (1966). *Monnaies crétoises du Ve au Ier siècle av. J.-C.* (Études crétoises 15). Paris: Geuthner.

LÉVÊQUE, P. (1957a). *Pyrrhos*. (BEFAR 185). Paris: De Boccard.

—— (1957b). 'Recherches nouvelles sur l'histoire d'Épire'. *RÉG* 70: 488–99.

—— (1998). 'L'État thessalien', *Topoi* 8: 267–9.

LÉVY, E. (1978). 'La monarchie macédonienne et le mythe d'une royauté démocratique'. *Ktéma* 5: 210–13.

LEWIS, D. M. (1962). 'The Federal Constitution of Keos'. *ABSA* 57: 1–4 = *Selected Papers in Greek and Near Eastern History* (Cambridge: Cambridge University Press, 1997), 22–8.

—— (1977). *Sparta and Persia*. Leiden: Brill.

—— (1997). *Selected Papers in Greek and Near Eastern History*. Cambridge: Cambridge University Press.

LINTOTT, A. (1982). *Violence, Civil Strife and Revolution in the Classical City*. London: Croom Helm.

—— (1992). 'Aristotle and Democracy'. *CQ* NS 42: 114–28 = J. Dunn and I. Harris (eds.), (1997). *Aristotle*, ii. 477–91. Cheltenham: Elgar.

—— (1997). 'The Theory of the Mixed Constitution at Rome', in J. Barnes and M. Griffin (eds.), *Philosophia Togata*, ii. *Plato and Aristotle at Rome*, 70–85. Oxford: Clarendon Press.

LLOYD, C. (1983). 'Greek Urbanity and the *Polis*', in R. Marchese (ed.), *Aspects of Graeco-Roman Urbanism*. (BAR int. series 188), 11–41. Oxford: British Archaeological Reports.

LLOYD, J. A., OWENS, E. J., and ROY, J. (1988). 'Tribe and Polis in the Chora of Megalopolis: Changes in Settlement Pattern in Relation to Synoecism', in *Proceedings of the 12th International Congress of Classical Archaeology* 4 (Athens: PUB), 179–82.

LOHMANN, H. (1992). 'Agriculture and Country Life in Classical Attica', in B. Wells (ed.), *Agriculture in Ancient Greece*, 29–57. Stockholm: Svenska Institutet i Athen.

LOMAS, K. (1993*a*). *Rome and the Western Greeks: Conquest and Acculturation in Southern Italy, 350 B.C.–A.D. 200*. London: Routledge.

—— (1993*b*). 'The City in South-east Italy: Ancient Topography and the Evolution of Urban Settlement, 600–300 BC'. *Accordia Research Papers* 4: 63–77.

—— (1997). 'Constructing "the Greek": Ethnic Identity in Magna Graecia', in T. J. Cornell and K. Lomas (eds.), *Gender and Ethnicity in Ancient Italy*, 31–42. London: Accordia Research Centre.

LONDEY, P. (1984). 'Philip II and the Delphic Amphictyony'. *MeditArch* 7: 25–34.

LORAUX, N. (1986). *The Invention of Athens: The Funeral Oration in the Classical City* (Eng. trans.). Cambridge, Mass.: Harvard University Press.

—— (1993). *The Children of Athena* (Eng. trans.). Princeton: Princeton University Press.

—— and VIDAL-NAQUET, P. (1979). 'La formation de l'Athènes bourgeoise: Essai d'historiographie', in R. R. Bolgar (ed.), *Classical Influences on Western Thought, 1650–1870*, 169–222. Cambridge: Cambridge University Press; trans. as 'The Formation of Bourgeois Athens', in P. Vidal-Naquet (ed.), *Politics, Ancient and Modern*, 82–140. Cambridge: Polity Press (1979).

MACDOWELL, D. M. (1963). *Athenian Homicide Law in the Age of the Orators*. Manchester: Manchester University Press.

—— (1971). *Aristophanes:* Wasps, *Edited with Introduction and Commentary*. Oxford: Clarendon Press.

—— (1986). *Spartan Law*. Edinburgh: Scottish Academic Press.

—— (1995). *Aristophanes and Athens*. Oxford: Clarendon Press.

McGLEW, J. F. (1993). *Tyranny and Popular Culture in Ancient Greece*. Ithaca, NY: Cornell University Press.

McINERNEY, J. (1994). 'Ethnos and Topography: The Rise of Phokian Power in the Fourth Century' (Ph.D. dissertation, Pennsylvania).

McKECHNIE, P. (1989). *Outsiders in the Greek Cities in the 4th century BC*. London: Routledge.

MADDOLI, G. (1982). 'Il concetto di Magna Grecia: Genesi di un concetto e realtà storico-politiche', in *Megale Hellas: Nome e immagine. Atti del 21° Convegno di studi sulla Magna Grecia*, 9–30. Taranto: Istituto per la storia e l'archeologia della Magna Grecia.

MAIER, F. G. (1994). 'Cyprus and Phoenicia', in D. M. Lewis, J. Boardman, S.

Hornblower, and M. Ostwald (eds.), *The Cambridge Ancient History*, 2nd edn., vi. 297–336. Cambridge: Cambridge University Press.

MALKIN, I. (1994*a*). *Myth and Territory in the Spartan Mediterranean*. Cambridge: Cambridge University Press.

—— (1994*b*). 'Inside and Outside: Colonization and the Formation of the Mother City', in B. d'Agostino and D. Ridgway (eds.), *Apoikia: Scritti in onore di Giorgio Buchner* (AnnArchStorAnt 1/Aion 16), 1–9.

MARCHETTI, P. (1977). 'A propos des comptes de Delphes sous les archontats de Théon (324/3) et de Caphis (327/6)'. *BCH* 101: 133–45.

MARROU, H. I. (1965). *Histoire de l'éducation dans l'antiquité*. Paris: Éditions du Seuil.

MARTIN, R. (1951). *Recherches sur l'agora grecque*. Paris: De Boccard.

—— (1974). *L'Urbanisme dans la Grèce antique*, 2nd edn. Paris: Picard.

—— (1980). 'L'espace dans les cités grecques', in *Architecture et société*, 9–41. Paris/Rome: CNRS/EFR.

MARTIN, T. R. (1985). *Sovereignty and Coinage in Classical Greece*. Princeton: Princeton University Press.

MARZOLFF, P. (1980). *Demetrias III.: Die deutschen archäologischen Forschungen in Thessalien*. Bonn: Habelt.

MASON, H. J. (1995). 'The End of Antissa'. *AJP* 116: 399–410.

MASSON, O. (1985). 'Cretica VII: Un groupe de noms crétois locaux: Τάσκος, τασκάνδας, etc.'. *BCH* 109: 195–7.

MATTINGLY, D. J. (1997). 'Dialogues of Power and Experience in the Roman Empire', in D. J. Mattingly (ed.), *Dialogues in Roman Imperialism: Power, Discourse and Discrepant Experience in the Roman Empire* (Journal of Roman Archaeology supp. 23), 7–26. Portsmouth, RI: Journal of Roman Archaeology.

MAY, J. M. F. (1939). *The Coinage of Damastion and the Lesser Coinages of the Illyro-Paeonian Region*. London: Oxford University Press.

MAZARAKIS AINIAN, A. (1997). *From Ruler's Dwellings to Temples*. Åström: Jonsered.

MEIER, C. (1980). *Die Entstehung des Politischen bei den Griechen*. Frankfurt: Suhrkamp.

—— (1990). *The Greek Discovery of Politics*. Cambridge, Mass.: Harvard University Press.

—— and VEYNE, P. (1988). *Kannten die Griechen die Demokratie?* Berlin: Wagenbach.

MEIGGS, R. (1964). 'A Note on the Population of Athens'. *CR* NS 14: 23.

—— (1972). *The Athenian Empire*. Oxford: Clarendon Press.

—— (1982). *Trees and Timber in the Ancient Mediterranean World*. Oxford: Clarendon Press.

—— and LEWIS, D. M. (1969). *A Selection of Greek Historical Inscriptions to the End of the Fifth Century B.C.* Oxford: Clarendon Press.

MELCHERT, H. C. (1993). *Lycian Lexicon*, 2nd edn. Chapel Hill.

MELONI, P. (1951). 'La tirannide di Euphrone in Sicione'. *Riv. di filol.* 79: 10–33.

MENDELS, D. (1984). 'Aetolia 331–301: Frustration, Political Power, and Survival'. *Historia* 33: 129–80.

MERKELBACH, R., and YOUTIE, H. C. (1968). 'Ein Michigan-Papyrus über Theramenes'. *ZPE* 2: 161–9.

MERSCH, A. (1997). 'Urbanisation of the Attic Countryside from the Late 8th Century to the 6th Century BC', in *Urbanization*, 45–62.

METZGER, H. (ed.) (1992). *Fouilles de Xanthos*, ix. *La Région nord du Létôon: Les sculptures. Les inscriptions gréco-lyciennes.* Paris: Klincksieck.

—— LAROCHE, E., DUPONT-SOMMER, A., and MAYRHOFER, M. (1979). *Fouilles de Xanthos*, vi. *La stèle trilingue du Létôon.* Paris: Klincksieck.

MILLER, M. C. (1997). *Athens and Persia in the Fifth Century BC: A Study in Cultural Receptivity.* Cambridge: Cambridge University Press.

MILLER, S. G. (1978). *The Prytaneion: Its Function and Architectural Form.* Berkeley and Los Angeles, Calif.: University of California Press.

—— (1988). 'The theorodokoi of the Nemean Games'. *Hesperia* 58: 147–63.

—— (1995a). 'Old Metroon and Old Bouleuterion in the Classical Agora of Athens', in *CPC Papers* 2: 133–56.

—— (1995b). 'Architecture as Evidence for the Identity of the Early *Polis*', in *CPC Acts* 2: 201–44.

MILLETT, P. (1985). 'Patronage and its Avoidance in Classical Athens', in A. Wallace-Hadrill (ed.), *Patronage in Ancient Society*, 15–48. London: Routledge.

MILOJČIĆ, V., and THEOCHARIS, D. (1976). *Demetrias I.: Die deutschen archäologischen Forschungen in Thessalien.* Bonn: Habelt.

MIRANDA, E. (1990). *Iscrizioni greche di Napoli.* Rome: Quasar.

MITCHELL, B. M. (1966). 'Cyrene and Persia'. *JHS* 86: 99–113.

—— (1974). 'Chronology of the Reign of Arkesilas III'. *JHS* 94: 174–8.

—— (1975). 'Polycrates and Samos'. *JHS* 95: 75–91.

MITCHELL, L. G. (1997a). *Greeks Bearing Gifts.* Cambridge: Cambridge University Press.

—— (1997b). 'Φιλία, εὔνοια and Greek Interstate Relations'. *Antichthon* 31: 28–44.

—— and RHODES, P. J. (1996). 'Friends and Enemies in Athenian Politics'. *G&R* 43: 11–30.

MOGGI, M. (1975). 'Συνοικίζειν in Tucidide'. *ASNPS* iii/5: 915–24.

—— (1976). *I sinecismi interstatali greci*, i. *Dalle origini al 338 a.c.* Pisa: Marlin.

MOMIGLIANO, A. (1935). 'Re e popolo in Macedonia prima di Alessandro'. *Athenaeum* 13: 3–21.

—— (1959). 'Atene nel III secolo a.C. e la scoperta di Roma nelle storie di Timeo di Tauromenio'. *RSI* 76: 529–56.

MOREL, J. P. (1983). 'Greek Colonisation in Italy and the West', in T. Hackens, N. D. Holloway, and R. R. Holloway (eds.), *The Crossroads of the Mediterranean*, 123–62. Louvain: Catholic University of Louvain Press.

MORETTI, L. (1957). 'Olympionikai: I vincitori negli antichi agoni olimpici', *Atti della Accademia Nazionale dei Lincei, Classe di scienze morali, stor. e filol., Memorie*, ser. 8, viii/2. 53–198. Rome.

—— (1976). *Iscrizioni storiche ellenistiche.* Florence: La Nuova Italia.

MORGAN, C. (1988). 'Corinth, the Corinthian Gulf and Western Greece during the Eighth Century BC'. *ABSA* 83: 313–38.

—— (1990). *Athletes and Oracles.* Cambridge: Cambridge University Press.

—— (1991). 'Ethnicity and Early Greek States: Historical and Material Perspectives'. *PCPhS* 37: 131–63.

—— (1994). 'The Evolution of a Sacral "Landscape": Isthmia, Perachora and the

Early Corinthian State', in S. Alcock and R. Osborne (eds.), *Placing the Gods*, 105–42. Oxford: Clarendon Press.

—— (1997). 'The Archaeology of Sanctuaries in Early Iron Age and Archaic Ethne: A Preliminary View', in Mitchell and Rhodes, *Development*, 168–98.

—— (1999). 'Cultural Subzones in Early Iron Age and Archaic Arkadia?', in *CPC Acts* 6: 382–456.

—— (2001). 'Ethne, Ethnicity and Early Greek States, ca. 1200–480: An Archaeological Perspective', in I. Malkin (ed.), *Ancient Perceptions of Greek Ethnicity*. Washington and Harvard: Center for Hellenic Studies/Harvard University Press, 75–112.

—— and COULTON, J. J. (1997). 'The Polis as a Physical Entity', in *CPC Acts* 4: 87–144.

—— and HALL, J. M. (1996). 'Achaian Poleis and Achaian Colonisation', in *CPC Acts* 3: 164–232.

—— and WHITELAW, T. (1991). 'Pots and Politics: Ceramic Evidence for the Rise of the Argive State'. *AJA* 95: 79–108.

MØRKHOLM, O. (1964). 'The Classification of Lycian Coins before Alexander the Great'. *JNG* 14: 65–76.

—— and NEUMANN, G. (1978). *Die lykische Münzlegende*. Göttingen: Vanderhoeck und Ruprecht.

—— and ZAHLE, J. (1972). 'The Coinage of Kuprlli'. *AArch* 43: 57–113.

—— —— (1976). 'The Coinages of the Lycian Dynasts'. *AArch* 47: 47–90.

MORLEY, N. D. G. (1996). *Metropolis and Hinterland: The City of Rome and the Italian Economy, 200 B.C.–A.D. 200*. Cambridge: Cambridge University Press.

MORRIS, I. (1986). 'Gift and Commodity in Archaic Greece'. *Man* 21: 1–17.

—— (1987). *Burial and Ancient Society*. Cambridge: Cambridge University Press.

—— (1991). 'The Early Polis as City and State', in J. Rich and A. Wallace-Hadrill (eds.), *City and Country in the Ancient World*, 24–57. London: Routledge.

—— (1994). 'Everyman's Grave', in A. L. Boegehold and A. C. Scafuro (eds.), *Athenian Identity and Civic Ideology*, 67–101. Baltimore, Md.: Johns Hopkins University Press.

MOSSÉ, C. (1969). *La Tyrannie dans la Grèce antique*. Paris: Presses Universitaires de France.

—— (1979). 'Citoyens actifs et citoyens "passifs" dans les cités grecques: Une approche théorique du problème'. *RÉA* 81: 241–9.

—— (1995). 'La classe politique à Athènes au IVème siècle', in W. Eder (ed.), *Die athenische Demokratie im 4. Jahrhundert v. Chr.*, 67–77. Stuttgart: Steiner.

MULGAN, R. G. (1977). *Aristotle's Political Theory*. Oxford: Clarendon Press.

MULLIEZ, D. (1997). 'La réforme d'Aleuas le Roux et ses avatars'. *Topoi* 7: 191–206.

MURAKAWA, K. (1957). 'Demiurgos'. *Historia* 6: 385–415.

MURRAY, O. (1988a). 'The Ionian Revolt', in J. Boardman, N. G. L. Hammond, D. M. Lewis, and M. Ostwald (eds.), *The Cambridge Ancient History*, 2nd edn., iv. 461–90. Cambridge: Cambridge University Press.

—— (1988b). 'Greek Forms of Government', in M. Grant and R. Kitzinger (eds.), *Civilization of the Ancient Mediterranean: Greece and Rome*, i. 439–86. New York: Scribner.

—— (ed.) (1990). *Sympotica*. Oxford: Clarendon Press.

—— (1993). *Early Greece*, 2nd edn. London: Fontana.

MUSTI, D. (1988). *Strabone e Magna Grecia*. Padua: Programma.

NAGY, G. (1985). 'Theognis and Megara: A Poet's Vision of his City', in Figueira and Nagy, *Theognis*, 22–81.

NENCI, G. (1953). *Pirro: Aspirazioni egemoniche ed equilibrio mediterraneo* (*Pubbl. fac. lett. fil.* 5/2). Turin: Università.

NEUMANN, G. (1979). *Neufunde lykischer Inschriften seit 1901*. Vienna: Österreichischen Akademie der Wissenschaften.

—— (1990). 'Die lykische Sprache', in *Götter, Heroen, Herrscher in Lykien*, 38–40. Vienna: Schroll.

NEWMAN, W. L. (1887–1902). *The Politics of Aristotle*. 4 vols.; Oxford: Clarendon Press.

NIELSEN, T. H. (1996a). 'Arkadia: City-ethnics and Tribalism', in *CPC Acts* 3: 117–63.

—— (1996b). 'Was there an Arkadian Confederacy in the Fifth Century B.C.?', in *CPC Papers* 3: 39–61.

—— (1996c). 'A Survey of Dependent *Poleis* in Classical Arkadia', in *CPC Papers* 3: 63–105.

—— (1996d). 'Πολλᾶν ἐκ πολίων: The Polis Structure of Arkadia in the Archaic and Classical Periods' (Ph.D. thesis, University of Copenhagen).

—— (1997). 'Triphylia: An Experiment in Ethnic Construction and Political Organisation', in *CPC Papers* 4: 129–62.

—— (1999). 'The Concept of Arkadia: The People, their Land and their Organisation', in *CPC Acts* 6: 16–79.

—— and ROY, J. (eds.) (1999). *Defining Ancient Arkadia* = *CPC Acts* 6.

NINIOU-KINDELE, B. (1990). 'Στοιχεία για την οδικήν σύνδεση της Λισσού με την Υρτακίνα και την Ελύρου'. Πεπραγμένα του ΣΤ' Διεθνούς Κρητολογικού Συνεδρίου. Α2: 49–58.

NIPPEL, W. (1980). *Mischverfassungstheorie und Verfassungsrealität in Antike und früher Neuzeit*. Stuttgart: Klett-Cotta.

NIXON, L., and PRICE, S. (1990). 'The Size and Resources of Greek Cities', in O. Murray and S. Price (eds.), *The Greek City from Homer to Alexander*, 137–70. Oxford: Clarendon Press.

NOSHY, I. (1968). 'Arkesilas III', in F. F. Gadallah (ed.), *Libya in History*, 53–78. Benghazi: University of Libya.

OAKLEY, J. H. (1992). 'An Athenian Red-figure Workshop from the Time of the Peloponnesian War', in F. Blondé and J.-Y. Perreault (eds.), *Les Ateliers de potiers dans le monde grec aux époques géométrique, archaïque et classique*, 195–203. Paris: De Boccard.

OBER, J. (1989). *Mass and Elite in Democratic Athens*. Princeton: Princeton University Press.

OGDEN, D. (1997). *The Crooked Kings of Ancient Greece*. London: Routledge.

OLIVERIO, G. (1933). *I conti dei demiurgi* (DAI 1/2). Bergamo: Istituto d'arti grafiche.

O'NEIL, J. L. (1995). *The Origins and Development of Ancient Greek Democracy*. Lanham, Md.: Rowman and Littlefield.

OOST, S. I. (1973). 'The Megara of Theagenes and Theognis'. *CPh* 68: 186–96.

OSBORNE, M. J. (1981–3). *Naturalization in Athens*. 4 vols. in 3; Brussels: Paleis der Academien.

OSBORNE, R. (1985). *Demos: The Discovery of Classical Attika*. Cambridge: Cambridge University Press.

—— (1987). *Classical Landscape with Figures*. London: George Philip.

—— (1994). 'Athenian Democracy: Something to Celebrate?'. *Dialogos: Hellenic Studies Review* 1: 48–58.

—— (1995). 'The Economics and Politics of Slavery at Athens', in A. Powell (ed.), *The Greek World*, 27–43. London and New York: Routledge.

—— (1996). *Greece in the Making, 1200–479 B.C.* London: Routledge.

—— (1997). 'Law and Laws: How Do We Join Up the Dots?' in Mitchell and Rhodes, *Development*, 74–82.

—— (1998). 'Early Greek Colonisation? The Nature of Greek Settlement in the West', in N. Fisher and H. van Wees (eds.), *Archaic Greece: New Approaches and New Evidence*, 251–67. London: Duckworth/The Classical Press of Wales.

ØSTBY, E. (1995a). 'I templi di Pallantion', in *AS Atene*, 68–9/51–2 [*Scavi di Pallantion*] for 1990–1: 53–93.

—— (1995b). 'Templi di Pallantion e dell'Arcadia', in *AS Atene*, 68–9/51–2 [*Scavi di Pallantion*] for 1990–1: 285–391.

OSTWALD, M. (1969). *Nomos and the Beginnings of Athenian Democracy*. Oxford: Clarendon Press.

—— (1986). *From Popular Sovereignty to the Sovereignty of Law*. Berkeley, Calif.: University of California Press.

OWENS, E. J. (1991). *The City in the Greek and Roman World*. London: Routledge.

PAGE, D. L. (1955). *Sappho and Alcaeus*. Oxford: Clarendon Press.

PANAYOTOU, A. (1986). 'An Inscribed Pithos Fragment from Aiane (W. Macedonia)'. *Kadmos* 25: 97–101.

PAPADOPOULOS, J. K. (1996). 'The Original Kerameikos of Athens and the Siting of the Classical Agora'. *GRBS* 37: 107–28.

PAPADOPOULOS, T. (1979). *Mycenaean Achaea*. Göteborg: Åström.

PAPAKONSTANTINOU-DIAMANTOROU, D. (1990). 'Χώρα Θεσσαλονίκης· Μια προσπάθεια οριοθέτησης'. in *Πόλις και χώρα στην αρχαία Μακεδονία και Θράκη. Μνήμη Δ. Λαζαρίδη*, 99–106. Thessaloniki: TAP.

PAPAKOSTA, L. (1991). 'Παρατηρήσεις σχετικά με την τοπογραφία του αρχαίου Αιγίου', in *Achaia und Elis*, 235–40.

PAPAPOSTOLOU, I. (1990). 'Ιστορικές μαρτυρίες και αρχαιολογικά ευρήματα της κλασσικής και της πρώιμης Ελληνιστικής πόλης των Πατρών', in K. G. Panitsas (ed.), *Τόμος τιμηικός Κ. Ν. Τριανταφύλλου*, i. 465–71. Patras: G. Petraki.

PAPAZOGLOU, F. (1978). *The Central Balkan Tribes in Pre-Roman Times*. Amsterdam: Hakkert.

—— (1986). 'Politarques en Illyrie'. *Historia* 35: 438–48.

PARASKEVAIDES, P. S. (1983). *Οι περιηγητές για τη Λέσβο*, 2nd edn. Athens: Vivliopoleio ton Vivliofilon.

PARKE, H. W. (1967). *The Oracles of Zeus: Dodona, Olympia, Ammon*. Oxford: Blackwell.

—— and BOARDMAN, J. (1957). 'The Struggle for the Tripod and the First Sacred War'. *JHS* 77: 276–82.

PARKER, R. (1983). *Miasma*. Oxford: Clarendon Press.

—— (1996). *Athenian Religion: A History*. Oxford: Clarendon Press.

—— (1998). *Cleomenes on the Acropolis*. Oxford: Clarendon Press.

PARKER, V. (1997). *Untersuchungen zum Lelantischen Krieg und verwandten Probleme der frühgriechischen Geschichte* (Historia Einzelschriften 109). Stuttgart: Steiner.

PARLANGELI, O. (1960). *Studi messapici*. Milan: Istituto Lombardo di Scienze e Lettere.

PARRY, G. (1969). *Political Elites*. London: Allen and Unwin.

PASHLEY, R. (1837). *Travels in Crete*. Cambridge: Pitt/London: John Murray.

PATTERSON, C. (1981). *Pericles' Citizenship Law of 451–50 BC*. New York: Arno Press.

PEARSON, L. (1987). *The Greek Historians of the West: Timaeus and his Predecessors*. Atlanta: Scholars Press.

PEDERSEN, H. (1945). *Lykisch und Hittitisch*. Copenhagen: Munksgaard.

PEDLEY, J. G. (1990). *Paestum*. London: Thames and Hudson.

PELLIZER, E. (1990). 'Outlines of a Morphology of Sympotic Entertainment', in O. Murray (ed.), *Sympotica*, 177–184. Oxford: Clarendon Press.

PERLMAN, P. (1992). 'One Hundred-citied Crete and the "Cretan Πολιτεία"'. *CPh* 87: 193–205.

—— (1995). '*Theorodokountes en tais polesin*: Panhellenic *Epangelia* and Political Status', in *CPC Acts* 2: 113–64.

PERROT, G. (1867). *L'Île de Crète: Souvenirs de voyage*. Paris: Hachette.

PETRIE, W. H. F. (1886). *Naukratis*, vol. i. London: Trübner and Co.

PETRONOTIS, A. (1973). *Η Μεγάλη Πόλις της Αρκαδίας*. Athens.

PETROPOULOS, M. (1987–8). 'Τρίτη ανασκαφική περίοδος στο Ανω Μαζαράκι (Ρακίτα) Αχαΐας', in Πρακτικά του Γ´ Διεθνούς Συνεδρίου Πελοποννησιακών Σπουδών, ii. 81–96. Athens.

—— (1990). 'Ἀρχαιολογικές έρευνες στην Αχαΐα', in K. G. Paritsas (ed.), *Τόμος τιμητικός Κ. Ν. Τριανταφύλλου*, i. 495–537. Patras: G. Petraki.

—— (1991). 'Τοπογραφικά της χώρας των Πατρέων', in *Achaia und Elis*, 249–58.

—— (1992–3). 'Περίπτερος αψιδωτός γεωμετρικός ναός στο Ανω Μαζαράκι (Ρακίτα) Πατρών', in Πρακτικά του Δ´ Διεθνούς Συνεδρίου Πελοποννησιακών Σπουδών, ii. 141–58. Athens.

—— (1994a). 'Ἀγροικίες Πατραϊκές', in *Structures rurales*, 405–24.

—— (1994b). 'Τα εργαστήρια τών ρωμαϊκών λυχναριών της Πάτρας και το Λυχνομαντείο' (Ph.D. thesis, University of Ioannina).

—— and RIZAKIS, A. D. (1994). 'Settlement Patterns and Landscape in the Coastal Area of Patras: Preliminary Report'. *JRA* 7: 183–207.

PICCIRILLI, L. (1974). 'Fliunte e il presunto colpo di stato democratico'. *ASNP* ser. iii/4: 59–70.

PIKOULAS, I. A. (1988). *Η νότια μεγαλοπολιτική χώρα από τον 8ο π.Χ. ως τον 4ο μ.Χ. αιώνα*. Athens: Horos.

—— (1995). *Οδικό δίκτυο και άμυνα*. Athens: Horos.

PLASSART, A. (1921). 'Inscriptions de Delphes: La liste des théorodoques'. *BCH* 45: 1–85.

PLAUMANN, G. (1913). 'ἑταῖροι'. *RE* viii/2. 1374–80.

POPE, M. (1988). 'Thucydides and Democracy'. *Historia* 37: 276–96.

POPHAM, M. R., SACKETT, L. H., and THEMELIS, P. G. (eds.) (1979–80). *Lefkandi*, i. *The Iron Age: The Settlement and the Cemeteries*. London: Thames and Hudson/ British School at Athens.

—— TOULOUPA, E., and SACKETT, L. H. (1982). 'The Hero of Lefkandi'. *Antiquity* 56: 169–74.

POUILLOUX, J. (1952). 'Promanties collectives et protocole delphique'. *BCH* 76: 484–513.

POWELL, A. (1988). *Athens and Sparta: Constructing Greek Political and Social History from 478 B.C.* London: Routledge.

—— and HODKINSON, S. (eds.) (1994). *The Shadow of Sparta*. London and New York: Routledge/ The Classical Press of Wales.

PRESTIANNI-GIALLOMBARDO, A. M., and TRIPODI, B. (1996). 'Iconografia monetale e ideologia reale macedone: I tipi del cavaliere nella monetazione di Alessandro I e di Filippo II'. *RÉA* 98: 311–55.

PRITCHETT, W. K. (1974). *The Greek State at War*, vol. ii. Berkeley, Calif.: University of California Press.

PURCELL, N. (1990). 'Mobility and the *Polis*', in O. Murray and S. Price (eds.), *The Greek City: From Homer to Alexander*, 29–58. Oxford: Clarendon Press.

QUINN, T. J. (1981). *Athens and Samos, Lesbos and Chios*. Manchester: Manchester University Press.

RAAFLAUB, K. (1983). 'Democracy, Oligarchy and the Concept of the "Free Citizen" in Late Fifth-century Athens'. *Political Theory* 11: 517–44.

—— (1989). 'Contemporary Perceptions of Democracy in Fifth-century Athens'. *C&M* 40: 33–70.

—— (1997). 'Soldiers, Citizens and the Evolution of the Early Greek *Polis*', in Mitchell and Rhodes, *Development*, 49–59.

RACKHAM, O., and MOODY, J. (1996). *The Making of the Cretan Landscape*. Manchester: Manchester University Press.

RAHE, P. A. (1980). 'The Selection of Ephors at Sparta'. *Historia* 29: 385–401.

RANDOLPH, B. (1687). *The Present State of the Islands in the Archipelago etc.* Oxford: Printed at the theater.

RAPP, G., and KRAFT, J. C. (1994). 'Holocene Coastal Change in Greece and Aegean Turkey', in P. N. Kardulias (ed.), *Beyond the Site: Regional Studies in the Aegean Area*, 69–90. Lanham, Md.: University Press of America.

RAUBITSCHEK, A. E. (1982). 'The Dedication of Aristokrates', in *Studies in Attic Epigraphy, History and Topography Presented to Eugene Vanderpool by Members of the American School of Classical Studies* (*Hesperia* supp. 19), 130–2. Princeton: American School of Classical Studies at Athens.

RAULIN, V. (1869). *Description physique de l'Isle de Crète*. Paris: Bertrand.

REDFIELD, J. M. (1986). 'The development of the Market in Archaic Greece', in B. L. Anderson and A. J. H. Latham (eds.), *The Market in History*, 29–58. London: Croom Helm.

RENFREW, C., and GIMBUTAS, M. (eds.) (1986). *Excavations at Sitagroi: A Prehistoric Village in North-east Greece* (Monumenta Archaeologica 13). Los Angeles: UCLA Institute of Archaeology.

—— and WAGSTAFF, M. (eds.) (1982). *An Island Polity: The Archaeology of Exploration in Melos*. Cambridge: Cambridge University Press.

REYES, A. T. (1994). *Archaic Cyprus*. Oxford: Clarendon Press.

REYNOLDS, J. M. (1981). 'Cirene e i libyi', in S. Stucchi (ed.), *Libyans and Greeks in Rural Cyrenaica* (Quaderni dell'archeologia di Libya 12), 378–83.

RHODES, P. J. (1972a). *The Athenian Boule*. Oxford: Clarendon Press.

—— (1972b). 'The Five Thousand in the Athenian revolution of 411 B.C.' *JHS* 92: 115–27.

—— (1979–80). 'Athenian Democracy after 403 B.C.' *CJ* 75: 305–23.

—— (1981a). *A Commentary on the Aristotelian Athenaion Politeia*. Oxford: Clarendon Press.

—— (1981b). 'The Selection of Ephors at Sparta'. *Historia* 30: 498–502.

—— (1992). 'The Athenian Revolution', in D. M. Lewis, J. Boardman, J. K. Davies, and M. Ostwald (eds.), *The Cambridge Ancient History*, 2nd edn., v. 62–95. Cambridge: Cambridge University Press.

—— (1993). 'The Greek Poleis: Demes, Cities, and Leagues', in *CPC Acts* 1: 161–82.

—— (1994). 'The Polis and the Alternatives', in D. M. Lewis, J. Boardman, S. Hornblower, and M. Ostwald (eds.), *The Cambridge Ancient History*, 2nd edn., vi. 565–91. Cambridge: Cambridge University Press.

—— (1995a). 'Epigraphical Evidence: Laws and Decrees', in *CPC Acts* 2: 91–112.

—— (1995b). 'Judicial Procedures in Fourth-century Athens: Improvement or Simply Change?', in W. Eder (ed.), *Die athenische Demokratie im 4. Jahrhundert v. Chr.*, 303–19. Stuttgart: Steiner.

—— with LEWIS, D. M. (1997). *The Decrees of the Greek States*. Oxford: Clarendon Press.

RIDGWAY, D. (1992). *The First Western Greeks*. Cambridge: Cambridge University Press.

RIHLL, T. E., and WILSON, A. G. (1991). 'Modelling Settlement Structures in Ancient Greece: New Approaches to the *Polis*', in J. Rich and A. Wallace-Hadrill (eds.), *City and Country in the Ancient World*, 59–95. London: Routledge.

RIZAKIS, A. D. (1992). *Paysages d'Achaie*, i. *Le Bassin du Peiros et la plaine occidentale*. Athens: KERA/Paris: De Boccard.

—— (1995). *Achaie*, i. *Sources textuelles et histoire régionale*. Athens: KERA/Paris: De Boccard.

ROBERTS, B. K. (1996). *Landscapes of Settlement*. London: Routledge.

ROBERTS, J. T. (1994). *Athens on Trial: The Antidemocratic Tradition in Western Thought*. Princeton: Princeton University Press.

ROBINSON, D. M. (ed.) (1929–52). *Excavations at Olynthus*. 14 vols.; Baltimore, Md.: Johns Hopkins University.

ROBINSON, E. S. G. (1928). 'Pseudoeginetica'. *NC* ser. 5: 172–98.

ROBINSON, E. W. (1997). *The First Democracies:. Early Popular Government outside Athens* (Historia Einzelschriften 107). Stuttgart: Steiner.

ROEBUCK, C. (1955). 'The Early Ionian League'. *CPh* 50: 26–40.

ROESCH, P. (1965). *Thespies et la Confédération béotienne*. Paris: De Boccard.

—— (1985). *Le Béotie antique*. Paris: CNRS.

ROMBOS, T. (1988). *The Iconography of Attic LGII Pottery*. Jonsered: Åström.

ROUSSEL, D. (1976). *Tribu et cité*. Paris: Les Belles Lettres.

380   *Bibliography*

ROUX, G. (1979). *L'Amphictionie, Delphes, et le temple d'Apollon au IVe siècle* (Collection de la Maison de l'Orient Méditerranéen, Sér. archéol. 6). Paris: De Boccard.

ROY, J. (1971). 'Arcadia and Boeotia in Peloponnesian Affairs, 370–62 B.C.' *Historia* 20: 569–99.

——(1972). 'Orchomenus and Clitor'. *CQ* NS 22: 78–80.

——(1974). 'Postscript on the Arcadian League'. *Historia* 23: 505–7.

——(1994). 'Thebes in the 360s BC', in D. M. Lewis, J. Boardman, S. Hornblower, and M. Ostwald (eds.), *The Cambridge Ancient History*, 2nd edn., vi. 187–208. Cambridge: Cambridge University Press.

——(1996). '*Polis* and Tribe in Classical Arkadia', *CPC Papers* 3: 107–12.

RUSCHENBUSCH, E. (1966). 'Ephialtes'. *Historia* 15: 369–76.

——(1979). *Athenische Innenpolitik im 5. Jahrhundert v. Chr.* Bamberg: aku.

——(1985). 'Die Zahl der griechischen Staaten und Arealgröße und Bürgerzahl der "Normalpolis"'. *ZPE* 59: 253–63.

RUTTER, N. K. (1979). *Campanian Coinage, 475–380 BC*. Edinburgh: Edinburgh University Press.

RUZÉ, F. (1983). 'Les tribus et la décision politique dans les cités grecques archaïques et classiques'. *Ktéma* 8 [1986]: 299–306.

RYFFEL H. (1949). *Metabolê Politeiôn: Der Wandel der Staatsverfassungen*. Bern: Haupt.

SAÏD, S. (1985). *Sophiste et tyran; ou, Le Problème du Prométhée enchaînée*. Paris: Klincksieck.

STE CROIX, G. E. M. DE (1972). *The Origins of the Peloponnesian War*. London: Duckworth.

——(1975). 'Political Pay outside Athens'. *CQ* NS 25: 48–52.

——(1981). *The Class Struggle in the Ancient Greek World*. London: Duckworth.

SAKELLARIOU, M. B. (1989). *The Polis-state: Definition and Origin*. Athens: KERA/ Paris: De Boccard.

SALLARES, R. (1991). *The Ecology of the Ancient Greek World*. London and Ithaca, NY: Duckworth and Cornell University Press.

SALMON, J. B. (1984). *Wealthy Corinth: A History of the City to 338 B.C.* Oxford: Clarendon Press.

——(1997). 'Lopping off the heads? Tyrants, Politics and the *Polis*', in Mitchell and Rhodes, *Development*, 60–73.

SALMON, P. (1978). *Étude sur la Confédération béotienne*. Brussels: Académie Royale.

SANTORO, C. (1982). *Nuovi studi messapici*. Galantina: Congedo Editore.

SARTORI, F. (1953). *Problemi di storia costituzionale italiota*. Rome: Bretschneider.

——(1957). *Le eterie nella vita politica ateniese del VI e V secolo a.-C.* Rome: Bretschneider.

SAUNDERS, T. J. (1993). 'Aristotle and Bagehot on Constitutional Deception', in H. D. Jocelyn and H. Hurt (eds.), *Tria Lustra* (Liverpool Classical Papers 3), 45–57. Liverpool.

SAVALLI, I. (1988). 'L'idéologie dynastique des poèmes grecs de Xanthos'. *AC* 47: 103–23.

SCAFURO, A. C. (1994). 'Introduction: Bifurcations and Intersections', in A. L. Boegehold and A. C. Scafuro (eds.), *Athenian Identity and Civic Ideology*, 1–20. Baltimore Md.: Johns Hopkins University Press.

SCHACHTER, A. (1981). *Cults of Boeotia*, vol. i. London: Institute of Classical Studies.

SCHAEFER, H. (1961). '*Πόλις μυρίανδρος*'. *Historia* 10: 292–317.

——(1962). '*Prostátes*'. *RE* supp. ix. 1287–304.

SCHALLIN, A. L. (1997). 'Urban Centres, Central Places and Nucleation in Greek Islands versus the Greek Mainland', in *Urbanization*, 17–44.

SCHAUS, G. P., and SPENCER, N. (1994). 'Notes on the Topography of Eresos'. *AJA* 98: 411–30.

SCHEID-TISSINIER, E. (1994). 'A propos du rôle et de la fonction de l'*ἵστωρ*'. *RPh* 68: 187–208.

SCHMIDT, M. (1858–64). *Lexicon Hesychii Alexandrini*. 4 vols.; Jena: F. Mauk.

SCHMITT, H. H. (1969). *Die Staatsverträge des Altertums*, vol. iii. Munich: Beck.

SCHÜTRUMPF, E. (1994). 'Aristotle on Sparta', in A. Powell and S. Hodkinson (eds.), *The Shadow of Sparta*, 323–45. London and New York: Routledge/The Classical Press of Wales.

SCHWEYER, A.-V. (1996). 'Le pays lycien'. *RA* 3–68.

SEAFORD, R. (forthcoming). 'Tragic Tyranny'.

SEAGER, R. (1967). 'Alcibiades and the Charge of Aiming at Tyranny'. *Historia* 16: 6–18.

SEALEY, R. (1960). 'Regionalism in Archaic Athens'. *Historia* 9: 155–80.

——(1964). 'Ephialtes'. *CPh* 59: 11–22.

——(1967). *Essays in Greek History*. New York: Manyland.

——(1976). *A History of the Greek City States, ca. 700–338 B.C.* Berkeley and Los Angeles: University of California Press.

——(1981). 'Ephialtes, *Eisangelia* and the Council', in G. S. Shrimpton and D. J. McCargar (eds.), *Classical Contributions: Studies in Honour of M. F. McGregor*, 125–34. Locust Valley, NY: Augustin.

SHEAR, T. L., Jr. (1973). 'The Athenian Agora: Excavations of 1971'. *Hesperia* 42: 121–79.

——(1994). '*Ἰσονόμους τ' Ἀθήνας ἐποιησάτην*: The Agora and Democracy', in Coulson et al., *Archaeology*, 225–48.

——(1995). 'Bouleuterion, Metroon and the Archives at Athens', in *CPC Papers* 2: 157–90.

SHEPHERD, G. (1995). 'The Pride of Most Colonials: Burial and Religion in the Sicilian Colonies', in T. Fischer-Hansen (ed.), *Ancient Sicily* (Acta Hyberborea 6), 51–82. Copenhagen: Museum Tusculanum.

SHERWIN WHITE, S. M. (1978). *Ancient Cos*. Göttingen: Vandenhoeck and Ruprecht.

——(1987). 'Seleucid Babylonia', in A. Kuhrt and S. Sherwin-White (eds.), *Hellenism in the East*, 1–31. Berkeley: University of California Press.

SHIPLEY, G. (1987). *A History of Samos 800–188 B.C.* Oxford: Clarendon Press.

SIGANIDOU, M. (1993). *La Civilisation grecque: Macédoine, royaume d'Alexandre le Grand*, Catalogue of the exhibition, Montreal, 7 May–19 Sept. 1993, 29–31. Athens: Kapon.

SIMON, E., HIRMER, M., and HIRMER, A. (1981). *Die griechischen Vasen*, 2nd edn. Munich: Hirmer.

SINCLAIR, R. (1987). *Democracy and Participation in Classical Athens*. Cambridge: Cambridge University Press.

SIX, J.-P. (1887). *Monnaies lyciennes*. Paris.

SJÖQVIST, E. (1973). *Sicily and the Greeks*. Ann Arbor: University of Michigan Press.

SKYDSGAARD, J. E. (1988). 'Transhumance in Ancient Greece', in C. R. Whittaker (ed.), *Pastoral Economies in Classical Antiquity* (*PCPhS* supp. 14), 75–86.

SLATER, P. (1968). *The Glory of Hera*. Boston: Beacon Press.

SMITH, C. J., and SERRATI, J. (eds.) (2000). *Sicily from Aeneas to Cicero: New Approaches in History and Archaeology*. Edinburgh: Edinburgh University Press.

SMITH, M. G. (1972). 'Complexity, Size and Urbanization', in P. J. Ucko, R. Tringham, and G. W. Dimbleby (eds.), *Man, Settlement and Urbanism*, 567–74. London: Duckworth.

SNODGRASS, A. M. (1971). *The Dark Age of Greece*. Edinburgh: Edinburgh University Press.

—— (1980). *Archaic Greece: The Age of Experiment*. London: Dent.

—— (1987). *An Archaeology of Greece: The Present State and Future Scope of a Discipline*. Berkeley: University of California Press.

—— (1990). 'Survey Archaeology and the Rural Landscape of the Greek City', in O. Murray and S. Price (eds.), *The Greek City from Homer to Alexander*, 113–36. Oxford: Clarendon Press.

—— (1994). 'The Nature and Standing of the Early Western Colonies', in G. R. Tsetskhladze and F. De Angelis (eds.), *The Archaeology of Greek Colonisation*, 1–10. Oxford: Oxford University Committee for Archaeology.

—— (1995). 'The Site of Askra', in P. Roesch and G. Argoud (eds.), *La Béotie antique*, 87–95. Paris: CNRS.

SORDI, M. (1958). *La lega tessala fino ad Alessandro Magno* (Studi ist. Ital. Stor. Ant. 15). Rome.

—— (1997). 'I *tagoi* tessali come suprema magistratura militare del *Koinon* tessalico', *Topoi* 7: 177–82.

SOUEREF, K. (1997). 'Ἐπισημάνσεις ἱστορικῆς τοπογραφίας για την περιοχή Τούμπα Θεσσαλονίκη', in Αφιέρωμα στον *N. G. L. Hammond*, 407–21. Thessaloniki: Hetaireia Makedonikon Spoudon.

See also Sueref, C.

SPENCE, I. G. (1993). *The Cavalry of Classical Greece*. Oxford: Clarendon Press.

SPENCER, N. (1993). '*Asty* and *chora* in early Lesbos' (Ph.D. Dissertation, King's College, London).

—— (1994). 'Towers and Enclosures of Lesbian Masonry in Lesbos: Rural Investment in the *Chora* of Archaic *Poleis*', in *Structures rurales*, 207–13.

—— (1995a). *A Gazetteer of Archaeological Sites in Lesbos* (BAR int. series 623). Oxford: British Archaeological Reports.

—— (1995b). 'Multi-dimensional Group Definition in the Landscape of Rural Greece', in N. Spencer (ed.), *Time, Tradition and Society in Greek Archaeology: Bridging the 'Great Divide'*, 24–42. London: Routledge.

—— (1995c). 'Early Lesbos between East and West: A "Grey Area" of Aegean Archaeology'. *ABSA* 90: 269–306.

SPIER, J. (1987). 'Lycian Coins in the "Decadrachm Hoard"', in I. Carradice (ed.), *Coinage and Administration in the Athenian and Persian Empires* (BAR int. series 343), 29–41. Oxford: British Archaeological Reports.

SPRATT, T. A. B. (1856). *Travels and Researches in Crete*. London: van Voorst.

SPYRIDAKIS, S. (1970). *Ptolemaic Itanos and Hellenistic Crete* (Univ. Cal. Publ. in History 82). Berkeley: University of California Press.

SPYROPOULOS, T. (1993). 'Νέα γλυπτά αποκτήματα του Αρχαιολογικού Μουσείου Τριπόλεως', in O. Palagia and W. Coulson (eds.), *Sculpture from Arcadia and Laconia*, 257–66. Oxford: Oxbow.

STAGAKIS, G. J. (1975). *Studies in the Homeric Society* (Historia Einzelschriften 26). Wiesbaden: Steiner.

STAHL, M. (1987). *Aristokraten und Tyrannen im archaischen Athen.* Stuttgart: Steiner.

STARR, C. G. (1977). *The Economic and Social Growth of Early Greece.* New York: Oxford University Press.

STEIN-HÖLKESKAMP, E. (1989). *Adelskultur und Polisgesellschaft.* Stuttgart: Steiner.

STEWART, C. T. (1958). 'The Size and Spacing of Cities: An Ecological Approach'. *American Geographical Review* 48: 222–45.

STILLE, A. (1994). *Excellent Cadavers.* London: Cape.

STOCKTON, D. (1990). *The Classical Athenian Democracy.* Oxford: Clarendon Press.

STROUD, R. S. (1984). 'The Gravestone of Socrates' Friend, Lysis'. *Hesperia* 53: 355–60.

STUCCHI, S. (1965). *L'Agora di Cirene*, vol. i. Rome: L'Erma di Bretschneider.

STUPPERICH, R. (1994). 'The Iconography of Athenian State Burials in the Classical Period', in Coulson *et al.*, *Archaeology*, 93–103.

SUEREF, C. (1993). 'Presupposti della colonizzazione lungo le coste epirote', in P. Cabanes (ed.), *L'Illyrie méridionale et l'Épire dans l'antiquité*, ii. *Actes du IIe colloque international de Clermont-Ferrand, 25–27 octobre 1990*, 29–46. Paris: De Boccard.

See also Soueref, K.

SVORONOS, J.-N. (1888). 'Monnaies crétoises inédites et incertaines'. *Revue numismatique*, 3rd ser. 6: 353–95.

——(1890). *Numismatique de la Crète ancienne.* Mâcon. Repr. with additions, Bonn, 1972: Habelt.

SWAIN, S. R. (1994). 'Man and Medicine in Thucydides'. *Arethusa* 27: 303–27.

TAUSEND, K. (1992). *Amphiktyonie und Symmachie* (Historia Einzelschriften 73). Stuttgart: Steiner.

TAYLOR, M. W. (1981). *The Tyrant Slayers: The Heroic Image in Fifth Century BC Athenian Art and Politics.* New York: Arno.

THEMELIS, P. G. (1983). 'An 8th Century Goldsmith's Workshop at Eretria', in R. Hägg (ed.), *The Greek Renaissance of the 8th Century BC*, 157–65. Stockholm: Åström.

THIRIET, F. (1959). *La Romanie vénitienne au Moyen Âge.* Paris: De Boccard.

THOMAS, R. (1989). *Oral Tradition and Written Record in Classical Athens.* Cambridge: Cambridge University Press.

——(1992). *Literacy and Orality in Ancient Greece.* Cambridge: Cambridge University Press.

THOMPSON, M., MØRKHOLM, O., and KRAAY, C. M. (1973). *An Inventory of Greek Coin Hoards.* New York: American Numismatic Society.

THOMPSON, W. E. (1970). 'The Politics of Phlius'. *Eranos* 68: 224–30.

THOMPSON, W. E. (1973). 'Observations on Spartan Politics'. *Rivista storica dell'antichità* 3: 47–58.

—— (1983). 'Arcadian Factionalism in the 360s'. *Historia* 32: 149–60.

TOMLINSON, R. A. (1972). *Argos and the Argolid*. London: Routledge and Kegan Paul.

TRAMPEDACH, K. (1994). *Platon, die Akademie und die zeitgenössische Politik* (Hermes Einzelschriften 66). Stuttgart: Steiner.

TRAVLOS, J. (1988). *Bildlexikon zur Topographie des antiken Attika*. Tübingen: Wasmuth.

TRÉHEUX, J. (1980). 'Sur les comptes du conseil à Delphes'. *BCH* 104: 519–24.

—— (1987). '*Koinon*'. *RÉA* 89: 39–46.

—— (1989). 'Sur les *probouloi* en Grèce'. *BCH* 113: 241–2.

TREUBER, O. (1887). *Geschichte der Lykier*. Stuttgart: Kohlhammer.

TRIGGER, B. (1972). 'Determinants of Urban Growth in Pre-industrial Societies', in P. J. Ucko, R. Tringham, and G. W. Dimbleby (eds.), *Man, Settlement and Urbanism*, 575–99. London: Duckworth.

TRITSCH, F. (1950). 'Lycian, Luwian, and Hittite'. *ArchOrient* 18/1–2: 494–518.

TSETSKHLADZE, G. R., and DE ANGELIS, F. (eds.) (1994). *The Archaeology of Greek Colonisation*. Oxford: Oxford University Committee for Archaeology.

TSIOLIS, V. (1995). 'El "Thersilion" de Megalópolis: Funciones y cronología'. *Gerión* 13: 47–68.

TUPLIN, C. J. (1985). 'Imperial Tyranny: Some Reflections on a Classical Greek Political Metaphor', in P. A. Cartledge and F. D. Harvey (eds.), *Crux: Essays in Greek History Presented to G. E. M. de Ste. Croix*, 348–75. Exeter: Imprint Academic/London: Duckworth.

—— (1993). *The Failings of Empire: A Reading of Xenophon* Hellenica *2. 3. 11–7. 5. 27* (Historia Einzelschriften 76). Stuttgart: Steiner.

TZIAPHALIAS, A. (1994). 'Δεκαπέντε χρόνια ανασκαφών στην αρχαία Λάρισα', in *Thessalia*, 153–78.

UGUZZONI, A., and GHINATTI, F. (1968). *Le tavole greche di Eraclea*. Rome: Bretschneider.

VALLET, G., and VOZA, G. (1984). *Dal neolitico all'era industriale nel territorio da Augusta a Siracusa*. Syracuse: Assessorato Regionale Beni Culturali e Ambientali—Soprintendenza alle Antichità per la Sicilia Orientale.

VAN ANDEL, TJ., and RUNNELS, C. (1987). *Beyond the Acropolis: A Rural Greek Past*. Stanford, Calif.: Stanford University Press.

—— (1995). 'The Earliest Farmers in Europe'. *Antiquity* 69/264: 481–500.

VAN DER LEEUW, S. E. (1981). 'Information Flows, Flow Structures and the Explanation of Change in Human Institutions', in S. E. van der Leeuw (ed.), *Archaeological Approaches to the Study of Complexity*, 229–312. Amsterdam: Albert Egges van Griffen Instituut voor Prae- en Protohistorie.

VAN GRONINGEN, B. A. (1966). *Theognis: Le Premier Livre*. Amsterdam: Noord-Hollandsche Uitg. Mij.

VAN WEES, H. (1992). *Status Warriors: War, Violence and Society in Homer and History*. Amsterdam: Gieben.

—— (1995*a*). 'Princes at Dinner: Social Event and Social Structure in Homer', in J. P. Crielaard (ed.), *Homeric Questions*, 147–82. Amsterdam: Gieben.

—— (1995*b*). 'Politics and the Battlefield. Ideology in Greek Warfare', in A. Powell (ed.), *The Greek World*, 153–78. London: Routledge.

—— (1998). 'Greeks Bearing Arms. The State, the Leisure Class, and the Display of Weapons in Archaic Greece', in N. Fisher and H. van Wees (eds.), *Archaic Greece: New Approaches and New Evidence*, 333–78. London: Duckworth/The Classical Press of Wales.

—— (1999). 'The Mafia of Early Greece: Violent Exploitation in the Seventh and Sixth Centuries BC', in K. Hopwood (ed.), *Organized Crime in Antiquity*, 1–51. London: Duckworth/The Classical Press of Wales.

VAPNARSKY, C. A. (1969). 'On Rank-size Distributions of Cities: An Ecological Approach'. *Economic Development and Cultural Change* 17: 584–95.

VELIGIANNI-TERZI, C. (1977). *Damiurgen: Zur Entwicklung einer Magistratur* (diss. phil. Heidelberg).

VELKOV, V., and DOMARADZKA, L. (1994). 'Kotys I (383/2–359 av. J.C.) et l'*emporion* Pistiros de Thrace'. *BCH* 118: 1–15.

VICKERS, M., and REYNOLDS, J. M. (1971–2). 'Cyrenaica 1962–72'. *ArchRep* 18: 33–4.

VLASTOS, G. (1953). 'Isonomia'. *AJP* 74: 337–66.

—— (1964). '*Isonomia Politikê*', in J. Mau and E. G. Schmidt (eds.), *Isonomia: Studien zur Gleichheitsvorstellung im griechischen Denken*, 1–35. Berlin: Akademie-Verlag.

—— (1973). *Platonic Studies*. Princeton: Princeton University Press.

VOKOTOPOULOU, J. (1986). Βίτσα· Τα νεκροταφεία μιας μολοσσικής κώμης. 3 vols.; Athens: Tameio Archaiologikon Poron kai Apallotrioseon.

VON DER LAHR, S. (1992). *Dichter und Tyrannen im archaischen Griechenland*. Munich: Tuduv.

VON FRITZ, K. (1954). *The Theory of the Mixed Constitution in Antiquity*. New York: Columbia University Press.

VON REDEN, S. (1995). *Exchange in Ancient Greece*. London: Duckworth.

VOZA, G. (1978). 'Eloro in età protoarcaica', in *Insediamenti coloniali greci in Sicilia nell'VIII. e VII. secolo a.C.* (Cronache di Archeologia 17), 134–5. Catania: Università di Catania, Istituto di Archeologia.

WADE-GERY, H. T. (1931). 'Eupatridai, Archons and Areopagus'. *CQ* 25: 1–11, 77–89.

—— (1958). *Essays in Greek History*. Oxford: Blackwell.

WAGSTAFF, J. M., and CHERRY, J. F. (1982). 'Settlement and Resources', in C. Renfrew and M. Wagstaff (eds.), *An Island Polity*, 246–63. Cambridge: Cambridge University Press.

WALBANK, F. W. (1957–79). *A Historical Commentary on Polybius*. 3 vols.; Oxford: Clarendon Press.

—— (1984). 'Monarchies and Monarchic Ideas', in F. W. Walbank, A. E. Astin, M. W. Frederiksen, and R. M. Ogilvie (eds.), *The Cambridge Ancient History*, 2nd edn., vii/1. 62–100. Cambridge: Cambridge University Press.

WALBANK, M. B. (1978). *Athenian Proxenies of the Fifth Century B.C.* Toronto: Stevens.

WARDLE, K. (1980). 'Excavations at Assiros, 1975–79'. *ABSA* 75: 229–67.

WATKIN, D. (1977). *Morality and Architecture*. Oxford: Clarendon Press.

WEBER, M. (1992). *Storia economica e sociale dell'antichità*, 2nd edn. (trans. B. S. Vigorita). Rome: Riuniti.

WEBSTER, J. (1996). 'Roman Imperialism and the "Post Imperial Age"', in J. Webster and N. Cooper (eds.), *Roman Imperialism: Post Colonial Perspectives*, 1–18. Leicester: Leicester University Press.

WEIL, R. (1960). *Aristote et l'histoire. Essai sur la 'Politique'*. Paris: Klincksieck.

WELWEI, K.-W. (1986). '"Demos" und "Plethos" in athenischen Volksbeschlüssen um 450 v. Chr.'. *Historia* 35: 177–91.

WENTKER, H. (1956). *Sizilien und Athen*. Heidelberg: Quelle & Meyer.

WEST, M. L. (1974). *Studies in Greek Elegy and Iambus*. Berlin: de Gruyter.

—— (1993). *Greek Lyric Poetry*. Oxford: Clarendon Press.

WESTBROOK, R. (1992). 'The Trial Scene in the *Iliad*'. *HSCPh* 94: 53–76.

WESTLAKE, H. D. (1935). *Thessaly in the Fourth Century BC*. London: Methuen.

WHEATLEY, P. (1972). 'The Concept of Urbanism', in P. J. Ucko, R. Tringham, and G. W. Dimbleby (eds.), *Man, Settlement and Urbanism*, 601–37. London: Duckworth.

WHIBLEY, L. (1896). *Greek Oligarchies: Their Character and Organisation*. London: Methuen.

WHITEHEAD, D. (1980). 'Euphron, Tyrant of Sicyon: An Unnoticed Problem in Xenophon *Hell.* 7. 3. 8'. *LCM* 5: 175–8.

—— (1982–3). 'Sparta and the Thirty Tyrants'. *AncSoc* 13–14: 105–30.

—— (1994). 'Site-classification and Reliability in Stephanus of Byzantium', in *CPC Papers* 1: 99–124.

WHITEHOUSE, R. D., and WILKINS, J. B. (1989). 'Greeks and Natives in South-east Italy: Approaches to the Archaeological Evidence', in T. C. Champion (ed.), *Centre and Periphery*, 102–26. London: Unwin Hyman.

WHITTAKER, C. R. (ed.) (1988). *Pastoral Economies in Classical Antiquity* (Cambridge Philological Society, supp. 14). Cambridge.

WILHELM, A. (1942). 'Proxenie und Euergesie', in *Attische Urkunden* (Sitz. Wien.), v. 220–5. Vienna: A. Holder.

—— (1950). *Griechische Epigramme aus Kreta* (*Symbolae Osloenses* supp. 13).

WILKIE, N. C. (1988). 'The Grevena Project, 1987'. *AJA* 92: 241.

—— ROSSER, J., SAVINA, M., and DOYLE, R. (1990). 'The Grevena Project, 1988–89'. *AJA* 94: 309.

WILL, E. (1977). Review of Cabanes (1976a). *RH* 257: 189–95.

—— (1979). *Histoire politique du monde hellénistique*, vol. i, 2nd edn. Nancy: Presses Universitaires.

WILLEMSEN, F., and BRENNE, S. (1991). 'Verzeichnis der Kerameikos-Ostraka'. *AM* 106: 147–56.

WILLETTS, R. F. (1955). *Aristocratic Society in Ancient Crete*. London: Routledge and Kegan Paul.

—— (1962). *Cretan Cults and Festivals*. London: Routledge and Kegan Paul.

—— (1967). *The Law Code of Gortyn*. Berlin: de Gruyter.

WILLIAMS, C. K. (1970). 'Corinth, 1969: Forum Area'. *Hesperia* 39: 1–39.

—— (1982). 'The Early Urbanization of Corinth'. *AS Atene* 60: 9–19.

—— (1995). 'Archaic and Classical Corinth', in *Corinto e l'Occidente: Atti del*

XXXIV Convegno di Studi sulla Magna Grecia, Taranto 7–11 ott. 1994, 31–45. Taranto: Istituto per la Storia e l'Archeologia della Magna Grecia.

WILSON, J. P. (2000). 'Ethnic and State Identity in the Greek Settlements in Southern Italy in the 8th and 7th Centuries BC', in E. Herring and K. Lomas (eds.), *The Emergence of State Identities in Italy in the 1ˢᵗ Millennium BC*, 31–44. London: Accordia Research Institute.

WISEMAN, J. (1978). *The Land of the Ancient Corinthians*. Göteborg: Åström.

WOOLF, G. (1993). 'Rethinking the *Oppida*'. *OJA* 2/2: 223–33.

WÖRLE, A. (1981). *Die politische Tätigkeit der Schüler Platons*. Göppingen: Kummerle.

WÖRRLE, M. (1991). 'Epigraphische Forschungen zur Geschichte Lykiens, IV'. *Chiron* 21: 203–39.

WRIGHT, J., CHERRY, J., DAVIS, J., MANTZOURANI, E., and SUTTON, S. (1990). 'The Nemea Valley Archaeological Project: A Preliminary Report'. *Hesperia* 59: 579–659.

WUENSCH, R. (1897). *IG* iii/3, appendix: 'Defixionum Tabellae'. Berlin: Reimer.

WYCHERLEY, R. E. (1957). *The Athenian Agora*, iii. *Literary and Epigraphical Testimonia*. Princeton: ASCSA.

ZAHLE, J. (1980). 'Lycian Tombs and Lycian Cities', in H. Metzger (ed.), *Actes du colloque sur la Lycie antique*, 37–49. Paris: Libr. d'Amérique et d'Orient Adrien Maisonneuve.

—— (1983). *Arkæologiske studiere i lykiske klippegrave*. Copenhagen: Museum Tusculanum.

—— (1989). 'Politics and Economy in Lycia during the Persian Period'. *RÉA* 91/1–2: 169–82.

ZAPHEIROPOULOS, N. (1956). Ἀνασκαφικαί ἔρευναι εἰς περιφέρειαν Φαρῶν Ἀχαΐας'. *Praktika* 193–201.

ZAPHEIROPOULOS, P. (1952). Ἀνασκαφικαί ἔρευναι εἰς περιφέρειαν Φαρῶν Ἀχαΐας'. *Praktika* 400–12.

ZEITLIN, F. I. (1990). 'Thebes: Theater of Self and Society in Athenian Drama', in J. J. Winkler and F. I. Zeitlin, *Nothing to Do with Dionysus?*, 130–67. Princeton: Princeton University Press.

ZHIVKOVA, L. (1973). *Das Grabmal von Kasanlak*. Sofia: Nauka.

ZIPF, G. K. (1949). *Human Behaviour and the Principle of Least Effort*. London: Hafner.

ZUCKER, F. (1952). *Studien zur Namenkunde vorhellenistischer und hellenistischer Zeit* (Sitzungsberichte der Deutschen Akademie der Wissenschaften zu Berlin. Klasse für Sprachen, Literatur und Kunst, Jahrgang 1951, No. 1).

Index

Index

polis (*cont.*):
  development different in W. Mediterranean 167–9
  emergence in west Crete 336–7
political organization 2, 24, 212–13
  changes in 29, 43
  evolution of 229–33, 252, 279
  fluidity of 252
  regional 23
  variation in 68
polypus 44
Polyrrhenia 336–7, 339–40, 347
poor, poverty 65, 131, 159
population 9–10, 87, 140, 168, 173, 207, 213–14, 240
  mixed 180, 232, 240; *see also* intermarriage
  population centres 24–5, 216
probouleusis 14 n. 39, 20 n. 53, 145, 150
production, economic 199–202
  see also land; wealth
proxenia 113–15, 297–9, 334
  proxeny decrees 26, 248, 297–305, 307

'rank size analysis' 218–19
regent, regency 92
regional identity 23–4
  merging of smaller groups in 255
  see also ethnic identity
religious association 331
  see also amphiktyony
religious authority 83, 146
representation 8, 231
republican regime 145
rivalry, dynastic 87

Sacred Wars:
  First 285
  Third 297
Salamis, Cyprian 291
  Evagoras, king of 116–18
Samos, Samians 12–13, 43, 85, 90–1, 102
sanctuaries and cult-places 23, 72–4, 138, 202, 206, 236, 281–5, 293–7, 317
  common 25–6
  sacred precincts (*temenea*) 88–9, 100, 206
  temples 72, 203
Scythia, Scythians 107
self-definition, Greek 168, 184–5
serfs 87–8, 96, 138, 150
settlement, overseas 172
  see also colonization
settlement patterns and organization 68–70, 96–8, 150, 189, 193, 197–211, 215–19, 224, 226–7, 240–1
  concentrations 197–204, 214, 228
  nucleation 208–10, 216–17, 269

rural settlement uncommon 204, 206
Sfakia (W. Crete) 330–1
  see also White Mountains
Sicels 176
Sicily 15, 181, 183
  see also Dionysius I; Gelon; Hieron; Syracuse
Sicyon 15, 321, 323–4
slaves, slavery 8–9, 140, 176
  freed slaves 181
  see also serfs
social change and mobility 44, 53, 60–3, 66–7, 79–81
Solon 119–20, 153, 155–7, 161, 165–6, 280
  economic reforms of 119
sortition: *see* lot
'sovereignty' 254
  problematic term 27 n. 62
space, and political organization 24, 207, 217–23, 230
Sparta 5–6, 12, 14–15, 20, 24, 82, 92, 101, 107, 155–6, 158, 160, 299, 308–10
  constitution 15, 245, 291; as 'mixed' 18 n. 50, 160
  dual kingship 15, 82–3, 107, 238, 251–2
  gerousia 18 n. 48, 20, 155, 160, 291; *see also* elders
  see also ephors
Spartocids: *see* Bosporan kingdom
stasis (civil strife) 9–10, 12, 30, 44, 80–1, 96, 101–2, 161, 165–6, 323–4
state 214
  formation of 256–7
  see also ethnē; polis
status, formal 175, 177, 182
Stephanus of Byzantium 328
symmachia, hegemonic 26–7
symposium 45, 46–9, 81
  poetry recited at 45, 48–9
synoikism 191, 193, 204, 206, 208–10, 229, 309, 336
  resynoikism 309 n. 5
Syracuse 13, 96, 98, 176
  democracy at 13, 96, 137–51
  tyranny at 140–1, 181

Tarentum (Taras) 174, 176
Tegea 30, 203, 308, 310, 312–15
tell sites 191, 223–8
Temenids of Argos 82, 267
territory 73, 98, 138, 149
  see also land
Theagenes, tyrant of Megara 38–42, 114
Thebes 11 n. 30, 12 n. 33, 28, 296, 302, 314, 317, 321–3
  Sacred Band 316
  see also Boeotia